Praise for *America's Best Colleges for B Students*

"This book contains practical information for any student searching for the right college 'fit' instead of simply trying to 'fit in' at the wrong college. From this small college's perspective, the 'solid B' student has the same chance as an A student to be successful in an environment where each is encouraged to develop his/her potential."

— Sandy Speed
Dean of Admission and Financial Aid
Schreiner University

"This book offers practical information and advice for students and parents alike. There is a great school out there for you — *America's Best Colleges for B Students* will help you find it!"

— Mark Campbell
Vice President for Enrollment Management
McKendree College

"At last, a college resource book for real students and real families. We hear so much about how only overachievers get into good schools that we forget that college isn't just about grades and tests scores; it's about learning, living and moving forward. This is something that all students need, regardless of their high school performance. Tamra Orr has given families the tools to help their young adults find the perfect college for them. An invaluable resource!"

— Teri Brown
Author of Day Tripping: Your Guide to Educational
Family Adventures

"Tamra Orr's refreshingly candid approach to the college search dispels the fear that B students and their families often face. An easy yet information-packed read!"

— Bethany Bierman
Assistant Director, Office of Undergraduate
Admissions
Augsburg College

"Many hard-working kids (this book calls them B students) don't think they're college material because they don't have high college boards or the highest grades. In short order, this book dispels that myth! Tamra Orr has gathered helpful insights and suggestions that will, thankfully, elevate the expectations of such students to achieve college success."

— Patrick J. O'Brien
Retired high school counselor, former Marquette
Northern California admissions representative and
current ACT ambassador

"This excellent 'advice' book is a must read for those students and their parents who want to understand and navigate the process and find the right match toward that important degree."

— Karen P. Condeni
Vice President and Dean of Enrollment
Ohio Northern University

"This book will be a terrific introduction to the college search process. The format offers helpful suggestions in a non-intimidating approach. For many high school students the college process becomes a seemingly insurmountable task. *America's Best Colleges for B Students* is a terrific introductory tool that outlines the basic steps to begin the college search process."

— Amanda (Mandy) Warhurst Webster
Senior Associate Director of Admission
Salve Regina University

"Tamra Orr's book is just what the 'not so perfect' student needs. The advice is to the point and incredibly useful. You don't have to attend a huge Ivy League school to get a superior education. Orr's book should be required reading for individuals of all ages who are thinking of attending college."

— Sandra Roy
Educator and author

Praise for *America's Best Colleges for B Students*

"What really makes a great student great? Is greatness limited to a letter grade on paper or a score on the SATs? There is so much more that factors into it like the sincere desire to not only succeed in the classroom, but succeed in life. There are some outstanding institutions of higher learning that understand that reality and offer programs from which B students will benefit the most as well as learning services that help them become better students. By offering an in-depth analysis of the best schools catering to the needs of real world students, this book will go far in helping families identify the best schools that suit individual needs. Education is not 'one size fits all,' and this book helps explain that — and will help anyone in search of higher education find the 'right fit.'"

— **Jennifer A. Fiorentino**
Director, Public Relations & Communications
Dean College

"With humor and insight, Tamra Orr sets the record straight about college admission, offering practical advice and hope to college-bound students. This book makes the important point that the college admission process doesn't need to be fraught with stress and anxiety. Many bright, interesting teens that underperformed in high school will recognize themselves in the pages of this book. Orr guides students in how to explore colleges where they can find themselves and achieve as never before."

— **Joan Casey**
College Planning Consultant
Educational Advocates

"Finally! A guide for motivated late bloomers — solid students who in the right environment will flourish. Tamra Orr has done her homework to provide you with the guidance and tips you need to find the college that's right for you — and help you succeed once you're there. Pack your suitcase for adventure and bring your drive, energy and personal commitment to achieve!"

— **Esther Goodcuff**
Associate Vice President for Enrollment Management
and Student Affairs
Adelphi University

America's Best Colleges *for* Students

Sixth Edition

A College Guide for Students Without Straight A's

TAMRA B. ORR

America's Best Colleges for B Students: A College Guide for Students without Straight A's
6th Edition
By Tamra B. Orr

Published by SuperCollege, LLC
2713 Newlands Avenue
Belmont, CA 94002
www.supercollege.com

Credits: Cover design TLC Graphics, www.TLCGraphics.com. Design: Monica Thomas. Cover photograph: istockphoto.com / © Bill Manning.

Trademarks: All brand names, product names and services used in this book are trademarks, registered trademarks or tradenames of their respective holders. SuperCollege is not associated with any college, university, product or vendor.

Disclaimers: The author and publisher have used their best efforts in preparing this book. It is intended to provide helpful and informative material on the subject matter. Some narratives and names have been modified for illustrative purposes. SuperCollege and the author make no representations or warranties with respect to the accuracy or completeness of the contents of the book and specifically disclaim any implied warranties or merchantability or fitness for a particular purpose. There are no warranties which extend beyond the descriptions contained in this paragraph. The accuracy and completeness of the information provided herein and the opinions stated herein are not guaranteed or warranted to produce any particular results. SuperCollege and the author specifically disclaim any responsibility for any liability, loss or risk, personal or otherwise, which is incurred as a consequence, directly or indirectly, of the use and application of any of the contents of this book.

ISBN-13: 978-1-61760-075-3

Manufactured in the United States of America
10 9 8 7 6 5 4 3 2 1

Library of Congress Cataloging-in-Publication Data
Orr, Tamra.
 America's best colleges for B students : a college guide for students without straight A's / by Tamra B. Orr. -- Sixth edition.
    pages cm
 ISBN 978-1-61760-075-3 (alk. paper)
1. College choice--United States--Directories. 2. Universities and colleges--United States--Directories. I. Title.
 LB2350.5.O77 2015
 378.73--dc23
                2015005903

*To my kids who brighten my life, my husband who enriches my life
and my parents who gave me life.*

CONTENTS

FOREWORD

If the prospect of receiving an A- in AP calculus keeps you up at night, this book is not for you. If, on the other hand, you are ecstatic about scoring that B in English, this book is exactly what you need!

One of the greatest myths about a college education is that you need to have straight A's or be the class valedictorian to get into an excellent college. The truth is that there are terrific colleges out there that want you — whether you are a B student or, gasp, even a C student. But don't assume that these colleges are looking for slackers. Quite the opposite: These schools know that good students don't always perform at their true potential in high school. For example:

- Maybe you didn't take high school seriously and only now have come to realize the importance of doing well academically.

- Maybe you managed your time poorly or were overcommitted with a job or activities.

- Maybe you were distracted by events in your life beyond your control.

- Maybe you were just bored with high school.

Whatever the reason, these schools know that your grades and test scores are not always reflective of who you are and how well you will do in college. So, if you are now committed to getting a college education and are willing to put in the time and effort to be a successful student, these colleges want you.

The key is: How do you find these colleges? What do you need to look for to make sure that you will excel? And how do you show the college that you are serious about getting a great education and will be an asset to their student body?

That's where this book will help. Here are just a few of the things that you will learn:

- How to identify colleges that accept students with less than perfect grades and test scores.

- What characteristics to look for in a college to ensure that you succeed academically as well as socially.

- How to best position yourself — both the positives and negatives — in the college application, essay and interview.

- Ways to pay for your education. (Scholarships are not just reserved for the A students. There are literally thousands also available for students based on non-academic skills and talents.)

- Tips for making that sometimes difficult transition from high school to college.

Tamra Orr has written this book just for you. She has been there, done that as a student like you without perfect grades or test scores. She knows there is no shame in being a B student. (In fact, Tamra knows how to present this as a huge positive to a college!) She also knows that just because you may not be in the "Ivy-League-Wannabe" crowd doesn't mean you are not motivated and committed to being successful.

Let her help you find that perfect college! We wish you the best in your journey!

— Gen and Kelly Tanabe
Authors of 14 books on college planning including
The Ultimate Guide to America's Best Colleges and
The Ultimate Scholarship Book

INTRODUCTION

Once upon a time, long, long ago, almost anyone who wanted to go to college and could find a way to afford it went to college. SAT just meant the past tense of "sit" and GPA was an odd combination of letters that might have been a neat abbreviation for "Grandpa." After World War II, tests and test scores started to gain in importance, but it would be some time before they would become the determining factor behind going to college. Sure, if you had a great SAT score or a really high GPA, it was easier to get scholarships or get the really BIG colleges to give you more than a glance. But I remember applying to colleges without much thought at all about my numbers (I'm dating myself now, as that was back in the late 1970s). I was too busy scoping out the campus, checking the ratio of guys to girls and, oh yeah, seeing what majors were offered. (I must say, however, that 30 years later, I can STILL tell you my SAT scores.)

The picture is quite different today. Getting into college is not only more expensive but also much tougher. Colleges have become so selective that even valedictorians with a 4.0 average and perfect SAT scores are being turned away from some of the Ivy League institutions.

Because of this, many students are ready to throw their hands in the air and say, "Okay, I get it! I don't have good enough numbers, so I obviously can't go to college. I'll just forget it!" If you are among these, realize this: You, yes YOU, are the reason for this book. It is designed to give you two things: help with what it takes to get into many colleges (and an overview of what happens after you do) and leads on which colleges are eagerly awaiting your application.

For starters, get rid of the myths/assumptions you might have about choosing a college. If you believe any of the following, take them from the "The Earth is Round" list (truth) and put them in the "Santa Claus/Tooth Fairy" list (fantasies). Here we go:

- You need a perfect GPA or SAT to get into a good college.

- The best way to pick a college is by reading the rankings in a magazine article/taking your best friend's recommendation/choosing the names you recognize the most.

- Traditional four-year colleges are the only ones employers will accept.

- Only the large colleges are worth attending.

- Your college should have more students than your high school does.

- Small colleges offer inferior classes, faculty and degrees.

  None of the above statements is true.

- A perfect score or transcript is not required at most colleges, as you will see as you read this book.

- The best way to select a college is to *not* accept someone else's opinion as absolute truth and to do your homework (yes, MORE homework) and find out which colleges best suit you and your preferences.

- While four-year colleges are the norm, there are many two-year programs and other options that are just as appealing to future employers.

- Small colleges often offer the conditions and student/teacher ratio that will ensure a high-quality, successful education. In no way are their classes, faculty or degrees inferior to those of the larger universities.

One of the biggest myths of all about college, of course, is that even if you find one that you like and will accept you, you will not be able to afford it. We will dispel that myth as well in Chapter Six.

You, standing right there in the middle of the library or bookstore (or at home scanning the intro because your parents told you, "READ THIS!"), you with the 2.9 or 3.1 GPA or the 1560 SAT score or 19 composite ACT, *can* go to a college or university. You can find yourself at a wonderful institution where you will make friends, have fun, grow up and yeah, learn a lot of stuff and get a degree. These colleges are not runners-up to the "good" places; they are wonderful schools that are willing to look beyond the numbers to the person standing behind them. They have admissions departments that give your scores some thought, and then put them down and search for the human being on the other side of the digits. And really, isn't that what you would want them to do anyway? You are certainly more than any group of numbers could possibly represent.

This book was written to guide you to lots of helpful information about 100 colleges and universities that want you to be a part of their student population. It will also show you how to:

- Make the best use of the time you still have left in high school

- Make a great impression on the college admissions department through both the essay and interview

- Explain those less-than-stellar numbers and let your strengths shine through

- Survive in college once you get there

Belonging is one of the strongest natural drives inside each and every person. You want to find a college where you are happy, comfortable and accepted. The administrations of these colleges want students who feel like they have found a new home. Let this book be your guide to that relationship.

SECTION ONE
CHOOSING

HOW TO CHOOSE
THE RIGHT COLLEGE
FOR YOU

CHAPTER ONE

WHERE TO FIND COLLEGES THAT WELCOME B STUDENTS

We Really Do Want You
(Or, Why Colleges Love B Students . . .)

Why would a college want you, the B STUDENT, instead of Ms. Straight A's or Mr. Perfect SAT Score? Easy! Colleges want diversity. They want all kinds of students and that means you too. You are so much more than your GPA or your ACT scores and most colleges realize that. They want you because you are curious, enthusiastic and interesting!

You want the chance to shine, and there are colleges that want to help you do it. Think about it for a moment. There are more than 3,400 four-year, accredited colleges and universities in this country. That's a lot of places to learn! You can be sure that there are many schools for everyone and there certainly are many choices for B students. Your statistics may make the search a little longer and a bit challenging but no less rewarding.

Nothing is as important to your educational success as finding a college where you feel comfortable. A key to success is being flexible and prepared to give the avenues open to you a fair chance. You have to be willing to look a little deeper and explore options, some of which you may not have thought of before. For instance, "Keep an open mind about going out of state," encourages Lynda McGee, college counselor at Downtown Magnets High School in Los Angeles. It is McGee's personal goal to find schools for all students. "Some students fear leaving the area, especially those in sunny California," she explains.

Judi Robinovitz, an educational consultant for more than 25 years, suggests that students be open to exploring colleges they may not already know about. "You have to dispel the notion that just because you have not heard of a college, it's a bad college," she says.

"There are no bad colleges," explains Patrick O'Brien, former admissions officer and consultant-ambassador for the ACT. "Remember, the 'best' school is the one that is best for you, not necessarily the ones that are highlighted in the books," says O'Brien.

But, why would a college be willing to take a chance on a student who doesn't have the kind of scores and grades thought to be required by a majority of colleges? It's simple: They have common sense.

First, a number of universities want a diverse student body roaming around their campuses. To achieve this, they have to broaden their ideas of what kind of student they will accept. Just as colleges accept people from all kinds of financial, ethnic, religious and racial backgrounds, they often will accept those with various levels of academic achievement.

Second, admissions officers often realize that while students may not have the most perfect numbers, they can still add greatly to the student body. They may be tremendous leaders, facilitators, speakers or organizers. They may exhibit strength in a variety of skills that can't be pinpointed with the average test score. For example, while a student may not perform well in math, he or she may excel in the humanities. These students can enrich the campus community in untold ways.

Last, colleges know that some students are genuinely working toward starting over, to changing their priorities and standards. Often this can be seen in school transcripts. Grades are improving with time; a new leaf has been turned over. Colleges recognize that some students really do go through difficult times such as the severe illness or death of a family member. Because of this, they are frequently willing to overlook some weak numbers and support that new dedication by accepting you into their college and giving you another way to continue your trend.

So the college that you assumed was out of reach because of your grades or test scores may actually be entirely possible if you can give them a reason for why you deserve to be there.

Looking Outside the Box

One secret to finding the right college is to look beyond the most popular schools that everyone you know is applying to and then to think outside of the box. Are there other colleges in your area? Before you start shaking your head because these "other" colleges aren't what you had in mind, at least do a little research. Look at their sites online, and check out the profiles at the end of this book. You can't say you don't like a place until you have enough information to know if you like it (otherwise known as innocent until proven guilty!).

Some schools that may be more open to B students include these:

- career-oriented colleges
- community colleges
- all men's colleges
- all women's colleges
- very small colleges

For many students, one of the best options remains the local community college. Yeah, you still have to live in your hometown, and most likely, still at home with your family, but you benefit from a good education while saving some big bucks for the future or for transferring to a four-year college. Community colleges are more open to students with B or C averages than some four-year institutions, so they can be a great solution for you.

But hey, you've heard some rumors about community colleges, right? You've heard them called everything from "Only Chance College" to "Harvard on the Highway." Like everything else, community colleges have a few myths surrounding them, and — here's a real surprise — most of them just aren't true. For instance:

- A degree from a community college is not as good as a university degree.

  That just doesn't make any sense. An apple is an apple. A degree is a degree. You did the work and earned the diploma. Is it the same thing as a degree from Harvard? Okay, maybe not, but most of the time it will still get you through the front door and into the job.

- The people who go to community college couldn't get in anywhere else.

  Not true. Students go to community college for a variety of reasons. Maybe it is more convenient and less expensive for some people because it allows them to keep working, giving them a chance to save money while providing a quality education that sometimes may even serve as a stepping stone to a traditional college.

- The faculty at community colleges is inferior to that of four-year institutions.

  The faculties and staff at community colleges and other colleges are quite comparable. They both have their degrees and years of experience to share with you.

- The credits from a community college will not transfer to other colleges.

  This is a myth. Credit hours from community colleges transfer in the same way that credit hours from four-year universities do.

COMMUNITY COLLEGE FACTS

Here are some of the current stats on community colleges, thanks to the helpful people at the American Association of Community Colleges (www. aacc.nche.edu):

Public institutions	992
Private institutions	96
Tribal institutions	35
TOTAL	1,123

12.4 million students currently enrolled

7.4 million for credit and 5 million for non-credit

46% of all U.S. undergraduates

41% of first-time freshmen

57% women; 43% men

61% part time; 39% full time

52% of African American undergrads

57% of Hispanic undergrads

43% of Asian/Pacific Islander undergrads

61% of Native American undergrads

Average tuition and fees: $3,347, and 58% of students receive some kind of financial aid.

More than 750,000 associate degrees

More than 450,000 two-year certificates

- Since community colleges cost so much less, they can't be any good.

Community colleges are fine institutions. The difference in tuition can be due to many reasons, but it is mainly because community colleges do not have the incredible overhead that residential colleges have.

In 2004, the American Association of Community Colleges conducted a survey to see what the hottest programs at these colleges were. The survey found that the top five fields to study were allied health (46.6 percent), skilled trades/industrial, public services, information technologies and business.

Go, Team, Go!

Remember that choosing a college is not usually an individual choice. Instead, it takes a team of people all working together, including your teachers, advisers, guidance counselors, principals, coaches and family members. You need help with a decision this big, because it is a complex one.

There are so many colleges that accept B students that it is important for you to consider several different elements when you start your search. Ask yourself these questions:

- What kind of student am I now, and what are my career plans for the future?

- What parts of school do I like the best and least now?

- What does the idea of success actually mean to me?

- Where do I see myself in two years? Five years? Ten years?

- What part of the country appeals most to me?

- Do I want a small, intimate college or a bustling, exciting university?

- What percentage of males and females would be ideal for me?

- What is the cost and how much financial aid does each school offer?

- What are the most popular majors and is mine on that list?

- Do I want to be involved in a sorority/fraternity?

- Will I have any scholarships or grants that affect where I can go?

- Do I want a philosophical or religious college?

You may not know the answers to all these questions yet. Many of them will only come after you have taken some tours, read your research and talked to your team. Giving them some thought now, however, will give you a head start.

What to Look for in a College

When you start your college search, you have to find a happy balance between being optimistic and realistic. Look at the GPA and ACT/SAT scores that each college lists and analyze those numbers in relationship to yours. If a college's cut-off on the SAT verbal score is 510 and yours is 520, go ahead and apply — it's a "safety" college. What if your score is 480? Give it a try — it's a "fairly good chance" college. How about a score of 410? Not likely — but you could still apply to this college; just don't hold your breath. Be willing to stretch a little and know that those numbers are not carved in stone but are general guidelines.

The colleges profiled in this book do more than just accept B students. They are dedicated to helping them. They may offer a first-year general studies, remedial or transition class to help get you started. Many offer on-campus writing clinics and tutoring services. When you get in touch with the representatives from these colleges, be prepared to ask them what services they might offer. Can you record lectures? Are there faculty advisers for each student? Are classes offered to help with the transition to college? Even if they don't have any plans in place (which is unlikely) your request might be just enough to implement one.

Let's take an up-close look at each of these options for a moment. It's important for you to think about which of these features is important to you and will help you succeed in college. Take notes so that when you contact a college rep or admissions officer, you can ask if these choices exist at the school:

TUTORING: A variety of types of tutoring are available on virtually every campus. The only question is what format you prefer. You can check into peer tutoring from either a classmate or friend; faculty tutoring from a willing professor; in-depth tutoring from a teacher's assistant or at special on-campus centers and clinics. While some tutors may charge a fee, most services tend to be free. When you speak with a college rep, ask what might be available if you should need extra assistance.

COUNSELING: While tutoring is helpful to understanding a certain assignment or class subject, counseling is a wider scope. A counselor will help you make bigger decisions like what major to choose, what classes to take and in what direction you should go to achieve your goal. An academic counselor will

A COLLEGE WHOSE DOOR IS ALWAYS OPEN

The core philosophy of the community college in America can be captured in the phrase "access and excellence." Community colleges, like all institutions of higher education, struggle to be excellent. But when it comes to "access," there is no struggle at all; community colleges are the access institutions of the 21st century.

The community college has emerged as the institution of the second chance — even the third and fourth chance. Community colleges take great pride in their "open-door philosophy," which means that any student who has graduated from high school or who has reached a certain age will be admitted. This philosophy and practice is remarkably different from those of most four-year colleges and universities. Historically, most four-year colleges and universities require that students meet certain criteria for admission, eliminating those who are under-prepared or unqualified to compete.

Community colleges are willing to give all applicants an opportunity to succeed regardless of their history. That does not mean that an unprepared student will be admitted into a very challenging program such as nursing or engineering technology. Instead, through assessment and advising, students who are not prepared for more challenging work will be guided into developmental education programs where they will receive special tutoring and courses in which they can develop the skills for more advanced work.

The focus of the community college — through its faculty and innovative programs and practices — is to help students succeed, regardless of their level of achievement when they enter.

— **TERRY O'BANION, former president of the League for Innovation in the Community College**

Chapter 1: Where to Find Colleges That Welcome B Students

not only help you reach academic goals, but he or she also will often help you with emotional and mental stress. To do your best academically, you need to be in good shape mentally. Counselors can recommend resources, give suggestions and tips, connect you with helpful mentors or organizations and much more.

CLASS SIZE AND PROFESSOR/STUDENT RATIO: One of the biggest advantages of small colleges is their small class size. While many universities, even the really large ones, state that their average class size is between 10 and 30, a number of small colleges have fewer students per class. Instead of 22:1 student to professor ratios, they may have 5:1. This can be good because your professors are much more likely to be aware of you; if you are struggling or having a problem, they will be more apt to recognize it and reach out. Small classes mean you can ask more questions and discuss things on a deeper level. It also frequently means that participation will play a role in your overall grade.

There are many positive things about small classes, but some students might say that small classes have a negative side as well. For example, if you miss class, professors know (in a class of several hundred, it is a lot less noticeable, believe me!). If your homework isn't turned in, it will be observed right away as well. Truthfully, these can be good things. Professors who notice you are getting behind can remind you to catch up before you've dug your hole so deep that it takes a miracle to pass the class.

Overall, small classes can make the transition from high school to college easier. You will not feel so much like a minnow floundering in a huge ocean. You will get to know your fellow classmates much easier and quicker if there are a half dozen in your class rather than hundreds. Smaller classes often create more of a sense of cooperation between students rather than competition. Instead of trying to do better than another person, you will only be trying to do better than you have done before — and that is the best kind of competition there is.

It's important to go beyond the statistics when you look at the numbers you find for professor/student ratio. Ask students who attend the school how much they interact with their professors and how much of an effort the professors make to help their students. More important than the ratio of professors to students is how involved the professors will be in your studies.

TEACHING STYLES: Another question to look into when choosing your college is what different teaching styles the school may offer. What emphasis does it have on lab time? Is there a period of internship? How much of class time is comprised of hands-on activities for kinesthetic learners? How much is pre-printed or written in forms that are student-friendly for visual learners? How much can be taped for auditory learners? Are there many field trips? All these options can make learning easier for many students. They are alternatives to the typical lecture/listen teaching format that has dominated your education up until now. Colleges offer new ways to learn and excel.

PASS/FAIL or CREDIT/NO CREDIT CLASSES: Not all colleges offer classes with pass/fail grading systems but a number of them have used it effectively, including the following: Millikin University, University of Iowa, University of Illinois, Ohio State University, Stanford University, Tufts University, University of California (Berkeley), Syracuse University, Pennsylvania State University, Pomona College and Grinnell College.

There are certainly a number of perks to this type of grading system. It often encourages students to explore classes that they might otherwise have ignored. For example, if you are an English major, you may not be brave enough to take an advanced math class because you will be surrounded by students who excel in math and competing with them might be overwhelming. However, if you know that you are only going to have to achieve a passing grade, you might be willing to go for it. With pass/fail, there is often less pressure on you; conversely, you may mistakenly think that you don't have to try at all (then you are just wasting everyone's time!).

In addition to regular classes, some types of learning fit the pass/fail system better than the traditional A, B, C, D and F. This is especially true for laboratory experiments, hands-on activities, thesis work and research.

Is there a downside to this type of grading system? Naturally. Some of these courses can't be counted toward your major. While taking a class that doesn't count toward your major may seem unwise, it can be a smart move. You might discover a new passion, interest or direction for your education. You might also discover that you are better at a subject than you had imagined. Pass/fail classes might even lead you to decide on a supplemental course of study, a double major— or you might even consider changing your major. Think of the pass/fail credit simply as an invitation to go down another new college pathway.

THE EMPHASIS ON FINAL EXAMS: Another option to explore is how much influence final exams have on your overall grades. If you are the type who suffers from test anxiety (more on that later) or just does not test well, you want to look for colleges that offer options to traditional testing. Maybe oral tests are possible. Maybe you can earn most of your grades through homework, class participation or other activities.

SUPPORT NETWORK AND LEVEL OF COMPETITION: Besides the formal support network provided by the school from tutoring and counseling, some colleges offer an informal support network. You will want to find out more about this. Do students tend to help each other or compete against each other? At some schools, students frequently work together on group projects or have study sessions together. At other schools, students work more independently. This is especially important if you learn better in a group environment.

SPECIAL PROGRAMS: Investigate what kind of special programs the colleges may offer. For example, some colleges offer co-op programs in which students are able to spend a semester gaining hands-on work experience with a company while earning credits. Most schools have study-abroad programs that allow some students to study internationally, but they vary in their size and scope. Special programs like these may appeal to you and may be just what you need to get motivated.

POSSIBLE AND POPULAR MAJORS: As you look through colleges listed in this book, take special note of the majors listed with each one. These are the most popular majors associated with the particular school. Why is it important to choose a college that features your major? It is just like going shopping. If you really want a pair of boot-cut jeans, you aren't going to go to a shoe store. You want to go where the clerks know what you are talking about and can lead you directly to many choices that fit your needs, right? It's the same thing with a college. If you want to be in computer tech, a college that specializes in art may not be the best choice. You want the school that is familiar with your major and can offer a strong faculty and curriculum in your choice.

You also want to check with a college rep for a school that interests you and ask if you can have a double major at that college (and not just CAN YOU, but will you get the support and guidance you need if you choose to) or can you create your own major. The more options you have, the better the chance of having a college education tailored to your unique needs and the stronger the possibility of overall success.

What if you are undecided about your major when you start your college search? Relax—you are far from being the only one. Make a list of the most likely areas you'd like to explore and then look to see which colleges offer them. It is a first step and that's where every journey begins.

Where to Find Out More about Colleges

- **College fairs.** Dozens or even hundreds of college representatives will come to your town for college fairs. This is your opportunity to ask questions and get a personal perspective from those associated with these colleges without leaving the city limits. Get a list of upcoming college fairs from your counselor or at http://www.nacacnet.org/college-fairs/.

- **College representatives at your school.** Be sure to meet representatives from colleges when they come to your school! You may be tempted to spend the time doing something else, but these events are designed to give you an opportunity to learn a lot about various colleges. You may also be meeting people who will eventually review your application, should you decide to submit one to any of the schools involved. If you make a good impression, your chances of admission may improve.

- **College catalogs/view books.** These may vary from a simple, colorful tri-fold pamphlet to a 40-page catalog, complete with DVD and/or CD, business cards with contact names, testimonials from students and dozens of photographs. Read them through carefully because they can answer many of your questions.

- **College websites.** Whether you look online at home, in the library or at school, take the time to look over the websites of some of the colleges you are interested in. They almost always have an FYI/FAQ section that will provide answers to basic questions. You also get a chance to see what the campus looks like, what some students have to say about the place (all glowing, of course!) and much more.

- **College alumni.** For great suggestions and insight into a college, see if you can get in touch with someone who actually attended it. It might be your cousin, your father's co-worker, someone your guidance counselor suggested or a person the college itself refers to you. Make a list of questions for that person ahead of time so you are sure to cover what you most want to know. If the person graduated more than a few years ago, some information might not be as current as you need, but you can still learn some important facts.

> My biggest piece of advice is that there IS a school for everyone and you WILL be accepted. Remember, you have power over your own life. Get connected with knowledgeable people, invest in books like this one and in the *Fiske's Guide* and Princeton Review's *361 Best Colleges*. Check out *U.S. News & World Report's* "A+ Schools for B Students."
>
> In your junior year, start making plans. Use the summer before your senior year the best way you can. Look for opportunities that open doors and windows for you—think big. If you can't find something, start your own. My son and his friends started a driveway sealing business and did great. Paint, mow lawns—show initiative. It will be a great topic for the essay you should be working on before summer ends.
>
> When school starts again, take the most challenging curriculum you are capable of handling. If your school is small and does not offer the more advanced courses, look elsewhere: go online, take distance learning classes or check out the community college.
>
> — **Shirley Bloomquist,** *MA,*
> *College and Educational Counselor*

- **College visits and tours.** While this topic will be discussed in greater depth later in this book, it is important to say at this point that college visits must be given the value that they deserve. Nothing makes a place come alive as much as visiting it. You can read about a university in every possible source, but you can't really know it until you visit it. That's when you can personally taste the cafeteria creations, hear the conversations in the student union and see the layout of the dorms in some of the residence halls. Go on a tour with your class, counselor, friends or family. The information you will gather is immeasurable.

- **College online virtual tours.** While going to a college in person is the best option, it is not always possible for a variety of reasons. In that case, be sure to at least go to a college's website and check out its virtual tour. You can get a better idea of whether this is the kind of place that calls to you — or not.

- **Guidance counselors.** These wonderful people can give you a lot of helpful information about individual colleges. They may have printed material, website suggestions, contact names and more. Just ask!

- **The school or local community library.** While this book is a great source for finding out about schools that welcome B and C students, there are tons more books out there that list college options. Check them out and look up the schools in which you are most interested. You'll find out useful information that can help you in your decision making. Spend some time just browsing through these books. You may encounter some colleges that you have not heard of before but that are intriguing possibilities.

- **Current college students.** Are there any students in your neighborhood or community already going to a college that interests you? Ask if you can meet for a snack and a chat and have all those questions you haven't been able to ask anyone else ready. Currently enrolled students are the real "been-there-done-that" experts. They will tell you the real truth about college life, not just what the writers of the college's marketing materials want you to know. If you can't find a college student in your area, go to the college and dialog with the students there. Can't get to the campus? Give the place a call and ask the admissions officer to connect you with some students.

- **Decoding college lingo 101.** When you are reading college literature (and believe me, you will get a TON of it), look for key words that will tell you more about how they evaluate applications. For example, they may say that they do a "comprehensive" review of a student's application. Typically, this means they will look beyond the numbers to things like background, extracurricular activities, essays, interviews, recommendations and more. Check online to see if the colleges you are interested in list information about their admissions process online; it might give you some great insight into how they make their decisions.

- **Right from admissions itself.** Skip the middle men and the media and go straight to the college's admissions office. Call and ask to speak with an admissions officer. Be honest. Explain your situation and ask what your chances of admission are or what you might be able to do to improve those chances. You might get some fantastic insider information (the legal kind!).

Visit Colleges Sooner Rather than Later

Don't wait a moment longer to go and visit schools. Seeing is believing! Reading about a place in a book or online is fine for background information, but it is a visit that will give you the true feel of the college's atmosphere, attitudes and activities. (To find out what college tours are like, check out the website www.campustours.com).

Patrick O'Brien, former admissions officer and consultant-ambassador for the ACT, says, "The more opportunities to visit college campuses as a junior or in the first part of senior year, the better. And don't just go for the standard college tour of the campus and facilities. Check out the dorms and dorm life," he advises. "Insist on visiting a class in a field of interest—it will show you how the college academic system really works."

Try not to visit colleges during summer, however. As O'Brien says, "Never visit a campus when school is not in session; that's like visiting your high school on a weekend—dullsville." Don't depend on Mom, Dad or your guidance counselor to contact the school for a tour either. Do it yourself; it shows that college that you have initiative.

When you go for a campus tour, take part of your college-finding team with you so that you can get their impressions of each place too. Don't spend your time exploring the things you can get from the school's website. Pretend you are an anthropologist from the future and study the place like we study primitive cultures today. Watch the students interact, check out the food sources, find out how the place accepts those from different ethnic, political or religious backgrounds, gays or married couples. Read the posters in the buildings and the bulletin boards in dorms. What announcements do they have? What are some of the upcoming events and activities? Do they have a choir, band or orchestra? How about a drama group? Hang out in the student union and see what goes on there. Is there a lot of diversity on the campus? Go by the bookstore and see what souvenirs you like. Check out the shopping area around the campus. Pick up a campus newspaper to read later.

Remembering all your impressions of the places you have seen will not be easy. After you have seen a couple of campuses, facts and opinions will begin to mesh and soon you will find yourself asking which college had that great library. Do you remember what campus had those huge trees and large green lawns? To prevent this from happening, make up a form to write down your thoughts as you tour a place. You can create a form that reminds you to give schools a score of 1 (horrible) to 10 (perfection itself), and that offers a spot for general comments, thoughts and questions to follow up on later.

On Page 15 is an example of the kind of form you could use. If you don't like it, my feelings aren't hurt. Create your own! Design it the way that fits best for you.

The Sky's the Limit

Once you start looking for colleges, you'll be overwhelmed at how many great choices there are. In fact, your problem may be that you have too many options!

After you have a list of colleges, the next step is to fill out the applications. This is your opportunity to make your case (why you should be accepted) to each college. While most colleges do look at the numbers from your GPA, SAT and ACT scores, they will also look to your character. They will want to know your aspirations, your passions, your level of responsibility and maturity and how you choose to spend your time. Who inspires you? Who influences you? What do you expect of yourself? College admissions officers see countless numbers of applications, many with high numbers, but it is the student that shows integrity, curiosity, originality and independence that will catch their eyes. Unlike grading those little #2 pencil-filled dots on the standardized tests, this kind of information is much harder to measure. The college application will go a long way to help paint that very unique portrait of you as a person.

But before we hit the application, let's take the next chapter to look at some things you can do now to make sure you maximize your time in high school and set yourself up to create the strongest application possible.

DON'T GET CAUGHT UP IN THE FRENZY

Many students get totally caught up in the college admissions frenzy without actually realizing that there are more than 4,000 colleges in the United States that have to stay open, so they are looking for students. In other words, you have a much better chance of getting in than you think.

Some advice for you:

- Remember that it is not what college you get into but what you do while you are there that matters the most.

- Even if you think you cannot get into a college, apply anyway.

- Make sure to apply to colleges other than just your favorite one. Even if you consider them a back-up plan, take the time to make a list and apply.

- Be true to yourself about what you want out of a college experience. If you really do not want one that is academically rigorous, that's totally fine. Just be up front about it.

- If one certain college is your dream but you don't fit the academic requirements, apply anyway. If you stand out in any way at all, you just may make it in after all.

— **LAURA JEANNE HAMMOND,**
Editor in Chief, *Next Step Magazine*

COLLEGE SCORE SHEET

Name of school: _____

Date visited: _____

Who went with me: _____

Contacts I made at the school: _____

_____

FOOD	1	2	3	4	5	6	7	8	9	10
CAMPUS	1	2	3	4	5	6	7	8	9	10
DORMS	1	2	3	4	5	6	7	8	9	10
GREEK	1	2	3	4	5	6	7	8	9	10
COMMUNITY	1	2	3	4	5	6	7	8	9	10
_____	1	2	3	4	5	6	7	8	9	10
_____	1	2	3	4	5	6	7	8	9	10

TOTAL SCORE: _____

Questions:

How does this place make me feel? _____

Best thing about this place: _____

_____

_____

Worst thing about this place: _____

_____

What is the city like? _____

_____

What special services are offered to help B students? _____

_____

Overall comments: _____

_____

_____

_____

Chapter 1: Where to
Find Colleges That
Welcome B Students

CHAPTER TWO

IT'S NEVER TOO LATE: TAKE THE NECESSARY STEPS TO MAKE A CHANGE FOR THE BETTER RIGHT NOW

Procrastination (pro-kras-ten-a-shun): that annoying habit that tends to follow us throughout our lives, convincing us that we can easily put off until tomorrow what we should be doing today (or yesterday) and not have to pay any consequences. (For an example, see the character of Scarlett O'Hara in the classic *Gone with the Wind*, who coined the phrase, "Fiddle-dee-dee, I'll think about it tomorrow!")

We've all done it. You will start the project/diet/chore/report/whatever tomorrow. Tomorrow, as little red-headed Annie reminded everyone in a relatively annoying song, is always a day away. It's eternally full of promise and potential. Unfortunately, when tomorrow arrives, it's today already, so we just repeat the mantra and everything is bumped one more time.

When it comes to getting ready for college, procrastination can be positively lethal. You already know that multiple forms have to be turned in early, from applications to financial aid requests. It doesn't stop there.

If your grades and test scores are not where you want them to be, there are no overnight miracles, potions or cures you can use. But there are steps you can take to brighten the picture a bit, especially if you are still in your sophomore or junior year.

Here is the list. Read it now (don't wait until tomorrow!) and you will already have a leg up on the competition. Some of these things are fairly simple; others take a lot of self-discipline. Fortunately, that is good practice for your college days ahead.

(1) Improve your grades ASAP.

Don't try to get out of improving your grades just because the school year is already partially over. Unless it's less then two weeks until summer vacation, there is still time to make a difference in that GPA. Here are some great ideas to try—TODAY, not tomorrow or next week. Don't be a Scarlett.

First of all, don't generalize your grades or the challenges of certain subject areas. If you're like most students (or human beings for that matter), you're stronger in some subjects than others. Think about which subjects give you the most trouble. Pinpoint the class or classes. Now narrow it down further. WHAT in that class is tough for you? In English, is it the reading or the writing? Is it the grammar or the composition? If it's science, is the difficulty in the lab or in reading the text? What formula or concept in math is bogging you down? If you can be specific about the problem, it is easier to find steps that will help you change things.

Once you know what issues are giving you the most trouble, do something about it. Here are just a few suggestions:

- Ask your teacher for help before or after class.

- Find a student who can help explain certain concepts.

- Join or create a study group.

- Get a tutor.

- Ask your parents for help.

What else can you do? If you are not already doing so, TAKE NOTES. By taking down what the teacher is saying and putting it in your own words, you are focusing and repeating key information. These notes should be as organized and neat as possible and then they should be read over at least once a day to make sure the material is sinking in. Studies have proven that you can learn far more reading short amounts of material each day rather than cramming lots of details in a few hours.

Go over your past tests, quizzes, worksheets and homework assignments. If you did something wrong on them, make sure you understand what it was. If you don't, then ask. There is nothing wrong with making mistakes if you turn around and use the experience for learning and understanding more.

Lastly, check to see if there is a way to earn some extra credit in the class where you are struggling. If there is, do it. It will help your overall grade and make a better impression on your teacher.

(2) Reorganize your priority list.

At the risk of sounding like your parents (and one day, you will realize how intelligent they really are), one of the most important steps you can take in high school is to make your studies a top priority. Does that mean that you will never see your friends and that you must give up any semblance of a social life? No. Instead, it simply means that when you think about your day, school should be high on the list, somewhere below breathing, eating and drinking, but way above watching *The Three Stooges* marathon on television.

If you have homework and your best friend calls and asks you to come over and hang out, give it some thought. Do your best to look beyond the fun of the moment to the potential reward down the road. It's not easy—but it is the mature thing to do (so be sure and let your parents know you made the responsible decision and earn a few brownie points in the process).

By making school a priority, other things will fall into line. Doing homework and studying for tests means better grades, and better grades mean a higher GPA and most likely a better performance on the SAT or ACT. In turn, both of those will strengthen your chances of getting into more colleges. Amanda (Mandy) Warhurst Webster, senior associate director of admissions at Salve Regina University, says, "Students must realize that the senior year is very important. You have to remain focused on academics and come in with a very strong first semester."

(3) Use your summers wisely.

Counting down the days to summer break is an educational tradition. Imagining how you are going to spend those long, hot, lazy summer days can keep you occupied for hours. Chances are that your plans include sleeping in, being with friends, finding a beach, exploring a career as a couch potato and generally doing as little as possible. Without ruling out those possibilities, why not include a few things that could actually raise your chance of college admission? Here are a few possibilities:

- **Get a job that will teach you important skills.** Colleges value students who work because it demonstrates responsibility and maturity. The skills you gain will also help you move up the ladder so that the next job you have will be better.

- **Read that list of books your English teacher handed out.** Doing this will not only give you a head start on the fall but will also help you prepare for the standardized tests.

- **Volunteer in your community.** Colleges like to see students who are involved and give back to their neighborhood or community. Plus, think of the sense of satisfaction that you'll receive from helping an elementary school child read or by making the life of a senior citizen less lonely.

- **Take a summer school class at your high school or a community college.** You can do this to review material from a class that you didn't do as well in or to get a jump start on your classes for the fall. The biggest question that college admissions officers ask when reviewing your application is this: Will you be able to handle the academic courses at this college? Show that you will by taking a class.

You still have lots of days to be lazy or sleep in, so find a balance.

Please remember that difficulty of admissions does NOT equal quality of education. Just because a school is really difficult to get accepted into does not guarantee that it is the highest quality or best fit for you. Keep an open mind. If you haven't heard of the college, it doesn't mean that it isn't a wonderful place. I am personally biased towards small colleges—they give you individual attention, professors and other administrators know your name and you have the chance to develop the academic self-confidence you need.

— **Judith Mackenzie,** *Mackenzie College Consulting*

(4) Start on that college essay NOW.

College essays (as you'll see in Chapter Four) can be extremely helpful in getting admitted to colleges. Don't wait to plan what you will say in an essay until you have to actually write it. Begin to brainstorm ideas and work on the basics you will need to know to write an outstanding essay. Don't put it off! That would be like waiting until the homecoming game to work on your tackling or waiting until the debate tournament to think about what position you are taking on an issue. Start now!

Brush up on basic English skills and start thinking about what ideas you might want to write about. Refer to the sample questions listed in Chapter Four and think about how you would answer each one. Go to the library and check out a book on writing a quality, winning college essay. Read the samples to get a feel for what admissions officers seem to prefer. Think how you would approach the same or similar topic. Line up your reasons, examples and anecdotes now, not later.

(5) Get to know your guidance counselor.

For many students, the guidance counselor is just one of those people in the background of your high school life. You rarely see him or her except on special occasions (or if you are in trouble). You have time to change all that! Schedule a visit with your guidance counselor. Ask for tips on how to improve your chances of getting into college. Ask for help in searching out the best options. A guidance counselor is a person that is there to help you, so make yourself accessible. Ask questions. Follow up on advice.

(6) Shed the fluff and take advanced placement, honors or college prep courses.

A number of colleges do some rearranging of your grades that you might not be aware of. They will look at the classes you took in high school, throw out the "fluff" classes and recalculate the "core" classes. Journalism, shop, drama, home economics—all gone. Only science, math and English might remain. For many students, this is an unpleasant surprise because the grades they got in their elective classes were the ones responsible for driving up their overall GPA. Knowing this, you might want to choose different classes for your junior and senior years. Throw out the easy classes and take advanced placement or college prep courses instead. Some suggestions include these classes: algebra, geometry, foreign language, laboratory science and English. The honest fact is that a B in a core class will benefit you more than an A in any fluff class.

Patrick O'Brien adds, "Junior year for many is like boot camp, or to say it another way, it's more like college while the frosh and sophomore years are more like middle school. It is a breakthrough year with greater opportunities but also greater challenges. More self-direction is expected," he adds. "You should expect it of yourself. Keep all things in balance."

Mark Campbell, vice president for enrollment management at McKendree College, advises high school students, "Don't be tempted to take the soft senior year. Continue to develop your writing!"

Here is a helpful chart for converting your grades over to the point system used for computing GPAs.

A	4.0
A-	3.7
B+	3.3
B	3.0
B-	2.7
C+	2.3
C	2.0
C-	1.7
D+	1.3
D	1.0
D-	0.7
F	0.0

(7) Get passionately involved in your community.

Another factor that can help you get accepted into college is a history of being actively involved in your community in some way. Don't wait until the summer of your senior year to do this. Start looking around now for ways to play a part in your community. Make sure that you are sincere; don't become involved just to impress the admissions departments of colleges. Do it to learn and explore, and to discover more about yourself. Find a place of service that is in an area of great interest to you. Then you will find your passion, and it will mean more to you than just wanting to look good on a piece of paper. And there's another plus—you will be able to write or talk about that passion in your essay or interview.

Some possible areas in which to get involved include volunteering at places such as these:

- schools
- crisis intervention centers
- homeless shelters
- park and recreation centers
- community gardens
- nursing homes
- libraries
- hunger relief centers
- humane society
- theatres

(8) Get a coach, tutor, mentor and/or study buddy.

Just like it is better to study several days before a test rather than several hours (or minutes!) before, why wait to find someone who can help you succeed in so many ways? If you are not doing well in a class, do not hesitate to ask for help. Talk to your teachers. Get a tutor. Find a student who will study with you. Hire a study coach. Learn from a mentor. Do what you need to do now to improve those grades, as well as your own enthusiasm, dedication and passion.

If the term "mentor" is new to you, here is some helpful information. A mentor is a guide and counselor, someone that gives advice and helps you think through decisions. The term "mentor" carries with it the connotation

THE TOP FIVE FACTS ABOUT LEARNING DISABILITIES

When someone has a learning disability, what he or she should be able to do is different from what he or she is able to do. Learning disabilities are invisible, life-long conditions. You can't tell by looking at a person that he or she has one, and learning disabilities can't be cured. One in every ten people has a learning disability.

A learning disability may mean you have difficulty with any of the following:

● spoken language

● written language

● coordination

● self-control

● organizational skills

● attention

● memory

FACT 1: People with LD are smart. People with LD have average to above average intelligence. Some people prefer to think of LD as a "different learning style" or a "learning difference." That's because you CAN learn, but the way in which you learn is different. You have a unique learning style.

FACT 2: There are many types of LD.

Dyslexia is usually thought of as a reading disability although it also means having problems using language in many forms.

Dyscalculia causes people to have problems doing arithmetic and understanding math concepts. Many people have issues with math, but a person with dyscalculia has a much more difficult time solving basic math problems.

Dysgraphia is a writing disorder that causes people to have difficulty forming letters or writing within a certain space.

Dyspraxia is a problem with the body's system of motion. Dyspraxia makes it difficult for a person to control and coordinate his or her movements.

Auditory memory and processing disability describes problems people have in understanding or remembering words or sounds because their brains don't understand language the way typical brains do.

FACT 3: LD is hereditary. No one knows the exact cause of LD but it is believed to be a problem with the central nervous system, meaning it is neurological. LD also tends to run in families. You may discover that one of your guardians or grandparents had trouble at school. LD is not caused by too much sugar, guardians who aren't strict enough or allergies.

FACT 4: LD must be assessed by a psychologist. Diagnosing LD involves a number of things. You and your guardians will be interviewed to find out what kind of problems you have had, how long you have had them and how seriously they have affected you. Your teachers should be interviewed as well.

You will be given several tests. These aren't the same kind of tests you take in school. Instead, the person testing you will ask you questions and get you to complete certain tasks. Once the tests are finished, the examiner looks at how you are doing at school and compares that with how you should be doing given how smart you are (your intelligence). If there is a difference between these that can't be explained by other reasons, then a diagnosis of LD is often made.

FACT 5: There is no cure for LD but lots can be done to help. One of the most important things you can do to help yourself is to understand what your particular LD is. It is also important for you to recognize and work on your strengths. Your guardians and teachers will help you learn about how to cope with your learning problems better by teaching strategies that can minimize their effect.

Source: Reprinted with permission from the Learning Disabilities Association of BC

that the person brings a certain knowledge that comes from wisdom and experience—in other words, a mentor is someone who "knows the ropes"—a friend, coach, tutor, teacher, counselor or even a relative that has been where you are. Research has shown that mentoring relationships can help students to develop work ethics and a sense of responsibility, as well as help raise self-esteem, strengthen communication skills and improve personal relationships. The skills that mentors can teach you will most likely help in high school and certainly in college.

(9) Make sure you aren't working "around" an undiagnosed learning disability.

If you have been continually struggling in school and it has been showing up in your grades and test scores, make sure that you have been tested for learning disabilities. It is possible that you have an undiagnosed issue that has caused you to develop a different learning style. Talk to your guidance counselor or family physician. Many of the colleges today welcome students with various learning disabilities and they have special programs geared especially for them.

Not sure what qualifies as a learning disability? It's a blanket term that covers everything from not being able to sit still in class to not being able to read very well. There are many people who dislike the phrase "learning disability." They believe that instead of calling areas of challenge "disabilities," people should realize that some students simply have found other approaches to gaining knowledge that are perhaps different from most people's ways of learning.

Review the information about learning disabilities from an organization called the Learning Disabilities Association of BC. Know the facts about learning disabilities.

Worried that learning disabilities will interfere with your education? There are many successful people who have made the "LD" list, such as Whoopi Goldberg, Magic Johnson, Nelson Rockefeller, Jay Leno and Charles Schwab. Not too shabby, eh? You wouldn't mind being in such good company, would you?

(10) Take classes at your local junior college.

Start your college career while you are still in high school by taking classes at your local junior or community college. Many of these institutions are open to the idea. Terry O'Banion, former president of the League for Innovation in the Community College, explains the possibilities. "In the last decade or so, many high schools and community colleges have created articulated programs to allow students enrolled in high school to take courses for community college credit," she says. "Called 'dual or concurrent enrollment,' the practice is very widespread and is likely to expand in the next few years.

"The practice emerged because able high school students often exhaust the supply of solid courses by their senior year; there is no reason to wait until they graduate from high school to begin taking college-level courses," adds O'Banion. "Additionally, community colleges and high schools in the same region share common purposes of preparing students for the workforce or for further education, and they can enhance that purpose by creating opportunities for high school students to take courses at the local community college to round out their schedules," she concludes.

Tonia Johnson, associate director of admission at Guilford College, also discourages students from leaving school early in their senior year. Just because you have all the credits you need doesn't mean you need to cut your year short. A better plan is to use this time to do something that will impress admissions officers. "Take courses somewhere, get involved in an internship, but use the time wisely," she says.

Regardless of the stage at which you need to make changes, don't look back at your mistakes: look forward to your possibilities. Making that difference can be enough to get your admissions application placed in the "accepted" pile instead of that other stack. Write out a list of the top ten things you want to change, pin it up and give it the attention it needs. You might be surprised at the results!

GETTING IN

BEYOND THE BASIC APPLICATION FORM: EXPLAINING WEAKNESSES AND BUILDING ON STRENGTHS

CHAPTER THREE

GPAS, SATS AND ACTS, OH MY!

Let's face it. If you're reading this book, it means those wonderful acronyms in the title of this chapter are not among your strong points. For one reason or another, your overall GPA or your test scores are just not that remarkable.

What can you do about that? One possibility is to check out the colleges that do not require standardized test scores as part of their admissions process. "What?" you ask in amazement. There are colleges that don't want those all important numbers? That's right. In fact, there are more than 700 of them and they can all be found at www.fairtest.org.

Why would some colleges choose not to rely on ACT and SAT scores? Here is how Fair Test explains it:

> "*Test scores are biased and unreliable.* Standardized college admissions tests are biased, imprecise and unreliable, and therefore should not be required for any college admissions process or scholarship award. If test scores are optional, students who feel that their strengths are reflected by their SAT or ACT scores can submit them, while those whose abilities are better demonstrated by grades, recommendations, a portfolio or a special project are assured that these will be taken into full account. Sometimes admissions officers use low test scores to automatically reject qualified candidates without even considering their schoolwork. That's simply not fair.

> "*Test scores are nearly useless in college admission.* Research shows that the SAT and ACT do not help colleges and universities make significantly better admissions decisions. The University of Chicago Press book, *The Case Against the SAT*, found that the SAT is 'statistically irrelevant' in college admission. It also proves that the SAT undermines the goal of diversity by reducing the number of qualified minority and lower-income students who are admitted."

If you are applying to a school that requires SAT or ACT scores, Fair Test encourages you to ask some important questions including these:

- How does your school use the SAT and/or ACT?

- Are cut-off scores used? If so, do they apply to general admissions or to particular programs?

- Does your school use any statistical formula which includes SAT/ACT scores to judge applicants' academic records?

- Do you take possible coaching into account when considering ACT or SAT scores?

- How does your college report SAT and ACT scores in handbooks and brochures?

- Does this college report simple averages or a range of scores? Does this include all entering students' scores in these figures, in compliance with the Good Practice Principles of the National Association for College Admission Counseling?

So, if all of this is true, why do most colleges rely so heavily on the results from standardized tests? It's a matter of "measurement." If you think about it, an A at a high school in Chicago may be different than an A at a high school in Los Angeles. In fact, an A at two high schools in the same school district or even with two different physics teachers at the same high school may be different. Because schools have varying ways of awarding grades and varying levels of difficulty, colleges need a uniform way to measure students. The SAT and ACT have become those measures. A great deal of importance is given to the scores achieved on them.

In fact, a good performance on college-entrance tests has become the focus of many a student's "free" time past the hours when the high school doors are closed for the day. In recent years, "test prep" has become more than just an option. It's a booming business! During the last few years, it has grown from $100 million to more than triple that. More and more students are putting out big bucks to prepare themselves to take the SAT.

So while standardized tests may be unreliable and not every college requires them, it doesn't look like they are going away anytime soon. If you are applying to a college that requires test scores, then you have little choice but to "bite the bullet" and take the test.

Meet the New Tests

As you probably know, most colleges consider test scores when making admission decisions. Let's take a look at these exams:

SAT Reasoning Test (www.collegeboard.com)

- The exam has three sections—Critical Reading, Math and Writing—each scored between 200 and 800 points for a total possible score of 2400.

- The Critical Reading section is 70 minutes long with two 25-minute sections and one 20-minute section. It contains reading comprehension, sentence completion and paragraph-length critical reading sections. This section replaces the old verbal section.

- The Math section is 70 minutes long with two 25-minute sections and one 20-minute section. It contains multiple-choice questions and student-produced responses on numbers and operations, algebra, geometry and statistics, probability and data analysis.

- The Writing section contains a 25-minute essay that is first and a 35-minute multiple choice section that has questions on identifying sentence errors, improving sentences and improving paragraphs.

ACT (www.actstudent.org)

- This exam has four multiple-choice tests and an optional Writing test. There is a score for each of the four tests (English, Math, Reading and Science) from 1 (low) to 36 (high), and the composite score is the average of the four test scores between 1 and 36.

- The English section has 75 questions in 45 minutes that test standard written English (punctuation, grammar and usage, sentence structure) and rhetorical skills (strategy, organization, style).

- The Mathematics section has 60 questions in 60 minutes that test pre-algebra (23 percent), elementary algebra (17 percent), intermediate algebra (15 percent), coordinate geometry (15 percent), plane geometry (23 percent) and trigonometry (7 percent).

- The Reading section has 40 questions in 35 minutes that test reading comprehension.

- The Science section has 40 questions in 35 minutes that test the "interpretation, analysis, evaluation, reasoning and problem-solving skills" of natural sciences.

- The optional Writing section has one essay prompt in 30 minutes that tests writing skills.

Tips for Getting a Higher Score

It goes without saying that doing well on the standardized college entrance exams (ACT/SAT) helps you get in the front door of most colleges. There are dozens of books to tell you how to do well on these standardized tests, so I will not attempt to do it here. Instead, here's a quick list of the most basic things you can do to assure that you do the best you can:

- Make a decision that the test is important to you and that you will give it time and effort.

- Get familiar with the test format so that this is not a surprise to you. Know what each test will cover. You can get free sample exams from the creators of the exams by going to www.collegeboard.com for the SAT and www.act.org for the ACT.

- Consider hiring a coach or tutor to help you prepare for the tests. There are intensive test preparation courses available from companies like Princeton Review (www.review.com) and Kaplan (www. kaplan.com), but there are also lower-cost options from community colleges and maybe even your high school.

- Go to the library or bookstore and start looking at all the test prep books. They come in several different formats. A recent trend is exciting novels of all kinds that entertain you while they introduce you to all of the vocabulary words you need to know for the test. Check the stories out at www.amazon.com or use a search engine to find "vocabulary SAT novels." The stories are so captivating that you completely forget that you are learning at the same time. SAT and ACT prep books are easy to find and will de-mystify the process for you.

- Check out websites on the Internet for test help. Just put "SAT test preparation" in the search box. Here are just a few of the many out there:

  www.review.com

  www.kaplan.com

  www.number2.com

  www.act-sat-prep.com

  www.4tests.com

  www.petersons.com

A last bit of advice before you take one of these standardized tests: Do not attempt to cram for them; it will never work. This is not that type of test. Instead go into the test well rested, following a good breakfast. Take the entire three hours and 35 minutes to complete it. Don't rush. If you get done early, just take the time to go back over your work. Don't panic when you see other students turning in their tests when you are far from done. Everyone has a different test pace, and getting done faster is not an indication of how anyone did. Know that you did the best you could and despite the scores, forge ahead. Colleges are waiting for you!

Taking the Credit; Taking the Blame

There will come a time within the application, essay or interview where you will be expected to either explain or discuss your SAT/ACT score and GPA. It's better to offer an explanation than to ignore your scores or GPA and hope that the admissions officers don't notice them. In fact, they will notice them, and without an explanation, they will have no reason to give you the benefit of the doubt.

Remember that admissions officers are human beings. They have made mistakes or struggled in some way in their lives. They will understand and listen, so take the time to explain honestly why you believe your numbers are not as high as you had hoped they would be.

Here is a list of the general do's and don'ts that you need to remember when discussing your less-than-stellar numbers. The key is to be honest at all times.

DO: Explain any circumstances that may have affected your numbers such as these:	DON'T:
frequent moves	whine
test anxiety or health issues	complain
learning disabilities	place blame on others (parents, teachers, etc.)
part-time jobs	adopt a "poor me" attitude
extenuating personal or family issues	be emotional

As you can see, it's important to take responsibility for your performance. Instead of making excuses or blaming others, state the facts and own up to how you did. There are legitimate and understandable reasons for not doing as well as you are capable of doing. Some of these reasons were listed above. But make sure that you do not confuse explanations with excuses. Not having a date to the spring formal is not a good reason.

Also have a balance between providing enough information to make your case but not so much information that your explanation is overwhelming. For example, you might write that having a severely ill parent affected your ability to concentrate on your studies for a semester, but you don't need to also provide the detail of every medical procedure your parent has had.

If your grades are low in a specific subject, explain this. You can describe how you have sought extra help in the subject or how you took a summer school class to make sure you really understood the material, but it's still a weak area. You can also explain that you plan to major in another subject area in which you are stronger when you reach college.

It's important as well to note any progress that you've made. If you have since improved your grades in a subject area or overall, indicate this and explain that you have a renewed commitment to your studies.

HOW WILL MY SAT ESSAY BE GRADED?

Each essay will be scored independently by two high school and college teachers. Neither scorer will know what points the other one gave. Each reader will assign the essay a score ranging from 1 to 6. Essays with a 6 are outstanding, with few to no errors at all. These essays are built on a main point that is supported by stories, examples and reasons. Essays with scores of 6 are organized, focused, coherent, smooth and are indicative of a wide vocabulary. But not every essay is a 6. Let's look at what other scores can mean:

- A score of 5 indicates that the essay is effective, without being stellar. It is effective with only a few grammar/usage/mechanics errors.

- Essays that are scored with a 4 are considered competent, but with some gaps in quality.

- An essay with a score of 3 is adequate but has a number of errors, including grammar/usage/mechanics, vocabulary, focus or development.

- A score of 2 means that the essay is seriously limited with a number of weaknesses.

- An essay that is scored with a 1 is severely flawed.

For more detailed information on how the scoring is done, check out the College Board website at www.collegeboard.com.

Once you have discussed this topic, you can move on to focus on your strengths instead. Without dwelling on the negative, you have the opportunity to highlight how much you have to offer the college.

Include a Resume to Highlight What You <u>Have</u> <u>Accomplished</u>

Many colleges will let you submit a resume. You may already have one on hand thanks to summer job searches. This can provide a beginning. The resume you used for looking for a summer part-time job might give you some quality information to use, but it probably will need changes before you share it with a college. Why? Two reasons: one, time has most likely passed since you wrote it and there may be new things to add, and two, your intention is different. You aren't trying to impress a potential employer so that he or she will give you a weekly paycheck. This time, the goal is to impress a college admissions officer and get you through the front door of the school.

Resumes are like the *Cliffs Notes* of your academic/educational and community life. They are the condensed version of the great stuff you have accomplished thus far. Resumes can be very effective. Here are some tips:

- Have high-quality paper.

- Choose a font size and style that is easy to read (at least 12 and below 18 and Arial, Times New Roman, Garamond or Franklin Gothic Book).

- Do not handwrite this resume. Even if you have to use the school or library computer, make sure this is neat and looks professional.

- Many word processing programs include a built-in resume wizard, so check and see if you can find one. This template walks you right through where to put what and then puts it in a format that looks great.

Here is what you need to include on your resume:

- full name

- current address

- telephone number (home and cell)

- email address

- all awards or honors you have earned

- all forms of community service

- all part-/full-time jobs

- references

- sports and extracurricular involvement—remember that these can be in school or outside of school!

One of the most important aspects of the resume is to include the pertinent details that truly explain what you have accomplished. For example, if you worked as a volunteer at a local children's day care center, include how many children you worked with and what responsibilities you held. This is the place where you can really shine in ways that your numbers do not reflect.

On Page 35 is an example of a typical type of resume you might want to include in your application. Look it over to see how you can adapt it to your needs.

After you have done all this hard work, don't blow it by not checking your spelling and grammar. The greatest resume will make a rotten impression if it has errors. Have someone else read over it before you finalize it. They may catch a mistake you missed—or remember something wonderful that you forgot to include.

A resume gives the opportunity to share with the college more than your grades and test scores. It gives them a snapshot of your achievements that will really help them understand what you have to offer.

A WORD ABOUT TEST ANXIETY

Feeling worried or pressured about taking a test is normal. Indeed, a slight edginess can often enhance your performance. However, if the worry turns into panic and/or fear and makes it almost impossible to study or take the test, you probably are suffering from test anxiety.

Test anxiety can strike before and/or during a test. It can make you feel physically sick, from a headache or nausea to faintness and hyperventilating. You might have a dry mouth, pounding heart or sweaty hands or be unusually emotional. It is often very difficult to concentrate at all.

How can you combat it? Here are some tips:

1. **Be prepared as much as possible for the test.** The SAT and ACT are cumulative exams that assess years of study in high school. They are not tests for which you can "cram." Get a good study guide and become familiar with what the SAT and ACT test. Try a few of the practice tests. Then relax and just do your best.

2. **Take good care of yourself.** Get enough sleep, eat healthy and get some regular exercise. Don't have any coffee before the test because caffeine increases your level of anxiety.

3. **Learn how to relax.** Sounds simple, but it can be challenging when your body and mind are trying to do just the opposite. Like with other things, practice is the key. Spend time learning how to think about each muscle group in your body. Start with your feet. Tighten them and then let them go. Work your way all the way up to your head. Breathe slowly and deeply.

4. **Replace negative thoughts with positive ones.** Instead of telling yourself, "I am just going to blow this entire test," say, "This may be a difficult test but I will do the best I can on it." Visualize yourself doing well on the test.

5. **When you are taking the test, remember those deep, slow breaths.** Be sure to read the test directions carefully. If you don't know a question, skip it and go back later.

6. **If you find yourself tensing up during the test, put down your pencil, take a few deep breaths, relax your neck and shoulders and then go back to it.** Go to another question or problem and come back to the one that made you anxious. Sometimes answering a few problems that you do know will help you remember the answer to the one that threw you a curve.

7. **When you are done, do something fun.** See a movie, go out to eat, meet with a friend or just take a well-deserved nap.

123 4th St.
Anytown, USA 10000

Phone 555-555-5555
Fax 555-555-5556
Email anystudent@aol.com

CHRIS SMITH

Community Involvement	Volunteered for six months (2015) at The Boys and Girls Club: helped organize and guide 30 children between the ages of 8 and 13 in multiple after-school activities. Learned skills of organization, teamwork, cooperation and discipline. Intern at Wheels Unlimited, my grandfather's bicycle repair shop, after school for two years (2013-2015). Learned how to serve customers, run a register and basic mechanics/engineering skills.
Extracurricular Activities	Participated in the Chess Club (2013) and the Debate Club (2014-2015). Director of the Drama Club (2014) and President of the Ski Club (2015).
Employment	June-August 2014 20 hours a week at Marin County Public Library June-August 2015 18 hours a week at the Community Theatre
Education	2012-2015 East County High School Summer 2014 Theatre Workshop Summer 2014 Sign Language 101 at St. Martin's Community College
References	Mr. Bob Smith, Youth Coordinator at the Boys and Girls Club, 555-222-1111 Mrs. Jean Youngblood, English/Language Arts Teacher, East County High School, 555-982-1120 Mr. Rod Cooper, High School Debate Coach, 555-888-1210 Miss Lindsay Francis, Professor of Sign Language, St. Martin's Community College, 555-333-0101
Awards received	Debate Team Regional First Prize, 2014 First Place, State Library Essay Contest, 2014 Heart of Gold, Volunteer Ribbon, 2015

CHAPTER FOUR

WINNING IN WRITING: THE ALL-IMPORTANT COLLEGE ESSAY

Not every college requires an essay, but most of them want to see one. If you are applying at one of the colleges that do not require ACT or SAT scores, for example, the college essay is extremely important. Bottom line: The chances are pretty good you will have to write an essay. And, putting aside your fears for a moment, you will come to realize that this is a good thing.

For many admissions officers, your essay is the first chance they get to see the real you. They already know your grades, test scores and what classes you have taken for the last four years, but they don't know YOU. Sure, they are looking at how well you remember those grammar and punctuation rules, as well as what kind of vocabulary you use, but they also want a glimpse of your personality, ambitions, talents, goals and dreams.

College essays have become such an important part of the admissions process that there are many books dedicated to showing you how to write them. Many also give sample essays to read from students who were accepted by colleges. One excellent book is *Accepted! 50 Successful College Admission Essays* by Gen Tanabe and Kelly Tanabe. Check out the many websites on the Net dedicated to the topic.

Be aware there are unscrupulous companies and people willing (for a price) to take the headache out of your hands and write the essay for you. Yes, you can buy your college essay. Is this ethical? What do you think? Not only is this wrong, but it also won't help you get into college. Purchased essays are never able to convey the real you to a college. Don't ask a friend or relative to write it for you either. The admissions officers are good at spotting styles that don't fit with students. Also consider that if you turn in something that reads like Ernest Hemingway, but your GPA in English class has always been a B or less, a red flag will pop up immediately.

But the best reason for writing your own essay is that regardless of your skill, you can write a successful essay that will reflect your personality and your passion for life. It's not as hard as you might imagine! Read on to learn how.

The questions and/or topics you might be given to write about in college essays vary a great deal in subject area. Regardless of the question, the point

TYPICAL ESSAY QUESTIONS

- Describe your most significant personal experience. How has it influenced you?

- Identify and discuss a problem facing your generation.

- What have you read that has had a special significance to you? Explain why.

- Describe a person or experience of particular importance to you.

- Describe the reasons that influenced you in selecting your intended major field of study.

- If you could travel through time and interview a prominent figure in the arts, politics, religion or science, whom would you choose and why?

- Describe your experience in living in a racially, culturally or ethnically diverse environment; what do you expect to need to know to live successfully in the multi-cultural society of the future?

- Make up a question, state it clearly and answer it. Feel free to use your imagination, recognizing that those who read it will not mind being entertained.

- Indicate what you consider your best qualities to be and describe how your college education will be of assistance to you in sharing these qualities and your accomplishments with others.

- Evaluate a significant experience, achievement or risk that you have taken and its impact on you.

- Indicate a person, character in fiction, a historical figure or a creative work (as in art, music, etc.) that has had a significant influence on you and describe that influence.

- Why do you want to spend two to six years of your life at a particular college, graduate school or professional school? How is the degree necessary to the fulfillment of your goals?

- Use this space to let us know something about you that we might not learn from the rest of your application.

- How have you grown and developed over the four years of your high school career?

- What is the biggest risk you have ever taken? Explain why you took it and what you learned afterward.

- Discuss some issue of personal, local or national concern and why it is important to you.

- Write about your favorite book or film and tell why it has influenced you.

- Relate the most humorous experience in your life.

- You have just finished writing your 300-page autobiography. Please submit page 217.

is to say who you are. You will show that in how you respond, what anecdotes you use, what examples you include and so on.

Essay Mistakes to Avoid from the Get Go

Remember that you want your essay to stand out from the others in the pile on that admission officer's desk. You want to make a favorable and memorable impression and you want the reader of the essay to feel as if he or she is getting to know you. To make sure that your essay sounds unique and individual, take care to avoid certain pitfalls; for example, don't respond with the answers that everyone else does. If you are asked to write about a book you have read, don't pick the one that all high school students were required to read. Pick something unusual or different, a book that tells the admissions personnel something about you for choosing it. It does not matter if the admissions officer has ever heard of it. What matters is how you explain why it was an important book to you.

If you are asked to write about an event in your life, go beyond just describing it. Show how it affected your life and how you are different because of it. The trick here is not writing what everyone else does. Along with Dr. Seuss essays, admissions officers weary of reading essays that focus on the "I've seen the light" philosophy. You lost the game, but achieved a goal. Your parents got divorced/took drugs and it taught you a lesson. You had this favorite teacher or coach. It's one thing to write about something that you learned from the experience, but it's over the top to write that you've found the purpose of life through these experiences. It's easy to think that you have to be profound and philosophical when you write this essay, but the truth is that admissions officers see more than enough of this approach.

Other things to avoid

Don't try to be cute by adding poetry or illustrations unless they directly relate to your topic or your specific talent, don't use unusually fancy paper and never handwrite the essay. While it is okay to be emotional, do not whine, complain or be sarcastic. Avoid using current films, actors or television shows for your examples, and don't try to sell yourself. Represent the special person you are, but don't sound like an overzealous salesman working on commission. Don't use anyone else's idea even if it is interesting. It won't sound like you and your support will sound hollow.

Be funny, be enthusiastic, be reflective—but make sure it is not something that you and 4,000 other students wrote about. Go beyond the expected and you will get noticed. The college essay is often the deciding factor in

---

THIS IS YOUR CHANCE!

Quite often, the college application essay is the perfect opportunity to tackle the subject of your less-than-stellar-quality test scores or GPA. Many times you can tie the question you are asked to write about to the subject of your strengths and weaknesses. If you can directly address the issue in your essay, do so. Look back over the list of the most commonly asked questions. Can you see how you could relate your strengths to the topic? For example, "Use this space to let us know something about you that we might not learn from the rest of your application." You could explain how you have been persistent, dedicated, strong, determined, creative or any other admirable trait through examples. You can show the admissions officers that while your numbers may not be the strongest they have seen, you are a bright, skilled and wonderful student that would be an excellent addition to any college. Think of the essay as your time to shine!

whether you are accepted or rejected. You want your words to push you over the top.

Putting Words on Paper

College essays are typically 250 to 500 words. That is about one to two pages of typing, double spaced. According to the Common Application (www.commonapp.org), that limit is a guideline because colleges do not actually count the words. They won't mind if it is a little shorter or longer because quality is far more important than quantity. "College admissions officers are far more concerned that the essay is well written, proofread (not just spell-checked), well thought out, etc. Do not get caught up in the 'micro' (words, spacing, font size, color of ink)," states the website. "They are looking for the 'macro': does the student write well and what can they learn about this person from his/her essay?" Their website has more helpful information on what you will find on many college application forms.

Once you know the question, sit down and brainstorm possible answers. Just let your mind wander around the topic and write it all down without judgment or self-censorship. When you have run out of ideas, start going through what you have. What looks best? Throw out the things you could only write a paragraph about and keep the ideas that you can build into several pages of examples and facts that support a topic sentence. Look for the ones that make you feel emotional; that probably means they impacted your life in some way. Then choose one.

Now, write out an outline, just like you have done for other papers and reports you've done in school. What are the main points you want to cover? What details go under each point? For example, imagine that you have been asked to write about something you have read that was significant to you. Some points you might want to cover include these: Why you chose to read the book, how you felt while reading it, what new perspectives or points of view the author taught you, what questions the material raised in your mind, what you learned from the experience.

Once your outline is done, it is time to write your first draft (and yes, that means there will be second, third and more drafts before you're done). Do not start your essay with any of the following opening sentences:

- My name is Kevin Jones and I . . .

- I was born in Los Angeles, California, and . . .

- My college admissions essay is going to be about . . .

- I am writing this because I really want to go to your college . . .

- This is the story of my life so far . . .

- I am such a great person that you will want to read my story . . .

- My parents, Jean and Jasper Carpenter, first moved . . .

These are boring lead-ins and you will most likely have lost the reader's attention in the very first paragraph. Start with something interesting, eye-catching and unique. Grab the admissions officer's attention by writing something that will make him or her put down that cup of coffee, sit up straight in the chair and want to read what comes next.

Your first draft should be written without worrying about grammar, spelling or punctuation. You want to get your best thoughts down first, without being slowed down by rules. In case you don't remember the basic structure from endless English classes, you need the minimum of a five-paragraph essay. It should look pretty much like this:

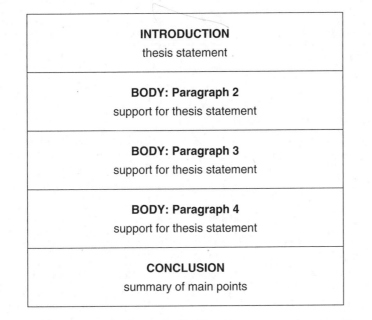

INTRODUCTION
thesis statement

BODY: Paragraph 2
support for thesis statement

BODY: Paragraph 3
support for thesis statement

BODY: Paragraph 4
support for thesis statement

CONCLUSION
summary of main points

When you are done, show the first draft to your friends and family. Ask their opinions. Should you give more detail? Was everything clear? Did it represent your personality? Is this how they would have imagined you answering the question? Listen carefully to their feedback so you can use it in your revisions.

Now write a second draft, pulling in any extra details you remembered and keeping others' comments in mind. This time, fix any spelling, grammar or punctuation errors. Share it with a favorite teacher or your guidance counselor. Get their comments. Go back to the desk. Go through it again, keeping the new feedback in mind. Run spell check (but do not depend on it) and print. You're ready.

What If I'm Not a Writer?

It is entirely possible that you are a whiz at math or a mad scientist, and writing just isn't your forte. If this is true, the college essay may be all that much more intimidating. So let's give your essay some thought before you begin to put words on paper.

Here are some ways to take your brilliant ideas and eventually come up with an essay. Which one sounds best to you?

- Get a tape recorder and tell what you would like to have in your essay. Consider this your first draft. Listen to it and refine it and when

LET ME EXPLAIN . . .

Remember in Chapter 3 how I talked about "taking the credit; taking the blame"? Let's return to this theme for a moment. An essay is one of your best opportunities to explain your grades. If you can do this clearly and honestly without resorting to whining and complaining, then you are doing yourself a huge favor.

Let's take a look at three partial sample essays that explain, in three very different ways, why these students' grades are less than stellar. Can you relate to what they say? How could you write your essay?

Example 1

Reaching and then maintaining high grades has always been a struggle for me. It wasn't that I didn't care about school, because I did. Basically, there were so many issues going on inside my house that I rarely had a moment to give to homework or studying. I have a younger brother named Kevin and he has cerebral palsy. He has to spend most of his time in a wheelchair and since both of my parents work, it is my job to take care of him as soon as I get home from school each afternoon. I don't mind doing it, but it really makes it hard for me to sit down and study for more than a few minutes at a time. Sometimes it also meant that I was up later than I should have been and then I was tired for class the next day.

Has your family experienced something that has made it harder for you to study and maintain good grades? It might be an illness or sickness, moving, divorce, a parent in the military, etc. Think about it for awhile. Maybe to help your family you have had to work two jobs. Perhaps you have had to help out in the family business. What are some reasons that you simply could not study or do as well in school as you had hoped?

Example 2

The only person that I can blame my poor grades on is me. For the first two years of high school, I just did not put the effort and time into my classes that they deserved. I spent most of my time playing sports and spending time with my friends. In my junior year, how-ever, that all changed. One of my best friends died in an automobile accident. It came as quite a shock to me. I guess, like a lot of other teenagers, I thought I was immortal and this accident proved me wrong. Moreover, it made me realize that time really is limited and if I wanted to go to college and pursue music, I had to start taking school a lot more seriously. Since that time, I have been working to make high school my first priority. It has not been easy and I am still struggling in a couple of my classes, but my GPA has steadily gone up.

Does this story sound familiar? Did something happen to you during your high school years that changed your perspective on things? Did you blow off school for a while and then something got your attention focused in a different direction? If you admit that once you didn't do so great but you're better now and why, it can be quite persuasive.

Example 3

My GPA is low for one reason and that is math. My teacher was very supportive and spent a great deal of extra time tutoring me but it never seemed to work. For whatever reason, math just continues to be incredibly difficult for me. As abysmal as I am at numbers, however, I excel with words. I love to read the writings of other authors as well as pen my own. I have kept journals since I was six years old and have written more than 100 short stories. I've won a number of local and regional contests and truly believe that my future will center on the publishing world. In the meantime, however, my math grades will keep pulling down my GPA and I will keep muddling my way through numbers while I am covering my notebooks with words.

Is there an area in which you stand out from the pack and another that is a constant struggle? Talk about it. Explain this challenge and what you have done to address it and even compensate for it. It is okay to honestly state that you are not as strong in one subject as you are in another. Show how you use that experience to fuel your productivity in areas where you do excel.

it centers on what you want to say, either type it as you listen or ask someone else to transcribe it for you.

- Sit down and talk to your parents or a special friend about your response to the essay question or topic. As you speak, have that person make a list or an outline of what points you mention. Once you have a basic roadmap, it can be easier to start writing the essay.

- Find some friends who are writers and ask for their tips, ideas and suggestions. Have one of them tutor you through the process as you write the essay.

- Get some books from the library that have sample essays and see if you can use them as inspiration.

- Ask your English teacher for some guidance in putting your ideas on paper.

- Check to see if the college you are applying to allows for some flexibility in the format of your essay. If so, you might be able to write it as a lab report or some other format that feels more comfortable to you. You might also see if a college will accept a verbal essay rather than a written one.

- Write the essay as best you can and then let someone who writes very well go over it for suggestions, corrections and revisions.

Out of Your Hands

It is done, gone and out of your hands. What happens to your essay now? That depends on the college. At least one person will read your essay. At smaller, more intimate colleges, it will probably be read by more than one person. Quite often the first person to see it is an admissions officer, commonly an alumnus of the college or someone with a strong background in education. If there are multiple readings, your essay passes next to another admissions officer or perhaps a director. At some colleges, it will even be presented to an entire admissions committee.

The college essay is important, so give it the time, attention and effort it deserves. In turn, the colleges will give your essay the time, attention and effort it deserves.

Winning in Admission—With Someone Else's Words

There is another important element of the admissions process that we don't want to overlook—personal reference letters. This time you don't have to sell yourself with your words; other people will do the job for you.

Whom should you ask to write a letter of reference? Common sense says to make it someone who likes you, right? Just don't make it your grandmother, best friend or boyfriend. Sure, they like you—even love you—but you need a letter that will show how a person has evaluated you as a potential student, not something about how you are the best granddaughter, friend or girlfriend in the world. Here are some potential people to ask:

- co-workers, employers or supervisors
- teachers
- coaches
- other school faculty
- your pastor
- karate instructor or sponsor of other activities outside of school
- if you have done volunteer work, ask the organization's leader

It may be tricky to ask someone at school for a letter of recommendation if you haven't done well in his/her class but don't rule it out. Explain to your teacher or counselor what you are trying to accomplish and you may find you have more of an ally than you had originally thought. If you have a reason for not performing to your full potential, let your teacher know. Explaining your circumstances can help your teacher write a more supportive letter that gives a fuller picture of who you are.

How do you go about asking for a letter of reference? Ask in person rather than by email or telephone. This way you can show how much it would mean to you to have this individual's personal recommendation.

Be sure to give the person plenty of time to write a quality letter. Don't walk up to your boss at the end of the shift and say, "Before I go home tonight, could you write a reference letter for me?" Ask weeks ahead if possible. If there are word limits or other restrictions on the letter's format, be sure to tell the person before he or she begins writing.

Some people may not know how to write a personal reference letter, so be ready to tell them what it should include. Provide a resume or summary of some of your achievements to help the different individuals that you ask to write letters, and include a stamped, addressed envelope to the school. The typical letter should be about one to two pages in length and should include these elements:

- The identity of the writer

- The writer's relationship to you (teacher/student; employer/ employee, etc.)

- Why the writer has chosen to recommend you as a potential candidate for college

- Examples and illustrations of the strong points that he or she has observed in you

- An overall evaluation of you as a student, community volunteer, all-around person

- A conclusion

Afterwards, always, always, always show your appreciation and gratitude for each person's help. A thank you note is really good manners, but a direct and sincere thank you face to face is great too.

CHAPTER FIVE

WINNING IN WORDS: THE ALSO-IMPORTANT COLLEGE INTERVIEW

You may or may not have won over those admissions officers or committee members with your written words, so now it's time to dazzle them with your verbal wit. The college interview is important as it is another chance to show a school just who you are, why you want to attend their college and why they should count themselves lucky to get you (in a humble fashion, of course). It is also another chance to explain why your numbers are not as high as they could be.

While not all colleges require an interview, if you are given the opportunity, take it. Interviews may be held at the college with an admissions officer, which requires a trip to the school. But sometimes interviews are conducted in your community by local alumni. You should look forward to the opportunity of an interview. In fact, you might find it easier to discuss issues face to face rather than on paper.

Of course, unlike the essay, an interview doesn't afford you the chance to brainstorm, outline, think about, mull over, ponder and weigh the questions. Your responses are going to be on the spot, so preparation is the key to not looking like a befuddled idiot desperately searching for the right answers.

What kinds of questions will you be asked during the interview? They are similar to the kinds of questions that are used as essay topics. But the essay has just one question to answer or one topic to explore. In the interview, however, you typically answer a number of questions and converse with an interviewer or panel for 15 minutes to an hour. Topics to be discussed are often divided into categories like school/classes, teachers, extracurricular activities, community, college and the world in general. Here are some typical examples. As you read these questions, think about how you would answer each one.

● How would you describe your high school?

● How do you fit into your school?

- If you could change one thing about your school, what would it be? Why?

- What has been your favorite/least favorite class in school?

- Who was your favorite/least favorite teacher in school? Why?

- How do you spend your free time and/or summers?

- Do you have a hobby of some kind? Tell me about it.

- Why are you interested in coming to this college?

- Where do you see yourself four years from now?

- What would you like to change about yourself?

- What are the three words that best describe you?

- What accomplishment are you most proud of?

- Why do you think you are a good match for this college?

- What do you think about _____ (current event, literature, art, music or other contemporary subject)?

Who will ask you these questions? It depends on the college. It may be an admissions officer, another student, faculty member, alumnus or panel of interviewers.

Keep in mind that a college interview is usually more like a casual chat over coffee, not a white-light-in-your-face interrogation. If you have a good sense of humor, the interview is the time to show it. If you have a talent, skill or ability that just did not fit on the application form or in your essay, speak now or forever hold your peace. If you can, find out if the interview is considered to be informational (just getting some facts about you and a time for questions and answers) or evaluative (part of the admissions criteria).

Feeling nervous as you go into the interview is understandable. In a way, it is a good thing because it will give you that extra boost of adrenaline you need to keep on your toes and pay attention. A person who isn't at least a little bit nervous may not do as well as one who is!

To make this less of a stressful event, practice what you are going to say ahead of time. Entertain your friends and family with it. Speak in front of the mirror or to an understanding guidance counselor. Prepare an answer for all the possible questions so you are ready, no matter which one the officer may ask.

The bottom line of the interview is simple—it is not the end all, be all of the admissions process. It will not usually make or break your acceptance. The person talking to you is a human being and may well have gone through the exact same thing you are going through right now. This means you will glimpse some compassion, empathy and even a smile during the interview. Relax, take a few deep breaths and let the special person that you are shine out!

According to the people at www.collegeboard.com, there are 13 things to avoid in a college interview. Are you paying attention? Here they are!

Don't:

- Be late

- Memorize speeches—instead sound natural and conversational

- Ask questions covered by the college catalog

- Chew gum

- Wear lots of cologne or perfume

- Swear or use too much slang

- Be arrogant—there's a fine line between being confident and boasting

- Lie—it will come back to haunt you

- Respond with only "yes" or "no" answers

- Tell the school it's your safety or last choice

- Be rude to the receptionist or any other staff you meet

- Bring a parent into the interview

- Refuse an interview

During the interview, more than your words count. While you don't have to come to the interview in a suit and tie or wear a dress, you shouldn't show up in shorts and tank top either. Be professional in your appearance. As you

HOW DO I RESPOND TO QUESTIONS LIKE "TELL ME ABOUT YOUR GREATEST FAILURE" OR "WHAT IS YOUR BIGGEST WEAKNESS?"

Contrary to what it may seem, these are not trick questions. They ask you to examine yourself closely and to be honest. Admissions officers often ask questions like these to draw out meaningful experiences in your life that show you have coped with a variety of challenges. To prepare for a question like this, just think a moment about what kind of difficult moments you have had to deal with in your life. Did your parents get divorced? Did you lose a friend? Think about what you have had to struggle with. Did you have trouble with a certain subject? How did you overcome your difficulty? What personality trait gives you the most trouble? What do you do about it? When you answer a question like this, you may just find out some amazing things about yourself that you had not realized yet!

YOUR INTERVIEW HOMEWORK

Remember those college brochures filled with pictures, statistics and text cultivating dust balls under your bed? Dig them out before your interview and do something really radical—read them! It is not necessary to read them cover to cover, but knowing such basic facts as where the school is located, what kind of environment it has, some of the courses it offers and some of the activities you may choose to participate in is a good idea. It does not impress interviewers to discover that students who are applying to their beloved alma mater do not even know what state it is located in or that the college is single sex. (There was an applicant who actually made it to the interview before he learned that the college he was applying to was an all-women school!)

Try to talk to relatives or friends who attend or have attended the college. They can give you insights into the college that are not found in the glossy brochures. The more you know the better.

Doing your homework will allow you to be able to ask intelligent questions. You are making the most important decision of your life so far. It makes sense that you would have a question or two about it. Having prepared questions not only helps create the two-way conversation dynamic, but it also demonstrates that you are serious about attending the college.

Not all questions are good questions, and in particular, avoid asking those obvious ones where the answers are on the first page of the college's brochure. Instead, the best questions to ask your interviewers are those that make them reflect on their own experiences, require them to do a little thinking and elicit an opinion. Making your interviewers think or express their opinions makes the interviews more interesting for them and makes your question seem insightful and probing. Some examples:

● What do you think about the X department?

● How did the small/large class size affect your education?

● How did X college prepare you for your career?

● What was the best opportunity you felt X university provided you?

● What is the best/worst aspect of X university or X city?

● If you had to do it again, what would you do differently?

Think of some more questions like these and write them on a list with the most interesting ones at the top. Take this list into the interviews and refer to them when the conversation begins to stall and when your interviewers ask you if you have any questions.

Reprinted with permission from Get into Any College by Gen and Kelly Tanabe

talk to the interviewer, sit up straight and don't fidget. Be sure to make eye contact. Never interrupt, and shake hands at the beginning and the end.

Your college interview is also a chance for you to ask questions. By doing so, you often show initiative and curiosity—two traits most colleges are looking for in their students. Ask if the officer has any advice for you, ask a question about your potential major or ask about dorm activities and college lifestyle. Find out if there will be a new student orientation program, what activities are available for freshmen, what part-time job opportunities there are in the area or end with a zinger like, "Is there anything you would like to know about me in order to help you make a fair and final decision about my application?"

The interview is a unique opportunity to establish rapport with a person who previously only knew you as numbers and words on paper. Use it wisely and show the interviewer(s) what a fantastic person you really are!

THE MOMENT OF TRUTH

What happens when the admissions officer asks you, "How do you explain the fact that your SAT score or GPA is a little less than wonderful?" First, expect it. That way you can prepare for it. If it doesn't happen, then whew! you are off the hook. If it does, you're ready. Second, be honest. Don't say there was a computer error or you really did better than that. Third, don't place blame. Don't try and put those numbers off on rotten teachers, stupid tests or unfair grading. On the other hand, you can explain with a truthful assessment of factors that have affected your life. Was there a crisis during that time? Did you have to work extra hours that cut into study time? Were you heavily involved with sports or other extracurricular activities? Did you find high school boring or stifling? Without accusing others, tell the interviewer why you believe those numbers do not represent your real potential.

What should you do if the admissions officer does not ask about your numbers? That's a judgment call, and the answer rests with your gut instinct. If the interview has gone really well and you feel like you have established a good rapport with the officer, explaining those numbers without being asked can be seen as admirable. If you have not clicked with the officer, however, and the interview has had some awkward pauses, you might want to just skip this so things don't go downhill.

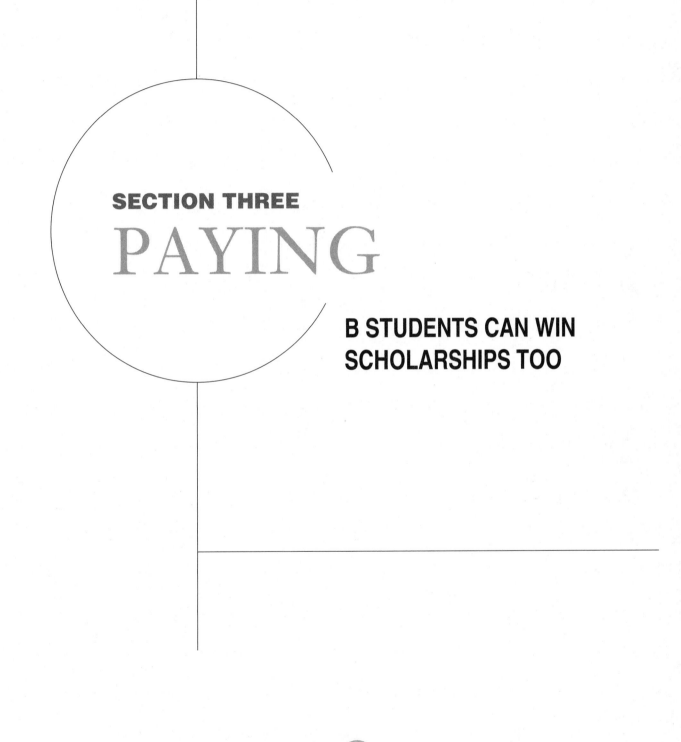

SECTION THREE

PAYING

B STUDENTS CAN WIN SCHOLARSHIPS TOO

B STUDENTS CAN WIN SCHOLARSHIPS TOO

"My GPA is not that hot . . . and my SAT scores were lousy because I had a temperature/didn't get enough sleep/forgot to prepare/had an argument with my boyfriend, so I wonder if I can even get into college. But heck, college costs thousands and thousands of dollars and my family cannot afford that. Why even apply? My parents don't have the money and scholarships only go to the straight A students anyway . . ."

Have you had that conversation with yourself? If so, you aren't the first and certainly won't be the last to do so. But be advised: Such thinking is a big mistake.

Without question, college costs a lot, and most families struggle to find enough money to pay for it. But those scholarships you keep hearing about are not just for the eggheads or overachievers who excelled in everything from U.S. history to trigonometry.

So who exactly gets scholarships besides those with high numbers? Let's take a look.

Students who show genuine financial need

And you thought growing up without a Porsche in the driveway was a bad thing? Scholarships were originally set up for these very students. They were put into place to support students' families financially so that college could be possible for many more than just those who can afford it. If your family has a genuine need to help you attend college, many scholarships may be available for you. The key to snatching one of them is simple: be honest about ALL your numbers, including finances; don't try to fudge those income levels. That isn't honest, and you will get caught. Also be prepared to show any extenuating circumstances behind those numbers. Was your mother laid off? Was there a medical emergency? Does your family have three kids in college already? These are important factors to include.

Students with a disability or illness

Not that you would wish for one, but if you happen to have a documented disability or illness, there is assistance for you because of it. A number of organizations support students with some kind of physical challenge. Scholarships are available from such sources as the Alexander Graham Bell Association, American Foundation for the Blind, Hemophilia Resources of America and the National Center for Learning Disabilities.

Students with specific majors

Already know what you want to do with the rest of your life? Countless organizations support young people who are pursuing certain careers. You must show that you are genuinely passionate about whatever field it might be, from digital photography to interior design. You will need to let the scholarship people know how you found out about the field, who mentored or inspired you, how your dedication grew and what skills you learned or developed. Have truthful, profound stories ready to share. Have you started your own business in this career already? Have you supported your fascination through volunteer work? Do you have recommendations from people in a related field? These are the factors that will help a committee select you above all others for that cash. Consider these examples: The American Nursery and Landscape Association has money for those who love flowers, trees and the outdoors. The Arabian Horse Foundation helps those who adore horses. Other organizations have money for those whose focus is cooking, construction, forestry, hospitality, the performing arts and more.

Students who show leadership

Are you known for taking charge and putting things together? Do you already have a few groupies that really like you? Scholarship committees are impressed with young people who have shown some form of leadership. If you have helped others by using your abilities in organization and guidance, or if you have inspired others, then this is the place to let it be known.

> **MYTH:**
> **YOU NEED STRAIGHT A'S TO WIN MONEY FOR COLLEGE**
>
> **The Truth:** While straight A's certainly don't hurt your chances of winning [scholarships and awards for college], you may be tempted to place too much importance on your grades. Many scholarships are based on criteria other than grades and are awarded for specific skills or talents such as linguistic, athletic or artistic ability. Even for scholarships in which grades are considered, GPA is often not the most important factor. What's more important is that you best match the qualities the scholarship committee seeks. Most students who win scholarships do not have the highest GPA. Don't let the lack of a perfect transcript prevent you from applying for scholarships.
>
> **— GEN AND KELLY TANABE,**
> *Get Free Cash for College*

What have you done? Show it, don't just tell it. Give concrete examples such as letters of recommendation, photographs and projects. Point out the responsibilities you have taken on and what they have taught you. Places like the Financial Service Centers of America, the Coca-Cola Scholars Foundation and Discover Card promote their own businesses by sharing their profits with students like you.

Students with particular religious backgrounds

If you have been wondering if God has been listening to those prayers, this might be your answer. To promote the growth and development of their religion or denomination, many church organizations offer students college scholarships. Okay, time for real honesty here. Do not try to get one of these scholarships or awards if the only times you go to church are to attend weddings, funerals and pray right before a major test. You have to be a true believer and show it through your active involvement with the church. Perhaps you lead a youth group, work in the church nursery, take classes from the pastor or participate in other areas of ministry. It is common to see scholarships from the Methodist, Catholic, Baptist and Presbyterian churches.

Students with superior athletic ability

Love to chase some kind of ball around? If you are the star football, basketball, baseball, tennis, golf or track star, chances are there is a college or organization that wants to give you the money to go to college. As Gen and Kelly Tanabe say in their book on scholarships, "Athletic scholarships are the Holy Grail. At their best, they can cover tuition and fees, room and board and books. That's not bad for doing something that you enjoy." Not sure if your sport is covered? Even the Ice Skating Institute of American Education Foundation and the National Archery Association have money to share. Check it out!

Students with a specific ethnic background

Time to look through your family tree. To celebrate their history and culture, some ethnic organizations are willing to give you money for school. This helps increase the number of minorities on campuses and also encourages students to go into professions they might have ignored or otherwise overlooked. Many groups are represented, including such organizations as the Sons of Norway and the National Italian American Foundation. Look for information regarding your heritage.

Students with hobbies

And your friends tried to say you were wasting your time! Not so. Scholarships are out there for young people who have serious hobbies. Of course, you have to show that you don't just pursue this hobby on rainy weekend afternoons, but that you are involved on a regular basis. You also want to prove dedication to this hobby by showing a consistent effort to improve the skills it takes to be good at what you do. Perhaps your hobby has even led you to awards and honors or to the creation of your own business.

WHERE TO FIND SCHOLARSHIPS

For most students, the hunt for scholarships is a short one. Many start with a scholarship book or head to the Internet. Unfortunately, most students end their search after exhausting these two sources.

Big mistake!

Books and the Internet are only the tip of the iceberg, and neither comes close to listing all the available scholarships. If you do your own detective work and canvass the community, you will uncover additional awards. Keep in mind that local scholarships may have smaller overall awards, but the chances of your winning them are much higher. Here's where to begin:

High school. The first stop in your scholarship hunt should be the high school counseling office. When an organization establishes a new scholarship (awards are created every year), high schools are the first places to get a notice. Over the years, most counseling offices have assembled a long list of scholarships. Don't reinvent the wheel if the counselor has already collected the information. Also remember that some high schools give out a set number of scholarships to their students each year and often less than that apply. In other words, all you would have to do to get the scholarship is fill out the papers!

Prospective colleges. Contact the financial aid office at every school you are interested in attending. Not only do the colleges themselves offer scholarships, but their financial aid offices also maintain lists of outside opportunities.

Civic and community organizations. Every community is home to dozens of civic organizations, such as the Rotary Club, Lions Club, Knights of Columbus, American Legion, Elks Club and VFW. Part of their mission is to support the community by awarding scholarships.

Businesses big and small. Many businesses such as newspapers, shopping malls, supermarkets and retailers offer scholarships to local students. For example, every Wal-Mart and Target store awards scholarships to students in the community. To find these opportunities, contact the manager at these businesses. You can get a list of businesses from the chamber of commerce or in the reference section of the public library.

Parent's employers/union. If your parents work for a large company, have them ask the human resources department about scholarships. If they are limited to the children of employees, there may be little competition for these awards. Also, if your parents are a member of a union, have them ask the union representative about scholarships.

Professional or trade associations. From accounting to zoology, every profession has its own associations, and many of these professional associations use scholarships to encourage students to enter the field. Start by looking at groups related to your future career.

Religious organizations. Your church or temple may offer scholarships to support members. If your local church does not have a scholarship program, check with the national headquarters.

Ethnic and cultural organizations. To promote a certain culture, develop leaders or encourage members to pursue higher education, many ethnic organizations sponsor scholarships.

WHERE TO FIND SCHOLARSHIPS

State and local governments. Make those tax dollars work for you by taking advantage of financial aid from state and local governments. Each state has a higher education agency that provides information on financial aid, and many administer state-based grant and loan programs. Closer to home, your county or city government may have awards for students in the community.

Private foundations and charities. As part of their mission to help the community, private foundations and charities often offer scholarships. To find these scholarships, visit your library and ask the reference librarian for a directory of local charities and foundations.

Friends and family. The more people who know you are looking for scholarships, the better. Friends and family members can be invaluable scholarship scouts as they go about their daily business. Scholarship opportunities have been uncovered on supermarket bulletin boards, standing in line at a bank, even on a bottle of aspirin. You never know where a scholarship will be publicized and who can help you to find it.

The Internet. Thousands of scholarships are just a click away. Websites such as Sallie Mae (www.salliemae.com/scholarships) make it easy to find scholarships free-of-charge. Although the Internet is a valuable resource, it is not a magic solution. Remember to use all the resources available to you.

Reprinted with permission from Sallie Mae How to Pay for College by Gen and Kelly Tanabe.

Discuss how this hobby has affected your life and what skills it has taught you. Be sure to include letters of recommendation from people who have seen what you are capable of. Do you spend hours doing graphic design on your computer? Have you sold some of your original logos to local companies? The Rhythm and Hues Studios might have money for you. Is photography all you can think about? Have you had your own displays at local stores? Do people call you to take pictures at their weddings or parties? Have your shots already popped up in the community newspaper? Talk to the National Press Photographers Foundation. Whatever your hobby, it's worth doing a little research to see if there are organizations with scholarships and awards for students just like you!

Students with parents who have generous employers

Check out your mom and/or dad's places of employment. It is not uncommon for businesses and corporations to include in their employee package some scholarship money for workers' children. Ask your parents to read through their employee handbooks again or just ask some questions. Who knows what hidden benefits your parent will find?

I hope you're convinced by now that just as colleges will happily take students with less-than-stellar grades and test scores, so will they just as happily take students who do not come from the wealthiest families. Financial aid is a huge part of college admissions and one that often means you can get that education you once told yourself was way out of reach. It's time to start an all-new conversation with yourself. Try something along these lines: "Hey, colleges really DO like me, and my family really CAN afford it now. So, what am I waiting for?" There you go.

Where Not to Find Scholarships

Watch out for scams. You already know this but it bears repeating: if it sounds too good to be true, it most likely is. Avoid any scholarship that asks you for payment, promises scholarships that NO ONE else has access to or asks for too much personal information like your Social Security number or bank account information.

Setting Your Priorities

Once you start searching for possible scholarships, you may easily find that there are so many that you are somewhat overwhelmed. Too many scholarships, too little time! It will help if you take time to prioritize them, i.e. decide which ones are the best fit for you. Ask yourself the following questions to help narrow down the list:

- How do you fit the mission or point of the award? Does it sound just like you or do you only match about 3 out of the 10 criteria?

- How much do academics count in each of the scholarships? Most organizations provide this information. If the only mention is a minimum GPA and yours is above that, you are set.

- How many awards are being given out? What are your overall chances of getting one?

- What is the scope of the competition? You will have a better chance of winning a scholarship that is only open to students in your county than one that is nationwide.

- How much is the award? Is it enough to make a difference? Consider the amount given, but don't just apply to the scholarships with the largest prizes because those often have the most competition.

Scholarship Essays

Scholarship essays and college admissions essays are not the same thing. When you are scheduling time to write your scholarship and college admissions essays, remember that the two are very different. While an admissions essay is geared to providing college admissions officers with an overall picture of who you are, the scholarship essay is targeted to the purpose of the scholarship itself. The people reading this are looking for something specific about you. For example, if you are applying for a sports scholarship, include information on the reason you play, what you have learned and how you have improved. If the scholarship is for future teachers, write about your experience with children and teaching or tutoring. Don't just list these things either in some kind of bulleted format. Instead, talk about the why, how or what behind it all.

How did you get involved? What new perspectives have you learned? Why do you want to pursue this further?

Time to recycle. You have been throwing your soda cans and water bottles in recycling containers for years now, so keep up the spirit and see if you can recycle any of your essays. The good news is that, naturally, this saves you time and effort. The bad news is that it isn't quite that simple. Before you decide to use Essay B for scholarship XYZ, make sure it actually fits. Read the question carefully and make sure you are addressing it specifically. You may be able to tweak certain parts of an essay and adapt something written for one college or scholarship to meet the criteria of others.

I hope you've seen from this chapter that scholarships are a possibility for any student, regardless of college-entrance exam scores or GPA. There are awards given for every background, talent or achievement. Many scholarship or award committees don't count grades or test scores as the most important factor. It is well worth taking some time to prioritize the scholarships you apply for. Then write the best application and essay that you can. With that combination, you have a good chance of winning funds for college.

Chapter 6: B Students Can Win Scholarships Too

SECTION FOUR
THE COLLEGES

A GUIDE TO THE COLLEGES THAT WELCOME B STUDENTS

A GUIDE TO THE COLLEGES THAT WELCOME B STUDENTS

As a B or C student, you have many options when it comes to finding a college that is right for you. In fact, there are far more colleges that want you than you could ever apply to in a single year. Your challenge will not be finding the right college but narrowing down your list of possibilities.

As you will see, not all colleges require certain GPAs or test scores to make it past the velvet rope. Now it's time to meet some of the schools that not only accept B and C students but that also embrace them. These colleges are competitive and offer the highest quality educations, but they also recognize that students like you have much to offer and are committed to ensuring your success.

How These Colleges Were Chosen

All the colleges and universities listed in this directory were chosen for several reasons.

● They each offer very high quality educations. Just because the colleges listed here accept students with less-than-perfect scores doesn't mean that they sacrifice quality. These schools are committed to preparing you for your future.

● B and C students are welcome. These colleges have test scores and GPA averages that fit well with the typical B student's range. In addition, the schools offer programs such as tutoring or mentoring that will help students succeed once they are in college.

● They are competitive. While not as selective as many of the colleges at the top of news magazines' lists, the schools listed here do have standards for admission. Because they generally draw from a smaller geographic area, community colleges are not included.

- They offer diversity. These schools represent all parts of the country and all sizes, from small to large.

ADELPHI UNIVERSITY

1 South Avenue, Garden City, NY 11530
Admissions: 516-877-3050 · Financial Aid: 516-877-3365
Email: admissions@adelphi.edu · Website: http://www.adelphi.edu

From the College

"Adelphi is a world class, modern university with excellent and highly relevant programs where students prepare for lives of active citizenship and professional careers. Through its schools and programs–the College of Arts and Sciences, Gordon F. Derner Institute of Advanced Psychological Studies, Honors College, Robert B. Willumstad School of Business, Ruth S. Ammon School of Education, The College of Nursing and Public Health, University College and the School of Social Work– the co-educational university offers undergraduate and graduate degrees as well as professional and educational programs for adults. Adelphi currently enrolls nearly 8,000 students from 43 states and 45 foreign countries. With its main campus in Garden City, New York, and centers in Manhattan, Hauppauge and Poughkeepsie, the university, chartered in 1896, maintains a commitment to liberal studies in tandem with rigorous professional preparation and active citizenship. Adelphi's lush 75 acre campus in historic Garden City has seven residence halls and is conveniently located 45 minutes from New York City, and just a few miles from some of Long Island's most beautiful beaches, parks and cultural centers. Adelphi's new recreation, sports, and performing arts complex has further enhanced a vibrant campus life.

"Students may join Adelphi's 80-plus student organizations, including fraternities, sororities and academic honor societies. Adelphi has outstanding NCAA Division I and II intercollegiate athletic teams, including its Division II national championship women's lacrosse team, as well as an array of intramural activities. Students also have free access to student counseling, career counseling, financial aid, mentoring and other life improvement services.

"Adelphi offers more than 100 undergraduate and graduate programs of study at its main Garden City campus, its three off-campus centers and via the web."

Campus Setting

Adelphi is a private, multipurpose university. Founded as a boys' preparatory school, it became a college in 1896, and gained university status in 1963. Its 75-acre campus is located in western Long Island, 20 miles from New York City. A four-year private institution, Adelphi University has an enrollment of 7,645 students. Besides a large, well-stocked library, the campus facilities also include: art gallery · bronze-casting foundry · sculpture and ceramics studios · theater · language labs · observatory. Adelphi University provides on-campus housing with 602 units that can accommodate 1,282 students. Housing options: coed dorms · special housing for disabled students. Recreation and sports facilities include: basketball, tennis and volleyball courts · baseball, lacrosse, soccer and softball fields · fitness center · swimming facility.

Student Life and Activities

The majority of students (77 percent) live off campus, which affects the on-campus social scene. In spite of this, students do find time to create their own recreational outlets. "Adelphi is what you make it," reports the student newspaper. If you want to meet people, there are plenty of opportunities. Students say, "There is a place for everyone to feel connected to the school no matter religion, race, gender or sexual orientation." Popular gathering spots include the University Center dining room, Post dining, commuter lounge, fire-side lounge, UC Plaza (when the weather is warm), New York City and Roosevelt Field Mall. Popular campus events include visual and

ADELPHI UNIVERSITY

Adelphi University
Garden City, NY (Pop. 22,546)
Location: Large town
Four-year private
Founded: 1896
Website: http://www.adelphi.edu

Students
Total enrollment: 7,645
Undergrads: 5,040
Freshmen: 918
Part-time students: 10%
From out-of-state: 10%
From public schools: 74%
Male/Female: 31%/69%
Live on-campus: 23%
In fraternities: 11%
In sororities: 9%
Off-campus employment rating: Good
Caucasian: 53%
African American: 11%
Hispanic: 13%
Asian: 8%
Hawaiian or Pacific Islander: <1%
Native American: <1%
Mixed (2+ ethnicities): 2%
International: 4%

Academics
Calendar: Semester
Student/faculty ratio: 12:1
Class size 9 or fewer: 11%
Class size 10-29: 72%
Class size 30-49: 16%
Class size 50-99: 2%
Class size 100 or more: -
Returning freshmen: 81%
Six-year graduation rate: 63%

Most Popular Majors
Nursing
Education
Business administration/management

performing arts exhibitions, Disabilities Awareness Week, International Week, Black History Month, Endowed Lectures Series, student theater and dance performances, concerts and performances by top music groups and comedians, lectures by U.N. Ambassadors, intercollegiate and intramural sports, Spring Fling Spring In/Spike It Festival, Homecoming and Career Day. Adelphi University has 80 official student organizations. Influential groups include Greeks, Circle K, Environmental Action Coalition, Christian Fellowship, African People Organization (APO), athletes, Caliber and La Union Latino. For those interested in sports, there are intramural teams such as: badminton · baseball · basketball · dodge ball · kick ball · flag football · soccer · volleyball. Adelphi University is a member of the Northeast Conference (Division I) and Northeast-10 Conference (Division II).

Academics and Learning Environment

Adelphi University has 315 full-time and 696 part-time faculty members, offering a student-to-faculty ratio of 12:1. The most common course size is 10 to 19 students. Adelphi University offers 104 majors with the most popular being nursing, education and business administration/management and least popular being French, philosophy and Spanish. The school has a general core requirement. Cooperative education is not offered. All first-year students must maintain a 2.0 GPA or higher to avoid academic probation. Other special academic programs that would appeal to a B student: self-designed majors · pass/fail grading option · independent study · double majors · dual degrees · accelerated study · honors program · internships · weekend college · distance learning.

B Student Support and Success

This school has offered a General Studies program since 1985. According to the university, it is designed for "motivated high school seniors who demonstrate the potential for academic success, but who have not met the traditional academic admission requirements. Counselors, faculty members and administrators identify potentially successful candidates on the basis of their applications and letters of recommendation, as well as through personal interviews." The program offers small classes and personal advisement for each student. At the end of the year, students who have met all of the requirements continue as sophomores in the school's other undergraduate programs.

Adelphi University provides a variety of support programs including dedicated guidance for: academic · career · personal · psychological · minority students · veterans · non-traditional students · family planning · religious. Adelphi also offers students remedial and refresher courses if they are struggling and need additional help. These courses include: reading · writing · math · study skills. Other remedial services include Computer lab, English conversation for international students. The average freshman year GPA is 3.2, and 81 percent of freshmen students return for their sophomore year. Among students who enter the workforce, approximately 88 percent enter a field related to their major within six months of graduation. Companies that most frequently hire graduates from Adelphi University include: NYC Public Schools ·

Enterprise Rent-A-Car · North Shore L.I.J. Health System · AHRC · Bethpage Federal Credit Union · Long Island Public Schools · JP Morgan Chase · KPMG · 1-800-Flowers · XL Capital Assurance · PricewaterhouseCoopers · Schwartz & Co · GEICO · Ernst & Young · Marcum & Kleigman · St. Francis Hospital · Winthrop University Hospital · Weiser.

Support for Students with Learning Disabilities

Students with learning disabilities will find support at Adelphi, through either requesting extra time for completing a degree, or a lightened course load. High school foreign language waivers are accepted. According to the school, writing, math and content labs are available for all students through the learning center and writing center. LD students can find assistance through Adelphi University's: tutors · learning center · testing accommodations · extended time for tests · take-home exam · oral tests · readers · typist/scribe · note-taking services · reading machines · tape recorders · texts on tape · early syllabus · diagnostic testing service · priority registration · waiver of math degree requirement. Individual or small group tutorials are also available in: time management · organizational skills · learning strategies · writing labs · study skills. An advisor/advocate from the Learning Disabilities Program is available to students.

How to Get Admitted

For admissions decisions, non-academic factors considered: interview · extracurricular activities · special talents, interests and abilities · character/personal qualities · volunteer work · work experience · state of residency · alumni relationship. A high school diploma is required, although a GED is also accepted for admissions consideration. SAT or ACT test scores are required of all applicants. *Academic units recommended:* 4 English, 3 Math, 3 Science, 2 Foreign Language.

Insight

"Our admissions process is holistic," says Esther Goodcuff, associate vice president for enrollment management and student affairs. "We carefully read every single piece of documentation in each application. Our General Studies program is not a remedial program but one that challenges students, while at the same time supports them. Our faculty does individual tutoring outside of class, and students are given an academic counselor to help with college transition issues." Goodcuff says that Adelphi's admissions department looks at trends in how students have been performing in high school, watching for an upward movement. "Letters of recommendation and the essay also give us a sense of just who you are," she adds. "We look for students who are highly motivated and truly want to do well."

How to Pay for College

To apply for financial aid, students should submit the following: Free Application for Federal Student Aid (FAFSA) · state aid form. Adelphi University participates in the Federal Work Study program. *Need-based aid programs include:* scholarships and grants · general need-based awards · Federal Pell grants · state scholarships and grants · college-based scholarships and grants · private scholarships and grants · United Negro College Fund · Endowed and restricted donor

ADELPHI UNIVERSITY

Admissions
Applicants: 8,654
Accepted: 5,897
Acceptance rate: 68.1%
Average GPA: 3.4
ACT range: 19-24
SAT Math range: 520-620
SAT Reading range: 500-600
SAT Writing range: 7-23
Top 10% of class: 26%
Top 25% of class: 64%
Top 50% of class: 92%

Deadlines
Early Action: 12/1
Early Decision: No
Regular Action: Rolling admissions
Common Application: Accepted

Financial Aid
In-state tuition: $30,840
Out-of-state tuition: $30,840
Room: Varies
Board: Varies
Books: $1,400
Freshmen receiving need-based aid: 75%
Undergrads rec. need-based aid: 63%
Avg. % of need met by financial aid: 22%
Avg. aid package (freshmen): $20,000
Avg. aid package (undergrads): $20,000
Avg. debt upon graduation: $32,692

Prominent Alumni
Thomas J. Donohue, president and CEO of the U.S. Chamber of Commerce; Jonathan Larson: writer, composer, and lyricist of 'Rent'; Alice Hoffman, best-selling novelist and author of more than 20 books.

School Spirit
Mascot: Panther
Colors: Brown and gold

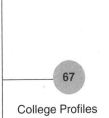

67

funds. *Non-need-based aid programs include:* scholarships and grants · state scholarships and grants · creative arts and performance awards · special achievements and activities awards · athletic scholarships.

AGNES SCOTT COLLEGE

141 East College Avenue, Decatur, GA 30030
Admissions: 800-868-8602, extension 6285 · Financial Aid: 404-471-6285
Email: admission@agnesscott.edu · Website: http://www.agnesscott.edu

From the College

"Agnes Scott College educates women to think deeply, live honorably and engage the intellectual and social challenges of their times. Students are drawn to Agnes Scott by its academic reputation, faculty and metropolitan Atlanta location, offering myriad cultural and experiential learning opportunities. A diverse and growing residential community of scholars, this highly selective liberal arts college presents its curriculum with international context. Study abroad is encouraged by offering faculty-led travel tied to classroom study to broaden understanding of cultural values and contrasts. A strong record of student achievement is found in the numbers of Agnes Scott students who earn prestigious scholarships and fellowships including Fulbright grants, Rhodes Scholarships, Thomas R. Pickering Foreign Affairs Fellowships and Benjamin A. Gilman International Scholarships. An array of experiential learning opportunities also encourages students to apply learning to career development. By challenging its students to demonstrate leadership in their education and serve their communities at home and abroad, Agnes Scott College delivers on its promise: The World for Women."

Campus Setting

Agnes Scott, founded in 1889, is a church-affiliated, liberal arts college for women. Its 100-acre campus is located in Decatur, six miles from downtown Atlanta. Campus buildings are Gothic and Victorian in style. A four-year private women's college, Agnes Scott College has an enrollment of 885 students. The school is also affiliated with the Presbyterian Church. The campus facilities include: art gallery · observatory · science center. Agnes Scott College provides on-campus housing with 446 units that can accommodate 795 students. Housing options: women's dorms · single-student apartments. Recreation and sports facilities include: physical activities building · swimming pool and diving facility · basketball courts · weight room · track and field.

Student Life and Activities

With 86 percent of students living on campus, there's always something going on. Popular gathering spots include the Alston Student Center and Eddie's Attic. Popular campus events include Writers' Festival, Spring Fling, Black Cat Week, Black Cat Formal, Cultural Events Series, Senior Investiture, Sophomore Family Weekend, Planetarium Shows, Fall Fest and Spring Fest. Agnes Scott College has 106 official student organizations. Popular groups on campus include the Programming Board, Committee of Student Multicultural Organizations, Masala-SACE and Witkaze, the Black Student Association. Athletically-minded students will enjoy intramural sports such as: running · cross-country · cycling · swimming · tennis · triathlon · yoga. Agnes Scott College is a member of the Great South Athletic Conference (Division III).

Academics and Learning Environment

Agnes Scott College has 70 full-time and 19 part-time faculty members, offering a student-to-faculty ratio of 11:1. The most common course size is 10 to 19 students, and Agnes Scott College offers 36 majors. The school has a general core requirement as well as a religion requirement. Cooperative education is not offered. All first-year students must maintain a 1.5 GPA or higher to avoid academic probation, and a minimum overall GPA of 2.0 is required to graduate. Other special academic

AGNES SCOTT COLLEGE

Agnes Scott College
Decatur, GA (Pop. 19,853)
Location: Small town
Four-year private women's college
Founded: 1889
Website: http://www.agnesscott.edu

Students
Total enrollment: 885
Undergrads: 885
Freshmen: 252
Part-time students: 2%
From out-of-state: 52%
From public schools: 75%
Male/Female: 1%/99%
Live on-campus: 86%
Off-campus employment rating: Excellent
Caucasian: 31%
African American: 33%
Hispanic: 9%
Asian: 4%
Mixed (2+ ethnicities): 6%
International: 12%

Academics
Calendar: Semester
Student/faculty ratio: 11:1
Class size 9 or fewer: 19%
Class size 10-29: 69%
Class size 30-49: 13%
Class size 50-99: -
Class size 100 or more: -
Returning freshmen: 82%
Six-year graduation rate: 64%

Most Popular Majors
Psychology
Social science
English language/literature

programs that would appeal to a B student: self-designed majors · pass/fail grading option · independent study · double majors · dual degrees · accelerated study · Phi Beta Kappa · internships.

B Student Support and Success

Besides being the setting for the horror flick "Scream 2," Agnes Scott offers smaller classes, often with fewer than a half dozen students. The school offers "talking study halls," centers where students can discuss homework assignments as a group. Every student is given an admission counselor who works from beginning to end on the application process. Agnes Scott features a Center for Writing and Speaking, a peer tutoring organization that helps students with both written and oral communication skills.

Agnes Scott College provides a variety of support programs including dedicated guidance for: academic · career · personal · psychological · minority students · non-traditional students · family planning · religious. The average freshman year GPA is 3.0, and 82 percent of freshmen students return for their sophomore year. After graduating, many enter the workforce and approximately 25 percent pursue a graduate degree. Among students who enter the workforce, approximately 45 percent enter a field related to their major within six months of graduation. Companies that most frequently hire graduates from Agnes Scott College include: Clinician · ERISA Pros · Florida Repertory Theatre · Georgia State University · Georgia Tech · Lindamood-Bell · Orlando Science Center · Parkview High School · RRISA · Savannah River Ecology Lab · Teach for America · Theater in the Square.

Support for Students with Learning Disabilities

For students with learning disabilities, Agnes Scott College will grant additional time to complete their degree. LD students will find the following programs at Agnes Scott College useful: tutors · testing accommodations · untimed tests · extended time for tests · oral tests · readers · typist/scribe · note-taking services · reading machines · tape recorders · texts on tape · early syllabus · priority registration · waiver of math degree requirement. Individual or small group tutorials are also available in: time management · organizational skills · learning strategies · writing labs · math labs · study skills. An advisor/advocate from the Office of Academic Advising and Student Disability Services is available to students.

How to Get Admitted

For admissions decisions, non-academic factors considered: interview · extracurricular activities · special talents, interests and abilities · character/personal qualities · volunteer work · work experience · geographical location · minority affiliation · alumni relationship. A high school diploma is required, although a GED is also accepted for admissions consideration. SAT or ACT test scores are required for some applicants. SAT Subject Test scores are required for some applicants. *According to the admissions office:* SAT Reasoning or ACT scores, interview with a college representative and graded writing sample required; international and home-schooled students must submit SAT Reasoning or ACT and SAT Subject tests. *Academic units recommended:* 4 English, 3 Math, 2 Science, 2 Social Studies, 2 Foreign Language.

How to Pay for College

To apply for financial aid, students should submit the following: Free Application for Federal Student Aid (FAFSA). Agnes Scott College participates in the Federal Work Study program. *Need-based aid programs include:* scholarships and grants · general need-based awards · Federal Pell grants · state scholarships and grants · college-based scholarships and grants · private scholarships and grants. *Non-need-based aid programs include:* scholarships and grants · general need-based awards · state scholarships and grants · creative arts and performance awards · special achievements and activities awards · special characteristics awards · tuition waivers for employees and their dependents.

AGNES SCOTT COLLEGE

Highlights

Admissions
Applicants: 1,077
Accepted: 896
Acceptance rate: 83.2%
Average GPA: 3.7
ACT range: 22-28
SAT Math range: 510-650
SAT Reading range: 500-660
SAT Writing range: 8-37
Top 10% of class: 40%
Top 25% of class: 67%
Top 50% of class: 91%

Deadlines
Early Action: 11/15
Early Decision: 11/1
Regular Action: 1/15 (priority)
3/15 (final)
Common Application: Accepted

Financial Aid
In-state tuition: $35,742
Out-of-state tuition: $35,742
Room: Varies
Board: Varies
Books: $1,000
Freshmen receiving need-based aid: 73%
Undergrads rec. need-based aid: 77%
Avg. % of need met by financial aid: 87%
Avg. aid package (freshmen): $32,641
Avg. aid package (undergrads): $32,875
Avg. debt upon graduation: $30,139

Prominent Alumni
Katherine Krill, CEO, Ann Taylor Stores Corporation; Jennifer Nettles, Grammy-winning country and folk musician; Jean Toal, Chief Justice, South Carolina Supreme Court.

School Spirit
Mascot: Scotties
Colors: Purple and white

ALBION COLLEGE

611 East Porter Street, Albion, MI 49224
Admissions: 800-858-6770 · Financial Aid: 517-629-0440
Email: admissions@albion.edu · Website: http://www.albion.edu

From the College

"Albion College offers a strong liberal arts curriculum with a purposeful focus on professional preparation in law, medicine, education, business management and the sciences. Consistently ranked among the top ten colleges for vibrant campus activities and opportunities for service and leadership, Albion also enjoys the support of its alumni, ranking 15th among all colleges and universities in annual giving. As a member of the Michigan Intercollegiate Athletics Association (MIAA), the oldest athletic conference in America, and NCAA Division III, a strong tradition of developing scholar-athletes continues as over 30 percent of all full-time students are involved in varsity athletics. A 144-acre preserve with nature trails and an interpretive center is located adjacent to campus along the Kalamazoo River. Recently, the college opened the Held Equestrian Center on 340 acres immediately south of the main campus."

Campus Setting

Albion, founded in 1835, is a church-affiliated, liberal arts college. Its 574-acre campus is located in south central Michigan, 65 miles from Detroit. Campus architecture includes both mid-nineteenth century and modern buildings. A four-year private institution, Albion College has an enrollment of 1,307 students. The school is also affiliated with the Methodist Church. The campus's facilities are: astronomical observatory · equestrian center · science complex. Albion College provides on-campus housing with 20 units that can accommodate 1,700 students. Housing options: coed dorms · women's dorms · fraternity housing · cooperative housing. Recreation and sports facilities include: aquatic center · basketball, racquetball, tennis and volleyball courts · equestrian center · field house with track · football stadium · recreation and wellness center · softball field.

Student Life and Activities

With 90 percent of students living on campus, social activities abound. Kellogg Center's popular events include Briton Bash, Party on Perry and Day of Woden. Albion College has 110 official student organizations, including fraternities and sororities. As for sports, there are intramural teams such as: basketball · canoe · dodgeball · football · kickball · racquetball · soccer · softball · swimming · tennis · Ultimate Frisbee · volleyball. Albion College is a member of the NCAA, Michigan Intercollegiate Athletic Association (Division III), Midwest Lacrosse Conference (Division III) and Intercollegiate Horse Show Association.

Academics and Learning Environment

When B students approach Albion College, many discover that a college's learning environment is just as important as the quality of its academic program. Albion College has 101 full-time and 41 part-time faculty members, offering a student-to-faculty ratio of 11:1. The most common course size is 10 to 19 students. Albion College offers 54 majors with the most popular being economics/management, biology and psychology. The school has a general core requirement. Cooperative education is not offered. All first-year students must maintain a 2.0 GPA or higher to avoid academic probation. Other special academic programs that would appeal to a B student: self-designed majors · pass/fail grading option · independent study · double majors · dual degrees · honors program · Phi Beta Kappa · internships.

B Student Support and Success

Albion wants its new students to transition well into college life and provides a First Year Experience, as others do. It offers Common Reading, followed up by presentations by the author, as well as a program called Student Orientation, Advising and Registration (SOAR). This takes place in May before the freshman year begins and is two days of touring the campus, meeting people, eating in the dining hall, speaking to faculty, planning student schedules and even registering for fall classes. The first three days of the first year center around get-acquainted activities such as skits, singing, lectures, ice cream breaks and comedians. Albion offers classes smaller than 20 students, and many undergrads speak highly of the casual and friendly attitudes of the faculty.

Albion College provides a variety of support programs including dedicated guidance for: academic · career · personal · psychological · minority students · military · veterans · non-traditional students · family planning · religious. Albion College recognizes that some students need extra preparation and therefore offers remedial and refresher courses in: reading · writing · math · study skills. The average freshman year GPA is 3.2, and 81 percent of freshmen students return for their sophomore year. Post graduation, many students enter the workforce, but approximately 48 percent pursue a graduate degree immediately. Out of the students who enter the workforce, approximately 52 percent enter a field related to their major within six months of their actual graduation. Companies that most frequently hire graduates from Albion College include: Baker Tilly Virchow Krause · PricewaterhouseCoopers LLP · JP Morgan Chase & Company.

Support for Students with Learning Disabilities

Those students with learning disabilities have the option of support programs offered by Albion College. In some cases, the college will grant additional time those students with learning disabilities who still desire to complete their degree. Another option for LD students is a lightened course load. The following programs are specifically geared towards students with learning disabilities: tutors · learning center · testing accommodations · extended time for tests · take-home exam · oral tests · readers · note-taking services · reading machines · tape recorders · texts on tape · videotaped classes · early syllabus · priority registration · waiver of math degree requirement. Individual or small group tutorials are also available in: time management · organizational skills · learning strategies · specific subject areas · writing labs · math labs · study skills. An advisor/advocate from the LD program is available to students.

How to Get Admitted

For admissions decisions, non-academic factors considered: interview · extracurricular activities · special talents, interests and abilities · character/personal qualities · volunteer work · work experience · state of residency · minority affiliation · alumni relationship. A high school diploma is required, although a GED is accepted for admissions consideration. SAT or ACT scores are required of all applicants. *Academic units recommended:* 4 English, 4 Math, 3 Science, 2 Social Studies, 2 Foreign Language.

ALBION COLLEGE

Highlights

Albion College
Albion, MI (Pop. 8,546)
Location: Large town
Four-year private
Founded: 1835
Website: http://www.albion.edu

Students
Total enrollment: 1,307
Undergrads: 1,307
Freshmen: 273
Part-time students: 3%
From out-of-state: 7%
Male/Female: 51%/49%
Live on-campus: 90%
Caucasian: 80%
African American: 3%
Hispanic: 3%
Asian: 2%
Hawaiian or Pacific Islander: <1%
Native American: <1%
Mixed (2+ ethnicities): 3%
International: 4%

Academics
Calendar: Semester
Student/faculty ratio: 11:1
Class size 9 or fewer: 22%
Class size 10-29: 69%
Class size 30-49: 8%
Class size 50-99: 1%
Class size 100 or more: -
Returning freshmen: 81%
Six-year graduation rate: 74%

Most Popular Majors
Economics/management
Psychology
Biology

ALBION COLLEGE

Admissions

Applicants: 4,430
Accepted: 2,498
Acceptance rate: 56.4%
Average GPA: 3.5
ACT range: 22-28
SAT Math range: 510-590
SAT Reading range: 520-580
SAT Writing range: Not reported
Top 10% of class: 21%
Top 25% of class: 52%
Top 50% of class: 84%

Deadlines

Early Action: 12/1
Early Decision: No
Regular Action: Rolling admissions
Common Application: Accepted

Financial Aid

In-state tuition: $36,872
Out-of-state tuition: $36,872
Room: $5,160
Board: $5,390
Books: $800
Freshmen receiving need-based aid: 79%
Undergrads rec. need-based aid: 71%
Avg. % of need met by financial aid: 80%
Avg. aid package (freshmen): $29,246
Avg. aid package (undergrads): $27,997
Avg. debt upon graduation: $37,191

Prominent Alumni

David Camp: U.S. House of Representatives, Chairman, Ways and Means Committee; Michigan's 4th District (R), Midland, MI; Denise Cortis Park: Director, Professor, Regents Research Scholar, Center for Vital Longevity, University of Texas, Dallas; Douglas Parker: Chief Executive Officer, American Airlines, Fort Worth, TX.

School Spirit

Mascot: Britons
Colors: Purple and gold
Song: *Fyte Onne*

How to Pay for College

To apply for financial aid, students should submit the following: Free Application for Federal Student Aid (FAFSA). Albion College participates in the Federal Work Study program. *Need-based aid programs include:* scholarships and grants · general need-based awards · Federal Pell grants · state scholarships and grants · college-based scholarships and grants · private scholarships and grants. *Non-need-based aid programs include:* scholarships and grants · state scholarships and grants · creative arts and performance awards · alumni affiliation scholarships.

ALBRIGHT COLLEGE

P.O. Box 15234, 13th and Bern Streets
Reading, PA 19612-5234
Admissions: 800-252-1856 · Financial Aid: 610-921-7515
Email: admission@alb.edu
Website: http://www.albright.edu

From the College

"Founded in 1856, Albright College is a selective, national liberal arts college enrolling 1,700 full-time undergraduates and more than 800 adult learners and graduate students. The college's flexible interdisciplinary curriculum, strengthened by a close-knit residential learning environment, encourages students to combine majors and disciplines to create individualized academic programs."

Campus Setting

Albright, founded in 1856, is a church-affiliated, liberal arts college. Its 118-acre campus is located at the edge of a residential section of Reading, 45 miles from Philadelphia. A four-year private institution, the school is also affiliated with the United Methodist Church. Beginning with a well-stocked library, the campus facilities include: art gallery · Holocaust resource center · media service center. Albright College provides on-campus housing with 19 units that can accommodate 1,192 students. Housing options: coed dorms · single-student apartments · special housing for international students. Recreation and sports facilities include: baseball, softball and practice fields · basketball, racquetball and tennis courts · stadium · gym · field house · fitness center · swimming pool.

Student Life and Activities

Sixty-nine percent of students living on campus, and the student body is a generally tight knit group. Campus Center, WAWA and residence halls are favorite gathering spots. Bingo, plays, and concerts are popular campus events. Albright College has 64 official student organizations. Greeks and athletes have a strong presence in student social life. For those interested in sports, there are intramural teams such as: basketball · football · racquetball · softball · volleyball · water polo. Albright College is a member of the Commonwealth Conference (Division III) and Middle Atlantic States Collegiate Athletic Conference (Division III).

Academics and Learning Environment

Albright has 113 full-time and 55 part-time faculty members and offers 53 majors. The school has a general core requirement. Cooperative education is available. All first-year students must maintain a 1.7 GPA or higher to avoid academic probation. Other special academic programs that would appeal to a B student: self-designed majors · pass/fail grading option · independent study · double majors · dual degrees · accelerated study · honors program · internships.

B Student Support and Success

At Albright, students have the ability to focus on a single field of study or combine several to create an individualized major. The

---

ALBRIGHT COLLEGE

Highlights

Albright College
Reading, PA (Pop. 88,102)
Location: Medium city
Four-year private
Founded: 1856
Website: http://www.albright.edu

Students
Total enrollment: 1,751
Undergrads: 1,751
Freshmen: 655
Part-time students: 2%
From out-of-state: 37%
From public schools: 83%
Male/Female: 44%/56%
Live on-campus: 69%
In fraternities: 14%
In sororities: 19%
Off-campus employment rating: Good
Caucasian: 62%
African American: 16%
Hispanic: 9%
Asian: 3%
Hawaiian or Pacific Islander: <1%
Native American: 1%
Mixed (2+ ethnicities): 1%
International: 3%

Academics
Calendar: 4-1-4 system
Student/faculty ratio: 13:1
Class size 9 or fewer: 13%
Class size 10-29: 74%
Class size 30-49: 12%
Class size 50-99: 1%
Class size 100 or more: -
Returning freshmen: 71%
Six-year graduation rate: 54%

Most Popular Majors
Business administration
Biology
Psychology

75

College Profiles

ALBRIGHT COLLEGE

Admissions
Applicants: 6,060
Accepted: 3,776
Acceptance rate: 62.3%
Average GPA: 3.4
ACT range: 20-25
SAT Math range: 470-570
SAT Reading range: 460-560
SAT Writing range: Not reported
Top 10% of class: 20%
Top 25% of class: 49%
Top 50% of class: 77%

Deadlines
Early Action: No
Early Decision: No
Regular Action: Rolling admissions
Common Application: Accepted

Financial Aid
In-state tuition: $37,320
Out-of-state tuition: $37,320
Room: $5,550
Board: $4,450
Books: $1,000
Freshmen receiving need-based aid: 89%
Undergrads rec. need-based aid: 93%
Avg. % of need met by financial aid: 79%
Avg. aid package (freshmen): $35,065
Avg. aid package (undergrads): $30,789
Avg. debt upon graduation: $26,252

Prominent Alumni
Bob Spitz, author of *New York Times* best seller, *The Beatles, the Biography*; Brent Hurley, founding member of YouTube; Ron Dissinger, Chief Financial Officer and Senior Vice President, Kellogg Company.

School Spirit
Mascot: Lions
Colors: Red and white
Song: *Hail Alma Mata*

America's
Best Colleges for
B Students

college offers a Learning Resource Center that is open daily for free individual tutoring or group sessions. A Writing Center gives students the chance to have their papers proofread and edited before they are turned in. The center offers workshops on time management, test taking tips, study skills and success strategies. Students with learning disabilities can contact the vice president of student services for individual arrangements. Class sizes average 15 to 20 with general classes slightly larger and advanced classes sometimes having fewer than 10 students.

Albright College provides a variety of support programs including dedicated guidance for: academic · career · personal · psychological · minority students · non-traditional students. The average freshman year GPA is 2.9, and 71 percent of freshmen students return for their sophomore year. After graduation, approximately 28 percent of students pursue a graduate degree. Among students who do go into the workforce, approximately 23 percent enter a field related to their major within six months of graduation. Companies that most frequently hire graduates from Albright College include: Accenture · Ernst & Young · Pfizer · Vanguard · SEI · PricewaterhouseCoopers · Federal Government · Lockheed Martin.

Support for Students with Learning Disabilities

Albright College supports learning disabled students by granting additional time to complete degrees, as well as a lightened course load. LD students might explore Albright's options, including: tutors · learning center · testing accommodations · extended time for tests · take-home exam · oral tests · readers · typist/scribe · note-taking services · texts on tape · early syllabus · priority registration. Individual or small group tutorials are also available in: organizational skills · learning strategies · specific subject areas · writing labs · study skills. An advisor/advocate from the LD program is available to students and is part of the admissions committee.

How to Get Admitted

For admissions decisions, non-academic factors considered: interview · extracurricular activities · special talents, interests and abilities · character/personal qualities · volunteer work · work experience · state of residency · alumni relationship. A high school diploma is required, although a GED is also accepted for admissions consideration. SAT or ACT test scores are considered, if submitted, but are not required. SAT Subject Test scores are not required. *Academic units recommended:* 4 English, 3 Math, 4 Science, 2 Social Studies, 3 Foreign Language.

How to Pay for College

To apply for financial aid, students should submit the following: Free Application for Federal Student Aid (FAFSA). Albright College participates in the Federal Work Study program. *Need-based aid programs include:* scholarships and grants · general need-based awards · Federal Pell grants · state scholarships and grants · college-based scholarships and grants · private scholarships and grants · Federal ACG/SMART grants. *Non-need-based aid programs include:* scholarships and grants · general need-based awards · state scholarships and grants · creative arts and performance awards · special achievements and activities awards · special characteristics awards.

ALCORN STATE UNIVERSITY

1000 ASU Drive #359, Alcorn State, MS 39096
Admissions: 601-877-6147 · Financial Aid: 601-877-6190
Email: ksampson@alcorn.edu · Website: http://www.alcorn.edu

From the College

"Alcorn State University is a Historically Black University that has been committed to academic excellence for over 140 years. Alcorn is a premier comprehensive land-grant university that develops diverse students into globally competitive leaders, and applies scientific research through collaborative partnerships that benefit the surrounding communities, state, nation and world. Alcorn was founded in 1871 and is the oldest public historically black land-grant institution in the United States and the second oldest state supported institution of higher learning in Mississippi.

"Alcorn offers graduate and undergraduate programs in agriculture, business, robotic engineering, science and mathematics, criminal justice, industrial technology, education, nursing and information technology among others. The University's academic programs are designed to challenge the mind, build intellectual integrity and create leaders of tomorrow. At Alcorn State University, education is a transformation: a discovery process in which students find voices and passions, learn to think critically and independently, gain new knowledge and build character."

Campus Setting

Alcorn State, founded in 1871, is the oldest historically black, land-grant university in the country. Its 1,756-acre campus is situated in Claiborne County, Mississippi, 90 miles southwest of Jackson. A four-year public institution, Alcorn State University has 3,848 students. Although not originally co-educational college, Alcorn State University has been co-ed since 1903. The school also has a library with 63,478 books. Alcorn State University provides on-campus housing with nine units that can accommodate 1,847 students. Housing options: women's dorms · men's dorms. Recreation and sports facilities include a sports complex.

Student Life and Activities

With 50 percent of students living on campus, there are lots of social activities both on-campus and off-campus. As reported by a school representative, "The social and cultural life on campus will continue to grow because we have created many new events for students." Popular on-campus gathering spots include the cafeteria and game room, and, off-campus, students typically gather at the Trace Theater. Favorite campus events include Probate Shows, concerts and Homecoming Week. Alcorn State University has 85 official student organizations, including Greek sororities and fraternities. Alcorn State University is a member of the NCAA and the Southwestern Athletic Conference (Division I, Football I-AA).

Academics and Learning Environment

Alcorn State University has 167 full-time and 52 part-time faculty members, offering a student-to-faculty ratio of 16:1. The most common course size is 10 to 19 students. Alcorn State University offers 75 majors with the most popular being biology, child development and business administration and least popular being general agriculture, history and applied science/technology. The school has a general core requirement. Cooperative education is available. All first-year students must maintain a 2.0 GPA or higher to avoid academic probation. Other special academic programs that would appeal to a B student: independent study · double majors · accelerated study · honors program · internships · distance learning.

ALCORN STATE UNIVERSITY

Alcorn State University
Lorman (Pop. 2,223)
Location: Rural
Four-year public
Founded: 1871
Website: http://www.alcorn.edu

Students
Total enrollment: 3,848
Undergrads: 3,157
Freshmen: 1,289
Part-time students: 13%
From out-of-state: 15%
From public schools: 99%
Male/Female: 35%/65%
Live on-campus: 50%
Caucasian: 3%
African American: 93%
Hispanic: 1%
Asian: <1%
Hawaiian or Pacific Islander: <1%
Native American: <1%
Mixed (2+ ethnicities): 1%
International: 1%

Academics
Calendar: Semester
Student/faculty ratio: 16:1
Class size 9 or fewer: 16%
Class size 10-29: 60%
Class size 30-49: 19%
Class size 50-99: 5%
Class size 100 or more: -
Returning freshmen: 68%
Six-year graduation rate: 35%

Most Popular Majors
Biology
Business administration
Child development

B Student Support and Success

This is primarily an African American college, although about eight percent of the students are Caucasian or of other ethnic backgrounds. Classes are small, and College for Excellence is offered for all freshmen, returning and transfer students. This program plans, supervises and coordinates all academic experiences of these students. It has an advising and tutoring staff and state-of-the-art computer labs. Professional advisors support students by helping them adjust to college life, teaching them about Alcorn and its policies, exploring career options and solving any problems that come along. Additionally, staff is available to teach good test-taking, studying and time management skills and to monitor progress. Students who need additional help in reading, writing or thinking skills are assisted so that they can quickly reach college-level proficiency.

Alcorn State University provides a variety of support programs including dedicated guidance for: academic · career · psychological. Additional counseling services include: alcohol/substance abuse. Annually, 68 percent of freshmen students return for their sophomore year. Approximately 39 percent of students pursue a graduate degree immediately after graduation. Among students who enter the workforce, approximately 40 percent enter a field related to their major within six months of graduation. Companies that most frequently hire graduates from Alcorn State University include: Cargill · Ameristar Casino/Hotel · Eastman Chemical · Entergy Operations · Enterprise Rent-A-Car · Ergon Refining · Department of Wildlife Fisheries and Parks · FDIC · Mississippi Department of Environmental Quality · Mississippi State Hospital · Primerica Financial Services · SUDA Rural Development · Sanderson Farms · Trustmark · Tyson Foods · USAE Corps of Engineers · USDA · U.S. Department of Energy · Walgreens · Wells Fargo Financial.

Support for Students with Learning Disabilities

Learning disabilities are supported at Alcorn thought a variety of programs including featuring additional time to complete a degree and giving credit for remedial classes. LD students can also use: remedial math · remedial English · remedial reading · tutors · extended time for tests · priority registration. Individual or small group tutorials are also available for time management and organizational skills. Writing and math labs are also offered.

How to Get Admitted

For admissions decisions, non-academic factors considered: interview · state of residency. A high school diploma is required, although a GED is also accepted for admissions consideration. SAT or ACT test scores are required for some applicants. SAT Subject Test scores are required for some applicants. *According to the admissions office:* Complete the College Prep Curriculum with: a minimum 3.2 GPA; minimum 2.5 GPA, minimum composite ACT score of 16 (combined SAT Reasoning score of 790), or rank in upper 50% of class and minimum composite ACT score of 16 (combined SAT Reasoning score of 790); minimum 2.0 GPA and minimum composite ACT score of 18 (combined SAT Reasoning score of 870). *Academic units recommended:* 4 English, 4 Math, 4 Science, 4 Social Studies, 1 Foreign Language.

How to Pay for College

To apply for financial aid, students should submit the following: Free Application for Federal Student Aid (FAFSA) · institution's own financial aid forms. Alcorn State University participates in the Federal Work Study program. *Need-based aid programs include:* scholarships and grants · general need-based awards · Federal Pell grants · state scholarships and grants · college-based scholarships and grants · private scholarships and grants. *Non-need-based aid programs include:* scholarships and grants · state scholarships and grants · athletic scholarships · ROTC scholarships.

ALCORN STATE UNIVERSITY

Highlights

Admissions
Applicants: 2,265
Accepted: 1,878
Acceptance rate: 82.9%
Average GPA: 3.0
ACT range: 16-19
SAT Math range: 410-480
SAT Reading range: 400-460
SAT Writing range: Not reported
Top 50% of class: 68%

Deadlines
Early Action: No
Early Decision: No
Regular Action: Rolling admissions
Common Application: Not accepted

Financial Aid
In-state tuition: $6,192
Out-of-state tuition: $15,433
Room: $5,902
Board: $2,748
Books: $1,510
Freshmen receiving need-based aid: 96%
Undergrads rec. need-based aid: 41%
Avg. % of need met by financial aid: 47%
Avg. aid package (freshmen): $14,589
Avg. aid package (undergrads): $14,554
Avg. debt upon graduation: $32,755

Prominent Alumni
Medgar Wiley Evers, civil rights martyr; Dr. Jesse E. McGee, cardiologist, National Black College Hall of Fame; Steve McNair, NFL quarterback, NCAA Football Recordholder, SWAC Hall of Fame.

School Spirit
Mascot: Brave
Colors: Purple and gold
Song: *Alcorn Ode*

ALFRED UNIVERSITY

1 Saxon Drive, Alfred, NY 14802-1205
Admissions: 800-541-9229 · Financial Aid: 607-871-2159
Email: admissions@alfred.edu · Website: http://www.alfred.edu

From the College

"Alfred University focuses on providing academically challenging programs in a student-centered environment in order to prepare well-educated, independent thinkers ready for lives of continuous intellectual and personal growth." This university states that it values "a learning environment that promotes open exchange of ideas, critical thinking, global awareness, technological literacy, intellectual honesty and community involvement; a work environment that promotes open communication, recognition of achievement and the development of personal potential; research and scholarship that advance the frontiers of knowledge, contribute to graduate and undergraduate teaching and demonstrate creativity in all fields of endeavor; diversity in people and cultures, ideas and scholarship; a campus that is safe, attractive and promotes health and wellness; and a caring community that respects each individual, fosters intellectual curiosity and growth, promotes and models good citizenship and encourages enlightened leadership."

Campus Setting

Pioneer Seventh Day Baptists founded Alfred University as a select school in 1836. Alfred became the first co-educational institution in New York State and the second in the nation. Students work and live on a scenic 232-acre hillside campus in Alfred, New York. Another 400 acres of recreational land is just minutes away. The nonsectarian university is comprised of the privately endowed College of Business, the College of Liberal Arts and Sciences and the New York State College of Ceramics (Kazuo Inamori School of Engineering and School of Art & Design). Bachelors, masters, advanced certificates and doctoral degrees are awarded as the culmination of Alfred University's academic and professional programs. A four-year private institution, Alfred University has an enrollment of 2,431 students. Campus facilities include: ceramic art museum · galleries · observatory · equestrian center · carillon. Alfred University provides on-campus housing with 26 units that can accommodate 1,461 students. Housing options: coed dorms · single-student apartments. Recreation and sports facilities include: artificial turf field for football, lacrosse, soccer and recreational use · tennis courts · fitness center · 6-lane swimming pool with 1 and 3 meter diving boards · gymnasium for basketball, volleyball and recreational use · racquetball/squash courts · tennis courts · equestrian center.

Student Life and Activities

With 76 percent of students living on campus, students always find something to do. Popular gathering spots include Powell Campus Center, Brick Lawn, the Bandstand, the Moka Joka and Terra Cotta. Favorite campus events include Hot Dog Day, Glam Slam and The Alfies. Alfred University has 65 official student organizations. The most popular are: Chamber singers · Habitat for Humanity · Kanakadea · Spectrum · Pet Pals · Student Activities Board · SAFE · Green Alfred · Alfred Steppas · AU Swing Society · Friday Night Live · Pirate Theater. Sports fans can enjoy intramural teams such as: basketball · soccer · racquetball · golf · volleyball. Alfred University is a member of the Empire Eight (Division III).

Academics and Learning Environment

Alfred University has 159 full-time and 59 part-time faculty members, offering a student-to-faculty ratio of 13:1. The most common course size is 10 to 19 students. Alfred University offers 65 majors with the most popular being art/design, mechanical engineering and business administration and least popular being philosophy, geology and global studies. The school has a general core requirement. Cooperative education is available. All first-year students must maintain a 2.0 GPA or higher to avoid academic probation, and a minimum overall GPA of 2.0 is required to graduate. Other special academic programs that would appeal to a B student: self-designed majors · pass/fail grading option · independent study · double majors · dual degrees · honors program · Phi Beta Kappa · internships.

B Student Support and Success

Rumored to have been the inspiration for the 1980s television series "Northern Exposure", this college is quiet and small but active. The school is especially known for its School of Engineering's glass and ceramic programs and is one of the few schools that offers a degree in Ceramic Engineering. Classes are typically less than 10 students. The general atmosphere appeals to the back-to-nature student who likes cold, snowy winters.

Alfred University provides a variety of support programs including dedicated guidance for: academic · career · personal · psychological · minority students · family planning. Additional counseling services include women's and wellness counseling. The average freshman year GPA is 2.6, and 75 percent of freshmen students return for their sophomore year. Companies that most frequently hire graduates from Alfred University include: Corning Inc. · Dresser Rand · Pratt and Whitney · Alfred University.

Support for Students with Learning Disabilities

If you have a learning disability, you might want to take advantage of specific support programs offered by Alfred University, such as additional time to complete your degree, and a lightened course load. High school foreign language waivers are accepted. According to the school, the progress of students receiving services from Special Academic Services is monitored. Students with learning disabilities will find the following programs at Alfred University useful: tutors · testing accommodations · untimed tests · extended time for tests · oral tests · readers · note-taking services · tape recorders · diagnostic testing service · waiver of math degree requirement. Individual or small group tutorials are also available in: time management · organizational skills · learning strategies · specific subject areas · writing labs · study skills. An advisor/advocate from the LD program is available to students.

How to Get Admitted

For admissions decisions, non-academic factors considered: interview · extracurricular activities · special talents, interests and abilities · character/personal qualities · volunteer work · work experience · state of residency · minority affiliation. A high school diploma is required, although a GED is also accepted for admissions consideration. SAT or ACT test scores are required of all applicants. SAT Subject Test scores are considered, if submitted, but are not

ALFRED UNIVERSITY

Highlights

Alfred University
Alfred (Pop. 5,237)
Location: Rural
Four-year private
Founded: 1836
Website: http://www.alfred.edu

Students
Total enrollment: 2,431
Undergrads: 1,960
Part-time students: 3%
From out-of-state: 20%
Male/Female: 49%/51%
Live on-campus: 76%
Off-campus employment rating: Poor
Caucasian: 66%
African American: 8%
Hispanic: 7%
Asian: 2%
Native American: <1%
Mixed (2+ ethnicities): 3%
International: 3%

Academics
Calendar: Semester
Student/faculty ratio: 13:1
Class size 9 or fewer: 20%
Class size 10-29: 63%
Class size 30-49: 14%
Class size 50-99: 2%
Class size 100 or more: 1%
Returning freshmen: 75%
Six-year graduation rate: 62%

Most Popular Majors
Art/design
Mechanical engineering
Business administration

81

College Profiles

ALFRED UNIVERSITY

Admissions
Applicants: 3,417
Accepted: 2,385
Acceptance rate: 69.8%
Placed on wait list: 91
Enrolled from wait list: 11
Average GPA: 3.2
ACT range: 21-27
SAT Math range: 500-600
SAT Reading range: 480-580
SAT Writing range: 2-15
Top 10% of class: 16%
Top 25% of class: 43%
Top 50% of class: 84%

Deadlines
Early Action: No
Early Decision: No
Regular Action: Rolling admissions
Common Application: Accepted

Financial Aid
In-state tuition: $28,774
Out-of-state tuition: $28,774
Room: $6,020
Board: $5,598
Books: $1,150
Freshmen receiving need-based aid: 82%
Undergrads rec. need-based aid: 81%
Avg. % of need met by financial aid: 83%
Avg. aid package (freshmen): $26,623
Avg. aid package (undergrads): $24,672
Avg. debt upon graduation: $33,467

Prominent Alumni
Joel Moskowitz, CEO of Ceradyne; Robert Klein, actor; William Schuster, NFL Referee.

School Spirit
Mascot: Saxons
Colors: Purple and gold
Song: *Hail to Thee Alfred*

required. *According to the admissions office:* There are no minimum requirements. Admission is determined on an individual basis. *Academic units recommended:* 4 English, 4 Math, 3 Science, 3 Social Studies, 1 Foreign Language.

Insight

Sue Goetschius, director of communications, says Alfred University has always been an institution "championing the underserved." Alfred was the first co-educational institution in New York State and among the first to enroll students regardless of ethnicity or religion. A large percentage of students today continue to be economically disadvantaged; more than 90 percent receive institutional financial aid, which is one reason why both *U.S. News & World Report* and the *Fiske Guide to Colleges* rate Alfred as being a good value. Another population the university has traditionally served is those whose high school records might not be the strongest, but who the admissions officers believe have the potential to do well. Goetschius explains, "Often, when I speak with our alumni, I hear the recurring theme, 'Alfred took a chance on me.'"

How to Pay for College

To apply for financial aid, students should submit the following: Free Application for Federal Student Aid (FAFSA) · institution's own financial aid forms · state aid form · Non-custodian (Divorced/ Separated) Parent's Statement · Business/Farm Supplement. Alfred University participates in the Federal Work Study program. *Need-based aid programs include:* scholarships and grants · general need-based awards · Federal Pell grants · state scholarships and grants · college-based scholarships and grants · private scholarships and grants. *Non-need-based aid programs include:* scholarships and grants · state scholarships and grants · creative arts and performance awards · leadership scholarships/grants.

ALMA COLLEGE

614 West Superior Street, Alma, MI 48801-1599
Admissions: 800-321-2562 · Financial Aid: 800-321-2562
Email: admissions@alma.edu · Website: http://www.alma.edu

From the College

"A residential college located in the middle of Michigan's Lower Peninsula, Alma College offers a personalized education with multiple paths and experiences leading to success. You may create new knowledge through academic research, expand your horizons through a global experience, supplement your academic work with service to others or internships or pursue artistic or athletic opportunities.

"A deep regard for students as individuals is fundamental to an Alma education, with small classes and many opportunities for one-on-one collaboration with dedicated faculty. Alma College recently put its strong student-centered philosophy front and center with the new Alma Commitment, offering a four-year graduation promise and a pledge that each interested student can participate in an experiential learning opportunity, such as an internship, research fellowship or study abroad, backed by $2,500 in Alma Venture funding from the college."

Campus Setting

Alma College, founded in 1886, is a selective, private liberal arts college that highlights personalized education, social responsibility and extraordinary achievements. Alma's undergraduates thrive on challenging academic program in a supportive, small-college environment emphasizing active, collaborative learning and close student-faculty interaction. Its 125-acre campus is within walking distance of downtown Alma, 40 miles from Saginaw, in the middle of Michigan's Lower Peninsula. Alma maintains a close relationship with the Presbyterian Church but also offers an environment that welcomes students of all religious backgrounds. A four-year private institution, Alma College has an enrollment of 1,419 students. In addition to a large, well-stocked library, the campus facilities include: planetarium · science center · center for exercise and health science. Alma College provides on-campus housing with 31 units that can accommodate 1,386 students. Housing options: coed dorms · women's dorms · sorority housing · fraternity housing. Recreation and sports facilities include: baseball, soccer and softball fields · basketball and volleyball courts · football, track and swimming pool stadium · tennis and recreation center.

Student Life and Activities

With 90 percent of students living on campus, there are always plentiful social activities. Popular gathering spots include Stone Recreation Center and Tyler-VanDusen Campus Center. Favorite campus events include Homecoming, All Nighter, Songfest and Honors Day. Alma College has 78 official student organizations. The most popular are: Ambassadors · Union Board · Student Congress · Students Offering Service · College Democrats · College Republicans · Amnesty International · Big Brothers/ Big Sisters · Model UN · Pride. Intramural teams include: basketball · dodgeball · softball · volleyball. Alma College is a member of the Michigan Intercollegiate Athletic Association (Division III).

Academics and Learning Environment

Alma College has 96 full-time and 70 part-time faculty members, offering a student-to-faculty ratio of 12:1. The most common course size is 10 to 19 students. Alma College offers 32 majors with the most popular being business administration, biology and education and least popular being physics, anthropology and philosophy.

ALMA COLLEGE

Highlights

Alma College
Alma, MI (Pop. 9,283)
Location: Small town
Four-year private
Founded: 1886
Website: http://www.alma.edu

Students
Total enrollment: 1,419
Undergrads: 1,419
Part-time students: 3%
From out-of-state: 12%
From public schools: 92%
Male/Female: 45%/55%
Live on-campus: 90%
In fraternities: 24%
In sororities: 30%
Off-campus employment rating: Good
Caucasian: 86%
African American: 2%
Hispanic: 3%
Asian: 2%
Native American: 1%
Mixed (2+ ethnicities): 2%
International: 1%

Academics
Calendar: 4-4-1 system
Student/faculty ratio: 12:1
Class size 9 or fewer: 26%
Class size 10-29: 66%
Class size 30-49: 7%
Class size 50-99: 2%
Class size 100 or more: -
Returning freshmen: 84%
Six-year graduation rate: 61%

Most Popular Majors
Business administration
Biology
Education

America's
Best Colleges for
B Students

The school has a general core requirement. Cooperative education is not offered. All first-year students must maintain a 2.0 GPA or higher to avoid academic probation, and a minimum overall GPA of 2.0 is required to graduate. Other special academic programs that would appeal to a B student: self-designed majors · pass/fail grading option · independent study · double majors · dual degrees · honors program · Phi Beta Kappa · internships.

B Student Support and Success

Alma College's Academic Effectiveness Program is designed for students who are struggling academically. A counselor works with each student to figure out the source of the problem and then develop a plan of action. The Center for Student Development also offers "Learning Lunches" each term on the topics of time management methods, note taking, classroom strategies, study skills, test taking strategies, test anxiety, preparing for employment and graduate school and pursuing internship options.

Alma College provides a variety of support programs including dedicated guidance for: academic · career · personal · minority students · non-traditional students · family planning · religious. Recognizing that some students may need extra preparation, Alma College offers remedial and refresher courses in: reading · writing · math · study skills. The average freshman year GPA is 2.9, and 84 percent of freshmen students return for their sophomore year. Among students who enter the workforce, approximately 42 percent enter a field related to their major within six months of graduation. Companies that most frequently hire graduates from Alma College include: AmeriCorps · Deloitte · Dow Corning · Ernst & Young · Hewitt Associates.

Support for Students with Learning Disabilities

If you're concerned about learning disabilities, Alma grants extra time to complete a degree, plus offers: tutors · learning center · testing accommodations · untimed tests · extended time for tests · take-home exam · oral tests · exam on tape or computer · readers · note-taking services · reading machines · tape recorders · early syllabus · priority registration · waiver of foreign language degree requirement. Individual or small group tutorials are also available in: time management · organizational skills · learning strategies · specific subject areas · writing labs · math labs · study skills. An advisor/advocate from the Academic and Career Planning is available to students and this person also sits on the admissions committee.

How to Get Admitted

For admissions decisions, non-academic factors considered: interview · extracurricular activities · special talents, interests and abilities · character/personal qualities · volunteer work · work experience · state of residency · alumni relationship. A high school diploma is required, although a GED is also accepted for admissions consideration. SAT or ACT test scores are required of all applicants. SAT Subject Test scores are not required. *According to the admissions office:* Minimum composite ACT score of 22 (combined SAT Reasoning score of 1030) and rank in top half of secondary school class required; minimum 3.0 GPA recommended. *Academic units recommended:* 4 English, 3 Math, 3 Science, 3 Social Studies, 2 Foreign Language.

How to Pay for College

To apply for financial aid, students should submit the following: Free Application for Federal Student Aid (FAFSA). Alma College participates in the Federal Work Study program. *Need-based aid programs include:* scholarships and grants · general need-based awards · Federal Pell grants · state scholarships and grants · college-based scholarships and grants. *Non-need-based aid programs include:* scholarships and grants · state scholarships and grants · creative arts and performance awards · special characteristics awards.

ALMA COLLEGE

Highlights

Admissions
Applicants: 2,554
Accepted: 1,772
Acceptance rate: 69.4%
Average GPA: 3.5
ACT range: 22-27
SAT Math range: 500-630
SAT Reading range: 460-640
SAT Writing range: 16-12
Top 10% of class: 27%
Top 25% of class: 53%
Top 50% of class: 84%

Deadlines
Early Action: No
Early Decision: No
Regular Action: Rolling admissions
Common Application: Accepted

Financial Aid
In-state tuition: $34,190
Out-of-state tuition: $34,190
Room: Varies
Board: Varies
Books: $926
Freshmen receiving need-based aid: 86%
Undergrads rec. need-based aid: 83%
Avg. % of need met by financial aid: 79%
Avg. aid package (freshmen): $25,442
Avg. aid package (undergrads): $24,779
Avg. debt upon graduation: $32,056

Prominent Alumni
Kim Taylor, managing director and president, Chicago Mercantile Exchange Clearing; Stephen Meyer, president, Welch Allyn.

School Spirit
Mascot: Scots
Colors: Maroon and cream

85

ALVERNO COLLEGE

P.O. Box 343922, Milwaukee, WI 53234-3922
Admissions: 800-933-3401 · Financial Aid: 800-933-3401
Email: admissions@alverno.edu · Website: http://www.alverno.edu

From the College

"Alverno College is a four-year independent, Catholic, liberal arts college for women that exists in order to promote the personal and professional development of its students. The college is known for its ability-based, assessment-as-learning approach to education, and has consulted with three U.S. presidential administrations on accountability and outcomes in higher education. In 2009 and 2010, U.S. Secretary of Education Arne Duncan praised Alverno as a school excelling in teacher preparation, and Wisconsin Governor Jim Doyle visited the college to observe it innovative teacher programs. The Alverno environment actively engages students in their education through hands-on practical learning and a highly developed off-campus internship program inherent to the curriculum, and provides students professional support in their educational endeavors including a professional advising office and a fully staffed career education center. Alverno College also employs the Diagnostic Digital Portfolio, a unique Web-based system which helps students process the feedback they receive from faculty, external assessors and peers. Alverno offers more than 35 major program areas of study, including graduate programs in education, nursing and business that are open to women and men."

Campus Setting

Alverno College, founded in 1887, is a four-year independent, Catholic, liberal arts college for women. Its 40-acre campus is located 12 miles from downtown Milwaukee and it has an enrollment of 2,605 students. The school is also affiliated with the Roman Catholic Church. In addition to a medium-sized library, the campus facilities include: art gallery · theatre · teaching, learning and technology center · clinical nursing skills lab · student-centered multimedia production facility · career center · international and intercultural center · communication resource center · math center. Alverno College provides on-campus housing with 184 units that can accommodate 252 students. Housing options are women's dorms. Recreation and sports facilities include: athletic training room · fields · fitness center · gymnasium · soccer and softball complex.

Student Life and Activities

The vast majority of students (89 percent) live off campus. Favorite student activities include: Community Day, Homecoming/Spirit Week, Boo Bash, Orientation, Weekly Roundtable Discussion, Alverno Idol, An Alverno Thanksgiving, Love Your Body Week, Alverno Presents Performing Art Series, Rotunda Ball and Backyard Bash. Alverno College has 37 official student organizations, including: Alpha, student newspaper, Alverno College Student Nurses Association, Alverno Student Education Organization, Artourage, Circle K, Hispanic Women of Alverno, Women of Asian Ethnicity, Psych Forum, Students in Free Enterprise, Inside Out literary journal, PAGE Board: Programming Activities and Great Events, Inferno Heat dance team, Student Athlete Advisory Council, Music Therapy Club and Team Green. Alverno College is a member of the Northern Athletics Conference (Division III).

Academics and Learning Environment

For the B student, the learning environment of a college is just as important as the quality of its academic program. Alverno College has 119 full-time and 150 part-time faculty members, offering a student-to-faculty ratio of 10:1. The most common course size is 10 to 19 students. Alverno College offers 52 majors with the most popular being nursing, elementary education and business management. The school has a general core requirement. Cooperative education is not offered. Other special academic programs that would appeal to a B student: self-designed majors · independent study · double majors · internships · weekend college · certificate programs.

B Student Support and Success

Alverno College offers a number of instructional services to help students achieve their academic goals. Basic courses in math, algebra, reading/writing, ESL and computer skills are offered. Communication and math resource centers are available, as well as peer and instructor tutoring. The college website states that the primary purpose of the Communication Resource Center is to help students with their writing, speaking or reading assignments by conferencing with them and responding to their individual questions and concerns. The center offers help with everything from prewriting skills (brainstorming, mapping, etc.) to revising, proofreading and editing.

Alverno College provides a variety of support programs including dedicated guidance for: academic · career · personal · psychological · religious. For those students who need extra preparation, Alverno College offers remedial and refresher courses in: reading · writing · math · study skills. Annually, 72 percent of freshmen students return for their sophomore year. Approximately 11 percent pursue a graduate degree immediately after graduation. Among students who enter the workforce, approximately 84 percent enter a field related to their major within six months of graduation. Companies that most frequently hire graduates from Alverno College include: Alverno College · Aurora Health Care · City of Milwaukee · Children's Hospital of Wisconsin · Community Memorial Hospital · Froedtert Hospital · Medical College of Wisconsin · M&I Corporation · Milwaukee Public Schools · Milwaukee County government · Northwestern Mutual · St. Luke's Medical Center · Waukesha Memorial Hospital · Wheaton Franciscan Healthcare.

Support for Students with Learning Disabilities

Students with learning disabilities may be interested in taking extra time to complete their degree, or taking a lighter course load. They may also want to check out Alverno's: remedial math · remedial English · remedial reading · tutors · learning center · extended time for tests · take-home exam · note-taking services · reading machines · tape recorders · early syllabus. Individual or small group tutorials are also available in: time management · organizational skills · learning strategies · specific subject areas · writing labs · math labs · study skills.

How to Get Admitted

For admissions decisions, non-academic factors considered: interview · extracurricular activities · special talents, interests and abilities · character/personal qualities · volunteer work · work experience · state of residency. A high school diploma is required, although a GED is also accepted for admissions consideration. SAT or ACT test scores are required of all applicants. SAT Subject Test scores

ALVERNO COLLEGE

Highlights

Alverno College
Milwaukee, WI (Pop. 597,867)
Location: Major city
Four-year private women's college
Founded: 1887
Website: http://www.alverno.edu

Students
Total enrollment: 2,536
From out-of-state: 2%
Male/Female: 0%/100%
Live on-campus: 11%
In sororities: 1%
Off-campus employment rating: Good
Caucasian: 55%
African American: 18%
Hispanic: 17%
Asian: 5%
Hawaiian or Pacific Islander: <1%
Native American: 1%
Mixed (2+ ethnicities): 3%
International: 1%

Academics
Calendar: Semester
Student/faculty ratio: 10:1
Class size 9 or fewer: 20%
Class size 10-29: 79%
Class size 30-49: 1%
Class size 50-99: -
Class size 100 or more: -
Returning freshmen: 72%
Six-year graduation rate: 39%

Most Popular Majors
Nursing
Business management
Elementary education

ALVERNO COLLEGE

Highlights

Admissions
Applicants: 643
Accepted: 418
Acceptance rate: 65.0%
Average GPA: 2.8
ACT range: 17-21
SAT Math range: Not reported
SAT Reading range: Not reported
SAT Writing range: Not reported

Deadlines
Early Action: No
Early Decision: No
Regular Action: Rolling admissions
Common Application: Not accepted

Financial Aid
In-state tuition: $23,784
Out-of-state tuition: $23,784
Room: Varies
Board: Varies
Books: Varies
Freshmen receiving need-based aid: 95%
Undergrads rec. need-based aid: 92%
Avg. aid package (freshmen): $17,696
Avg. aid package (undergrads): $15,791
Avg. debt upon graduation: $41,405

Prominent Alumni
Sister Joel Read, President-Emerita, Alverno College, education reformist; Stephanie Arends, Superior Court Judge, State of Washington; Cathy Rick, chief nursing officer, Veteran's Health Administration.

School Spirit
Mascot: Inferno
Colors: Red and white and black
Song: *Where All Belong*

are not required. *Academic units recommended:* 4 English, 3 Math, 3 Science, 3 Social Studies, 2 Foreign Language.

How to Pay for College

To apply for financial aid, students should submit the following: Free Application for Federal Student Aid (FAFSA) · institution's own financial aid forms. Alverno College participates in the Federal Work Study program. *Need-based aid programs include:* scholarships and grants · general need-based awards · Federal Pell grants · state scholarships and grants · college-based scholarships and grants · private scholarships and grants · Federal Nursing scholarships. *Non-need-based aid programs include:* scholarships and grants · state scholarships and grants · alumni.

America's
Best Colleges for
B Students

ANGELO STATE UNIVERSITY

2601 West Avenue North, San Angelo, TX 76909
Admissions: 800-946-8627 · Financial Aid: 800-933-6299
Email: admissions@angelo.edu · Website: http://www.angelo.edu

From the College

"Angelo State University provides a strong academic experience while offering significant financial support to students. As a result, the university's academic quality and low student-faculty ratio (18-1) prepare students for success in their chosen professions or acceptance to graduate and professional school, such as medicine and law. Because of major scholarship and gift aid support which does not have to be repaid like many academic loans, ASU boasts one of the nation's lowest student debt burdens upon graduation.

"The school emphasizes producing students who can think critically, adapt to a changing world and succeed in various environments. ASU appeals to those who want a more rigorous academic experience through the school's Honors Program, and to those who want to study abroad through the International Studies Program that provides a more global experience while keeping costs within reach.

"ASU has the only Physics Department in Texas ranked in the top 20 among undergraduate programs nationwide and a nationally recognized Biology Department which has the first department in the nation to have its biology honor society named the top chapter in the nation a record six times.

"The university is organized with six colleges: Business; Education; Liberal and Fine Arts; Nursing and Allied Health; Sciences; and Graduate Studies as well as 19 academic departments. Those departments offer 43 undergraduate programs, 21 graduate programs, including a doctorate, and one associate degree as more than 100 majors. As a member of the Texas Tech University System, ASU provides options for a variety of pre-professional and two-plus-two and four-plus-one programs with Texas Tech. ASU draws students from practically every county in Texas (221 of 254) as well as from 44 states and 24 countries. With more than half of its graduates as first generation college students, ASU is attuned to the academic and social needs of a new generation of college students.

"Along with ASU's academic offerings, it also provides a 268-acre campus that features an attractive and safe setting for a college education. ASU's campus facilities are valued at over $376 million and include the Math-Computer Science Building, which houses one of the most sophisticated computer systems in the state; the Junell Center/Stephens Arena, one of the top facilities in all of NCAA Division II athletics; and the Houston-Harte University Center, the center of campus student life. Additionally, the university operates 6,000 additional acres in farm and ranch lands that also serve as home for ASU's Management, Instruction and Research Center as well as the Food Safety and Product Development Laboratory.

"Thanks to funding by the Robert G. and Nona K. Carr Scholarship Foundation, ASU has scholarships that benefit one in every six students with grants ranging from $2,000 to $6,000. Established in 1978 exclusively to benefit needy and deserving ASU students, the Carr Foundation today holds assets of more than $96 million. For the 2013-14 academic year, approximately $4 million in Carr Scholarships were awarded to ASU students."

Campus Setting

Founded in 1928, Angelo State University is the second-largest campus in the Texas Tech University System. ASU's 268-acre main campus is located in San Angelo, the center of a community of 100,000 where West Texas meets the Hill Country. A comprehensive public university, Angelo State offers programs leading to bachelor's,

ANGELO STATE UNIVERSITY

Highlights

Angelo State University
San Angelo, TX (Pop. 95,887)
Location: Medium city
Four-year public
Founded: 1928
Website: http://www.angelo.edu

Students
Total enrollment: 6,536
Undergrads: 5,546
Freshmen: 1,589
Part-time students: 15%
From out-of-state: 2%
From public schools: 96%
Male/Female: 46%/54%
Live on-campus: 35%
In fraternities: 2%
In sororities: 1%
Off-campus employment rating: Good
Caucasian: 55%
African American: 8%
Hispanic: 30%
Asian: 1%
Hawaiian or Pacific Islander: <1%
Native American: <1%
Mixed (2+ ethnicities): 2%
International: 3%

Academics
Calendar: Semester
Student/faculty ratio: 18:1
Class size 9 or fewer: 6%
Class size 10-29: 60%
Class size 30-49: 25%
Class size 50-99: 8%
Class size 100 or more: 1%
Returning freshmen: 55%
Six-year graduation rate: 28%

Most Popular Majors
Interdisciplinary studies
Business/marketing
Psychology

master's and doctoral degrees. ASU is recognized for its academic programs in agriculture, educator preparation, nursing, physics, computer science/computer gaming and field biology. A four-year public institution, Angelo State University has a large, well-stocked library and a planetarium. The university provides on-campus housing with seven units that can accommodate 2,060 students. Housing options include: coed dorms · single-student apartments · special housing for disabled students. Recreation and sports facilities include: arena · center for human performance · intramural fields · tennis courts · baseball complex · lake house.

Student Life and Activities

Most students (65 percent) live off campus. According to a school representative, "The university social network centers around the Houston Harte University Center. With multiple flat screen televisions, Direct TV lounge areas, gaming systems, ping pong, pool, card tables and DVD rentals, the UC is a bee hive of activity. The UC also shows current films during regular movie nights which offer free popcorn and drinks for students. Also available in the University Center is a popular food court with national vendors, ranging from Chick-fil-A to Starbucks Coffee. The UC houses the Student Government Association, student organizations, the University Book Store and a branch of the Concho Educators Federal Credit Union branch. With multiple coed and gender specific sports, the program sees thousands of student participants throughout the year. Angelo State also sponsors 100 student-led organizations with many receiving national recognition for outstanding achievement, service and participation."

On campus, students gather at Houston Harte University Center, ASU Lake Facility and Lake House, ASU intramural fields, Center for Human Performance, disk golf course, University Mall and Baptist Student Ministries Center. Off campus, San Angelo River Walk, Lake Nasworthy, Fast Eddie's, Starbucks, Bakerstreet Coffee, Hastings, Sunset Mall, Scrub Pub and Buffalo Wild Wings are popular gathering spots. Popular campus events include Rambunctious Weekend, Homecoming, Ram Jam, West Texas Medical Associate Moon Lectures, football, baseball, Midnight Madness and planetarium shows. Popular campus groups include Tri Beta Biological Honor Society, Block and Bridle, Intramural and Recreation Program and the Society of Physics Students. Those hoping to join a sports team can check out the intramural teams: basketball · boxing · flag football · gymnastics · handball · indoor soccer · martial arts · racquetball · softball · tennis · Ultimate Frisbee · wrestling · volleyball. Angelo State University is a member of the Lone Star Conference (Division II).

Academics and Learning Environment

For the B student, the learning environment of a college is just as important as the quality of its academic program. Angelo State University has 281 full-time and 70 part-time faculty members, offering a student-to-faculty ratio of 18:1. The most common course size is 20 to 29 students. Angelo State University offers 68 majors with the most popular being psychology, interdisciplinary studies and business/marketing, and least popular being drama, foreign languages and math. The school has a general core requirement. Cooperative education is not offered. All first-year students must maintain a 2.0 GPA or higher to avoid academic probation, and a minimum overall GPA of 2.5 is required to graduate. Other special academic programs that would appeal to a B student: independent study · double majors · honors program · internships · distance learning.

B Student Support and Success

Angelo State University provides a variety of support programs including dedicated guidance for: academic · career · personal · psychological · veterans. Recognizing that some students may need extra preparation, Angelo State University offers remedial and refresher courses in: reading · writing · math · study skills. Annually, 55 percent of freshmen students return for their sophomore year. The average freshman year GPA is 2.5. Companies that most frequently hire graduates from Angelo State University include: Enterprise Rent-a-Car · Orix · Raytheon · school districts · USAA.

Support for Students with Learning Disabilities

Students with learning disabilities will find the following programs at Angelo State University useful: remedial math · remedial English · remedial reading · learning center · extended time for tests · oral tests · note-taking services · tape recorders · diagnostic testing service. Individual or small group tutorials are also available.

How to Get Admitted

For admissions decisions, non-academic factors considered: state of residency. A high school diploma is required, although a GED is also accepted for admissions consideration. SAT or ACT test scores are required of all applicants. SAT Subject Test scores are not required. *According to the admissions office:* Minimum SAT Reasoning score of 820 (composite ACT score of 17) is required. *Academic units recommended:* 4 English, 4 Math, 4 Science, 3.5 Social Studies, 2 Foreign Language.

Insight

Preston Lewis, director of communications and marketing, says that while ASU welcomes students graduating in the top 10 percent of their graduating class, the university has, as a strategic move, paid special attention to recruiting students in the top 11 percent to 25 percent of their graduating class as well. Special scholarships are targeted to students graduating in this range. More than half of students are first-generation college students. Lewis states, "We are accustomed to welcoming not just students but their families into the college experience."

How to Pay for College

To apply for financial aid, students should submit the following: Free Application for Federal Student Aid (FAFSA). Angelo State University participates in the Federal Work Study program. *Need-based aid programs include:* scholarships and grants · general need-based awards · Federal Pell grants · state scholarships and grants · college-based scholarships and grants · private scholarships and grants · Federal Nursing scholarships · Carr Academic Scholarships. *Non-need-based aid programs include:* scholarships and grants · state scholarships and grants · athletic scholarships · ROTC scholarships · Carr Merit Scholarships.

ANGELO STATE UNIVERSITY

Highlights

Admissions
Applicants: 2,599
Accepted: 2,092
Acceptance rate: 80.5%
Average GPA: Not reported
ACT range: 17-23
SAT Math range: 440-540
SAT Reading range: 420-520
SAT Writing range: Not reported
Top 10% of class: 10%
Top 25% of class: 35%
Top 50% of class: 72%

Deadlines
Early Action: No
Early Decision: No
Regular Action: Rolling admissions
Common Application: Not accepted

Financial Aid
In-state tuition: $4,700
Out-of-state tuition: $15,560
Room: $4,100
Board: $2,700
Books: $1,500
Freshmen receiving need-based aid: 71%
Undergrads rec. need-based aid: 69%
Avg. % of need met by financial aid: 65%
Avg. aid package (freshmen): $10,759
Avg. aid package (undergrads): $10,579
Avg. debt upon graduation: $24,360

Prominent Alumni
Satcha Pretto, Univision Network Anchor; Dr. Arnoldo De Leon, Nationally recognized historian on Mexican American History; Grant Teaff, Executive Director, American Football Coaches Association; Ronnie Hawkins, Lt. Gen., U.S. Air Force.

School Spirit
Mascot: Rams and Rambelles
Colors: Blue and gold
Song: *In Time to Come*

91

College Profiles

ANNA MARIA COLLEGE

Highlights

Anna Maria College
Paxton, MA (Pop. 4,386)
Location: Rural
Four-year private
Founded: 1946
Website: http://www.annamaria.edu

Students
Total enrollment: 1,432
Undergrads: 1,037
Freshmen: 318
Part-time students: 22%
From out-of-state: 24%
Male/Female: 45%/55%
Live on-campus: 54%
Off-campus employment rating: Good
Caucasian: 69%
African American: 9%
Hispanic: 9%
Asian: 1%
Native American: 1%
Mixed (2+ ethnicities): 2%

Academics
Calendar: Semester
Student/faculty ratio: 12:1
Class size 9 or fewer: 30%
Class size 10-29: 69%
Class size 30-49: -
Class size 50-99: -
Class size 100 or more: -
Returning freshmen: 61%
Six-year graduation rate: 48%

Most Popular Majors
Criminal justice

92

America's
Best Colleges for
B Students

ANNA MARIA COLLEGE

50 Sunset Lane, Paxton, MA 01612
Admissions: 508-849-3360
Financial Aid: 800-344-4586, extension 366
Email: admission@annamaria.edu
Website: http://www.annamaria.edu

From the College

"Anna Maria College recognizes its obligation to serve its immediate community, the Commonwealth of Massachusetts, the nation and the world through the provision of education, the preservation of learning and the sponsorship of research. Rooted in the Roman Catholic tradition of higher education, Anna Maria College is maintained and operated in conformity with the values of the Judeo-Christian tradition and in keeping with the ideals of its foundresses, the Sisters of Saint Anne. These ideals, which reflect the development of the total human being, also include increasing access to quality education, educational innovation and respect for practical skills.

"Anna Maria offers its undergraduate students a program integrating a liberal arts education, coupled with strong career preparation. For graduate students, the college offers an education fostering high standards of personal development and professional achievement, as well as a mature sense of responsibility."

Campus Setting

Anna Maria is a church-affiliated, liberal arts college. Founded in 1946 as a college for women, it began admitting men in 1973. Its 180-acre campus is set on the grounds of a 19th century estate, eight miles from Worcester. A four-year private institution, Anna Maria College offers campus facilities including: art gallery · art studio classrooms · dark room. Anna Maria College provides on-campus housing with 207 units that can accommodate 396 students. Housing options include: coed dorms · special housing for disabled students. Recreation and sports facilities include an activities center.

Student Life and Activities

Just over half of the students (54 percent) live off campus, but social life is active. "You can go to each room/floor of the dorm and be a welcome guest," reports the editor of the student newspaper. Students also appreciate Worcester's big nightlife. On campus, students gather in the Spiritwoods Pub and the dorm lobby; off campus, Sooney's Restaurant, Ralph's Diner and the Tipperary Pub are popular. Favorite activities include men's soccer games, men's and women's basketball games, Spring Weekend, the Variety Show and productions by the Drama and New England Theater Company. Anna Maria College has 13 official student organizations. The Ski Club, the Drama Club, the History Club and intramural sports are influential on campus life. Anna Maria College is a member of the Commonwealth Coast Conference (Division III).

Academics and Learning Environment

Anna Maria College has 52 full-time and 171 part-time faculty members, offering a student-to-faculty ratio of 12:1. The most common course size is 10 to 19 students. Anna Maria College offers 42 majors with the most popular being criminal justice and least popular being Spanish, English and art therapy. The school has a general core requirement. Cooperative education is not offered. All first-year students must maintain a 2.0 GPA or higher to avoid academic probation. Other special academic programs that would appeal to a B student: self-designed majors · pass/fail grading option · independent study · double majors · dual degrees · accelerated study · internships · certificate programs.

B Student Support and Success

Anna Maria College offers an $8,000 scholarship based upon involvement in the high school community and the community at large. Anna Maria does not require minimum scores on the SAT. In addition, the admissions department states that there are many B and C students who are highly involved in their high school and are welcomed at Anna Maria.

Anna Maria College provides a variety of support programs including dedicated guidance for: academic · career · personal · psychological. Recognizing that some students may need extra preparation, Anna Maria offers remedial courses in: reading · writing · math · study skills. The average freshman year GPA is 3.0, and 61 percent of freshmen students return for their sophomore year.

Support for Students with Learning Disabilities

Students with learning disabilities may take advantage of specific support programs, including individual or small group tutorials.

How to Get Admitted

For admissions decisions, non-academic factors considered: interview · extracurricular activities · special talents, interests and abilities · character/personal qualities · volunteer work · work experience · state of residency · alumni relationship. A high school diploma is required, although a GED is also accepted for admissions consideration. SAT or ACT test scores are required of all applicants. SAT Subject Test scores are not required. *According to the admissions office:* Minimum combined SAT Reasoning score of 900, rank in top half of secondary school class and minimum 2.5 GPA recommended. Academic unit: 4 English, 3 Math, 3 Science, 2 Social Studies, 2 Foreign Language.

How to Pay for College

To apply for financial aid, students should submit the following: Free Application for Federal Student Aid (FAFSA) · state aid form. Anna Maria College participates in the Federal Work Study program. *Need-based aid programs include:* scholarships and grants · general need-based awards · Federal Pell grants · state scholarships and grants · college-based scholarships and grants · private scholarships and grants · Federal Nursing scholarships · United Negro College Fund. *Non-need-based aid programs include:* scholarships and grants · general need-based awards · state scholarships and grants · special achievements and activities awards · special characteristics awards.

ANNA MARIA COLLEGE

Highlights

Admissions
Applicants: 1,902
Accepted: 1,287
Acceptance rate: 67.7%
Average GPA: Not reported
ACT range: 16-22
SAT Math range: 410-510
SAT Reading range: 400-480
SAT Writing range: Not reported

Deadlines
Early Action: No
Early Decision: No
Regular Action: Rolling admissions
Common Application: Accepted

Financial Aid
In-state tuition: $31,920
Out-of-state tuition: $31,920
Room: Varies
Board: Varies
Books: $500
Avg. aid package (freshmen): $27,361
Avg. aid package (undergrads): $22,228

Prominent Alumni
Edward Davis, fomer police commissioner of the Boston Police Department; Brendan Doherty, former superintendent of the Rhode Island State Police.

School Spirit
Mascot: AMCAT
Colors: Maroon and white

ARIZONA STATE UNIVERSITY

Admissions Services, P.O. Box 870112, Tempe, AZ 85287-0112
Admissions: 480-965-7788 · Financial Aid: 855-278-5080
Email: admissons@asu.edu · Website: http://www.asu.edu

From the College

"Arizona State University's Tempe campus welcomes students pursuing a wide range of majors including business, liberal arts, engineering and the sciences. Modern classrooms and high-tech laboratories create a dynamic and engaging learning environment. The newly expanded fitness complex allows students to take a break from their studies and focus on their health, while the Sun Devil Athletics facilities, performing arts venues, museums and vibrant downtown Tempe location complement this diverse university environment.

"ASU's vision is to establish ASU as the model for a New American University, measured not by who we exclude, but by who we include and how they succeed; pursuing research and discovery that benefits the public good and assuming major responsibility for the economic, social, and cultural vitality and health and well-being of the community. ASU champions intellectual and cultural diversity, and is home to students from all 50 states and more than 150 countries. Its research is inspired by real-world application, blurring the boundaries that traditionally separate academic disciplines."

Campus Setting

Arizona State University is a public, comprehensive university. Founded as a normal school in 1885, it gained university status in 1958. ASU is known as "One University in Many Places." ASU has four distinctive campuses throughout metropolitan Phoenix located on over 1,960 acres. At the Tempe campus, ASU focuses on research and graduate education along with an undergraduate education that is analytic and preparatory for graduate or professional school or employment. At the Polytechnic campus, ASU focuses on learning through an applied approach to professional and technological programs that meet business and societal needs and an emphasis on technical education that is a direct preparation for the workforce. At the West campus, ASU focuses on interdisciplinary liberal arts education with professional programs that connect to the community. Through the Downtown Phoenix campus, ASU is focused on programs with a direct urban and public connection.

A four-year public institution, Arizona State University has an enrollment of 48,739 students. ASU features: art, anthropology, geology, history and sports museums · early childhood development lab · herbarium · robotics lab · semiconductor clean room · high-resolution electron microscope facility · solar research facilities · Biodesign Institute · Institute of Sustainability · arboretum · Gammage. Arizona State University provides a variety of housing options including: coed dorms · sorority housing · fraternity housing · single-student apartments · married-student apartments. Recreation and sports facilities include: aquatic area · athletic fields.

Student Life and Activities

Most students (77 percent) live off campus. Students gather around the notable landmarks on campus such as Grady Gammage Memorial Auditorium, Palm Walk, which is lined by 111 palm trees, Charles Trumbull Hayden Library, the University Club Building and University Bridge. Popular campus events include Homecoming, Family Weekend, World Festival, Devil's in Disguise, Passport to ASU, Final's Breakfast, A Week, MLK Day of Service and Cesar Chavez Day of Service. Arizona

State University has 673 official student organizations. The most popular are: religious, minority and international student groups and music, theatre, political, service and special-interest groups. The school's intramural teams include: badminton · basketball · dodgeball · flag football · floor hockey · golf · racquetball · sand volleyball · soccer · softball · table tennis · tennis · Ultimate Frisbee · Wiffle ball · wrestling. Arizona State University is a member of the Member of Pacific-12 Conference (Division I, Football I-A).

Academics and Learning Environment

Arizona State University has 1914 full-time and 220 part-time faculty members, offering a student-to-faculty ratio of 22:1. The most common course size is 10 to 19 students. Arizona State University offers 270 majors with the most popular being psychology, business/management/marketing and communication/media. The school has a general core requirement. Cooperative education is available. All first-year students must maintain a 1.6 GPA or higher to avoid academic probation, and a minimum overall GPA of 2.0 is required to graduate. Other special academic programs that would appeal to a B student: pass/fail grading option · independent study · double majors · dual degrees · accelerated study · honors program · internships · distance learning certificate programs.

B Student Support and Success

Like other colleges, ASU offers First Year Experience for freshmen. According to the college, this program is designed to "provide a strong foundation for all first-year students and students in transition that will foster their academic and personal success. We will achieve this mission by providing academic support services, opportunities for the exchange of ideas, workshops, generating and supporting research and scholarship, hosting visiting scholars and practitioners, faculty interaction within living and learning communities, administering a website and student involvement opportunities with the university community." The Learning Resource Center offers tutoring to help students develop study skills and strategies. This nationally certified program offers tutoring in more than 100 courses, either in a group or individual settings. Peer coaching teaches time management, study habits and test-taking skills. The program also includes software training and Academic Skills Workshops.

Arizona State University provides a variety of support programs for the B student, including: academic · career · personal · psychological · minority students · military · veterans · non-traditional students · family planning · religious. The average freshman year GPA is 2.9, and 84 percent of freshmen students return for their sophomore year. Companies that most frequently hire graduates from Arizona State University include: American Express · Banner Health System · Boeing Co. · Chandler Public Schools · Charles Schwab and Co. · General Dynamics · Gilbert Public Schools · Honeywell · Intel · KPMG LLP · Kyrene School District · Maricopa County · Mesa Public Schools · Peoria Unified School District · PricewaterhouseCoopers LLP · State of Arizona · Target · Teach for America · University of Phoenix.

ARIZONA STATE UNIVERSITY

Highlights

Arizona State University
Tempe, AZ (Pop. 166,842)
Location: Major city
Four-year public
Founded: 1885
Website: http://www.asu.edu

Students
Total enrollment: 48,739
Undergrads: 38,735
Freshmen: 7,286
Part-time students: 10%
From out-of-state: 35%
Male/Female: 56%/44%
Live on-campus: 23%
In fraternities: 8%
In sororities: 13%
Off-campus employment rating: Excellent
Caucasian: 57%
African American: 4%
Hispanic: 18%
Asian: 7%
Hawaiian or Pacific Islander: <1%
Native American: 1%
Mixed (2+ ethnicities): 4%
International: 7%

Academics
Calendar: Other
Student/faculty ratio: 22:1
Class size 9 or fewer: 10%
Class size 10-29: 56%
Class size 30-49: 16%
Class size 50-99: 12%
Class size 100 or more: 6%
Returning freshmen: 84%
Six-year graduation rate: 60%

Most Popular Majors
Psychology
Business/management/marketing
Communication/media

ARIZONA STATE UNIVERSITY

Admissions
Applicants: 21,770
Accepted: 17,465
Acceptance rate: 80.2%
Average GPA: 3.5
ACT range: 22-28
SAT Math range: 520-650
SAT Reading range: 500-620
SAT Writing range: Not reported
Top 10% of class: 31%
Top 25% of class: 63%
Top 50% of class: 90%

Deadlines
Early Action: No
Early Decision: No
Regular Action: Rolling admissions
Common Application: Not accepted

Financial Aid
In-state tuition: $9,343
Out-of-state tuition: $23,136
Room: $6,150
Board: $3,158
Books: $1,040
Freshmen receiving need-based aid: 60%
Undergrads rec. need-based aid: 60%
Avg. % of need met by financial aid: 59%
Avg. aid package (freshmen): $13,755
Avg. aid package (undergrads): $12,688
Avg. debt upon graduation: $21,137

Prominent Alumni
Al Michaels, NBC Sports Commentator; Kate Spade, designer/owner, Kate Spade LLC; Phil Mickelson, professional golfer.

School Spirit
Mascot: Sparky
Colors: Maroon and gold
Song: *Fight Devils*

Support for Students with Learning Disabilities

Learning disabled students may take advantage of ASU's support programs including additional time to complete a degree and a lightened course load. According to the school, there are no special admissions requirements for students with disabilities and they must meet the same requirements as any other student. Students who utilize alternative format, i.e. digital electronic files are encouraged to register early with the DRC, which is separate from the university process. The school's philosophy is that students with disabilities are no less capable than any other student.

Students with learning disabilities will find the following programs at Arizona State University useful: tutors · testing accommodations · extended time for tests · take-home exam · oral tests · exam on tape or computer · readers · typist/scribe · note-taking services · reading machines · early syllabus · waiver of math degree requirement. Individual or small group tutorials are also available in: time management · organizational skills · learning strategies · specific subject areas · writing labs · math labs · study skills. An advisor/advocate from the Disability Resources Center is available to students.

How to Get Admitted

A high school diploma is required, although a GED is also accepted for admissions consideration. SAT or ACT test scores are required of all applicants. *According to the admissions office:* Minimum combined SAT Reasoning score of 1040 (composite ACT score of 22), rank in top quarter of secondary school class or minimum 3.0 GPA recommended of in-state applicants; minimum combined SAT Reasoning score of 1110 (composite ACT score of 24), rank in top quarter of secondary school class or minimum 3.0 GPA recommended of out-of-state applicants. *Academic units recommended:* 4 English, 4 Math, 3 Science, 1 Social Studies, 2 Foreign Language.

How to Pay for College

To apply for financial aid, students should submit the following: Free Application for Federal Student Aid (FAFSA). Arizona State University participates in the Federal Work Study program. *Need-based aid programs include:* scholarships and grants · general need-based awards · Federal Pell grants · state scholarships and grants · college-based scholarships and grants · private scholarships and grants. *Non-need-based aid programs include:* scholarships and grants · state scholarships and grants · creative arts and performance awards · special achievements and activities awards · athletic scholarships · ROTC scholarships.

AUBURN UNIVERSITY

108 Mary Martin Hall, Auburn, AL 36849
Admissions: 800-282-8769 · Financial Aid: 334-844-4634
Email: admissions@auburn.edu · Website: http://www.auburn.edu

From the College

"Auburn University has provided instruction, research and outreach for more than 150 years, and is among a distinctive group of universities designated as Land, Sea and Space Grant institutions. AU has more than 250,000 graduates and provides 140 degree programs to more than 25,000 graduate and undergraduate students. Graduates include six NASA astronauts, the head of the Kennedy Space Center, the nation's first and only class of undergraduate wireless engineers, dozens of CEOs, world-famous architects and several authors and journalists. AU emphasizes international education, is at the forefront of engineering, transportation technology and veterinary medicine, achieves global impact through modern agricultural, extension and forestry/wildlife programs, and fulfills critical research and national shortages through pharmaceutical, sciences, mathematics, education, nursing and human sciences offerings."

Campus Setting

Auburn is a multipurpose, land-grant university. It was founded as a private, liberal arts institution in 1856 and came under state control in 1872. Its 1,871-acre campus is located in Auburn. A four-year public institution, Auburn University has an enrollment of 24,864 students. Although not originally a co-educational college, Auburn University has been co-ed since 1892. In addition to a large, well-stocked library, the campus facilities include: art museum · herbarium · research center · research institute · flight simulators · animal clinics · special centers · laboratories. Auburn University provides on-campus housing that can accommodate 3,986 students. Housing options include: coed dorms · women's dorms · sorority housing · fraternity housing · single-student apartments · special housing for disabled students. Recreation and sports facilities include: aquatic center · coliseum · fitness and weight rooms · golf course · track · racquetball and tennis courts.

Student Life and Activities

Most students (79 percent) live off campus. Popular campus gathering spots include the Student Center, concourse, downtown cafes and restaurants, main library, cafeteria and residence halls. Popular campus events include A-Day, Freshman Convocation, freshmen leadership programs, Greek Recruitment, Greek Sing, Greek Week, Splash Into Spring, University Program Council-sponsored entertainment, Holiday Tree Lighting, Tiger Nights, Burn the (Georgia) Bulldogs, Homecoming Week, student government elections, outdoor and international movies, Rolling Toomer's Corner, athletics events, Step Shows & Tiger-Stomp, service opportunities/events, Welcome Week, Beat Bama Parade, Beat Bama Food Drive and Black History Month. Auburn University has 447 official student organizations. The most popular are: G.A.N.G. Student Ministries · Gay Straight Alliance · Historic Preservation Guild · Agriculture Ambassadors · American Institute of Chemical Engineers · Association of Certified Fraud Examiners · Mock Trial Competition Team · Public Relations Council of Alabama. For those interested in sports, there are intramural teams such as: badminton · cycling · lacrosse · rowing · rugby · sailing · soccer · table tennis · tennis · volleyball · water polo · water skiing · wrestling. Auburn University is a member of the Southeastern Conference (Division I, Football I-A).

AUBURN UNIVERSITY

Auburn University
Auburn, AL (Pop. 56,908)
Location: Large town
Four-year public
Founded: 1856
Website: http://www.auburn.edu

Students
Total enrollment: 24,864
Undergrads: 19,799
Freshmen: 4,522
Part-time students: 9%
From out-of-state: 37%
From public schools: 88%
Male/Female: 51%/49%
Live on-campus: 21%
In fraternities: 21%
In sororities: 31%
Off-campus employment rating: Excellent
Caucasian: 85%
African American: 7%
Hispanic: 3%
Asian: 2%
Native American: 1%
International: 1%

Academics
Calendar: Semester
Student/faculty ratio: 18:1
Class size 9 or fewer: 9%
Class size 10-29: 55%
Class size 30-49: 21%
Class size 50-99: 9%
Class size 100 or more: 7%
Returning freshmen: 89%
Six-year graduation rate: 68%

Most Popular Majors
Biomedical sciences
Finance
Psychology

Academics and Learning Environment

Auburn University has 1,184 full-time and 179 part-time faculty members, offering a student-to-faculty ratio of 18:1. The most common course size is 20 to 29 students. Auburn University offers 300 majors with the most popular being finance, biomedical sciences and psychology, and least popular being business/marketing education, music and economics. The school has a general core requirement. Cooperative education is available. All first-year students must maintain a 1.5 GPA or higher to avoid academic probation, and a minimum overall GPA of 2.0 is required to graduate. Other special academic programs that would appeal to a B student: independent study · double majors · dual degrees · accelerated study · honors program · Phi Beta Kappa · internships · distance learning certificate programs.

B Student Support and Success

Auburn's network of academic advisors is by department or major. Advisors assist students with selecting classes and career planning, and they also give general advice. Some department heads provide information about their departments to prospective applicants as well. Learning Communities bring together first-year students in the same major to take certain required classes as a group. This enables students to easily form study groups and to navigate classes cooperatively. Departments also offer help that is basic to a student's field of study. For example, the Auburn Office of Engineering Student Services provides tutoring for freshmen and transfer engineering students who need assistance in entry-level math, chemistry and physics classes. The tutoring is done by volunteer upperclassmen in group or one-on-one sessions.

Auburn University provides a variety of support programs including dedicated guidance for: academic · career · personal · psychological · minority students · military · veterans · non-traditional students · family planning. Additional counseling services include: sexual assault. The average freshman year GPA is 3.0, and 89 percent of freshmen students return for their sophomore year. Among students who enter the workforce, approximately 81 percent enter a field related to their major within six months of graduation. Companies that most frequently hire graduates from Auburn University include: Alabama Power · AmSouth Bank · Baptist Health System · Cargill Steel Corporation · Chevron · Colonial Bank · DMJM Harris · Ernst & Young · Exxon Mobil · Georgia Pacific · Honeywell · IBM · Kimley-Horn & Associates · KMPG · Lockheed Martin · Lennar Homes · Merrill Lynch · Michelin North America · Milliken & Company · Northrop Grumman · Pepsico · PricewaterhouseCoopers · Proctor & Gamble · Regions Bank · Sony · Southern Company · Weyerhaeuser.

Support for Students with Learning Disabilities

Students with learning disabilities may want to take additional time to complete their degrees or lighten their course loads. In addition, the Program for Students with Disabilities offers a variety of Assistive Technology for students with learning disabilities. Text-to-speech software and electronic text are available for students with reading disabilities. Kurweil 3000, a scanning and reading software, and Dragon Naturally Speaking, a speech-to-text software, are available for student use in two locations on campus. Individual training is offered for students who may benefit from the use of assistive technology. Students with learning disabilities will find the following programs at Auburn University useful: tutors · learning center · testing accommodations · extended time for tests · oral tests · readers · typist/scribe · note-taking services · reading machines · early syllabus · diagnostic testing service · priority registration · waiver of math degree requirement. Individual or small group tutorials are also available in: time management · organizational skills · learning strategies · specific subject areas · writing labs · math labs · study skills. An advisor/advocate from the Program for Students with Disabilities is available to students.

How to Get Admitted

For admissions decisions, non-academic factors considered: extracurricular activities · special talents, interests and abilities · character/personal qualities · volunteer work · work experience · geographical location · alumni relationship. A high school diploma is required, although a GED is also accepted for admissions consideration. SAT or ACT test scores are required of all applicants. SAT Subject Test scores are recommended but not required. *According to the admissions office:* Math units must include algebra I, algebra II, and one unit of analysis, calculus, geometry or trigonometry. Science units must include biology and a physical science. Minimum composite ACT score of 18 and minimum 2.5 GPA required of in-state applicants; minimum composite ACT score of 22 and minimum 2.5 GPA required of out-of-state applicants. *Academic units recommended:* 4 Social Studies, 1 Foreign Language.

How to Pay for College

To apply for financial aid, students should submit the following: Free Application for Federal Student Aid (FAFSA). Auburn University participates in the Federal Work Study program. *Need-based aid programs include:* scholarships and grants · general need-based awards · Federal Pell grants · state scholarships and grants · college-based scholarships and grants · private scholarships and grants · Federal Nursing scholarships. *Non-need-based aid programs include:* scholarships and grants · general need-based awards · state scholarships and grants · athletic scholarships · ROTC scholarships.

AUBURN UNIVERSITY

Highlights

Admissions
Applicants: 15,745
Accepted: 13,027
Acceptance rate: 82.7%
Average GPA: 3.7
ACT range: 24-30
SAT Math range: 540-650
SAT Reading range: 520-620
SAT Writing range: 6-30
Top 10% of class: 29%
Top 25% of class: 60%
Top 50% of class: 86%

Deadlines
Early Action: on a rolling basis beginning October 1
Early Decision: No
Regular Action: Rolling admissions
Common Application: Not accepted

Financial Aid
In-state tuition: $10,200
Out-of-state tuition: $27,384
Room: $6,892
Board: $5,286
Books: $1,200
Freshmen receiving need-based aid: 37%
Undergrads rec. need-based aid: 38%
Avg. % of need met by financial aid: 45%
Avg. aid package (freshmen): $9,889
Avg. aid package (undergrads): $10,492
Avg. debt upon graduation: $26,990

Prominent Alumni
Kathy Thornton, astronaut; Don Logan, CEO, Time Warner Cable; Rheta Grimsley Johnson, syndicated columnist.

School Spirit
Mascot: Tigers
Colors: Orange and blue
Song: *War Eagle*

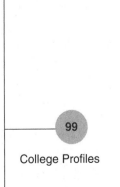

99

AUGSBURG COLLEGE

2211 Riverside Avenue South, Minneapolis, MN 55454
Admissions: 612-330-1001 · Financial Aid: 800-458-1721
Email: admissions@augsburg.edu · Website: http://www.augsburg.edu

From the College

"As the Evangelical Lutheran Church in America's (ELCA) most diverse and only urban institution, Augsburg strives to educate both traditional and non-traditional students, offering undergraduate degrees in over 50 major areas of study. The college also grants six graduate degrees, among them the Master of Science in Physician Assistant Studies, the state's only Physician Assistant training program. Augsburg's 3,700 students come from diverse religious, cultural and ethnic backgrounds. The college also is a nationally recognized leader in providing services to students with physical and learning disabilities. This on-campus diversity is enhanced by Augsburg's location at the crossroads of the Twin Cities' most diverse neighborhoods. The college's location also provides access for Augsburg's students to participate in community service and internship experiences that not only enhance their classroom learning but also prepare them for life's work in a multi-cultural society."

Campus Setting

Augsburg, founded in 1869, is a church-affiliated, liberal arts college. Its 24-acre campus is located one mile from downtown Minneapolis. A four-year private institution, Augsburg College has an enrollment of 3,554 students. Although not originally a co-educational college, Augsburg College has been co-ed since 1874. The school is also affiliated with the Evangelical Lutheran Church in America. In addition to a large, well-stocked library, the campus facilities include: art gallery · auditorium · chapel. Augsburg College provides on-campus housing with 525 units that can accommodate 1,050 students. Housing options: coed dorms · single-student apartments · special housing for disabled students. Recreation and sports facilities include: athletic, baseball, football, soccer and softball fields · basketball and volleyball courts · cross-country park · ice arena · stadium.

Student Life and Activities

Most students (60 percent) live off campus. Favorite social spots include: Daily Chapel, Annual Homecoming Weekend, Velkommen Jule and Campus Kitchens. Augsburg College has 40 official student organizations. The most popular are: art club · business organization · Goliard Society of Medievalists · International Student Organization · Queer and Straight in Unity · College Democrats · College Republicans · Association for Computing Machinery · Chemistry Society. For those interested in sports, there are intramural teams such as: basketball · broomball · fantasy football · flag football · hockey/skating · kickball · pickleball · powderpuff football · soccer · softball · Ultimate Frisbee · volleyball. Augsburg College is a member of the Minnesota Intercollegiate Athletic Conference (Division III).

Academics and Learning Environment

Augsburg College has 195 full-time and 208 part-time faculty members, offering a student-to-faculty ratio of 16:1. The most common course size is 20 to 29 students. Augsburg College offers 51 majors with the most popular being management, nursing and psychology and least popular being medieval studies, women's studies and computational economics. The school has a general core requirement as well as a religion requirement. Cooperative education is not offered. All first-year students must maintain a 2.0 GPA or higher to avoid academic probation, and a minimum overall GPA of 2.0 is required to graduate. Other special academic programs that would appeal to a B student include: self-designed majors · pass/fail grading option · independent study · double majors · dual degrees · accelerated study · honors program · Phi Beta Kappa · internships · weekend college.

B Student Support and Success

Support for academic success is provided through tutoring, academic skills coaching, supplemental instruction and the math, public speaking and writing labs. Augsburg's TRiO/Student Support Services program helps students who are 1) low-income, 2) first-generation enrollees or 3) disabled (learning or physical) to achieve their bachelor's degrees. StepUp provides ongoing support to students in chemical recovery who are willing and able to progress toward an academic degree while remaining clean and sober. Students live together in separate, chemical-free housing. The Center for Learning and Adaptive Student Services (CLASS) assists academically qualified students with learning, attention, psychiatric or other cognitive disabilities reach their individual potential through services and accommodations, while the Access Center supports students with documented physical disabilities.

Augsburg College provides a variety of support programs including dedicated guidance for: academic · career · personal · psychological · minority students · religious. The average freshman year GPA is 2.9, and 80 percent of freshmen students return for their sophomore year. Among students who enter the workforce, approximately 85 percent enter a field related to their major within six months of graduation. Companies that most frequently hire graduates from Augsburg College include: Target Corporation · Cargill · KPMG International · Best Buy · Anoka Hennepin School District · Hennepin County Social Services · Wells Fargo Bank.

Support for Students with Learning Disabilities

Learning disabled students are allowed to take extra time to complete a degree. According to the Augsburg, The Center for Learning and Adaptive Student Services (CLASS) at Augsburg College provides accommodations and academic support to students with any of a broad range of specific cognitive and psychological disabilities, including dyslexia, ADHD and Asperger syndrome. CLASS also serves students with psychiatric disabilities such as anxiety disorder, depression and PTSD, and those with acquired or developmental neurological conditions in which the primary impact is on cognitive function. Students with learning disabilities will find the following programs at Augsburg College useful: tutors · learning center · testing accommodations · extended time for tests · take-home exam · oral tests · readers · note-taking services · reading machines · tape recorders · waiver of math degree requirement. Individual or small group tutorials are also available in: time management · organizational skills · learning strategies · writing labs · math labs · study skills. An advisor/advocate from the Center for Learning and Adaptive Student Services is available to students.

How to Get Admitted

For admissions decisions, non-academic factors considered: interview · extracurricular activities · special talents, interests and abilities ·

AUGSBURG COLLEGE

Highlights

Augsburg College
Minneapolis (Pop. 387,753)
Location: Major city
Four-year private
Founded: 1869
Website: http://www.augsburg.edu

Students
Total enrollment: 3,554
From out-of-state: 17%
Male/Female: 45%/55%
Live on-campus: 40%
Off-campus employment rating: Fair
Caucasian: 60%
African American: 9%
Hispanic: 6%
Asian: 7%
Hawaiian or Pacific Islander: <1%
Native American: 1%
Mixed (2+ ethnicities): 4%
International: 2%

Academics
Calendar: Semester
Student/faculty ratio: 16:1
Class size 9 or fewer: 30%
Class size 10-29: 66%
Class size 30-49: 3%
Class size 50-99: -
Class size 100 or more: -
Returning freshmen: 78%
Six-year graduation rate: 65%

Most Popular Majors
Management
Nursing
Psychology

AUGSBURG COLLEGE

Admissions
Applicants: 2,218
Accepted: 1,196
Acceptance rate: 53.9%
Average GPA: 3.0
ACT range: 20-25
SAT Math range: 490-590
SAT Reading range: 495-623
SAT Writing range: Not reported
Top 10% of class: 13%
Top 25% of class: 37%
Top 50% of class: 75%

Deadlines
Early Action: No
Early Decision: No
Regular Action: Rolling admissions
Common Application: Accepted

Financial Aid
In-state tuition: $33,766
Out-of-state tuition: $33,766
Room: $4,707
Board: $3,802
Books: $1,000
Avg. aid package (freshmen): $28,263
Avg. aid package (undergrads): $24,604

Prominent Alumni
Peter Agre, Nobel Prize winner in chemistry; Lute Olson, NCAA National Champion, basketball coach with University of Arizona; Devean George, former professional basketball player, Los Angeles Lakers and Dallas Mavericks.

School Spirit
Mascot: Auggies
Colors: Maroon and gray
Song: *Auggie War Song*

character/personal qualities · volunteer work · work experience · state of residency · minority affiliation · alumni relationship. A high school diploma is required, although a GED is also accepted for admissions consideration. SAT or ACT test scores are required of all applicants. SAT Subject Test scores are considered, if submitted, but are not required. *According to the admissions office:* Minimum composite ACT score of 22, rank in top half of secondary school class and minimum 2.5 GPA recommended. *Academic units recommended:* 4 English, 4 Math, 4 Science, 4 Social Studies, 3 Foreign Language.

Insight

"At Augsburg, we realize that grades are only one measure of success," says Bethany Bierman, assistant director of the Office of Undergraduate Admissions. She notes that one of the college's graduates received a D in high school chemistry and went on to receive a Nobel Prize in chemistry! The college is an intentionally diverse community, and with that comes students from a range of academic backgrounds. The admissions officers do a thorough review of an application, but grades are not the only basis on which students are accepted. Applicants can demonstrate that they are qualified for Augsburg by the extracurricular activities in which they are involved, including work positions or volunteer work. The difficulty of courses a student has selected in high school is also considered. Additionally, letters of recommendation that focus on the character of the student tell the admissions officers a great deal.

"Ultimately, Augsburg seeks to accept students who want to use their gifts to make a difference in the world," she says. Bierman states that the school's overall philosophy is that it is "more concerned with the quality and character of the alumni we produce than the incoming GPA of our students. As long as we know that students are working to their full potential, taking their academic work seriously and are seeking to make a difference in their community, we are proud of them, regardless of grades that are B's or C's."

How to Pay for College

To apply for financial aid, students should submit the following: Free Application for Federal Student Aid (FAFSA). Augsburg College participates in the Federal Work Study program. *Need-based aid programs include:* scholarships and grants · general need-based awards · Federal Pell grants · state scholarships and grants · college-based scholarships and grants · private scholarships and grants · Federal Nursing scholarships. *Non-need-based aid programs include:* scholarships and grants · state scholarships and grants · creative arts and performance awards · special achievements and activities awards · special characteristics awards.

BELLARMINE UNIVERSITY

2001 Newburg Road, Louisville, KY 40205
Admissions: 800-274-4723 · Financial Aid: 502-272-8124
Email: admissions@bellarmine.edu · Website: http://www.bellarmine.edu

From the College

"Bellarmine University is an independent Catholic university educating students of many faiths, ages, nations and cultures, and with respect for each individual's intrinsic value and dignity. The school educates students through undergraduate and graduate programs in the liberal arts and professional studies.

"Here we seek to foster a thoughtful, informed consideration of serious ideas, values and issues, time-honored and contemporary, across a broad range of compelling concerns that are regional, national and international. Thus we strive to be worthy of our foundational motto: 'In Veritatis Amore, In the Love of Truth'.

"Our lush 137-acre campus currently comprises more than 30 buildings including the W.L. Lyons Brown Library, the Norton Health Science Center and halls that are home to the nursing, education, and the arts and sciences. Bellarmine has six residence halls (with a seventh currently under construction), a chapel, campus center and university quadrangle. Our recreational facilities include indoor and outdoor tennis courts; fitness center; golf course and athletic fields including a state-of-the-art Frazier Stadium that's home to lacrosse, soccer, field hockey and track and field. Our campus on three hills and our award-winning architecture evoke the beautiful Italian hill towns of Tuscany, birthplace of our patron."

Campus Setting

Bellarmine, founded in 1950, is a private university, affiliated with the Roman Catholic Church. After merging with Ursuline College in 1968, Bellarmine became coed. Colleges/Schools include: Arts and Sciences, the Donna and Allan Lansing School of Nursing & Health Sciences, the W. Fielding Rubel School of Business, the Annsley Frazier Thornton School of Education and the School of Continuing and Professional School. Its 135-acre campus is located in Louisville. A four-year institution, Bellarmine University has an enrollment of 3,419 students. The campus features a large library, as well as the Thomas Merton Center. Bellarmine University provides on-campus housing with 1,127 units. Housing options include: coed dorms · women's dorms · men's dorms · special housing for disabled students. Recreation and sports facilities include: baseball and softball fields · golf course · gymnasium · recreation and fitness center · soccer stadium · tennis courts · track.

Student Life and Activities

Most students (57 percent) live off campus. Popular gathering spots include Campus Center, SAC and Bardstown Road. Favorite campus events include: Hillside, Relay for Life, Family Weekend, Ball on the Bell, Homecoming, Pioneer Dance, Senior Week and Flow Hip-Hop Dance Show. Bellarmine University has 76 official student organizations. The most popular are: jazz club · student theatre · dance team · Student Ambassadors · Students for Social Justice · Students for Life · University Radio Association · Colleges Against Cancer · Students for Organ Donation · education club · Friendly English Society · philosophy club · Communication Association · math club · Accounting Association · Association for Computing Machinery · psychology club · biology club · chemistry club · Clinical Laboratory Science Society · Pre-Physical Therapy Association · Association of Cardiopulmonary Science · Association of Nursing Students · Physical Therapy Association · University Democrats · University Republicans · political science club · Mock Trial · Pre-Law Society. For those interested

BELLARMINE UNIVERSITY

Bellarmine University
Louisville (Pop. 253,128)
Location: Medium city
Four-year private
Founded: 1950
Website: http://www.bellarmine.edu

Students
Total enrollment: 3,419
Undergrads: 2,593
Freshmen: 773
Part-time students: 8%
From out-of-state: 38%
From public schools: 69%
Male/Female: 36%/64%
Live on-campus: 43%
In fraternities: 1%
In sororities: 1%
Off-campus employment rating: Excellent
Caucasian: 83%
African American: 4%
Hispanic: 3%
Asian: 2%
Hawaiian or Pacific Islander: <1%
Native American: <1%
Mixed (2+ ethnicities): 2%
International: 2%

Academics
Calendar: Semester
Student/faculty ratio: 12:1
Class size 9 or fewer: 10%
Class size 10-29: 75%
Class size 30-49: 15%
Class size 50-99: 1%
Class size 100 or more: -
Returning freshmen: 80%
Six-year graduation rate: 66%

Most Popular Majors
Nursing
Psychology
Business administration

in sports, there are intramural teams such as: basketball · flag football · golf · soccer · tennis · volleyball. Bellarmine University is a member of the NCAA, Eastern College Athletic Conference Lacrosse (Division I) and the Great Lakes Valley Conference (Division II).

Academics and Learning Environment

Bellarmine University has 155 full-time and 235 part-time faculty members, offering a student-to-faculty ratio of 12:1. The most common course size is 10 to 19 students. Bellarmine University offers 50 majors with the most popular being nursing, business administration and psychology. The school has a general core requirement as well as a religion requirement. Cooperative education is not offered. All first-year students must maintain a 2.0 GPA or higher to avoid academic probation. Other special academic programs that would appeal to a B student include: self-designed majors · independent study · double majors · dual degrees · accelerated study · honors program · internships · certificate programs.

B Student Support and Success

This college's Academic Resource Center is the place for help with classes and college careers. There are tutors available for the 100- and 200-level classes, both in individual and group study sessions. The staff at ARC helps to analyze students' essays to improve grammar, style and formatting. Bellarmine also offers a one-hour credit course called Freshman Focus. It helps freshmen make the transition to college. This program includes reading, writing, discussion and out-of-class activities. The focus of the course is increasing a student's self-awareness and sense of purpose when it comes to his/her education and making important decisions about academic and social lives. Students are graded (A to F) in this class.

Bellarmine University provides multiple support programs including: academic · career · personal · psychological · religious. The average freshman year GPA is 3.1, and 80 percent of freshmen students return for their sophomore year. While many enter the workforce after graduation, approximately 25 percent pursue a graduate degree immediately after graduation. Among students who find employment, approximately 80 percent enter a field related to their major within six months of graduation. Companies that most frequently hire graduates from Bellarmine University include: Abercrombie and Fitch · AIG · AmeriCorps · Baptist East Hospital · Bellarmine University · Deloitte · Department of the Navy · Ernst and Young · Evanston Hospital · Frazier Arms Museum · GE Industrial · Girl Scouts of Kentuckiana · Hardin Memorial Hospital · Heaven Hills Distillery · Kessler Company · Kosair Hospital · Jefferson County Public Schools · Jewish Hospital · Mayor of Louisville · Norton Hospital · Old Towne Mortgage · Rescare · Saint Xavier High School · Sherman Williams · Strothman and Company · United Parcel Service · U.S. Bank · Wells Fargo · William M. Mercer Company.

Support for Students with Learning Disabilities

Students with learning disabilities can access a variety of support programs, and according to the school, LD advisor/advocates can meet with faculty on an individual basis. LD students can utilize: tutors · learning center · untimed tests · extended time for tests ·

take-home exam · oral tests · readers · note-taking services · reading machines · tape recorders · texts on tape · videotaped classes · early syllabus. Individual or small group tutorials are also available in: time management · organizational skills · learning strategies · specific subject areas · writing labs · math labs · study skills. An advisor/advocate from the Counseling Center is available to students.

How to Get Admitted

For admissions decisions, non-academic factors considered: interview · extracurricular activities · special talents, interests and abilities · character/personal qualities · volunteer work · work experience · geographical location · minority affiliation · alumni relationship. A high school diploma is required, although a GED is also accepted for admissions consideration. SAT or ACT test scores are required of all applicants. SAT Subject Test scores are not required. *According to the admissions office:* Minimum combined SAT Reasoning score of 1000 (composite ACT score of 21), rank in top half of secondary school class and minimum 2.5 GPA recommended. *Academic units recommended:* 4 English, 4 Math, 4 Science, 3 Social Studies, 2 Foreign Language.

How to Pay for College

To apply for financial aid, students should submit the following: Free Application for Federal Student Aid (FAFSA). Bellarmine University participates in the Federal Work Study program. *Need-based aid programs include:* scholarships and grants · general need-based awards · Federal Pell grants · state scholarships and grants · college-based scholarships and grants · private scholarships and grants. *Non-need-based aid programs include:* scholarships and grants · general need-based awards · state scholarships and grants · creative arts and performance awards · special achievements and activities awards · special characteristics awards · athletic scholarships · ROTC scholarships.

BELLARMINE UNIVERSITY

Highlights

Admissions
Applicants: 4,160
Accepted: 3,943
Acceptance rate: 94.8%
Average GPA: 3.5
ACT range: 22-27
SAT Math range: 490-590
SAT Reading range: 490-590
SAT Writing range: Not reported
Top 10% of class: 25%
Top 25% of class: 54%
Top 50% of class: 82%

Deadlines
Early Action: 11/1
Early Decision: No
Regular Action: Rolling admissions
Common Application: Accepted

Financial Aid
In-state tuition: $36,290
Out-of-state tuition: $36,290
Room: $6,580
Board: $4,120
Books: $692
Freshmen receiving need-based aid: 84%
Undergrads rec. need-based aid: 75%
Avg. % of need met by financial aid: 73%
Avg. aid package (freshmen): $29,188
Avg. aid package (undergrads): $27,406
Avg. debt upon graduation: $28,071

Prominent Alumni
Dr. James Heck, inventor of drug Cancidas; Angela Mason, co-founder, ITS Services; Joseph P. Clayton, former CEO/chairman, Sirius Satellite Radio.

School Spirit
Mascot: Knights
Colors: Scarlet and silver
Song: *On Knights of Bellarmine*

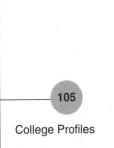

Bowie State University
Bowie, MD (Pop. 56,129)
Location: Large town
Four-year public
Founded: 1865
Website: http://www.bowiestate.edu

Students
Total enrollment: 6,398
Undergrads: 5,195
Freshmen: 25
Part-time students: 16%
From out-of-state: 13%
From public schools: 95%
Male/Female: 78%/22%
Live on-campus: 18%
In fraternities: 3%
In sororities: 10%
Caucasian: 4%
African American: 85%
Hispanic: 3%
Asian: 2%
Hawaiian or Pacific Islander: <1%
Native American: <1%
Mixed (2+ ethnicities): 3%
International: 3%

Academics
Calendar: Semester
Student/faculty ratio: 16:1
Class size 9 or fewer: 8%
Class size 10-29: 81%
Class size 30-49: 11%
Class size 50-99: -
Class size 100 or more: -
Returning freshmen: 39%
Six-year graduation rate: 37%

Most Popular Majors
Business administration
Computer science
Education

BOWIE STATE UNIVERSITY

14000 Jericho Park Road, Bowie, MD 20715-9465
Admissions: 877-772-6943 · Financial Aid: 301-860-3540
Email: ugradadmissions@bowiestate.edu
Website: http://www.bowiestate.edu

From the College

"Building on its image as a student-centered institution, Bowie State University will provide its diverse student population with a course of study that ensures a broad scope of knowledge and understanding that is deeply rooted in expanded research activities. The university excels in teacher education and will become the premier teacher of teachers."

Campus Setting

Bowie State, founded in 1865, is a public university of liberal arts and technology studies. Its 312-acre campus is located in Bowie, 22 miles from Washington, DC. A four-year public institution, Bowie State University is a historically black university with 6,398 students. Bowie State University provides on-campus housing with 1,400 units that can accommodate 1,400 students. Housing options: coed dorms · women's dorms · men's dorms · single-student apartments. Recreation and sports facilities include a gymnasium.

Student Life and Activities

Most students live off campus. However, Bowie State University has 71 official student organizations. The most popular are: gospel choir · university singers · jazz ensemble · concert, marching and pep bands · departmental and political clubs · honor societies · team managers. Bowie State University is a member of the Central Intercollegiate Athletic Association (Division II).

Academics and Learning Environment

Bowie State University has 216 full-time and 192 part-time faculty members, and a student to faculty ration of 16:1. The most common course size is 20 to 29 students. Bowie State University offers 37 majors with the most popular being business administration, computer science and education and least popular being English, mathematics and fine/performing arts. The school has a general core requirement. Cooperative education is not offered. All first-year students must maintain a 2.0 GPA or higher to avoid academic probation, and a minimum overall GPA of 2.0 is required to graduate. Other special academic programs that would appeal to a B student include: pass/fail grading · independent study · double majors · honors program · internships · distance learning certificate programs.

B Student Support and Success

Bowie's Writing Center helps students with English class assignments. The school also has a Student Success and Retention Center. The center assists students through programs and activities that "foster student academic, social and personal development." It is focused on helping freshmen transition into college life with the aid of placement testing, mentoring and tutorial services. In addition to these services, Bowie State sponsors the Freshman Seminar course. It is designed to help each student pursue academic excellence and includes lessons about the college's history and its contribution to Maryland. Students learn to critically analyze specific readings that introduce them to concepts in liberal arts and to broaden their understanding of global awareness, critical thinking and oral and written communication skills. According to the college, "The goal is for students to become academically, personally and socially successful within and beyond the intellectual community." Mentoring is popular at Bowie State. Mentors are matched with students to help foster a strong relationship that "promotes academic success, retention and the successful graduation of students." Peer mentors are paired with six freshmen based on academic majors. KEAP, or Knowledge Enriched through Academic Performance, helps students with issues like poor grades and poor attendance. Students with a GPA of 2.0 or lower are required to take part in KEAP.

Bowie State University provides a variety of support programs including dedicated guidance for: academic · career · personal · psychological · minority students · military. Recognizing that some students may need extra preparation, Bowie State University offers remedial and refresher courses in: reading · writing · math · study skills. The average freshman year GPA is 2.5, and 39 percent of freshmen students return for their sophomore year.

Support for Students with Learning Disabilities

Students with learning disabilities are often given extra time to complete a degree, as well as lighter course loads. LD students can also access: tutors · learning center · testing accommodations · extended time for tests · take-home exam · oral tests · typist/scribe · note-taking services · reading machines · early syllabus · priority registration. Individual or small group tutorials are also available in: organizational skills · writing labs · math labs. An advisor/advocate from the Disability Support Services is available to students.

How to Get Admitted

For admissions decisions, non-academic factors considered: extracurricular activities · state of residency. A high school diploma is required, although a GED is also accepted for admissions consideration. SAT or ACT test scores are required of all applicants. *According to the admissions office:* Minimum combined SAT Reasoning score of 900 and minimum 2.2 GPA required of in-state applicants; minimum combined SAT Reasoning score of 950 and minimum 2.6 GPA required of out-of-state applicants.

How to Pay for College

To apply for financial aid, students should submit the following: Free Application for Federal Student Aid (FAFSA) · institution's own financial aid forms. Bowie State University participates in the Federal Work Study program. *Need-based aid programs include:* scholarships and grants · general need-based awards · Federal Pell grants · state scholarships and grants · college-based scholarships and grants · private scholarships and grants. *Non-need-based aid programs include:* scholarships and grants · general need-based awards · state scholarships and grants · creative arts and performance awards · athletic scholarships · ROTC scholarships.

BOWIE STATE UNIVERSITY

Highlights

Admissions
Applicants: 3,986
Accepted: 2,063
Acceptance rate: 51.8%
Average GPA: Not reported
ACT range: 17-20
SAT Math range: 400-470
SAT Reading range: 410-490
SAT Writing range: 390-470

Deadlines
Early Action: No
Early Decision: No
Regular Action: Rolling admissions
Common Application: Not accepted

Financial Aid
In-state tuition: $4,969
Out-of-state tuition: $15,545
Room: $6,702
Board: $3,730
Books: $1,100
Freshmen receiving need-based aid: 83%
Undergrads rec. need-based aid: 83%
Avg. % of need met by financial aid: 46%
Avg. aid package (freshmen): $8,250
Avg. aid package (undergrads): $8,287

Prominent Alumni
Christa McAuliffe, space shuttle Challenger astronaut; Joanne Benson, Maryland State Assembly delegate; James Proctor, Jr., Maryland State Assembly delegate; Judge William Missouri, Maryland Circuit Court Judge.

School Spirit
Mascot: Bulldog
Colors: Black and gold

107

BOWLING GREEN STATE UNIVERSITY

110 McFall Center, Bowling Green, OH 43403
Admissions: 866-246-6732 · Financial Aid: 419-372-2651
Email: choosebgsu@bgsu.edu · Website: http://www.bgsu.edu

From the College

"Bowling Green State University provides exceptional educational opportunities inside and outside the classroom that prepare students for lifelong intellectual growth, career development, lives of engaged citizenship and leadership in a global society. Through academic, research, public and private partnerships, BGSU students enrich their classroom learning with real-world experiences such as service learning, co-ops, practicums and internships, education abroad, fieldwork, undergraduate research and community involvement. BGSU emphasizes discovery, creativity, real-world experiences, achievement, collaboration and a culture of respect in a welcoming, supportive community."

Campus Setting

Bowling Green State is a public university. Founded as a teacher-training institution in 1910, it began granting bachelor's degrees in 1929. Programs are offered through the Colleges of Arts and Sciences, Business Administration, Education and Human Development, Health and Human Services, Musical Arts and Technology. Its 1,338-acre campus is located in Bowling Green, 25 miles south of Toledo. A four-year public institution, Bowling Green State University has an enrollment of 16,958 students. The campus facilities include: musical arts building · planetarium · life science building. Bowling Green State University provides on-campus housing with 47 units that can accommodate 6,806 students. Housing options: coed dorms · sorority housing · fraternity housing · single-student apartments · special housing for disabled students · special housing for international students. Recreation and sports facilities include: field house · golf course · ice arena · outdoor and indoor recreation centers · football field · baseball field · soccer field · softball field · basketball and volleyball arena · indoor and outdoor track · swimming pool · indoor and outdoor tennis courts.

Student Life and Activities

Just over half of the students (56 percent) live off campus. Intramural sports include: broomball · curling · flag football · golf scramble · indoor soccer · racquetball · softball · tennis · volleyball · wallyball. Bowling Green State University is a member of the Western Collegiate Hockey Association (Division I) and the Mid-America Conference (Division I).

Academics and Learning Environment

Bowling Green State University has 750 full-time and 315 part-time faculty members, offering a student-to-faculty ratio of 18:1. The most common course size is 10 to 19 students. Bowling Green State University offers 256 majors with the most popular being liberal studies, early childhood education and individualized studies. The school has a general core requirement. Cooperative education is available. All first-year students must maintain a 1.5 GPA or higher to avoid academic probation, and a minimum overall GPA of 2.0 is required to graduate. Other special academic programs that would appeal to a B student include: self-designed majors · pass/fail grading option · independent study · double majors · dual degrees · accelerated study · honors program · Phi Beta Kappa · internships · distance learning.

B Student Support and Success

Bowling Green offers the Office of Academic Enhancement (ACEN), which is dedicated to providing advice and academic support to new students so that they can make a smooth transition from high school to college. Students can find tutoring, mentoring and individualized academic assistance through ACEN, so that they can achieve academic success. In addition to this, Bowling Green has a Study Skills Center that features computer software, course content video cassettes, a "How to Succeed in…"series of manuals, study tips brochures and charts and tests from various classes. Mentor groups are available for students who are struggling in their coursework. These groups meet once a week for 50-minute sessions. The mentors are students who have earned an A in the course he/she is helping with. Students who are enrolled in a math or statistics course are also encouraged to utilize the Math and Stats Tutoring Center. Students can get help on any course writing needed through the Writing Center. The school offers a class called ACEN 100, which is a College Reading/Learning Skills course. It is designed to improve the basic reading and learning habits of students in topics like vocabulary, note taking, comprehension, time management, test taking and critical thinking.

Bowling Green State University provides a variety of support programs including: academic · career · personal · psychological · minority students · military · veterans · non-traditional students · family planning. Recognizing that some students may need extra preparation, Bowling Green State University offers remedial and refresher courses in: reading · writing · math · study skills. The average freshman year GPA is 2.9, and 70 percent of freshmen students return for their sophomore year. Companies that most frequently hire graduates from Bowling Green State University include: American Electric Power Company · American Greetings · Applied Materials · Avery Dennison Corporation · Battele · C.H. Robinson Worldwide · Cleveland Clinic · Coca-Cola Enterprises · Cooper Tire · Dana Corporation · Dietrich Metal Framing · Disney · FirstEnergy Corporation · Eaton · Emerson Electric Company · Ernst & Young · Ford Motor Company · Frito-Lay · GE · Goodrich Corporation · Goodyear Tire & Rubber Company · Honda · Kohl's Corporation · Lowe's Companies · Macy's · Marathon Oil Corporation · Maritz Research · Marriott · Mead Westvaco · Medtronic · Monsanto Company · National City Corporation · NCR Corporation · Newell Rubbermaid · Owens Corning · Owens-Illinois · Parker Hannifin Corporation · Progressive · Rockwell Automation · Science Applications International Corporation · Scotts Company · Sherwin-Williams Company · Social Security Administration · Target Corporation · Turner Construction Company · Wells Fargo · Westfield Insurance.

Support for Students with Learning Disabilities

Students with learning disabilities are often granted additional time to complete their degree. High school foreign language and math waivers are accepted. According to the school, all services are provided on the basis of documented need to ensure equal access. LD students can also access: tutors · learning center · testing accommodations · extended time for tests · take-home exam · oral tests · exam on tape or computer · readers · typist/scribe · note-taking

BOWLING GREEN STATE UNIVERSITY

Highlights

Bowling Green State University
Bowling Green, OH (Pop. 31,384)
Location: Large town
Four-year public
Founded: 1910
Website: http://www.bgsu.edu

Students
Total enrollment: 16,958
Undergrads: 14,477
Freshmen: 4,308
Part-time students: 8%
From out-of-state: 14%
From public schools: 89%
Male/Female: 44%/56%
Live on-campus: 44%
In fraternities: 8%
In sororities: 12%
Off-campus employment rating: Good
Caucasian: 78%
African American: 10%
Hispanic: 4%
Asian: 1%
Hawaiian or Pacific Islander: <1%
Native American: <1%
Mixed (2+ ethnicities): 2%
International: 2%

Academics
Calendar: Semester
Student/faculty ratio: 18:1
Class size 9 or fewer: 17%
Class size 10-29: 54%
Class size 30-49: 20%
Class size 50-99: 6%
Class size 100 or more: 2%
Returning freshmen: 70%
Six-year graduation rate: 54%

Most Popular Majors
Early childhood education
Liberal studies
Individualized studies

109

College Profiles

BOWLING GREEN STATE UNIVERSITY

Admissions

Applicants: 15,689
Accepted: 11,370
Acceptance rate: 72.5%
Average GPA: 3.3
ACT range: 20-25
SAT Math range: 450-560
SAT Reading range: 460-560
SAT Writing range: 1-7
Top 10% of class: 12%
Top 25% of class: 34%
Top 50% of class: 70%

Deadlines

Early Action: No
Early Decision: No
Regular Action: Rolling admissions
Common Application: Not accepted

Financial Aid

In-state tuition: $9,096
Out-of-state tuition: $16,404
Room: $5,160
Board: $3,084
Books: $1,278
Freshmen receiving need-based aid: 71%
Undergrads rec. need-based aid: 69%
Avg. % of need met by financial aid: 75%
Avg. aid package (freshmen): $12,988
Avg. aid package (undergrads): $13,285
Avg. debt upon graduation: $30,057

Prominent Alumni

Leon Bibb; Bernie Casey; Tim Conway.

School Spirit

Mascot: Falcons
Colors: Brown and orange
Song: *Forward Falcons*

services · reading machines · tape recorders · texts on tape · early syllabus · priority registration · waiver of math degree requirement. Individual or small group tutorials are also available in: time management · organizational skills · specific subject areas · writing labs · math labs · study skills. An advisor/advocate from the Disability Services is available to students.

How to Get Admitted

For admissions decisions, non-academic factors considered: interview · extracurricular activities · special talents, interests and abilities · character/personal qualities · volunteer work · work experience · state of residency · minority affiliation · alumni relationship. A high school diploma is required, although a GED is also accepted for admissions consideration. SAT or ACT test scores are required of all applicants. *Academic units recommended:* 4 English, 3 Math, 3 Science, 3 Social Studies, 2 Foreign Language.

How to Pay for College

To apply for financial aid, students should submit the following: Free Application for Federal Student Aid (FAFSA). Bowling Green State University participates in the Federal Work Study program. *Need-based aid programs include:* scholarships and grants · general need-based awards · Federal Pell grants · state scholarships and grants · college-based scholarships and grants · private scholarships and grants · Federal Nursing scholarships. *Non-need-based aid programs include:* scholarships and grants · general need-based awards · state scholarships and grants · creative arts and performance awards · special achievements and activities awards · special characteristics awards · athletic scholarships · ROTC scholarships.

BRADLEY UNIVERSITY

1501 West Bradley Avenue, Peoria, IL 61625
Admissions: 800-447-6460 · Financial Aid: 309-677-3089
Email: admissions@bradley.edu · Website: http://www.bradley.edu

From the College

"Bradley University is a private, independent university offering undergraduate and graduate programs in the liberal and fine arts, the sciences, business, communications, education, engineering and the health sciences. The school features 100 undergraduate and 30 graduate programs. This residential campus of 6,000 students blends large-school opportunities with a small-school personality. Bradley students experience a balance of academic and co-curricular opportunities that emphasize collaboration, teamwork and active learning. This experience provides an integration of a liberal arts education, professional preparation and personal and social development. Located just three hours from Chicago and St. Louis, Bradley is committed to serving central Illinois through its research, creative production and outreach programs."

Campus Setting

Bradley, founded in 1897, is a private, coeducational, comprehensive university. Programs are offered through the Foster Colleges of Business Administration, the Slane College Communications and Fine Arts, the College of Education and Health Sciences, the College of Engineering and Technology, the College of Liberal Arts and Sciences and the Graduate School. Its 85-acre campus is located in a residential area of Peoria, Illinois. A four-year institution, Bradley University has an enrollment of 5,459 students. Bradley's campus has a global communications center and two art galleries. The school provides on-campus housing with 30 units that can accommodate 2,850 students. Housing options: coed dorms · sorority housing · fraternity housing · single-student apartments · married-student apartments. Recreation and sports facilities include: student recreation center · softball fields · soccer fields · outdoor tennis courts · outdoor basketball courts.

Student Life and Activities

With 68 percent of students living on campus, there are plenty of social activities, including an active calendar of theatre and musical performances. The new Markin Student Recreation Center and Greek houses are favorite gathering spots. Popular campus events include Late Night BU, Homecoming, Sibling's Weekend, Parents' Weekends and Welcome Week activities. Bradley University has 240 official student organizations. Popular groups on campus include Student Activities Council, student government, men's basketball team and Greek life. For those interested in sports, there are intramural teams such as: 5K run · badminton · basketball · billiards · bowling · diving · flag football · golf · indoor soccer · racquetball · soccer · softball · swimming · table tennis · volleyball · walleyball · wrestling. Bradley University is a member of the Missouri Valley Conference (Division I).

Academics and Learning Environment

Bradley University has 351 full-time and 244 part-time faculty members, offering a student-to-faculty ratio of 12:1. The most common course size is 10 to 19 students. Bradley University offers 105 majors with the most popular being communications, mechanical engineering and nursing and least popular being religious studies, environmental science physics and engineering physics. The school has a general core requirement. Cooperative education is available. All first-year students must maintain a 2.0 GPA or higher to avoid academic probation. Other special academic programs

111

College Profiles

BRADLEY UNIVERSITY

Highlights

Bradley University
Peoria, IL (Pop. 115,234)
Location: Medium city
Four-year private
Founded: 1897
Website: http://www.bradley.edu

Students
Total enrollment: 5,459
Undergrads: 4,855
Freshmen: 1,085
Part-time students: 5%
From out-of-state: 13%
Male/Female: 48%/52%
Live on-campus: 68%
In fraternities: 33%
In sororities: 27%
Off-campus employment rating: Fair
Caucasian: 74%
African American: 7%
Hispanic: 6%
Asian: 4%
Hawaiian or Pacific Islander: <1%
Native American: 1%
International: 1%

Academics
Calendar: Semester
Student/faculty ratio: 12:1
Class size 9 or fewer: 25%
Class size 10-29: 59%
Class size 30-49: 13%
Class size 50-99: 3%
Class size 100 or more: 1%
Returning freshmen: 88%
Six-year graduation rate: 78%

Most Popular Majors
Communications
Mechanical engineering
Nursing

that would appeal to a B student include: self-designed majors · pass/fail grading option · independent study · double majors · dual degrees · honors program · internships · certificate programs.

B Student Support and Success

Bradley's website states, "We encourage students to apply who feel that they can demonstrate both the academic ability to succeed and the potential to contribute to the total educational experience at Bradley. While our students perform above national averages in strong college preparation curriculums, we do not have a stated minimum rank, grade point average (GPA) or ACT or SAT score. We also recognize that rank and GPA can only be considered meaningful in the context of the quality of the high school attended and the classes that a student takes. It is also very important to our admissions review committee that our students balance academic ability with the other qualities that lead to success at Bradley. Social skills, communications skills, leadership, community service and unique experiences are important qualities in our admission and scholarship review. Finally, different academic areas have different admission requirements."

Bradley University offers specific programs for: academic · career · psychological · minority students. The average freshman year GPA is 2.9, and 88 percent of freshmen students return for their sophomore year. Approximately 13 percent of graduates return for a graduate degree. Among students who pursue employment, approximately 97 percent enter a field related to their major within six months of graduation. Companies that most frequently hire graduates from Bradley University include: OSF Saint Francis Medical Center · Caterpillar Inc. · Menards Inc. · Enterprise Rent-A-Car · Sargent & Lundy LLC · Nordstrom Inc. · Liberty Mutual Insurance Co. · Chicago Public School District 299 · Peoria Public School District 150 · Target Corp. · ConAgra Foods Inc. · Bradley University.

Support for Students with Learning Disabilities

Students with learning disabilities may take advantage of the school's Center for Learning Assistance, which provides "select coordinated accommodations" as defined by standardized national service-delivery models. This includes the provision of a contact person, generic support services, peer tutors and student referral service for off-campus testing resources. These services are available only during the academic year. LD students can also access: tutors · learning center · untimed tests · extended time for tests · tape recorders · videotaped classes · early syllabus. Individual or small group tutorials are also available in: time management · organizational skills · learning strategies · writing labs · math labs · study skills. An advisor/advocate from the LD program is available to students.

How to Get Admitted

For admissions decisions, non-academic factors considered: interview · extracurricular activities · special talents, interests and abilities · character/personal qualities · volunteer work · work experience · geographical location · minority affiliation · alumni relationship. A high school diploma is required, although a GED is also accepted for admissions consideration. SAT or ACT test scores are required of all applicants. SAT Subject Test scores are not required. *Academic units recommended:* 5 English, 4 Math, 3 Science, 3 Social Studies, 2 Foreign Language.

How to Pay for College

To apply for financial aid, students should submit the following: Free Application for Federal Student Aid (FAFSA). Bradley University participates in the Federal Work Study program. *Need-based aid programs include:* scholarships and grants · general need-based awards · Federal Pell grants · state scholarships and grants · college-based scholarships and grants · private scholarships and grants. *Non-need-based aid programs include:* scholarships and grants · state scholarships and grants · creative arts and performance awards · special achievements and activities awards · special characteristics awards · athletic scholarships.

BRADLEY UNIVERSITY

Highlights

Admissions
Applicants: 8,969
Accepted: 6,004
Acceptance rate: 66.9%
Average GPA: 3.7
ACT range: 23-28
SAT Math range: 510-630
SAT Reading range: 500-640
SAT Writing range: Not reported
Top 10% of class: 30%
Top 25% of class: 64%
Top 50% of class: 91%

Deadlines
Early Action: No
Early Decision: No
Regular Action: Rolling admissions
Common Application: Accepted

Financial Aid
In-state tuition: $30,500
Out-of-state tuition: $30,500
Room: $5,460
Board: $3,960
Books: $1,050
Freshmen receiving need-based aid: 48%
Undergrads rec. need-based aid: 70%
Avg. % of need met by financial aid: 68%
Avg. aid package (freshmen): $18,282
Avg. aid package (undergrads): $18,933

Prominent Alumni
Ray LaHood, U.S. Secretary of Transportation; Aaron Schock, youngest congressman in the U.S. House of Representatives, Illinois,18th District; Rene C. Byer, winner of the Pulitzer Prize, senior photographer, *Sacramento Bee.*

School Spirit
Colors: Red and white
Song: *Hail Red and White*

BRIDGEWATER STATE UNIVERSITY

131 Summer Street, Bridgewater, MA 02325
Admissions: 508-531-1237 · Financial Aid: 508-531-1341
Email: admission@bridgew.edu
Website: http://www.bridgew.edu

From the College

"Bridgewater State College is the comprehensive public college of Southeastern Massachusetts and has a dual mission: to educate the residents of Southeastern Massachusetts and the Commonwealth, and to use its intellectual, scientific and technological resources to support and advance the economic and cultural life of the region. While maintaining its historical focus on the preparation of teachers, Bridgewater today provides a broad range of baccalaureate degree programs through its School of Arts and Sciences, its School of Education and Allied Studies and new School of Management and Aviation Science, which includes the only four-year Aviation program at a public college in New England. In recent years, Bridgewater has renovated its library, built a new residence hall and is building a $98.7 million science facility."

Campus Setting

Bridgewater, founded in 1840, is a public college of liberal arts and professional studies. Its 235-acre campus is located in Bridgewater, 28 miles south of Boston. A four-year institution, Bridgewater State College has an enrollment of 11,417 students. The school also has a library with 319,764 books. It provides on-campus housing with eight units capable of accommodating 2,804 students. Housing options: coed dorms · single-student apartments. Recreation and sports facilities include: athletic and football fields · baseball and softball parks · gymnasium · tennis courts.

Student Life and Activities

Most students (65 percent) live off campus. Popular gathering spots are the campus center, the Rat and Cenzio's. Favorite campus activities include Winterfest, Springfest and Homecoming. Bridgewater State College has 181 official student organizations. Circle K, WBIM, the Program Committee and the Student Government Association have strong presences on campus. Bridgewater State College is a member of the ECAC (Division I, Football I-AA), Little East Conference (Division III), Massachusetts State College Athletic Conference (Division III), New England Football Conference (Division III), New England Alliance, New England Women's Lacrosse Alliance (Division III) and Pilgrim Wrestling League (Division III).

Academics and Learning Environment

Bridgewater State College has 321 full-time and 454 part-time faculty members, offering a student-to-faculty ratio of 20:1. The most common course size is 20 to 29 students. Bridgewater State College offers 47 majors. The most popular include psychology, criminal justice and management. The least popular are philosophy, American politics and chemistry/geology. The school has a general core requirement. Cooperative education is not offered. All first-year students must maintain a 2.0 GPA or higher to avoid academic probation, and a minimum overall GPA of 2.0 is required to graduate. Other special academic programs that would appeal to a B student: independent study · double majors · accelerated study · honors program · internships · distance learning.

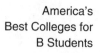

B Student Support and Success

Bridgewater offers the Academic Achievement Center (AAC), which features learning assistance programs and is home to Second Language Services, the Office of Disability Resources, Tutoring Services, the Writing Studio, Mathematics Services, Study and Research Services and the Communication Laboratory. The college also provides a Core Curriculum that is a skill centered, outcomes-based general education course, designed to help all students prepare for learning in their chosen fields. It is made up of four areas: skills requirements (writing, logical reasoning, mathematical reasoning and spoken communication); core distribution requirements (arts, humanities, natural and social and behavioral sciences, global culture, multiculturalism, quantitative reasoning and the U.S. Constitution); seminars (writing/speaking intensive courses) and requirements in the major (connecting the core curriculum to each major).

Bridgewater State College provides a variety of support programs including: academic · career · personal · psychological · minority students · family planning · religious. Annually, 81 percent of freshmen students return for their sophomore year. Companies that most frequently hire graduates from Bridgewater State College include: Accenture · Advanced Rehabilitation System · Bayer Diagnostic · Boston Biomedical · Braintree Rehabilitation Hospital · Brown & Co. · Delta Airlines · Department of Social Services · Fidelity Investments · FleetBoston · Foxboro Company · General Dynamics · Gillette Company · Health South · Investors Bank & Trust · LEC Environment Consulting Little · Mass General Hospital · Massachusetts House of Representatives · May Institute · Meditech · Midwest Express Airline · New England Cable News · Northeast Rehabilitation Hospital · PBS Consultants · PricewaterhouseCoopers · Providence Journal · Putnam Investments · Springborn Laboratories · State Street · Stone and Webster · United States Department of Labor · WCVB TV 5 · Wells Fargo Financial · WPEP 1570 AM.

Support for Students with Learning Disabilities

Students coping with a type of learning disabilities may be granted additional time to complete a degree and/or lighten the average course load. LD students may also access: tutors · learning center · testing accommodations · untimed tests · extended time for tests · take-home exam · oral tests · readers · note-taking services · tape recorders · early syllabus · priority registration · waiver of math degree requirement. Individual or small group tutorials are also available in: time management · organizational skills · learning strategies · specific subject areas · writing labs · math labs · study skills. An advisor/advocate from the LD program is available to students.

How to Get Admitted

For admissions decisions, non-academic factors considered: extracurricular activities · special talents, interests and abilities · character/personal qualities · volunteer work · work experience · state of residency · minority affiliation · alumni relationship. A high school diploma is required, although a GED is also accepted for admissions consideration. SAT or ACT test scores are required of all applicants. SAT

BRIDGEWATER STATE UNIVERSITY

Highlights

Bridgewater State University
Bridgewater, MA (Pop. 25,185)
Location: Large town
Four-year public
Founded: 1840
Website: http://www.bridgew.edu

Students
Total enrollment: 11,417
Undergrads: 9,684
Part-time students: 17%
From out-of-state: 5%
Male/Female: 42%/58%
Live on-campus: 35%
Off-campus employment rating: Excellent
Caucasian: 80%
African American: 8%
Hispanic: 5%
Asian: 2%
Hawaiian or Pacific Islander: <1%
Native American: <1%
Mixed (2+ ethnicities): 3%
International: <1%

Academics
Calendar: Semester
Student/faculty ratio: 20:1
Class size 9 or fewer: 10%
Class size 10-29: 71%
Class size 30-49: 18%
Class size 50-99: 1%
Class size 100 or more: -
Returning freshmen: 81%
Six-year graduation rate: 54%

Most Popular Majors
Psychology
Criminal justice
Management

College Profiles

BRIDGEWATER STATE UNIVERSITY

Highlights

Admissions
Applicants: 6,170
Accepted: 4,525
Acceptance rate: 73.3%
Placed on wait list: 673
Enrolled from wait list: 126
Average GPA: 3.2
ACT range: 20-22
SAT Math range: 460-560
SAT Reading range: 450-550
SAT Writing range: Not reported

Deadlines
Early Action: 11/15
Early Decision: No
Regular Action: Rolling admissions
Common Application: Accepted

Financial Aid
In-state tuition: $910
Out-of-state tuition: $7,050
Room: $6,540
Board: $3,388
Books: $1,000
Freshmen receiving need-based aid: 69%
Undergrads rec. need-based aid: 64%
Avg. aid package (freshmen): Not reported
Avg. aid package (undergrads): Not reported

Prominent Alumni
Jeff Corwin, actor and TV host; Lou Gorman, former general manager of the Boston Red Sox; Ann Hobson Pilot, principal harpist of the Boston Symphony Orchestra and the Boston Pops.

School Spirit
Mascot: Bears
Colors: Crimson and white

Subject Test scores are not required. *Academic units recommended*: 4 English, 3 Math, 3 Science, 1 Social Studies, 2 Foreign Language.

How to Pay for College

To apply for financial aid, students should submit the following: Free Application for Federal Student Aid (FAFSA). Bridgewater State College participates in the Federal Work Study program. *Need-based aid programs include*: scholarships and grants · general need-based awards · Federal Pell grants · state scholarships and grants · college-based scholarships and grants · private scholarships and grants. *Non-need-based aid programs include*: scholarships and grants · state scholarships and grants.

America's
Best Colleges for
B Students

BRYANT UNIVERSITY

1150 Douglas Pike, Smithfield, RI 02917-1291
Admissions: 800-622-7001 · Financial Aid: 800-248-4036
Email: admission@bryant.edu · Website: http://www.bryant.edu

From the College

"Bryant was established in 1863, and is a small, private university in New England that focuses on helping students build knowledge, develop character and achieve success—as they define it. The College of Arts and Sciences and the College of Business integrate business, liberal arts and technology to distinguish the Bryant educational experience. This integration ensures that students become well-rounded individuals with the analytical, problem-solving, business, and communication skills to successfully compete and contribute in a complex, global environment.

"Bryant enrolls 3,400 undergraduate and more than 400 graduate students with 112 tenured and tenure-track, full-time faculty. More than 3,000 individuals and businesses benefit on an annual basis from professional education and consulting services offered by Bryant's Executive Development Center and the John H. Chafee Center for International Business.

"Bryant offers undergraduate programs in actuarial mathematics, business administration with seven concentrations available, communication, economics, environmental science, global studies, history, information technology, international business, literary and cultural studies, mathematics and statistics, politics and law, psychology and sociology. Bryant's Graduate School of Business offers master's degrees in business administration (MBA), information systems (MSIS), taxation (MST) and professional accountancy (MPAc). All of Bryant's academic programs are accredited by the New England Association of Schools and Colleges (NEASC). The College of Business is accredited by AACSB International-The Association to Advance Collegiate Schools of Business, a distinction earned by less than 10 percent of business colleges worldwide."

Campus Setting

Founded in 1863, Bryant University is a four-year private liberal arts university with a College of Business and a College of Arts and Sciences. Its 420-acre campus is located in Smithfield, Rhode Island, 12 miles from Providence. The campus facilities include: theatre · food court · Interfaith Center. Bryant University provides on-campus housing with 1,036 units that can accommodate 2,882 students. Housing options: coed dorms · women's dorms · special housing for disabled students. Recreation and sports facilities include: athletic fields · baseball and softball complex · gymnasium · natatorium · recreation and wellness center · rugby field · sports arena · stadium · weight room.

Student Life and Activities

Eighty-one percent of students live on campus. According to the editor of the student newspaper, they (the student organization) try very hard to increase the social aspect of college life. Popular gathering places are Lupo's, The Living Room, The Strand, Thayer Street, The Junction and Parente's. Popular events on campus are semi-formals, MSU Extravaganza Night, commencement, convocation, ISO UN Festival, Parents' Weekend, Spring Weekend, Special Olympics and the Festival of Lights. Bryant University has 96 official student organizations. Influential groups on campus are the Student Programming Board, rugby teams, Student Senate and Greek organizations. For those interested in sports, there are intramural teams such

BRYANT UNIVERSITY

Bryant University
Smithfield (Pop. 20,613)
Location: Large town
Four-year private
Founded: 1863
Website: http://www.bryant.edu

Students
Total enrollment: 3,454
Undergrads: 3,287
Freshmen: 890
Part-time students: 3%
From out-of-state: 89%
Male/Female: 42%/58%
Live on-campus: 81%
In fraternities: 6%
In sororities: 7%
Off-campus employment rating: Fair
Caucasian: 74%
African American: 4%
Hispanic: 6%
Asian: 4%
Hawaiian or Pacific Islander: <1%
Native American: <1%
Mixed (2+ ethnicities): <1%
International: 7%

Academics
Calendar: Semester
Student/faculty ratio: 16:1
Class size 9 or fewer: 5%
Class size 10-29: 50%
Class size 30-49: 45%
Class size 50-99: -
Class size 100 or more: -
Returning freshmen: 90%
Six-year graduation rate: 82%

Most Popular Majors
Marketing
Finance
Management

as: basketball · flag football · floor hockey · indoor soccer · inner-tube water polo · softball · volleyball. Bryant University is a member of the Northeast Conference (Division I).

Academics and Learning Environment

Bryant University has 165 full-time and 133 part-time faculty members, offering a student-to-faculty ratio of 16:1. The most common course size is 30 to 39 students. Bryant University offers 38 majors with the most popular being marketing, finance and management and least popular being history and literary/cultural studies. The school has a general core requirement. Cooperative education is not offered. All first-year students must maintain a 2.0 GPA or higher to avoid academic probation, and a minimum overall GPA of 2.0 is required to graduate. Other special academic programs that would appeal to a B student include: independent study · double majors · dual degrees · honors program · internships.

B Student Support and Success

Bryant College provides extra help to students through the Academic Center for Excellence (ACE). Each year, more than 1,600 students use its services to help with class performance. ACE's philosophy is that college students are not born with good study skills and habits, and like anything else in life, they require practice on a regular basis. Even students who have great study skills in high school may find that they need extra help in college. According to the college, ACE's primary goal is to "help students become self-reliant, independent, confident learners so that they may successfully meet the demands of their chosen academic curricula." They do this through both a tutoring program and study skills instruction in group sessions provided by a combination of staff, peer tutors and faculty. Along with ACE, Bryant offers a Writing Center. Here you can learn and polish the skills of written communication through one-on-one consultations with staff and tutors. Access is provided through ACE to workshops and printed materials that are helpful tools in honing writing skills.

Bryant University provides a variety of support programs including dedicated guidance for: academic · career · personal · psychological · minority students · non-traditional students · family planning · religious. The average freshman year GPA is 2.8, and 90 percent of freshmen students return for their sophomore year. Approximately 22 percent of students pursue a graduate degree following graduation. Among students who enter the workforce, approximately 76 percent enter a field related to their major within six months of graduation. Companies that most frequently hire graduates from Bryant University include: State Street Corporation · Target · TJX · DiSanto Priest & Co. · Liberty Mutual · FedEx Freight · PricewaterhouseCoopers · Hartford Insurance Group · Fidelity Investments · CVS · Ernst & Young · Mercer · Liberty Mutual · Ross Stores · Hanover Insurance · Travelers · Cambridge Associates · Citizens Bank · Wolfe & Co. · Boston Celtics · Pepsi Bottling Group · Raytheon · Towers Watson.

Support for Students with Learning Disabilities

Bryant University supports students with learning disabilities by offering: tutors · learning center · testing accommodations · extended time for tests · reading machines · tape recorders. Individual or small group tutorials are also available in: time management · organizational skills · learning strategies · specific subject areas · writing labs · math labs · study skills. An advisor/advocate from the LD program is available to students.

How to Get Admitted

For admissions decisions, non-academic factors considered: interview · extracurricular activities · special talents, interests and abilities · character/personal qualities · volunteer work · work experience · geographical location · minority affiliation · alumni relationship. A high school diploma is required, although a GED is also accepted for admissions consideration. SAT or ACT test scores are required of all applicants. SAT Subject Test scores are not required. *According to the admissions office:* The average GPA of admitted students is 3.4 and the average SAT Reasoning score is 1150 (composite ACT score is 25). *Academic units recommended:* 4 English, 4 Math, 3 Science, 2 Foreign Language.

How to Pay for College

To apply for financial aid, students should submit the following: Free Application for Federal Student Aid (FAFSA). Bryant University participates in the Federal Work Study program. *Need-based aid programs include:* scholarships and grants · general need-based awards · Federal Pell grants · state scholarships and grants · college-based scholarships and grants · private scholarships and grants. *Non-need-based aid programs include:* scholarships and grants · state scholarships and grants · athletic scholarships · ROTC scholarships · minority status scholarships.

BRYANT UNIVERSITY

Highlights

Admissions
Applicants: 6,013
Accepted: 4,603
Acceptance rate: 76.6%
Placed on wait list: 97
Average GPA: 3.3
ACT range: 23-27
SAT Math range: 540-630
SAT Reading range: 510-590
SAT Writing range: 2-23
Top 10% of class: 18%
Top 25% of class: 50%
Top 50% of class: 88%

Deadlines
Early Action: 12/3
Early Decision: 11/15
Regular Action: 2/1 (final)
Notification of admission by: 3/23
Common Application: Accepted

Financial Aid
In-state tuition: $38,199
Out-of-state tuition: $38,199
Room: $8,277
Board: $5,825
Books: $1,300
Freshmen receiving need-based aid: 68%
Undergrads rec. need-based aid: 65%
Avg. % of need met by financial aid: 53%
Avg. aid package (freshmen): $23,109
Avg. aid package (undergrads): $22,549
Avg. debt upon graduation: $44,580

Prominent Alumni
Kristian P. Moor, President and CEO, Chartis Insurance; Ian Morris, President and CEO, Marketleader Inc.; Sharon Garavel Corporate Vice President, GE Capital.

School Spirit
Mascot: Bulldogs
Colors: Black, gold and white

119

Caldwell University
Caldwell (Pop. 7,239)
Location: Large town
Four-year private
Founded: 1939
Website: http://www.caldwell.edu

Students
Total enrollment: 2,182
Undergrads: 1,576
Freshmen: 457
Part-time students: 17%
From out-of-state: 13%
Male/Female: 31%/69%
Live on-campus: 32%
In fraternities: 1%
In sororities: 4%
Off-campus employment rating: Excellent
Caucasian: 46%
African American: 16%
Hispanic: 14%
Asian: 2%
Hawaiian or Pacific Islander: <1%
Native American: <1%
Mixed (2+ ethnicities): 1%
International: 5%

Academics
Calendar: Semester
Student/faculty ratio: 11:1
Class size 9 or fewer: 36%
Class size 10-29: 58%
Class size 30-49: 6%
Class size 50-99: -
Class size 100 or more: -
Returning freshmen: 90%
Six-year graduation rate: 55%

CALDWELL UNIVERSITY

120 Bloomfield Avenue, Caldwell, NJ 07006
Admissions: 973-618-3500 · Financial Aid: 973-618-3221
Email: admissions@caldwell.edu
Website: http://www.caldwell.edu

From the College

"Founded in 1939 by the Sisters of St. Dominic, Caldwell University is a Catholic institution in the Judeo-Christian tradition with a heritage of over seven centuries of Dominican commitment to higher education. Serving a diverse population of all ages, Caldwell University provides a liberal arts education which promotes spiritual, aesthetic and intellectual growth. Upon this foundation, the college offers career-related programs which prepare its graduates to take advantage of opportunities in a complex society."

Campus Setting

Caldwell is a church-affiliated, liberal arts college. Founded as a college for women in 1939, it adopted coeducation in 1986. Its 70-acre campus is located in Caldwell, 20 miles from New York City. The school is also affiliated with the Roman Catholic Church. Caldwell University provides on-campus housing with 191 units that can accommodate 515 students. Housing options: coed dorms.

Student Life and Activities

More than half of the students live off campus. Students spend time at events such as: Diversity Day, Homecoming and Founder's Day. Caldwell University has 29 official student organizations. The most popular are: choral groups · drama club · jazz and pep bands · music ensembles · musical theatre · service groups · Spanish club · business club · team managers. Caldwell University is a member of the NCAA (Division II) and the Central Atlantic Collegiate Conference (Division II).

Academics and Learning Environment

Caldwell University has 88 full-time and 122 part-time faculty members, offering a student-to-faculty ratio of 11:1. The most common course size is 2 to 9 students. Caldwell University offers 48 majors and has a general core requirement as well as a religion requirement. Cooperative education is not offered. All first-year students must maintain a 2.0 GPA or higher to avoid academic probation. Other special academic programs that would appeal to a B student include: self-designed majors · pass/fail grading option · independent study · double majors · accelerated study · honors program · internships · weekend college · distance learning certificate programs.

B Student Support and Success

A variety of support services are available through Caldwell's Academic Support Center. Individual and group tutoring is offered on both a scheduled and drop-in basis. The Writing Center has regular hours also and focuses on helping students become independent critical thinkers and writers. In addition, an online writing lab is another option students may access. Students work with peer or professional tutors and there is no charge for these sessions. A supplemental instruction program is offered during the year in courses that serve large numbers of freshman or sophomores. This course focuses on skills needed to better understand lectures, develop study strategies and prepare for exams. Workshops on note taking, textbook reading, time management and test taking strategies are offered throughout the year.

Caldwell University provides a variety of support programs including dedicated guidance for: academic · personal · non-traditional students. Additional counseling services include: Alcohol/substance abuse counseling. Recognizing that some students may need extra preparation, Caldwell University offers remedial and refresher courses in: reading · writing · math · study skills. The average freshman year GPA is 2.8, and 90 percent of freshmen students return for their sophomore year. While many students enter the workforce, approximately 20 percent pursue a graduate degree immediately after graduation. Among students who enter the workforce, approximately 76 percent enter a field related to their major within six months of graduation. Companies that most frequently hire graduates from Caldwell University include: Xerox · Ricoh · Cosmair Inc. · Horizon Blue Cross/Blue Shield · Boards of Education.

Support for Students with Learning Disabilities

Students with learning disabilities may take additional time to complete their degree or take a lighter course load. High school foreign language and math waivers are accepted. LD students can also access: remedial math · remedial English · remedial reading · special classes · tutors · learning center · untimed tests · extended time for tests · oral tests · readers · note-taking services · reading machines · tape recorders. Individual or small group tutorials are also available in: time management · organizational skills · learning strategies · writing labs · math labs.

How to Get Admitted

For admissions decisions, non-academic factors considered: interview · extracurricular activities · special talents, interests and abilities · character/personal qualities · volunteer work · work experience · state of residency. A high school diploma is required, although a GED is also accepted. SAT or ACT test scores are required of all applicants. SAT Subject Test scores are considered, if submitted, but are not required. *Academic units recommended:* 4 English, 2 Math, 2 Science, 2 Foreign Language.

How to Pay for College

To apply for financial aid, students should submit the following: Free Application for Federal Student Aid (FAFSA) · institution's own financial aid forms · state aid form. Caldwell University participates in the Federal Work Study program. *Need-based aid programs include:* scholarships and grants · general need-based awards · Federal Pell grants · state scholarships and grants · college-based scholarships and grants · private scholarships and grants. *Non-need-based aid programs include:* scholarships and grants · state scholarships and grants · creative arts and performance awards · special achievements and activities awards · special characteristics awards · athletic scholarships.

CALDWELL UNIVERSITY

Highlights

Admissions
Applicants: 2,894
Accepted: 1,912
Acceptance rate: 66.1%
Average GPA: 3.5
ACT range: 16-24
SAT Math range: 420-550
SAT Reading range: 410-520
SAT Writing range: 1-10
Top 10% of class: 10%
Top 25% of class: 25%
Top 50% of class: 62%

Deadlines
Early Action: 12/1
Early Decision: No
Regular Action: Rolling admissions
Common Application: Accepted

Financial Aid
In-state tuition: $28,900
Out-of-state tuition: $28,900
Room: Varies
Board: Varies
Books: $2,000
Freshmen receiving need-based aid: 97%
Undergrads rec. need-based aid: 90%
Avg. % of need met by financial aid: 73%
Avg. aid package (freshmen): $24,409
Avg. aid package (undergrads): $20,047
Avg. debt upon graduation: $25,381

Prominent Alumni
Arline Friscia, member of the New Jersey General Assembly and Mary Jo Codey, former First Lady of the State of New Jersey.

School Spirit
Mascot: Cougars
Colors: Red and white

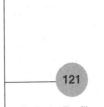

121

CAMPBELL UNIVERSITY

P.O. Box 546, Buies Creek, NC 27506
Admissions: 800-334-4111, extension 1290
Financial Aid: 800-334-4111, extension 1310
Email: admissions@campbell.edu · Website: http://www.campbell.edu

From the College

"Campbell University is a university of the liberal arts, sciences and professions that is committed to helping students develop an integrated Christian personality characterized by a wholeness of body, mind and spirit. Campbell is a Baptist university affiliated with the Baptist State Convention of North Carolina. Both in and out of the classroom, the university endeavors to present Christian principles to students and to foster their application to daily life.

"Located in Buies Creek, a rural, residential community in Harnett County, Campbell University has an 850-acre campus. Raleigh, the state's capital, and Fayetteville are less than thirty miles from campus. Within about an hour's driving time students can enjoy the benefits of the Research Triangle Park, the cities of Durham and Chapel Hill. Campbell has been named 'The Safest Campus in North Carolina,' by USA Today.

"Campbell is fully accredited by the Southern Association of Colleges and Schools (SACS), Commission on Colleges, as a Level V Institution. Campbell also has accredited and nationally recognized graduate programs in business, divinity, education, law and pharmacy.

"Affiliated with the Atlantic Sun Conference, Campbell features competitive Division I Varsity athletics. The Fighting Camels men's sports include: basketball, baseball, cross-country, golf, soccer, tennis, track, wrestling and football. Campbell's women's sports include: basketball, cheerleading, cross-country, golf, soccer, softball, tennis, track, volleyball and swimming.

"Campbell's total enrollment is over 2,800 undergraduate and 1,700 graduate students. In an average year, the student body comes from over 90 North Carolina counties, all 49 other states and 50 countries. Eighty percent of the student body comes from North Carolina."

Campus Setting

Campbell is a church-affiliated university. It was founded as an academy in 1887, became a four-year college in 1961 and gained university status in 1979. Its 850-acre campus is located in Buies Creek, 30 miles from Raleigh and Fayetteville. A four-year private institution, Campbell University has an enrollment of 6,189 students. The school is also affiliated with the Baptist Church. Campus facilities include: drug information center · museum and exhibit hall · nature trail · golf course. Campbell University provides on-campus housing accommodating 2,100 students. Housing options: women's dorms · men's dorms · single-student apartments · married-student apartments · special housing for disabled students. Recreation and sports facilities include: fitness facilities · natatorium · student centers · weight rooms · track · intramural fields.

Student Life and Activities

Most students live off campus, but popular gathering spots include: Wallace Student Center, Quiznos, Coffee Society and Buffaloe Lanes. Favorite campus events include Welcome Week, Homecoming/Parent's Weekend, Spring Fling, Mr. Campbell Pageant and the Spring Formal. Campbell University has 50 official student organizations. The Baptist Student Union, the Student Government Association, men's and women's basketball and soccer teams, football and Kappa Psi (pharmacy fraternity) influence student life. For those interested in sports, there are intramural teams such as: baseball · basketball · flag football · softball · volleyball. Campbell University is a member of the Atlantic Sun Conference (Division I), Northeast Conference (Division I) and Pioneer League (Football).

Academics and Learning Environment

Campbell University offers a student-to-faculty ratio of 18:1 and 63 majors. The school has a general core requirement as well as a religion requirement. Cooperative education is available. All first-year students must maintain a 1.4 GPA or higher to avoid academic probation, and a minimum overall GPA of 2.0 is required to graduate. Other special academic programs that would appeal to a B student include: independent study · double majors · accelerated study · honors program · internships · distance learning.

B Student Support and Success

Both group and peer tutoring are available at Campbell University, and the school also has a Writing Center. Student support services include workshops on study skills, test taking skills, time management and test anxiety. The school has a program known as the Early Alert System, which puts students in contact with the appropriate campus resources in order to help them to meet their educational goals. Faculty and staff members refer students who are struggling in their academic work, as well as those who are missing class often or who are having trouble adjusting to campus life. The Early Alert System helps to make sure that every student is able to take full advantage of the educational opportunities available at Campbell. Campbell University provides dedicated guidance for: academic · career · personal · psychological · veterans · non-traditional students · religious. Additional counseling services include: major. Annually, Companies that most frequently hire graduates from Campbell University include: Bank of America · BB&T · Enterprise Rent-a-Car · Merrill Lynch · Wachovia.

Support for Students with Learning Disabilities

Learning disabled students may take lighter course loads, plus access: remedial math · remedial English · tutors · testing accommodations · extended time for tests · take-home exam · oral tests · readers · note-taking services · tape recorders · texts on tape · early syllabus · priority registration · waiver of math degree requirement. Individual or small group tutorials are also available in: time management · organizational skills · learning strategies · specific subject areas · writing labs · study skills. An advisor/advocate from the Student Support Services is available to students.

How to Get Admitted

For admissions decisions, non-academic factors considered: interview · extracurricular activities · special talents, interests and abilities · character/personal qualities · volunteer work · work experience · state of residency · alumni relationship. A high school diploma is required, although a GED is also accepted for admissions consideration. SAT or ACT test scores are required of all applicants. SAT Subject Test scores are recommended but not required. SAT Reasoning score of 950 (composite ACT score of 20) required. *According to the admissions office:* Math units must include algebra II and geometry. Social studies units must include 1 unit of U.S. history. *Academic units recommended:* 2 Foreign Language.

CAMPBELL UNIVERSITY

Highlights

Campbell University
Buies Creek (Pop. 2,215)
Location: Rural
Four-year private
Founded: 1887
Website: http://www.campbell.edu

Students
Total enrollment: 6,189
Undergrads: 4,589
From out-of-state: 20%
Male/Female: 50%/50%
Live on-campus: Not reported
Off-campus employment rating: Fair
Caucasian: 55%
African American: 17%
Hispanic: 6%
Asian: 2%
Hawaiian or Pacific Islander: <1%
Native American: 1%
Mixed (2+ ethnicities): 2%
International: 2%

Academics
Calendar: Semester
Student/faculty ratio: 18:1
Class size 9 or fewer: 32%
Class size 10-29: 45%
Class size 30-49: 13%
Class size 50-99: 10%
Class size 100 or more: 1%
Returning freshmen: 77%
Six-year graduation rate: 55%

123

College Profiles

CAMPBELL UNIVERSITY

Highlights

Admissions
Applicants: 11,714
Accepted: 8,199
Acceptance rate: 70.0%
Average GPA: Not reported
ACT range: 17-27
SAT Math range: 385-645
SAT Reading range: 380-655
SAT Writing range: Not reported

Deadlines
Early Action: No
Early Decision: No
Regular Action: Rolling admissions
Common Application: Not accepted

Financial Aid
In-state tuition: $26,550
Out-of-state tuition: $26,550
Room: $4,500
Board: $5,160
Books: Varies
Undergrads receiving need-based or merit-based aid: 100%
Avg. aid package (freshmen): Not reported
Avg. aid package (undergrads): Not reported

Prominent Alumni
Bob Etheridge, U.S. Congressman; Elaine Marshall, North Carolina Secretary of State; Eugene McDaniel, U.S. Representative.

School Spirit
Mascot: Fighting Camels
Colors: Orange and black

How to Pay for College

To apply for financial aid, students should submit the following: Free Application for Federal Student Aid (FAFSA). Campbell University participates in the Federal Work Study program. *Need-based aid programs include:* scholarships and grants · general need-based awards · Federal Pell grants · state scholarships and grants · college-based scholarships and grants · private scholarships and grants. *Non-need-based aid programs include:* scholarships and grants · general need-based awards · state scholarships and grants · athletic scholarships · ROTC scholarships.

CARROLL COLLEGE

1601 North Benton Avenue, Helena, MT 59625-0002
Admissions: 800-992-3648 · Financial Aid: 800-992-3648
Email: enroll@carroll.edu · Website: http://www.carroll.edu

From the College

"Carroll College is a Catholic diocesan liberal arts college dedicated to making a difference. Most Carroll faculty, staff and students choose to volunteer their time to help others. It's called service learning, and it's a foundation of the Carroll College experience. The commitment to selfless service naturally extends to the classroom. Because of faculty support, Carroll students enjoy high acceptance rates to medical schools and law and business graduate programs.

"The philosophy of putting students first applies to every department on campus, from student housing and community life to class registration and financial aid. Carroll ensures a student's education is 'Non scholae sed vitae—not for school alone but for life.'"

Campus Setting

Carroll, founded in 1909, is a church-affiliated, liberal arts college. Its 63-acre campus is located in central Helena, on the eastern slope of the Rocky Mountains. A four-year private institution, Carroll College has an enrollment of 1,431 students. Although not originally a co-educational college, Carroll College has been co-ed since 1944. The school is also affiliated with the Roman Catholic Church. The campus facilities include: performing arts center · arts lab · dance studio · engineering lab · observatory · seismograph station · science labs · nursing lab · fitness center. Carroll College provides on-campus housing with 435 units that can accommodate 830 students. Housing options: coed dorms · single-student apartments.

Student Life and Activities

Just over half (57 percent) of students live on campus, and they enjoy Search Weekend, Senior Retreat, Community Halloween Events for Children, Jr./Sr. Banquet and Softball Weekend. Carroll College has 37 official student organizations. The most popular are: Astronomy · Gay-Straight Alliance · Health Services · Music · Psychology · SAVE · Student Ambassadors · Students for a Just Society · Outdoor Club · Cadet Corps · CC Student Nurses Association · Circle K · College Democrats · College Republicans · Dance Team · Education · Engineers Without Borders. Carroll College is a member of the Frontier Conference (NAIA).

Academics and Learning Environment

Carroll College has 88 full-time and 75 part-time faculty members, offering a student-to-faculty ratio of 12:1. The most common course size is 10 to 19 students. Carroll College offers 31 majors. The most popular are business administration, elementary education and biology, while the least favorite majors are foreign languages, computer science and arts. The school has a general core requirement as well as a religion requirement. Cooperative education is not offered. All first-year students must maintain a 2.0 GPA or higher to avoid academic probation, and a minimum overall GPA of 2.0 is required to graduate. Other special academic programs that would appeal to a B student: self-designed majors · pass/fail grading option · independent study · double majors · dual degrees · accelerated study · honors program · internships.

125

CARROLL COLLEGE

Highlights

Carroll College
Helena, MT (Pop. 29,134)
Location: Medium city
Four-year private
Founded: 1909
Website: http://www.carroll.edu

Students
Total enrollment: 1,431
Undergrads: 1,431
Part-time students: 6%
From out-of-state: 64%
From public schools: 84%
Male/Female: 42%/58%
Live on-campus: 57%
Off-campus employment rating: Fair
Caucasian: 79%
African American: 1%
Hispanic: 4%
Asian: 1%
Hawaiian or Pacific Islander: <1%
Native American: 1%
Mixed (2+ ethnicities): 1%
International: 2%

Academics
Calendar: Semester
Student/faculty ratio: 12:1
Class size 9 or fewer: 28%
Class size 10-29: 60%
Class size 30-49: 10%
Class size 50-99: 2%
Class size 100 or more: -
Returning freshmen: 81%
Six-year graduation rate: 67%

Most Popular Majors
Business administration
Elementary education
Biology

B Student Support and Success

The Learning Commons exists to provide students with free opportunities to strengthen their academic skills through peer tutoring and study skills assistance. Carroll also offers supplemental instruction in some of the most difficult courses, and Writing Center assistants help tutor anyone struggling in English classes. Carroll's philosophy is based on the Four Pillars: Integrated Knowledge, Lifelong Skills, Enduring Values and Gateway Experiences. In addition, the Walter Young Center offers personal counseling for emotional challenges facing students. Anyone needing assistance in a class can also be matched with an academic coach for additional help and resources.

Carroll College provides a variety of support programs including dedicated guidance for: academic · career · personal · psychological · religious. Recognizing that some students may need extra preparation, Carroll College offers remedial and refresher courses in: reading · writing · math · study skills. The average freshman year GPA is 3.2, and 81 percent of freshmen students return for their sophomore year. Approximately 22 percent of graduates pursue a graduate degree immediately after graduation. One year after graduation, the school reports that three percent of graduates have entered graduate school. Among students who enter the workforce, approximately 35 percent enter a field related to their major within six months of graduation. Companies that most frequently hire graduates from Carroll College include: Galusha Higgins Galusha · Anderson ZurMuehlen · Helena School District · Mountain West Bank · DA Davidson.

Support for Students with Learning Disabilities

Students with learning disabilities are supported by additional time to complete a degree, as well as lighter course loads. LD students may take advantage of services including: tutors · learning center · extended time for tests · oral tests · readers · note-taking services · waiver of math degree requirement. Individual or small group tutorials are also available in: writing labs · math labs. An advisor/advocate from the LD program is available to students.

How to Get Admitted

For admissions decisions, non-academic factors considered: interview · extracurricular activities · special talents, interests and abilities · character/personal qualities · volunteer work · work experience · state of residency · alumni relationship. A high school diploma is required, although a GED is also accepted for admissions consideration. SAT or ACT test scores are required of all applicants. SAT Subject Test scores are required for some applicants. *According to the admissions office:* Minimum composite ACT score of 21 (combined SAT Reasoning score of 1000) and minimum 2.5 GPA recommended. *Academic units recommended:* 4 English, 3 Math, 2 Science, 2 Social Studies, 2 Foreign Language.

How to Pay for College

To apply for financial aid, students should submit the following: Free Application for Federal Student Aid (FAFSA). Carroll College participates in the Federal Work Study program. *Need-based aid* programs include: scholarships and grants · general need-based awards · Federal Pell grants · state scholarships and grants · college-based scholarships and grants · private scholarships and grants. *Non-need-based aid programs include:* scholarships and grants · state scholarships and grants · athletic scholarships · ROTC scholarships.

CARROLL COLLEGE

Highlights

Admissions
Applicants: 3,279
Accepted: 1,740
Acceptance rate: 53.1%
Average GPA: 3.6
ACT range: 22-27
SAT Math range: 510-610
SAT Reading range: 490-620
SAT Writing range: 3-20
Top 10% of class: 25%
Top 25% of class: 61%
Top 50% of class: 90%

Deadlines
Early Action: 12/1
Early Decision: No
Regular Action: Rolling admissions
Common Application: Accepted

Financial Aid
In-state tuition: $28,670
Out-of-state tuition: $28,670
Room: $4,552
Board: $4,398
Books: $1,000
Freshmen receiving need-based aid: 72%
Undergrads rec. need-based aid: 65%
Avg. % of need met by financial aid: 71%
Avg. aid package (freshmen): $19,174
Avg. aid package (undergrads): $19,599
Avg. debt upon graduation: $26,931

Prominent Alumni
Casey Fitzsimmons, former member of the Detroit Lions; Raymond Hunthausen, former Archbishop of Seattle.

School Spirit
Mascot: Fighting Saints
Colors: Purple and vegas gold

127

College Profiles

CHAMPLAIN COLLEGE

163 South Willard Street, Burlington, VT 05401
Admissions: 800-570-5858 · Financial Aid: 800-570-5858
Email: admission@champlain.edu · Website: http://www.champlain.edu

From the College

"Founded in 1878, Champlain College is a private college overlooking Lake Champlain in Burlington, VT, with additional campuses in Montreal and Dublin. Our career-driven approach to education prepares students for professional life beginning with their first semester. Students choose from more than 80 subject areas, including undergraduate majors, minors, specializations, graduate degrees and certificate programs."

Campus Setting

An educational pioneer since 1878, Champlain is a college where students and faculty don't just respond to opportunities, they create them. "We've introduced new fields of study, like Game Design and Computer and Digital Forensics, and offer majors with a specific focus, like e-Business Management, Digital Filmmaking and Public Relations. Champlain's three-dimensional education, another pioneering concept, integrates relevant, professionally focused studies with a rigorous Core curriculum and practical Life Skills program," describes a representative. A four-year private institution located on 21-acres in Burlington, Champlain College has an enrollment of 3,275 students. In addition to a small library, the campus also has a business and technology center. Champlain College provides on-campus housing with 473 units that can accommodate 1,361 students. Housing options: coed dorms · special housing for international students. Recreation and sports facilities include: fitness center · gymnasium.

Student Life and Activities

Less than half (42 percent) of students live off campus. According to the editor of the student newspaper, Burlington, Vermont, is a small but active college town along the shore of Lake Champlain with lots of clubs, activities, skiing, hiking and water sports. A popular gathering place on campus is the IDX Student Life Center. Champlain College has 40 official student organizations. The most popular are: Get Real (service club) · World Drummers' Club · book club · children's club · criminal justice club · e-gaming club · Heritage Society · psychology club · software engineering club · social work club · computer forensics club · international club · URGE · Speak Easy · Student Alumni Association · MusicMakers. For those interested in sports, there are intramural teams such as: basketball · crew · dance · golf · hiking · ice hockey · indoor soccer · lacrosse · rock climbing · rafting · ice climbing · Zumba · snowboarding · Ultimate Frisbee · volleyball.

Academics and Learning Environment

Champlain College has 103 full-time and 306 part-time faculty members, offering a student-to-faculty ratio of 14:1. The most common course size is 10 to 19 students. Champlain College offers 56 majors. Digital forensics, game art/design/development and psychology are the most popular. The school has a general core requirement. Cooperative education is not offered. All first-year students must maintain a 2.0 GPA or higher to avoid academic probation, and a minimum overall GPA of 2.0 is required to graduate. Other special academic programs that would appeal to a B student include: self-designed majors · independent study · double majors · dual degrees · accelerated study · honors program · internships · distance learning certificate programs.

B Student Support and Success

Champlain offers a number of different centers to help students become and stay academically strong. At the Advising and Registration Center, or ARC, academic advisors provide one-on-one help to students who are choosing courses and planning their majors. At the Student Life Office, various academic support labs in accounting/math, writing and computers are offered as well as peer tutoring and counseling. The school also has Career Services and Health Services departments to help with planning and to give support.

Champlain College provides a variety of support programs including dedicated guidance for: academic · career · personal · minority students · non-traditional students. The average freshman year GPA is 3.0, and 79 percent of freshmen students return for their sophomore year. Approximately eight percent of graduates pursue a graduate degree immediately after graduation. Among students who enter the workforce, approximately 85 percent enter a field related to their major within six months of graduation. Companies that most frequently hire graduates from Champlain College include: IBM · KPMG · IDX Systems Corp. · Chittenden Bank · General Dynamics · Marsh Management · US Immigration and Naturalization Services (INS).

Support for Students with Learning Disabilities

Students with learning disabilities will be supported by a number of programs including: tutors · testing accommodations · untimed tests · extended time for tests · oral tests · note-taking services · early syllabus · priority registration.

How to Get Admitted

For admissions decisions, non-academic factors considered: interview · extracurricular activities · special talents, interests and abilities · character/personal qualities · volunteer work · work experience · state of residency · geographical location · alumni relationship. A high school diploma is required, although a GED is also accepted for admissions consideration. SAT or ACT test scores are required of all applicants. SAT Subject Test scores are required for some applicants. *According to the admissions office:* Minimum 2.0 GPA and essay required. *Academic units recommended:* 4 English, 4 Math, 4 Science, 2 Social Studies, 2 Foreign Language.

How to Pay for College

To apply for financial aid, students should submit the following: Free Application for Federal Student Aid (FAFSA) · institution's own financial aid forms · state aid form · Non-custodian (Divorced/Separated) Parent's Statement. Champlain College participates in the Federal Work Study program. *Need-based aid programs include:* scholarships and grants · general need-based awards · Federal Pell

CHAMPLAIN COLLEGE

Highlights

Champlain College
Burlington, VT (Pop. 42,282)
Location: Medium city
Four-year private
Founded: 1878
Website: http://www.champlain.edu

Students
Total enrollment: 3,275
Undergrads: 2,868
Freshmen: 689
Part-time students: 19%
From out-of-state: 80%
Male/Female: 60%/40%
Live on-campus: 58%
Off-campus employment rating: Good
Caucasian: 70%
African American: 3%
Hispanic: 4%
Asian: 1%
Hawaiian or Pacific Islander: <1%
Native American: <1%
Mixed (2+ ethnicities): 2%
International: 1%

Academics
Calendar: Semester
Student/faculty ratio: 14:1
Class size 9 or fewer: 18%
Class size 10-29: 82%
Class size 30-49: -
Class size 50-99: -
Class size 100 or more: -
Returning freshmen: 79%
Six-year graduation rate: 57%

Most Popular Majors
Digital forensics
Game art/design/development
Psychology

129

CHAMPLAIN COLLEGE

Highlights

Admissions
Applicants: 5,097
Accepted: 3,574
Acceptance rate: 70.1%
Placed on wait list: 75
Enrolled from wait list: 31
Average GPA: 3.0
ACT range: 22-28
SAT Math range: 490-620
SAT Reading range: 500-620
SAT Writing range: 3-22
Top 10% of class: 15%
Top 25% of class: 39%
Top 50% of class: 68%

Deadlines
Early Action: No
Early Decision: 11/15
Regular Action: 11/15 (priority)
1/31 (final)
Notification of admission by: 12/15
Common Application: Accepted

Financial Aid
In-state tuition: $32,800
Out-of-state tuition: $32,800
Room: $8,500
Board: $5,250
Books: $1,000
Freshmen receiving need-based aid: 78%
Undergrads rec. need-based aid: 68%
Avg. % of need met by financial aid: 63%
Avg. aid package (freshmen): $22,628
Avg. aid package (undergrads): $19,612

Prominent Alumni
Rusty DeWees, actor.

School Spirit
Colors: Blue and white

grants · state scholarships and grants · college-based scholarships and grants · private scholarships and grants. *Non-need-based aid programs include:* state scholarships and grants.

CHOWAN UNIVERSITY

One University Place, Murfreesboro, NC 27855
Admissions: 888-4-CHOWAN · Financial Aid: 252-398-1229
Email: enroll@chowan.edu
Website: http://www.chowan.edu

From the College

"Chowan University offers a personal liberal arts education in a rural, church-related setting, with regionally acclaimed programs in biology, psychology, criminal justice, graphic communication, business administration, teacher education, history and physical education. Personal attention from faculty and staff gives each student his or her best opportunity for success."

Campus Setting

Chowan, founded in 1848, is a private, church-affiliated, liberal arts college. Its 300-acre campus is located in Murfreesboro, 60 miles from Norfolk. A four-year institution, Chowan University has an enrollment of 1,367 students. Although not originally a co-educational college, Chowan University has been co-ed since 1931. The school is also affiliated with the Baptist Church. The school also has a library with 200,000 books. Chowan University provides on-campus housing with 800 units that can accommodate 1,020 students. Housing options: women's dorms · men's dorms · special housing for disabled students.

Student Life and Activities

Eighty-five percent of students live on campus, and popular events include Homecoming and Snow Ball. Some of the most popular student organizations include: Concert, jazz and pep bands · chorus · singing group · Chowan Players · Ambassadors · Campus Program Board · team managers · Order of the Silver Feather · creative writing, education, history, imaging technology, physical education, psychology, women's and science clubs. For those interested in sports, there are intramural teams such as: basketball · dodgeball · flag football · football · in-line hockey · indoor soccer · indoor volleyball · roller hockey · Ultimate Frisbee. Chowan University is a member of the NCAA (Division II), NCCAA and CIAA.

Academics and Learning Environment

Chowan University has 62 full-time and 29 part-time faculty members, and offers a student-to-faculty ratio of 16:1. Chowan University offers 28 majors with the most popular being business administration, physical education and psychology. The least popular are religion, music and mathematics. The school has a general core requirement as well as a religion requirement. Cooperative education is not offered. All first-year students must maintain a 1.5 GPA or higher to avoid academic probation, and a minimum overall GPA of 2.0 is required to graduate. Other special academic programs that would appeal to a B student: self-designed majors ·

CHOWAN UNIVERSITY

Highlights

Chowan University
Murfreesboro, NC (Pop. 2,813)
Location: Rural
Four-year private
Founded: 1848
Website: http://www.chowan.edu

Students
Total enrollment: 1,367
Undergrads: 1,361
Freshmen: 593
Part-time students: 6%
From out-of-state: 63%
From public schools: 89%
Male/Female: 47%/53%
Live on-campus: 85%
In fraternities: 15%
In sororities: 15%
Off-campus employment rating: Good
Caucasian: 21%
African American: 70%
Hispanic: 3%
Asian: <1%
Hawaiian or Pacific Islander: <1%
Native American: <1%
Mixed (2+ ethnicities): 4%
International: 1%

Academics
Calendar: Semester
Student/faculty ratio: 16:1
Class size 9 or fewer: 28%
Class size 10-29: 49%
Class size 30-49: 22%
Class size 50-99: 1%
Class size 100 or more: -
Returning freshmen: 48%
Six-year graduation rate: 25%

Most Popular Majors
Business administration
Physical education
Psychology

131

CHOWAN UNIVERSITY

Admissions

Applicants: 4,617
Accepted: 2,487
Acceptance rate: 53.9%
Average GPA: 2.6
ACT range: 14-17
SAT Math range: 340-440
SAT Reading range: 360-430
SAT Writing range: Not reported
Top 10% of class: 3%
Top 25% of class: 11%
Top 50% of class: 39%

Deadlines

Early Action: No
Early Decision: No
Regular Action: 8/1 (priority)
Common Application: Not accepted

Financial Aid

In-state tuition: $22,700
Out-of-state tuition: $22,700
Room: $4,100
Board: $4,130
Books: $850
Freshmen receiving need-based aid: 86%
Undergrads rec. need-based aid: 88%
Avg. % of need met by financial aid: 60%
Avg. aid package (freshmen): Not reported
Avg. aid package (undergrads): Not reported

Prominent Alumni

Fred Banks, former player for the Miami Dolphins; Jerry Holmes, former player for the New York Jets; Curtis Whitley, former player for the Oakland Raiders.

School Spirit

Mascot: Hawks
Colors: Blue and white

independent study · double majors · honors program · internships · distance learning.

B Student Support and Success

Chowan offers its entire student body a tutoring program located in the campus library. Students request a tutor in any area of study by filling out an online tutor request form. Student tutors work one on one with students to provide this service four nights a week at no cost. Chowan also has Camp 121, a tutoring center that gives students a quiet space for individual studying between the hours of 9 and 5. Individual and group study sessions are frequently held at Camp 121 as well.

Chowan University provides dedicated guidance for academic, career and religion. The average freshman year GPA is 2.4.

Support for Students with Learning Disabilities

Students with learning disabilities may want to look into support programs, including: remedial math · tutors · learning center · un-timed tests · extended time for tests · oral tests · note-taking services · tape recorders · early syllabus · priority registration. Individual or small group tutorials are also available in: time management · organizational skills · learning strategies · specific subject areas · writing labs · math labs · study skills. An advisor/advocate from the LD program is available to students.

How to Get Admitted

For admissions decisions, non-academic factors considered: interview · extracurricular activities · special talents, interests and abilities · character/personal qualities · volunteer work · work experience · state of residency · geographical location · alumni relationship. A high school diploma is required, although a GED is also accepted for admissions consideration. SAT or ACT test scores are required of all applicants. SAT Subject Test scores are not required. *Academic units recommended:* 4 English, 3 Math, 2 Science, 3 Social Studies, 2 Foreign Language.

How to Pay for College

To apply for financial aid, students should submit the following: Free Application for Federal Student Aid (FAFSA). Chowan University participates in the Federal Work Study program. *Need-based aid programs include:* scholarships and grants · general need-based awards · Federal Pell grants · state scholarships and grants · college-based scholarships and grants · private scholarships and grants. *Non-need-based aid programs include:* scholarships and grants · general need-based awards · state scholarships and grants · athletic scholarships · church-related · leadership · and regional scholarships/grants.

CHRISTOPHER NEWPORT UNIVERSITY

1 Avenue of the Arts, Newport News, VA 23606-3072
Admissions: 800-333-4268 · Financial Aid: 800-333-4268
Email: admit@cnu.edu · Website: http://www.cnu.edu

From the College

"Christopher Newport University (CNU) is dedicated to the ideals of scholarship, leadership and service. We celebrate the values inherent in the liberal arts and sciences and live as a community of honor transforming hearts and minds. Led by Paul Trible, a former U.S. senator, CNU has more than doubled the size of its freshman class, increased the SAT average by more than 200 points, dramatically enhanced the number of faculty and seen applications increase by more than 700 percent. As our faculty grows, CNU will maintain a freshman class of 1,200, driving down the average class size from 24 to 14.

"We offer outstanding academics; promote service, honor and leadership; and provide rich opportunities for undergraduate research - a rare occurrence at many schools. Superb teaching, personal attention and faculty-student mentorship allow creativity and excellence to flourish. CNU students develop the qualities of mind and spirit to lead lives of significance, thanks to a curriculum that stimulates intellectual inquiry and fosters civic responsibility. Each fall the President's Leadership Program accepts approximately 400 high-achieving freshmen who have exhibited leadership characteristics in their schools and communities.

"Through the four-year Honors Program, academically talented students enjoy a rich educational experience, participating in challenging courses and cultural/intellectual activities. Additional signature programs prepare students for career success. Through the Pre-Med and Pre-Health Program, qualified students may apply for early acceptance to Eastern Virginia Medical School (EVMS). Students successful in this competitive process receive, before the end of their sophomore year, guaranteed admission to EVMS after graduating from CNU (without having to take the MCAT). Led by a legal, constitutional and political history scholar, the Pre-Law Program helps students gain admission to the nation's top 25 law schools. The Master of Arts in Teaching allows students to earn a graduate degree with just one additional year of study beyond the bachelor's degree. Through Learning Communities, freshmen enroll in at least three courses with the same 15-30 students. Courses are based on an academic interest, satisfy graduation requirements and smooth the transition into college by connecting like-minded students. All freshmen are assigned a core faculty advisor who mentors them for two years, provides academic support, helps with course selection, and introduces campus resources and engagement opportunities. The university promotes study abroad for all students, sponsoring international study programs for cross-cultural education and growth. This includes a permanent relationship with the University of Oxford and dozens of smaller, faculty-led programs.

"Faculty and students interact on a beautiful 260-acre campus. CNU has completed nearly $1 billion in capital construction over the past decade with additional projects under way. The Mariners' Museum Library, which contains the Western Hemisphere's largest maritime collection, is housed in CNU's Paul and Rosemary Trible Library and provides an incomparable resource for students, faculty and researchers. Across campus, students make their mark in 200-plus activities - from academic groups to social, athletic and beyond. High achievers in both the classroom and on the field of play, the university's student-athletes help make CNU athletics one of the nation's most successful NCAA Division III programs."

CHRISTOPHER NEWPORT UNIVERSITY

Christopher Newport University
Newport News, VA (Pop. 180,726)
Location: Medium city
Four-year public
Founded: 1960
Website: http://www.cnu.edu

Students
Total enrollment: 5,232
Undergrads: 5,094
Freshmen: 1,591
Part-time students: 3%
From out-of-state: 9%
Male/Female: 43%/57%
Live on-campus: 71%
In fraternities: 8%
In sororities: 8%
Off-campus employment rating: Excellent
Caucasian: 75%
African American: 8%
Hispanic: 5%
Asian: 2%
Hawaiian or Pacific Islander: <1%
Native American: <1%
Mixed (2+ ethnicities): 5%
International: <1%

Academics
Calendar: Semester
Student/faculty ratio: 16:1
Class size 9 or fewer: 3%
Class size 10-29: 65%
Class size 30-49: 27%
Class size 50-99: 1%
Class size 100 or more: 3%
Returning freshmen: 84%
Six-year graduation rate: 66%

Most Popular Majors
Psychology
Biology
Communication studies

Campus Setting

Christopher Newport, founded in 1960, is a comprehensive, public university. Programs are offered through the College of Arts and Humanities, College of Natural and Behavioral Sciences and the College of Social Sciences. Its 260-acre campus is located in Newport News, midway between Williamsburg and Norfolk. A four-year institution, Christopher Newport University has an enrollment of 5,232 students. In addition to a large, well-stocked library, the campus facilities include: art gallery · center for the arts · center for sports and convocation. Christopher Newport University provides on-campus housing with 1,022 units that can accommodate 3,708 students. Housing options: coed dorms · single-student apartments. Recreation and sports facilities include: field house · fitness center · grass field · artificial turf · tennis courts.

Student Life and Activities

Seventy-one percent of students live on campus and enjoy a wide variety of social activities, including the David Student Center, the Ferguson Center for the Arts concerts/performances, Fall Fest, Spring Fest, Captain's Ball, Campus Tie Dye, Homecoming, Pancake Breakfast, Food 4 Thought, Day of Service and Padeia. Christopher Newport University has 200 official student organizations. The most popular are: Ballroom Dancing Society · College Music Educators National Conference · Campus Girl Scouts · Virginia Association of Teachers of English · Student Honor Educators and Assistants · Student Virginia Education Association · classics club · French club · Students in Free Enterprise · Campus Activities Board · Circle K · Gay-Straight Student Union · Social Work Association · sociology club · Direct Marketing Association · Society for Human Resource Management · accounting club · economics and finance club · mathematics club · Model UN · College Republicans · Young Democrats · biology club · chemistry club · psychology club · Association for Computing Machinery · Institute of Electric and Electronic Engineers. For those interested in sports, there are intramural teams such as: badminton · basketball · flag football · soccer · softball · tennis · volleyball. Christopher Newport University is a member of the Capital Athletic Conference (Division III), USA South Athletic Conference (Division III) and the Mid-Atlantic Intercollegiate Sailing Association (MAISA).

Academics and Learning Environment

Christopher Newport University has 268 full-time and 148 part-time faculty members, offering a student-to-faculty ratio of 16:1. The most common course size is 10 to 19 students. Christopher Newport University offers 41 majors. Biology, communication studies and psychology are the most popular choices. The least popular are American studies, integrative biology and German. The school has a general core requirement. Cooperative education is not offered. All first-year students must maintain a 2.0 GPA or higher to avoid academic probation. Other special academic programs include: self-designed majors · pass/fail grading option · independent study · double majors · dual degrees · honors program · internships.

B Student Support and Success

Christopher Newport College provides academic advising and counseling/career services to their students. Their Writing Center offers help to students who are writing papers or projects. In addition, the school has a Learning Communities program for first-year students. This program involves 18 to 24 students who live together, take two classes together and build strong relationships with the community. This arrangement provides support for the transition from home to college, while also giving each participant a peer mentor to learn from as well as help with setting up study groups, test review sessions, informal group tutoring and more.

Christopher Newport University provides a variety of support programs including dedicated guidance for: academic · career · personal · minority students · religious. The average freshman year GPA is 2.9, and 84 percent of freshmen students return for their sophomore year. Many students enter the workforce, and approximately 28 percent pursue a graduate degree immediately after graduation.

Support for Students with Learning Disabilities

Students coping with learning disabilities may find assistance in programs such as: extended time for tests · oral tests · note-taking services · tape recorders. Individual or small group tutorials are also available in specific subject areas (writing and math).

How to Get Admitted

For admissions decisions, non-academic factors considered: interview · extracurricular activities · special talents, interests and abilities · character/personal qualities · volunteer work · work experience · geographical location · alumni relationship. A high school diploma is required, although a GED is also accepted for admissions consideration. SAT or ACT test scores are required for some applicants. SAT Subject Test scores are not required. *According to the admissions office:* Rank in top half of secondary school class and minimum 3.0 GPA required. *Academic units recommended:* 4 English, 4 Math, 4 Science, 4 Social Studies, 3 Foreign Language.

How to Pay for College

To apply for financial aid, students should submit the following: Free Application for Federal Student Aid (FAFSA). Christopher Newport University participates in the Federal Work Study program. *Need-based aid programs include:* scholarships and grants · general need-based awards · Federal Pell grants · state scholarships and grants · college-based scholarships and grants · private scholarships and grants. *Non-need-based aid programs include:* scholarships and grants · general need-based awards · state scholarships and grants · creative arts and performance awards · ROTC scholarships · President's Leadership Program.

CHRISTOPHER NEWPORT UNIVERSITY

Highlights

Admissions
Applicants: 7,016
Accepted: 4,141
Acceptance rate: 59.0%
Placed on wait list: 1,639
Enrolled from wait list: 137
Average GPA: 3.7
ACT range: 23-28
SAT Math range: 530-620
SAT Reading range: 540-630
SAT Writing range: Not reported
Top 10% of class: 20%
Top 25% of class: 53%
Top 50% of class: 91%

Deadlines
Early Action: 12/1
Early Decision: 11/15
Regular Action: 11/15 (priority)
2/1 (final)
Notification of admission by: 3/15
Common Application: Accepted

Financial Aid
In-state tuition: $11,646
Out-of-state tuition: $21,974
Room: $6,564
Board: $3,750
Books: $1,218
Freshmen receiving need-based aid: 45%
Undergrads rec. need-based aid: 44%
Avg. % of need met by financial aid: 62%
Avg. aid package (freshmen): $8,036
Avg. aid package (undergrads): $8,381
Avg. debt upon graduation: $27,324

Prominent Alumni
Randall Munroe, creator, XKCD.com; Bradford Wood, CFO, St. Louis Cardinals; Perry Moss, president, Rubicon Global.

School Spirit
Mascot: Captain Chris
Colors: Royal blue and silver
Song: *Go Captains*

135

COASTAL CAROLINA UNIVERSITY

P.O. Box 261954, Conway, SC 29528-6054
Admissions: 800-277-7000 · Financial Aid: 843-349-2313
Email: admissions@coastal.edu · Website: http://www.coastal.edu

From the College

"Coastal Carolina University is a public, comprehensive, liberal arts institution. The university offers baccalaureate programs to approximately 8,867 undergraduate students in 55 fields of study including acclaimed programs in marine science, resort tourism and professional golf management. Graduate programs include an M.B.A. Waties Island, 1,062 acres of pristine barrier island on the Atlantic coast, provides a natural laboratory for extensive study in the sciences. Students enjoy a nationally competitive NCAA I athletic program that includes football, an inspiring cultural calendar and a tradition of community interaction fueled by more than 100 student clubs and organizations."

Campus Setting

Coastal Carolina University, founded in 1954, is a public, comprehensive university. Its 630-acre campus is located in Conway, nine miles from Myrtle Beach. A four-year institution, Coastal Carolina University has a total enrollment of 9,478 students. The campus features a marine science and wetland biology lab. Coastal Carolina University provides on-campus housing with 1,029 units that can accommodate 3,290 students. Housing options: coed dorms · single-student apartments · special housing for disabled students. Recreation and sports facilities include: athletic fields · basketball and volleyball courts · weight room.

Student Life and Activities

Over half (61 percent) of students live off campus. As reported by a school representative, "'Cliques' are prominent, social and cultural life is up and coming. OSAL, Residence Life and Multicultural Student Services are working to enhance cultural diversity and awareness. Popular gathering spots include the CINO Grille, Student Center game room, volleyball court in front of the Woods community, campus recreation center, Broadway at the Beach, Coastal Ale House and the beach. Popular campus events include football games/tailgating, late night bingo in the commons, Casino Night in the fall, CINO Day in the spring, Homecoming week events, Greek week events, Greek formals, step shows, diversity programs, intramural sports, basketball games, baseball games and game show nights. Coastal Carolina University has 185 official student organizations. Popular groups on campus include Greeks, athletes, STAR members, Leadership Challenge members, Coastal Productions Board, honor societies, the Chanticleer, CCU Customs, gospel choir and intramural teams. For those interested in sports, there are intramural teams such as: badminton · basketball · dodgeball · football · flag football · golf · pickleball · soccer · softball · Wiffle ball · volleyball · water polo. Coastal Carolina University is a member of the Big South Conference (Division I).

Academics and Learning Environment

Coastal Carolina University has 406 full-time and 265 part-time faculty members, offering a student-to-faculty ratio of 17:1. The most common course size is 20 to 29 students. Coastal Carolina University offers 46 majors with the most popular being management, marketing and communication and least popular being intelligence/ national security studies, physics and economics (B.A.). The school has a general core requirement. Cooperative education is available. All first-year students must maintain a 2.0 GPA or higher to avoid academic probation, and a minimum overall GPA of 2.0 is required to graduate. Other special academic programs that would appeal to a B student include: self-designed majors · pass/fail grading option · independent study · double majors · dual degrees · accelerated study · honors program · internships · distance learning certificate programs.

B Student Support and Success

At Coastal Carolina, professional academic advising and peer mentoring are available. The school also has a course called UNIV 110, which is designed to develop critical thinking and research skills, to provide community support during the first semester of enrollment and to acquaint students with the school's resources. Tutoring sessions are offered and there is even a Grammar Hotline to call. The UNIV 110 course, also known as a "First Year Experience," involves peers, faculty and staff and other members within the community. Students play an active part in forums, workshops, discussions, readings, case studies and community service projects. This includes assignments that might come in various forms, ranging from quizzes, tests and journals to presentations, portfolios and writing projects. In the end, UNIV 110 helps students to develop a clearer and more comprehensive academic and career development plan for the future.

Coastal Carolina University provides a variety of support programs including dedicated guidance for: academic · career · personal · psychological · minority students · veterans · non-traditional students · family planning. The average freshman year GPA is 2.9, and 63 percent of freshmen students return for their sophomore year. Approximately 15 percent of graduates pursue a graduate degree immediately after graduation. Among students who enter the workforce, approximately 73 percent enter a field related to their major within six months of graduation. Companies that most frequently hire graduates from Coastal Carolina University include: City of Myrtle Beach · Coastal Carolina University · Horry County Government · Horry County Schools · Horry Telephone.

Support for Students with Learning Disabilities

Students with learning disabilities may choose to take a lightened course load. High school foreign language waivers are accepted. According to the school, all students who register are requested to participate in a coaching relationship with the counselor where an academic plan is developed and followed and there are meetings with the student throughout the first semester. Meetings include time management, organization, specific areas of weakness (i.e. reading, math, writing), tutoring and study group. Students with learning disabilities will find the following programs at Coastal Carolina University useful: remedial math · special classes · tutors · learning center · testing accommodations · untimed tests · extended time for tests · take-home exam · oral tests · readers · typist/scribe · note-taking services · reading machines · tape recorders · texts on tape · videotaped classes · early syllabus · priority registration · priority seating. Individual or small group tutorials are also available in: time management · organizational skills · learning strategies · specific subject areas · writing labs · math labs · study skills. An advisor/advocate from the LD program is available to students.

COASTAL CAROLINA UNIVERSITY

Highlights

Coastal Carolina University
Conway, SC (Pop. 18,688)
Location: Small town
Four-year public
Founded: 1954
Website: http://www.coastal.edu

Students
Total enrollment: 9,478
Undergrads: 8,867
Freshmen: 2,808
Part-time students: 9%
From out-of-state: 53%
From public schools: 92%
Male/Female: 46%/54%
Live on-campus: 39%
In fraternities: 3%
In sororities: 6%
Off-campus employment rating: Excellent
Caucasian: 69%
African American: 20%
Hispanic: 4%
Asian: 1%
Hawaiian or Pacific Islander: <1%
Native American: <1%
Mixed (2+ ethnicities): 3%
International: 1%

Academics
Calendar: Semester
Student/faculty ratio: 17:1
Class size 9 or fewer: 10%
Class size 10-29: 62%
Class size 30-49: 26%
Class size 50-99: 2%
Class size 100 or more: -
Returning freshmen: 63%
Six-year graduation rate: 46%

Most Popular Majors
Management
Communication
Marketing

137

College Profiles

COASTAL CAROLINA UNIVERSITY

Highlights

Admissions
Applicants: 14,050
Accepted: 9,014
Acceptance rate: 64.2%
Average GPA: 3.4
ACT range: 19-24
SAT Math range: 460-550
SAT Reading range: 450-540
SAT Writing range: Not reported
Top 10% of class: 10%
Top 25% of class: 33%
Top 50% of class: 70%

Deadlines
Early Action: No
Early Decision: No
Regular Action: 12/1 (priority)
7/1 (final)
Common Application: Not accepted

Financial Aid
In-state tuition: $9,960
Out-of-state tuition: $23,300
Room: $5,440
Board: $3,000
Books: $1,142
Freshmen receiving need-based aid: 73%
Undergrads rec. need-based aid: 72%
Avg. % of need met by financial aid: 48%
Avg. aid package (freshmen): $9,685
Avg. aid package (undergrads): $9,417
Avg. debt upon graduation: $33,882

Prominent Alumni
Mike Tolbert, fullback, Carolina Panthers;
Dustin Johnson, professional golfer,
PGA; Elise Testone, singer/songwriter.

School Spirit
Mascot: Chanticleers
Colors: Bronze and coastal teal

How to Get Admitted

For admissions decisions, non-academic factors considered: interview · extracurricular activities · special talents, interests and abilities · character/personal qualities · alumni relationship · geographical location. A high school diploma is required, although a GED is also accepted for admissions consideration. SAT or ACT test scores are required of all applicants. SAT Subject Test scores are considered, if submitted, but are not required. *According to the admissions office:* Sliding scale with minimum combined SAT Reasoning score of 960 (composite ACT score of 21) and minimum 3.0 GPA required. *Academic units recommended:* 4 English, 4 Math, 3 Science, 2 Social Studies, 2 Foreign Language.

How to Pay for College

To apply for financial aid, students should submit the following: Free Application for Federal Student Aid (FAFSA). Coastal Carolina University participates in the Federal Work Study program. *Need-based aid programs include:* scholarships and grants · general need-based awards · Federal Pell grants · state scholarships and grants · college-based scholarships and grants · private scholarships and grants. *Non-need-based aid programs include:* scholarships and grants · general need-based awards · state scholarships and grants · creative arts and performance awards · athletic scholarships.

COE COLLEGE

1220 First Avenue, NE, Cedar Rapids, IA 52402
Admissions: 877-225-5863 · Financial Aid: 877-225-5863
Email: admission@coe.edu · Website: http://www.coe.edu

From the College

"Coe College's mission is to provide students an education of superior quality that prepares graduates for satisfying lives in a global society. Coe believes that a liberal arts education allows students to discover their real talents and interests, while developing the skills, abilities and habits of mind that will make possible a successful career in any field of endeavor, including ones that do not yet exist. The Coe Plan, an innovative and unique program grounded in the liberal arts, is designed to ensure that Coe students make an effective transition from college to career. Coe is one of the few private liberal arts institutions in the country to make practical, real-world experience, such as internships, off-campus study and research projects, a requirement for graduation. Nursing students reap the benefits of one-on-one clinical experiences at a top 100 hospital located across the street from campus, students majoring in the sciences complete high-level research projects with faculty and students from all majors work in the largest undergraduate, student-run writing center in the country, located on Coe's campus."

Campus Setting

Coe, founded in 1851, is a church-affiliated, liberal arts college. Its 60-acre campus is located a mile from downtown Cedar Rapids. A four-year private institution, Coe College has an enrollment of 1,420 students. Although not originally a co-educational college, Coe College has been co-ed since 1853. In addition to a large, well-stocked library, the campus facilities include: music studio · GIS/GPS lab. Coe College provides on-campus housing with 20 units that can accommodate 1,186 students. Housing options: coed dorms · women's dorms · men's dorms · sorority housing · fraternity housing · single-student apartments. Recreation and sports facilities include: baseball, soccer and softball fields · basketball courts · cross-country course · field house · football and volleyball stadiums · racquetball center · swimming pool.

Student Life and Activities

Eighty-six percent of students live on campus. Hot spots on and off campus include the Pub, the Piano Lounge, Library Quad, TKE House, Mahoney's, Moose McDuffies and Brewed Awakenings. Blindspot, athletic events, plays, Presidential Ball and Homecoming are the most popular social events of the year. Coe College has 81 official student organizations. Students groups who influence campus life include Greeks, Cosmos, athletes and the Senate. For those interested in sports, there are intramural teams such as: basketball · flag football · floor hockey · racquetball · soccer · softball · squash · tennis · Ultimate Frisbee · volleyball. Coe College is a member of the Iowa Intercollegiate Athletic Conference (Division III).

Academics and Learning Environment

Coe College has 93 full-time and 74 part-time faculty members, offering a student-to-faculty ratio of 11:1. The most common course size is 10 to 19 students. Coe College offers 51 majors. The most popular majors are business administration, psychology and nursing. The least popular are German, French and philosophy. The school has a general core requirement. Cooperative education is available. All first-year students must maintain a 2.0 GPA or higher to avoid academic probation. Other special academic programs that would appeal to a B student: self-designed majors · pass/fail

COE COLLEGE

Coe College
Cedar Rapids, IA (Pop. 128,119)
Location: Medium city
Four-year private
Founded: 1851
Website: http://www.coe.edu

Students
Total enrollment: 1,420
Undergrads: 1,420
Freshmen: 389
Part-time students: 5%
From out-of-state: 53%
Male/Female: 46%/54%
Live on-campus: 86%
In fraternities: 12%
In sororities: 13%
Off-campus employment rating: Excellent
Caucasian: 76%
African American: 4%
Hispanic: 5%
Asian: 2%
Native American: <1%
Mixed (2+ ethnicities): 3%
International: 4%

Academics
Calendar: 4-4-1 system
Student/faculty ratio: 11:1
Class size 9 or fewer: 27%
Class size 10-29: 67%
Class size 30-49: 5%
Class size 50-99: 1%
Class size 100 or more: -
Returning freshmen: 79%
Six-year graduation rate: 67%

Most Popular Majors
Business administration
Psychology
Nursing

grading option · independent study · double majors · accelerated study · honors program · Phi Beta Kappa · internships.

B Student Support and Success

Like a growing number of colleges today, Coe offers a First Year Seminar to help students transition from high school to college. This program emphasizes learning basic writing skills and offers a number of different classes to take to get these skills. To support this, the college has a Writing Center plus a Speaking Center for stronger oral presentations. The college also provides an Academic Achievement Program that offers an umbrella of services. Academic assistance includes tutoring, advising, helping with study skills, getting supplemental instruction, reading assistance and math help. Several types of counseling are offered, including peer, personal, career and substance abuse. In addition, Coe offers the TRANSITIONS program, a half-credit course that helps students "improve skills necessary for successful performance in college," including the topics of study skills, time management, self motivation and personal responsibility.

Coe College provides a variety of support programs including guidance in academic, career, personal, psychological, family planning, minority students and religion. Remedial and refresher courses are available in: reading · writing · math · study skills. Annually, 79 percent of freshmen students return for their sophomore year. Approximately 20 percent of students pursue a graduate degree right after graduation. One year after graduation, the school reports that 25 percent of graduates have entered graduate school. Among students who enter the workforce, approximately 63 percent enter a field related to their major within six months of graduation. Companies that most frequently hire graduates from Coe College include: Aegon USA · branch offices of McGladry and Pullen · Deloitte · Principal Financial Group · Rockwell-Collins · U.S. Department of Labor · University of Iowa Hospitals and Clinics · various school districts throughout the region.

Support for Students with Learning Disabilities

Students with learning disabilities may take advantage of additional time to complete their degree, as well as a lightened course load. LD students may access: remedial reading · tutors · learning center · testing accommodations · untimed tests · extended time for tests · take-home exam · oral tests · note-taking services · tape recorders · early syllabus. Individual or small group tutorials are also available in: time management · organizational skills · learning strategies · specific subject areas · writing labs · math labs · study skills. An advisor/advocate from the LD program is available to students. This member also sits on the admissions committee.

How to Get Admitted

For admissions decisions, non-academic factors considered: interview · extracurricular activities · special talents, interests and abilities · character/personal qualities · volunteer work · work experience · state of residency · alumni relationship. A high school diploma is required, although a GED is also accepted for admissions consideration. SAT or ACT test scores are required of all applicants. *According to the admissions office:* Minimum composite ACT score of

20 (combined SAT Reasoning score of 940), rank in top two-fifths of secondary school class and minimum 3.0 GPA recommended. *Academic units recommended:* 4 English, 3 Math, 3 Science, 3 Social Studies, 2 Foreign Language.

How to Pay for College

To apply for financial aid, students should submit the following: Free Application for Federal Student Aid (FAFSA). Coe College participates in the Federal Work Study program. *Need-based aid programs include:* scholarships and grants · general need-based awards · Federal Pell grants · state scholarships and grants · college-based scholarships and grants · private scholarships and grants. *Non-need-based aid programs include:* scholarships and grants · general need-based awards · state scholarships and grants · creative arts and performance awards · special achievements and activities awards · special characteristics awards · ROTC scholarships.

COE COLLEGE

Highlights

Admissions
Applicants: 2,972
Accepted: 1,834
Acceptance rate: 61.7%
Average GPA: 3.6
ACT range: 23-28
SAT Math range: 495-670
SAT Reading range: 493-693
SAT Writing range: 18-23
Top 10% of class: 31%
Top 25% of class: 61%
Top 50% of class: 91%

Deadlines
Early Action: 12/10
Early Decision: No
Regular Action: Rolling admissions
Common Application: Accepted

Financial Aid
In-state tuition: $36,990
Out-of-state tuition: $36,990
Room: $3,730
Board: $4,500
Books: $1,000
Freshmen receiving need-based aid: 86%
Undergrads rec. need-based aid: 82%
Avg. % of need met by financial aid: 82%
Avg. aid package (freshmen): $30,087
Avg. aid package (undergrads): $28,412
Avg. debt upon graduation: $31,660

Prominent Alumni
Fred Jackson, Running Back, Buffalo Bills; Dr. T.J. Kiczenski, Research Associate Glass Research Group, Corning, Inc., inventor; Ronald T.Y. Moon, Former Chief Justice, Hawaii Supreme Court.

School Spirit
Mascot: Kohawks
Colors: Crimson and Vegas Gold

COLLEGE OF IDAHO

2112 Cleveland Boulevard, Caldwell, ID 83605-4432
Admissions: 800-224-3246 · Financial Aid: 800-224-3246
Email: admissions@collegeofidaho.edu
Website: http://www.collegeofidaho.edu

From the College

"The College of Idaho is a place where you can complete your degree in four years, with a high job placement rate. If you plan to attend graduate school, the College of Idaho has a very positive record for acceptance and placement rates at some of the most reputable programs in the country. We offer small classes (12:1 student to faculty ratio), faculty who care about you as a person, internships, an academic calendar which encourages international travel and opportunities to participate in community-based classes and projects. The college was recently ranked the 20th best college in the U.S. for "More Things to Do on Campus" by the Princeton Review and is regularly ranked in various publications as a top college in the Pacific Northwest. The College of Idaho's location in "the Treasure Valley' allows for outdoor opportunities that include skiing, hiking, climbing, rafting, kayaking and exploring the desert. Located minutes from metropolitan Boise, the college is easily accessible by air or automobile."

Campus Setting

The College of Idaho is a liberal arts institution founded in 1891. Its 50-acre campus is located in Caldwell, 25 miles west of Boise. A four-year private institution, Idaho College has an enrollment of 1,059 students. Campus facilities include: movie theater · activities center · chapel · gem and mineral collection · museum of natural history · planetarium · herbarium · student center. Idaho College provides on-campus housing with 347 units that can accommodate 577 students. Housing options: coed dorms · fraternity housing · single-student apartments · special housing for disabled students. Recreation and sports facilities include: activities center · stadium.

Student Life and Activities

Just over half (62 percent) of students live on campus. According to the school, "There are many activities going on during the school year. The Student Involvement Office helps students discover how to get involved in activities on campus and in the community. From athletics to theater or music, the opportunities are limitless for students to be involved." Students gather at McCain Student Union, Simplot Dining Hall, local coffee shops, restaurants, Albertson's Athletic Center and the Center on the Grove in Boise. Homecoming, Caldwell Fine Art Programs, Theater Productions, Langroise Trio, Greek Formal, Liberal Art Lectures, Potters Clay, A.L.A.S. Cultural Dinners, Late Night Campus Ministry, Finals Breakfasts, Berger's Bench, Spring Fling, Rosenthal Art Gallery, student government activities, C of I Student Research Conference, Cinco de Mayo Celebration, Comedy in the Pub, Phreakin' Phrenzies, Film Festivales, Greek Week, Winter Fest, sporting activities, intermural activities and Outdoor Program are popular events. College of Idaho has 50 official student organizations. The most popular are: Music, theatre, political, service and special-interest groups · art club · Spanish club · Writers Co · math club · Philo Tech Society · Pre Health Prof. Club · C of I Chem Society · engineering club · space aeronautics club · music club · swing dance · Young Democrats · Young Republicans · Students Economic Freedom · Big Brothers/Sisters · Circle K · Pep Band · cheer squad · men's lacrosse · gay/straight alliance. Sports include intramural teams such as: badminton · baseball · basketball · bowling · dodgeball · flag football · Frisbee ·

lacrosse · soccer · softball · volleyball. College of Idaho is a member of the Cascade Collegiate Conference (NAIA).

Academics and Learning Environment

College of Idaho has 75 full-time and 38 part-time faculty members, offering a student-to-faculty ratio of 12:1. The most common course size is 10 to 19 students. College of Idaho offers 31 majors with the most popular being health, business and history and least popular being elementary education, religion and sports/fitness center management. The school has a general core requirement. Cooperative education is available. All first-year students must maintain a 2.0 GPA or higher to avoid academic probation, and a minimum overall GPA of 2.0 is required to graduate. Other special academic programs that would appeal to a B student include: self-designed majors · pass/fail grading option · independent study · double majors · dual degrees · honors program · internships.

B Student Support and Success

At the College of Idaho, new students participate in the First Year Experience, which is geared to provide "living and learning experiences that facilitates a successful transition to a college community centered on exacting scholarship and life-long learning." The program includes a First Year Theme and Book in which a theme is chosen and then a book supporting that theme is read before the fall semester begins. From there, discussions of the book are held, as well as guest speakers, films, debates, theatrical productions and even special tie-in menus in the dining halls.

College of Idaho provides guidance programs for: academic · career · personal · psychological · minority students · military · non-traditional students · family planning · religious. Additional counseling services include: peer counseling. Remedial and refresher courses are offered in: reading · writing · math · study skills. Annually, 83 percent of freshmen students return for their sophomore year. Companies that most frequently hire graduates from College of Idaho include: Micron Computers · Inclusion · Caldwell Public Schools · College of Santa Fe · Univ. of Nevada - Las Vegas · Idaho National Laboratory · AstraZeneca · Planned Parenthood of Idaho Inc. · Sapidyne Instruments Inc. · J. R. Simplot Company · Center Point · United Way · ConAgra Foods · Bureau of Reclamation Job Corps · Prudential Financial · Northwestern Mutual Financial Network · Provarity · Gem State Developmental Center Inc. · Boise, Meridian, Kuna, Vallivue and Caldwell School Districts.

Support for Students with Learning Disabilities

Learning disabled students are supported by the College of Idaho through lighter course loads and additional time to complete a degree. LD students may also find support through: remedial math · tutors · learning center · testing accommodations · untimed tests · extended time for tests · take-home exam · oral tests · readers · note-taking services · reading machines · tape recorders · early syllabus · diagnostic testing service · priority registration · waiver of foreign language and math degree requirement. Individual or small group tutorials are also available in: time management · organizational skills · learning strategies · specific subject areas · writing labs · math labs · study skills. An advisor/advocate from the LD program

COLLEGE OF IDAHO

Highlights

College of Idaho
Caldwell, ID (Pop. 47,668)
Location: Large town
Four-year private
Founded: 1891
Website: http://www.collegeofidaho.edu

Students
Total enrollment: 1,059
Undergrads: 1,042
Freshmen: 299
Part-time students: 4%
From out-of-state: 17%
Male/Female: 42%/58%
Live on-campus: 62%
In fraternities: 15%
In sororities: 22%
Off-campus employment rating: Good
Caucasian: 62%
African American: 1%
Hispanic: 15%
Asian: 3%
Hawaiian or Pacific Islander: <1%
Native American: 1%
Mixed (2+ ethnicities): 1%
International: 8%

Academics
Calendar: 4-1-4 system
Student/faculty ratio: 12:1
Class size 9 or fewer: 28%
Class size 10-29: 54%
Class size 30-49: 15%
Class size 50-99: 2%
Class size 100 or more: -
Returning freshmen: 83%
Six-year graduation rate: 64%

Most Popular Majors
Business
Health
History

143

College Profiles

COLLEGE OF IDAHO

Highlights

Admissions
Applicants: 1,388
Accepted: 901
Acceptance rate: 64.9%
Average GPA: 3.6
ACT range: 22-27
SAT Math range: 480-600
SAT Reading range: 470-630
SAT Writing range: 2-24
Top 10% of class: 25%
Top 25% of class: 56%
Top 50% of class: 88%

Deadlines
Early Action: 11/15
Early Decision: No
Regular Action: Rolling admissions
Common Application: Accepted

Financial Aid
In-state tuition: $24,200
Out-of-state tuition: $24,200
Room: $3,340
Board: $2,704
Books: $1,200
Freshmen receiving need-based aid: 74%
Undergrads rec. need-based aid: 71%
Avg. % of need met by financial aid: 92%
Avg. aid package (freshmen): $24,707
Avg. aid package (undergrads): $23,706
Avg. debt upon graduation: $27,607

Prominent Alumni
Dr. Mary Shorb, co-discoverer of vitamin B-12; Joe Albertson- founder, Albertson's supermarket chain; Kris McDivitt- co-founder, Patagonia Outerwear.

School Spirit
Mascot: Coyotes
Colors: Purple and gold
Song: *Hail College of Idaho*

is available to students. This member also sits on the admissions committee.

How to Get Admitted

For admissions decisions, non-academic factors considered: interview · extracurricular activities · special talents, interests and abilities · character/personal qualities · volunteer work · work experience · state of residency · alumni relationship. A high school diploma is required, although a GED is also accepted for admissions consideration. SAT or ACT test scores are required of all applicants. SAT Subject Test scores are not required. *According to the admissions office:* Minimum 3.0 GPA and SAT of 1000 or ACT of 20 for regular admission. Provisional admission also considered. *Academic units recommended:* 4 English, 4 Math, 3 Science, 4 Social Studies, 3 Foreign Language.

How to Pay for College

To apply for financial aid, students should submit the following: Free Application for Federal Student Aid (FAFSA) · institution's own financial aid forms. College of Idaho participates in the Federal Work Study program. *Need-based aid programs include:* scholarships and grants · general need-based awards · Federal Pell grants · state scholarships and grants · college-based scholarships and grants · private scholarships and grants. *Non-need-based aid programs include:* scholarships and grants · general need-based awards · state scholarships and grants · creative arts and performance awards · special achievements and activities awards · athletic scholarships · ROTC scholarships.

COLLEGE OF ST. MARY

7000 Mercy Road, Omaha, NE 68106
Admissions: 800-926-5534 · Financial Aid: 800-926-5534
Email: enroll@csm.edu · Website: http://www.csm.edu

From the College

"The only women's university in a five-state Mid-western region, College of Saint Mary (CSM) is a Catholic college dedicated to the education of women in an environment that calls forth potential and fosters leadership. CSM offers 30 programs of study, including education, nursing, applied psychology, forensic science and women's studies, with divisions in professional studies, arts and sciences and health professions. Since 1923, CSM has remained dedicated to its original mission: the education of women for leadership, service and success. While CSM is committed to undergraduate education, graduate programs in education, the health professions and organizational leadership enable professionals in the area to reach their career and personal goals while still working full-time.

"CSM offers innovative programs unavailable elsewhere in the region. A specially designed residence hall, Mothers Living and Learning, allows single mothers and their children to live on campus while the mother pursues her degree. Education students directly teach at-risk children while learning to instruct math and science effectively in our Operation SMART program, a partnership with Girls, Inc. of Omaha. An agreement with the Peter Kiewit Institute encourages women studying math and science at CSM to enter into the engineering profession. This '2 + 3' program allows a CSM student to receive a CSM bachelor's degree in Math or Science and a Master's Degree from the University of Nebraska in engineering in just five years.

"Over 90 percent of CSM students receive financial aid, and CSM has several unique scholarship programs. Through donor support, the McAuley Scholarship program provides full tuition and fees for 15 women at any one time who are currently receiving public assistance, such as food stamps or housing subsidies. The Marie Curie Scholars Program, funded by a grant from the National Science Foundation, provides significant financial support for academically talented, but financially challenged, students who plan to study biology, chemistry or mathematics.

"Campus life is rich and exciting. CSM fields competitive NAIA teams in basketball, cross country, softball, volleyball and soccer. The new Hixson-Lied Commons offers a coffee shop, chairs for studying or chatting, wireless internet and rooms where student organizations can meet. The Achievement Center, also located in the Commons, is a place where students can build study skills, receive tutoring in a variety of subjects and find help searching for internships and jobs.

"Omaha's midtown development, Aksarben Village, is emerging just across the street from campus; soon students will close to new restaurants, retail stores and a movie theatre. Our Lied Fitness Center offers free, on-campus workout facilities including a swimming pool, and the Keystone Trail and Papio Creek winds across the edge of campus, offering a place to run, walk or bike.

"In the classroom, students combine a liberal arts core with practical learning opportunities, career-specific skills, leadership development and community service. Our service learning program sponsors annual winter, spring and summer break trips where students travel to locations such as the U.S.-Mexico border and China to learn while serving."

Campus Setting

The College of Saint Mary, founded in 1923, is a private, church-affiliated university for women. Its 25-acre campus is located in a suburban section of Omaha. A four-year

COLLEGE OF ST. MARY

Highlights

College of St. Mary
Omaha (Pop. 421,570)
Location: Major city
Four-year private women's college
Founded: 1923
Website: http://www.csm.edu

Students
Total enrollment: 970
Undergrads: 735
Freshmen: 139
Part-time students: 13%
From out-of-state: 38%
From public schools: 87%
Male/Female: 1%/99%
Live on-campus: 32%
Off-campus employment rating: Good
Caucasian: 77%
African American: 6%
Hispanic: 12%
Asian: 2%
Hawaiian or Pacific Islander: <1%
Native American: <1%
Mixed (2+ ethnicities): 3%
International: 1%

Academics
Calendar: Semester
Student/faculty ratio: 7:1
Class size 9 or fewer: 35%
Class size 10-29: 57%
Class size 30-49: 8%
Class size 50-99: -
Class size 100 or more: -
Returning freshmen: 79%
Six-year graduation rate: 40%

Most Popular Majors
Nursing
Business
Biology

college, College of St. Mary has an enrollment of 970 students. The school is also affiliated with the Roman Catholic Church. The campus facilities include: chapel · auditorium · art gallery · fitness center. College of St. Mary provides on-campus housing with 168 units that can accommodate 275 students. Housing options: women's dorms. Recreation and sports facilities include: fitness center · parks.

Student Life and Activities

Most students (68 percent) live off campus. Popular events include Welcome Days, Queen of Hearts Celebration, Annual Powder Puff Football Competition, Spirit of Service Day, Hypnotist/Mentalist, Homecoming/Heritage Week Events and Casino Night. CSM has 20 official student organizations. The most popular are: Residence Hall Council (RHC) · Student Education Association of Nebraska (SEAN) · Student Nurses Association (SNA) · Student Occupational Therapy Association (SOTA) · Student Paralegal Association · Student Senate · Campus Activities Board (CAB) · Dance Team · Do Unto Others (DUO) Board · Golden S · Math and Science Club · Green Team · Peer Review Board · Social Sciences Organization · Students Against Violence (SAV) · Multicultural Association of Students (MAS) · Phi Beta Lambda. For those interested in sports, there are intramural teams such as: bowling · volleyball. CSM is a member of the Midlands Collegiate Athletic Conference (NAIA).

Academics and Learning Environment

College of St. Mary has 61 full-time and 140 part-time faculty members, offering a student-to-faculty ratio of 7:1. The most common course size is 10 to 19 students. CSM offers 34 majors. Nursing, business and biology are the most popular, while math, chemistry and theology are the least. The school has a general core requirement as well as a religion requirement. Cooperative education is not offered. All first-year students must maintain a 2.0 GPA or higher to avoid academic probation. Other special academic programs that would appeal to a B student include: pass/fail grading option · independent study · double majors · dual degrees · accelerated study · honors program · internships · weekend college · distance learning certificate programs.

B Student Support and Success

The Achievement Center at the College of Saint Mary helps students develop self-confidence, effective study skills, a strong resume, job search strategies and "unique gifts and talents." Tutoring and testing services are available and the website offers multiple support links to developing a variety of skills in multiple subjects.

College of St. Mary provides a variety of support programs including dedicated guidance for: academic · career · personal · psychological · minority students · non-traditional students · religious. Recognizing that some students may need extra preparation, CSM offers remedial and refresher courses in: reading · writing · math · study skills. The average freshman year GPA is 3.2, and 79 percent of freshmen students return for their sophomore year. Approximately 71 percent of students enter a field related to their major within six months of graduation. Companies that most frequently hire graduates from College of St. Mary include: Alegent Healthcare · Bergan Mercy Medical Center · Children's Hospital

· Creighton Medical Center · Immanuel Hospital · Omaha Public Schools · Union Pacific Railroad.

Support for Students with Learning Disabilities

If necessary, the college will grant a lightened course load and additional time to students with learning disabilities to complete their degree. LD students might also access: remedial math · remedial English · tutors · learning center · testing accommodations · extended time for tests · take-home exam · oral tests · readers · note-taking services · reading machines · tape recorders · videotaped classes · early syllabus · diagnostic testing service · priority registration. Individual or small group tutorials are also available in: time management · organizational skills · learning strategies · specific subject areas · study skills.

How to Get Admitted

For admissions decisions, non-academic factors considered: extracurricular activities · state of residency. A high school diploma is required, although a GED is also accepted for admissions consideration. SAT Subject Test scores are not required. *According to the admissions office:* Minimum composite ACT score of 18 and a minimum 2.0 GPA required. *Academic units recommended:* 4 English, 3 Math, 3 Science, 2 Social Studies.

How to Pay for College

To apply for financial aid, students should submit the following: Free Application for Federal Student Aid (FAFSA). College of St. Mary participates in the Federal Work Study program. *Need-based aid programs include:* scholarships and grants · general need-based awards · Federal Pell grants · state scholarships and grants · college-based scholarships and grants · private scholarships and grants. *Non-need-based aid programs include:* scholarships and grants · state scholarships and grants · creative arts and performance awards · athletic scholarships.

COLLEGE OF ST. MARY

Highlights

Admissions
Applicants: 347
Accepted: 189
Acceptance rate: 54.5%
Average GPA: 3.6
ACT range: 20-26
SAT Math range: Not reported
SAT Reading range: Not reported
SAT Writing range: Not reported
Top 10% of class: 28%
Top 25% of class: 51%
Top 50% of class: 87%

Deadlines
Early Action: No
Early Decision: No
Regular Action: Rolling admissions
Common Application: Not accepted

Financial Aid
In-state tuition: $27,984
Out-of-state tuition: $27,984
Room: Varies
Board: Varies
Books: $1,098
Freshmen receiving need-based aid: 90%
Undergrads rec. need-based aid: 92%
Avg. % of need met by financial aid: 69%
Avg. aid package (freshmen): $20,514
Avg. aid package (undergrads): $18,855
Avg. debt upon graduation: $40,026

School Spirit
Mascot: Flames
Colors: Blue and gold

COLLEGE OF THE ATLANTIC

105 Eden Street, Bar Harbor, ME 04609
Admissions: 800-528-0025 · Financial Aid: 207-801-5645
Email: inquiry@coa.edu · Website: http://www.coa.edu

From the College

"Located between the Atlantic Ocean and Acadia National Park, College of the Atlantic offers two degrees: a BA and MPhil, both in Human Ecology. In pursuit of this degree, students consider their individual passions to create their own academic trajectories, integrating knowledge from all academic disciplines and personal experience to fulfill the mission of Human Ecology: investigating and improving relationships between humans and our social, natural, built and virtual communities. COA's small size and individualized curriculum encourages tutorials, intensive seminar-style classes and frequent faculty-student interchanges.

"Having one major means that COA has no departments and no departmental requirements; classes are interdisciplinary. Coursework consists of readings, usually from primary sources, as well as active investigation. These efforts culminate in a term-long senior project. As part of coursework and/or senior projects, recent students have participated in international meetings on climate change, investigated the impact of big box stores (resulting in first-in-the-nation legislation for Maine), used GIS maps to educate local towns on impending planning decisions and prepared an emergency system for a California town, and more.

"Beyond this, COA is a democratic institution, with students involved on all levels of governance and a weekly campus meeting to discuss current campus issues and decisions. Major decisions must be brought to this All-College Meeting; committees that filter into the governance structure include participation by students. Opportunities for travel abound; students must complete a one-term internship, which usually takes them off-campus and often abroad. The college offers a residency term in Mexico and another in Quebec. International connections on campus are extensive, as COA has one of the highest percentages of international students of any college.

"COA is the first college to become carbon neutral; new student residences are outfitted with composting toilets; the kitchen serves food from the college's organic farm. Now, COA offers one of the very few undergraduate green and socially responsible business programs and a Food Systems Program that connects COA's organic farm to an organic research center in the United Kingdom and a graduate school in Germany."

Campus Setting

College of the Atlantic was founded in 1969 on the premise that education should go beyond understanding the world as it is, to enabling students to actively shape its future. Classes focus on understanding the relationships between humans and our environment - and improving those relationships: in policy, the arts, science and a multitude of category-defying fields. According to the college, "We call this Human Ecology. Classes are truly interdisciplinary, learning hands-on and active, relationships are emphasized. Students are expected to shape their own individual path to their degree, and are encouraged to go to the source and do their own creative thinking in the hopes that they may help shape a more sustainable and just future."

A four-year private institution, College of the Atlantic has an enrollment of 370 students. Campus facilities include: art gallery · natural history museum · GIS laboratory · green graphics lab · applied human ecology center · watershed coalition · media design studio · video editing lab · organic community garden · ceramics studio · equipment for outdoor leadership including kayaks, canoes, cross-country skis, snowshoes and climbing equipment. College of the Atlantic provides on-campus housing with 15 units that can accommodate 150 students. Housing options: coed dorms.

Student Life and Activities

More than half of the students (58 percent) live off campus. A school representative notes, "Acadia National Park is in our backyard, so students often go hiking, kayaking, biking and skiing in the park. We're right on the ocean and a group of students do swim - year-round! There are several musical groups on campus at all times - currently they include a number of rock bands, a bluegrass band, several jazz ensembles and a few classical music groups. All find venues at which to perform during the year." Popular gathering spots also include the dock and the Shrine, as well as Deering Common, the new campus center. Off-campus gathering spots are usually student homes. Popular campus events include Bar Island Swim, The Nature of Halloween, Annual National Toboggan Championships, Earth Day, Coffeehouse performances, Ultimate Frisbee, 24-hour plays, Film festivals, Aurora Ball-ealis (a staff-created party for students, staff and faculty), cricket, soccer, ice hockey, Fandango (an international cultural show with humor, music, dance; also a philanthropic fundraiser), Faculty-Staff-Senior Tug of War, Winter Carnival and Green Graduation. College of the Atlantic has 14 official student organizations. Popular groups on campus range from SustainUS, to the international cultural organization that creates Fandango, to a meditation group. For those interested in sports, there are intramural teams such as: basketball · bicycling · canoeing · climbing · cricket · hiking · ice hockey · kayaking · rock climbing · sailing · SCUBA diving · skiing/cross-country · snowshoeing · soccer · softball · Ultimate Frisbee · volleyball · water polo.

Academics and Learning Environment

College of the Atlantic has 29 full-time and 13 part-time faculty members, offering a student-to-faculty ratio of 10:1. The most common course size is 10 to 19 students. College of the Atlantic offers a single degree, human ecology, although students design their own major among arts and design, environmental sciences and human studies. The school does not have a general core requirement. Cooperative education is available. Other special academic programs that would appeal to a B student include: self-designed majors · pass/fail grading option · independent study · internships.

B Student Support and Success

"At COA, we focus on a student's creativity, desire to do something, as well as their innate interest in learning."

College of the Atlantic provides dedicated guidance for: academic · career · personal · psychological · minority students · family planning · religious. Annually, 81 percent of freshmen students return for their sophomore year. Approximately 10 percent of students pursue a graduate degree immediately after graduation. One year after graduation, the school reports that 16 percent of graduates have entered graduate school. Among students who enter the workforce, approximately 90 percent enter a field related to their major within six months of graduation. Companies that most frequently hire graduates from College of the Atlantic include:

COLLEGE OF THE ATLANTIC

Highlights

College of the Atlantic
Bar Harbor, ME (Pop. 5,235)
Location: Rural
Four-year private
Founded: 1969
Website: http://www.coa.edu

Students
Total enrollment: 370
Undergrads: 362
Freshmen: 126
Part-time students: 5%
From out-of-state: 86%
From public schools: 63%
Male/Female: 33%/67%
Live on-campus: 42%
Off-campus employment rating: Fair
Caucasian: 69%
African American: 1%
Hispanic: 5%
Asian: 2%
Native American: 1%
Mixed (2+ ethnicities): 2%
International: 15%

Academics
Calendar: Trimester
Student/faculty ratio: 10:1
Class size 9 or fewer: 27%
Class size 10-29: 73%
Class size 30-49: -
Class size 50-99: -
Class size 100 or more: -
Returning freshmen: 81%
Six-year graduation rate: 69%

Most Popular Majors
Human ecology

149

College Profiles

COLLEGE OF THE ATLANTIC

Admissions
Applicants: 455
Accepted: 333
Acceptance rate: 73.2%
Average GPA: 3.6
ACT range: 25-33
SAT Math range: 530-640
SAT Reading range: 580-690
SAT Writing range: 2-58
Top 10% of class: 10%
Top 25% of class: 69%
Top 50% of class: 95%

Deadlines
Early Action: No
Early Decision: 12/1
Regular Action: 2/15 (final)
Notification of admission by: 4/1
Common Application: Accepted

Financial Aid
In-state tuition: $39,942
Out-of-state tuition: $39,942
Room: $6,000
Board: $3,300
Books: $600
Freshmen receiving need-based aid: 91%
Undergrads rec. need-based aid: 89%
Avg. % of need met by financial aid: 95%
Avg. aid package (freshmen): $39,625
Avg. aid package (undergrads): $35,649
Avg. debt upon graduation: $19,285

Prominent Alumni
Congresswoman Chellie Pingree, First District Congresswoman from Maine; Greg Stone, Vice President of Conservation International, influential in creating the world's largest marine sanctuary in Kiribati, the Phoenix Islands; Nell Newman, founder, Newman's Own Organics.

School Spirit
Mascot: Black Flies

New England Aquarium · Maine State Department of Education · National Park Service.

Support for Students with Learning Disabilities

At College of the Atlantic, learning disabled students may take advantage of additional time to complete their degree or a lightened course load. Credit is given for remedial courses taken. High school foreign language waivers are accepted. Students with learning disabilities will find the following programs at College of the Atlantic useful: remedial English · remedial reading · special classes · tutors · testing accommodations · untimed tests · extended time for tests · take-home exam · oral tests · readers · note-taking services · reading machines · tape recorders · texts on tape · early syllabus · priority registration. Individual or small group tutorials are also available in: time management · organizational skills · learning strategies · specific subject areas · writing labs · math labs · study skills. An advisor/advocate from the LD program is available to students. This member also sits on the admissions committee.

How to Get Admitted

For admissions decisions, non-academic factors considered: interview · extracurricular activities · special talents, interests and abilities · character/personal qualities · volunteer work · work experience · geographical location · minority affiliation · alumni relationship. A high school diploma is required, although a GED is also accepted for admissions consideration. SAT or ACT test scores are considered, if submitted, but are not required. SAT Subject Test scores are considered, if submitted, but are not required. *According to the admissions office:* Recommended rank in top quarter of secondary school class or minimum 3.0 GPA. *Academic units recommended:* 4 Math, 3 Science, 5 Social Studies, 2 Foreign Language.

How to Pay for College

To apply for financial aid, students should submit the following: Free Application for Federal Student Aid (FAFSA) · institution's own financial aid forms · Non-custodian (Divorced/Separated) Parent's Statement. College of the Atlantic participates in the Federal Work Study program. *Need-based aid programs include:* scholarships and grants · general need-based awards · Federal Pell grants · state scholarships and grants · college-based scholarships and grants · private scholarships and grants. *Non-need-based aid programs include:* scholarships and grants · state scholarships and grants.

America's
Best Colleges for
B Students

COLORADO STATE UNIVERSITY

1062 Campus Delivery, Fort Collins, CO 80523
Admissions: 970-491-6909 · Financial Aid: 970-491-6321
Email: admissions@colostate.edu · Website: http://www.colostate.edu

From the College

"Founded in 1870 and established as a land-grant institution, Colorado State is a fully accredited public university recognized for its excellence in academic programs from the baccalaureate to the postgraduate level. Our land-grant mission of teaching, research and outreach means that we're dedicated to service - serving you, our students, first. Colorado State offers more than 150 programs of study within eight colleges allowing you to shape a course of study that best meets your personal and professional goals. The university emphasizes the importance of active learning providing opportunities for field experience, laboratory research, internships and study abroad. As a student at Colorado State, you will learn side by side with faculty mentors who are recognized internationally as leaders in their fields.

"Colorado State University is located in the center of Fort Collins, a city of about 131,000 people. Fort Collins provides a unique blend of big city advantages and small town friendliness. There are several shopping malls, hundreds of restaurants, multiple movie complexes, a regional cultural center, natural areas and miles of bike trails. Close to campus are Rocky Mountain National Park, the Poudre River and Horsetooth Reservoir. These recreation areas, as well as many others close by, offer endless opportunities for outdoor activities - such as skiing, snowboarding, hiking, camping, white water rafting and boating. And the city's agreeable climate of 300 days of sunshine a year enables you to take year-round advantage of the spectacular surroundings."

Campus Setting

Colorado State is a public university. Founded in 1870, it became a land-grant college in 1879 and was granted university status in 1957. Its 586-acre main campus is located in Fort Collins, Colorado at the foot of the Rocky Mountains, 65 miles north of Denver. A four-year public institution, Colorado State University has an enrollment of 31,256 students. Campus facilities include: art gallery · center for the arts · historic costume and textile museum. Colorado State University provides on-campus housing with 3,923 units that can accommodate 6,635 students. Housing options: coed dorms · single-student apartments · married-student apartments · special housing for disabled students · special housing for international students. Recreation and sports facilities include: arena · basketball and recreational centers · lacrosse, soccer and softball fields · gymnasium · stadium · tennis courts · inline hockey rink · climbing wall · swimming pool.

Student Life and Activities

Most students (75 percent) live off campus. CSU Rams maintain an active social life; whether enjoying live music in the vibrant local nightlife or attending one of the many cultural events held on campus, there's no shortage of opportunities to unwind. The hot spots for students are Lory Student Center, Morgan Library, Mugs Coffee Lounge and any of the numerous bars and restaurants in Old Town Fort Collins. CSU/CU (football) Rocky Mountain Showdown, Homecoming, Commencement, Ag day, Monfort lecture series, President's Fall Address and University Picnic, Spring Career Fair and Business Day are popular events. Colorado State University has 611 official student organizations. Student Government has a widespread influence on

COLORADO STATE UNIVERSITY

Colorado State University
Fort Collins, CO (Pop. 148,612)
Location: Medium city
Four-year public
Founded: 1870
Website: http://www.colostate.edu

Students
Total enrollment: 31,256
Undergrads: 23,798
Freshmen: 5,798
Part-time students: 13%
From out-of-state: 25%
From public schools: 88%
Male/Female: 49%/51%
Live on-campus: 25%
In fraternities: 7%
In sororities: 9%
Off-campus employment rating: Excellent
Caucasian: 74%
African American: 2%
Hispanic: 9%
Asian: 2%
Hawaiian or Pacific Islander: <1%
Native American: <1%
Mixed (2+ ethnicities): 3%
International: 3%

Academics
Calendar: Semester
Student/faculty ratio: 17:1
Class size 9 or fewer: 11%
Class size 10-29: 51%
Class size 30-49: 20%
Class size 50-99: 12%
Class size 100 or more: 7%
Returning freshmen: 87%
Six-year graduation rate: 65%

Most Popular Majors
Business administration
Human development/family studies
Health/exercise science

campus, as do many other academic and social groups. For those interested in sports, there are intramural teams such as: basketball · bowling · disc golf · dodgeball · flag football · golf · kickball · indoor triathlon · paintball · racquetball · soccer · softball · Ultimate Frisbee · volleyball · water polo. Colorado State University is a member of the Mountain West Conference (Division I, Football I-A).

Academics and Learning Environment

Colorado State University has 984 full-time and 25 part-time faculty members, offering a student-to-faculty ratio of 17:1. The most common course size is 10 to 19 students. Colorado State University offers 220 majors with the most popular being business administration, health/exercise science and human development/family studies and least popular being agricultural economics, wildlife biology and fishery biology. The school has a general core requirement. Cooperative education is available. All first-year students must maintain a 2.0 GPA or higher to avoid academic probation. Other special academic programs that would appeal to a B student include: pass/fail grading option · independent study · double majors · dual degrees · accelerated study · honors program · Phi Beta Kappa · internships · distance learning certificate programs.

B Student Support and Success

Colorado State's Academic Advancement Center is available for low income and/or first generation students and those who have disabilities. These students are also eligible for the Mentoring for Leadership Program. A peer mentoring program, it connects students with upper class mentors and campus resources. Tutoring is available through the Center and is built around the philosophy that "with the right study strategies and resources to clarify content any student can raise their course grade." Tutors assist students with finding study strategies that work for their course and explain content that students may have not completely understood in lecture.

Colorado State University provides dedicated guidance for: academic · career · personal · psychological · minority students · military · veterans · non-traditional students · family planning · religious. The average freshman year GPA is 2.9, and 87 percent of freshmen students return for their sophomore year.

Support for Students with Learning Disabilities

Students with learning disabilities may take advantage of additional time to complete their degree, or a lightened course load. LD students can also access: tutors · testing accommodations · extended time for tests · take-home exam · exam on tape or computer · readers · typist/scribe · note-taking services · reading machines · tape recorders · early syllabus · diagnostic testing service · waiver of math degree requirement. Individual or small group tutorials are also available in: time management · organizational skills · learning strategies · specific subject areas · writing labs · math labs · study skills. An advisor/advocate from the Resources for Disabled Students is available to students.

How to Get Admitted

For admissions decisions, non-academic factors considered: extracurricular activities · special talents, interests and abilities · character/personal qualities · volunteer work · work experience · state of residency · geographical location · alumni relationship. A high school diploma is required, although a GED is also accepted for admissions consideration. SAT or ACT test scores are required of all applicants. *Academic units recommended:* 4 English, 4 Math, 3 Science, 2 Social Studies, 2 Foreign Language.

How to Pay for College

To apply for financial aid, students should submit the following: Free Application for Federal Student Aid (FAFSA). Colorado State University participates in the Federal Work Study program. *Need-based aid programs include:* scholarships and grants · general need-based awards · Federal Pell grants · state scholarships and grants · college-based scholarships and grants · private scholarships and grants. *Non-need-based aid programs include:* scholarships and grants · general need-based awards · state scholarships and grants · creative arts and performance awards · special characteristics awards · athletic scholarships · ROTC scholarships.

COLORADO STATE UNIVERSITY

Highlights

Admissions
Applicants: 17,970
Accepted: 13,914
Acceptance rate: 77.4%
Average GPA: 3.6
ACT range: 22-27
SAT Math range: 510-630
SAT Reading range: 510-620
SAT Writing range: Not reported
Top 10% of class: 22%
Top 25% of class: 52%
Top 50% of class: 88%

Deadlines
Early Action: 12/1
Early Decision: No
Regular Action: Rolling admissions
Common Application: Accepted

Financial Aid
In-state tuition: $7,494
Out-of-state tuition: $23,347
Room: $4,956
Board: $5,820
Books: $1,126
Freshmen receiving need-based aid: 48%
Undergrads rec. need-based aid: 52%
Avg. % of need met by financial aid: 67%
Avg. aid package (freshmen): $11,492
Avg. aid package (undergrads): $11,806
Avg. debt upon graduation: $23,726

Prominent Alumni
Bill Ritter, Jr., governor, Colorado; Mary Cleave, astronaut and associate administrator, Science Mission Directorate, NASA; Yusef Komunyakaa, Pulitzer Prize winning poet.

School Spirit
Mascot: Rams
Colors: Green and gold

COPPIN STATE UNIVERSITY

Highlights

Coppin State University
Baltimore (Pop. 621,342)
Location: Major city
Four-year public
Founded: 1900
Website: http://www.coppin.edu

Students
Total enrollment: 3,612
Undergrads: 3,127
From out-of-state: 23%
Male/Female: 26%/74%
Live on-campus: Not reported
Off-campus employment rating: Fair
Caucasian: 1%
African American: 83%
Hispanic: 2%
Asian: <1%
Hawaiian or Pacific Islander: <1%
Native American: <1%
Mixed (2+ ethnicities): 2%
International: 8%

Academics
Calendar: Semester
Student/faculty ratio: 14:1
Class size 9 or fewer: 11%
Class size 10-29: 50%
Class size 30-49: 21%
Class size 50-99: 11%
Class size 100 or more: 7%
Returning freshmen: 65%
Six-year graduation rate: 15%

Most Popular Majors
Psychology
Management science
Criminal justice

COPPIN STATE UNIVERSITY

2500 West North Avenue, Baltimore, MD 21216-3698
Admissions: 800-635-3674 · Financial Aid: 410-951-3636
Email: admissions@coppin.edu
Website: http://www.coppin.edu

From the College

"A comprehensive, urban, liberal arts institution with a commitment to teaching, research and continuing service to its community, Coppin State University provides educational access and diverse opportunities for students with a high potential for success and for students whose promise may have been hindered by a lack of social, personal or financial opportunity. Powered by information technology as the centerpiece for achieving its institutional goals, Coppin State University embodies urban education and public service."

Campus Setting

Coppin State, founded in 1900, is a public university. Its 45-acre campus is located in Baltimore. A four-year institution, Coppin State University is a historically black university with 3,612 students. Coppin State University provides on-campus housing with 2 units that can accommodate 650 students. Housing options: coed dorms · special housing for disabled students. Recreation and sports facilities include: physical education complex · tennis courts.

Student Life and Activities

Most students live off campus. Coppin State University has a number of official student organizations, including: Coppin Models · Coppin Players · choir · dance ensemble · marching band · Dancing Divas · The Main Attraction · Akira Anime and Video Game Club · Grove Phi Groove Social Fellowship Inc. · Entertainment Management Student Union · American Humanics Student Association · Social Work Association · Green Coppin Coalition · Chi Eta Phi Nursing Sorority · Student Rehabilitation Counseling · The Talented Tenth Social Sciences Club · psychology club · sports management club · STEM Club. There are intramural teams such as: basketball · flag football · softball · tennis · volleyball. Coppin State University is a member of the NCAA (Division I) and Mid-Eastern Athletic Conference (Division I, Football I-AA).

Academics and Learning Environment

Coppin State University has 159 full-time and 173 part-time faculty members, offering a student-to-faculty ratio of 14:1. Coppin State University offers 40 majors with the most popular being psychology, management science and criminal justice and least popular being history and philosophy. The school has a general core requirement. Cooperative education is available. All first-year students must maintain a 1.2 GPA or higher to avoid academic probation. Other special academic programs that would appeal to a B student include: independent study · double majors · dual degrees · accelerated study · honors program · internships · weekend college · distance learning.

B Student Support and Success

Coppin offers a variety of Student Support Services with one-on-one help. They also require that each new student take a one-semester Freshman Seminar course. Students may receive help at the Academic Resource Center, which features four labs with basic, intermediate and advanced levels of instruction and tutoring at no cost. Coppin's Student Support Services includes academic advising with assistance in course selection and career planning. It also offers individual and group tutoring services, computer-assisted instruction and informational workshops on topics like study skills, computer literacy, test taking and note taking. Coppin has a series of video-assisted instruction in courses like algebra and writing.

Coppin State University offers support programs for: academic · career · personal · psychological · minority students. Additional counseling services include: substance abuse counseling and veterans' counseling. Recognizing that some students may need extra preparation, Coppin State University offers remedial and refresher courses in: reading · writing · math · study skills. The average freshman year GPA is 2.0, and 70 percent of freshmen students return for their sophomore year. Among students who enter the workforce, approximately 70 percent enter a field related to their major within six months of graduation. Companies that most frequently hire graduates from Coppin State University include: Baltimore City Public Schools · Baltimore County Public Schools · Social Security Administration · Baltimore City Department of Social Services.

Support for Students with Learning Disabilities

Students with learning disabilities may take advantage of specific support programs including: remedial math · remedial English · remedial reading · tutors · learning center · untimed tests · extended time for tests · note-taking services · waiver of math degree requirement. An advisor/advocate from the Student Support Services is available to students.

How to Get Admitted

For admissions decisions, non-academic factors considered: interview · extracurricular activities · special talents, interests and abilities · character/personal qualities · volunteer work · work experience · geographical location · minority affiliation · alumni relationship. A high school diploma is required, although a GED is also accepted for admissions consideration. SAT or ACT test scores are required of all applicants. *According to the admissions office:* Minimum composite ACT score of 18 (combined SAT Reasoning score of 900) and minimum 2.5 GPA required.

How to Pay for College

To apply for financial aid, students should submit the following: Free Application for Federal Student Aid (FAFSA). Coppin State University participates in the Federal Work Study program. *Need-based aid programs include:* scholarships and grants · general need-based awards · Federal Pell grants · state scholarships and grants · college-based scholarships and grants · private scholarships and grants · Federal Nursing scholarships · United Negro College Fund. *Non-need-based aid programs include:* scholarships and grants · general need-based awards · state scholarships and grants · athletic scholarships.

COPPIN STATE UNIVERSITY

Highlights

Admissions
Applicants: 5,980
Accepted: 2,153
Average GPA: Not reported
ACT range: Not reported
SAT Math range: 400-470
SAT Reading range: 410-480
SAT Writing range: Not reported

Deadlines
Early Action: No
Early Decision: No
Regular Action: Rolling admissions
Common Application: Accepted

Financial Aid
In-state tuition: $6,502
Out-of-state tuition: $11,763
Room: Varies
Board: Varies
Books: Varies
Undergrads receiving need-based or merit-based aid: 95%
Avg. aid package (freshmen): Not reported
Avg. aid package (undergrads): Not reported

Prominent Alumni
Bishop L. Robinson, first African American Police Commissioner of Baltimore; Larry Stewart, former NBA player; Verda Welcome, former Maryland state senator.

School Spirit
Mascot: Eagle
Colors: Royal blue and gold

155

College Profiles

CORNELL COLLEGE

600 First Street SW, Mount Vernon, IA 52314-1098
Admissions: 800-747-1112 · Financial Aid: 877-579-4049
Email: admissions@cornellcollege.edu
Website: http://www.cornellcollege.edu

From the College

"Cornell College is a private, liberal arts college recognized for its personalized and intellectually engaging undergraduate education. Our distinctiveness begins in the classroom with our One Course at a Time (OCAAT) academic calendar and extends onto the campus where there is a strong sense of community, mentoring relationships between faculty and students and opportunities to lead and volunteer. Cornell College was founded in 1853, and the historic 129-acre campus is home of a diverse student body of 1,200 who come from 48 states and 20 countries, including 19 percent domestic students of color, and five percent international students. The academic calendar provides students with creativity and depth in each course where students and their professor spend 3 1/2 weeks focusing their time and effort. Instead of balancing 4-6 courses, Cornell students delve deeply into the material exploring a range of perspectives and taking advantage of the flexibility, which provides time for extended discussions, lab experience virtually every day in the sciences and field work whenever possible.

"In addition to the engagement in the classroom, Cornell students find OCAAT also provides them with the flexibility to be fully engaged outside of class through more than 100 clubs and organizations, varsity athletics and an array of performing arts organizations. The flexibility also provides students with a breadth of study abroad opportunities (students typically study in more than 20 countries each year), internships (which may be done virtually anywhere), research on and off campus within students major fields of interests, and through independent study."

Campus Setting

Cornell College, founded in 1853, is a private, national liberal arts college located in the historic community of Mount Vernon, Iowa. The 129-acre campus is situated 15 miles east of Cedar Rapids, 20 miles north of Iowa City, and approximately 200 miles west of Chicago. Cornell was the first college in the country to have the entire campus listed with the National Register of Historic Places. Cornell was also the second college in the country to adopt the block plan, or One Course at a Time, an academic calendar in which students devote themselves to just one subject for three-and-a-half-week course terms. A four-year institution, Cornell College has an enrollment of 1,180 students. The school is also affiliated with the United Methodist Church. Campus facilities include: theatre · museum · geology center. Cornell College provides on-campus housing with 12 units that can accommodate 1,083 students. Housing options: coed dorms · women's dorms · men's dorms · single-student apartments. Recreation and sports facilities include: athletic fields · baseball diamond · football, soccer and softball fields · basketball and volleyball courts · gymnasium · indoor and outdoor track · multi-sports center · racquetball courts · strength training center · wrestling facility · weight room.

Student Life and Activities

Ninety percent of students live on campus. In addition to the events scheduled at Cornell, students also take advantage of performances, bands, etc. that visit the Cedar

Rapids and Iowa City area. Students also use 'block breaks' for visits to many of the regional cities including Chicago, Minneapolis, St. Louis, Kansas City and Indianapolis. Student organization such as the mountaineering and outdoors clubs will also use these extended weekends for trips to the Rockies or to Minnesota and Wisconsin for camping and hiking. Favorite gathering spots include the Ratt, the Commons and Pfeiffer Lounge and Scores Sports Bar and Grill. Well-attended events include Student Symposium, Music Mondays, Homecoming, Knock Your Block Off, New Student Orientation Events and music and theatre concerts. Athletic contests for most sports are the most popular social events of the school year. Cornell College has 122 official student organizations. Groups which influence student life include the media, PAAC - Performing Arts and Activities Council, the non-national fraternities and sororities, athletics, multicultural groups and theatre and music organizations. For those interested in sports, there are intramural teams such as: badminton · bowling · basketball · dodge ball · floor hockey · football · indoor soccer · racquetball · softball · Ultimate Frisbee · volleyball · wallyball · wrestling. Cornell College is a member of the Midwest Conference (Division III).

Academics and Learning Environment

Cornell College has 89 full-time and 27 part-time faculty members, offering a student-to-faculty ratio of 12:1. The most common course size is 10 to 19 students. Cornell College offers 39 majors. Psychology, economics/business and biology are the most popular majors. Russian, Latin American Studies and German are the least. The school has a general core requirement. Cooperative education is available. All first-year students must maintain a 2.0 GPA or higher to avoid academic probation. Other special academic programs that would appeal to a B student include: self-designed majors · independent study · double majors · dual degrees · Phi Beta Kappa · internships · certificate programs.

B Student Support and Success

Cornell has a first-year-only course that helps new students acclimate to doing college-level work. It includes a writing emphasis course, student mentors and a full advising system. Instructors help students develop skills in writing, reading comprehension, oral communication, information literacy, creativity, research and mathematics. They also show students how to build independent work habits. A lot of personal attention is given to help students be successful in a rather intense program.

Cornell College provides dedicated guidance for: academic · career · personal · psychological · minority students · non-traditional students · family planning · religious. The average freshman year GPA is 3.1, and 85 percent of freshmen students return for their sophomore year. Approximately 23 percent pursue a graduate degree immediately after graduation. One year after graduation, the school reports that 55 percent of graduates have entered graduate school. Among students who enter the workforce, approximately 50 percent enter a field related to their major within six months of graduation. Companies that most frequently hire graduates from Cornell College include: GE Healthcare · Department of Defense · Country Insurance · National Student Leadership Council · Uni-

CORNELL COLLEGE

CORNELL COLLEGE

Admissions
Applicants: 2,716
Accepted: 1,436
Acceptance rate: 52.9%
Placed on wait list: 142
Enrolled from wait list: 43
Average GPA: 3.5
ACT range: 24-30
SAT Math range: 540-690
SAT Reading range: 535-685
SAT Writing range: 10-40
Top 10% of class: 38%
Top 25% of class: 66%
Top 50% of class: 91%

Deadlines
Early Action: 12/1
Early Decision: 11/1
Regular Action: Rolling admissions
Common Application: Accepted

Financial Aid
In-state tuition: $37,275
Out-of-state tuition: $37,275
Room: $3,800
Board: $4,700
Books: $800
Freshmen receiving need-based aid: 78%
Undergrads rec. need-based aid: 75%
Avg. % of need met by financial aid: 84%
Avg. aid package (freshmen): $32,040
Avg. aid package (undergrads): $30,087
Avg. debt upon graduation: $27,227

Prominent Alumni
Christopher Carney, representative, U.S. Congress; Dr. Lawrence Dorr, Director of Dorr Arthritis Institute at Centinela Hospital, CA; Dr. Campbell McConnell, economist, educator and author.

School Spirit
Mascot: Rams
Colors: Purple and white

versity of Iowa · San Francisco Ballet · Toyota Financial Services · Van Meter Industrial Inc. · Mercy Hospital · Denver Public Schools · Chicago Public Schools · Integrated DNA Technologies · Target Corporation · Bank One · AEGON/Life Investors · Allied Insurance · Ernst & Young · Iowa Department of Natural Resources · KPMG LLP · Mutual of Omaha · Principal Financial Group · Rockwell Collins · Wells Fargo.

Support for Students with Learning Disabilities

Students with learning disabilities may take advantage of specific support programs offered by Cornell College. High school foreign language waivers are accepted. LD students may choose to explore: tutors · learning center · testing accommodations · untimed tests · extended time for tests · take-home exam · exam on tape or computer · typist/scribe · note-taking services · tape recorders · early syllabus · priority registration. Individual or small group tutorials are also available in: time management · organizational skills · learning strategies · specific subject areas · writing labs · math labs · study skills. An advisor/advocate from the LD program is available to students.

How to Get Admitted

For admissions decisions, non-academic factors considered: interview · extracurricular activities · special talents, interests and abilities · character/personal qualities · volunteer work · work experience · geographical location · minority affiliation · alumni relationship. A high school diploma is required, although a GED is also accepted for admissions consideration. SAT or ACT test scores are required of all applicants. SAT Subject Test scores are considered, if submitted, but are not required. *Academic units recommended:* 4 English, 3 Math, 3 Science, 3 Social Studies, 2 Foreign Language.

How to Pay for College

To apply for financial aid, students should submit the following: Free Application for Federal Student Aid (FAFSA) · institution's own financial aid forms · Non-custodian (Divorced/Separated) Parent's Statement. Cornell College participates in the Federal Work Study program. *Need-based aid programs include:* scholarships and grants · general need-based awards · Federal Pell grants · state scholarships and grants · college-based scholarships and grants · private scholarships and grants · ACG · SMART · TEACH grants. *Non-need-based aid programs include:* scholarships and grants · general need-based awards · state scholarships and grants · creative arts and performance awards.

America's
Best Colleges for
B Students

DEAN COLLEGE

99 Main Street, Franklin, MA 02038
Admissions: 508-541-1508 · Financial Aid: 508-541-1518
Email: admission@dean.edu · Website: http://www.dean.edu

From the College

"Dean College offers what you expect to find—safe, residential campus, athletic programs, clubs and activities, wireless network, scholarships and financial aid—but with
an atmosphere that is a little more patient, a bit more nurturing. The college bridges
the leap between high school and university by offering two- or four-year degrees
from a New England campus guided by a passionate faculty. Proof that sometimes
the smartest distance between two points isn't a straight line."

Campus Setting

Dean College, founded in 1865, is a private, coed institution offering Associate and
Baccalaureate degrees. The 140-acre campus is located in Franklin. A four-year institution, Dean College has an enrollment of 1,300 students. Dean College provides
on-campus housing with 507 units that can accommodate 935 students. Housing
options: coed dorms · women's dorms · special housing for disabled students. Recreation and sports facilities include: field · fitness center · golf course · gymnasium.

Student Life and Activities

Almost all students (89 percent) live on campus. A popular on-campus gathering
spot is the Campus Center. Favorite campus events include Cabaret Night, Spring
Weekend, Dance Team and Dance Company shows and Family Weekend. Dean
College has 25 official student organizations. The most popular are: dance team ·
drama club · criminal justice club · SORT Leaders · Community Advisors · Student
Ambassadors · Community Outreach · Emerging Leaders · Orientation and Welcome
Leaders. For those interested in sports, there are intramural teams such as: badminton
· basketball · soccer · softball · volleyball. Dean College is a member of the NJCAA
and the Northeast Football Conference.

Academics and Learning Environment

For the B student, the learning environment of a college is just as important as the
quality of its academic program. Dean College has 31 full-time and 107 part-time
faculty members, offering a student-to-faculty ratio of 16:1. The most common course
size is 10 to 19 students. Dean College offers 24 majors. Dance is the most popular and
arts/entertainment management is the least. The school has a general core requirement. Cooperative education is not offered. All first-year students must maintain a
1.8 GPA or higher to avoid academic probation. Other special academic programs
include: independent study · accelerated study · honors program · internships.

B Student Support and Success

A quote from Dean College offers these words regarding their staff and programs:
"Dean College provides a level of academic support that goes above and beyond the
norm found in higher education today. Our full-time academic advisors are completely
dedicated to helping students through their time at Dean and thus do not have any
faculty responsibilities. Faculty, meanwhile, are required to submit progress reports
on every student periodically during the semester. In addition, Dean offers a comprehensive learning center that provides students with opportunities for personalized,
drop-in or peer-tutoring services according to their academic needs."

159

College Profiles

DEAN COLLEGE

Highlights

Dean College
Franklin, MA (Pop. 32,065)
Location: Large town
Four-year private
Founded: 1865
Website: http://www.dean.edu

Students
Total enrollment: 1,300
Undergrads: 1,300
Freshmen: 544
Part-time students: 17%
From out-of-state: 53%
Male/Female: 53%/47%
Live on-campus: 89%
Off-campus employment rating: Good
Caucasian: 43%
African American: 15%
Hispanic: 6%
Asian: 1%
Hawaiian or Pacific Islander: <1%
Native American: <1%
Mixed (2+ ethnicities): 3%
International: 11%

Academics
Calendar: Semester
Student/faculty ratio: 16:1
Class size 9 or fewer: 13%
Class size 10-29: 76%
Class size 30-49: 11%
Class size 50-99: -
Class size 100 or more: -
Returning freshmen: 62%
Six-year graduation rate: 62%

Most Popular Majors
Dance

Dean College provides programs with dedicated guidance for: academic · personal · psychological · veterans · non-traditional students · family planning. Dean College offers remedial and refresher courses in: reading · writing · math · study skills. The average freshman year GPA is 2.7, and 62 percent of freshmen students return for their sophomore year. Approximately 98 percent pursue a graduate degree immediately after graduation. Among students who enter the workforce, approximately 86 percent enter a field related to their major within six months of graduation.

Support for Students with Learning Disabilities

Dean College offers students with learning disabilities the chance to take a lighter course load, as well extra time to complete a degree. High school foreign language waivers are accepted. Dean College's Arch Program provides many services to student with learning and/or physical disabilities. Some additional programs that might be helpful include: special classes · tutors · learning center · extended time for tests · oral tests · readers · note-taking services · reading machines · tape recorders · texts on tape. Individual or small group tutorials are also available in: time management · organizational skills · learning strategies · specific subject areas · writing labs · math labs · study skills. An advisor/advocate from the Dean Arch Program is available to students. This member also sits on the admissions committee.

How to Get Admitted

For admissions decisions, non-academic factors considered: interview · extracurricular activities · special talents, interests and abilities · character/personal qualities · volunteer work · work experience · state of residency · alumni relationship. A high school diploma is required, although a GED is also accepted for admissions consideration. SAT or ACT test scores are required of all applicants. SAT Subject Test scores are considered, if submitted, but are not required. *According to the admissions office:* No minimum admissions requirements. *Academic units recommended:* 4 English, 3 Math, 3 Science, 3 Social Studies, 1 Foreign Language.

Insight

"Dean College is more focused on a student's future than we are on his/her past. While we are not about open enrollment, we are about providing students with opportunity and helping them to reposition their academic profile in the hopes of transferring to the school of choice. Applicants need to show us academic potential in the admissions process. If we can identify academic potential (be it through improving grades, SAT scores, recommendations, etc.) we feel that Dean's supportive learning environment and structure can help harness that potential and position students for what is near in their academic lives.

"Dean College helps students get into four-year schools and more often than not, we help them get into four-year schools that academically are at least one level higher than what their profile would have allowed them to get into as incoming freshmen. Dean College is made for the B or C student who aspires to transfer to a higher level school as we foster the type of initial accomplishment, growth and confidence necessary for them to ultimately pursue and complete a bachelor's degree at a four-year institution."

How to Pay for College

To apply for financial aid, students should submit the following: Free Application for Federal Student Aid (FAFSA). Dean College participates in the Federal Work Study program. *Need-based aid programs include:* scholarships and grants · general need-based awards · Federal Pell grants · state scholarships and grants · college-based scholarships and grants · private scholarships and grants. *Non-need-based aid programs include:* scholarships and grants · state scholarships and grants · creative arts and performance awards · athletic scholarships.

DEAN COLLEGE

Highlights

Admissions
Applicants: 2,594
Accepted: 1,773
Acceptance rate: 68.4%
Average GPA: 2.4
ACT range: 15-19
SAT Math range: 370-470
SAT Reading range: 380-480
SAT Writing range: 1-2
Top 10% of class: 4%
Top 25% of class: 11%
Top 50% of class: 22%

Deadlines
Early Action: 12/1
Early Decision: No
Regular Action: Rolling admissions
Common Application: Accepted

Financial Aid
In-state tuition: $34,390
Out-of-state tuition: $34,390
Room: $9,325
Board: $5,435
Books: $1,000
Freshmen receiving need-based aid: 78%
Undergrads rec. need-based aid: 74%
Avg. % of need met by financial aid: 29%
Avg. aid package (freshmen): $24,602
Avg. aid package (undergrads): $23,345
Avg. debt upon graduation: $16,692

Prominent Alumni
William Green, CEO, Accenture; Richard Belzer, actor; Jay T. Jenkins, Broadway choreographer.

School Spirit
Mascot: Bulldogs
Colors: Cardinal red, black and white

161

DEPAUL UNIVERSITY

1 East Jackson Boulevard, Chicago, IL 60604-2287
Admissions: 800-433-7285 · Financial Aid: 312-362-8610
Email: admission@depaul.edu · Website: http://www.depaul.edu

From the College

"DePaul University is the nation's largest Catholic university, with over 24,000 students and about 300 programs of study. We prepare our students to succeed in the global community through an experience-based, multicultural education that draws on our broad array of partnerships. Classes are small and taught by knowledgeable faculty members who take full advantage of the city's corporate, cultural and community resources. We are nationally recognized for the strength of our service-learning curriculum and for the academic rigor and prominence of our programs. More than 98 percent of classes are taught by faculty members, not teaching assistants, while 90 percent of classes have 40 or fewer students. All full-time faculty members teach, and those who teach graduate students also teach undergraduates. Many faculty members are nationally recognized in their field, yet they are accessible and approachable, taking an active interest in our students' aspirations. Theory and experience are blended throughout the curriculum.

"Nearly half of all our undergraduates complete at least one internship before graduation, putting us among the top 10 universities nationally in providing such experience. DePaul meshes seamlessly with Chicago's commercial and artistic communities, offering students unparalleled access to internships and learning opportunities with many of the nation's top corporations and organizations as well as a rich array of cultural events and institutions. An example is DePaul's recent partnership with Cinespace Chicago to provide students with film and television production experience in the midst of the city's premier movie studio. In 2012, DePaul established the Alliance for Health Sciences with Rosalind Franklin University of Medicine and Science and has created 3+ programs leading to graduate degrees in medicine, pharmacology and more. The alliance also provides internships, student research opportunities and academic enrichment to support DePaul's rapid program and enrollment growth in health sciences. Our Steans Center, one of a handful of endowed service-learning programs in the nation, coordinates courses that teach students while simultaneously helping more than 400 organizations throughout the metropolitan area. Students tap such connections for internships, mentors, class projects, professional contacts and more. DePaul is one of 62 universities nationwide, and the only one in Illinois, to qualify for the Community Engagement citation given by the Carnegie Foundation for the Advancement of Teaching. Its faculty and staff forge global and local educational partnerships impacting key ethical and social justice issues.

"DePaul's service-learning focus is a key element of our mission, which is to provide a high quality, values-based education to a wide range of students, with particular attention to first-generation students and those from disadvantaged backgrounds. Our student body is diverse; 37 percent of all undergraduates are of color; about 33 percent of freshmen are first-generation students from families where neither parent holds a college degree. DePaul maintains high standards for admission; 25 percent of incoming freshmen graduated in the top 10 percent of their class. About 36 percent of all freshmen are from outside Illinois. International students represent about six percent of the student body and come from more than 90 nations. This wide range of backgrounds and perspectives enables students to learn from each other through our discussion- and project-oriented approach. Students admitted under DePaul's test-optional policy succeed at similar rates to students who submit the ACT or

SAT. Of DePaul's 160,000 living alumni, about 100,000 reside in the metropolitan area, providing students with a network locally and around the world."

Campus Setting

DePaul's partnerships throughout Chicago allow it to provide an exceptional educational experience that is vibrant, pragmatic and socially engaged. Classes are small and taught by knowledgeable, experienced faculty members who take advantage of Chicago's corporate, cultural and community resources. DePaul is nationally recognized for service learning and the academic rigor and prominence of its programs. Founded in 1898 by the Congregation of the Mission (Vincentians), DePaul's tradition of providing a quality education to students from a wide range of backgrounds, with particular attention to first-generation students, has led to one of the nation's most diverse student bodies. With nine colleges and schools, DePaul has campuses in Chicago's Loop and Lincoln Park neighborhoods and four suburbs and degree programs in six nations. It is part of the BIG EAST Conference in Division I sports.

A four-year private institution, DePaul University has an enrollment of 24,414 students. Although not originally a co-educational college, DePaul University has been co-ed since 1911. The school is also affiliated with the Roman Catholic Church. Campus facilities include: Environmental Science and Chemistry Building (gold LEED-certified · 2009) · Digital Cinema laboratory with motion-capture system · Green-screen studio · converged newsroom · Theatre · Art Museum · Biological and Environmental Science Building · Student Center · Performing Arts Center · Recording Studio · Marketing Research Center · Welcome Center. DePaul University provides on-campus housing with 1,114 units that can accommodate 2,677 students. Housing options: coed dorms · single-student apartments · special housing for disabled students · special housing for international students. Recreation and sports facilities include: athletic center · fitness center (multi-level · multi-purpose) · rugby field · soccer field · softball field.

Student Life and Activities

Most students (83 percent) live off campus. According to a school representative, "DePaul University has a very diverse student population with an active social life. Students have over 300 student organizations to choose from with a wide array of interests. If students want to start their own club, the process is very simple." Popular events are Loop Campus FEST and Homecoming. DePaul University has 313 official student organizations. "About six percent of our students are involved in Greek life. Student organizations include DePaul Activities Board (DAB), Blue Crew (pep club and biggest club on campus) DePaul Men's a Cappella, DeFRAG, club sports and intramurals," describes a school representative. Intramural teams include: badminton · basketball · 5-on-5 floor hockey · 4-on-4 flag football · football · kickball · racquetball · soccer · softball · table tennis · tennis · Ultimate Frisbee · volleyball · water polo. DePaul University is a member of the Big East Conference (Division I).

DEPAUL UNIVERSITY

Highlights

DePaul University
Chicago (Pop. 2,714,856)
Location: Major city
Four-year private
Founded: 1898
Website: http://www.depaul.edu

Students
Total enrollment: 24,414
Undergrads: 16,420
Freshmen: 2,894
Part-time students: 17%
From out-of-state: 36%
From public schools: 77%
Male/Female: 46%/54%
Live on-campus: 17%
In fraternities: 3%
In sororities: 9%
Off-campus employment rating: Good
Caucasian: 56%
African American: 8%
Hispanic: 17%
Asian: 7%
Hawaiian or Pacific Islander: <1%
Native American: <1%
Mixed (2+ ethnicities): 4%
International: 3%

Academics
Calendar: Quarter
Student/faculty ratio: 16:1
Class size 9 or fewer: 15%
Class size 10-29: 59%
Class size 30-49: 25%
Class size 50-99: 1%
Class size 100 or more: -
Returning freshmen: 85%
Six-year graduation rate: 70%

Most Popular Majors
Psychology
Accounting
Finance

163

DEPAUL UNIVERSITY

Admissions
Applicants: 19,957
Accepted: 11,948
Acceptance rate: 59.9%
Average GPA: 3.7
ACT range: 23-28
SAT Math range: 520-630
SAT Reading range: 530-630
SAT Writing range: Not reported
Top 10% of class: 25%
Top 25% of class: 57%
Top 50% of class: 89%

Deadlines
Early Action: 11/15
Early Decision: No
Regular Action: 11/15 (priority)
2/1 (final)
Notification of admission by: 3/15
Common Application: Accepted

Financial Aid
In-state tuition: $34,390
Out-of-state tuition: $34,390
Room: Varies
Board: Varies
Books: $1,104
Freshmen receiving need-based aid: 71%
Undergrads rec. need-based aid: 70%
Avg. % of need met by financial aid: 62%
Avg. aid package (freshmen): $22,215
Avg. aid package (undergrads): $20,252
Avg. debt upon graduation: $26,848

Prominent Alumni
Richard M. Daley, Former Mayor of Chicago; James M. Jenness, Chairman of the Board, Kellogg Co.; Anne R. Pramaggiore, President and CEO of ComEd.

School Spirit
Mascot: Blue Demons
Colors: Royal blue and scarlet
Song: *DePaul Fight Song*

America's
Best Colleges for
B Students

Academics and Learning Environment

DePaul University has 975 full-time and 969 part-time faculty members, offering a student-to-faculty ratio of 16:1. The most common course size is 20 to 29 students. DePaul University offers 225 majors with the most popular being finance, psychology and accounting and least popular being e-business and physics. The school has a general core requirement as well as a religion requirement. Cooperative education is available. All first-year students must maintain a 2.0 GPA or higher to avoid academic probation. Other special academic programs that would appeal to a B student include: self-designed majors · pass/fail grading option · independent study · double majors · dual degrees · accelerated study · honors program · internships · weekend college · distance learning certificate programs.

B Student Support and Success

Student Support Services at DePaul is a program that is open to students who demonstrate a need for academic support and meet one of the following three requirements: 1) is from a low income as defined by the U.S. Department of Education, 2) is from a family from which neither parent has a bachelor's degree or 3) has a documented physical or learning disability. SSS provides advising, academic assistance and mentoring to undergrads meeting the above requirements. Students are assigned an advisor who will help develop an educational plan, select courses and find resources to help with financing the student's education. SSS also offers individual tutoring and group study opportunities in a variety of subjects. Workshops are offered each quarter to help with learning on topics such as memory, active learning, note taking and test preparation.

DePaul University provides a variety of support programs for: academic · career · personal · psychological · minority students · military · veterans · non-traditional students · family planning · religious. Recognizing that some students may need extra preparation, DePaul University offers remedial and refresher courses in: reading · writing · math · study skills. The average freshman year GPA is 3.2, and 85 percent of freshmen students return for their sophomore year. Approximately 22 percent of students pursue a graduate degree right after graduation. Among students who enter the workforce, approximately 42 percent enter a field related to their major within six months of graduation. Companies that most frequently hire graduates from DePaul University include: DePaul University · Deloitte · Target · Federal Reserve Bank of Chicago · JP Morgan Chase · PricewaterhouseCoopers · Sears Holding Corporation · Abbott Laboratories · Nordstrom · Harris Bank · Teach for America · AmeriCorps · Children's Memorial Hospital · KPMG · Kraft · TCF Bank.

Support for Students with Learning Disabilities

According to the school, The PLuS (Productive Learning Strategies) Program is a free, year-round, comprehensive program serving all learning disabled and/or AD/HD students with a diagnosis within the last 3-5 years. All students receive extended time on exams, priority registration, course selection advising and advocacy. Weekly meetings with LD Specialists available by student request for a fee. LD Specialists monitor progress, work on time management, organization, reading comprehension and written language skills and strategies. Availability is limited, and a student may be temporarily placed on a waiting list. Students with learning disabilities will find the following programs at DePaul University useful: remedial math · remedial English · tutors · untimed tests · extended time for tests · take-home exam · readers · typist/scribe · early syllabus · waiver of math degree requirement. Individual or small group tutorials are also available in: time management · organizational skills · learning strategies · writing labs · math labs. An advisor/advocate from the PLuS (Productive Learning Strategies) is available to students.

How to Get Admitted

For admissions decisions, non-academic factors considered: interview · extracurricular activities · special talents, interests and abilities · character/personal qualities · volunteer work · work experience · geographical location · religious affiliation/commitment · minority affiliation · alumni relationship. A high school diploma is required, although a GED is also accepted for admissions consideration. SAT or ACT test scores are required for some applicants. *Academic units recommended:* 4 English, 3 Math, 3 Science, 2 Foreign Language.

How to Pay for College

To apply for financial aid, students should submit the following: Free Application for Federal Student Aid (FAFSA). DePaul University participates in the Federal Work Study program. *Need-based aid programs include:* scholarships and grants · general need-based awards · Federal Pell grants · state scholarships and grants · college-based scholarships and grants · private scholarships and grants · Federal Academic Competitiveness Grant · Federal Smart Grant · Federal TEACH Grant. *Non-need-based aid programs include:* scholarships and grants · state scholarships and grants · creative arts and performance awards · athletic scholarships · ROTC scholarships.

DREW UNIVERSITY

36 Madison Avenue, Madison, NJ 07940-1493
Admissions: 973-408-3739 · Financial Aid: 973-408-3112
Email: cadm@drew.edu · Website: http://www.drew.edu

From the College

"Drew, a traditional small liberal arts college, combines the classic liberal arts tradition with innovative programming across the curriculum and upholds the highest intellectual standards. Drew seeks to promote diversity, civic engagement and social responsibility both in and out of the classroom. Located on nearly 200 acres known by students as "the Forest," Drew's campus is 30 miles west of midtown Manhattan. Students take advantage of this location by studying in New York City on programs like the Wall Street Semester, the Art Semester and the United Nations Semester, all directed by Drew faculty. Drew offers the full range of traditional majors in the liberal arts, along with several cutting-edge interdisciplinary and area-studies programs, as well as many opportunities for study abroad, including the unique and popular Drew International Seminars and semester-long programs in London and Brussels run by Drew's own faculty. Because of Drew's location, students benefit from internship opportunities at corporate headquarters, research laboratories, foundations, charitable organizations and government agencies. Drew's low student-to-faculty ratio and small class size enable its faculty to develop close mentoring relationships with students."

Campus Setting

Drew, founded in 1867, is a private university. Its 186-acre campus is located in Madison, 27 miles from New York City. Many of its buildings date from the 19th and early 20th centuries. A four-year institution, Drew University has an enrollment of 2,291 students. Although not originally a co-educational college, Drew University has been co-ed since 1943. It provides on-campus housing with 778 units that can accommodate 1,477 students. Housing options: coed dorms · special housing for disabled students. Recreation and sports facilities include: athletic center · baseball and softball fields · stadium.

Student Life and Activities

With 77 percent of students living on campus, students frequent The Other End Coffee House and The Pub. Drew Forum Lecture Series, Fall Sports Weekend, Family Weekend, First Annual Picnic, Holiday Ball, JamFest a Capella concert, Med-Fest - That Medieval Thing, Mr. Drew and Reunion Weekend are popular campus events. Drew University has 85 official student organizations. The most popular are: 36 Madison Avenue (male a capella group) · American Civil Liberties Union · All of the Above · Alliance (LBGTQ student association) · Alpha Phi Omega · Ariel · art club · art history club · Bridging our Anthropology Students · Center Pub Association · cheerleading club · Circle K · College Chorale · College Democrats · College Republicans · comic book club · Commuters · Conversation Partners · Environmental Action League · dance club · dance team · Health Organization · improv group · Organization of Anime · Chemistry Society · Uganda Initiative · Dramatic Society · Model UN · shooting team · Extracurricular Activities Board · fashion club · Francophone Association · gaming club · Graduate Student Association · Green Key Tour Guides · Habitat for Humanity · Honduras Project · Residence Halls Living council · neuroscience club · Music Society · On a Different Note · Orientation Committee · Peer Assistance and Referral · Pre-Health Society · service organization · psychology club · Residence Association · Smith Political Science and Pre-Law · sociology club · Students for a Democratic Society · Students for Life · That Medieval Thing ·

America's
Best Colleges for
B Students

The Other End · Theo School Environmental Group · Theological Student Association · University Program Board · Volunteer Resource Center · Women's Concerns Club. For those interested in sports, there are intramural teams such as: basketball · billiards · flag football · indoor soccer · soccer · softball · tennis. Drew University is a member of the Landmark Conference (Division III).

Academics and Learning Environment

Drew University has 149 full-time and 122 part-time faculty members, offering a student-to-faculty ratio of 10:1. The most common course size is 10 to 19 students. Drew University offers 47 majors with the most popular being political science, psychology and economics. Least favorites include physics, classics and Chinese studies. The school has a general core requirement. Cooperative education is available. All first-year students must maintain a 2.0 GPA or higher to avoid academic probation. Other special academic programs that would appeal to a B student include: self-designed majors · pass/fail grading option · independent study · double majors · accelerated study · honors program · Phi Beta Kappa · internships.

B Student Support and Success

Peer tutors are available for all courses taught in any given semester at Drew University. The campus also features a Writing Center where students can learn more about the writing process and bring reports, papers and other written material to receive feedback in the form of impartial and helpful responses. At the center, students can find out more about organizing papers, the process of revisions, grammar techniques, writing speeches and resumes and looking at proper word choice.

Drew University provides support programs for: academic · career · personal · psychological · minority students · non-traditional students · family planning · religious. The average freshman year GPA is 2.9, and 76 percent of freshmen students return for their sophomore year. Approximately 28 percent of students pursue a graduate degree immediately after graduation. Companies that most frequently hire graduates from Drew University include: Chubb · ACNielsen Bases · Datacor · Morgan Stanley · JP Morgan Chase · Japan Exchange and Teaching Program (JETS) · Merck Pharmaceuticals · Peace Corps · Johnson & Johnson · Berlitz Publishing · Weil Cornell Medical Center · Memorial Sloan-Kettering Cancer Center · Teach for America · New York Life.

Support for Students with Learning Disabilities

Drew University offers learning disabled students additional time to complete their degree and/or a lightened course load. LD students may also look into: tutors · testing accommodations · extended time for tests · take-home exam · note-taking services · tape recorders · early syllabus. Individual or small group tutorials are also available in: time management · organizational skills · learning strategies · specific subject areas · writing labs · study skills.

How to Get Admitted

For admissions decisions, non-academic factors considered: interview · extracurricular activities · special talents, interests and abilities · character/personal qualities · volunteer work · work experience ·

DREW UNIVERSITY

Highlights

Drew University
Madison, NJ (Pop. 16,128)
Location: Small town
Four-year private
Founded: 1867
Website: http://www.drew.edu

Students
Total enrollment: 2,291
Undergrads: 1,493
Freshmen: 400
Part-time students: 4%
From out-of-state: 32%
Male/Female: 38%/62%
Live on-campus: 77%
Off-campus employment rating: Fair
Caucasian: 55%
African American: 10%
Hispanic: 14%
Asian: 5%
Hawaiian or Pacific Islander: <1%
Native American: <1%
Mixed (2+ ethnicities): 3%
International: 3%

Academics
Calendar: Semester
Student/faculty ratio: 10:1
Class size 9 or fewer: 19%
Class size 10-29: 71%
Class size 30-49: 9%
Class size 50-99: -
Class size 100 or more: -
Returning freshmen: 76%
Six-year graduation rate: 69%

Most Popular Majors
Political science
Psychology
Economics

DREW UNIVERSITY

Highlights

Admissions
Applicants: 3,430
Accepted: 2,656
Acceptance rate: 77.4%
Average GPA: 3.4
ACT range: 21-27
SAT Math range: 500-610
SAT Reading range: 490-610
SAT Writing range: 3-29
Top 10% of class: 31%
Top 25% of class: 62%
Top 50% of class: 89%

Deadlines
Early Action: No
Early Decision: 12/1
Regular Action: Rolling admissions
Common Application: Accepted

Financial Aid
In-state tuition: $44,232
Out-of-state tuition: $44,232
Room: $7,914
Board: $4,388
Books: $1,128
Freshmen receiving need-based aid: 73%
Undergrads rec. need-based aid: 69%
Avg. % of need met by financial aid: 77%
Avg. aid package (freshmen): $32,235
Avg. aid package (undergrads): $33,354
Avg. debt upon graduation: $25,526

Prominent Alumni
Leo H. Grohowski, Chief Investment Officer, BNY Mellon; The Honorable M. Teresa Ruiz, Member, New Jersey State Senate; Emilia Fabricant, Executive Vice President, Aeropostale, Inc.

School Spirit
Mascot: Rangers
Colors: Green and blue

state of residency. A high school diploma is not required for admissions consideration. SAT or ACT test scores are considered, if submitted, but are not required. SAT Subject Test scores are not required. *Academic units recommended:* 4 English, 3 Math, 2 Science, 2 Social Studies, 2 Foreign Language.

How to Pay for College

To apply for financial aid, students should submit the following: Free Application for Federal Student Aid (FAFSA) · CSS/Financial Aid PROFILE. Drew University participates in the Federal Work Study program. *Need-based aid programs include:* scholarships and grants · general need-based awards · Federal Pell grants · state scholarships and grants · college-based scholarships and grants · private scholarships and grants. *Non-need-based aid programs include:* scholarships and grants · general need-based awards · state scholarships and grants · creative arts and performance awards · special characteristics awards.

168

DREXEL UNIVERSITY

3141 Chestnut Street, Philadelphia, PA 19104-2875
Admissions: 800-237-3935 · Financial Aid: 215-895-2537
Email: enroll@drexel.edu · Website: http://www.drexel.edu

From the College

"Drexel, as Philadelphia's technological, cooperative education university, was the first university to mandate students to own computers and the first to operate a fully wireless campus. Technology is integrated into every aspect of the university. Drexel focuses on experiential learning through its cooperative education program, one of the nation's largest and oldest. The service-learning initiative complements cooperative education by allowing students to utilize the resources of Philadelphia as a 'living laboratory.' Drexel's thriving multidisciplinary research enterprise has erased boundaries between academic specialties. As a comprehensive university, Drexel includes the nation's largest private medical school and newest law school."

Campus Setting

Drexel is a comprehensive national research university founded in 1891 to provide educational opportunities to women and men from all walks of life. Drexel offers 73 undergraduate majors in disciplines including arts and sciences, business, education, engineering and biomedicine, information science and technology, media arts, nursing and health professions. The University's undergraduates comprise traditional students, adult students and online students around the world. Undergraduate studies at Drexel are distinguished by The Drexel Co-op, in which most students alternate classroom study with up to three 6-month periods of full-time professional employment in their field of interest. A four-year private institution, Drexel University has an enrollment of 25,500 students. In addition to a large, well-stocked library, the campus also has galleries. Drexel University offers housing for 4,200 students. Housing options: coed dorms · sorority housing · fraternity housing · special housing for disabled students · special housing for international students. Recreation and sports facilities include: athletic center · fields · tennis courts.

Student Life and Activities

Most students (65 percent) live off campus. Basketball games are a popular campus event. Drexel University has 363 official student organizations. Greeks and athletes have a strong presence in student social life. For those interested in sports, there are intramural teams such as: aerobics · badminton · basketball · billiards · darts · equestrian sports · flag football · floor hockey · rock climbing · soccer · softball · skiing · squash · table tennis · tennis · Ultimate Frisbee · volleyball. Drexel University is a member of the Colonial Athletic Association (Division I).

Academics and Learning Environment

Drexel University has 1,061 full-time and 953 part-time faculty members, offering a student-to-faculty ratio of 11:1. The most common course size is 10 to 19 students. Drexel University offers 145 majors. Engineering, business administration and health professions are the most popular. Appropriate technology, unified science and anthropology are the least. The school does not have a general core requirement. Cooperative education is available. All first-year students must maintain a 2.0 GPA to avoid academic probation. Other special academic programs that would appeal to a B student include: self-designed majors · pass/fail grading option · independent study · double majors · dual degrees · accelerated study · honors program · internships · weekend college · distance learning certificate programs.

169

College Profiles

DREXEL UNIVERSITY

Highlights

Drexel University
Philadelphia, PA (Pop. 1,536,471)
Location: Major city
Four-year private
Founded: 1891
Website: http://www.drexel.edu

Students
Total enrollment: 25,500
Undergrads: 15,876
Freshmen: 3,116
Part-time students: 18%
From out-of-state: 50%
From public schools: 70%
Male/Female: 54%/46%
Live on-campus: 35%
In fraternities: 9%
In sororities: 8%
Off-campus employment rating: Excellent
Caucasian: 58%
African American: 7%
Hispanic: 6%
Asian: 12%
Hawaiian or Pacific Islander: 1%
Native American: <1%
Mixed (2+ ethnicities): 2%
International: 11%

Academics
Calendar: Quarter
Student/faculty ratio: 11:1
Class size 9 or fewer: 26%
Class size 10-29: 59%
Class size 30-49: 10%
Class size 50-99: 3%
Class size 100 or more: 2%
Returning freshmen: 85%
Six-year graduation rate: 65%

Most Popular Majors
Engineering
Business administration
Health professions

B Student Support and Success

Free tutoring is available to all students of the College of Nursing and Health Professions, the School of Public Health and non-medical students of the College of Medicine. Some tutoring is individualized, while other situations include group settings. The Student Counseling Center helps students with personal issues, including making the adjustment to university life. At different times throughout the year, workshops on study skills, stress management, assertiveness training and sexual health are offered. The center provides academic skills testing, and counselors can help students to establish an individualized time-management system to improve study skills and test taking abilities and to reduce test anxiety.

Drexel University provides dedicated guidance for: academic · career · personal · psychological · minority students · non-traditional students. Additional counseling services include: General Psycho-therapy for range of psychological disorders. Recognizing that some students may need extra preparation, Drexel University offers remedial and refresher courses in: reading · writing · math · study skills. The average freshman year GPA is 2.9, and 85 percent of freshmen students return for their sophomore year. Among students who enter the workforce, approximately 56 percent enter a field related to their major within six months of graduation. Companies that most frequently hire graduates from Drexel University include: Lockheed Martin · Glaxosmithkline · The Vanguard Group · DuPont · Boeing · Deloitte · Independence Blue Cross · Merck · Rohm and Haas · PSE&G · Susquehanna International · PECO.

Support for Students with Learning Disabilities

For students coping with learning disabilities, Drexel offers the usual options of additional time to complete a degree and/or taking a less demanding course load. According to the school, students must self-identify and request services in order to receive accom-modations. LD students may also access: tutors · learning center · testing accommodations · extended time for tests · take-home exam · oral tests · readers · typist/scribe · note-taking services · reading machines · tape recorders · texts on tape · early syllabus · diagnos-tic testing service · priority registration. Individual or small group tutorials are also available in: time management · organizational skills · learning strategies · specific subject areas · writing labs · math labs · study skills.

How to Get Admitted

For admissions decisions, non-academic factors considered: interview · extracurricular activities · special talents, interests and abilities · character/personal qualities · volunteer work · work experience · state of residency · alumni relationship. A high school diploma is required, although a GED is also accepted for admissions consid-eration. SAT or ACT test scores are required of all applicants. SAT Subject Test scores are recommended but not required. *Academic units recommended:* 3 Math, 1 Science, 1 Foreign Language.

How to Pay for College

To apply for financial aid, students should submit the following: Free Application for Federal Student Aid (FAFSA). Drexel University participates in the Federal Work Study program. *Need-based aid* programs include: scholarships and grants · general need-based awards · Federal Pell grants · state scholarships and grants · college-based scholarships and grants · private scholarships and grants · United Negro College Fund. *Non-need-based aid programs include:* scholarships and grants · state scholarships and grants · creative arts and performance awards · athletic scholarships · ROTC scholarships · alumni affiliation scholarships.

DREXEL UNIVERSITY

Highlights

Admissions
Applicants: 40,586
Accepted: 30,382
Acceptance rate: 74.9%
Average GPA: 3.6
ACT range: 24-29
SAT Math range: 580-680
SAT Reading range: 540-640
SAT Writing range: 8-36
Top 10% of class: 34%
Top 25% of class: 65%
Top 50% of class: 92%

Deadlines
Early Action: No
Early Decision: 11/15
Regular Action: Rolling admissions
Common Application: Accepted

Financial Aid
In-state tuition: $35,135
Out-of-state tuition: $35,135
Room: $8,730
Board: $5,685
Books: $2,000
Freshmen receiving need-based aid: 64%
Undergrads rec. need-based aid: 65%
Avg. % of need met by financial aid: 56%
Avg. aid package (freshmen): Not reported
Avg. aid package (undergrads): Not reported

Prominent Alumni
Ramani Ayer, former CEO of the Hartford Financial Services; Elaine Garzarelli, financial analyst; George Campbell, president of the Cooper Union.

School Spirit
Mascot: Dragons
Colors: Blue and gold

171

DUQUESNE UNIVERSITY

600 Forbes Avenue, Pittsburgh, PA 15282
Admissions: 800-456-0590 · Financial Aid: 412-396-6607
Email: admissions@duq.edu · Website: http://www.duq.edu

From the College

"Duquesne is consistently ranked among America's top Catholic universities for its faculty and 134-year tradition of academic excellence. A co-educational university on a self-contained campus with views of Pittsburgh's skyline and rivers, the university has 10,011 students representing nearly every state and 82 nations. Some 87 percent of incoming freshman are drawn from the top half of their high school class. Duquesne offers undergraduate and graduate degree programs in natural and environmental sciences, leadership, business, nursing, health sciences, pharmacy, law, education, music and the liberal arts."

Campus Setting

Duquesne, founded in 1878, is a church-affiliated university. Its 49.5-acre campus overlooks downtown Pittsburgh. A four-year private institution, Duquesne University has an enrollment of 9,904 students and has been co-ed since 1909. Campus facilities include: recording complex · recital hall · music electronic studio · keyboard lab · music technology center · music control lab · academic research center for pharmaceutical information · pharmaceutical technology center · pharmacy manufacturing lab · phenomenology center · health sciences cadaver lab · nurse-managed wellness center · business school investment center · liberal arts living-learning communities · center for nursing research · confocal microscopes · mass spectrometry facilities · 400-and 500-MHZ NMR spectrometers · electron microscopes · x-ray diffraction spectrometers · research center for pharmacy care - pharmacy wellness and disease management program · patient simulation lab · Claufield digital media center · nurse managed wellness center · center for health care diversity · power center for fitness and recreation. Duquesne University provides on-campus housing with 1,742 units that can accommodate 3,453 students. Housing options: coed dorms · sorority housing · fraternity housing · single-student apartments · married-student apartments · special housing for disabled students. Recreation and sports facilities include: basketball, tennis and volleyball courts · football, lacrosse and soccer fields · aerobics and yoga studios · weight training and cardio equipment centers · hockey rink · swimming pool · indoor and outdoor tracks.

Student Life and Activities

A little over half (61 percent) of students live on campus and enjoy such fun spots as Nite Spot, Starbucks, Power Recreation Center, The Red Ring, the South Side, the Carnegie Museum and music venues, Heinz Field, PNC Park, Warhol Museum, Heinz Hall, Benedum, Cultural District and Station Square. Popular events include Orientation, Carnival / AutumnFest, International Student Week, Christmas Ball, Freshman Parent Weekend, Greek Week, Bluffstock, Light Up the Night, Multi-Cultural Unity Banquet, Commuter Day, Spotlight Musical Theater Shows, Program Council Major Concert and NiteSpot Late Night Programs. Duquesne University has 200 official student organizations. Student Government, Campus Ministry and Greeks influence student life. Intramural teams include: basketball · indoor soccer · non-tackle football · racquetball · outdoor soccer · tennis · volleyball · cornhole · dodgeball · kickball · street hockey · Wiffle ball. Duquesne University is a member of the Atlantic 10 Conference (Division I) and the Northeast Conference (Division I for football).

Academics and Learning Environment

Duquesne University has 489 full-time and 502 part-time faculty members, offering a student-to-faculty ratio of 14:1. The most common course size is 10 to 19 students. Duquesne University offers 158 majors. Nursing, accounting and biology are the most popular choices, while rhetoric, world literature and classical languages are the least. The school has a general core requirement as well as a religion requirement. Cooperative education is not offered. All first-year students must maintain a 1.8 GPA or higher to avoid academic probation, and a minimum overall GPA of 2.0 is required to graduate. Other special academic programs that would appeal to a B student include: self-designed majors · pass/fail grading option · independent study · double majors · dual degrees · accelerated study · honors program · internships · weekend college · distance learning certificate programs.

B Student Support and Success

At Duquesne's Michael P. Weber Learning Skills Center, students will find three programs that are designed to help them achieve academic success: Individualized Study Skills Assistance, College Success Credit Courses and tutoring. Individualized Study Skills Assistance teaches students about reading, note taking, organizing information, listening, test taking and more. The program is designed to assist students in understanding how to learn more effectively and efficiently. Tutoring is done on a one-to-one basis on in small-group settings and is free for all students. Study skills classes can also be taken for college course credit.

Duquesne University provides dedicated guidance for: academic · career · personal · psychological · minority students · veterans · non-traditional students · religious. Duquesne University offers remedial and refresher courses in: reading · writing · math · study skills. Other remedial services include test prep, foreign language training and ESL tutorials. The average freshman year GPA is 3.3, and 88 percent of freshmen students return for their sophomore year. Approximately 21 percent pursue a graduate degree immediately after graduation. One year after graduation, the school reports that 38 percent of graduates have entered graduate school. Approximately 60 percent enter a field related to their major within six months of graduation. Companies that most frequently hire graduates from Duquesne University include: U.S. Department of Energy · PNC Bank · Genco Supply Chain · Verizon · Henderson.

Support for Students with Learning Disabilities

Duquesne University offers learning disabled students additional time to complete their degree and/or a lightened course load. LD students can also utilize: tutors · learning center · testing accommodations · extended time for tests · oral tests · readers · typist/scribe · note-taking services · tape recorders · texts on tape · early syllabus · priority registration. Individual or small group tutorials are also available in: time management · organizational skills · learning strategies · specific subject areas · writing labs · math labs · study skills.

How to Get Admitted

For admissions decisions, non-academic factors considered: interview · extracurricular activities · special talents, interests and abilities ·

DUQUESNE UNIVERSITY

Highlights

Duquesne University
Pittsburgh (Pop. 307,484)
Location: Major city
Four-year private
Founded: 1878
Website: http://www.duq.edu

Students
Total enrollment: 9,904
Undergrads: 5,970
Freshmen: 1,790
Part-time students: 4%
From out-of-state: 27%
Male/Female: 41%/59%
Live on-campus: 61%
In fraternities: 17%
In sororities: 21%
Off-campus employment rating: Good
Caucasian: 84%
African American: 4%
Hispanic: 3%
Asian: 2%
Hawaiian or Pacific Islander: <1%
Native American: <1%
Mixed (2+ ethnicities): 2%
International: 4%

Academics
Calendar: Semester
Student/faculty ratio: 14:1
Class size 9 or fewer: 13%
Class size 10-29: 56%
Class size 30-49: 23%
Class size 50-99: 5%
Class size 100 or more: 3%
Returning freshmen: 88%
Six-year graduation rate: 76%

Most Popular Majors
Nursing
Accounting
Biology

173

DUQUESNE UNIVERSITY

Highlights

Admissions
Applicants: 6,793
Accepted: 5,033
Acceptance rate: 74.1%
Average GPA: 3.7
ACT range: 22-27
SAT Math range: 530-620
SAT Reading range: 520-600
SAT Writing range: 3-25
Top 10% of class: 27%
Top 25% of class: 60%
Top 50% of class: 89%

Deadlines
Early Action: 12/1
Early Decision: 11/1
Regular Action: Rolling admissions
Common Application: Not accepted

Financial Aid
In-state tuition: $30,070
Out-of-state tuition: $30,070
Room: $6,044
Board: $5,040
Books: $1,000
Freshmen receiving need-based aid: 73%
Undergrads rec. need-based aid: 70%
Avg. % of need met by financial aid: 77%
Avg. aid package (freshmen): $24,965
Avg. aid package (undergrads): $23,753
Avg. debt upon graduation: $26,119

Prominent Alumni
M. Joy Drass, M.D. President, Georgetown University Hospital; John Clayton, NFL Analyst, ESPN; Marianne Cornetti, internationally-acclaimed opera singer.

School Spirit
Mascot: Duke
Colors: Red and blue
Song: *Fight Song*

character/personal qualities · volunteer work · work experience · state of residency · minority affiliation · alumni relationship. A high school diploma is required, although a GED is also accepted for admissions consideration. SAT or ACT test scores are required of all applicants. SAT Subject Test scores are not required. *According to the admissions office:* Minimum combined SAT Reasoning score of 1000 (minimum composite ACT score of 22) and minimum 3.0 GPA recommended. *Academic units recommended:* 4 English, 2 Math, 2 Science, 2 Social Studies, 2 Foreign Language.

How to Pay for College

To apply for financial aid, students should submit the following: Free Application for Federal Student Aid (FAFSA) · institution's own financial aid forms. Duquesne University participates in the Federal Work Study program. *Need-based aid programs include:* scholarships and grants · general need-based awards · Federal Pell grants · state scholarships and grants · college-based scholarships and grants · private scholarships and grants · United Negro College Fund. *Non-need-based aid programs include:* scholarships and grants · state scholarships and grants · athletic scholarships · ROTC scholarships · music and drama scholarships/grants.

America's
Best Colleges for
B Students

EARLHAM COLLEGE

801 National Road West, Richmond, IN 47374
Admissions: 765-983-1600 · Financial Aid: 765-983-1217
Email: admission@earlham.edu · Website: http://www.earlham.edu

From the College

"At Earlham, we believe learning is a pathway to lives of consequence. We expect our students to be fully present: to think rigorously, value directness and genuineness and actively seek insights from differing perspectives. Our Quaker tradition produces distinctively Earlham qualities. Our students are astute, transparent, ready to build consensus and able to discern the 'signal from the noise.' These qualities are essential for success, whether in medicine, business, education or into fields and careers that have yet to be invented. Nowhere is the world closer than it is here at Earlham. We are consistently ranked among the top liberal arts colleges for enrolling the highest percentage of international students. Our students represent 81 countries. It is impossible to come to our campus and not leave with a wider perspective and an intellectual framework that is rich in global content."

Campus Setting

Earlham, founded in 1847, is a church-affiliated, liberal arts college. Its 800-acre campus is located in Richmond, 45 miles west of Dayton, Ohio. A four-year private institution, Earlham College has an enrollment of 1,164 students. The school is also affiliated with the Society of Friends Church. The campus has a large library and a natural history museum. Earlham College provides on-campus housing with 507 units that can accommodate 1,052 students. Housing options: coed dorms · women's dorms · men's dorms · special housing for disabled students · special housing for international students.

Student Life and Activities

Virtually all students (96 percent) live on campus, and enjoy events such as Sunsplash, Homecoming, Parent's Weekend, Little Sibs Weekend, Air Guitar, Springfest, Africa fest, Latino fest and Kwanzaa. Earlham College has 70 official student organizations. The most popular are: Action Against Rape · campus ministries · choral groups · concert band · dance · drama/theatre · jazz band · The Committee for Justice in the Middle East · Dance Alloy · College Democrats · Environmental Action Coalition · Equestrian Program · Progressive Union · Volunteer Exchange · Young Friends · economic club · Active Minds · Figure Drawing · Gamers United · geology club · Hunt Seat Equestrian Team · Mock Trial · Model UN · outdoors club · Poet heads Anonymous · psychology club · Rowntree Records · Agricultural Program & Miller Farm · Spectrum · Stop Laughing · Student Activities Board · Student Executive Council · Student Filmmakers Guild · Student Nominating Committee · Student Organizations Council · Westwood Tutoring · AIDS Coalition · Women's Center · Amnesty International · Anime · A cappella group · business club. Intramural teams include: basketball · non-tackle football · racquetball · soccer. Earlham College is a member of the Heartland Collegiate Athletic Conference.

Academics and Learning Environment

Earlham College has 102 full-time and 17 part-time faculty members, offering a student-to-faculty ratio of 10:1. The most common course size is 10 to 19 students. Earlham College offers 37 majors with the most popular being psychology, biology and interdisciplinary and least popular being studies in computer science, engineering and international studies. The school has a general core requirement. Coopera-

EARLHAM COLLEGE

Highlights

Earlham College
Richmond, IN (Pop. 36,599)
Location: Large town
Four-year private
Founded: 1847
Website: http://www.earlham.edu

Students
Total enrollment: 1,164
Undergrads: 1,064
Freshmen: 271
Part-time students: 3%
From out-of-state: 65%
Male/Female: 45%/55%
Live on-campus: 96%
Off-campus employment rating: Good
Caucasian: 52%
African American: 14%
Hispanic: 6%
Asian: 4%
Native American: 1%
Mixed (2+ ethnicities): <1%
International: 18%

Academics
Calendar: Semester
Student/faculty ratio: 10:1
Class size 9 or fewer: 37%
Class size 10-29: 52%
Class size 30-49: 8%
Class size 50-99: 3%
Class size 100 or more: -
Returning freshmen: 89%
Six-year graduation rate: 71%

Most Popular Majors
Psychology
Biology
Interdisciplinary

tive education is not offered. All first-year students must maintain a 2.0 GPA or higher to avoid academic probation, and a minimum overall GPA of 2.0 is required to graduate. Other special academic programs include: self-designed majors · independent study · double majors · dual degrees · accelerated study · internships.

B Student Support and Success

Based on Quaker traditions and orientation, Earlham College is considered a high-level liberal arts school. Class discussions are more common than lectures here. The Center for Academic Enrichment offers free peer tutoring to all students and has regular information on study skills. A Writing Lab is available for those having trouble with any aspect of the writing process, from brainstorming the initial idea to making the final edits. The Office of Student Development centers its programs and policies on the belief that "life outside the classroom influences a student's growth and development as much as the academic experience." According to the college's website, "Student Development designs, implements and evaluates programs and services in the following areas: student success, wellness, recreational sports, career development, counseling, athletics, residence life, student activities, campus safety and security, health services, service learning, alcohol and drug education and conduct."

Earlham College provides support programs for: academic · career · personal · psychological · minority students · family planning · religious. The average freshman year GPA is 2.8, and 89 percent of freshmen students return for their sophomore year. Approximately 27 percent pursue a graduate degree immediately after graduation. Companies that most frequently hire graduates from Earlham College include: Teach for America · Peace Corps · Intel · Outward Bound · AmeriCorps.

Support for Students with Learning Disabilities

Students with learning disabilities may be able to take advantage of additional time to finish their degrees, as well as take a lighter load of courses. An adviser from the LD program is available to students on an individual basis to meet with faculty and/or students 3-5 times a semester. Total number of peer tutors available to work with LD students varies. Students with learning disabilities can also access: extended time for tests · take-home exam · exam on tape or computer · note-taking services · reading machines · tape recorders · priority registration · waiver of math degree requirement. Individual or small group tutorials are also available in: time management · organizational skills · learning strategies · specific subject areas · writing labs · study skills. An advisor/advocate from the Center for Academic Enrichment is available to students.

How to Get Admitted

For admissions decisions, non-academic factors considered: interview · extracurricular activities · special talents, interests and abilities · character/personal qualities · volunteer work · work experience · alumni relationship. A high school diploma is required, although a GED is also accepted for admissions consideration. SAT or ACT test scores are considered, if submitted, but are not required. SAT Subject Test scores are considered, if submitted, but are not required. *According to the admissions office:* High consideration is given to a student's academic achievement and preference is given to students with a minimum 3.0 GPA who rank in the top quarter of their secondary school class. *Academic units recommended:* 4 English, 4 Math, 4 Science, 4 Social Studies, 4 Foreign Language.

How to Pay for College

To apply for financial aid, students should submit the following: Free Application for Federal Student Aid (FAFSA). Earlham College participates in the Federal Work Study program. *Need-based aid programs include:* scholarships and grants · general need-based awards · Federal Pell grants · state scholarships and grants · college-based scholarships and grants · private scholarships and grants. *Non-need-based aid programs include:* scholarships and grants · state scholarships and grants · minority student scholarships/grants.

EARLHAM COLLEGE

Highlights

Admissions
Applicants: 1,890
Accepted: 1,204
Acceptance rate: 63.7%
Placed on wait list: 190
Enrolled from wait list: 54
Average GPA: 3.5
ACT range: 26-31
SAT Math range: 560-640
SAT Reading range: 590-700
SAT Writing range: 11-36
Top 10% of class: 29%
Top 25% of class: 60%
Top 50% of class: 92%

Deadlines
Early Action: 12/1
Early Decision: 11/1
Regular Action: 1/1 (priority)
2/15 (final)
Notification of admission by: 3/1
Common Application: Accepted

Financial Aid
In-state tuition: $42,000
Out-of-state tuition: $42,000
Room: $4,400
Board: $4,200
Books: $1,200
Freshmen receiving need-based aid: 73%
Undergrads rec. need-based aid: 64%
Avg. % of need met by financial aid: 87%
Avg. aid package (freshmen): $38,405
Avg. aid package (undergrads): $36,142
Avg. debt upon graduation: $28,353

Prominent Alumni
Michael C. Hall, actor, *Six Feet Under*; Frances Moore Lappe, author, *Diet for a Small Planet*.

School Spirit
Mascot: Quakers
Colors: Maroon and white

ECKERD COLLEGE

4200 54th Avenue South, St. Petersburg, FL 33711
Admissions: 727-864-8331 · Financial Aid: 727-864-8334
Email: admissions@eckerd.edu · Website: http://www.eckerd.edu

From the College

"Eckerd College is the only private, national, liberal arts college in Florida that is located on a waterfront setting in St. Petersburg. It offers a commitment to teaching and mentoring and innovative educational programs attracting students of all ages from 47 states and 35 countries, creating a rich international diversity of cultural and ethnic backgrounds. Eckerd students are engaged in their education through small classes, independent and collaborative research, internships, study abroad, volunteer service and campus activities. The mission of Eckerd College is to provide excellent, innovative undergraduate liberal arts education and lifelong learning programs in the unique Florida environment, within the context of a covenant relationship with the Presbyterian Church (U.S.A.)"

Campus Setting

Eckerd, founded in 1958, is a church-affiliated college of liberal arts and sciences. Its 188-acre campus is located on Boca Ciega Bay in St. Petersburg, 25 miles from Tampa. A four-year private institution, Eckerd College has an enrollment of 1,821 students. Campus facilities include: chapel auditorium · marine science laboratory · art and music centers. Eckerd College provides on-campus housing with 788 units that can accommodate 1,501 students. Housing options: coed dorms · women's dorms · single-student apartments · special housing for disabled students. Recreation and sports facilities include: baseball and softball fields · tennis courts.

Student Life and Activities

The majority of students (85 percent) live on campus. As reported by a school official, "the key characteristics of student life at Eckerd include: a focus upon Eckerd as a genuine community of learning and of caring where students thrive socially, physically, intellectually and spiritually and where students participate in shaping campus life; the availability on campus of a wide array of social, cultural, entertainment and recreational programs and activities where students may interact with other students, with faculty, and with staff, enriching their classroom learning; great opportunities for service-learning locally, nationally and globally through a variety of co-curricular service programs, course-based service-learning experiences, alternative Spring Break service trips and service abroad; career and graduate school preparation that includes engaged and field-based learning opportunities and internships, career exploration and counseling resources and student directed campus life initiatives that help to ready our graduates for success in graduate and professional schools, in the workplace and as citizens; through ASPEC, access to the wisdom and career and personal insights of a sophisticated group of senior professionals, retired statespersons, physicians, lawyers, artists and others; proximity to beaches and marine activities, including fishing, sailing, and water skiing directly from campus; access to the cultural resources of the vibrant Tampa Bay region and the unique natural ecosystems of Florida's Gulf coast."

Popular campus events include Festival of Cultures, Chinese New Year, Festival of Hope, Family Weekend, Kappa Karnival, Fall Ball, Spring Cruise, Earth Day Celebration, Take Back The Night, Givers Banquet, Health Fair and Career Day. Eckerd College has 90 official student organizations. The most popular are: creative writing club · Students in Free Enterprise · art club · anime club · cinema club · dance squad · a cappella · jazz club · sewing club · Theatre Troupe · Alliance of Concerned

Individuals · Amnesty International · Best Buddies · Circle K · Coalition for Community Justice · Earth Society · garden club · Homeless Outreach · Students for a Free Tibet · marketing club · management club · law club · Model UN · Young Democrats · Association of Environmental Professionals · Bipedal Society · Herpetological Society · Sustainable Campus Task Force · ECWAD Health Squad · pre-health club · psychology club · Association for Computing Machinery · Triton Software · Ale Connoisseurs · Palmetto Productions · SAVEGAME · Spirit Bank · Tofun Club · Iota Counsel · Women's Resource Center. For those interested in sports, there are intramural teams such as: basketball · cricket · disc golf · dodgeball · equestrian sports · field hockey · flag football · kayaking · kickball · kiteboarding · martial arts · sand volleyball · soccer · softball · surfing · swimming club · tennis club · Ultimate Frisbee · wakeboarding. Eckerd College is a member of the Sunshine State Conference (Division II).

Academics and Learning Environment

Eckerd College has 117 full-time and 52 part-time faculty members, offering a student-to-faculty ratio of 12:1. The most common course size is 20 to 29 students. Eckerd College offers 39 majors. Marine science, environmental studies and psychology are favorites, while ancient studies, comparative literature and women's/gender studies are less so. The school has a general core requirement. Cooperative education is not offered. All first-year students must maintain a 1.6 GPA or higher to avoid academic probation, and a minimum overall GPA of 2.0 is required to graduate. Other special academic programs that would appeal to a B student include: self-designed majors · pass/fail grading option · independent study · double majors · dual degrees · accelerated study · honors program · Phi Beta Kappa · internships.

B Student Support and Success

Eckerd believes in support for struggling students. Faculty advisors are like mentors and provide continuing support and counsel through the student's years. Freshmen choose a mentor from a list of professionals who lead what is called Autumn Term at Eckerd. First-year students report to the school three weeks before returning students and take part in a course (for credit) that provides a thorough introduction to the campus and its resources as well as academic requirements and policies. Following the freshman year, students can choose a new mentor who specializes in their area of academic interest. Graduates receive more than the official academic transcript. They also get a co-curricular transcript that includes all of the out-of-class activities in which the student has been involved, including volunteer work, sports, leadership positions and club involvement. This transcript can be used to supplement applications for jobs, graduate work or other postgraduate plans.

Eckerd College provides dedicated guidance for: academic · career · personal · psychological · minority students · family planning · religious. Annually, 83 percent of freshmen students return for their sophomore year. Among students who enter the workforce, approximately 33 percent enter a field related to their major within six months of graduation. Companies that most frequently hire graduates from Eckerd College include: Apple Inc. · Bank of

ECKERD COLLEGE

Eckerd College
St. Petersburg, FL (Pop. 246,541)
Location: Medium city
Four-year private
Founded: 1958
Website: http://www.eckerd.edu

Students
Total enrollment: 1,821
Undergrads: 1,821
Freshmen: 453
Part-time students: 2%
From out-of-state: 85%
Male/Female: 40%/60%
Live on-campus: 85%
Off-campus employment rating: Good
Caucasian: 78%
African American: 2%
Hispanic: 8%
Asian: 1%
Hawaiian or Pacific Islander: <1%
Native American: 1%
Mixed (2+ ethnicities): 3%
International: 5%

Academics
Calendar: 4-1-4 system
Student/faculty ratio: 12:1
Class size 9 or fewer: 12%
Class size 10-29: 78%
Class size 30-49: 9%
Class size 50-99: 1%
Class size 100 or more: -
Returning freshmen: 83%
Six-year graduation rate: 66%

Most Popular Majors
Marine science
Environmental studies
Psychology

ECKERD COLLEGE

Admissions
Applicants: 3,509
Accepted: 2,534
Acceptance rate: 72.2%
Placed on wait list: 47
Enrolled from wait list: 20
Average GPA: 3.3
ACT range: 23-28
SAT Math range: 510-600
SAT Reading range: 520-620
SAT Writing range: Not reported

Deadlines
Early Action: 11/15
Early Decision: No
Regular Action: Rolling admissions
Common Application: Accepted

Financial Aid
In-state tuition: $38,242
Out-of-state tuition: $38,342
Room: $5,310
Board: $5,240
Books: $1,200
Freshmen receiving need-based aid: 67%
Undergrads rec. need-based aid: 59%
Avg. % of need met by financial aid: 86%
Avg. aid package (freshmen): $30,336
Avg. aid package (undergrads): $30,880
Avg. debt upon graduation: $32,605

Prominent Alumni
Dennnis Lehane, author; Brian Sabean, general manager, San Francisco Giants; Aaron O'Connell, quantum physicist.

School Spirit
Mascot: Triton
Colors: Teal, black, navy and white

America · Discovery Channel · Ernst & Young · Federal Trade Commission · Florida Department of Environmental Protection · Florida Humanities Council · Franklin Templeton · Lab Corp. · Morgan Stanley · National Institute on Aging · National Park Service · National Science Foundation · Peace Corps · Raymond James Financial · Sierra Club · Southern DataCOMM Inc. · Tampa Bay Devil Rays · Tech Data · Toronto Raptors · Tropicana-Pepsi · United States Geological Survey · UPS · Verizon · Wachovia Securities · Walt Disney World.

Support for Students with Learning Disabilities

Students with learning disabilities may take advantage of Eckerd's individual or small group tutorials.

How to Get Admitted

For admissions decisions, non-academic factors considered: interview · extracurricular activities · special talents, interests and abilities · character/personal qualities · volunteer work · work experience · state of residency · alumni relationship. A high school diploma is required, although a GED is also accepted for admissions consideration. SAT or ACT test scores are required of all applicants. *According to the admissions office:* Demanding and rigorous high school curriculum required. *Academic units recommended:* 4 English, 3 Math, 3 Science, 2 Social Studies, 2 Foreign Language.

How to Pay for College

To apply for financial aid, students should submit the following: Free Application for Federal Student Aid (FAFSA). Eckerd College participates in the Federal Work Study program. *Need-based aid programs include:* scholarships and grants · general need-based awards · Federal Pell grants · state scholarships and grants · college-based scholarships and grants · private scholarships and grants. *Non-need-based aid programs include:* scholarships and grants · state scholarships and grants · creative arts and performance awards · special achievements and activities awards · athletic scholarships · ROTC scholarships.

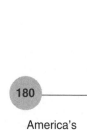

ELMIRA COLLEGE

One Park Place, Elmira, NY 14901
Admissions: 800-935-6472 · Financial Aid: 607-735-1728
Email: admissions@elmira.edu · Website: http://www.elmira.edu

From the College

"Elmira College is a traditional, fully residential liberal arts college with a historical association with Mark Twain. In all majors, even several pre-professional programs, students complete a foundation in liberal arts and sciences. Ninety percent of students are traditional college age and live on campus in dormitories, apartments and houses. Forty percent of students study abroad. Intensive study is required in six-week spring term in April and May. Numerous student traditions bring students and faculty together. In coursework, emphasis is on writing; on campus, strong emphasis is on activities, including 26 athletic teams. All students attend performing arts events, and complete community service and internships."

Campus Setting

Elmira is a private, liberal arts college. Founded as a women's college in 1855, it adopted coeducation in 1969. Its 42-acre campus is located in a residential area of Elmira. A four-year institution, Elmira College has an enrollment of 1,542 students. Elmira College provides on-campus housing with 17 units that can accommodate 1,241 students. Housing options: coed dorms · women's dorms · single-student apartments. Recreation and sports facilities include: ice arena · 2 gymnasiums · indoor tennis courts · racquetball courts · recreational pool · fitness center · 6 squash courts · 3 playing fields (one with lights) · Eldridge Park Stadium (softball) · Elmira Country Club (golf).

Student Life and Activities

With 94 percent of students living on campus, the editor of the student newspaper reports, "The entertainment-based organizations do an excellent job of bringing fun and educational acts to campus. There is always something going on around campus every weekend. If you are looking for a college where everyone knows your name, this is the one you are looking for!" Mackenzies, the Branch, Kingsbury's, Sheehans, the Arnot Mall and Harris Hill are favorite hang-outs. May Days, Holiday Weekend, Honors & Recognition Banquet, Octagon Fair and Mountain Day are a few of the favorite events. Elmira College has 103 official student organizations. Student Association, Residence Life, the Octagon, Student Activities Board, Big Event Committee and the Guys & Girls House have widespread influence on campus life. Intramural teams include: basketball · bowling · flag football · racquetball · softball · step aerobics · turkey trot · volleyball · water aerobics. Elmira College is a member of the ECAC, Empire Eight (Division III).

Academics and Learning Environment

Elmira College has 100 full-time and 85 part-time faculty members, offering a student-to-faculty ratio of 10:1. The most common course size is 10 to 19 students. Elmira College offers 42 majors with the most popular being elementary education, nursing and business administration and least popular being foreign language, classical studies and philosophy/religion. The school has a general core requirement. Cooperative education is not offered. All first-year students must maintain a 2.0 GPA or higher to avoid academic probation, and a minimum overall GPA of 2.0 is required to graduate. Other special academic programs include: self-designed majors · pass/fail grading option · independent study · double majors · dual degrees · accelerated

ELMIRA COLLEGE

Elmira College
Elmira, NY (Pop. 28,987)
Location: Large town
Four-year private
Founded: 1855
Website: http://www.elmira.edu

Students
Total enrollment: 1,542
Undergrads: 1,408
Part-time students: 16%
From out-of-state: 41%
Male/Female: 28%/72%
Live on-campus: 94%
Off-campus employment rating: Fair
Caucasian: 67%
African American: 3%
Hispanic: 3%
Asian: 1%
Hawaiian or Pacific Islander: <1%
Native American: <1%
Mixed (2+ ethnicities): 2%
International: 4%

Academics
Calendar: Other
Student/faculty ratio: 10:1
Class size 9 or fewer: 24%
Class size 10-29: 70%
Class size 30-49: 5%
Class size 50-99: -
Class size 100 or more: -
Returning freshmen: 75%
Six-year graduation rate: 63%

Most Popular Majors
Elementary education
Business administration
Nursing

study · honors program · Phi Beta Kappa · internships · distance learning certificate programs.

B Student Support and Success

In addition to small class sizes (12 or less usually), Elmira also offers a special writing class during the fall term of a student's first year. It is held on Saturdays and comes with a tutor. Elmira states that the class is designed to "hone one of the most important skills you will ever develop in your life: the ability to communicate clearly in writing." The college holds that this special program will help students develop good academic habits by making studying a part of weekend plans. Their final comment says it all: "And finally, we care enough about your academic development to get up and teach on Saturday."

Elmira College provides support programs for: academic · career · personal · psychological · family planning · religious. The average freshman year GPA is 3.0, and 75 percent of freshmen students return for their sophomore year. Approximately 52 percent pursue a graduate degree immediately after graduation. Among students who enter the workforce, approximately 83 percent enter a field related to their major within six months of graduation. Companies that most frequently hire graduates from Elmira College include: Blackbaud · Cornell University · Blue Shield · Tribune Television Co. · Bose Inc. · Federal Bureau of Investigation · US Armed Forces · National Cancer Institute · AmeriCorps · Ford Motor Co. · Fidelity Investments · CIGNA · NYS Inspector General · Deloitte · MCI-North America · Delta Airlines · Morgan Stanley · Merrill Lynch · Panasonic · Wyeth Labs · Newell-Rubbermaid · Wells Fargo Financial Services · Unilever · Maersk · HSBC Financial Services · Pfizer Inc. · Corning Inc. · Walt Disney World · Xerox Corporation · Deutsch Bank NY · Federal Reserve Bank of New York.

Support for Students with Learning Disabilities

Students with learning disabilities may take additional time to complete their degree or choose a lightened course load. LD students may also explore the options of: tutors · testing accommodations · untimed tests · extended time for tests · take-home exam · oral tests · readers · note-taking services · reading machines · tape recorders · early syllabus · diagnostic testing service · waiver of math degree requirement · waiver of foreign language degree requirement. Individual or small group tutorials are also available in: time management · organizational skills · learning strategies · specific subject areas · writing labs · math labs · study skills. An advisor/advocate from the disability services office is available to students.

How to Get Admitted

For admissions decisions, non-academic factors considered: interview · extracurricular activities · special talents, interests and abilities · character/personal qualities · volunteer work · work experience · state of residency · geographical location · minority affiliation · alumni relationship. A high school diploma is required, although a GED is also accepted for admissions consideration. SAT or ACT test scores are required of all applicants. SAT Subject Test scores are not required. *Academic units recommended:* 4 English, 3 Math, 3 Science, 3 Social Studies, 2 Foreign Language.

How to Pay for College

To apply for financial aid, students should submit the following: Free Application for Federal Student Aid (FAFSA) · state aid form. Elmira College participates in the Federal Work Study program. *Need-based aid programs include:* scholarships and grants · general need-based awards · Federal Pell grants · state scholarships and grants · college-based scholarships and grants · private scholarships and grants. *Non-need-based aid programs include:* scholarships and grants · state scholarships and grants · special achievements and activities awards · special characteristics awards · ROTC scholarships.

ELMIRA COLLEGE

Highlights

Admissions
Applicants: 2,302
Accepted: 1,836
Acceptance rate: 79.8%
Placed on wait list: 50
Enrolled from wait list: 12
Average GPA: 3.2
ACT range: Not reported
SAT Math range: 470-580
SAT Reading range: 470-580
SAT Writing range: Not reported
Top 10% of class: 28%
Top 25% of class: 58%
Top 50% of class: 84%

Deadlines
Early Action: No
Early Decision: 11/15
Regular Action: Rolling admissions
Common Application: Accepted

Financial Aid
In-state tuition: $36,600
Out-of-state tuition: $36,600
Room: $6,300
Board: $5,500
Books: $600
Freshmen receiving need-based aid: 88%
Undergrads rec. need-based aid: 84%
Avg. % of need met by financial aid: 78%
Avg. aid package (freshmen): $30,064
Avg. aid package (undergrads): $29,925
Avg. debt upon graduation: $27,426

Prominent Alumni
Susan Douglas, author; Robert Gottleib, founder, Trident Media, literary agent; Alair Townsend, former deputy mayor of NYC, financial columnist.

School Spirit
Mascot: Soaring Eagle
Colors: Purple and gold
Song: *Elmira College Alma Mater*

ENDICOTT COLLEGE

376 Hale Street, Beverly, MA 01915
Admissions: 978-921-1000 · Financial Aid: 800-325-1114 (out-of-state)
Email: admissio@endicott.edu · Website: http://www.endicott.edu

From the College

"Endicott College is the first college in the nation to require all students to complete yearly internships. Today, Endicott remains dedicated to that vision and every student completes a first-year experience program, three work-experience internships and a senior thesis. Endicott's competency-based curriculum exposes students to their field of study early in the program. Master programs are offered in business, computer science, education, interior design and nursing. The core emphasizes research, communication, creative and analytic skills. The mission emphasizes values, community service, technological competency, diversity, international awareness and ultimately, lives open to change."

Campus Setting

Endicott is a private, liberal and professional studies institution which offers baccalaureate and graduate-level programs. Founded in 1939 as a women's college, it became coeducational in 1994. Its 231-acre campus is located in Beverly, 20 miles north of Boston. A four-year institution, Endicott College has an enrollment of 5,287 students. Campus facilities include: museum · center for the arts · student-run restaurant · cyber-cafe. Endicott College provides on-campus housing with 938 units that can accommodate 2,006 students. Housing options: coed dorms · women's dorms · single-student apartments · special housing for disabled students · special housing for international students. Recreation and sports facilities include: baseball and softball fields · climbing walls · field house · fitness center · gymnasium · practice fields · racquetball and tennis courts · stadium · track · skating rink (off campus) · aerobics studio · nature trails · moored sailboats.

Student Life and Activities

With 82 percent of students living on campus, popular gathering spots include the Callahan Center (student center), the Post Center (athletic facilities), the Center for the Arts and private beaches. Popular campus events include Homecoming/Family Weekend, Annual Regatta and the Festival of Lights. Endicott College has 60 official student organizations. The most popular are: ALANA · America's Institute for Graphic Art · Amnesty International · Arts Council · Athletic Training Club · book club · Campus Activities Board · Commuter Student Association · drama club · education club · Dance Repertory Ensemble · Harmonic Overtones · Oratory Society · Rock Band · Biotech Society · Environmental Society · investment club · Musicians Collective · Singers · fitness club · Friendship Club · Gay Straight Alliance · Hall Council · International Interior Design Association · Law & Justice Club · math and computer science club · Ocean 2 Ocean · outdoor adventure club · physical education club · Political Debate Society · psychology and human services club · REACH Peer Education · Rotaract Service Club · Shipmates · Student Athletic Advisory Council · Student Nurses Association · Student Peace Alliance. Intramural teams include: baseball · dodgeball · flag football · floor hockey · kickball · racquetball · soccer · volleyball. Endicott College is a member of the NCAA, Commonwealth Coast Conference (Division III), ECAC, Intercollegiate Horse Show Association, New England Football Conference (Division III), North Eastern Collegiate Volleyball Association (Division III) and North Eastern Collegiate Hockey Association.

Academics and Learning Environment

Endicott College has 94 full-time and 299 part-time faculty members, offering a student-to-faculty ratio of 14:1. The most common course size is 20 to 29 students. Endicott College offers 52 majors. Business administration, sport management and hospitality management are typically most popular. History, political science and international studies are the least. The school has a general core requirement. Cooperative education is not offered. All first-year students must maintain a 1.8 GPA or higher to avoid academic probation. Other special academic programs that would appeal to a B student include: self-designed majors · independent study · accelerated study · honors program · internships · distance learning certificate programs.

B Student Support and Success

Endicott offers students access to an extensive computer lab, plus the availability of the Scangas Center for Media and Learning where workshops and training sessions are taught throughout the year. The Academic Technology Workshops provide tips on common software packages. The college also offers FYE 101 (first year experience), which is a one-credit class taught by faculty and staff, addressing the challenges incoming students face and strategies on how to meet them. This course helps students to learn and use social skills, to find academic resources, to become familiar with college policies and to follow procedures. According to the website, "The program is designed to promote student learning and development, improve student satisfaction and success and encourage engagement in the life of the college which is fostered by connections with the Endicott community. Ultimately, we expect that by the end of the first year, students will have increased self-confidence, stronger academic and professional skills, and will be involved and committed to the 'Endicott Experience'."

Endicott College provides dedicated guidance for: academic · career · personal · psychological · minority students · family planning · religious. Annually, 81 percent of freshmen students return for their sophomore year. Approximately 18 percent pursue a graduate degree right after graduation.

Support for Students with Learning Disabilities

Students with learning disabilities may want to look into the following programs: tutors · learning center · testing accommodations · untimed tests · extended time for tests · take-home exam · oral tests · readers · note-taking services · tape recorders · priority registration · waiver of foreign language degree requirement. Individual or small group tutorials are also available in: time management · organizational skills · learning strategies · specific subject areas · writing labs · math labs · study skills. An advisor/advocate from the LD program is available to students.

How to Get Admitted

For admissions decisions, non-academic factors considered: interview · extracurricular activities · special talents, interests and abilities · character/personal qualities · volunteer work · work experience · geographical location · minority affiliation · alumni relationship. A high school diploma is required, although a GED is also accepted

ENDICOTT COLLEGE

Highlights

Endicott College
Beverly, MA (Pop. 40,286)
Location: Large town
Four-year private
Founded: 1939
Website: http://www.endicott.edu

Students
Total enrollment: 5,287
Undergrads: 2,852
Freshmen: 702
Part-time students: 11%
From out-of-state: 55%
From public schools: 80%
Male/Female: 41%/59%
Live on-campus: 82%
Off-campus employment rating: Good
Caucasian: 80%
African American: 2%
Hispanic: 3%
Asian: 1%
Hawaiian or Pacific Islander: <1%
Native American: <1%
Mixed (2+ ethnicities): 2%
International: 2%

Academics
Calendar: 4-1-4 system
Student/faculty ratio: 14:1
Class size 9 or fewer: 14%
Class size 10-29: 81%
Class size 30-49: 5%
Class size 50-99: -
Class size 100 or more: -
Returning freshmen: 81%
Six-year graduation rate: 70%

Most Popular Majors
Business
Sport management
Hospitality management

185

College Profiles

ENDICOTT COLLEGE

Highlights

Admissions
Applicants: 3,732
Accepted: 2,682
Acceptance rate: 71.9%
Placed on wait list: 40
Enrolled from wait list: Not reported
Average GPA: 3.2
ACT range: 21-25
SAT Math range: 500-590
SAT Reading range: 480-570
SAT Writing range: 1-17
Top 10% of class: 15%
Top 25% of class: 39%
Top 50% of class: 81%

Deadlines
Early Action: No
Early Decision: No
Regular Action: Rolling admissions
Notification of admission by: 11/1
Common Application: Accepted

Financial Aid
In-state tuition: $28,994
Out-of-state tuition: $28,994
Room: $9,648
Board: $4,266
Books: $1,146
Freshmen receiving need-based aid: 70%
Undergrads rec. need-based aid: 64%
Avg. % of need met by financial aid: 63%
Avg. aid package (freshmen): $19,514
Avg. aid package (undergrads): $20,065
Avg. debt upon graduation: $40,090

Prominent Alumni
Lee Bryant, actress; Sara O'Meara, Nobel Peace Prize nominee.

School Spirit
Mascot: Gulls
Colors: Blue and green

for admissions consideration. SAT or ACT test scores are required for some applicants. *Academic units recommended:* 4 English, 3 Math, 2 Science, 2 Social Studies.

How to Pay for College

To apply for financial aid, students should submit the following: Free Application for Federal Student Aid (FAFSA) · institution's own financial aid forms · Non-custodian (Divorced/Separated) Parent's Statement. Endicott College participates in the Federal Work Study program. *Need-based aid programs include:* scholarships and grants · general need-based awards · Federal Pell grants · state scholarships and grants · college-based scholarships and grants · private scholarships and grants. *Non-need-based aid programs include:* scholarships and grants · general need-based awards · state scholarships and grants · creative arts and performance awards · special achievements and activities awards · special characteristics awards · ROTC scholarships.

America's
Best Colleges for
B Students

EVERGREEN STATE COLLEGE

2700 Evergreen Parkway, NW, Olympia, WA 98505
Admissions: 360-867-6170 · Financial Aid: 360-867-6205
Email: admissions@evergreen.edu · Website: http://www.evergreen.edu

From the College

"Evergreen State College in Olympia, Washington is a public, liberal arts college where coordinated, team-taught, interdisciplinary programs—combining a range of topics around a central theme—replace disconnected courses. Faculty members write narrative evaluations to assess student work, rather than reducing performance and progress to a letter grade. The curriculum promotes engagement and collaboration, rather than competition. Students have the freedom, and accountability, to design their education to meet their personal and career goals, without the limits of formalized majors or rigid requirements. The curriculum is redesigned every year, and upper division students can propose individual learning contracts to further customize their learning experience.

"While in many ways Evergreen breaks the mold of traditional higher education—and in doing so opens up opportunities for students with a wide range of learning styles and career goals—the college delivers a high level of academic rigor. The National Survey of Student Engagement, sponsored by the Pew Charitable Trusts, notes that Evergreen students tend to read more, prepare more extensively for class, make more presentations and engage more actively with faculty and each other than at the vast majority of colleges and universities nationwide. Students have opportunities for research, hands-on field study, community service, internships and study abroad. Evergreen is one of just three institutions on the West Coast included in the book Colleges That Change Lives by former *New York Times* education editor Loren Pope.

"Evergreen is located in the state capital of Olympia. Students can easily access the urban life of Seattle or Portland, or the recreational opportunities of the Pacific Ocean, Mount Rainier and the Olympic National Park, all within a one- to two-hour drive. Evergreen's forested 1,000-acre campus features a half-mile of saltwater beach on Puget Sound, a Native American longhouse, an organic farm and award-winning, environmentally friendly architecture in its newest classroom and office complex. With a strong commitment to sustainability in operations, curriculum and policy, Evergreen has been noted as one of the nation's top 'green' colleges.

"The vast majority of Evergreen's 4,800 students are undergraduates studying the liberal arts and the sciences, including natural and physical sciences. The college also offers graduate programs in education, environmental study, Public administration and teaching."

Campus Setting

Evergreen State College, founded in 1967, is a public college. Its 1,000-acre campus is located on Puget Sound. A four-year institution, Evergreen State College has an enrollment of 4,398 students. Campus facilities include: gallery · animation and design studio · art annex · ceramics studio · metal shop · photography studios and darkrooms · wood shop · education and cultural center · organic farm and community gardens · science labs. Evergreen State College provides on-campus housing with 950 units that can accommodate 990 students. Housing options: coed dorms · single-student apartments · married-student apartments · special housing for disabled students · special housing for international students. Recreation and sports facilities include: aerobic and dance rooms · fields · gymnasium · outdoor and indoor climbing walls · racquetball courts · sports pavilion · swimming pool · weight rooms.

EVERGREEN STATE COLLEGE

Evergreen State College
Olympia, WA (Pop. 47,698)
Location: Large town
Four-year public
Founded: 1967
Website: http://www.evergreen.edu

Students
Total enrollment: 4,398
Undergrads: 4,087
Part-time students: 8%
From out-of-state: 43%
Male/Female: 47%/53%
Live on-campus: 20%
Off-campus employment rating: Fair
Caucasian: 66%
African American: 5%
Hispanic: 7%
Asian: 2%
Hawaiian or Pacific Islander: <1%
Native American: 2%
Mixed (2+ ethnicities): 7%
International: <1%

Academics
Calendar: Quarter
Student/faculty ratio: 23:1
Class size 9 or fewer: 17%
Class size 10-29: 51%
Class size 30-49: 25%
Class size 50-99: 8%
Class size 100 or more: -
Returning freshmen: 71%
Six-year graduation rate: 54%

America's
Best Colleges for
B Students

Student Life and Activities

Most students (80 percent) live off campus. "There's an independent streak at Evergreen," explains one senior. "The academic approach - interdisciplinary programs, freedom to create your own academic pathway, individual learning contracts - attracts people who like to take a different approach to things. There's a definite 'green' and activist feel on campus, and there's a lot less concern about who's wearing what or who belongs to what group than you'd see at some schools. Beyond campus, lots of students hang out in downtown Olympia, where there are more restaurants, coffee shops and brew pubs. And yes, it rains a lot here."

Popular on-campus gathering spots include Red Square, the library, the student-run Flaming Eggplant Café and the Evergreen woods and beach. Popular off-campus gathering spots in Olympia include Old School Pizza, The Capital Theatre, Rainy Day Records, Le Voyeur Café and Lounge, Last Word Books, the New Moon Café, The Brotherhood Lounge, Caffé Vita, the Northern All Ages Venue and Olympia's many city parks. Popular campus events include Synergy (Sustainability Conference), Graduation, Harvest Festival, Day of Presence/Day of Absence, Longhouse Native Arts Fair, Lunar New Year Festival, Rachel Carson Forum, Chibi Chibi Con and the Willi Unsoeld Seminar. The Evergreen State College has 58 official student organizations. Groups that have a strong presence in student social life include the Geoduck Student Union, KAOS, the Women's Resource Center, S&A Productions, Black Student Union, Riot to Follow Productions, Transgender Resources and Education Xtravaganza and Circus Resurgence. Intramural teams include: basketball · soccer · volleyball · wrestling. The Evergreen State College is a member of the NAIA and the Cascade Collegiate Conference.

Academics and Learning Environment

For the B student, the learning environment of a college is just as important as the quality of its academic program. Evergreen State College has 166 full-time and 66 part-time faculty members, offering a student-to-faculty ratio of 23:1. The most common course size is 20 to 29 students. Evergreen State College offers 58 majors. The school does not have a general core requirement. Cooperative education is not offered. Other special academic programs include: self-designed majors · independent study · double majors · dual degrees · accelerated study · internships · weekend college.

B Student Support and Success

Evergreen has a unique style of teaching that will appeal to students who do not excel in traditional classrooms that are facilitated by the typical lecture/listen methods. This college designs classes so that there is a balance between seminars, hands-on learning and off-campus exploration. Weeklong field trips are not uncommon here. The college also offers a program called Individual Learning Contracts. This allows students to do advanced academic study in an area they already have a background in, working independently and meeting weekly with a sponsor. Evergreen also has an extensive study abroad program for students.

Evergreen State College provides a variety of support programs including: academic · career · personal · psychological · minority students · veterans · family planning. Additional counseling services include: addictive behavior specialist. Annually, 71 percent of freshmen students return for their sophomore year. Companies that most frequently hire graduates from Evergreen State College include: AmeriCorps · National Park Service · Quinault Indian Nation · Senior Services for South Sound · South Puget Sound Community College · Tacoma School District · United States Military · University of Washington · Washington State Department of Corrections · Washington State Department of Ecology · Washington State Department of Fish and Wildlife · Washington State Department of Natural Resources · Washington State Department of Social and Health Services.

Support for Students with Learning Disabilities

Taking extra time to complete a degree or carrying a lighter course load are both options for learning disabled students. According to the school, depending on the nature of your disability and how it impacts your educational experience, services and accommodations provided on an individually determined basis may include: accessible facilities, alternative testing, accessible parking, sign language interpreters/CART, note takers, priority registration, adaptive equipment/assistive technology, books on tape, tutorial assistance from KEY Student Services and the Learning Resource Center, counseling referrals and peer support and advocacy. Students with learning disabilities may also want to explore the options: tutors · learning center · testing accommodations · extended time for tests · take-home exam · typist/scribe · note-taking services · reading machines · tape recorders · priority registration · waiver of math degree requirement. Individual or small group tutorials are also available in: time management · organizational skills · learning strategies · specific subject areas · writing labs · math labs · study skills. An advisor/advocate from the Access Services is available to students.

How to Get Admitted

For admissions decisions, non-academic factors considered: interview · extracurricular activities · volunteer work · work experience · state of residency. A high school diploma is required, although a GED is also accepted for admissions consideration. SAT or ACT test scores are required of all applicants. SAT Subject Test scores are not required. *According to the admissions office:* Minimum 2.0 GPA required. *Academic units recommended:* 4 English, 3 Math, 2 Science, 3 Social Studies, 2 Foreign Language.

How to Pay for College

To apply for financial aid, students should submit the following: Free Application for Federal Student Aid (FAFSA) · institution's own financial aid forms. Evergreen State College participates in the Federal Work Study program. *Need-based aid programs include:* scholarships and grants · general need-based awards · Federal Pell grants · state scholarships and grants · college-based scholarships and grants · private scholarships and grants. *Non-need-based aid programs include:* scholarships and grants · state scholarships and grants · special achievements and activities awards · special characteristics awards · athletic scholarships.

EVERGREEN STATE COLLEGE

Highlights

Admissions
Applicants: 1,583
Accepted: 1,537
Acceptance rate: 97.1%
Average GPA: 3.0
ACT range: 20-27
SAT Math range: 450-580
SAT Reading range: 500-630
SAT Writing range: 4-20
Top 10% of class: 10%
Top 25% of class: 23%
Top 50% of class: 54%

Deadlines
Early Action: No
Early Decision: No
Regular Action: Rolling admissions
Common Application: Not accepted

Financial Aid
In-state tuition: $7,833
Out-of-state tuition: $19,920
Room: Varies
Board: Varies
Books: $1,026
Freshmen receiving need-based aid: 59%
Undergrads rec. need-based aid: 65%
Avg. % of need met by financial aid: 63%
Avg. aid package (freshmen): $8,740
Avg. aid package (undergrads): $9,236
Avg. debt upon graduation: $19,401

Prominent Alumni
Matt Groening, cartoonist, creator of *Life in Hell*, *The Simpsons* and *Futurama*; Robert McChesney, media scholar and co-founder of Free Press; Lynda Barry, graphic novelist and cartoonist.

School Spirit
Mascot: Geoducks
Colors: Forest and white
Song: *The Geoduck Fight Song*

189

College Profiles

FAIRMONT STATE UNIVERSITY

1201 Locust Avenue, Fairmont, WV 26554
Admissions: 800-641-5678, extension 2
Financial Aid: 800-641-5678, extension 2
Email: admit@fairmontstate.edu · Website: http://www.fairmontstate.edu

From the College

"Fairmont State University, including Pierpont Community and Technical College, which is a division of the university, offers a wide variety of graduate, bachelor and associate degrees. The mission of FSU is to provide opportunities for individuals to achieve their professional and personal goals and discover roles for responsible citizenship that promote the common good. The mission of Pierpont C&TC is to provide opportunities for learning, training and further education that enrich the lives of individuals and promote the economic growth of our service region and state. With a 120-acre main campus in Fairmont, West Virginia, FSU is part of the state's growing high technology corridor, including a metro area of about 50,000 residents. The FSU main campus is within a short drive of larger cities such as Pittsburgh, Pennsylvania, and opportunities for outdoor recreation in West Virginia. FSU serves a 13-county region with facilities including the Robert C. Byrd National Aerospace Education Center in Bridgeport, West Virginia. The main campus is home to the West Virginia Folklife Center. A recent project between Pierpont C&TC and Braxton County High School has created the nation's first rural Early College High School, allowing students to earn a certificate or an associate degree while they are in high school. FSU offers many evening and online classes to accommodate non-traditional students."

Campus Setting

Fairmont State, founded in 1865, is a public university of the arts and sciences. It was founded as a private teacher training school, became state-supported in 1867 and began offering bachelor's degrees in 1943. Programs are offered through the Schools of Business and Economics, Education and Health and Human Performance, Fine Arts, Health Careers, Languages and Literatures, Science and Mathematics, Social Science and Technology. Its 89-acre campus is located in Fairmont, 75 miles south of Pittsburgh. A four-year institution, Fairmont State University has an enrollment of 4,232 students. In addition to a large, well-stocked library, the campus also has a West Virginia folklife center. Fairmont State University provides on-campus housing with 424 units that can accommodate 1,068 students. Housing options: coed dorms · women's dorms · men's dorms · single-student apartments · married-student apartments. Recreation and sports facilities include: arena center · fields · tracks.

Student Life and Activities

Most students (79 percent) live off campus. Popular campus events include Celebration of Ideas Lecture Series, Live at Lunch Music Series, Women of WV Art Expo, annual blood drive, activities fair, majors fair, career fair, education career fair, Banned Book Week, Alcohol, Substance Abuse and Sexuality Awareness Week and the talent contest series. Fairmont State University has 81 official student organizations. The most popular are: Collegiate Singers · ballroom dancing club · American Choral Directors Association · Percussion Ensemble · Music Educators National Conference · Spanish club · Student Graphics Organization · American Institute of Architecture Students · Student Historical Society · Masquers Club · Bisexual Gay & Lesbian Students & Friends · Honors Association · Non-traditional Student Society · Residence Life Club · Students In Free Enterprise · Students Taking Action In Nature's Defense · American Sign Language/Deaf Culture Club · American Association of University Women · Political Science Association · College Republicans · Young

Democrats · Society for Human Resource Management · Falcon Financial Group · Student Accountant Society · Family & Consumer Sciences Association · Health Information Technology Association · American Chemical Society Student Affiliates · Forensic Science Club · Student Behavioral Science Association · Student Medical Laboratory Technology Association · Student Nurses Association · Student Veterinary Technician Association · Outdoor Adventure Club · Student Athlete Advisory Committee · Technology Education Collegiate Association (TECA) · Community & Technical EMS Association · Information Systems Student Organization · Society of Automotive Engineers · American Society of Civil Engineers · American Society of Interior Designers · American Society of Mechanical Engineers · American Society of Safety Engineers. For those interested in sports, there are intramural teams such as: baseball · basketball · billiards · cornhole · dodgeball · football · golf · horseshoes · softball · table tennis · tennis · Texas hold'em · volleyball. Fairmont State University is a member of the NCAA (Division II) and the Mountain East Conference.

Academics and Learning Environment

Fairmont State University has 169 full-time and 130 part-time faculty members. The most common course size is 20 to 29 students. Fairmont State University offers 47 majors with the most popular being business administration, criminal justice and education. History, studio art and contemporary fine arts technology are the least popular. The school has a general core requirement. Cooperative education is available. All first-year students must maintain a 2.0 GPA or higher to avoid academic probation, and a minimum overall GPA of 2.0 is required to graduate. Other special academic programs that would appeal to a B student include: independent study · double majors · accelerated study · honors program · internships · weekend college · distance learning.

B Student Support and Success

Fairmont is two schools in one. Here you can earn an associate degree through Fairmont State Community and Technical College; then get a bachelor's degree at the university. The student-to-faculty ratio at Fairmont is about 17:1, and average class size is 22 students. Tutoring is free for all students through the Tutorial Services Program, although the majority of students are limited to 10 hours per semester. (Students with documented learning disabilities may get additional sessions.) Virtually all subject areas are covered. Fairmont also offers a cutting-edge program called Supplemental Instruction. It is based on the experience of past students and is designed to help enrollees with courses that have been historically proven to be the most difficult. The course is free and is taught by faculty-recommended students.

Fairmont State University provides a variety of support programs including: academic · career · personal · psychological · minority students · military · veterans. Fairmont State University offers remedial and refresher courses in: reading · writing · math · study skills. The average freshman year GPA is 2.4, and 61 percent of freshmen students return for their sophomore year. Approximately 17 percent pursue a graduate degree after graduating. One year after graduation, the school reports that 22 percent of graduates have

FAIRMONT STATE UNIVERSITY

Highlights

Fairmont State University
Fairmont, WV (Pop. 18,737)
Location: Small town
Four-year public
Founded: 1865
Website: http://www.fairmontstate.edu

Students
Total enrollment: 4,232
Undergrads: 3,966
Freshmen: 1,591
Part-time students: 13%
From out-of-state: 10%
From public schools: 94%
Male/Female: 45%/55%
Live on-campus: 21%
In fraternities: 2%
In sororities: 2%
Off-campus employment rating: Good
Caucasian: 86%
African American: 5%
Hispanic: 2%
Asian: <1%
Hawaiian or Pacific Islander: <1%
Native American: <1%
Mixed (2+ ethnicities): 2%
International: 2%

Academics
Calendar: Semester
Student/faculty ratio: 17:1
Class size 9 or fewer: 18%
Class size 10-29: 61%
Class size 30-49: 16%
Class size 50-99: 5%
Class size 100 or more: -
Returning freshmen: 61%
Six-year graduation rate: 34%

Most Popular Majors
Business administration
Education
Criminal justice

191

FAIRMONT STATE UNIVERSITY

Highlights

Admissions
Applicants: 2,799
Accepted: 1,861
Acceptance rate: 66.5%
Average GPA: 3.3
ACT range: 18-23
SAT Math range: 420-520
SAT Reading range: 410-520
SAT Writing range: Not reported
Top 10% of class: 13%
Top 25% of class: 39%
Top 50% of class: 74%

Deadlines
Early Action: No
Early Decision: No
Regular Action: Rolling admissions
Common Application: Not accepted

Financial Aid
In-state tuition: $5,824
Out-of-state tuition: $12,288
Room: $4,026
Board: $3,446
Books: $1,000
Freshmen receiving need-based aid: 71%
Undergrads rec. need-based aid: 76%
Avg. % of need met by financial aid: 64%
Avg. aid package (freshmen): $8,385
Avg. aid package (undergrads): $8,360
Avg. debt upon graduation: $23,051

Prominent Alumni
Ira Robinson, first chairman of the Federal Radio Commission; Richard Louis Skinner, inspector general, U.S. Department of Homeland Security.

School Spirit
Mascot: Falcon
Colors: Maroon, tan, and white
Song: *College on the Hill*

entered graduate school. Among students who enter the workforce, approximately 80 percent enter a field related to their major within six months of graduation. Companies that most frequently hire graduates from Fairmont State University include: Department of Veterans Affairs · Federal Bureau of Prisons · Marion County Board of Education · Monongalia General Hospital · Mylan Pharmaceuticals · Taylor County Board of Education · United Hospital Center · WVU Hospitals.

Support for Students with Learning Disabilities

At Fairmont, students with learning disabilities may take additional time to complete their degrees, as well as carry a lighter course load. Students with learning disabilities may also benefit from: remedial math · remedial English · remedial reading · tutors · learning center · testing accommodations · extended time for tests · oral tests · readers · typist/scribe · note-taking services · reading machines · tape recorders · texts on tape · early syllabus · diagnostic testing service · special bookstore section · priority registration. Individual or small group tutorials are also available in: time management · organizational skills · learning strategies · specific subject areas · writing labs · math labs · study skills. An advisor/advocate from the LD program is available to students. This member also sits on the admissions committee.

How to Get Admitted

For admissions decisions, non-academic factors considered: state of residency. A high school diploma is required, although a GED is also accepted for admissions consideration. SAT or ACT test scores are required of all applicants. *According to the admissions office:* Minimum composite ACT score of 18 and minimum 2.0 GPA required.

How to Pay for College

To apply for financial aid, students should submit the following: Free Application for Federal Student Aid (FAFSA). Fairmont State University participates in the Federal Work Study program. *Need-based aid programs include:* scholarships and grants · general need-based awards · Federal Pell grants · state scholarships and grants · college-based scholarships and grants · private scholarships and grants. *Non-need-based aid programs include:* scholarships and grants · state scholarships and grants · creative arts and performance awards · athletic scholarships.

America's
Best Colleges for
B Students

FISK UNIVERSITY

1000 17th Avenue North, Nashville, TN 37208-3051
Admissions: 800-443-FISK · Financial Aid: 615-329-8585
Email: admit@fisk.edu · Website: http://www.fisk.edu

From the College

"Founded in 1866, the university is co-educational, private and one of America's premier historically black universities. The first black college to be granted a chapter of Phi Beta Kappa Honor Society, Fisk serves a diverse student body with students from 40 states and six foreign countries. The focal point of the 40-acre campus and architectural symbol of the university is Jubilee Hall, the first permanent building for the education of blacks in the South, named for the internationally renowned Fisk Jubilee Singers. From its earliest days, Fisk faculty and alumni have been among America's intellectual leaders providing leadership in several fields including medicine, science, art, humanities, religion, literature, sociology and philosophy. Fisk alumni include W. E. B. Du Bois, the first black Ph.D. from Harvard, great social critic and co-founder of the NAACP. In proportion to its size, Fisk continues to contribute a higher percentage of African American alumni to the ranks of scholars pursuing doctoral degrees than any other institution in the United States."

Campus Setting

Fisk, founded as the Fisk School in 1866, is a church-affiliated liberal arts university. Its 40-acre campus, listed with the National Register of Historical Landmarks, is located on a hill overlooking downtown Nashville. A four-year private institution, Fisk University is a historically black university with 620 students. Fisk University provides on-campus housing with 460 units that can accommodate 850 students. Housing options: coed dorms · women's dorms · men's dorms.

Student Life and Activities

As reported by a school representative, Fisk University is "primarily a residential campus, with many academic and co-curricular activities, great exposure to diverse cultures (Caribbean, South American, African) and a domestically diverse student population (40 U.S. states represented)." The Campus Grove is a popular on-campus gathering spot. Favorite campus events include Homecoming, Greek Step Show and Competition and the Spring Arts Festival. Fisk University has 85 official student organizations. Popular groups on campus include Greek fraternities and sororities and the Jubilee Singers. Fisk University is a member of the NAIA.

Academics and Learning Environment

For the B student, the learning environment of a college is just as important as the quality of its academic program. Fisk University has 49 full-time and 26 part-time faculty members, offering a student-to-faculty ratio of 10:1. The most common course size is 2 to 9 students. Fisk University offers 21 majors. The top favorites

Highlights

Fisk University
Nashville (Pop. 609,644)
Location: Major city
Four-year private
Founded: 1866
Website: http://www.fisk.edu

Students
Total enrollment: 620
Undergrads: 580
Freshmen: 183
Part-time students: 4%
From out-of-state: 79%
From public schools: 89%
Male/Female: 38%/62%
Live on-campus: 61%
In fraternities: 18%
In sororities: 23%
Off-campus employment rating: Excellent
Caucasian: 1%
African American: 83%
Hispanic: <1%
Asian: <1%
Native American: <1%
Mixed (2+ ethnicities): 2%
International: 4%

Academics
Calendar: Semester
Student/faculty ratio: 10:1
Class size 9 or fewer: 56%
Class size 10-29: 35%
Class size 30-49: 8%
Class size 50-99: 1%
Class size 100 or more: -
Returning freshmen: 85%
Six-year graduation rate: 59%

Most Popular Majors
Psychology
English
Business administration

FISK UNIVERSITY

Highlights

Admissions
Applicants: 1,746
Accepted: 795
Acceptance rate: 45.5%
Average GPA: 3.0
ACT range: 17-22
SAT Math range: 400-570
SAT Reading range: 410-540
SAT Writing range: 4-15
Top 10% of class: 18%
Top 25% of class: 46%
Top 50% of class: 81%

Deadlines
Early Action: No
Early Decision: No
Regular Action: Rolling admissions
Common Application: Accepted

Financial Aid
In-state tuition: $19,240
Out-of-state tuition: $19,240
Room: $5,752
Board: $4,408
Books: Varies
Freshmen receiving need-based aid: 98%
Undergrads rec. need-based aid: 90%
Avg. % of need met by financial aid: 75%
Avg. aid package (freshmen): $14,181
Avg. aid package (undergrads): $12,920
Avg. debt upon graduation: $6,147

Prominent Alumni
Dr. W.E.B. Du Bois; Nikki Giovanni; Dr. John Hope Franklin.

School Spirit
Mascot: Bulldogs

are psychology, English and business administration. The school has a general core requirement. Cooperative education is not offered. All first-year students must maintain a 2.0 GPA or higher to avoid academic probation. Other special academic programs that would appeal to a B student include: self-designed majors · pass/fail grading option · independent study · double majors · honors program · Phi Beta Kappa · internships.

B Student Support and Success

The Core Curriculum is really the heart of Fisk's education program. It centers around eight multicultural and interdisciplinary courses and is designed to help students grasp oral and written communication skills, logical and critical thinking, knowledge of the arts, history and literature and the processes and methods of science.

Fisk University provides support programs including: academic · personal · psychological · religious. Fisk University offers remedial and refresher courses in: reading · writing · math · study skills. The average freshman year GPA is 2.5, and 85 percent of freshmen students return for their sophomore year. A year after graduation, Fisk reports 40 percent of graduates enter graduate school. Among students who enter the workforce, approximately 12 percent enter a field related to their major within six months of graduation.

Support for Students with Learning Disabilities

Students with learning disabilities should know that high school foreign language and math waivers are accepted. They may find additional support through: tutors · learning center · untimed tests · extended time for tests · oral tests · readers. Individual or small group tutorials are also available in: time management · organizational skills · learning strategies · specific subject areas · writing labs · math labs · study skills.

How to Get Admitted

For admissions decisions, non-academic factors considered: interview · extracurricular activities · special talents, interests and abilities · character/personal qualities · volunteer work · work experience · state of residency · geographical location · alumni relationship. A high school diploma is required, although a GED is also accepted for admissions consideration. SAT or ACT test scores are required of all applicants. SAT Subject Test scores are considered, if submitted, but are not required. *According to the admissions office:* Math units should include algebra and plane geometry. *Academic units recommended:* 4 English, 3 Math, 1 Science, 3 Social Studies, 1 Foreign Language.

How to Pay for College

To apply for financial aid, students should submit the following: Free Application for Federal Student Aid (FAFSA) · Student Eligibility Report. Fisk University participates in the Federal Work Study program. *Need-based aid programs include:* scholarships and grants · general need-based awards · Federal Pell grants · state scholarships and grants · college-based scholarships and grants · private scholarships and grants · United Negro College Fund. *Non-need-based aid programs include:* scholarships and grants · state scholarships and grants.

FLAGLER COLLEGE

74 King Street, St. Augustine, FL 32084
Admissions: 800-304-4208, extension 220
Financial Aid: 800-304-4208, extension 225
Email: admiss@flagler.edu · Website: http://www.flagler.edu

From the College

"The aim of Flagler College is to provide a supportive and challenging environment in which students acquire knowledge, exercise good citizenship and adhere to high standards. The principal focus of the college's academic program is undergraduate education in selected liberal and pre-professional studies; thus, the role of teaching is central to the college's mission. The purposes of the academic program are to provide opportunities for general and specialized learning; to assist students in preparing for careers and to aid qualified students in pursuing graduate and professional studies. The objectives of the student life program at Flagler are to establish appropriate standards of conduct and to promote activities that will contribute to the development of self-discipline, integrity and leadership. Flagler College was established as a memorial to Henry M. Flagler. The Hotel Ponce de Leon, built by Mr. Flagler, serves as a reminder of his enterprise, diligence and commitment to high standards. The college is pledged to the preservation and use of this facility and other historic and architecturally unique campus structures."

Campus Setting

Flagler, founded in 1968, is a private, liberal arts college. Its administration building is located in the former Ponce de Leon Hotel, a Spanish-style former luxury resort now listed on the National Register of Historic Places. Its 44-acre campus is located in the center of St. Augustine. A four-year institution, Flagler College has an enrollment of 2,839 students, and has been co-ed since 1971. Campus facilities include: art gallery · art building · auditorium · communication building · student center. Flagler College provides on-campus housing with six units that can accommodate 1,034 students. Housing options: women's dorms · men's dorms. Recreation and sports facilities include: baseball, soccer and softball fields · gymnasium · tennis courts.

Student Life and Activities

More than half of the students (65 percent) live off campus. Popular gathering spots include the student center, West Lawn, Ponce Hall breezeway, local coffee shops, cafes and beaches. Favorite campus events include Midnight Breakfast, Mu Fest, Spring and Winter Formal, sports team competitions, surfing, speaker forums and literary presentations. Flagler College has 39 official student organizations. Popular groups on campus include the artistic organizations and theatre groups. The school's intramural teams include: badminton · bowling · football · tennis · Ultimate Frisbee · volleyball · surfing. Flagler College is a member of the NCAA (Division II).

Academics and Learning Environment

Flagler College has 106 full-time and 116 part-time faculty members, offering a student-to-faculty ratio of 17:1. The most common course size is 20 to 29 students. Of the college's 24 majors, the most popular are business administration, psychology and education. The least favorite include Spanish, philosophy/religion and liberal studies. The school has a general core requirement. Cooperative education is not offered. All first-year students must maintain a 2.0 GPA or higher to avoid academic probation. Other special academic programs include: independent study · double majors · dual degrees · internships.

FLAGLER COLLEGE

Highlights

Flagler College
St. Augustine, FL (Pop. 13,407)
Location: Small town
Four-year private
Founded: 1968
Website: http://www.flagler.edu

Students
Total enrollment: 2,839
Undergrads: 2,839
Part-time students: 3%
From out-of-state: 36%
From public schools: 78%
Male/Female: 41%/59%
Live on-campus: 36%
Off-campus employment rating: Excellent
Caucasian: 76%
African American: 4%
Hispanic: 8%
Asian: 1%
Hawaiian or Pacific Islander: <1%
Native American: <1%
Mixed (2+ ethnicities): 3%
International: 3%

Academics
Calendar: Semester
Student/faculty ratio: 17:1
Class size 9 or fewer: 5%
Class size 10-29: 90%
Class size 30-49: 4%
Class size 50-99: -
Class size 100 or more: -
Returning freshmen: 67%
Six-year graduation rate: 63%

Most Popular Majors
Business administration
Psychology
Education

B Student Support and Success

Flagler College was established as a memorial to Henry M. Flagler, and in accordance with his high standards, the college adheres to strict requirements on values. They have a strong attendance policy, prohibit alcohol and inter-dorm visitation and put a heavy emphasis on social justice and service. According to their website, "The objectives of the student life program at Flagler are to establish appropriate standards of conduct and to promote activities that will contribute to the development of self-discipline, integrity and leadership."

Flagler College provides a variety of support programs including dedicated guidance for: academic · career · personal · psychological. Recognizing that some students may need extra preparation, Flagler College offers remedial and refresher courses in: reading · writing · math · study skills. The average freshman year GPA is 2.8, and 67 percent of freshmen students return for their sophomore year. Companies that most frequently hire graduates from Flagler College include: Deloitte · Duval County Schools · The Gap · Hertz Corporation · KPMG · Palm Beach County Schools · Pulte Homes · Regency Centers · Ring Power · St. John's County Schools · YMCA.

Support for Students with Learning Disabilities

Flagler allows students with learning disabilities to take additional time to complete their degree, as well as pursue a lighter course load. According to the school, services for students with disabilities are determined on an individual basis according to the documented significant limitation of the disability. The admission process, while allowing for reasonable accommodations, still looks for students who are otherwise qualified. Students with learning disabilities may also want to look into: remedial math · remedial English · remedial reading · tutors · testing accommodations · extended time for tests · take-home exam · oral tests · readers · typist/scribe · note-taking services · reading machines · tape recorders · early syllabus · diagnostic testing service · waiver of math degree requirement. Individual or small group tutorials are also available in: time management · organizational skills · learning strategies · writing labs · math labs · study skills. An advisor/advocate from the Office of Services for Students with Disabilities is available to students.

How to Get Admitted

For admissions decisions, non-academic factors considered: interview · extracurricular activities · special talents, interests and abilities · character/personal qualities · volunteer work · geographical location · minority affiliation · alumni relationship. A high school diploma is required, although a GED is also accepted for admissions consideration. SAT or ACT test scores are required of all applicants. SAT Subject Test scores are recommended but not required. *According to the admissions office:* Minimum SAT Reasoning scores of 500 in critical reading, math, and writing (composite ACT score of 21) required. *Academic units recommended:* 4 English, 4 Math, 3 Science, 3 Social Studies, 2 Foreign Language.

How to Pay for College

To apply for financial aid, students should submit the following: Free Application for Federal Student Aid (FAFSA) · institution's own financial aid forms · state aid form. Flagler College participates in the Federal Work Study program. *Need-based aid programs include:* scholarships and grants · general need-based awards · Federal Pell grants · state scholarships and grants · college-based scholarships and grants · private scholarships and grants. *Non-need-based aid programs include:* scholarships and grants · general need-based awards · state scholarships and grants · creative arts and performance awards · special characteristics awards · athletic scholarships.

FLAGLER COLLEGE

Highlights

Admissions
Applicants: 5,396
Accepted: 2,691
Acceptance rate: 49.9%
Placed on wait list: 474
Enrolled from wait list: 31
Average GPA: 3.5
ACT range: 20-25
SAT Math range: 460-550
SAT Reading range: 470-580
SAT Writing range: 1-9
Top 10% of class: 9%
Top 25% of class: 31%
Top 50% of class: 67%

Deadlines
Early Action: No
Early Decision: 12/1
Regular Action: 1/15 (priority)
3/1 (final)
Notification of admission by: 3/30
Common Application: Accepted

Financial Aid
In-state tuition: $16,180
Out-of-state tuition: $16,180
Room: $4,290
Board: $4,710
Books: $1,000
Freshmen receiving need-based aid: 61%
Undergrads rec. need-based aid: 64%
Avg. % of need met by financial aid: 59%
Avg. aid package (freshmen): $12,178
Avg. aid package (undergrads): $11,619
Avg. debt upon graduation: $24,526

Prominent Alumni
Robert Strang, CEO, Investigative Management Group; Laura Neall, vice president of communications, The PGA Tour; Charles Tinlin, judge, St. Johns County Court.

School Spirit
Mascot: Lion
Colors: Crimson and gold

197

FLORIDA AGRICULTURAL & MECHANICAL UNIVERSITY

Lee Hall, Suite 400, Tallahassee, FL 32307
Admissions: 866-642-1198 · Financial Aid: 866-238-2318
Email: ugrdadmissions@famu.edu · Website: http://www.famu.edu

From the College

"Florida Agricultural and Mechanical University (FAMU) is an 1890 land-grant institution dedicated to the advancement of knowledge, resolution of complex issues and the empowerment of citizens and communities. The university provides a student-centered environment consistent with its core values. The faculty is committed to educating students at the undergraduate, graduate, doctoral and professional levels by preparing graduates to apply their knowledge, critical thinking skills and creativity in their service to society. FAMU's distinction as a doctoral/research institution will continue to provide mechanisms to address emerging issues through local and global partnerships. Expanding upon the university's land-grant status, it will enhance the lives of constituents through innovative research, engaging cooperative extension and public service. While the university continues its historic mission of educating African Americans, FAMU embraces persons of all races, ethnic origins and nationalities as life-long members of the university community."

Campus Setting

Florida Agricultural and Mechanical University, founded in 1887, is a public, historically black university. Its 419-acre campus is located in Tallahassee. A four-year institution, Florida A&M has 10,743 students. It provides on-campus housing with units accommodating 2,697 students. Housing options: coed dorms · women's dorms · men's dorms · single-student apartments · married-student apartments · special housing for disabled students.

Student Life and Activities

Most students (73 percent) live off campus. A school representative stated, "FAMU is the largest single-campus HBCU in the United States. It has a diverse student population, and provides many opportunities for students to pursue an array of academic and social interests." Popular campus events include Be Out Day, SGA campaign rallies Rattler Cinema, Game Night, drive-in movies, Homecoming, Rattler Pride Award, Make a Difference, Volunteer Day and the Essence Fashion Show. Florida A&M University has 135 official student organizations. The most popular are: Marching and pep bands · musical and drama groups · drill team · literary guild · team managers · academic and special-interest groups. Florida A&M University is a member of the Mid-Eastern Athletic Conference (Division I, Football I-AA) and Northeast Conference (Division I, Football I-AA).

Academics and Learning Environment

Florida A&M University has 549 full-time and 184 part-time faculty members, offering a student-to-faculty ratio of 17:1. The most common course size is 20 to 29 students. Florida A&M University offers 105 majors. Business administration, criminal justice and nursing are most popular, while least popular includes French, art education and technology education. The school has a general core requirement. Cooperative education is available. All first-year students must maintain a 2.0 GPA or higher to avoid academic probation, and a minimum overall 2.0 GPA is required to graduate. Other special academic programs include: pass/fail grading option ·

198

independent study · double majors · accelerated study · honors program · internships · distance learning.

B Student Support and Success

While academics are very important at Florida A&M, the school also seeks students with diverse backgrounds, believing that other skills and talents students may possess can benefit the university. Applicants may demonstrate their strengths through the admission essay. Florida A&M University provides a variety of support programs for: academic · career · personal · psychological · minority students · military · veterans · non-traditional students. Recognizing that some students may need extra preparation, Florida A&M University offers remedial and refresher courses in: reading · writing · math · study skills. The average freshman year GPA is 2.3, and 79 percent of freshmen students return for their sophomore year. Approximately 33 percent of students pursue a graduate degree immediately after graduation. Among students who enter the workforce, approximately 30 percent enter a field related to their major within six months of graduation.

Support for Students with Learning Disabilities

Students with learning disabilities may take extra time to complete their degree and/or take a lightened course load. High school foreign language and math waivers are accepted. According to the school, "The Center of Disability Accessibility and Resources (CeDAR) at Florida A&M University provides unique and comprehensive services and accommodations for students with learning and physical disabilities who desire to pursue college level studies. We identify participants' level of abilities and provide services that include assessment, prescriptive plans of study, academic advisement and individualized counseling."

Students with learning disabilities will find the following programs at Florida A&M University useful: remedial math · remedial English · remedial reading · special classes · tutors · learning center · testing accommodations · extended time for tests · oral tests · exam on tape or computer · readers · note-taking services · reading machines · tape recorders · texts on tape · early syllabus · special bookstore section · priority registration · waiver of math degree requirement · waiver of foreign language degree requirement. Individual or small group tutorials are also available in: time management · organizational skills · learning strategies · specific subject areas · writing labs · math labs · study skills. An advisor/advocate from the CeDAR-Center of Disability Accessibility and Resources is available to students. This member also sits on the admissions committee.

How to Get Admitted

For admissions decisions, non-academic factors considered: extracurricular activities · special talents, interests and abilities · character/personal qualities · volunteer work · work experience · alumni relationship. A high school diploma is required, although a GED is also accepted for admissions consideration. SAT or ACT test scores are required of all applicants. *According to the admissions office:* Minimum SAT Reasoning scores of 460 in both critical reading and math and 440

FLORIDA AGRICULTURAL & MECHANICAL UNIVERSITY

Highlights

Florida Agricultural & Mechanical University
Tallahassee (Pop. 186,971)
Location: Medium city
Four-year public
Founded: 1887
Website: http://www.famu.edu

Students
Total enrollment: 10,743
Undergrads: 8,930
Freshmen: 1,145
Part-time students: 10%
From out-of-state: 20%
From public schools: 85%
Male/Female: 39%/61%
Live on-campus: 27%
In fraternities: 2%
In sororities: 3%
Off-campus employment rating: Fair
Caucasian: 3%
African American: 94%
Hispanic: 1%
Asian: 1%
Native American: <1%
Mixed (2+ ethnicities): <1%
International: 1%

Academics
Calendar: Trimester
Student/faculty ratio: 17:1
Class size 9 or fewer: 13%
Class size 10-29: 42%
Class size 30-49: 32%
Class size 50-99: 11%
Class size 100 or more: 1%
Returning freshmen: 79%
Six-year graduation rate: 40%

Most Popular Majors
Business administration
Criminal justice
Nursing

199

College Profiles

FLORIDA AGRICULTURAL & MECHANICAL UNIVERSITY

Admissions
Applicants: 5,028
Accepted: 2,263
Acceptance rate: 45.0%
Average GPA: 3.3
ACT range: 18-22
SAT Math range: 430-510
SAT Reading range: 430-520
SAT Writing range: 1-5
Top 10% of class: 16%
Top 25% of class: 46%
Top 50% of class: 84%

Deadlines
Early Action: No
Early Decision: No
Regular Action: Rolling admissions
Common Application: Not accepted

Financial Aid
In-state tuition: $18,714
Out-of-state tuition: $30,656
Room: $5,060
Board: $3,980
Books: Varies
Freshmen receiving need-based aid: 86%
Undergrads rec. need-based aid: 85%
Avg. % of need met by financial aid: 70%
Avg. aid package (freshmen): $14,262
Avg. aid package (undergrads): $13,039
Avg. debt upon graduation: $31,251

Prominent Alumni
Dr. LaSalle D. Laffall, Jr., surgeon; Anika Noni Rose, actress; William Packer, movie producer.

School Spirit
Mascot: Rattlers
Colors: Orange and green
Song: *FAMU Alma Mater*

in writing (composite ACT scores of 19 in both English and math and 18 in writing) and minimum 2.5 GPA required.

How to Pay for College

To apply for financial aid, students should submit the following: Free Application for Federal Student Aid (FAFSA). Florida A&M University participates in the Federal Work Study program. *Need-based aid programs include:* scholarships and grants · general need-based awards · Federal Pell grants · state scholarships and grants · college-based scholarships and grants · private scholarships and grants · Federal Nursing scholarships · United Negro College Fund. *Non-need-based aid programs include:* scholarships and grants · state scholarships and grants · creative arts and performance awards · athletic scholarships · ROTC scholarships.

FLORIDA SOUTHERN COLLEGE

111 Lake Hollingsworth Drive, Lakeland, FL 33801-5698
Admissions: 800-274-4131 · Financial Aid: 800-205-1600
Email: fscadm@flsouthern.edu · Website: http://www.flsouthern.edu

From the College

"Florida Southern College is a comprehensive college with a liberal arts core offering 50 majors and distinctive graduate programs in business administration, education and nursing. The college's mission is to prepare students to make positive and consequential contributions to our world, and our 14:1 student-faculty ratio allows for the personalized instruction and mentoring relationships that reflect our "engaged learning" approach to educational preparation. Engaged learning at Florida Southern refers to a range of pedagogical practices oriented around the student as an active, creative participant in academic endeavors.

"We require our 2,400 undergraduate and graduate students to contribute significantly to the learning process in and out of the classroom. Engaged learning encompasses an array of student-faculty collaborative research, performance, service learning, study abroad and internship opportunities. Numerous fine and performing arts options are available to our students as well. Students' performances and gallery exhibitions enhance cultural life throughout Central Florida. Our students are also service-oriented, logging more than 10,000 hours of community service annually.

"Forty percent of our undergraduates study abroad, and this year's offerings include summer programs in 10 countries (e.g. China, New Zealand and Austria); and semester programs in England, Northern Ireland and Spain. Students enrolled in May Option for the international business and international financial management courses will study multinational and local corporations in China for three weeks."

Campus Setting

Florida Southern College, founded in 1883, is a private, comprehensive United Methodist-affiliated college. The college maintains its commitment to academic excellence through 50 undergraduate programs and distinctive graduate programs in business administration, education and nursing. Its 113-acre campus, within an hour of Tampa and Orlando, is located in Lakeland. A four-year private institution, Florida Southern College has an enrollment of 2,395 students. Campus facilities include: art galleries · center for Florida history · hall of fames · planetarium · auditorium · visitor center · theatres · nursing building · technology center · wellness center · nuclear magnetic resonance imagine instrument · virtual patient simulation lab · garden. Florida Southern College provides on-campus housing with 833 units that can accommodate 1,712 students. Housing options: coed dorms · women's dorms · men's dorms · sorority housing · fraternity housing · single-student apartments · married-student apartments · special housing for disabled students. Recreation and sports facilities include: gymnasium · tennis courts · intramural fields · wellness center · swimming pool.

Student Life and Activities

About three-quarters of students live on campus. As reported by a school representative, "Our 113-acre campus is busy and active, engaged in learning about our world and living life to the fullest in classrooms, around campus and in the companies and national and international organizations that welcome FSC students as interns and volunteers." The campus is abuzz with activity day and night. On campus, students gather in Tutu's Cyber Cafe, the Hollis Wellness Center and Pool, Badcock Garden, The Terrace Cafe and the Field House. Off campus, students shop and go out

FLORIDA SOUTHERN COLLEGE

Florida Southern College
Lakeland, FL (Pop. 99,999)
Location: Medium city
Four-year private
Founded: 1883
Website: http://www.flsouthern.edu

Students
Total enrollment: 2,395
Undergrads: 2,192
Freshmen: 655
Part-time students: 3%
From out-of-state: 41%
From public schools: 82%
Male/Female: 41%/59%
Live on-campus: 79%
In fraternities: 37%
In sororities: 32%
Off-campus employment rating: Good
Caucasian: 72%
African American: 6%
Hispanic: 9%
Asian: 2%
Hawaiian or Pacific Islander: <1%
Native American: <1%
Mixed (2+ ethnicities): 4%
International: 5%

Academics
Calendar: Semester
Student/faculty ratio: 14:1
Class size 9 or fewer: 26%
Class size 10-29: 60%
Class size 30-49: 14%
Class size 50-99: -
Class size 100 or more: -
Returning freshmen: 78%
Six-year graduation rate: 58%

Most Popular Majors
Business administration
Biology
Nursing

for dinner at Lakeside Village and downtown Lakeland shops and restaurants, walking/biking the paths around Lake Hollingsworth or venturing 30-45 minutes away for Tampa/Orlando attractions and the nation's best beaches. Popular campus events include the Fairwell Festival, the Founders Week Ball and celebrations, the Festival of Fine Arts performances, art shows at the Melvin Gallery and the Florida Lecture Series. Florida Southern College has 85 official student organizations. Popular groups on campus include fraternities and sororities and athletic teams. For those interested in sports, there are intramural teams such as: 5K walk/run · basketball · billiards · bowling · dodgeball · free throw · golf · indoor volleyball · rock/paper/scissors · soccer · softball · swimming · table tennis · tailgate triathlon · tennis singles · Ultimate Frisbee · Wiffle ball. Florida Southern College is a member of the Sunshine State Conference (Division II).

Academics and Learning Environment

Florida Southern College has 119 full-time and 103 part-time faculty members, offering a student-to-faculty ratio of 14:1. The most common course size is 10 to 19 students. Florida Southern College offers 53 majors with the most popular being business administration, biology and nursing and least popular being humanities, art history and computer science/math. The school has a general core requirement as well as a religion requirement. Cooperative education is not offered. All first-year students must maintain a 2.0 GPA or higher to avoid academic probation. Other special academic programs include: self-designed majors · pass/fail grading option · independent study · double majors · honors program · internships.

B Student Support and Success

The Academic Support Services at Florida Southern College hopes to "foster the development of life skills and habits of academic excellence." It helps students make the transition to college life through offering specific orientation programs, customizing help sessions to identify needs and provide resources and supplying referrals.

Florida Southern College provides dedicated guidance for: academic · career · personal · psychological · minority students · religious. Additional counseling services include: non-traditional student. The average freshman year GPA is 3.1, and 78 percent of freshmen students return for their sophomore year. Approximately 26 percent pursue a graduate degree right after graduation. Among students who enter the workforce, approximately 70 percent enter a field related to their major within six months of graduation. Companies that most frequently hire graduates from Florida Southern College include: Enterprise Rent-A-Car · GEICO Direct · Lakeland Regional Health Systems · Polk County Public Schools · Publix Super Markets · Pulte Homes · State of Florida · U.S. Army · Walt Disney World · Watson Clinic.

Support for Students with Learning Disabilities

According to the school, Florida Southern College does not modify any courses or requirements for LD students. Students with learning disabilities may access extended time for taking tests and individual or small group tutorials.

How to Get Admitted

For admissions decisions, non-academic factors considered: interview · extracurricular activities · special talents, interests and abilities · character/personal qualities · volunteer work · work experience · state of residency · religious affiliation/commitment · minority affiliation · alumni relationship. A high school diploma is required, although a GED is also accepted for admissions consideration. SAT or ACT test scores are required of all applicants. SAT Subject Test scores are not required. *According to the admissions office:* Minimum combined SAT Reasoning score of 1050 (composite ACT score of 23), minimum 3.0 GPA in academic college-preparatory courses and rank in the upper half of secondary school class required. *Academic units recommended:* 2 Foreign Language.

How to Pay for College

To apply for financial aid, students should submit the following: Free Application for Federal Student Aid (FAFSA) · institution's own financial aid forms. Florida Southern College participates in the Federal Work Study program. *Need-based aid programs include:* scholarships and grants · general need-based awards · Federal Pell grants · state scholarships and grants · college-based scholarships and grants · private scholarships and grants. *Non-need-based aid programs include:* scholarships and grants · general need-based awards · state scholarships and grants · creative arts and performance awards · special achievements and activities awards · special characteristics awards · athletic scholarships · ROTC scholarships · community service and leadership scholarships/grants.

FLORIDA SOUTHERN COLLEGE

Highlights

Admissions
Applicants: 4,963
Accepted: 2,476
Acceptance rate: 49.9%
Average GPA: 3.6
ACT range: 18-23
SAT Math range: 510-590
SAT Reading range: 500-590
SAT Writing range: 3-17
Top 10% of class: 20%
Top 25% of class: 56%
Top 50% of class: 81%

Deadlines
Early Action: No
Early Decision: 12/1
Regular Action: Rolling admissions
Common Application: Accepted

Financial Aid
In-state tuition: $29,340
Out-of-state tuition: $29,340
Room: $5,250
Board: $1,310
Books: $1,230
Freshmen receiving need-based aid: 73%
Undergrads rec. need-based aid: 73%
Avg. % of need met by financial aid: 73%
Avg. aid package (freshmen): $23,958
Avg. aid package (undergrads): $23,599
Avg. debt upon graduation: $33,191

Prominent Alumni
Abdalla Salem El-Badri, secretary general, OPEC; Fred Lewis, former chief justice, Florida Supreme Court; James Carl France, president, International Speedway Corporation.

School Spirit
Mascot: Moccasins
Colors: Red and white

203

FLORIDA STATE UNIVERSITY

A2500 University Center, 282 Champions Way, Tallahassee, FL 32306
Admissions: 850-644-6200 · Financial Aid: 850-644-5871
Email: admissions@admin.fsu.edu · Website: http://www.fsu.edu

From the College

"Florida State University is an internationally recognized teaching and research institution committed to preparing our students for a life that balances knowledge, creativity, leadership and contribution. Designated as a Carnegie Research University (very high research activity), Florida State offers more than 320 undergraduate, graduate and professional degree programs, including medicine and law.

"Our students have the opportunity to conduct research alongside Nobel laureates and Pulitzer Prize winners, Guggenheim Fellows, members of the National Academy of Sciences and American Academy of Arts and Sciences and other globally recognized teachers and researchers. Through the efforts of our Office of Undergraduate Research, students partner with faculty who share their academic interests, and who encourage them to design and conduct original research projects. Through the Office of National Fellowships, Florida State has become a leader among the state's public universities by setting records in the award of national fellowships and scholarships for our students. We offer state-of-the-art teaching techniques in our technologically enhanced classrooms and wireless networking community.

"Our innovative student services include a comprehensive campus-wide leadership learning program, a center for community and global-based learning through service and an award-winning career center. World-class cultural events, championship athletics, extensive recreational facilities and a friendly, close-knit University community enrich student life and extend learning well beyond the classroom.

"Our diverse student body hails from all fifty states and more than 130 countries, and our numerous international programs throughout the world include year-round programs in Florence, Italy; London, England; Panama City, Panama and Valencia, Spain."

Campus Setting

Florida State, founded in 1851, is a public, comprehensive university. Its 463-acre campus is located within a mile of downtown Tallahassee. A four-year institution, Florida State University has an enrollment of 40,909 students. Although not originally a co-educational college, Florida State University has been co-ed since 1947. The campus facilities include: library · conservatory · museums · marine laboratory · oceanographic institute · magnetic field laboratory · developmental research school · Challenger space center · planetarium · accelerators · super computers. Florida State University provides on-campus housing with 3,548 units that can accommodate 6,387 students. Housing options: coed dorms · women's dorms · sorority housing · fraternity housing · single-student apartments · married-student apartments · special housing for disabled students. Recreation and sports facilities include: football, lacrosse, soccer and softball fields · racquetball and tennis courts · swimming pool · indoor and outdoor tracks · basketball arena.

Student Life and Activities

Eighty percent of students live off campus. Popular on-campus gathering spots include the Student Union, Student Life Center and Landis Green. Popular campus events include Seven Days of Opening Nights, Market Wednesday, LEAD - In at the Rez, President's Retreat, speakers series, FSUnity Day, Earth Day, Dance Marathon, Flying High Circus, Parents' Weekend, Homecoming Festivities & Parade, PowWow,

President's Ice Cream Social, Last Call Before Fall and Seminole Sensation Week. Florida State University has 550 official student organizations. The most popular are: Music ensembles · marching and pep bands · baton twirling · drill team · theatre and dance groups · debate groups · team managers · other academic and special-interest groups. There are intramural teams available: basketball · beach volleyball · billiards · bowling · disc golf · flag football · homerun derby · horseshoes · kickball · racquetball · speedball · soccer · softball · swimming · table tennis · tennis · volleyball · walleyball · Wiffleball. Florida State University is a member of the Atlantic Coast Conference (Division I, Football I-A).

Academics and Learning Environment

Florida State University has 1,272 full-time and 398 part-time faculty members, offering a student-to-faculty ratio of 26:1. The most common course size is 20 to 29 students. Florida State University offers 503 majors with the most popular being finance, English and psychology. The school has a general core requirement. Cooperative education is available. All first-year students must maintain a 2.0 GPA or higher to avoid academic probation, and a minimum overall GPA of 2.0 is required to graduate. B students might want to research this list: pass/fail grading option · independent study · double majors · dual degrees · accelerated study · honors program · Phi Beta Kappa · internships · distance learning certificate programs.

B Student Support and Success

Although this is a rather large college, its staff and faculty care about the students and their success. FSU's Center for Academic Retention and Enhancement provides preparation, orientation and academic support programming for students who may be facing unique challenges because of cultural, economic or educational circumstances. A program called SSSMO, or Students Supporting Students Mentoring Organization, offers mentors that help students in becoming acclimated to the school. They also act as role models in academic areas and in leadership.

Florida State University provides dedicated guidance for: academic · career · personal · psychological · minority students · military · veterans · non-traditional students · family planning · religious. Recognizing that some students may need extra preparation, Florida State University offers remedial and refresher courses in: reading · writing · math · study skills. The average freshman year GPA is 3.1, and 92 percent of freshmen students return for their sophomore year. After college? It's true that many students enter the workforce, approximately 35 percent pursue a graduate degree immediately after graduation. Out of the amount of students who enter the workforce, approximately 70 percent of them enter a field related to their major within six months of graduation. Some companies that most frequently hire graduates from Florida State University are: Abercrombie & Fitch · Ameriprise Financial Services · Babies 'R Us · City Furniture · CSX Transportation · Deloitte · Dirt Devil/Hoover · E & J GALLO · Ernst & Young · Florida Auditor General · GEICO · Harris Corporation · IBM · KPMG · Lockheed Martin · Macy's Florida · Marriott International Corp. · NOAA · Northwestern Mutual Financial Network · Pulte Homes

FLORIDA STATE UNIVERSITY

Highlights

Florida State University
Tallahassee (Pop. 186,971)
Location: Medium city
Four-year public
Founded: 1851
Website: http://www.fsu.edu

Students
Total enrollment: 40,909
Undergrads: 32,528
Freshmen: 6,048
Part-time students: 11%
From out-of-state: 12%
From public schools: 89%
Male/Female: 45%/55%
Live on-campus: 20%
In fraternities: 16%
In sororities: 22%
Off-campus employment rating: Good
Caucasian: 66%
African American: 9%
Hispanic: 17%
Asian: 3%
Hawaiian or Pacific Islander: <1%
Native American: <1%
Mixed (2+ ethnicities): 2%
International: 1%

Academics
Calendar: Semester
Student/faculty ratio: 26:1
Class size 9 or fewer: 12%
Class size 10-29: 50%
Class size 30-49: 23%
Class size 50-99: 9%
Class size 100 or more: 6%
Returning freshmen: 92%
Six-year graduation rate: 77%

Most Popular Majors
Finance
English
Psychology

205

College Profiles

FLORIDA STATE UNIVERSITY

Highlights

Admissions
Applicants: 29,579
Accepted: 16,803
Acceptance rate: 56.8%
Average GPA: 3.9
ACT range: 25-29
SAT Math range: 550-640
SAT Reading range: 560-640
SAT Writing range: 5-43
Top 10% of class: 42%
Top 25% of class: 77%
Top 50% of class: 97%

Deadlines
Early Action: No
Early Decision: No
Regular Action: 1/15 (final)
Common Application: Accepted

Financial Aid
In-state tuition: $6,467
Out-of-state tuition: $21,633
Room: $6,160
Board: $4,048
Books: $1,000
Freshmen receiving need-based aid: 55%
Undergrads rec. need-based aid: 55%
Avg. % of need met by financial aid: 49%
Avg. aid package (freshmen): $8,694
Avg. aid package (undergrads): $9,033
Avg. debt upon graduation: $22,772

Prominent Alumni
Meg Crofton, president, Walt Disney World; Sara Blakely, entrepreneur and creator/owner, Spanx; Todd Combs, investment manager, Berkshire Hathaway.

School Spirit
Mascot: Seminoles
Colors: Garnet and gold
Song: *Alma Mater - High Over Towering Pines*

· Protivit, Rachlin, Cohen & Holtz LLP · Regions Financial Organization · Schlumberger · Sears Holdings Corporation · Shell Oil · Software Architects · State of Florida · Target Corporation · Teach for America · U.S. Armed Forces · Wachovia · Woseley North America.

Support for Students with Learning Disabilities

Students with learning disabilities may want to investigate programs specifically geared towards them, which are available through Florida State University. After discussing whether its appropriate or not, the college may grant additional time to LD students so that they can finish their degree. A lightened course load is another option open to LD students. Students with learning disabilities will find the following programs very appealing: testing accommodations · extended time for tests · take-home exam · oral tests · exam on tape or computer · readers · typist/scribe · note-taking services · reading machines · tape recorders · texts on tape · early syllabus · diagnostic testing service · priority registration · priority seating · waiver of math degree requirement. Individual or small group tutorials are also available in: time management · organizational skills · learning strategies · writing labs · math labs · study skills. An advisor/advocate from the Student Disability Resource Center is available to students.

How to Get Admitted

For admissions decisions, non-academic factors considered: extracurricular activities · special talents, interests and abilities · character/personal qualities · volunteer work · work experience · geographical location · alumni relationship. A high school diploma is required, although a GED is also accepted for admissions consideration. SAT or ACT test scores are required of all applicants. SAT Subject Test scores are not required. *Academic units recommended:* 4 English, 4 Math, 4 Science, 2 Social Studies, 4 Foreign Language.

How to Pay for College

To apply for financial aid, students should submit the following: Free Application for Federal Student Aid (FAFSA). The Florida State University participates in the Federal Work Study program. *Need-based aid programs include:* scholarships and grants · general need-based awards · Federal Pell grants · state scholarships and grants · college-based scholarships and grants · private scholarships and grants. *Non-need-based aid programs include:* scholarships and grants · general need-based awards · state scholarships and grants · athletic scholarships.

America's
Best Colleges for
B Students

FORT LEWIS COLLEGE

1000 Rim Drive, Durango, CO 81301
Admissions: 877-FLC-COLO · Financial Aid: 800-352-7512
Email: admission@fortlewis.edu
Website: http://www.fortlewis.edu

From the College

"Fort Lewis College is a public four-year liberal arts college in Durango, Colorado. We offer more than 100 academic specialties backed by the 'big picture' of the liberal arts. Real-world experiences through internships, service learning, study abroad and undergraduate research launch students into professional careers.

"Fort Lewis College is also known for its spectacular setting, outdoor opportunities and Colorado lifestyle. Located at 6,872 feet on a mesa overlooking the Animas River Valley, the campus sits at the foot of the San Juan Mountains and the headwaters of the Colorado Plateau, where the region's mountains, deserts, rivers and canyons serve as both classrooms and playgrounds."

Campus Setting

Fort Lewis, founded in 1911, is a public, liberal arts college. Its 350-acre campus is located on a mesa overlooking Durango's business district, in southwestern Colorado. Fort Lewis College provides on-campus housing with 887 units that can accommodate 1,521 students. Housing options: coed dorms · single-student apartments · married-student apartments · special housing for disabled students. Recreation and sports facilities include: center · fields · gymnasium · outdoor track · pool.

Student Life and Activities

As reported by a school representative, "Fort Lewis is a welcoming, friendly and open community that is very accepting of all kinds of students, ages, traditions and religions." Popular gathering places for students are the Clock Tower, the Amphitheater, the Student Life Center, the River Rock Café and John F. Reed Library patio. Common Reading Experience lecture series and Halloween, Hozhoni Days, Tri-the-Rim, Skyfest, Homecoming and varsity soccer games are popular events on campus. Fort Lewis College has 65 official student organizations. Outdoor Adventurers, Native Americans and soccer players are all influential groups on campus. For those interested in sports, there are intramural teams such as: badminton · basketball · cornhole · dodgeball · flag football · golf · kickball · soccer · tennis · Ultimate Frisbee · volleyball. The college is a member of the Rocky Mountain Athletic Conference (Division II).

Academics and Learning Environment

Fort Lewis College has 158 full-time and 70 part-time faculty members, offering a student-to-faculty ratio of 21:1. The most common course size is 20 to 29 students. Fort Lewis College offers 30 majors. Business, exercise science and biology are most popular; gender/women's studies, south west/Native American/indigenous studies and humanities are least. The school has a general core requirement. All first-year students must maintain a 2.0 GPA or

FORT LEWIS COLLEGE

Fort Lewis College
Durango, CO (Pop. 17,216)
Location: Small town
Four-year public
Founded: 1911
Website: http://www.fortlewis.edu

Students
Total enrollment: 4,028
Undergrads: 4,028
Freshmen: 1,371
Part-time students: 8%
From out-of-state: 48%
Male/Female: 51%/49%
Live on-campus: 38%
Off-campus employment rating: Fair
Caucasian: 57%
African American: 1%
Hispanic: 9%
Asian: <1%
Hawaiian or Pacific Islander: <1%
Native American: 22%
Mixed (2+ ethnicities): 6%
International: 2%

Academics
Calendar: Semester
Student/faculty ratio: 21:1
Class size 9 or fewer: 22%
Class size 10-29: 53%
Class size 30-49: 22%
Class size 50-99: 3%
Class size 100 or more: -
Returning freshmen: 65%
Six-year graduation rate: 37%

Most Popular Majors
Business
Exercise science
Biology

207

College Profiles

FORT LEWIS COLLEGE

Highlights

Admissions
Applicants: 2,560
Accepted: 2,240
Acceptance rate: 87.5%
Average GPA: 3.2
ACT range: 20-25
SAT Math range: 475-580
SAT Reading range: 470-570
SAT Writing range: Not reported
Top 10% of class: 10%
Top 25% of class: 32%
Top 50% of class: 65%

Deadlines
Early Action: 1/15
Early Decision: No
Regular Action: Rolling admissions
Common Application: Accepted

Financial Aid
In-state tuition: $5,544
Out-of-state tuition: $16,072
Room: $4,400
Board: $4,450
Books: $1,208
Freshmen receiving need-based aid: 63%
Undergrads rec. need-based aid: 60%
Avg. % of need met by financial aid: 89%
Avg. aid package (freshmen): $12,131
Avg. aid package (undergrads): $12,420
Avg. debt upon graduation: $21,843

Prominent Alumni
Christopher Schauble, news anchor and co-host of "Today in L.A", former actor in "West Wing"; Scott Tipton, U.S. House of Representatives, Raymond Boucher, attorney and partner for Kiesel Boucher Larson.

School Spirit
Mascot: Skyhawks
Colors: Blue and gold

America's
Best Colleges for
B Students

higher to avoid academic probation. Other special academic programs that would appeal to a B student include: self-designed majors · independent study · double majors · accelerated study · honors program · internships · distance learning.

B Student Support and Success

The Academic Success Program at Fort Lewis is free to all college students. It allows students to network with other learning support programs on campus and offers fall and winter symposiums to help first-year students acclimate to college life. An Early Alert System is available for students who are struggling and small study groups are set up across campus. The Algebra Alcove helps students in their math classes, including the provision of problem-solving classes and supplemental instruction. A Writing Center is offered for "building better writers."

Fort Lewis College provides dedicated guidance for: academic · career · personal · psychological · minority students · veterans · non-traditional students · family planning · religious. The average freshman year GPA is 2.5, and 65 percent of freshmen students return for their sophomore year. Companies that most frequently hire graduates from Fort Lewis College include: Department of Defense · Durango Mountain Resort · First National Bank · Hyatt · IBM · KPMG · Mercury Payment Systems · police departments · school districts · Wells Fargo Bank.

Support for Students with Learning Disabilities

Students with learning disabilities may want to learn more about Fort Lewis's support programs including: extended time for tests · oral tests · readers · note-taking services · tape recorders. Individual or small group tutorials are also available in: specific subject areas · writing labs · math labs. An advisor/advocate from the Academic Success Program is available to students.

How to Get Admitted

For admissions decisions, non-academic factors considered: interview · extracurricular activities · special talents, interests and abilities · character/personal qualities · volunteer work · work experience · state of residency · alumni relationship. A high school diploma is required, although a GED is also accepted for admissions consideration. SAT or ACT test scores are required of all applicants. SAT Subject Test scores are not required. *According to the admissions office:* Computer science and modern languages courses recommended. Admissions based on an index of standardized test scores and GPA. *Academic units recommended:* 4 English, 4 Math, 3 Science, 2 Social Studies, 1 Foreign Language.

How to Pay for College

To apply for financial aid, students should submit the following: Free Application for Federal Student Aid (FAFSA). Fort Lewis College participates in the Federal Work Study program. *Need-based aid programs include:* scholarships and grants · general need-based awards · Federal Pell grants · state scholarships and grants · college-based scholarships and grants · private scholarships and grants. *Non-need-based aid programs include:* scholarships and grants · general need-based awards · state scholarships and grants · creative arts and performance awards · athletic scholarships.

GEORGE MASON UNIVERSITY

4400 University Drive, Fairfax, VA 22030
Admissions: 703-993-2400 · Financial Aid: 703-993-2353
Email: admissions@gmu.edu
Website: http://www.gmu.edu

From the College

"George Mason at its core is innovative, diverse, entrepreneurial and accessible. Mason is committed to being a university for the world, a place where we work across cultures, bringing new perspectives and solutions to the world's most pressing problems and preparing our students to navigate in the world.

"Mason is innovative: we question current thinking and try new ideas. We honor time-tested academic principles while striving to create new forms of education that serve our students better and new paths of research that can uncover solutions to the world's greatest challenges. Mason professors conduct groundbreaking research in areas such as cancer, climate change, international policy and politics, national and international security, the biosciences and computer game design. Our professors are well-known leaders in their fields who routinely welcome undergraduates to actively participate in their research.

"Mason is diverse: we bring together a multitude of people and ideas in everything that we do. Our culture of inclusion, our multidisciplinary approach and our global perspective make us more effective educators and scholars. Mason has programs in more than 30 countries, with reciprocal relationships with universities in Russia, Korea, China and Germany. Mason's undergraduates come from all 50 states and 125 countries.

"Mason is entrepreneurial: we put ideas into action. We educate students to create as well as carry out jobs; become agents of positive change and add value through government or business, for profit or nonprofit organizations, academia or the arts. We pursue discoveries that can make a difference in the world, and help our community thrive socially, economically and culturally.

"And Mason is accessible: we are an open and welcoming community that partners with public and private organizations in our region and around the world. Mason students have opportunities to advance their careers both inside and outside the classroom, including internships at nationally and internationally recognized companies and organizations ranging from *National Geographic* to the White House. Work and internship opportunities run the gamut: foreign embassies, wildlife preserves, network news programs, global IT organizations. Through a first-of-its-kind partnership with the Smithsonian, Mason offers students the chance to spend a semester at one of the most advanced conservation research centers in the world, and complete a minor in applied conservation studies in just that one semester.

"Mason occupies a unique position in the higher education marketplace. With strong undergraduate and graduate degree programs, Mason students are routinely recognized with national and international scholarships and awards. Every day, Mason students can be found lobbying Congress on educational issues, pioneering outreach programs for disadvantaged children or collecting oral histories in the U.S. Holocaust Memorial Museum. The prospects of internships, research and employment here are unmatched anywhere else. Many Mason graduates continue employment at places where they interned; 70 percent of alumni remain in the area to take advantage of the outstanding job market. A George Mason University education is an excellent investment: students who earn a bachelor's degree receive the highest starting salary of all public schools in Virginia. In addition, Mason students earn the highest median annual wages of all Virginia four-year degree institutions."

GEORGE MASON UNIVERSITY

George Mason University
Fairfax, VA (Pop. 23,461)
Location: Small town
Four-year public
Founded: 1972
Website: http://www.gmu.edu

Students

Total enrollment: 33,917
Undergrads: 21,990
Freshmen: 2,694
Part-time students: 22%
From out-of-state: 20%
From public schools: 90%
Male/Female: 48%/52%
Live on-campus: 27%
In fraternities: 11%
In sororities: 10%
Off-campus employment rating: Excellent
Caucasian: 46%
African American: 10%
Hispanic: 11%
Asian: 18%
Hawaiian or Pacific Islander: <1%
Native American: <1%
Mixed (2+ ethnicities): 5%
International: 4%

Academics

Calendar: Semester
Student/faculty ratio: 16:1
Class size 9 or fewer: 7%
Class size 10-29: 52%
Class size 30-49: 25%
Class size 50-99: 12%
Class size 100 or more: 4%
Returning freshmen: 87%
Six-year graduation rate: 66%

Most Popular Majors

Psychology
Communication
Biology

Campus Setting

George Mason, founded in 1972, is a public university. Programs are offered through the College of Humanities and Social Sciences, the College of Education and Human Development, the Volgenau School of Information Technology and Engineering, the College of Visual and Performing Arts, the Institute for Conflict Analysis and Resolution, the College of Health and Human Services, the College of Science, the School of Management, the School of Public Policy and the School of Law. Its 677-acre main campus is located in Fairfax, 18 miles from Washington, DC. A four-year institution, George Mason University has an enrollment of 33,917 students. In addition to a large, well-stocked library, the campus facilities include: astronomy observatory · research buildings · biomedical research lab · performing arts and conservation and research centers. George Mason University provides on-campus housing with 2,136 units that can accommodate 6,083 students. Housing options: coed dorms · single-student apartments · special housing for disabled students. Recreation and sports facilities include: recreation/athletic, baseball and track complexes · aquatics and fitness center · field house · tennis courts.

Student Life and Activities

Most students (73 percent) live off campus. As reported by a school official, "Mason students have a wide range of places to go, including Old Towne Fairfax and Washington, DC. Mason also has a variety of student organizations and activities." Favorite gathering places include the Student Union, the Johnson Center, Rathskeller Sports Bar, Jazzman's Cafe and Fat Tuesday's. Favorite campus events include Welcome Week, New Student Days, Patriot Days, Homecoming, Mason Day, International Week, Mason Madness and Pride Week. George Mason University has 461 official student organizations. Influential groups include Greeks, Campus Ministries, Student Government, International Clubs and various athletic groups. For those interested in sports, there are intramural teams such as: basketball · cricket · football · golf · soccer · softball · swimming · table tennis · tennis · track and field · volleyball. George Mason University is a member of the Colonial Athletic Association (Division I), Eastern College Athletic Conference (Division I), Eastern Intercollegiate Volleyball Association (Division I), IC4A and Atlantic 10.

Academics and Learning Environment

George Mason University has 1,222 full-time and 1,239 part-time faculty members, offering a student-to-faculty ratio of 16:1. The most common course size is 20 to 29 students. George Mason University offers 184 majors. The most popular are psychology, communication and biology, while the least are computational/data sciences, environmental science and Russian/Eurasian studies. The school has a general core requirement. Cooperative education is available. All first-year students must maintain a 2.0 GPA or higher to avoid academic probation. Other special academic programs that would appeal to a B student include: self-designed majors · pass/fail grading option · independent study · double majors · dual degrees · accelerated study · honors program · internships · distance learning certificate programs.

B Student Support and Success

Learning Services at George Mason encompasses many different methods to help support students who are struggling academically. Study skills workshops are offered on topics such as concentration, procrastination, academic skills, motivation and goal setting. Tutor Referral matches students with peer tutors (which charge varying fees). Services are confidential, and use of these services does not become part of the student's academic record.

George Mason University provides a variety of support programs including: academic · career · personal · psychological · minority students · military · veterans · non-traditional students · family planning · religious. Additional counseling services include: international student advising · alcohol, drug and health · sexual assault. George Mason University offers remedial and refresher courses in: reading · writing · math · study skills. Other remedial services include miscellaneous life skills. The average freshman year GPA is 3.0, and 87 percent of freshmen students return for their sophomore year. Companies that most frequently hire graduates from George Mason University include: BB&T Bank · Booz Allen Hamilton · Computer Sciences Corporation · Cotton and Company · Deloitte · Enterprise Rent-A-Car · Ernst & Young · FBI · Fairfax County Government · Fairfax County Public Schools · Freddie Mac · George Mason University · IBM · INOVA Health Care System · KPMG · Lockheed Martin · ManTech · Navy Federal Credit Union · Northern Virginia Community College · Northrop Grumman · PricewaterhouseCoopers · Science Applications International Corporation (SAIC) · U.S. Army · U.S. Department of Justice · U.S. Investigations Services · Virginia Hospital Center.

Support for Students with Learning Disabilities

Students with learning disabilities may take additional time to complete their degree or a lightened course load. According to the school, Mason has an Office of Disability Services (ODS) that is available to assist all students with disabilities. Please note that disability-specific services are not available through ODS and that counseling and tutorial services are available to all Mason students through other departments outside of ODS. Students with learning disabilities may also utilize: learning center · testing accommodations · extended time for tests · take-home exam · oral tests · readers · typist/scribe · note-taking services · reading machines · tape recorders · texts on tape · early syllabus · priority registration.

How to Get Admitted

For admissions decisions, non-academic factors considered: extracurricular activities · special talents, interests and abilities · character/personal qualities · volunteer work · work experience · state of residency · alumni relationship. A high school diploma is required, although a GED is also accepted for admissions consideration. SAT or ACT test scores are required for some applicants. SAT Subject Test scores are recommended but not required. *According to the admissions office:* Written personal statement required. SAT Reasoning/ACT scores recommended. *Academic units recommended:* 4 English, 4 Math, 3 Science, 4 Social Studies, 3 Foreign Language.

GEORGE MASON UNIVERSITY

Highlights

Admissions
Applicants: 20,805
Accepted: 12,905
Acceptance rate: 62.0%
Placed on wait list: 2,228
Enrolled from wait list: 252
Average GPA: 3.7
ACT range: 24-28
SAT Math range: 530-630
SAT Reading range: 520-620
SAT Writing range: Not reported
Top 10% of class: 20%
Top 25% of class: 56%
Top 50% of class: 94%

Deadlines
Early Action: 11/1
Early Decision: No
Regular Action: 11/1 (priority)
1/15 (final)
Notification of admission by: 4/1
Common Application: Not accepted

Financial Aid
In-state tuition: $10,657
Out-of-state tuition: $30,235
Room: $6,000
Board: $4,100
Books: Varies
Freshmen receiving need-based aid: 51%
Undergrads rec. need-based aid: 52%
Avg. % of need met by financial aid: 59%
Avg. aid package (freshmen): $12,367
Avg. aid package (undergrads): $11,901
Avg. debt upon graduation: $26,710

Prominent Alumni
Ken Cuccinelli, 2010 Attorney General for Commonwealth of Virginia; Deborah Hersman, nominated by President Obama to chair National Transportation Safety Board; Zainab Salbi, president/founder, Women for Women International.

School Spirit
Mascot: The Patriot
Colors: Green and gold
Song: *GMU Alma Mater*

211

How to Pay for College

To apply for financial aid, students should submit the following: Free Application for Federal Student Aid (FAFSA). George Mason University participates in the Federal Work Study program. *Need-based aid programs include:* scholarships and grants · general need-based awards · Federal Pell grants · state scholarships and grants · college-based scholarships and grants · private scholarships and grants. *Non-need-based aid programs include:* scholarships and grants · general need-based awards · state scholarships and grants · creative arts and performance awards · athletic scholarships · ROTC scholarships.

GEORGIA REGENTS UNIVERSITY

1120 15th Street, Augusta, GA 30912
Admissions: 706-737-1632 · Financial Aid: 706-737-1431
Email: admissions@gru.edu · Website: http://www.gru.edu

From the College

"GRU is a public metropolitan university with the atmosphere of a small liberal arts college, plus a supportive staff and a diverse student body. It offers personal one-on-one attention from the faculty, and a friendly, supportive staff who cares about student success. It also features the beauty of a historic campus with new technology-rich academic buildings. All of this, plus the more than 200 faculty, 300 staff and 6,300 diverse students make Georgia Regents University a truly unique place to be."

Campus Setting

Georgia Regents is a public, comprehensive university. Founded as a postgraduate academy in 1783, it became a junior college in 1925, was incorporated into the state university system in 1958, and began granting four-year degrees in 1967. Its 72-acre campus is located on a former plantation in Augusta. A four-year institution, Georgia Regents University has an enrollment of 6,741 students. Campus facilities include: history museum · golf course. Georgia Regents University provides on-campus housing with 162 units that can accommodate 508 students. Housing options: single-student apartments.

Student Life and Activities

Most students (93 percent) live off campus. Georgia Regents University has 66 official student organizations. The most popular are: choir · concert and pep bands · jazz ensemble · drama guild · team managers. Georgia Regents University is a member of the Peach Bell Conference (Division II) and Division I Golf.

Academics and Learning Environment

Georgia Regents University has 259 full-time and 154 part-time faculty members, offering a student-to-faculty ratio of 18:1. The most common course size is 20 to 29 students. Georgia Regents University offers 48 majors with the most popular being biology, psychology and early childhood education and least popular being Spanish, art and music performance. The school has a general core requirement. Cooperative education is available. All first-year students must maintain a 1.3 GPA or higher to avoid academic probation. Other special academic programs that would appeal to a B student include: independent study · double majors · dual degrees · honors program · Phi Beta Kappa · internships · distance learning certificate programs.

B Student Support and Success

Georgia Regents offers an extensive First Year Experience to help new students transition to college life. Its goal is "to increase retention and help students successfully progress toward graduation."

GEORGIA REGENTS UNIVERSITY AUGUSTA

Highlights

Georgia Regents University Augusta
Augusta, GA (Pop. 195,844)
Location: Medium city
Four-year public
Founded: 1925
Website: http://www.gru.edu

Students
Total enrollment: 6,741
Undergrads: 5,961
Part-time students: 30%
From out-of-state: Not reported
Male/Female: 38%/62%
Live on-campus: 7%
In fraternities: 1%
In sororities: 1%
Off-campus employment rating: Good
Caucasian: 56%
African American: 26%
Hispanic: 4%
Asian: 3%
Hawaiian or Pacific Islander: <1%
Native American: <1%
Mixed (2+ ethnicities): 4%
International: 1%

Academics
Calendar: Semester
Student/faculty ratio: 18:1
Class size 9 or fewer: 11%
Class size 10-29: 65%
Class size 30-49: 22%
Class size 50-99: 2%
Class size 100 or more: -
Returning freshmen: 67%
Six-year graduation rate: 22%

Most Popular Majors
Biology
Psychology
Early childhood education

213

College Profiles

GEORGIA REGENTS UNIVERSITY AUGUSTA

Highlights

Admissions
Applicants: 2,424
Accepted: 1,316
Acceptance rate: 54.3%
Average GPA: 3.0
ACT range: 18-22
SAT Math range: 440-540
SAT Reading range: 440-540
SAT Writing range: Not reported

Deadlines
Early Action: No
Early Decision: No
Regular Action: Rolling admissions
Common Application: Not accepted

Financial Aid
In-state tuition: $5,512
Out-of-state tuition: $17,126
Room: Varies
Board: Varies
Books: Varies
Freshmen receiving need-based aid: 70%
Undergrads rec. need-based aid: 63%
Avg. aid package (freshmen): $1,219
Avg. aid package (undergrads): $1,511
Avg. debt upon graduation: $7,779

Prominent Alumni
Leila Denmark, co-developer of the pertussis vaccine; Dr. No-Hee Park, dean of the UCLA School of Dentistry; Garret Siler, former NBA basketball player.

School Spirit
Mascot: Jaguars
Colors: Blue and white

Participants take classes with other first year students, live together at University Village, have a close support group with mentors, get together for study sessions, attend campus social and athletic events and act as a part of a social support system that helps students meet others and share experiences with others.

Georgia Regents University provides many different support programs for students, including: academic · career · personal · minority students · military · veterans. Recognizing that some students may need extra preparation, Georgia Regents University offers remedial and refresher courses in: reading · writing · math · study skills. Annually, 67 percent of freshmen students return for their sophomore year. Companies that most frequently hire graduates from GRU include: Georgia State Merit System · Governor's Intern Program · Southtrust Bank · Georgia Department of Audits.

Support for Students with Learning Disabilities

Learning disabled students are often granted extra time to complete their degrees, as well as a lighter course load. LD students can access: remedial math · remedial English · remedial reading · learning center · testing accommodations · extended time for tests · take-home exam · oral tests · readers · typist/scribe · note-taking services · reading machines · tape recorders · diagnostic testing service · priority registration. Individual or small group tutorials are also available in: time management · organizational skills · learning strategies · writing labs · math labs · study skills. An advisor/advocate from the Testing & Disability Service is available to students.

How to Get Admitted

For admissions decisions, non-academic factors considered: state of residency. A high school diploma is required, although a GED is also accepted for admissions consideration. SAT or ACT test scores are required of all applicants. *According to the admissions office:* Admission based on eligibility index of standardized test scores and GPA; minimum eligibility index of 1830 required.

How to Pay for College

To apply for financial aid, students should submit the following: Free Application for Federal Student Aid (FAFSA). Georgia Regents University participates in the Federal Work Study program. *Need-based aid programs include:* scholarships and grants · general need-based awards · Federal Pell grants · state scholarships and grants · college-based scholarships and grants · private scholarships and grants. *Non-need-based aid programs include:* scholarships and grants · general need-based awards · state scholarships and grants · creative arts and performance awards · special achievements and activities awards · special characteristics awards · athletic scholarships · ROTC scholarships.

America's
Best Colleges for
B Students

GOUCHER COLLEGE

1021 Dulaney Valley Road, Baltimore, MD 21204
Admissions: 800-468-2437, extension 6100 · Financial Aid: 410-337-6141
Email: admissions@goucher.edu · Website: http://www.goucher.edu

From the College

"Goucher College is a small college with a big view of the world and intellectual community without boundaries. Here, students are prepared to embark on a life of inquiry and discovery, creativity and analytical thinking. Goucher students are able to put their learning into action through collaborative research in the natural sciences, guest residencies of renowned professors, service-learning programs that support local communities, internships and international study.

"Building on these strengths, our vision for a liberal arts education grows from the understanding that in the 21st century, every academic inquiry and intellectual endeavor has a global context. In all of our 31 majors, we encourage our students to explore their intellectual interests in ways that transcend the boundaries of traditional disciplines. Goucher's well-known study-abroad requirement comes with a great deal of curricular flexibility and a $1,200 stipend to help defray travel costs.

"Another asset is its soon-to-open Athenaeum: Part high-tech library, part public forum, part art gallery, part café and many others. The Athenaeum assumes an integrated, harmonious place within a pedestrian-friendly, architecturally unified campus. The world-class lecturers who visit this campus every year give our students the opportunity to step up and ask important questions of important people.

"The college's environmental initiatives, both curricular and extracurricular, have derived much of their direction and momentum from the suggestions and activities of our students. Representing 45 states and 27 countries, our students arrive at Goucher prepared to excel academically and eager to take advantage of the many resources offered on campus and in nearby Baltimore and Washington, DC. Our 287-acre campus boasts comfortable residence halls, a modern athletic complex and playing fields, stables and miles of wooded trails."

Campus Setting

Goucher is a selective, independent, coeducational institution dedicated to the interdisciplinary traditions of the liberal arts and a broad international perspective on education. Founded as a college for women in 1885, it adopted coeducation in 1987. Its 287-acre campus is located in Towson, eight miles north of the center of Baltimore. A four-year institution, Goucher College has an enrollment of 2,111 students. In addition to a large, well-stocked library, the campus also has an athenaeum. Goucher College provides on-campus housing with 659 units that can accommodate 1,210 students. Housing options: coed dorms · women's dorms · men's dorms · special housing for disabled students. Recreation and sports facilities include: cardio fitness center · racquetball courts · weight room and equipment room · swimming pool.

Student Life and Activities

The majority (84 percent) of students live on campus. As reported by a school official, "Goucher is more than just a residential college. It's a living and learning community in which the lines between those two key elements become blurred by design. Many of our residence halls have classrooms built into them. Some of the houses within them are centered on themes that inspire students to come together to study, hold club meetings, participate in activities and just enjoy one another's company. And all over campus, from the academic buildings to the dining halls to the student coffeehouse and beyond, there is a discernible energy of people sharing their ideas and

GOUCHER COLLEGE

Highlights

Goucher College
Towson, MD (Pop. 55,197)
Location: Large town
Four-year private
Founded: 1885
Website: http://www.goucher.edu

Students
Total enrollment: 2,111
Undergrads: 1,449
Freshmen: 478
Part-time students: 2%
From out-of-state: 81%
From public schools: 66%
Male/Female: 34%/66%
Live on-campus: 84%
Off-campus employment rating: Good
Caucasian: 68%
African American: 9%
Hispanic: 7%
Asian: 3%
Hawaiian or Pacific Islander: <1%
Native American: <1%
Mixed (2+ ethnicities): 4%
International: 2%

Academics
Calendar: Semester
Student/faculty ratio: 9:1
Class size 9 or fewer: 17%
Class size 10-29: 78%
Class size 30-49: 5%
Class size 50-99: 1%
Class size 100 or more: -
Returning freshmen: 86%
Six-year graduation rate: 68%

Most Popular Majors
Psychology
Communication
Management

perspectives, their learning and their lives. Once you are here, you won't have to go far to find a stellar array of cultural, social and education events. Throughout every year, Goucher's calendar is packed with lectures, readings and performances by internationally renowned guests and homegrown talent alike. There are more than 60 student-run clubs here. There's an active Student Government Association, plus 17 varsity sports teams and several intramural sports clubs, not to mention language clubs, political organizations, music groups and religious and art organizations. Across our whole campus, every day, you'll find people coming together around the interests they share. So, wherever you hail from or plan to go, you will find a way to explore your passions, as well as a community of people interested in what you have to share."

Popular gathering spots on-campus include The Gopher Hole and the library at the Aethenaeum. Off campus, students frequent the Inner Harbor and Fells Point. Popular campus events include The Kratz Center for Creative Writing Guest Speaker and Writer-in-Residence, Blind Date Ball, Spring Gala, Fusion Diversity Celebration, The Henry and Ruth Blaustein Rosenberg Lecture-Performance, The Janet and Avery Fisher Music Residency, Get Into Goucher Day, The Women Writing About Women Symposium, Dancers in Action Concerts, Choregraphie Antique Dance History Ensemble Concerts, The Mid-Atlantic Creative Nonfiction Summer Writers Conference and The Burke Jane Austen Scholar-in-Residence Lecture. Goucher College has 60 official student organizations. The Women's Interest Group, Umoja-African American group, the Quindecim and the Student Government Association have a strong presence in the school social life. For those interested in sports, there are intramural teams such as: basketball · lightweight football · racquetball · softball · Ultimate Frisbee. Goucher College is a member of the Landmark Athletic Conference (Division III).

Academics and Learning Environment

Goucher College has 138 full-time and 64 part-time faculty members, offering a student-to-faculty ratio of 9:1. The most common course size is 10 to 19 students. Goucher College offers 42 majors with the most popular being psychology, communication and management and least popular being computer science, women's studies, and physics. The school has a general core requirement. Cooperative education is available. All first-year students must maintain a set GPA to avoid academic probation. Other special academic programs that would appeal to a B student include: self-designed majors · pass/fail grading option · independent study · double majors · dual degrees · Phi Beta Kappa · internships · distance learning.

B Student Support and Success

Goucher's Academic Center for Excellence (ACE) is for all students and is based on the premise that each student has the ability to learn and successfully complete all college course work. Individual help in study skills is provided by mentors who are successful students that have been trained in peer counseling. They meet with students one or two times a week. Others work with students on issues like time management, procrastination prevention, organizational skills, memory and concentration, note and test taking strategies and test preparation. Study Skills Workshops are offered repeatedly on these same subjects. In addition to these services, Goucher offers supplemental instruction in the sciences and humanities. Study groups meet regularly with an instructor and work together as a team to better understand the material. A drop-in Math Lab is offered on campus Sunday through Thursday, and a Writing Center, although not part of ACE, is available to help students at all stages of the writing process.

Goucher College provides dedicated guidance for: academic · career · personal · psychological · minority students · veterans · non-traditional students · family planning · religious. Additional counseling services include: academic. Annually, 86 percent of freshmen students return for their sophomore year. Approximately 80 percent of students who are employed are in a field related to their major within six months of graduation. Companies that most frequently hire graduates from Goucher College include: Ameri-Corps · Baltimore City Public Schools · Baltimore County public schools · Goucher College · Johns Hopkins University · Lockheed Martin · Office of Senators/Representatives · Pierce Promotions and Event Management · University of Maryland.

Support for Students with Learning Disabilities

Students with learning disabilities may take advantage of additional time to complete their degree or pursue a lightened course load.

How to Get Admitted

For admissions decisions, non-academic factors considered: interview · extracurricular activities · special talents, interests and abilities · character/personal qualities · volunteer work · work experience · geographical location · minority affiliation · alumni relationship. A high school diploma is required, although a GED is also accepted for admissions consideration. SAT or ACT test scores are considered, if submitted, but are not required. *Academic units recommended:* 4 English, 4 Math, 3 Science, 3 Social Studies, 4 Foreign Language.

How to Pay for College

To apply for financial aid, students should submit the following: Free Application for Federal Student Aid (FAFSA) · CSS/Financial Aid PROFILE · Non-custodian (Divorced/Separated) Parent's Statement · Business/Farm Supplement. Goucher College participates in the Federal Work Study program. *Need-based aid programs include:* scholarships and grants · general need-based awards · Federal Pell grants · state scholarships and grants · college-based scholarships and grants · private scholarships and grants. *Non-need-based aid programs include:* scholarships and grants · state scholarships and grants · creative arts and performance awards.

GOUCHER COLLEGE

Highlights

Admissions
Applicants: 3,466
Accepted: 2,505
Acceptance rate: 72.3%
Placed on wait list: 160
Enrolled from wait list: 2
Average GPA: 3.2
ACT range: 23-28
SAT Math range: 500-620
SAT Reading range: 510-660
SAT Writing range: 11-32
Top 10% of class: 31%
Top 25% of class: 58%
Top 50% of class: 88%

Deadlines
Early Action: 12/1
Early Decision: 11/15
Regular Action: 2/1 (priority)
Notification of admission by: 4/1
Common Application: Accepted

Financial Aid
In-state tuition: $39,808
Out-of-state tuition: $39,808
Room: $6,798
Board: $4,066
Books: $1,000
Freshmen receiving need-based aid: 73%
Undergrads rec. need-based aid: 64%
Avg. % of need met by financial aid: 75%
Avg. aid package (freshmen): $29,709
Avg. aid package (undergrads): $29,199
Avg. debt upon graduation: $27,921

Prominent Alumni
Sarah Tilghman Hughes, federal judge, only woman to swear in a U.S. president (Lyndon B. Johnson); Zeke Berzoff-Cohen, founder/executive director, The Intersection; Bradford Shellhammer, co-founder, Fab.com.

School Spirit
Mascot: Gophers
Colors: Blue and gold

GRANITE STATE COLLEGE

Highlights

Granite State College

Location: Small town
Four-year public
Founded: 1972
Website: http://www.granite.edu

Students

Total enrollment: 2,058
Undergrads: 1,797
From out-of-state: 7%
Male/Female: 30%/70%
Live on-campus: 0%
Off-campus employment rating: Good
Caucasian: 82%
African American: 1%
Hispanic: 2%
Asian: 1%
Hawaiian or Pacific Islander: <1%
Native American: 1%
Mixed (2+ ethnicities): 2%
International: <1%

Academics

Calendar: Trimester
Student/faculty ratio: 10:1
Class size 9 or fewer: 50%
Class size 10-29: 50%
Class size 30-49: -
Class size 50-99: -
Class size 100 or more: -
Returning freshmen: 81%
Six-year graduation rate: 54%

Most Popular Majors

Individualized studies
Business
Behavioral science

Eight Old Suncook Road, Concord, NH 03301
Admissions: 603-513-1339 · Financial Aid: 603-513-1392
Email: ask.granite@granite.edu
Website: http://www.granite.edu

From the College

"Granite State College is the University System of New Hampshire's statewide college for adults of all ages. Innovative programs and flexible scheduling make it possible for students to balance responsibilities such as work and family while earning a college degree. Nine centers, many satellite classroom locations and an online Virtual Center make higher education accessible, engaging, and convenient. GSC faculty are experienced teachers with years of practical experience in their fields. Self-design Bachelor of Arts and Bachelor of Science degrees, along with a strong independent study program, match educational outcomes to students' individual interests and backgrounds."

Campus Setting

Founded in 1972, the mission of the college is to provide the citizens of the state with access to public higher education. Access is achieved in a number of ways. Granite State College operates nine Centers located strategically throughout the state and offers classes, advising and administrative services to students who live and work in each area. GSC delivers its programs and courses in formats that meet the needs of part-time students who are balancing family and work with their educational responsibilities. This includes classes offered in the evenings, during the weekends, totally online and through a hybrid or blended format. A four-year public institution, Granite State College has an enrollment of 1,797 students. Granite State College does not have on-campus housing for students.

Student Life and Activities

All students (100 percent) live off campus. Most students are adults and have established ties to the community and are not interested in college-based social events or activities. Students tend to remain focused on degree goals until graduation. Granite State College has two official student organizations: Alumni Learner Association · Green Team.

Academics and Learning Environment

Granite State College has 185 part-time faculty members, offering a student-to-faculty ratio of 10:1. The most common course size is 2 to 9 students. Granite State College offers 14 majors. Individualized studies, business and behavioral science are the top choices. Least popular are information technology, criminal justice and early childhood education. The school has a general core requirement. Cooperative education is available. All first-year students must maintain a 2.0 GPA or higher to avoid academic probation, and a minimum overall GPA of 2.0 is required to graduate. Other special academic programs include: self-designed majors · independent study · double majors · dual degrees · accelerated study · internships · distance learning.

B Student Support and Success

At this college, students can design their own bachelor's degree programs. Orientation sessions are offered year round, and academic advisors focus on helping enrollees prepare for tests, study and take notes. Academic Resource Coordinators provide additional academic services. The college's Academic Resource Center offers students computers, books, study sheets and multiple resources. In addition, skills assessments help students choose the best courses in writing and math. Regular workshops are offered throughout the year and cover the professional focus to personal support. Granite focuses on a set of core values in order to meet the educational needs of its students.

Granite State College provides a support programs for: academic · career · veterans · non-traditional students. Additional counseling services include: Financial aid counseling. Annually, 81 percent of freshmen students return for their sophomore year. Among students who are employed, approximately 94 percent enter a field related to their major within six months of graduation.

Support for Students with Learning Disabilities

If necessary, Granite State College will grant additional time to students with learning disabilities to complete their degree, plus offers programs such as: tutors · extended time for tests · take-home exam · readers · note-taking services · tape recorders · texts on tape · early syllabus · waiver of math degree requirement. Individual or small group tutorials are also available in: specific subject areas · writing labs · math labs · study skills. An advisor/advocate from the LD program is available to students.

How to Get Admitted

For admissions decisions, non-academic factors considered: interview · state of residency. A high school diploma is required, although a GED is also accepted for admissions consideration.

How to Pay for College

To apply for financial aid, students should submit the following: Free Application for Federal Student Aid (FAFSA) · institution's own financial aid forms. Granite State College participates in the Federal Work Study program. *Need-based aid programs include:* scholarships and grants · general need-based awards · Federal Pell grants · state scholarships and grants · college-based scholarships and grants · private scholarships and grants · New Hampshire Adult Student Aid Program. *Non-need-based aid programs include:* scholarships and grants · state scholarships and grants.

GRANITE STATE COLLEGE

Highlights

Admissions
Applicants: 267
Accepted: 267
Acceptance rate: 100%
Average GPA: Not reported
ACT range: Not reported
SAT Math range: Not reported
SAT Reading range: Not reported
SAT Writing range: Not reported

Deadlines
Early Action: No
Early Decision: No
Regular Action: Rolling admissions
Common Application: Not accepted

Financial Aid
In-state tuition: $8,550
Out-of-state tuition: $9,450
Room: Varies
Board: Varies
Books: $900
Freshmen receiving need-based aid: 91%
Undergrads receiving need-based or merit-based aid: 70%
Avg. aid package (freshmen): 90%
Avg. aid package (undergrads): Not reported

College Profiles

GREEN MOUNTAIN COLLEGE

1 Brennan Circle, Poultney, VT 05764-1199
Admissions: 802-287-8208 · Financial Aid: 802-287-8210
Email: admiss@greenmtn.edu · Website: http://www.greenmtn.edu

From the College

"Green Mountain College takes the environment as the unifying theme underlying the academic and social experience of the campus. Through a broad range of liberal arts and career-focused majors and a service-oriented student affairs program, the college fosters ideals of environmental responsibility, public service, international understanding and life-long intellectual, physical and spiritual development. Drawing on its rich and varied history, the College is committed to a spirit of adventure and leadership in undergraduate higher education."

Campus Setting

Green Mountain, founded in 1834, is a private college offering specialized programs in the fields of business and education. Its 155-acre campus is located in Poultney, 20 miles from Rutland. A four-year institution, Green Mountain College has an enrollment of 851 students, and has been co-ed since 1974. The school is also affiliated with the United Methodist Church. Green Mountain College provides on-campus housing that can accommodate 657 students. Housing options: coed dorms · single-student apartments · cooperative housing. Recreation and sports facilities include: gymnasium · playing fields · soccer and softball fields · swimming pool · weight room.

Student Life and Activities

Eighty-seven percent of students live on campus, and popular gathering spots include the Pub House, the Lake House and A.J.'s. Popular campus events include the spring concert. Green Mountain College has 56 official student organizations. The most popular are: America Reads · chorus · Do Everything Club (substance-free group) · drama and dance groups · educational policy committee · education and psychology clubs · judicial board · music guild · research groups · student life committee · volunteer groups · business association · New England Explorers · outing club. For those interested in sports, there are intramural teams such as: basketball · floor hockey · golf · rugby · snowboarding · soccer · softball · Ultimate Frisbee · volleyball.

Academics and Learning Environment

Green Mountain College has 42 full-time and 39 part-time faculty members, offering a student-to-faculty ratio of 14:1. The most common course size is 10 to 19 students. Out of Green Mountain College's 22 majors, the most popular is environmental studies. The school has a general core requirement. Cooperative education is not offered. All first-year students must maintain a 1.7 GPA or higher to avoid academic probation, and a minimum overall GPA of 2.0 is required to graduate. Other special academic programs that would appeal to a B student: self-designed majors · pass/fail grading option · independent study · double majors · dual degrees · honors program · internships · distance learning certificate programs.

B Student Support and Success

Green Mountain College provides a variety of support programs including dedicated guidance for: academic · career · personal · psychological · minority students · family planning · religious. Recognizing that some students may need extra preparation,

Green Mountain College offers remedial and refresher courses in: reading · writing · math · study skills. Annually, 69 percent of freshmen students return for their sophomore year.

Support for Students with Learning Disabilities

Green Mountain College offers students with learning disabilities extra time to complete their degree, as well as the option of taking a lightened course load. LD students may also want to look into: remedial math · tutors · learning center · extended time for tests · take-home exam · oral tests · readers · note-taking services · reading machines · tape recorders · texts on tape · early syllabus · priority registration · waiver of math degree requirement. Individual or small group tutorials are also available in: time management · organizational skills · learning strategies · specific subject areas · writing labs · math labs · study skills.

How to Get Admitted

For admissions decisions, non-academic factors considered: interview · extracurricular activities · special talents, interests and abilities · character/personal qualities · volunteer work · work experience · state of residency. A high school diploma is required, although a GED is also accepted for admissions consideration. SAT or ACT test scores are recommended but not required. SAT Subject Test scores are considered, if submitted, but are not required. *Academic units recommended:* 4 English, 4 Math, 4 Science, 3 Social Studies, 3 Foreign Language.

Insight

Sandra Bartholomew is the dean of enrollment management at Green Mountain College. She says the average GPA for incoming classes is about 3.0 and that GMC students are "passionate, committed and highly functioning young people who place a high value on interactive experiences that connect classroom learning with the real world." Academic programs are field-based and interdisciplinary. With small class sizes and a "talented, experienced" faculty (over 90 percent of professors at GMC have terminal degrees) students thrive on a campus that "values individuality and community." Results from the 2008 National Survey of Students Engagement (NSSE) show that students give GMC high marks compared to peer institutions in level of academic challenge, degree of active and collaborative learning, number of enriching educational experiences and degree of student/faculty interaction.

How to Pay for College

To apply for financial aid, students should submit the following: Free Application for Federal Student Aid (FAFSA) · state aid form · Scholarship forms. Green Mountain College participates in the Federal Work Study program. *Need-based aid programs include:* scholarships and grants · general need-based awards · Federal Pell grants · state scholarships and grants · college-based scholarships and grants · private scholarships and grants. *Non-need-based aid programs include:* scholarships and grants · general need-based awards · state

GREEN MOUNTAIN COLLEGE

Green Mountain College
Poultney, VT (Pop. 1,595)
Location: Rural
Four-year private
Founded: 1834
Website: http://www.greenmtn.edu

Students
Total enrollment: 851
Undergrads: 601
Freshmen: 167
Part-time students: 5%
From out-of-state: 91%
Male/Female: 44%/56%
Live on-campus: 87%
Off-campus employment rating: Fair
Caucasian: 62%
African American: 6%
Hispanic: 2%
Asian: 2%
Hawaiian or Pacific Islander: <1%
Native American: 1%
Mixed (2+ ethnicities): 2%
International: 4%

Academics
Calendar: Semester
Student/faculty ratio: 14:1
Class size 9 or fewer: 16%
Class size 10-29: 76%
Class size 30-49: 8%
Class size 50-99: -
Class size 100 or more: -
Returning freshmen: 69%
Six-year graduation rate: 39%

Most Popular Majors
Environmental studies

221

GREEN MOUNTAIN COLLEGE

Highlights

Admissions
Applicants: 773
Accepted: 584
Acceptance rate: 75.5%
Average GPA: 2.7
ACT range: Not reported
SAT Math range: 440-570
SAT Reading range: 480-630
SAT Writing range: Not reported

Deadlines
Early Action: 11/1
Early Decision: No
Regular Action: 3/1 (priority)
Common Application: Accepted

Financial Aid
In-state tuition: $32,594
Out-of-state tuition: $32,594
Room: Varies
Board: Varies
Books: $980
Freshmen receiving need-based aid: 81%
Undergrads rec. need-based aid: 79%
Avg. % of need met by financial aid: 69%
Avg. aid package (freshmen): $28,913
Avg. aid package (undergrads): $26,475
Avg. debt upon graduation: $33,448

Prominent Alumni
Catherine Villafranco Parker, vice president of Wainwright Bank & Trust Company; Lloyd Bartholomew, head of the gastroenterology section at the Mayo Clinic.

School Spirit
Mascot: Eagle
Colors: Green and gold
Song: *This Green Place*

scholarships and grants · creative arts and performance awards · special achievements and activities awards.

222

GUILFORD COLLEGE

5800 West Friendly Avenue, Greensboro, NC 27410
Admissions: 800-992-7759 · Financial Aid: 336-316-2165
Email: admission@guilford.edu · Website: http://www.guilford.edu

From the College

"Guilford College draws on Quaker and liberal arts traditions to produce lifelong learners and agents of change in the world. Student-centered instruction nurtures each individual amid an intentionally diverse community. A values-rich educational experience explores the ethical dimension of knowledge and promotes honesty, compassion, integrity, courage and respect for the individual. A challenging academic program fosters critical and creative thinking through analysis, inquiry, communication, consensus building, problem solving and leadership. A global perspective values people of other cultures and the natural environment in which we all live. Service opportunities forge a connection between thought and action."

Campus Setting

Guilford, founded in 1837, is a church-affiliated college. Its 300-acre campus is located in northwest Greensboro in the Piedmont section of North Carolina. Campus architecture reflects a Georgian Colonial influence. A four-year private institution, Guilford College has an enrollment of 2,302 students. The school is also affiliated with the Society of Friends Church. Campus facilities include: art gallery · language lab · science center · observatory. Guilford College provides on-campus housing with 11 units that can accommodate 1,043 students. Housing options: coed dorms · women's dorms · men's dorms · single-student apartments · special housing for international students. Recreation and sports facilities include: athletic center · fields · field house · golf club · gymnasium · park · physical education center · swimming pool · tennis courts.

Student Life and Activities

Three-quarters (77 percent) of students live on campus. They enjoy spending time at the Student Union, gazebo and the lake. Popular campus events include Serendipity Spring Festival and the Eastern Music Festival. Guilford College has 45 official student organizations. The most popular are: Expressions in Dance · cooking club · organic gardening · photo club · poetry club · Fancy Feet and Fingers · Campus Activities Board · Community Aids Awareness Project · Forevergreen · French club · German club · Gender Equality Now · GPeace · Pride · Project Community · Community Senate · College Democrats · forensic biology club · health science cub · history club · psychology club · archery club · outdoors club. For those interested in sports, there are intramural teams such as: baseball · basketball · bowling · cheerleading · non-tackle football · rugby · soccer · softball · table tennis · tennis · volleyball · water polo. Guilford College is a member of the Old Dominion Athletic Conference (Division III).

Academics and Learning Environment

Guilford College has 118 full-time and 69 part-time faculty members, offering a student-to-faculty ratio of 15:1. The most common course size is 10 to 19 students. Of Guilford College's 37 majors, the most popular are business/marketing, social sciences and psychology. The school has a general core requirement. Cooperative education is available. All first-year students must maintain a 2.0 GPA or higher to avoid academic probation. Other special academic programs include: self-designed majors · pass/fail grading option · independent study · double majors · dual degrees · honors program · internships · weekend college · certificate programs.

223

College Profiles

GUILFORD COLLEGE

Highlights

Guilford College
Greensboro, NC (Pop. 277,080)
Location: Medium city
Four-year private
Founded: 1837
Website: http://www.guilford.edu

Students
Total enrollment: 2,302
Undergrads: 2,302
Freshmen: 444
Part-time students: 16%
From out-of-state: 43%
From public schools: 75%
Male/Female: 44%/56%
Live on-campus: 77%
Off-campus employment rating: Fair
Caucasian: 61%
African American: 24%
Hispanic: 5%
Asian: 3%
Hawaiian or Pacific Islander: <1%
Native American: <1%
Mixed (2+ ethnicities): 3%
International: 2%

Academics
Calendar: 4-1-4 system
Student/faculty ratio: 15:1
Class size 9 or fewer: 12%
Class size 10-29: 82%
Class size 30-49: 5%
Class size 50-99: -
Class size 100 or more: -
Returning freshmen: 68%
Six-year graduation rate: 57%

Most Popular Majors
Business/marketing
Social sciences
Psychology

America's
Best Colleges for
B Students

B Student Support and Success

At Guilford, the SAT is optional. Writing samples and an interview are required when a student does not submit standardized test scores. It is home to a high school preparation school with 100 students. In a required first-year class, students are taken on campus tours, shown various resources and helped to transition to college life.

Guilford College provides dedicated guidance for: academic · career · personal · psychological · minority students · veterans · non-traditional students · family planning · religious. Additional counseling services include: first-year transitional counseling. Guilford College offers remedial and refresher courses in: reading · writing · math · study skills. Other remedial services include science. The average freshman year GPA is 2.9, and 68 percent of freshmen students return for their sophomore year. Of those who are employed, approximately 65 percent enter a field related to their major within six months of graduation. Companies that most frequently hire graduates from Guilford College include: AmeriCorps Vista · banking industry · Friends Schools (various) · Guilford College · Guilford County · Guilford County Schools · Konica Minolta Manufacturing · Moses Cone Hospital · Peace Corps · People Inc. of Southwest Virginia · Rockingham County · Vanity Fair.

Support for Students with Learning Disabilities

Guilford College permits students with learning disabilities to take additional time to complete their degree and /or carry a lightened course load. High school foreign language and math waivers are accepted. Students with learning disabilities may also want to explore: special classes · tutors · learning center · testing accommodations · untimed tests · extended time for tests · take-home exam · oral tests · readers · note-taking services · reading machines · tape recorders. Individual or small group tutorials are also available in: time management · organizational skills · learning strategies · specific subject areas · study skills. An advisor/advocate from the Disability Services is available to students. This member also sits on the admissions committee.

How to Get Admitted

For admissions decisions, non-academic factors considered: interview · extracurricular activities · special talents, interests and abilities · character/personal qualities · volunteer work · work experience · geographical location · religious affiliation/commitment · minority affiliation · alumni relationship. A high school diploma is required, although a GED is also accepted for admissions consideration. SAT or ACT test scores are considered, if submitted, but are not required. SAT Subject Test scores are considered, if submitted, but are not required. *According to the admissions office:* Minimum 2.0 GPA required. *Academic units recommended:* 4 English, 3 Math, 3 Science, 3 Social Studies, 2 Foreign Language.

Insight

"We have a multi-layer approach to student success," says the Guilford staff. The First Year Program addresses the needs of first year Guilford students from the time they are admitted to the college until they declare their major. To assist the students in their transition into college life, the First Year Program coordinates all contact with the students during the summer prior to their first year. Through CHAOS (Guilford College's Orientation Program), First Year Experience classes and the FYE lab, the First Year Program steers students to target issues of diversity, academic success and the new student experience.

"The Learning Commons is ready to help students become more efficient and self-directed learners," says the college staff. The LC offers faculty tutors and peer tutors, in group or individual sessions. Faculty tutors help students with quantitative skills, writing, reading, study skills, test taking and time management. Students are active in three peer tutoring groups: Writing Studio peer tutors (students can help brainstorm a paper, discuss the focus and support in a paper a student has written or give feedback on a draft); Chemistry 911 (students can get help with intro-level chemistry courses); and a large Student Tutoring Service (tutoring in specific courses across the curriculum). While Guilford doesn't have a special program for students with disabilities, the college does have useful services for these students.

"Many students do well academically in spite of frustrating 'glitches,'" says the staff. The retention rate for students with learning disabilities is approximately the same as that of the college in general. The staff reports that students who do best are generally those who work hard, who consult with advisors to carefully plan/balance classes and schedules and who are good self-advocates. The staff also says that students with learning differences often know themselves well as learners and so they regularly "offer us new ideas and strategies and fresh insights into methods that work."

According to the college, Guilford is looking for students who have challenged themselves academically, who have been involved in their high school and home communities and who have shown leadership and the potential to be successful in the college's academic environment. Students should show a desire to be successful in college.

"Drive to succeed goes a long way to making us feel that a student can make a difference in our environment," says the staff. Grades are relative to the school environment. The college wants to see that a student has given a strong effort in a challenging course setting.

"The grade alone does not tell the whole story. We look at the school setting, the course title and level. We want hard-working students who have the desire to be successful at Guilford and to graduate," says the staff.

How to Pay for College

To apply for financial aid, students should submit the following: Free Application for Federal Student Aid (FAFSA) · CSS/Financial Aid PROFILE · Non-custodian (Divorced/Separated) Parent's Statement · Business/Farm Supplement. Guilford College participates in the Federal Work Study program. *Need-based aid programs include:* scholarships and grants · general need-based awards · Federal Pell grants · state scholarships and grants · college-based scholarships and grants · private scholarships and grants. *Non-need-based aid programs include:* scholarships and grants · state scholarships and grants · special achievements and activities awards.

GUILFORD COLLEGE

Highlights

Admissions
Applicants: 3,030
Accepted: 2,066
Acceptance rate: 68.2%
Placed on wait list: 101
Enrolled from wait list: 2
Average GPA: 3.2
ACT range: 20-26
SAT Math range: 490-600
SAT Reading range: 480-620
SAT Writing range: 4-17
Top 10% of class: 11%
Top 25% of class: 33%
Top 50% of class: 69%

Deadlines
Early Action: Rolling
Early Decision: No
Regular Action: Rolling admissions
Common Application: Accepted

Financial Aid
In-state tuition: $33,050
Out-of-state tuition: $33,050
Room: Varies
Board: Varies
Books: $1,600
Freshmen receiving need-based aid: 85%
Undergrads rec. need-based aid: 85%
Avg. % of need met by financial aid: 83%
Avg. aid package (freshmen): $25,729
Avg. aid package (undergrads): $20,980
Avg. debt upon graduation: $24,255

Prominent Alumni
M.L. Carr, NBA player, coach and executive; Rick Goings, CEO, Tupperwave Corporation; Howard Coble, congressman.

School Spirit
Mascot: Quakers
Colors: Dark red and grey

225

GUSTAVUS ADOLPHUS COLLEGE

800 West College Avenue, St. Peter, MN 56082
Admissions: 800-487-8288 · Financial Aid: 800-487-8288
Email: admission@gustavus.edu · Website: http://www.gustavus.edu

From the College

"The oldest Lutheran college in Minnesota, Gustavus was founded in 1862 by Swedish Lutheran immigrants and named for Swedish King Gustav II Adolf. Gustavus Adolphus College is affiliated with the Evangelical Lutheran Church in America. Throughout its history, it has valued its Lutheran and Swedish heritages. The Gustavus culture derives from our founding traditions and offers a distinctiveness of feeling and deed on the campus and in the greater world.

"At Gustavus, students receive personal attention in small-sized classes and engage in collaborative research with their professors. The college is fully accredited and known for its strong music, science, writing, athletics, study-abroad and service-learning programs. We maintain a chapter of Phi Beta Kappa and our annual Mayday! Peace Conference, an event devoted to topics relating to human rights and social justice. Gustavus is internationally recognized for its annual Nobel Conference. This signature event was launched in 1965 following a gathering on campus of 26 Nobel laureates for the dedication of the Nobel Hall of Science in 1963. The conference brings cutting-edge science issues to the attention of the public, engages world-renowned science speakers and provides opportunities to explore the moral and societal impact of scientific issues.

"Gustavus holds the conviction that religious faith enriches and informs learning and is a fundamental notion underpinning our emphasis on community, ethics and service. While strongly Lutheran in tradition and character, conformity to that specific faith tradition is not expected.

"We embrace the notion that true leadership expresses itself in service to others, and affirm the classical ideal of a liberating education, an education that frees one to serve God and humanity to the best of one's ability."

Campus Setting

Gustavus Adolphus, founded in 1862, is a church-affiliated, private liberal arts college. Its 340-acre campus is located in St. Peter, 60 miles southwest of Minneapolis-St. Paul. A four-year institution, Gustavus Adolphus College has an enrollment of 2,455 students. The school is also affiliated with the Lutheran Church. Gustavus Adolphus College provides on-campus housing with 20 units that can accommodate 2,081 students. Housing options: coed dorms · single-student apartments. Recreation and sports facilities include: arboretum · baseball, soccer and softball field · basketball, volleyball and indoor/outdoor tennis courts · country club · football stadium · gymnastics studio · ice rink · natatorium · track complex.

Student Life and Activities

The majority (85 percent) of students live on campus. According to the student newspaper, campus organizations try to make up for Gustavus' small-town atmosphere, and their success is apparent in how few students leave for the weekend—very few. Greek events and successful varsity sports offer many reasons to stick around. The favorite on-campus gathering spot is The Dive, a non-alcoholic dance club. Off campus, students frequent local bars and house parties. Popular events on campus include Nobel Conference, MayDay! Conference, Christmas in Christ Chapel, Honors Day and Building Bridges. Gustavus Adolphus College has 120 official student organizations. Greeks and athletes have a widespread influence on campus life. For those interested in sports, there are intramural teams such as: badminton · basketball · broomball · flag football · golf · hockey · racquetball · soccer · softball · tennis · Ultimate Frisbee · volleyball · walleyball. Gustavus Adolphus College is a member of the Minnesota Intercollegiate Athletic Conference (Division III).

Academics and Learning Environment

Gustavus Adolphus College has 201 full-time and 51 part-time faculty members, offering a student-to-faculty ratio of 11:1. The most common course size is 10 to 19 students. Gustavus Adolphus College offers 48 majors. The most popular are business administration, biology and education and least popular are Russian, German and Japanese studies. The school has a general core requirement as well as a religion requirement. Cooperative education is not offered. All first-year students must maintain a 1.8 GPA or higher to avoid academic probation. Other special academic programs include: self-designed majors · independent study · double majors · dual degrees · honors program · Phi Beta Kappa · internships.

B Student Support and Success

Gustavus Adolphus offers a Writing Center for one-on-one consultation and help with reading and interpreting assignments. The Advising Center helps coordinate meetings between students, advisors and professors to make the most of career help.

Gustavus Adolphus College provides a variety of support programs including: academic · career · personal · psychological · minority students · family planning · religious. The average freshman year GPA is 3.3, and 91 percent of freshmen students return for their sophomore year. After college, 26 percent return for a graduate degree. Approximately 31 percent of graduates working are in a field related to their majors within six months of graduation. Companies that most frequently hire graduates from Gustavus Adolphus College include: Federated Insurance · Liberty Mutual · Mayo Clinic · Target.

Support for Students with Learning Disabilities

According to Gustavus Adolphus College, Disability Services offers counseling and accommodations to all students who self-identify and provide documentation. Students must also meet with the Disability Services Coordinator and register with Disability Services. One-on-one peer tutoring is also available as well as designated tutors to serve students with LD in the Writing Center. Additional services include a computer with the Kurzweil system installed. Students with learning disabilities will find the following programs at Gustavus Adolphus College useful: tutors · learning center · testing accommodations · extended time for tests · take-home exam · oral tests · exam on tape or computer · readers · typist/scribe · note-taking services · proofreading services · reading machines · tape recorders · texts on tape · early syllabus · special bookstore section · priority registration · waiver of foreign language degree requirement. Individual or small group tutorials are also available in: time management · organizational skills · learning strategies · specific subject areas · writing labs · math labs · study skills. An advisor/advocate from the Disability Services/Advising and Counseling is available to students.

GUSTAVUS ADOLPHUS COLLEGE

Highlights

Gustavus Adolphus College
Saint Peter, MN (Pop. 11,427)
Location: Small town
Four-year private
Founded: 1862
Website: http://www.gustavus.edu

Students
Total enrollment: 2,455
Undergrads: 2,455
Freshmen: 610
Part-time students: 1%
From out-of-state: 19%
From public schools: 93%
Male/Female: 46%/54%
Live on-campus: 85%
In fraternities: 11%
In sororities: 12%
Off-campus employment rating: Excellent
Caucasian: 84%
African American: 2%
Hispanic: 3%
Asian: 4%
Native American: <1%
Mixed (2+ ethnicities): 3%
International: 3%

Academics
Calendar: 4-1-4 system
Student/faculty ratio: 11:1
Class size 9 or fewer: 18%
Class size 10-29: 66%
Class size 30-49: 16%
Class size 50-99: 1%
Class size 100 or more: -
Returning freshmen: 91%
Six-year graduation rate: 82%

Most Popular Majors
Business administration
Biology
Education

227

College Profiles

GUSTAVUS ADOLPHUS COLLEGE

Highlights

Admissions
Applicants: 4,804
Accepted: 3,037
Acceptance rate: 63.2%
Average GPA: 3.6
ACT range: 24-30
SAT Math range: 530-660
SAT Reading range: 550-680
SAT Writing range: Not reported
Top 10% of class: 33%
Top 25% of class: 67%
Top 50% of class: 95%

Deadlines
Early Action: 11/1
Early Decision: No
Regular Action: Rolling admissions
Common Application: Accepted

Financial Aid
In-state tuition: $39,550
Out-of-state tuition: $39,550
Room: $5,950
Board: $3,300
Books: $900
Freshmen receiving need-based aid: 78%
Undergrads rec. need-based aid: 72%
Avg. % of need met by financial aid: 89%
Avg. aid package (freshmen): $31,847
Avg. aid package (undergrads): $30,614
Avg. debt upon graduation: $26,818

Prominent Alumni
James M. McPherson; Peter Krause; Margaret Anderson Kelliher.

School Spirit
Mascot: Gus the Lion
Colors: Black and gold
Song: *Gustie Rouser*

How to Get Admitted

For admissions decisions, non-academic factors considered: interview · extracurricular activities · special talents, interests and abilities · character/personal qualities · volunteer work · work experience · state of residency · geographical location · minority affiliation · alumni relationship. A high school diploma is required, although a GED is also accepted for admissions consideration. SAT or ACT test scores are considered, if submitted, but are not required. *According to the admissions office:* Rank in top third of secondary school class recommended. *Academic units recommended:* 4 English, 4 Math, 3 Science, 2 Social Studies, 3 Foreign Language.

How to Pay for College

To apply for financial aid, students should submit the following: Free Application for Federal Student Aid (FAFSA) · institution's own financial aid forms · CSS/Financial Aid PROFILE. Gustavus Adolphus College participates in the Federal Work Study program. *Need-based aid programs include:* scholarships and grants · general need-based awards · Federal Pell grants · state scholarships and grants · college-based scholarships and grants · private scholarships and grants. *Non-need-based aid programs include:* scholarships and grants · general need-based awards · state scholarships and grants · creative arts and performance awards · special achievements and activities awards · special characteristics awards · ROTC scholarships.

America's
Best Colleges for
B Students

HAMPDEN-SYDNEY COLLEGE

P.O. Box 667, Hampden-Sydney, VA 23943
Admissions: 800-755-0733 · Financial Aid: 434-223-6119
Email: hsapp@hsc.edu · Website: http://www.hsc.edu

From the College

"Hampden-Sydney College's spirit lies in its sense of community and its preservation of tradition. HSC is all about seeking to form good men and good citizens in an atmosphere of sound learning. Challenged by the curriculum and guided by the professors, students can get help when they need it because classes are small. The greatest advantage of small-college life is that everyone can be involved. Athletics, debating, publications, fraternity life—all are part of the education process. Many students enjoy the outdoors: hunting, fishing, camping and hiking. Public service, leadership and volunteerism are developed through opportunities to participate in the HSC Volunteer Fire Department, The Wilson Center for Leadership, community service projects with the local community and 'Beyond the Hill' community service trips to Belize, Honduras and other service-oriented trips abroad. In addition to the college's own study abroad programs, HSC students are eligible to participate and earn academic credit in approved foreign-study programs in Europe, Central and South America, South and East Asia, the Middle East and the Virginia program at Oxford. In addition, the HSC faculty develops May Term Abroad programs in special topics in their discipline. Past programs have included European Union Studies in France, Economics/Political Science/Culture studies in Eastern Europe, Tropical Biology in Mexico, Theatre in Scotland, Language Immersion in Spain and Area Studies in Egypt. The total experience at the college produces a man well-suited for the challenges of a job, the demands of social service and the pleasure of personal endeavors."

Campus Setting

Hampden-Sydney, founded in 1775, is a private, liberal arts college for men. Its 1,340-acre campus, including Federal style architecture, is located 65 miles southwest of Richmond. A four-year men's college, Hampden Sydney College has an enrollment of 1,070 students. The school is also affiliated with the Presbyterian Church. Campus facilities include: museum · center for leadership · athletic hall of fame. Hampden Sydney College provides on-campus housing with 51 units that can accommodate 1,122 students. Housing options: men's dorms · fraternity housing · single-student apartments · married-student apartments · special housing for international students. Recreation and sports facilities include: field house · gymnasium · fitness center · indoor swimming pool.

Student Life and Activities

With 95 percent of students living on campus, there are plenty of popular gathering spots including The Tiger Inn, Kirby Field House, Main Street Lanes and Macado's. Popular campus events include Family Weekend, Homecoming Concert, Symposium, Music Festival, Greek Week, ODAC Basketball and Signing of the Honor Code. Hampden-Sydney College has 68 official student organizations. The most popular are: Film, French, philosophy, psychology and Spanish clubs · Animation Society · WWHS-FM · Pre-Business Society · Pre-Healthy Society · Pre-Law Society · College Democrats · College Republicans · athletic club · Outsiders Club · Madisonian Society · Ambassadorial Committee · Volunteer Fire Department · Good Men Good Citizens · Student Admissions Committee · Student Development Committee · Student Museum Board · Future Educators Club · Union-Philanthropic Society · Society

HAMPDEN-SYDNEY COLLEGE

Hampden-Sydney College
Hampden-Sydney, VA (Pop. 1,450)
Location: Rural
Four-year private men's college
Founded: 1775
Website: http://www.hsc.edu

Students
Total enrollment: 1,070
Undergrads: 1,070
Freshmen: 292
Part-time students: Not reported
From out-of-state: 29%
From public schools: 67%
Male/Female: 100%/ 0%
Live on-campus: 95%
In fraternities: 34%
Off-campus employment rating: Fair
Caucasian: 81%
African American: 8%
Hispanic: 2%
Asian: 2%
Hawaiian or Pacific Islander: <1%
Native American: 1%
Mixed (2+ ethnicities): 5%
International: <1%

Academics
Calendar: Semester
Student/faculty ratio: 11:1
Class size 9 or fewer: 32%
Class size 10-29: 65%
Class size 30-49: 3%
Class size 50-99: -
Class size 100 or more: -
Returning freshmen: 77%
Six-year graduation rate: 62%

Most Popular Majors
Economics
History
Economics/business

for the Preservation of Southern Heritage. For those interested in sports, there are intramural teams such as: clay target · dodgeball · fly fishing · lacrosse · rugby · skiing · soccer · snowboarding · volleyball. Hampden-Sydney College is a member of the Old Dominion Athletic Conference (Division III).

Academics and Learning Environment

Hampden-Sydney College has 92 full-time and 15 part-time faculty members, offering a student-to-faculty ratio of 11:1. The most common course size is 10 to 19 students. Hampden-Sydney College's 27 majors include the popular economics, history and economics/business, and the less popular fine arts, German and applied computational physics. The school has a general core requirement. Cooperative education is available. All first-year students must maintain a 1.5 GPA or higher to avoid academic probation, and a minimum overall GPA of 2.0 is required to graduate. Other special academic programs that would appeal to a B student: independent study · double majors · dual degrees · honors program · Phi Beta Kappa · internships.

B Student Support and Success

Hampden-Sydney College offers a number of services for the B student. The Advising Program is for all freshmen. They are assigned an Academic Advisor who, in turn, helps with class selection, study skills development and transitioning to college life. Pre Term Workshops are offered before the fall semester begins to help students develop and improve academic skills and tutoring is available in a number of different courses, Academic Skills Workshops are offered weekly on topics such as goal setting, time management, note taking, reading skills, active learning, test taking and preparation, charting academic progress and dealing with stress.

Hampden-Sydney College provides a variety of support programs including: academic · career · personal · psychological · minority students · religious. The average freshman year GPA is 2.7, and 77 percent of freshmen students return for their sophomore year. Approximately 25 percent go after a graduate degree right after graduation. One year after graduation, the school reports that 32 percent of graduates have entered graduate school. Among those students who are employed, approximately 30 percent enter a field related to their major within six months of graduation. Companies that most frequently hire graduates from Hampden-Sydney College include: AIG SunAmerica Securities · Anheuser-Busch · Blue Ridge Outdoors Magazine · Ferguson Enterprises · HomeTown Realty · JP Morgan · McGuire Woods LLP · Merrill Lynch · Morgan Stanley · Signature Government Solutions · Suntrust · Swiss Finance Academy · U.S. Senate, Congress and Representatives · Wachovia · the White House · Youth Service International.

Support for Students with Learning Disabilities

According to Hampden-Sydney College, most services in the Academic Success office are available to all students, regardless of whether a disability has been identified (testing and course accommodations excluded). Students with learning disabilities may also look into: tutors · learning center · extended time for tests · oral tests · note-taking services · reading machines · tape recorders · texts on tape · videotaped classes · waiver of math degree requirement. Individual or small group tutorials are also available in: time management · organizational skills · learning strategies · specific subject areas · writing labs · math labs · study skills. An advisor/advocate from the LD program is available to students.

How to Get Admitted

For admissions decisions, non-academic factors considered: interview · extracurricular activities · character/personal qualities · volunteer work · work experience · state of residency · minority affiliation · alumni relationship. A high school diploma is required, although a GED is also accepted for admissions consideration. SAT or ACT test scores are required of all applicants. SAT Subject Test scores are recommended but not required. *According to the admissions office:* Rank in top two-fifths of secondary school class and minimum GPA 3.0 recommended, and a minimum 2.0 GPA is required. *Academic units recommended:* 4 English, 4 Math, 3 Science, 1 Social Studies, 3 Foreign Language.

How to Pay for College

To apply for financial aid, students should submit the following: Free Application for Federal Student Aid (FAFSA) · CSS/Financial Aid PROFILE · state aid form. Hampden-Sydney College participates in the Federal Work Study program. *Need-based aid programs include:* scholarships and grants · general need-based awards · Federal Pell grants · state scholarships and grants · college-based scholarships and grants · private scholarships and grants. *Non-need-based aid programs include:* scholarships and grants · general need-based awards · state scholarships and grants · special achievements and activities awards · ROTC scholarships.

HAMPDEN-SYDNEY COLLEGE

Highlights

Admissions
Applicants: 2,623
Accepted: 1,439
Acceptance rate: 54.9%
Average GPA: 3.4
ACT range: 22-27
SAT Math range: 510-615
SAT Reading range: 495-600
SAT Writing range: Not reported
Top 10% of class: 13%
Top 25% of class: 28%
Top 50% of class: 85%

Deadlines
Early Action: 1/15
Early Decision: 11/15
Regular Action: 3/1 (final)
Notification of admission by: 4/15
Common Application: Accepted

Financial Aid
In-state tuition: $38,018
Out-of-state tuition: $38,018
Room: Varies
Board: Varies
Books: $1,298
Freshmen receiving need-based aid: 19%
Avg. % of need met by financial aid: 79%
Avg. aid package (freshmen): $28,503
Avg. aid package (undergrads): $29,135
Avg. debt upon graduation: $28,651

Prominent Alumni
Dr. Eugene Hickcock, U.S. Deputy Secretary of Education; Dr. Randall Chitwood, chairman of surgery, East Carolina University; Scott Cooper, director, Crazy Heart.

School Spirit
Mascot: Tiger
Colors: Garnet and gray

231

HAMPTON UNIVERSITY

100 East Queen Street, Hampton, VA 23668
Admissions: 800-624-3328 · Financial Aid: 800-624-3341
Email: admit@hamptonu.edu · Website: http://www.hamptonu.edu

From the College

"Students at Hampton University say that Hampton is a school of rich tradition, family values and excellent education. Hampton is a comprehensive multicultural and historically black institution dedicated to the promotion of world-class learning, building of character and preparation of promising students of all backgrounds for positions of leadership and service. In addition, its strong liberal arts curriculum provides students with a panoramic view. . . a map of the universe. Others say that Hampton students have a certain attitude and flare about themselves that you will not see on other campuses. He or she is poised, considerate, self-sufficient, driven and a leader. Lastly, the historic campus where Booker T. Washington graduated is unique and sits on the waterfront and provides a living and learning atmosphere like no other. Hampton University, our home by the sea, is a blend of past traditions with innovative twenty-first century teaching and research."

Campus Setting

Hampton, founded in 1868, is a historically-black, private, liberal arts university. Programs are offered through the Schools of Business, Engineering and Technology, Liberal Arts and Education, Nursing, Pharmacy, and Science, and through the College of Continuing Education and the Graduate College. Its 314-acre campus, including buildings listed with the National Register of Historic Places, is located within 40 miles of Jamestown, Yorktown and Williamsburg. A four-year institution, Hampton University has 4,622 students. Campus facilities include: museum · chapel. Hampton University provides on-campus housing with 22 units that can accommodate 3,066 students. Housing options: coed dorms · women's dorms · men's dorms. Recreation and sports facilities include a gymnasium.

Student Life and Activities

Well more than half (56 percent) of students live on campus. The social and cultural atmosphere of the Hampton University community is one characterized by African-American unity. In addition, Hampton encourages academic as well as social development and the importance of reaching out to the community surrounding the campus. On campus, students gather at the student union and the library; off campus, Ogden Circle and Hampden Harbor are popular hangouts. Popular annual events include Homecoming, the Black Family Conference, the Mass Media Arts Symposium and Career Day. Hampton University has 110 official student organizations. The Student Government Association, the Student Christian Association and the Greek community are among the groups that have a widespread influence on campus life. Intramural teams include: basketball. Hampton University is a member of the Mid-Eastern Athletic Conference (Division I, Football I-AA).

Academics and Learning Environment

Hampton University has 323 full-time and 90 part-time faculty members, offering a student-to-faculty ratio of 10:1. The most common course size is two to nine students. Hampton University offers 90 majors. The most popular are biology, psychology and business administration. The school has a general core requirement. Cooperative education is available. All first-year students must maintain a 2.0 GPA or higher to avoid academic probation, and a minimum overall GPA of 2.0 is required to graduate.

Other special academic programs that would appeal to a B student include: pass/fail grading option · independent study · double majors · dual degrees · accelerated study · honors program · Phi Beta Kappa · internships · distance learning.

B Student Support and Success

Student Support Services is a federally funded program that, like many others, helps to support students as long as they meet one or more of three criteria: 1) come from a family where neither parent has a college degree, 2) come from a low-income family or 3) have a documented learning or physical disability. This program provides educational support service through counseling, tutoring and educational and career seminars. The overall goal is to develop and implement educational services and activities that will motivate and assist students toward the achievement of their academic, career, social and personal goals.

Hampton University provides dedicated guidance for: academic · career · personal · military · veterans · non-traditional students · religious. Hampton University offers remedial and refresher courses in: reading · writing · math · study skills. The average freshman year GPA is 3.3, and 76 percent of freshmen students return for their sophomore year. While many enter the workforce, approximately 46 percent pursue a graduate degree right after graduation. One year after graduation, the school reports that 12 percent of graduates have entered graduate school. Among students who enter the workforce, approximately 26 percent enter a field related to their major within six months of graduation. Companies that most frequently hire graduates from Hampton University include: Daimler Chrysler · Johnson and Johnson · Lockheed Martin.

Support for Students with Learning Disabilities

Students with learning disabilities may take advantage of a lightened course load. High school foreign language waivers are accepted. Students with learning disabilities will find the following programs helpful: remedial math · remedial English · remedial reading · special classes · tutors · testing accommodations · untimed tests · extended time for tests · oral tests · readers · typist/scribe · note-taking services · reading machines · tape recorders · texts on tape · diagnostic testing service · priority registration · priority seating · waiver of foreign language degree requirement. Individual or small group tutorials are also available in: time management · organizational skills · learning strategies · specific subject areas · writing labs · math labs · study skills. An advisor/advocate from the LD program is available to students.

How to Get Admitted

For admissions decisions, non-academic factors considered: extracurricular activities · special talents, interests and abilities · character/personal qualities · volunteer work · work experience · state of residency · alumni relationship. A high school diploma is required, although a GED is also accepted for admissions consideration. SAT or ACT test scores are required for some applicants. *According to the admissions office:* Test optional policy for applicants with a minimum 3.3 GPA or rank in the top 10% of their secondary school class. One recommendation from a teacher in a core subject area recommended

HAMPTON UNIVERSITY

Highlights

Hampton University
Hampton, VA (Pop. 136,836)
Location: Medium city
Four-year private
Founded: 1868
Website: http://www.hamptonu.edu

Students
Total enrollment: 4,622
Undergrads: 3,742
Freshmen: 1,301
Part-time students: 7%
From out-of-state: 79%
From public schools: 90%
Male/Female: 36%/64%
Live on-campus: 56%
In fraternities: 5%
In sororities: 4%
Off-campus employment rating: Good
Caucasian: 4%
African American: 92%
Hispanic: 1%
Asian: 1%
Hawaiian or Pacific Islander: <1%
Native American: <1%
Mixed (2+ ethnicities): <1%
International: 1%

Academics
Calendar: Semester
Student/faculty ratio: 10:1
Class size 9 or fewer: 30%
Class size 10-29: 55%
Class size 30-49: 14%
Class size 50-99: 1%
Class size 100 or more: -
Returning freshmen: 76%
Six-year graduation rate: 68%

Most Popular Majors
Biology
Psychology
Business administration

233

HAMPTON UNIVERSITY

Highlights

Admissions
Applicants: 15,337
Accepted: 5,529
Acceptance rate: 36.1%
Average GPA: 3.3
ACT range: 18-23
SAT Math range: 460-540
SAT Reading range: 460-550
SAT Writing range: Not reported
Top 10% of class: 20%
Top 25% of class: 45%
Top 50% of class: 89%

Deadlines
Early Action: 11/1
Early Decision: No
Regular Action: 11/1 (priority)
3/1 (final)
Common Application: Accepted

Financial Aid
In-state tuition: $19,548
Out-of-state tuition: $19,548
Room: $5,040
Board: $4,652
Books: $1,100
Freshmen receiving need-based aid: 63%
Undergrads rec. need-based aid: 55%
Avg. % of need met by financial aid: 35%
Avg. aid package (freshmen): $5,730
Avg. aid package (undergrads): $5,623
Avg. debt upon graduation: $9,878

Prominent Alumni
Booker T. Washington; Wanda Sykes;
Charles E. Phillips.

School Spirit
Mascot: Pirate
Colors: Reflex blue and white
Song: *Hampton: A Song of Service, Love and Loyalty*

of test optional applicants. *Academic units recommended:* 2 Foreign Language.

How to Pay for College

To apply for financial aid, students should submit the following: Free Application for Federal Student Aid (FAFSA). Hampton University participates in the Federal Work Study program. *Need-based aid programs include:* scholarships and grants · general need-based awards · Federal Pell grants · state scholarships and grants · college-based scholarships and grants · private scholarships and grants · ACG and SMART grants. *Non-need-based aid programs include:* scholarships and grants · state scholarships and grants · athletic scholarships · ROTC scholarships.

America's
Best Colleges for
B Students

HARTWICK COLLEGE

1 Hartwick Drive, Oneonta, NY 13820-4020
Admissions: 888-HARTWICK · Financial Aid: 888-427-8942
Email: admissions@hartwick.edu · Website: http://www.hartwick.edu

From the College

"As a small, private, liberal arts college, Hartwick College focuses on fostering collaborative student-faculty relationships: Our faculty bring the latest insights from the world into the classroom to deepen student learning. The college's setting upon a hill overlooking Oneonta, New York, features the close relationships expected from a college of 1,550 students with a student-to-faculty ratio of 11:1.

"Our Connecting the Classroom to the World philosophy puts an emphasis on experiential learning so that students are prepared to continuously shape and reshape their future. When our students study abroad, complete an internship, collaborate with a professor on a research project or work in the local community, their learning translates into an education that changes lives. More than 60 percent of Hartwick students gain first-hand experience either studying off-campus or completing an internship. Hartwick faculty lead off-campus programs all over the world during our January Term, which allows students to broaden their horizons. Our academic calendar, centered on the four-week January Term, not only enables students to travel the world, but also offers opportunities to undertake a topic-focused class, do an internship, perform directed research or complete a senior capstone project.

"Our nearby Pine Lake Environmental Campus has also provided residential and curricular opportunities for students to investigate the importance of sustainability since 1972. The entire Hartwick community from academic to residential life and athletics now embraces a longstanding commitment to experiential learning through our Connecting the Classroom to the World approach to a liberal arts education."

Campus Setting

Hartwick, founded in 1797, is a private college. Its 425-acre campus is located in Oneonta, New York. A four-year institution, Hartwick College has an enrollment of 1,615 students, and provides on-campus housing with 11 units that can accommodate 1,203 students. Housing options: coed dorms · sorority housing · fraternity housing · single-student apartments. Recreation and sports facilities include: grass and turf fields · gymnasium · racquetball and squash courts · stable (off-campus) · stadium · swimming pool · fitness room.

Student Life and Activities

Seventy-seven percent of students live on campus. Popular gathering spots include the Dewar Student Union and the Yager Hall foyer by the entrance to the library. Popular campus events include Taste of Hartwick, Holiday Ball, Time to Unwind during Exam Week, Habitat for Humanity Spring Break Challenge, OH Fest-Oneonta State/Hartwick concert and fair, Last Day of Clash Bash, Midnight Madness and Breakfast of Champions. Hartwick College has 66 official student organizations. The most popular are: BiGala+ · Circle K · Women's Center · Amnesty International · Habitat for Humanity · fraternities · sororities · academic honor societies · Tri-Beta · Honor Society · Orchesis Dance Club · Untitled Art Club. For those interested in sports, there are intramural teams such as: basketball · dodgeball · flag football · volleyball · soccer. Hartwick College is a member of the Mid-American Conference (Division I for men's soccer), Collegiate Water Polo Association (Division I for women) and Empire Eight (Division III).

HARTWICK COLLEGE

Hartwick College
Oneonta, NY (Pop. 13,840)
Location: Small town
Four-year private
Founded: 1797
Website: http://www.hartwick.edu

Students
Total enrollment: 1,615
Undergrads: 1,615
Freshmen: 528
Part-time students: 2%
From out-of-state: 32%
From public schools: 86%
Male/Female: 41%/59%
Live on-campus: 77%
In fraternities: 3%
In sororities: 5%
Off-campus employment rating: Fair
Caucasian: 69%
African American: 6%
Hispanic: 6%
Asian: 2%
Hawaiian or Pacific Islander: <1%
Native American: 1%
International: 3%

Academics
Calendar: 4-1-4 system
Student/faculty ratio: 11:1
Class size 9 or fewer: 22%
Class size 10-29: 70%
Class size 30-49: 8%
Class size 50-99: -
Class size 100 or more: -
Returning freshmen: 72%
Six-year graduation rate: 58%

Most Popular Majors
Business
Nursing
Biology

Academics and Learning Environment

Hartwick College has 112 full-time and 89 part-time faculty members, offering a student-to-faculty ratio of 11:1. The most common course size is 10 to 19 students. Hartwick College offers 35 majors. The top choices are business, nursing and biology. The least are medical technology, music and languages. The school has a general core requirement. Cooperative education is available. All first-year students must maintain a 2.0 GPA or higher to avoid academic probation. Other special academic programs include: self-designed majors · independent study · double majors · dual degrees · accelerated study · honors program · internships.

B Student Support and Success

Hartwick's Academic Center for Excellence assigns each incoming student to a professional advisor. Together they discuss academic progress and course selection. Other ACE staff members are available to advise students in related areas such as schedule changes and degree planning. Tutoring is available in most subject areas simply by filling out a request form. Supplemental instructors also help with courses that are considered especially challenging. They organize group tutoring sessions and work one on one inside the classroom. If a student's overall GPA falls below 2.0, he/she must sign a probationary agreement. All students on probation are to be involved in one of three programs: Close Scrutiny (a weekly one on one with a professional staff member); College Success (a small group weekly meeting to discuss issues of concern and develop strategies for academic success); or regular meetings with professional staff (to ensure students are staying on track).

Hartwick College provides a variety of support programs including academic · career · personal · psychological · family planning. Annually, 72 percent of freshmen students return for their sophomore year. Companies that most frequently hire graduates from Hartwick College include: Agilent · HP · IBM · PricewaterhouseCoopers · Bassett Hospitals · local and regional school districts.

Support for Students with Learning Disabilities

Hartwick College grants additional time or a lighter course load to students with learning disabilities. High school foreign language and math waivers are accepted. LD students may also explore the options of: tutors · learning center · extended time for tests · readers · typist/scribe · note-taking services · proofreading services · tape recorders · priority seating. Individual or small group tutorials are also available in: time management · organizational skills · learning strategies · specific subject areas · writing labs · study skills. An advisor/advocate from the LD program is available to students.

How to Get Admitted

For admissions decisions, non-academic factors considered: interview · extracurricular activities · special talents, interests and abilities · character/personal qualities · volunteer work · work experience · geographical location · alumni relationship. A high school diploma is required, although a GED is also accepted for admissions consideration. SAT or ACT test scores are required for some applicants. SAT Subject Test scores are considered, if submitted, but are not required. *According to the admissions office:* Grades, strength of curriculum and secondary school class rank are all considered. *Academic units recommended:* 4 English, 3 Math, 3 Science, 2 Social Studies, 3 Foreign Language.

How to Pay for College

To apply for financial aid, students should submit the following: Free Application for Federal Student Aid (FAFSA) · International Student's Certification of Finances. Hartwick College participates in the Federal Work Study program. *Need-based aid programs include:* scholarships and grants · general need-based awards · Federal Pell grants · state scholarships and grants · college-based scholarships and grants · private scholarships and grants. *Non-need-based aid programs include:* scholarships and grants · state scholarships and grants · creative arts and performance awards · special achievements and activities awards · athletic scholarships.

HARTWICK COLLEGE

Highlights

Admissions
Applicants: 5,392
Accepted: 4,542
Acceptance rate: 84.2%
Placed on wait list: 71
Enrolled from wait list: Not reported
Average GPA: 3.2
ACT range: 23-27
SAT Math range: 510-610
SAT Reading range: 500-620
SAT Writing range: 5-21
Top 10% of class: 20%
Top 25% of class: 47%
Top 50% of class: 86%

Deadlines
Early Action: No
Early Decision: 11/1
Regular Action: Rolling admissions
Common Application: Accepted

Financial Aid
In-state tuition: $39,260
Out-of-state tuition: $39,260
Room: $5,680
Board: $5,120
Books: $700
Freshmen receiving need-based aid: 87%
Undergrads rec. need-based aid: 82%
Avg. % of need met by financial aid: 79%
Avg. aid package (freshmen): $33,006
Avg. aid package (undergrads): $30,926
Avg. debt upon graduation: $29,904

Prominent Alumni
Scott Adams, cartoonist; Cyrus Mehri, civil rights attorney; Christopher Knight, art critic.

School Spirit
Mascot: Hawks
Colors: Blue and white

237

HIGH POINT UNIVERSITY

833 Montlieu Avenue, High Point, NC 27262-3598
Admissions: 800-345-6993 · Financial Aid: 336-841-9124
Email: admiss@highpoint.edu · Website: http://www.highpoint.edu

From the College

"Situated on 320 acres in the heart of North Carolina's Piedmont Triad, High Point University combines the warmth and intimacy of a small liberal arts college with the academic offerings and amenities of a large state university. With over 4,000 students representing 41 states and 37 countries, the High Point University student body is both diverse and dynamic. Most classes have enrollments of less than 20, allowing students to interact with instructors who are well-trained career teachers, not graduate assistants. Students may earn academic credit by participating in internships or by traveling abroad and studying in such locations as England, Mexico, Scotland and China. High Point University also offers 14 NCAA Division I athletic programs and numerous extracurricular opportunities. It is ranked by US News and World Report at #3 among regional colleges in the south, while Forbes ranks it in the top seven percent among America's Best Colleges. Parade Magazine also lists HPU in the top 25 private schools in the nation."

Campus Setting

High Point University, founded in 1924, is private liberal arts institution affiliated with the United Methodist Church. Its 320-acre campus is located in High Point, within a close proximity to Greensboro and Winston-Salem, NC. A four-year institution, High Point University has an enrollment of 4,199 students. Campus facilities include: Fine arts, convocation and university centers · schools of communication and commerce. High Point University provides on-campus housing with 19 units that can accommodate 2,855 students. Housing options: coed dorms · women's dorms · men's dorms · sorority housing · fraternity housing · single-student apartments. Recreation and sports facilities include: baseball and soccer fields · stadium.

Student Life and Activities

The majority (85 percent) of students live on campus. As reported by a school representative, "At High Point University, campus life encourages wholeness and empowers students by creating a strong sense of self, of camaraderie, of community. In fact, students, faculty and staff emphasize-always-the unity of the High Point experience, whether they're playing sports; watching their favorite team; rehearsing for a play; meeting a deadline for a campus publication; debating a political issue; painting The Rock or gliding across the Greensward in pursuit of a lazy, floating disk. The foundation of community is Residential Life. In a typical year two-thirds of the entering freshman come from states other than North Carolina; one-third, from more than 500 miles away. As a result, students tend to stay on campus over the weekends. In fact, even students who could easily go home often don't because their friends at High Point don't and because there is much to do on campus and off. Each semester, the Student Activities Board, an agency of the Student Government Association, sponsors a variety of entertainment, including comedians, concerts, dances, excursions, film nights and major campus events, such as Homecoming, Family Weekend and Spring Fling. Among the most popular student activities are film nights at local theaters. The Student Activities Board splits the cost of the ticket and provides transportation for students without cars."

Popular on-campus gathering spots include the University Center and Slane Student Center. Popular campus events include New Student Orientation, Homecoming, Snow Ball Dance, Spring Fling, Greek Week, Campus Life Award Ceremony, Derby Day and Panther Palooza. High Point University has 109 official student organizations. The most popular are: Art League · Cabaret · Spotlight Players · Tower Players · wind ensemble · University Singers · Community Affairs Board · Student Activities Board · American Humanics · home furnishings club · interior design club · Panhellenic Council · Intrafraternity Council · Craven Investment Club · biology club · criminal justice club · pre-law club · judicial board · psychology club · Student Senate. For those interested in sports, there are intramural teams such as: basketball · flag football · soccer · Ultimate Frisbee · volleyball. High Point University is a member of the Big South Conference (Division I).

Academics and Learning Environment

High Point University has 236 full-time and 117 part-time faculty members, offering a student-to-faculty ratio of 15:1. The most common course size is 10 to 19 students. High Point University offers 51 majors with the most popular being business administration, education and communication. The school has a general core requirement as well as a religion requirement Cooperative education is available. All first-year students must maintain a 2.0 GPA or higher to avoid academic probation. Other special academic programs include: self-designed majors · pass/fail grading option · independent study · double majors · dual degrees · honors program · internships · distance learning.

B Student Support and Success

The Academic Services Center at High Point "strives to foster the academic growth and development" of its students, according to its website. Tutoring is available at no charge year round. Walk-in tutoring promotes group tutoring, while individual tutoring can be scheduled with a simple request form. In addition, supplemental instruction puts a tutor in classrooms to listen and take notes and then help students with those classes. For communication classes, Writing Fellows review students' essays to help them improve their work.

High Point University provides a number of support programs including academic · career · personal · psychological · minority students · military · veterans · non-traditional students · family planning · religious. High Point University offers remedial and refresher courses in: reading · writing · math · study skills. The average freshman year GPA is 2.9, and 75 percent of freshmen students return for the following year. Of the students who enter the work force, 36 percent enter a field related to their major within six months of graduation. Companies that most frequently hire graduates from High Point University include: BB&T · Bank of America · Barnes and Noble · BellSouth · CIGNA Government Services · Citi Group · Coca Cola Consolidated · MassMutual Financial Group · Novant Health · United Airlines · Wachovia.

Support for Students with Learning Disabilities

High Point University allows students with learning disabilities to take extra time to complete degrees, as well as pursue a lighter course load. Credit is given for remedial courses taken. High school foreign

HIGH POINT UNIVERSITY

Highlights

High Point University
High Point, NC (Pop. 106,586)
Location: Medium city
Four-year private
Founded: 1924
Website: http://www.highpoint.edu

Students
Total enrollment: 4,199
Undergrads: 3,999
Freshmen: 1,160
Part-time students: 1%
From out-of-state: 79%
From public schools: 60%
Male/Female: 41%/59%
Live on-campus: 85%
In fraternities: 13%
In sororities: 36%
Off-campus employment rating: Good
Caucasian: 84%
African American: 6%
Hispanic: 3%
Asian: 1%
Hawaiian or Pacific Islander: <1%
Native American: 1%
Mixed (2+ ethnicities): 1%
International: 1%

Academics
Calendar: Semester
Student/faculty ratio: 15:1
Class size 9 or fewer: 20%
Class size 10-29: 70%
Class size 30-49: 10%
Class size 50-99: -
Class size 100 or more: -
Returning freshmen: 75%
Six-year graduation rate: 62%

Most Popular Majors
Business administration
Communication
Education

239

College Profiles

HIGH POINT UNIVERSITY

Highlights

Admissions
Applicants: 6,598
Accepted: 4,757
Acceptance rate: 72.1%
Placed on wait list: 301
Enrolled from wait list: 177
Average GPA: 3.2
ACT range: 21-26
SAT Math range: 490-590
SAT Reading range: 490-580
SAT Writing range: 3-17
Top 10% of class: 22%
Top 25% of class: 51%
Top 50% of class: 80%

Deadlines
Early Action: 11/8
Early Decision: 11/1
Regular Action: Rolling admissions
Common Application: Not accepted

Financial Aid
In-state tuition: $27,775
Out-of-state tuition: $27,775
Room: $5,350
Board: $6,130
Books: $1,500
Freshmen receiving need-based aid: 46%
Undergrads rec. need-based aid: 49%
Avg. % of need met by financial aid: 53%
Avg. aid package (freshmen): $13,266
Avg. aid package (undergrads): $1,825
Avg. debt upon graduation: $20,192

Prominent Alumni
Tubby Smith, Kentucky basketball coach; James Doolittle, CEO Emeritus, Time-Warner Cable; Dr. Nido R. Qubein, motivational speaker, businessman, university president.

School Spirit
Mascot: Panthers
Colors: Purple and white

language and math waivers are accepted. According to the school, the program remains flexible to meet the needs of students with all types of disabilities. Audio textbooks conversion is completed on campus. Students may meet individually with the program director to address areas not covered by their disability accommodations (self-advocacy, study and social skills, campus involvement, etc.).

Students with learning disabilities may also find these programs helpful: remedial math · remedial English · remedial reading · tutors · learning center · testing accommodations · extended time for tests · take-home exam · oral tests · exam on tape or computer · readers · typist/scribe · note-taking services · reading machines · tape recorders · priority registration · priority seating. Individual or small group tutorials are also available in: time management · organizational skills · learning strategies · specific subject areas · writing labs · math labs · study skills. An advisor/advocate from the Academic Services Center is available to students. This member also sits on the admissions committee.

How to Get Admitted

For admissions decisions, non-academic factors considered: interview · extracurricular activities · special talents, interests and abilities · character/personal qualities · volunteer work · work experience · state of residency. A high school diploma is required, although a GED is also accepted for admissions consideration. SAT or ACT test scores are required of all applicants. SAT Subject Test scores are not required. *According to the admissions office:* Minimum combined SAT Reasoning score of 900, rank in top half of secondary class and minimum 2.0 GPA in college-preparatory courses recommended. *Academic units recommended:* 4 English, 4 Math, 3 Science, 3 Social Studies, 3 Foreign Language.

How to Pay for College

To apply for financial aid, students should submit the following: Free Application for Federal Student Aid (FAFSA) · state aid form. High Point University participates in the Federal Work Study program. *Need-based aid programs include:* scholarships and grants · general need-based awards · Federal Pell grants · state scholarships and grants · college-based scholarships and grants · private scholarships and grants. *Non-need-based aid programs include:* scholarships and grants · general need-based awards · state scholarships and grants · creative arts and performance awards · athletic scholarships.

240

HILBERT COLLEGE

5200 South Park Avenue, Hamburg, NY 14075-1597
Admissions: 800-649-8003 · Financial Aid: 716-649-7900
Email: admissions@hilbert.edu · Website: http://www.hilbert.edu

From the College

"A private, four-year institution in the Catholic, Franciscan tradition, Hilbert encourages personal and organizational change through vision and hope, and creates a meaningful undergraduate educational experience based in the liberal arts. Hilbert's challenging academic programs are taught by professors who bring in-depth theoretical and practical experience to the classroom, which is balanced with student internship opportunities. New academic concentrations have been added in family violence, forensic investigation, rehabilitation services and sports management. Known for its law and justice programs, Hilbert's new economic crime investigation lab is one of only a few computer crime and forensic training labs for undergraduates in the country to give students hands-on training in the field. In addition, Hilbert has new, apartment-style student residences, and updated athletic and administrative facilities."

Campus Setting

Hilbert is a private, Catholic, Franciscan college. Founded in 1957, it adopted coeducation in 1969. Its 49-acre campus is located in the town of Hamburg, 10 miles from Buffalo. A four-year institution, Hilbert College has an enrollment of 1,069 students. In addition to a small library, the campus also has a legal research lab. Hilbert College provides on-campus housing with 150 units that can accommodate 304 students. Housing options: coed dorms · single-student apartments. Recreation and sports facilities include: baseball, lacrosse, soccer and softball fields · fitness center · gym.

Student Life and Activities

Almost three-quarters of the students (71 percent) live off campus. Popular gathering spots include the campus center pool room, the commuter locker room, gym, residence halls and the campus pond. Eagerly anticipated social events include Wellness Week, Parent's Weekend Homecoming, Halloween Dance, Medieval Dinner and Quad Party. Hilbert College has 20 official student organizations. Student Government and the Adventurer Club have a strong presence in student social life. For those interested in sports, there are intramural teams such as: basketball · football · fitness · lacrosse. Hilbert College is a member of the Allegheny Mountain Collegiate Conference (Division III), ECAC (Division III) and North United Volleyball Conference (Division III).

Academics and Learning Environment

Hilbert College has 47 full-time and 81 part-time faculty members, offering a student-to-faculty ratio of 13:1. Hilbert College offers 24 majors. Currently, the top choices are criminal justice, business administration and forensic science, while least popular are rehabilitation studies, digital media/communications and paralegal studies. The school has a general core requirement as well as a religion requirement. Cooperative education is not offered. All first-year students must maintain a 1.5 GPA or higher to avoid academic probation, and a minimum overall GPA of 2.0 is required to graduate. Other special academic programs that would appeal to a B student include: independent study · honors program · internships · distance learning.

HILBERT COLLEGE

Hilbert College
Hamburg, NY (Pop. 56,936)
Location: Major city
Four-year private
Founded: 1957
Website: http://www.hilbert.edu

Students
Total enrollment: 1,069
Undergrads: 1,019
Freshmen: 187
Part-time students: 13%
From out-of-state: 6%
From public schools: 90%
Male/Female: 45%/55%
Live on-campus: 29%
Off-campus employment rating: Good
Caucasian: 72%
African American: 9%
Hispanic: 2%
Asian: <1%
Hawaiian or Pacific Islander: <1%
Native American: 2%
Mixed (2+ ethnicities): 3%
International: 1%

Academics
Calendar: Semester
Student/faculty ratio: 13:1
Class size 9 or fewer: 31%
Class size 10-29: 67%
Class size 30-49: 2%
Class size 50-99: 1%
Class size 100 or more: -
Returning freshmen: 75%
Six-year graduation rate: 39%

Most Popular Majors
Criminal justice
Business administration
Forensic science

B Student Support and Success

Hilbert College provides a variety of support programs including: academic · career · personal · psychological · minority students · military · veterans · non-traditional students · religious. Hilbert College offers remedial and refresher courses in: reading · writing · math · study skills. The average freshman year GPA is 3.1, and 75 percent of freshmen students return for their sophomore year. Approximately 17 percent of students pursue a graduate degree right after graduation. After one year, 21 percent are in graduate school. Among students who enter the workforce, approximately 80 percent enter a field related to their major within six months of graduation. Companies that most frequently hire graduates from Hilbert College include: Federal government agencies (U.S. Customs · INS · Border Patrol · FBI · Secret Service) · local and state government courts and police agencies · M&T Bank · HSBC · National Fuel · Fisher-Price · Carlton Technologies · law firms · human services agencies.

Support for Students with Learning Disabilities

Hilbert College gives LD students more time to complete their degrees, as well as the option of taking a lighter load. These students may also want to explore: remedial math · remedial English · tutors · extended time for tests · oral tests · readers · note-taking services · tape recorders · waiver of foreign language degree requirement. Individual or small group tutorials are also available in: time management · organizational skills · learning strategies · specific subject areas · writing labs · math labs · study skills. An advisor/advocate from the LD program is available to students.

How to Get Admitted

For admissions decisions, non-academic factors considered: interview · extracurricular activities · special talents, interests and abilities · character/personal qualities · volunteer work · work experience · state of residency. A high school diploma is required, although a GED is also accepted for admissions consideration. SAT or ACT test scores are considered, if submitted, but are not required. SAT Subject Test scores are not required. *According to the admissions office:* Average GPA of admitted students is 3.0. *Academic units recommended:* 4 English, 3 Math, 3 Science, 3 Social Studies, 1 Foreign Language.

Insight

Paula Witherell, public relations director, says that Hilbert offers a supportive campus where every student matters. Its philosophy is that since it was founded by the Franciscan Sisters of St. Joseph congregation, it "embraces the values of St. Francis of Assisi: respect, service, hope, vision, joy, integrity, compassion and peace."

How to Pay for College

To apply for financial aid, students should submit the following: Free Application for Federal Student Aid (FAFSA) · state aid form. Hilbert College participates in the Federal Work Study program. *Need-based aid programs include:* scholarships and grants · general need-based awards · Federal Pell grants · state scholarships and grants · college-based scholarships and grants · private scholarships and grants. *Non-need-based aid programs include:* scholarships and grants · state scholarships and grants.

HILBERT COLLEGE

Highlights

Admissions
Applicants: 865
Accepted: 703
Acceptance rate: 81.3%
Average GPA: 3.1
ACT range: 18-21
SAT Math range: 430-540
SAT Reading range: 400-510
SAT Writing range: Not reported
Top 10% of class: 4%
Top 25% of class: 19%
Top 50% of class: 50%

Deadlines
Early Action: No
Early Decision: No
Regular Action: Rolling admissions
Common Application: Not accepted

Financial Aid
In-state tuition: $19,300
Out-of-state tuition: $19,300
Room: $4,000
Board: $1,070
Books: $750
Freshmen receiving need-based aid: 88%
Undergrads rec. need-based aid: 83%
Avg. % of need met by financial aid: 67%
Avg. aid package (freshmen): $15,206
Avg. aid package (undergrads): $14,423
Avg. debt upon graduation: $19,319

School Spirit
Mascot: Hawks
Colors: Blue and white

243

HIRAM COLLEGE

P.O. Box 67, Hiram, OH 44234
Admissions: 800-362-5280 · Financial Aid: 330-569-5107
Email: admission@hiram.edu · Website: http://www.hiram.edu

From the College

"Hiram College offers distinctive programs. About half of Hiram's students study abroad at some point during their four years. Recently, a group of 19 students led by two faculty members traveled around the world to study climate change, stopping in nine different locations. Common study abroad destinations include France, China, Mexico, Guatemala, Costa Rica, the Galapagos Islands and several African countries. Because Hiram students receive credits for the courses taught by Hiram faculty on these trips, studying abroad will not impede progress in their majors or delay graduation.

"Another unique aspect of a Hiram education is our academic calendar, known as the Hiram Plan. Our semesters are divided into 12-week and 3-week periods. Students usually enroll in three courses during each 12-week period, and one intensive course during the 3-week period. Many students spend the 3-week on study abroad trips or taking unusual courses not typically offered during the 12-week period. Our small classes encourage interaction between students and their professors. Students can work with professors on original research projects and often participate in musical groups and intramural sports teams alongside faculty members."

Campus Setting

Hiram College, founded in 1850, is a private, residential, liberal arts college located in Hiram, Ohio, southeast of Cleveland. A four-year institution, Hiram College has an enrollment of 1,395 students. The school is also affiliated with the Christian Church (Disciples of Christ). Hiram College provides on-campus housing that can accommodate 1,040 students. Housing options: coed dorms · women's dorms · special housing for disabled students · cooperative housing.

Student Life and Activities

The vast majority of students (82 percent) live on campus. Hangouts include Hiram Advance, Kennedy Center, Student Union, the new dining hall, Hiram College Library, Athletic Facilities and Gery's Down Under. Popular events include Celebrating Excellence at Hiram and Education that Works Conference. Hiram College has 90 official student organizations. The most popular include the chamber orchestra, dance team, jazz ensemble, marching band, Democratic Club, Republican Club, Students Against Social Injustice, Investment Club and chemistry and education club. Hiram College is a member of the North Coast Athletic Conference (Division III).

Academics and Learning Environment

Hiram College has 79 full-time and 60 part-time faculty members, offering a student-to-faculty ratio of 12:1. Hiram College offers 32 majors and the top favorites are biology, management and biomedical humanities. The school has a general core requirement. Cooperative education is not offered. All first-year students must maintain a 2.0 GPA or higher to avoid academic probation. Other special academic programs that would appeal to a B student include: self-designed majors · pass/fail grading option · independent study · double majors · dual degrees · accelerated study · Phi Beta Kappa · internships · weekend college.

B Student Support and Success

Hiram offers hands-on experiences in academics as well as off-campus study programs. Student Academic Services provides a variety of assistance programs including online time management tips and free peer tutoring with fellow students who excel in the class the student finds to be a challenge. The Writing Center offers information, services and programs to help students write more efficiently and effectively, as well as to foster a love and respect for language. Trained writing assistants are available by appointment. Along with these services, the college provides test-taking tips.

Hiram College provides a variety of support programs including dedicated guidance for: academic · career · personal · psychological · minority students · veterans · non-traditional students · family planning · religious. Annually, 78 percent of freshmen students return for their second year, and 23 percent pursue a graduate degree immediately after graduation. One year after graduation, the school reports that 40 percent of graduates have entered graduate school. Among students who are employed, approximately 23 percent enter a field related to their major within six months of graduation. Companies that most frequently hire graduates from Hiram College include: Case Western Reserve Medical Research Laboratories · Progressive Insurance · KeyLink · Berea Children's Home · Enterprise · Penske.

Support for Students with Learning Disabilities

Students with learning disabilities may find the following programs quite helpful: tutors · testing accommodations · extended time for tests · take-home exam · oral tests · note-taking services · early syllabus. Individual or small group tutorials are also available in: time management · organizational skills · learning strategies · specific subject areas · writing labs · math labs · study skills. An advisor/advocate from the LD program is available to students.

How to Get Admitted

For admissions decisions, non-academic factors considered: interview · extracurricular activities · special talents, interests and abilities · character/personal qualities · volunteer work · state of residency · alumni relationship. A high school diploma is required, although a GED is also accepted for admissions consideration. SAT or ACT test scores are required of all applicants. *Academic units recommended:* 4 English, 4 Math, 3 Science, 2 Social Studies, 2 Foreign Language.

How to Pay for College

To apply for financial aid, students should submit the following: Free Application for Federal Student Aid (FAFSA). Hiram College participates in the Federal Work Study program. *Need-based aid programs include:* scholarships and grants · general need-based awards · Federal Pell grants · state scholarships and grants · college-based scholarships and grants · private scholarships and grants. *Non-need-based aid programs include:* scholarships and grants · general need-based awards · state scholarships and grants · creative arts and

HIRAM COLLEGE

Highlights

Hiram College
Hiram, OH (Pop. 1,407)
Location: Rural
Four-year private
Founded: 1850
Website: http://www.hiram.edu

Students
Total enrollment: 1,395
From out-of-state: 24%
Male/Female: 45%/55%
Live on-campus: 82%
In fraternities: 10%
In sororities: 10%
Off-campus employment rating: Good
Caucasian: 71%
African American: 13%
Hispanic: 4%
Asian: 1%
Hawaiian or Pacific Islander: <1%
Native American: <1%
Mixed (2+ ethnicities): 2%
International: 4%

Academics
Calendar: Other
Student/faculty ratio: 12:1
Class size 9 or fewer: 34%
Class size 10-29: 63%
Class size 30-49: 3%
Class size 50-99: -
Class size 100 or more: -
Returning freshmen: 75%
Six-year graduation rate: 66%

Most Popular Majors
Biology
Management
Biomedical humanities

245

HIRAM COLLEGE

Highlights

Admissions
Applicants: 1,279
Accepted: 1,112
Acceptance rate: 96.9%
Average GPA: 3.3
ACT range: 19-25
SAT Math range: 450-580
SAT Reading range: 430-600
SAT Writing range: 450-560
Top 10% of class: 20%
Top 25% of class: 46%
Top 50% of class: 74%

Deadlines
Early Action: No
Early Decision: No
Regular Action: Rolling admissions
Common Application: Accepted

Financial Aid
In-state tuition: $29,065
Out-of-state tuition: $29,065
Room: $4,820
Board: $5,040
Books: Varies
Freshmen receiving need-based or merit-based aid: 100%
Avg. aid package (freshmen): Not reported
Avg. aid package (undergrads): Not reported

Prominent Alumni
Julie Cunningham, president and CEO of the Conference of Minority Transportation Officials; James A. Garfield, 20th President of the United States; Lucretia Rudolph Garfield, First Lady of the United States.

School Spirit
Mascot: Terriers

performance awards · special achievements and activities awards · special characteristics awards.

246

HOLLINS UNIVERSITY

P.O. Box 9707, Roanoke, VA 24020
Admissions: 800-456-9595 · Financial Aid: 540-362-6332
Email: huadm@hollins.edu · Website: http://www.hollins.edu

From the College

"Founded in 1842, Hollins was the first chartered women's college in Virginia. Today it is a small university with an undergraduate program for women and an array of graduate programs for men and women. Some of Hollins' distinctions include a nationally ranked creative writing program, one of the oldest study abroad programs in the country and extensive opportunities for internships and faculty/student research. Through the university's Batten Leadership Institute, students can earn a certificate in leadership studies through a program that combines classes, skills-building groups and leadership projects on and off campus. Hollins' program of seminars for first-year students is designed to encourage creative problem solving and to introduce students to the university's collaborative learning environment."

Campus Setting

Hollins, founded in 1842, is an independent liberal arts university dedicated to academic excellence and humane values. Hollins offers undergraduate liberal arts education for women, selected graduate programs for men and women and community outreach initiatives. Its 475-acre campus is located in Roanoke. A four-year private women's college, Hollins University has an enrollment of 750 students. Campus facilities include: visual arts center · museum · fitness center · equestrian center · science building · swim center · climbing wall. Hollins University provides on-campus housing with 553 units that can accommodate 679 students. Housing options: women's dorms · single-student apartments · special housing for disabled students · special housing for international students. Recreation and sports facilities include: aerobics studio · climbing wall · fields · gymnasium · riding ring · swimming pool · tennis court · weight room.

Student Life and Activities

Three-quarters (79 percent) of students live on campus. "Many students spend a majority of their time at other colleges," reports the editor of the student newspaper. "Most students road trip and participate in other school's activities." Popular on-campus gathering spots include the Moody Student Center, Front Quad and Tinker Beach. Off-campus, students gather at the Roanoke City Market and Grandin Village. Popular campus events include fall and spring theatre and dance productions, Ring Night, Fall Formal, Tinker Day, Spring Cotillion and MayFest. Hollins University has 31 official student organizations. Hollins Activities Board is an influential group on campus. Intramural teams include: outdoor program. Hollins University is a member of the Old Dominion Athletic Conference (Division III).

Academics and Learning Environment

Hollins University has 70 full-time and 25 part-time faculty members, offering a student-to-faculty ratio of 8:1. The most common course size is two to nine students. Hollins University offers 34 majors with the most popular being English, biology and studio art. The least popular are chemistry, classical studies and music. The school has a general core requirement. Cooperative education is not offered. All first-year students must maintain a 1.8 GPA or higher to avoid academic probation, and a minimum overall GPA of 2.0 is required to graduate. Other special academic programs that would appeal to a B student include: self-designed majors · pass/fail

247

College Profiles

HOLLINS UNIVERSITY

Highlights

Hollins University
Roanoke, VA (Pop. 97,469)
Location: Medium city
Four-year private women's college
Founded: 1842
Website: http://www.hollins.edu

Students
Total enrollment: 750
Undergrads: 580
Freshmen: 153
Part-time students: 4%
From out-of-state: 49%
From public schools: 85%
Male/Female: 1%/99%
Live on-campus: 79%
Off-campus employment rating: Good
Caucasian: 71%
African American: 10%
Hispanic: 6%
Asian: 3%
Hawaiian or Pacific Islander: <1%
Native American: <1%
Mixed (2+ ethnicities): 3%
International: 5%

Academics
Calendar: 4-1-4 system
Student/faculty ratio: 8:1
Class size 9 or fewer: 48%
Class size 10-29: 50%
Class size 30-49: 2%
Class size 50-99: -
Class size 100 or more: -
Returning freshmen: 67%
Six-year graduation rate: 59%

Most Popular Majors
English
Studio art
Biology

grading option · independent study · double majors · dual degrees · accelerated study · honors program · Phi Beta Kappa · internships.

B Student Support and Success

While Hollins is listed as an all-women college, men do account for one percent of the student body. Help for students is available through the Center for Learning Excellence, which is made up of a Writing Center and a Quantitative Reasoning Center.

Hollins University provides dedicated guidance for: academic · career · personal · psychological · minority students · non-traditional students · family planning · religious. Hollins University offers remedial and refresher courses in: reading · writing · math · study skills. The average freshman year GPA is 3.0 and 67 percent of freshmen students return for their sophomore year.

Companies that most frequently hire graduates from Hollins University include: Abercrombie and Fitch · Abraham Clark High School · Alcoa · American Institutes for Research · AmeriCorps NCCC · Ann Taylor Loft · Apple · Bankers Life and Casualty · Brown and Jennings PLC · Buc and Beardsley · Carillon · Carolinas Healthcare System · Center for Career Development & Ministry/ Bertuccis · Center for Digital Imaging Arts/Boston University · Cherish Our Children International · Christ Tabernacle · Cincinnati Children's Hospital Medical Center · Community Support Services · Compass Group · Core Team Specialist · Covington City Public Schools · Cracker Barrel · Dallas Area Habitat for Humanity/AmeriCorps National Direct · Faith Christian Church · FBI · Federal Deposit Insurance Corp. · Gaston Gators/Jesse Brown's Adventure · GEICO · Hampton Roads Academy · Hearing Health Associates · HICAPS Inc. · Hollins University · Hollins University/ Eleanor D. Wilson Museum · Hurt Park Elementary · James River High School · JET Program · Killington Ski Resort · KONE Inc. · Lexmark · Mariner Media Inc. · Mary Kay/Shadowbox · Metro Restaurant · Museum of Science and Industry · New York State Board of Law Examiners · Nordstrom · Novo Nordisk · Our Daily Beast · Paradise Farms · Patient Access Network Foundation · Richmond Animal League · Roanoke City DSS · Roanoke City Public Schools · Selecto Scientific.

Support for Students with Learning Disabilities

Hollins University gives learning disabled students extra time to complete their degree, plus the option to carry a much lighter course load. According to the school, a student requesting accommodation and support services needs to provide a diagnostic report which clearly identifies a learning disability based on testing and evaluation. These students may also find the following programs very useful: tutors · learning center · testing accommodations · untimed tests · extended time for tests · take-home exam · oral tests · readers · note-taking services · tape recorders · waiver of math degree requirement. Individual or small group tutorials are also available in: time management · organizational skills · learning strategies · specific subject areas · writing labs · math labs · study skills. An advisor/advocate from the Academic Services is available to students.

How to Get Admitted

For admissions decisions, non-academic factors considered: interview · extracurricular activities · special talents, interests and abilities · character/personal qualities · volunteer work · work experience · state of residency · alumni relationship. A high school diploma is required, although a GED is also accepted for admissions consideration. SAT or ACT test scores are required of all applicants. *According to the admissions office:* Minimum combined SAT Reasoning score of 1000, rank in top two-fifths of secondary school class, and minimum 3.0 GPA recommended.

How to Pay for College

To apply for financial aid, students should submit the following: Free Application for Federal Student Aid (FAFSA) · state aid form. Hollins University participates in the Federal Work Study program. *Need-based aid programs include:* scholarships and grants · general need-based awards · Federal Pell grants · state scholarships and grants · college-based scholarships and grants · private scholarships and grants. *Non-need-based aid programs include:* scholarships and grants · general need-based awards · state scholarships and grants · creative arts and performance awards.

HOLLINS UNIVERSITY

Highlights

Admissions
Applicants: 824
Accepted: 571
Acceptance rate: 69.3%
Average GPA: 3.5
ACT range: 21-27
SAT Math range: 470-580
SAT Reading range: 500-640
SAT Writing range: 3-30
Top 10% of class: 24%
Top 25% of class: 54%
Top 50% of class: 83%

Deadlines
Early Action: 12/1
Early Decision: 11/1
Regular Action: Rolling admissions
Common Application: Accepted

Financial Aid
In-state tuition: $33,660
Out-of-state tuition: $33,660
Room: Varies
Board: Varies
Books: $1,000
Freshmen receiving need-based aid: 79%
Undergrads rec. need-based aid: 77%
Avg. % of need met by financial aid: 80%
Avg. aid package (freshmen): $32,308
Avg. aid package (undergrads): $30,402
Avg. debt upon graduation: $30,660

Prominent Alumni
Annie Dillard, author and Pulitzer Prize winner; Ann Compton, ABC News Washington correspondent; Natasha Trethewey, U.S. Poet Laureate.

School Spirit
Colors: Green and gold
Song: *The Green and the Gold*

249

HOOD COLLEGE

401 Rosemont Avenue, Frederick, MD 21701
Admissions: 800-922-1599 · Financial Aid: 301-696-3411
Email: admission@hood.edu · Website: http://www.hood.edu

From the College

"Hood College was founded in 1893, and is an independent, liberal arts college providing a residential experience for undergraduate women and men, and a professionally oriented graduate school. Located on 50 acres in the middle of historic Frederick, Maryland, and within an hour's drive of Washington, DC, and Baltimore, Hood is consistently ranked as one of the nation's best and most affordable colleges. In this closely-knit community, students and professors know each other by name. Hood maintains a vibrant community that responds to the intellectual, professional and personal goals of individual students of diverse races, ethnicities and ages. Stressing high-quality undergraduate research and internship opportunities, Hood provides a university-like education in a small college setting."

Campus Setting

The college's 50-acre campus is located in Frederick, MD, one hour from Washington, DC, and Baltimore, MD. A four-year private institution, Hood College has an enrollment of 2,393 students, and has been co-ed since 2003. The school is also affiliated with the Congregational (United Church of Christ). In addition to a large, well-stocked library, the campus facilities include: observatory · child development laboratory school. Hood College provides on-campus housing with 410 units that can accommodate 828 students. Housing options: coed dorms · women's dorms · single-student apartments · special housing for disabled students. Recreation and sports facilities include: multi-sport turf field (field hockey · lacrosse · soccer) · softball field · aquatics center · gymnasium · fitness center.

Student Life and Activities

Just over half (56 percent) of the students at Hood College live on campus. Popular gathering spots include The Whitaker Student Union on campus and Baker Park or Cunningham Falls off campus. Popular campus events include The Messiah performed by the Hood Choir, Policies for Dollars, Liberation Weekend, May Madness Week, Crab Feast, Midnight Breakfast Weekend Blockbuster Movies, Junior Ring Ceremony, Strawberry Breakfast, and Welcome Back Week featuring the Foam Bash. Hood College has 79 official student organizations. Popular groups on campus include the Student Government Association, the Campus Activities Board and the House Forum. For those interested in sports, there are intramural teams such as: basketball · billiards · football · soccer · table tennis · volleyball. Hood College is a member of the Middle Atlantic Conference (Division III).

Academics and Learning Environment

Hood College has 93 full-time and 164 part-time faculty members, offering a student-to-faculty ratio of 12:1. The most common course size is 10 to 19 students. Hood College offers 45 majors with the most popular being psychology, management and biology, and least popular being French, music and German. The school has a general core requirement. Cooperative education is not offered. All first-year students must maintain a 2.0 GPA or higher to avoid academic probation. Other special academic programs include: self-designed majors · pass/fail grading option · independent study · double majors · dual degrees · honors program · internships · certificate programs.

B Student Support and Success

Academic Services focuses on helping students who are having trouble in specific courses as well as those who want to be more effective learners. Freshmen and sophomores are advised by a special group of faculty. Once a major is declared, students are reassigned to an advisor in that subject. Assessment of skills and knowledge is available through a Basic Skills Inventory. The results are studied so that students can be encouraged to take remedial courses before entering the college classroom. For example, should a student find that he/she would benefit from a review of math foundations before enrolling in a college math course, algebra review classes are available. In addition, classroom teaching, tutoring, videos, computer software and printed materials are provided. Individualized programs are also sometimes offered.

Hood College provides dedicated guidance for: academic · career · personal · psychological · minority students · military · veterans · non-traditional students · family planning · religious. The average freshman year GPA is 2.8, and 78 percent of freshmen students return for their sophomore year. Approximately 38 percent of graduates return to pursue another degree immediately after graduation. One year after graduation, the school reports that 40 percent of graduates have entered graduate school. Among students who enter the workforce, approximately 42 percent enter a field related to their major within six months of graduation. Companies that most frequently hire graduates from Hood College include: Bechtel Corporation · Booz Allen Hamilton · Frederick County Public Schools · Invitrogen/Life Technologies · National Cancer Institute · NSA · USARIMIID.

Support for Students with Learning Disabilities

Hood College provides extra time to students with learning disabilities to complete their degree, as well as the option of a lightened course load. Students with learning disabilities may also find the following programs useful: remedial math · remedial English · special classes · tutors · testing accommodations · untimed tests · extended time for tests · oral tests · note-taking services · reading machines · tape recorders · priority registration · waiver of math degree requirement. Individual or small group tutorials are also available in: time management · organizational skills · learning strategies · specific subject areas · writing labs · math labs · study skills. An advisor/advocate from the LD program is available to students.

How to Get Admitted

For admissions decisions, non-academic factors considered: interview · extracurricular activities · special talents, interests and abilities · character/personal qualities · volunteer work · work experience · state of residency. A high school diploma is required, although a GED is also accepted for admissions consideration. SAT or ACT test scores are required for some applicants. SAT Subject Test scores are considered, if submitted, but are not required. *According to the admissions office:* Minimum combined SAT Reasoning score of 1000 (500 in both critical reading and math), rank in top fifth of secondary school class and minimum 3.0 GPA required. SAT Reasoning optional for students with minimum 3.26 secondary school

HOOD COLLEGE

Highlights

Hood College
Frederick, MD (Pop. 66,382)
Location: Large town
Four-year private
Founded: 1893
Website: http://www.hood.edu

Students
Total enrollment: 2,393
Undergrads: 1,387
Freshmen: 308
Part-time students: 9%
From out-of-state: 34%
From public schools: 82%
Male/Female: 34%/66%
Live on-campus: 56%
Off-campus employment rating: Excellent
Caucasian: 65%
African American: 12%
Hispanic: 8%
Asian: 3%
Hawaiian or Pacific Islander: <1%
Native American: <1%
Mixed (2+ ethnicities): 4%
International: 3%

Academics
Calendar: Semester
Student/faculty ratio: 12:1
Class size 9 or fewer: 25%
Class size 10-29: 70%
Class size 30-49: 5%
Class size 50-99: -
Class size 100 or more: -
Returning freshmen: 78%
Six-year graduation rate: 66%

Most Popular Majors
Management
Psychology
Biology

251

College Profiles

HOOD COLLEGE

Admissions

Applicants: 1,686
Accepted: 1,366
Acceptance rate: 81.0%
Average GPA: 3.5
ACT range: 18-25
SAT Math range: 460-580
SAT Reading range: 450-580
SAT Writing range: 1-13
Top 10% of class: 12%
Top 25% of class: 45%
Top 50% of class: 77%

Deadlines

Early Action: No
Early Decision: No
Regular Action: Rolling admissions
Common Application: Accepted

Financial Aid

In-state tuition: $33,620
Out-of-state tuition: $33,620
Room: $6,080
Board: $1,590
Books: $1,200
Freshmen receiving need-based aid: 85%
Undergrads rec. need-based aid: 85%
Avg. % of need met by financial aid: 74%
Avg. aid package (freshmen): $28,041
Avg. aid package (undergrads): $26,534
Avg. debt upon graduation: $26,890

Prominent Alumni

Marcia Coyle, Washington Bureau Chief, *National Law Journal*; Dr. Joy Dubost, Director of Nutrition and Healthy Living, National Restaurant Association, National Spokesperson for the American Dietetic Association; Beverley Swaim-Staley, Maryland State Secretary of Transportation.

School Spirit

Mascot: Blazer
Colors: Navy and gray

GPA. *Academic units recommended:* 4 English, 4 Math, 4 Science, 1 Social Studies, 3 Foreign language.

How to Pay for College

To apply for financial aid, students should submit the following: Free Application for Federal Student Aid (FAFSA). Hood College participates in the Federal Work Study program. *Need-based aid programs include:* scholarships and grants · general need-based awards · Federal Pell grants · state scholarships and grants · college-based scholarships and grants · private scholarships and grants. *Non-need-based aid programs include:* scholarships and grants · general need-based awards · state scholarships and grants · creative arts and performance awards · ROTC scholarships.

HOWARD UNIVERSITY

2400 Sixth Street, NW, Washington, DC 20059
Admissions: 800-822-6363 · Financial Aid: 800-433-3243
Email: admission@howard.edu · Website: http://www.howard.edu

From the College

"Howard University is a comprehensive, research-oriented, predominantly African American university providing an educational experience at reasonable cost to students of high academic potential. Particular emphasis is placed upon providing educational opportunities for African Americans, and for other historically disenfranchised groups. It is a place where students come to study, free of oppression of any type, stripe or kind; and a university which engenders and nurtures an environment that celebrates African American culture in all its diversity. It educates students and prepares them for important leadership positions and responsibility in an increasingly complex world."

Campus Setting

Howard University, founded in 1867, is a private doctoral/research-extensive institution with 12 schools and colleges: the Graduate School of Arts and Sciences; the Schools of Business, Communications, Divinity, Education, Law and Social Work; and the Colleges of Arts and Sciences, Dentistry, Engineering, Architecture and Computer Sciences, Medicine and Pharmacy, Nursing and Allied Health Sciences. Its 89-acre campus is located in the North West section of Washington, DC. A four-year institution, Howard University is a historically black university with 10,002 students. In addition to a large, well-stocked library, the campus facilities include: art gallery · hospital · museum · international affairs and research centers. Howard University provides on-campus housing with 5,000 units that can accommodate 6,500 students. Housing options: coed dorms · women's dorms · men's dorms · single-student apartments · married-student apartments.

Student Life and Activities

Just over half (55 percent) of students live on campus. Popular campus events include the Homecoming Program, Spring Black Arts Festival, Week-end at the Mecca, Commencement Week, Convocation, Residence Hall Week, International Student Night, Howard's Musical Productions and the James Porter Colloquium. Howard University has 225 official student organizations. The most popular are: Gospel choir · marching and pep bands · string ensemble · jazz society · dance group · drama groups · chess club · debate group · team managers · state and city geographical clubs · other academic and professional clubs. For those interested in sports, there are intramural teams such as: badminton · basketball · bowling · soccer · softball · table tennis. Howard University is a member of the NCAA.

Academics and Learning Environment

Howard University has 1,064 full-time and 456 part-time faculty members, offering a student-to-faculty ratio of 10:1. The most common course size is 2 to 9 students. Howard University offers 110 majors with the most popular being biology, psychology and journalism and least popular being German, classical civilization and French. The school has a general core requirement. Cooperative education is available. All first-year students must maintain a 2.0 GPA or higher to avoid academic probation. Other special academic programs that would appeal to a B student include: self-designed majors · pass/fail grading option · independent study · double majors · dual degrees · accelerated study · honors program · Phi Beta Kappa · internships · distance learning certificate programs.

253

College Profiles

HOWARD UNIVERSITY

Highlights

Howard University
Washington, DC (Pop. 632,323)
Location: Major city
Four-year private
Founded: 1867
Website: http://www.howard.edu

Students
Total enrollment: 10,002
Undergrads: 6,688
From out-of-state: 96%
Male/Female: 33%/67%
Live on-campus: 55%
In fraternities: 2%
In sororities: 1%
Off-campus employment rating: Good
Caucasian: 1%
African American: 91%
Hispanic: <1%
Asian: 1%
Hawaiian or Pacific Islander: <1%
Native American: 2%
Mixed (2+ ethnicities): <1%
International: 3%

Academics
Calendar: Semester
Student/faculty ratio: 10:1
Class size 9 or fewer: 37%
Class size 10-29: 44%
Class size 30-49: 15%
Class size 50-99: 3%
Class size 100 or more: 1%
Returning freshmen: 83%
Six-year graduation rate: 63%

Most Popular Majors
Biology
Journalism
Psychology

B Student Support and Success

Howard assigns undergraduates an academic advisor during their first week of school. The Center for Academic Reinforcement assists students with academic difficulties, conducts pre-orientation programs for entering freshmen, offers three-credit-hour courses in mathematics, verbal, study skills and reading and recently provided 2,000 tutoring and laboratory assistance sessions.

Howard University provides dedicated guidance for: academic · career · personal · psychological · minority students · veterans · non-traditional students · family planning · religious. Howard University offers remedial and refresher courses in: reading · writing · math · study skills. Annually, 84 percent of freshmen students return for their sophomore year. Approximately 40 percent pursue a graduate degree right after graduation. A year after graduating, 60 percent of students have entered graduate school. Among students who are employed, approximately 65 percent enter a field related to their major within six months of graduation.

Companies that most frequently hire graduates from Howard University include: ABC Disney · Allstate Insurance · American Power Conversion · Ameriprise Financial · Amica Mutual Insurance · Applied Materials · AT&T · Avis Budget Group · AXA-Advisors · Bearingpoint Inc. · Bechtel · Bloomingdale's · Booz Allen & Hamilton · Brown Shoe Co. · Cardinal Health · Carrier Corporation · Central Intelligence Agency · CGI · Cintas Corporation · CISCO · Compton Unified · Defense Contract Audit Agency · Defense Information Systems Agency · DFI International · Government Services · DMG Securities Inc. · Domino's Pizza · DRAFTFCB · Easton Area School District · ECHOSTAR Communications · Eli Lilly · ESPN · Enterprise Rent-A-Car · Ernst & Young · Fairbanks North Star Borough SD · Fairfax County Fire and Rescue Department · Alexandra City · Fairfax County Public Schools · FDIC · Ford Motor Company · Freddie Mac · Friendship Public Charter School · Gap Inc. · Geico · General Services Administration · Girl Scout Council of the Nation's Capital · Goldman Sachs · Hartford Financial Services · Illinois Tool Works · Institute for Defense Analysis · JC Penny Company Inc. · Johnson & Johnson · JP Morgan · Kennedy Krieger Institute · Lehman Brothers · M & T Bank · Marsh Inc. · Mediaedgeicia · Memorial Sloan Kettering · Miami-Dade County Public Schools · Microsoft · Missile Defense Agency · Montgomery County Public Schools · NASA · National Geospatial Intelligence Agency · National Security Agency · NAVAIR · Naval Inventory Control Point · Naval Surface Warfare Center · Newark Public Schools · Newell Rubbermaid · Northern Trust · Northrop Grumman Corp · Oak Ridge Institute for Science and Education · PEPCO Energy Services Inc. · Pepsi Bottling Group · Prudential Mortgage Capital Group · Radford Army Ammunition for Alliant · Raytheon Company · Safeway · Shakespeare Theater Company · Siemens Corporation · Southern Company · Sprint · Stockamp & Associates · Stryker Medical · Andersen Corporation · T-Mobile · Talbots · Tandberg · Target · Target Corporation · The Walt Disney Company · U. S. Department of Health and Human Services · U.S. Dept. of State · U.S. Dept. of the Treasury · Bureau of the Public Debt · U.S. Secret Service.

Support for Students with Learning Disabilities

According to Howard University, admission requirements for LD students are the same as those for regular students. These students may find other programs helpful, including: testing accommodations · extended time for tests · take-home exam · substitution of courses · readers · note-taking services · tape recorders · texts on tape · early syllabus · priority registration · waiver of math degree requirement. An advisor/advocate from the Special Students Services is available to students.

How to Get Admitted

For admissions decisions, non-academic factors considered: extracurricular activities · special talents, interests and abilities · volunteer work · work experience · state of residency · alumni relationship. A high school diploma is required, although a GED is also accepted for admissions consideration. SAT or ACT test scores are required of all applicants. SAT Subject Test scores are considered, if submitted, but are not required. *Academic units recommended:* 4 English, 2 Math, 3 Science, 2 Social Studies, 2 Foreign Language.

How to Pay for College

To apply for financial aid, students should submit the following: Free Application for Federal Student Aid (FAFSA) · institution's own financial aid forms. Howard University participates in the Federal Work Study program. *Need-based aid programs include:* scholarships and grants · general need-based awards · Federal Pell grants · state scholarships and grants · college-based scholarships and grants · private scholarships and grants · Federal Nursing scholarships. *Non-need-based aid programs include:* scholarships and grants · general need-based awards · state scholarships and grants · creative arts and performance awards · athletic scholarships · ROTC scholarships.

HOWARD UNIVERSITY

Highlights

Admissions
Applicants: 11,687
Accepted: 5,727
Acceptance rate: 49.0%
Average GPA: Not reported
ACT range: 21-26
SAT Math range: 480-590
SAT Reading range: 490-590
SAT Writing range: 480-580

Deadlines
Early Action: 11/1
Early Decision: No
Regular Action: Rolling admissions
Common Application: Accepted

Financial Aid
In-state tuition: $22,884
Out-of-state tuition: $22,884
Room: Varies
Board: $1,914
Books: Varies
Avg. aid package (freshmen): $26,657
Avg. aid package (undergrads): $24,655

Prominent Alumni
Edward Brooke, senator; Douglas Wilder, governor, former U.S. senator, former governor of Virginia, mayor of Richmond; Thurgood Marshall.

School Spirit
Mascot: Bison
Colors: Red, white and blue
Song: *Alma Mater*

255

INDIANA STATE UNIVERSITY

200 North Seventh Street, Terre Haute, IN 47809-9989
Admissions: 812-237-2121 · Financial Aid: 800-841-4744
Email: admissions@indstate.edu · Website: http://www.indstate.edu

From the College

"Indiana State University integrates teaching and research for high-achieving, goal-oriented students who seek opportunities for personal, professional and intellectual growth on a diverse, civically engaged campus. From their first day, our students are challenged by high-quality, experiential academic programs and are supported by personal attention from our faculty and staff who inspire students to create and apply knowledge through dynamic partnerships with the community and the world. Our graduates are valued for their demonstrated knowledge and expertise, active citizenship and leadership qualities."

Campus Setting

Indiana State, founded in 1865, is a public university. Programs are offered through the Colleges of Arts and Sciences; Business; Education; Nursing, Health and Human Services; Technology and School of Graduate Studies. Its 92-acre campus is located on the north side of Terre Haute's downtown business district, 71 miles from Indianapolis. A four-year institution, Indiana State University has an enrollment of 12,114 students. Campus facilities include: art gallery · music hall · museum · civic center · observatory. Indiana State University provides on-campus housing with 2,397 units that can accommodate 3,761 students. Housing options: coed dorms · women's dorms · men's dorms · sorority housing · fraternity housing · single-student apartments · married-student apartments · special housing for disabled students. Recreation and sports facilities include: arena · cross country course · softball and soccer complex · tennis club and complex.

Student Life and Activities

Most students (64 percent) live off campus. Because Terre Haute is a rural community, students often have to make their own fun. The Student Union Board sponsors movies, bands and lectures. There's a strong music scene in the Midwest, so a lot of great acts pass through. Bloomington and Indianapolis are each an hour away and are further repositories of culture. On campus, the food court and Student Recreation Center are favorite spots. For night life, students head to the 4th Quarter or the Verve (for live music), the Indiana Theatre (a historic movie house), Sonka's Irish Pub, The Coffee Grounds, Seventh and Elm Bar and Grill and the Ballyhoo. The most popular events on campus are Homecoming, Men's and Women's basketball, Battle of the Bands, Theatrefest, the Convocation Series, International Film Series, Trike Race in fall and Tandem Race in spring. Indiana State University has 152 official student organizations. Greeks, international students, Union Board and the Afro-American Cultural Center influence life on campus. For those interested in sports, there are intramural teams such as: badminton · basketball · pickleball · racquetball · soccer · softball · swimming · tennis · track and field · volleyball. Indiana State University is a member of the Gateway Football Conference (Division I, Football I-AA) and Missouri Valley Conference (Division I).

Academics and Learning Environment

For the B student, the learning environment of a college is just as important as the quality of its academic program. Indiana State University has 468 full-time and 203 part-time faculty members, offering a student-to-faculty ratio of 19:1. The most common course size is 20 to 29 students. Indiana State University offers 121 majors, and the top favorites include elementary education, early childhood education and criminology. The school has a general core requirement. Cooperative education is available. All first-year students must maintain a 2.0 GPA or higher to avoid academic probation, and a minimum overall GPA of 2.5 is required to graduate. Other special academic programs that would appeal to a B student include: independent study · double majors · dual degrees · accelerated study · honors program · internships · distance learning.

B Student Support and Success

The Student Academic Services Center at Indiana State helps in several ways. The Mentoring Program's primary goal, according to the college, is to "assist first-year students so that they may benefit from additional support, encouragement and services." Staff members are updated weekly on each student's progress and adjustment to college life. Students sign a Mentoring Contract at the beginning of the process. A professional advisement staff is always available for help or advice. The school offers a tutoring program for all general studies classes on either a drop-in or appointment basis. Additionally, students are invited to take University 101-Learning in the University Community, a two-credit hour elective that helps with the transition to the college. Students can learn study strategies, critical thinking and writing skills while being introduced to campus resources and services. The course also discusses the history of the school and the community around it.

Indiana State University provides a variety of support programs including dedicated guidance for: academic · career · personal · psychological · minority students · veterans. Each year, 61 percent of freshmen return for their second year. Approximately 10 percent pursue a graduate degree immediately after graduation. A year after graduation, 17 percent of graduates have gone on to graduate school. Companies that most frequently hire ISU graduates include: Federal Mutual Insurance · State Farm Insurance · Cummins Inc. · Enterprise Rent-A-Car · Deloitte · Union Hospital · Turner Construction · General Motors · Eli Lilly & Company.

Support for Students with Learning Disabilities

Indiana State University permits additional time to complete a degree, and lighter course loads to students learning disabilities. These students may also want to explore other options including: tutors · learning center · testing accommodations · extended time for tests · take-home exam · oral tests · exam on tape or computer · readers · note-taking services · tape recorders · texts on tape · early syllabus · waiver of math degree requirement. Individual or small group tutorials are also available in: time management · organizational skills · learning strategies · specific subject areas · writing labs · math labs · study skills. An advisor/advocate from the LD program is available to students.

How to Get Admitted

For admissions decisions, non-academic factors considered: interview · extracurricular activities · special talents, interests and abilities · character/personal qualities · state of residency. A high school diploma is required, although a GED is also accepted for admissions

INDIANA STATE UNIVERSITY

Highlights

Indiana State University
Terre Haute, IN (Pop. 61,112)
Location: Medium city
Four-year public
Founded: 1865
Website: http://www.indstate.edu

Students
Total enrollment: 12,114
Undergrads: 10,076
Part-time students: 14%
From out-of-state: 16%
Male/Female: 46%/54%
Live on-campus: 36%
Off-campus employment rating: Excellent
Caucasian: 67%
African American: 18%
Hispanic: 3%
Asian: 1%
Hawaiian or Pacific Islander: <1%
Native American: <1%
Mixed (2+ ethnicities): 3%
International: 6%

Academics
Calendar: Semester
Student/faculty ratio: 19:1
Class size 9 or fewer: 11%
Class size 10-29: 56%
Class size 30-49: 24%
Class size 50-99: 7%
Class size 100 or more: 2%
Returning freshmen: 61%
Six-year graduation rate: 39%

Most Popular Majors
Elementary education
Early childhood education
Criminology

INDIANA STATE UNIVERSITY

Highlights

Admissions
Applicants: 10,709
Accepted: 9,245
Acceptance rate: 86.3%
Average GPA: 3.1
ACT range: 16-22
SAT Math range: 410-520
SAT Reading range: 400-510
SAT Writing range: Not reported
Top 10% of class: 9%
Top 25% of class: 28%
Top 50% of class: 68%

Deadlines
Early Action: No
Early Decision: No
Regular Action: 7/1 (priority)
8/15 (final)
Common Application: Not accepted

Financial Aid
In-state tuition: $8,216
Out-of-state tuition: $18,146
Room: Varies
Board: Varies
Books: $1,170
Freshmen receiving need-based or merit-based aid: 92%
Avg. aid package (freshmen): Not reported
Avg. aid package (undergrads): Not reported

Prominent Alumni
Anton 'Tony' Hulman George, president of Indianapolis Motor Speedway; Bruce Baumgartner, Olympic Wrestler, Coach, currently Director of Athletics at Edinboro University of Pennsylvania; Larry Bird, Boston Celtics MVP, Olympic gold medalist, former Head Coach of the Indiana Pacers and NBA Coach of the Year, currently president of Indiana Pacers.

School Spirit
Mascot: Sycamore Sam
Colors: Blue and white
Song: *March On*

consideration. SAT or ACT test scores are required of all applicants. SAT Subject Test scores are considered, if submitted, but are not required. *According to the admissions office:* Indiana Core 40 curriculum, rank in top half of secondary school class and minimum 2.0 GPA required; minimum combined SAT Reasoning score of 800 recommended. *Academic units recommended:* 2 English, 8 Math, 8 Science, 2 Social Studies, 2 Foreign Language.

How to Pay for College

To apply for financial aid, students should submit the following: Free Application for Federal Student Aid (FAFSA). Indiana State University participates in the Federal Work Study program. *Need-based aid programs include:* scholarships and grants · general need-based awards · Federal Pell grants · state scholarships and grants · college-based scholarships and grants · private scholarships and grants. *Non-need-based aid programs include:* scholarships and grants · general need-based awards · state scholarships and grants · creative arts and performance awards · athletic scholarships · ROTC scholarships · alumni affiliation scholarships · art scholarships · minority status scholarships · state/district residency scholarships/grants.

INDIANA UNIVERSITY BLOOMINGTON

107 South Indiana Avenue, Bloomington, IN 47405-7000
Admissions: 812-855-0661 · Financial Aid: 812-855-0321
Email: iuadmit@indiana.edu · Website: http://www.iub.edu

From the College

"Indiana University Bloomington finds that the most common response for students choosing IU over similar schools are the reputation of our academic and extracurricular opportunities; flexibility in curricula, especially for exploratory students; a variety of academic and extracurricular opportunities; access to faculty and current technology; beauty of campus; an institutional philosophy of personal attention; a friendly and diverse college town and the promise of a true college experience."

Campus Setting

Indiana University Bloomington, founded in 1820, is a public, comprehensive institution. Programs are offered through the College of Arts and Sciences, the Division of Labor Studies, Henry Radford Hope School of Fine Arts, Hutton Honors College, Jabobs School of Music, Kelley School of Business, School of Continuing Studies, School of Education, School of Health, Physical Education, and Recreation, School of Informatics, School of Journalism, School of Law, School of Library and Information Science, School of Nursing, School of Optometry, School of Public and Environmental Affairs, School of Social Work, University Division and the University Graduate School. Its 1,928-acre campus is located in the city of Bloomington, 45 miles from Indianapolis.

A four-year institution, Indiana University Bloomington has an enrollment of 46,817 students, and has been co-ed since 1867. Campus facilities include: anthropology, art, folklore and history museums · musical arts center · auditorium · arboretum · outdoor educational center · observatories. Indiana University Bloomington provides on-campus housing accommodating 12,871 students. Housing options include: coed dorms · women's dorms · men's dorms · sorority housing · fraternity housing · single-student apartments · married-student apartments · special housing for disabled students · special housing for international students · cooperative housing. Recreation and sports facilities include: baseball, field hockey, football, soccer and softball fields · basketball and volleyball courts · football and soccer stadium · cross-country course · field house · golf course · gymnasium · indoor track and field complex · rowing center · tennis center · volleyball court · wrestling facility · water polo · swimming and diving facility.

Student Life and Activities

More than half of students (73 percent) live off campus. Some popular on-campus gathering spots include the Memorial Union and the recreational sports center, while off-campus students gather at the Bloomington Bagel Company and the Village Deli. Students participate in events including the IU Little 500 Bicycle race, Homecoming Parade and IU Dance Marathon. The most popular student organizations are: choral group · concert band · dance · drama · theatre · jazz band · marching band · music ensembles · music theatre · opera · symphony orchestra · AIESEC student organization · Apparel Merchandising Organization · French and Italian Graduate Student Organization · Indiana University Mongolian Student Organization · NELC Graduate Student Organization · Graduate Employees Organization · Cinephile Film Arts Organization · Student Philanthropy Organization · Cigarette Clean Up Organization. Indiana University Bloomington is a member of the Big Ten Conference (Division I, Football I-A) and Collegiate Water Polo Association (Division I).

INDIANA UNIVERSITY BLOOMINGTON

Indiana University Bloomington
Bloomington, IN (Pop. 81,963)
Location: Medium city
Four-year public
Founded: 1820
Website: http://www.iub.edu

Students
Total enrollment: 46,817
Undergrads: 36,862
Freshmen: 7,658
Part-time students: 16%
From out-of-state: 38%
Male/Female: 49%/51%
Live on-campus: 28%
In fraternities: 21%
In sororities: 23%
Off-campus employment rating: Good
Caucasian: 74%
African American: 4%
Hispanic: 4%
Asian: 4%
Hawaiian or Pacific Islander: <1%
Native American: <1%
Mixed (2+ ethnicities): 3%
International: 10%

Academics
Calendar: Semester
Student/faculty ratio: 18:1
Class size 9 or fewer: 12%
Class size 10-29: 52%
Class size 30-49: 19%
Class size 50-99: 11%
Class size 100 or more: 7%
Returning freshmen: 90%
Six-year graduation rate: 77%

Most Popular Majors
Finance
Accounting
Marketing

Academics and Learning Environment

Indiana University Bloomington has 2,014 full-time and 367 part-time faculty members, offering a student-to-faculty ratio of 18:1. The most common course size is 20 to 29 students. Indiana University Bloomington offers 436 majors. Finance, marketing and accounting are the most popular choices. The school has a general core requirement. Cooperative education is available. All first-year students must maintain a 2.0 GPA or higher to avoid academic probation. Other special academic programs that would appeal to a B student include: self-designed majors · pass/fail grading option · independent study · double majors · dual degrees · accelerated study · honors program · Phi Beta Kappa · internships · distance learning certificate programs.

B Student Support and Success

The Student Academic Center of Indiana University is focused on helping with any problems students might have. According to the college, its philosophy is "student support, student respect and student success." Study Smarter Workshops cover a wide field of topics, including learning from returned exams, improving reading speed and catching up in a course when all hope seems gone. Supplemental Instruction offers small group study sessions guided by fellow students who have already taken the same course and have been recommended by the professor. Here, students can review content, ask questions, discuss issues and learn effective reading and study strategies. The Phoenix Program serves students who have been put on academic probation. It offers several courses to help these individuals get back on track. Those who do are later offered the chance to serve as peer mentors to others. Individualized Academic Assessment and Assistance is offered to students who are not sure about their strengths and weaknesses or exactly what kind of help they need. This free assessment program is done on a walk-in or appointment basis. Outreach Services is a program of mini-workshops or presentations that are offered in the residence halls, fraternity houses, classes or organizations on topics such as test taking and time management. Non-Credit Programs and Services is an hour-long, individual session that can help students identify and target areas causing academic stress. The Right Start Program is for freshmen who are not familiar with campus/college life (first-generation students, or students from small towns or high schools, etc.). It offers an orientation to the college life and culture of IU through resources in small seminar groups. This is a full semester course that earns the student two credit hours and teaches lessons about the campus, college lifestyles and study skills.

Indiana University Bloomington provides dedicated guidance for: academic · career · personal · psychological · minority students · military · veterans · non-traditional students · family planning · religious. Indiana University Bloomington offers remedial and refresher courses in: reading · writing · math · study skills. Each year, 90 percent of freshmen students return for their sophomore year.

Support for Students with Learning Disabilities

Indiana University Bloomington allows learning disabled students to take a lighter course load. Also, according to the school, Disability Services for Students (DSS) provides a welcoming and supportive environment for students with disabilities at Indiana University Bloomington and ensures they have equal access to all available opportunities. DSS coordinates the implementation of support services, empowers students to achieve their personal and academic goals and promotes awareness by educating the university community. Students with learning disabilities will find the following programs at Indiana University Bloomington useful: testing accommodations · extended time for tests · take-home exam · oral tests · readers · typist/scribe · note-taking services · reading machines · tape recorders · priority registration · waiver of math degree requirement. Individual or small group tutorials are also available in: time management · organizational skills · learning strategies · study skills. An advisor/advocate from the Learning Disability Services/ Disability Services for Students is available to students.

How to Get Admitted

For admissions decisions, non-academic factors considered: interview · extracurricular activities · special talents, interests and abilities · character/personal qualities · volunteer work · work experience · geographical location · minority affiliation · alumni relationship. A high school diploma is required, although a GED is also accepted for admissions consideration. SAT or ACT test scores are required of all applicants. SAT Subject Test scores are recommended but not required. *According to the admissions office:* Minimum 3.0 GPA recommended; rank in top two-fifths of secondary school class recommended for state residents; rank in top third of secondary school class recommended for out-of-state applicants. Preference given to Indiana residents who score above the state average and to non-residents who score above the national average on SAT Reasoning/ACT tests. *Academic units recommended:* 4 English, 4 Math, 3 Science, 3 Social Studies, 3 Foreign Language.

How to Pay for College

To apply for financial aid, students should submit the following: Free Application for Federal Student Aid (FAFSA). Indiana University Bloomington participates in the Federal Work Study program. *Need-based aid programs include:* scholarships and grants · general need-based awards · Federal Pell grants · state scholarships and grants · college-based scholarships and grants · private scholarships and grants. *Non-need-based aid programs include:* scholarships and grants · state scholarships and grants · creative arts and performance awards · special achievements and activities awards · special characteristics awards · athletic scholarships.

INDIANA UNIVERSITY BLOOMINGTON

Highlights

Admissions
Applicants: 37,826
Accepted: 27,300
Acceptance rate: 72.2%
Average GPA: 3.6
ACT range: 24-30
SAT Math range: 540-660
SAT Reading range: 520-630
SAT Writing range: 7-29
Top 10% of class: 35%
Top 25% of class: 70%
Top 50% of class: 95%

Deadlines
Early Action: No
Early Decision: No
Regular Action: Rolling admissions
Common Application: Not accepted

Financial Aid
In-state tuition: $10,388
Out-of-state tuition: $33,241
Room: Varies
Board: Varies
Books: $1,500
Freshmen receiving need-based aid: 45%
Undergrads rec. need-based aid: 44%
Avg. % of need met by financial aid: 87%
Avg. aid package (freshmen): $12,206
Avg. aid package (undergrads): $11,744
Avg. debt upon graduation: $27,619

Prominent Alumni
Joshua Bell, violinist; Kevin Kline, actor; Jane Pauley, broadcaster.

School Spirit
Mascot: Hoosiers
Colors: Cream and crimson
Song: *Indiana, Our Indiana*

261

INDIANA UNIVERSITY OF PENNSYLVANIA

1011 South Drive, Indiana, PA 15705
Admissions: 800-442-6830 · Financial Aid: 724-357-2218
Email: admissions-inquiry@iup.edu · Website: http://www.iup.edu

From the College

"Indiana University of Pennsylvania was established in 1875 and is the only doctoral research university in the Pennsylvania State System of Higher Education. IUP has a long tradition of academic excellence and receives frequent accolades, including designation as one of The Best 379 Colleges in the 2015 edition of a Princeton Review book by that name. The university provides an intellectually challenging experience to more than 14,000 students at three campuses, all easily accessible from Pittsburgh and the Middle Atlantic region. Academic offerings include more than 130 undergraduate majors with a variety of internship and study abroad programs, nearly 60 master's degree programs and 11 doctoral degrees. Unusual opportunities for research at all levels and the Robert E. Cook Honors College provide special challenges for academic growth. The variety and quality of instruction are characteristic of a big university, yet at IUP, close, one-to-one relationships develop within the teaching framework, and a strong sense of community prevails."

Campus Setting

Indiana University of Pennsylvania, founded in 1875, is a public, comprehensive institution. Programs are offered through the Colleges of Business, Education, Fine Arts, Health and Human Services, Humanities and Social Sciences, Natural Sciences and Mathematics and the School of Continuing Education. Its 374-acre campus is located in western Pennsylvania, 65 miles from Pittsburgh. A four-year institution, Indiana University Pennsylvania has an enrollment of 14,728 students. Campus facilities include: art museum · natural history museum · lodge · farm · co-generation plant · sailing base. Indiana University Pennsylvania provides on-campus housing with 1,981 units that can accommodate 4,076 students. Housing options: coed dorms · single-student apartments · special housing for disabled students · special housing for international students. Recreation and sports facilities include: field house · natatorium · stadium.

Student Life and Activities

Most students (68 percent) live off campus. Indiana University of Pennsylvania has 307 official student organizations. The most popular are: choral and instrumental ensembles · jazz, marching and pep bands · residence hall association · drill team · team managers · departmental, service and special-interest groups. For those interested in sports, there are intramural teams such as: basketball · bench press · bowling · flag football · golf · racquetball · soccer · softball · volleyball · walleyball · water polo · wrestling. Indiana University of Pennsylvania is a member of the Pennsylvania State Athletic Conference (Division II).

Academics and Learning Environment

Indiana University of Pennsylvania has 625 full-time and 98 part-time faculty members, offering a student-to-faculty ratio of 18:1. The most common course size is 20 to 29 students. Indiana University of Pennsylvania's 117 majors include the popular nursing, criminology and communications media and less popular French,

America's
Best Colleges for
B Students

physics education and economics/mathematics. The school has a general core requirement. Cooperative education is not offered. All first-year students must maintain a 2.0 GPA or higher to avoid academic probation, and a minimum overall GPA of 2.0 is required to graduate. Other special academic programs that would appeal to a B student include: pass/fail grading option · independent study · double majors · dual degrees · accelerated study · honors program · internships · weekend college · distance learning.

B Student Support and Success

IU offers credit courses that help students cope with the demands of college. Through the Learning Enhancement Center, a student can take classes on such topics as learning strategies, vocabulary expansion, reading skills for college study and introduction to college math. The center provides tutoring, supplemental instruction, workshops and a campus-wide academic support program to help all levels of students. The Writing Center offers tutoring by other students on a drop-in basis. The center also sponsors writing workshops with subjects such Internet use in research and resume writing. If a student's GPA falls below 2.0, he/she is placed on academic probation and must implement an Academic Recovery Plan, which is designed to help students make progress toward academic good standing.

Indiana University of Pennsylvania provides dedicated guidance for: academic · career · personal · psychological · minority students · military · veterans · non-traditional students · family planning. Indiana University of Pennsylvania offers remedial and refresher courses in: reading · writing · math · study skills. Annually, 73 percent of freshmen students return for their sophomore year.

Support for Students with Learning Disabilities

Indiana University of Pennsylvania offers students with learning disabilities a variety of support programs including: remedial math · remedial reading · learning center · testing accommodations · extended time for tests · take-home exam · oral tests · readers · note-taking services · reading machines · tape recorders · priority registration. Individual or small group tutorials are also available in: time management · organizational skills · learning strategies · specific subject areas · writing labs · math labs · study skills. An advisor/advocate from the LD program is available to students.

How to Get Admitted

For admissions decisions, non-academic factors considered: interview · extracurricular activities · special talents, interests and abilities · character/personal qualities · volunteer work · work experience · state of residency. A high school diploma is required, although a GED is also accepted for admissions consideration. SAT or ACT test scores are required of all applicants. SAT Subject Test scores are not required. *Academic units recommended:* 4 English, 3 Math, 3 Science, 3 Social Studies, 2 Foreign Language.

INDIANA UNIVERSITY OF PENNSYLVANIA

Highlights

Indiana University of Pennsylvania
Indiana, PA (Pop. 13,953)
Location: Small town
Four-year public
Founded: 1875
Website: http://www.iup.edu

Students
Total enrollment: 14,728
Undergrads: 12,471
Freshmen: 3,896
Part-time students: 6%
From out-of-state: 6%
Male/Female: 45%/55%
Live on-campus: 32%
In fraternities: 7%
In sororities: 6%
Off-campus employment rating: Good
Caucasian: 78%
African American: 10%
Hispanic: 3%
Asian: 1%
Hawaiian or Pacific Islander: <1%
Native American: <1%
Mixed (2+ ethnicities): 3%
International: 4%

Academics
Calendar: Semester
Student/faculty ratio: 18:1
Class size 9 or fewer: 8%
Class size 10-29: 53%
Class size 30-49: 25%
Class size 50-99: 12%
Class size 100 or more: 2%
Returning freshmen: 73%
Six-year graduation rate: 50%

Most Popular Majors
Criminology
Nursing
Communications media

INDIANA UNIVERSITY OF PENNSYLVANIA

Admissions
Applicants: 9,367
Accepted: 8,476
Acceptance rate: 90.5%
Average GPA: Not reported
ACT range: Not reported
SAT Math range: 440-540
SAT Reading range: 440-530
SAT Writing range: Not reported
Top 10% of class: 8%
Top 25% of class: 23%
Top 50% of class: 58%

Deadlines
Early Action: No
Early Decision: No
Regular Action: Rolling admissions
Common Application: Not accepted

Financial Aid
In-state tuition: $6,820
Out-of-state tuition: $17,050
Room: $5,312
Board: $2,456
Books: $1,100
Freshmen receiving need-based aid: 75%
Undergrads rec. need-based aid: 71%
Avg. % of need met by financial aid: 53%
Avg. aid package (freshmen): $9,234
Avg. aid package (undergrads): $8,726
Avg. debt upon graduation: $37,457

Prominent Alumni
Bonnie Harbison Anderson; Terry Dunlap; Chad Hurley.

School Spirit
Mascot: Crimson Hawks
Colors: Crimson and grey
Song: *Hail Indiana*

How to Pay for College
To apply for financial aid, students should submit the following: Free Application for Federal Student Aid (FAFSA). Indiana University of Pennsylvania participates in the Federal Work Study program. *Need-based aid programs include:* scholarships and grants · general need-based awards · Federal Pell grants · state scholarships and grants · college-based scholarships and grants · private scholarships and grants · United Negro College Fund. *Non-need-based aid programs include:* scholarships and grants · general need-based awards · state scholarships and grants · creative arts and performance awards · athletic scholarships · ROTC scholarships.

LAKE FOREST COLLEGE

555 North Sheridan Road, Lake Forest, IL 60045
Admissions: 800-828-4751 · Financial Aid: 847-735-5103
Email: admissions@lakeforest.edu · Website: http://www.lakeforest.edu

From the College

"A highly selective, undergraduate, liberal arts institution, the 107-acre campus is located 30 miles north of downtown Chicago in a suburb along Lake Michigan. The college takes full advantage of its proximity to one of the world's most dynamic cities, offering unmatched academic, cultural, internship, mentorship and employment resources. Its faculty is committed to teaching and, as the college's mission statement reads, 'We know our students by name.' Lake Forest College prepares students to become responsible citizens of the global community and celebrates the personal growth that accompanies the quest for excellence."

Campus Setting

Lake Forest College, founded in 1857, is a private liberal arts school. Its 107-acre campus is located in Lake Forest, one-half mile from Lake Michigan and 30 miles north of Chicago. A four-year institution, Lake Forest College has an enrollment of 1,622 students. Lake Forest College provides on-campus housing that accommodates 1,269 students. Housing options: coed dorms · women's dorms · single-student apartments. Recreation and sports facilities include: basketball, handball and racquetball courts · ice rink · softball field · swimming pool · weight rooms · indoor track · batting and golf cages · dance and aerobic studio · cardio equipment · gymnasium · multipurpose indoor courts with three surfaces.

Student Life and Activities

Nearly three-quarters (72 percent) of students live on campus. "With a very diverse student body many of the organizations provide activities for others to get to know the various cultures represented on campus. Soup & Stories is an extremely popular program where students have the opportunity to speak to the campus community about their life experiences in a casual informal setting where soup is served. With a student body of 1,575 students of all class years get to know each other and become a tight-knit community. Most all students stay on campus for the weekends and there is a lot to do," reports a school representative.

Popular gathering spots include Mohr Student Center, Sports and Fitness Center and the library. Homecoming and Family Weekend, Spring Concert, Relay for Life, theatre performances and athletic events are popular events during the school year. Lake Forest College has 50 official student organizations. Popular groups on campus include international groups, the entertainment team, Greek life, athletes and theater performers. Intramural teams include: ball hockey · basketball · broom ball · flag football · indoor soccer · table tennis · racquetball · volleyball. Lake Forest College is a member of the Midwest Conference (Division III), Northern Collegiate Hockey Association and Midwest Collegiate Hockey Association.

Academics and Learning Environment

Lake Forest College has 99 full-time and 79 part-time faculty members, offering a student-to-faculty ratio of 13:1. The most common course size is 10 to 19 students. Lake Forest College's 34 majors include the most popular psychology, communication and biology and least popular religion, area studies and Latin American studies. The

LAKE FOREST COLLEGE

Lake Forest College
Lake Forest, IL (Pop. 19,375)
Location: Small town
Four-year private
Founded: 1857
Website: http://www.lakeforest.edu

Students
Total enrollment: 1,622
Undergrads: 1,594
Freshmen: 403
Part-time students: 1%
From out-of-state: 34%
From public schools: 70%
Male/Female: 42%/58%
Live on-campus: 72%
In fraternities: 7%
In sororities: 11%
Off-campus employment rating: Good
Caucasian: 58%
African American: 6%
Hispanic: 14%
Asian: 5%
Hawaiian or Pacific Islander: <1%
Native American: <1%
Mixed (2+ ethnicities): 3%
International: 10%

Academics
Calendar: Semester
Student/faculty ratio: 13:1
Class size 9 or fewer: 11%
Class size 10-29: 80%
Class size 30-49: 7%
Class size 50-99: 1%
Class size 100 or more: -
Returning freshmen: 82%
Six-year graduation rate: 64%

Most Popular Majors
Communication
Psychology
Biology

school has a general core requirement. Cooperative education is not offered. All first-year students must maintain a 2.0 GPA or higher to avoid academic probation. Other special academic programs that would appeal to a B student: self-designed majors · pass/fail grading option · independent study · double majors · dual degrees · accelerated study · honors program · Phi Beta Kappa · internships.

B Student Support and Success

Insight from Lake Forest College includes the following: "We offer a comprehensive Academic Resource Center, which provides tutorial support open to all students. The program is coordinated by a Learning Resource Specialist. The college also supports a strong Writing Center, seminars in time management and study skills development.

"The personal interview is strongly recommended and is the best resource for assessing a student's potential to flourish at Lake Forest. We value students who are committed to community and campus involvement, who have a clear understanding of why they have applied to Lake Forest and whose needs are well matched with the college. In addition to the interview, students should strive to take a challenging high school curriculum, including honors or advanced placement courses when possible.

"We consider the rigor of a student's high school curriculum in contest to the grade point average and we read transcripts carefully. In this regard, we can appreciate strengths and weaknesses of each individual student, including a consideration of B or even C grades. There is a 'story' behind each transcript and we seek to understand a student's academic journey through the personal interview."

Lake Forest College provides dedicated guidance for: academic · career · personal · psychological · minority students · family planning · Annually, 82 percent of freshmen students return for their sophomore year. Approximately 21 percent pursue a graduate degree immediately after graduation. A year after graduation, 24 percent of graduates have entered graduate school. Among students who are employed, approximately 79 percent enter a field related to their major within six months of graduation. Companies that most frequently hire graduates from Lake Forest College include: Abbott Laboratories · Accenture · Brunswick · Chicago Historical Society · Coyote Logistics · IMC Global · LaSalle Financial · Medline · Morgan Stanley · Northern Trust · SBC · Teach for America · Wells Fargo Financial.

Support for Students with Learning Disabilities

Lake Forest College offers learning disabled students a lighter course load. These students may also access: tutors · learning center · testing accommodations · extended time for tests · take-home exam · oral tests · readers · typist/scribe · note-taking services · reading machines · tape recorders · texts on tape · early syllabus · priority registration. Individual or small group tutorials are also available in: time management · organizational skills · learning strategies · specific subject areas · writing labs · math labs · study skills. An advisor/advocate from the LD program is available to students.

How to Get Admitted

For admissions decisions, non-academic factors considered: interview ·
extracurricular activities · special talents, interests and abilities ·
character/personal qualities · volunteer work · work experience ·
state of residency · geographical location · alumni relationship. A
high school diploma is required, although a GED is also accepted
for admissions consideration. SAT or ACT test scores are required
for some applicants. *According to the admissions office:* Accelerated
courses recommended. *Academic units recommended:* 4 English, 4
Math, 4 Science, 4 Social Studies, 3 Foreign Language.

How to Pay for College

To apply for financial aid, students should submit the following: Free
Application for Federal Student Aid (FAFSA) · institution's own
financial aid forms. Lake Forest College participates in the Federal
Work Study program. *Need-based aid programs include:* scholarships
and grants · general need-based awards · Federal Pell grants · state
scholarships and grants · college-based scholarships and grants ·
private scholarships and grants. *Non-need-based aid programs include:*
scholarships and grants · general need-based awards · state scholarships and grants · creative arts and performance awards · special
achievements and activities awards · special characteristics awards.

LAKE FOREST COLLEGE

Highlights

Admissions
Applicants: 3,684
Accepted: 2,110
Acceptance rate: 57.3%
Placed on wait list: 10
Enrolled from wait list: 8
Average GPA: 3.6
ACT range: 23-28
SAT Math range: 510-620
SAT Reading range: 510-620
SAT Writing range: 510-610
Top 10% of class: 24%
Top 25% of class: 58%
Top 50% of class: 91%

Deadlines
Early Action: 11/15
Early Decision: 12/1
Regular Action: 2/15 (priority)
Notification of admission by: 3/10
Common Application: Accepted

Financial Aid
In-state tuition: $40,448
Out-of-state tuition: $40,448
Room: $4,480
Board: $5,000
Books: Varies
Freshmen receiving need-based aid: 79%
Undergrads rec. need-based aid: 78%
Avg. % of need met by financial aid: 83%
Avg. aid package (freshmen): $34,695
Avg. aid package (undergrads): $33,571
Avg. debt upon graduation: $31,909

Prominent Alumni
Richard Armstrong, Director, Solomon
R. Guggenheim Foundation; Sig Gissler,
Administrator, Pulitzer Prizes.

School Spirit
Mascot: Boomer: Black Bear
Colors: Red and black

267

LONGWOOD UNIVERSITY

201 High Street, Farmville, VA 23909
Admissions: 800-281-4677, extension 2 · Financial Aid: 800-281-4677
Email: admissions@longwood.edu · Website: http://www.longwood.edu

From the College

"Longwood University offers a truly distinctive combination - the opportunities, diversity and affordability of a public university, along with the warmth and spirit of a smaller college. All students participate in internships or research projects to gain relevant work-related experience. Longwood is committed to providing students with the technological, communication and human relation skills necessary to succeed."

Campus Setting

Longwood, founded in 1839, is public university. Its 160-acre campus is located in Farmville, 60 miles west of Richmond. A four-year institution, Longwood University has an enrollment of 4,960 students, and has been co-ed since 1976. Longwood University has 2,025 units capable of holding 2,955 students. Housing options: coed dorms · women's dorms · sorority housing · fraternity housing · single-student apartments · special housing for disabled students · special housing for international students. Recreation and sports facilities include: basketball, racquetball and tennis courts · field hockey, lacrosse, softball and soccer fields · gymnasium · weight room.

Student Life and Activities

Nearly three-quarters (71 percent) of students live on campus. Popular on-campus gathering spots include Stubbs Lawn or Wheeler Lawn. Popular campus events include October Fest, Spring Weekend and Theme Mixers. Longwood University has 184 official student organizations. The most popular are: Camerata Singers · gospel choir · Lancer Productions · Longwood Company of Dancers · Blue Heat (dancers) · Ambassadors · Longwood Players · Music Educators National Conference · modern foreign language club · National Student Speech/Language/Hearing Association · history club · Honor Board · Campus Safety Escort Service · Groups and Individuals Volunteering Efforts · Habitat for Humanity · Orientation Leaders · Peer Helpers/Peer Mentors · Big Sibling Program · Students Advocating for a Fearless Environment · Student Educators for Active Leadership · Unity Alliance · Wellness Advocates · Intrafraternity Council · Pan-Hellenic Council · Independent Innovators · math club · Accounting Association · American Marketing Association · political science club · Judicial Board · Athletic Trainers Association · Therapeutic Recreation · biology club · chemistry club. Intramural teams include: air hockey · basketball · bowling · flag football · indoor soccer · indoor volleyball · sand volleyball · softball · spades · table tennis. Longwood University is a member of the Big South Conference (Division I) and Northern Pacific Field Hockey Conference (Division I).

Academics and Learning Environment

Longwood University has 238 full-time and 50 part-time faculty members, offering a student-to-faculty ratio of 18:1. The most common course size is 20 to 29 students. Longwood University offers 34 majors. Liberal studies, business administration and psychology are the most popular. Least popular are modern foreign languages, economics and chemistry. The school has a general core requirement. Cooperative education is not offered. All first-year students must maintain a 2.0 GPA or higher to avoid academic probation, and a minimum overall GPA of 2.0 is required to graduate.

Other special academic programs include: pass/fail grading option · independent study · double majors · dual degrees · accelerated study · honors program · internships · distance learning.

B Student Support and Success

Longwood College offers a Learning Center that is located in the Greenwood Library. It features a speaking center, as well as a writing center and open labs. There is no charge for any of the services offered, and sessions are on a drop-in basis.

Longwood University provides dedicated guidance for: academic · career · personal · psychological · family planning · religious. Each year, 80 percent of freshmen students return for their sophomore year. Companies that most frequently hire graduates from Longwood University include: America Online · AT&T · BB&T · Capital One · Circuit City · Deloitte · Dominion Virginia Power · DuPont · Federal Reserve Bank · Goodman & Company · Johnson & Johnson · Kraft Foods · KPMG · Microsoft Corporation · Philip Morris · State Farm Insurance · SunTrust · Wachovia.

Support for Students with Learning Disabilities

Longwood University offers additional time to students with learning disabilities to complete their degree, as well as a lightened course load. These students may also want to access the options of: tutors · learning center · testing accommodations · extended time for tests · take-home exam · readers · typist/scribe · note-taking services · reading machines · tape recorders · texts on tape · priority seating · waiver of math degree requirement. Individual or small group tutorials are also available in: time management · organizational skills · learning strategies · specific subject areas · writing labs · math labs · study skills. An advisor/advocate from the Office of Disability Support Services is available to students.

How to Get Admitted

For admissions decisions, non-academic factors considered: extracurricular activities · special talents, interests and abilities · character/personal qualities · volunteer work · geographical location · minority affiliation · alumni relationship. A high school diploma is required, although a GED is also accepted for admissions consideration. SAT or ACT test scores are required of all applicants. SAT Subject Test scores are not required. *According to the admissions office:* Minimum combined SAT Reasoning score of 1000, rank in top half of secondary school class and minimum 3.0 GPA required. *Academic units recommended:* 4 English, 4 Math, 4 Science, 2 Social Studies, 4 Foreign Language.

How to Pay for College

To apply for financial aid, students should submit the following: Free Application for Federal Student Aid (FAFSA). Longwood University participates in the Federal Work Study program. *Need-based aid programs include:* scholarships and grants · general need-based awards · Federal Pell grants · state scholarships and grants · college-based scholarships and grants · private scholarships and grants. *Non-*

Highlights

Longwood University
Farmville, VA (Pop. 8,161)
Location: Small town
Four-year public
Founded: 1839
Website: http://www.longwood.edu

Students
Total enrollment: 4,960
Undergrads: 4,497
Freshmen: 1,205
Part-time students: 8%
From out-of-state: 3%
From public schools: 92%
Male/Female: 34%/66%
Live on-campus: 71%
In fraternities: 22%
In sororities: 22%
Off-campus employment rating: Fair
Caucasian: 78%
African American: 8%
Hispanic: 5%
Asian: 1%
Hawaiian or Pacific Islander: <1%
Native American: <1%
Mixed (2+ ethnicities): 3%
International: 1%

Academics
Calendar: Semester
Student/faculty ratio: 18:1
Class size 9 or fewer: 16%
Class size 10-29: 65%
Class size 30-49: 18%
Class size 50-99: 1%
Class size 100 or more: -
Returning freshmen: 80%
Six-year graduation rate: 63%

Most Popular Majors
Liberal studies
Business administration
Psychology

269

LONGWOOD UNIVERSITY

Highlights

Admissions
Applicants: 4,055
Accepted: 3,299
Acceptance rate: 81.4%
Average GPA: 3.4
ACT range: 19-23
SAT Math range: 460-540
SAT Reading range: 460-550
SAT Writing range: Not reported
Top 10% of class: 10%
Top 25% of class: 33%
Top 50% of class: 73%

Deadlines
Early Action: 12/1
Early Decision: No
Regular Action: Rolling admissions
Common Application: Accepted

Financial Aid
In-state tuition: $20,836
Out-of-state tuition: $34,606
Room: $3,702
Board: $3,108
Books: $1,000
Freshmen receiving need-based aid: 53%
Undergrads rec. need-based aid: 52%
Avg. % of need met by financial aid: 80%
Avg. aid package (freshmen): $13,173
Avg. aid package (undergrads): $13,155
Avg. debt upon graduation: $26,465

Prominent Alumni
Becky A. Bailey Ph.D., founder/president of Loving Guidance Inc., recognized expert in childhood education and developmental psychology; Thomas I. Dewitt, president/CEO, SNVC, L.C.; William E. Todd, ambassador to the Kingdom of Cambodia.

School Spirit
Mascot: Lancers
Colors: Blue and white
Song: *Alma Mater*

need-based aid programs include: scholarships and grants · general need-based awards · state scholarships and grants · creative arts and performance awards · athletic scholarships · ROTC scholarships.

LUTHER COLLEGE

700 College Drive, Decorah, IA 52101-1045
Admissions: 563-387-1287 · Financial Aid: 563-387-1018
Email: admissions@luther.edu · Website: http://www.luther.edu

From the College

"Luther offers more than 60 majors, minors, pre-professional and special programs leading to the bachelor of arts degree. A Phi Beta Kappa chapter attests to the academic excellence of the college. Forty states and 56 countries are represented in the nearly 2,500-member student body. The campus is built on the rolling wooded hills and rugged limestone cliffs of northeast Iowa's bluff country. The scenic Upper Iowa River flows through the lower portion of the 200-acre central campus. The college owns an additional 800 acres adjoining the central campus which are devoted to environmental research, biological studies and recreation."

Campus Setting

Luther is a church-affiliated, liberal arts college. Founded as a college for men in 1861, it adopted coeducation in 1936. Its 200-acre campus is located in Decorah, 15 miles south of the Minnesota border. A four-year private institution, Luther College has an enrollment of 2,466 students. The school is affiliated with the Lutheran Church ELCA. Luther College provides on-campus housing with 11 units that can accommodate 2,134 students. Housing options: coed dorms · single-student apartments · married-student apartments. Recreation and sports facilities include: fitness center · indoor track · intramural fields · disc golf course.

Student Life and Activities

The vast majority (84 percent) of students live on campus. Students flock to events including Homecoming, Flamingo Ball, Family Weekend, Christmas at Luther, Ethnic Arts Festival, Center Stage Series, major concerts and guest speakers. Luther College has 90 official student organizations. The most popular are: Aurora (women's choir) · Cantorei · Cathedral Choir · Collegiate Chorale · Collegium Musicum · concert band · dance team · jazz band · jazz orchestra · Nordic Choir · Norsemen (men's choir) · opera workshop · Performing Arts Council · SPIN Theatre · symphony orchestra · varsity band · wind and percussion ensemble · Athletes Serving Others · Chess Club · College Democrats · College Republicans · entrepreneurship club · Model UN · PRIDE · Secular Student Society · Student Activities Council · Students Helping Our Community · chemistry club · Environmental Concerns Organization · health sciences club · Pre-Registered Nurses. For those interested in sports, there are intramural teams such as: running clubs, flag football, floor hockey, sand volleyball, Ultimate Frisbee, and Wii bowling leagues. Luther College is a member of the Iowa Intercollegiate Athletic Conference (Division III).

Academics and Learning Environment

Luther College has 180 full-time and 77 part-time faculty members, offering a student-to-faculty ratio of 12:1. The most common course size is 10 to 19 students. Luther College's 40 majors include the popular biology, management and music and the far less popular Africana studies, Scandinavian studies and women/gender studies. The school has a general core requirement as well as a religion requirement. Cooperative education is not offered. All first-year students must maintain a 1.8 GPA or higher to avoid academic probation, and a minimum overall GPA of 2.0 is required to graduate. Other special academic programs that would appeal to a B student include:

LUTHER COLLEGE

Luther College
Decorah, IA (Pop. 8,109)
Location: Small town
Four-year private
Founded: 1861
Website: http://www.luther.edu

Students
Total enrollment: 2,466
Undergrads: 2,466
Part-time students: 2%
From out-of-state: 69%
From public schools: 90%
Male/Female: 43%/57%
Live on-campus: 84%
In fraternities: 1%
In sororities: 2%
Off-campus employment rating: Good
Caucasian: 85%
African American: 2%
Hispanic: 3%
Asian: 2%
Native American: <1%
Mixed (2+ ethnicities): 2%
International: 6%

Academics
Calendar: 4-1-4 system
Student/faculty ratio: 12:1
Class size 9 or fewer: 16%
Class size 10-29: 76%
Class size 30-49: 7%
Class size 50-99: 1%
Class size 100 or more: -
Returning freshmen: 87%
Six-year graduation rate: 76%

Most Popular Majors
Biology
Music
Management

self-designed majors · pass/fail grading option · independent study · double majors · dual degrees · honors program · Phi Beta Kappa · internships · certificate programs.

B Student Support and Success

This Lutheran college has a Student Academic Support Center. The goals of the center include assisting students in becoming self-confident critical thinkers and learners, helping with peer tutoring, linking students to helpful resources and meeting the needs of all students who need any kind of academic assistance. Luther offers a class called Critical Reading and Learning Strategies (GS110) that helps students become better readers through the description, interpretation and evaluation of different texts. Additionally, the Learning and Study Skills Inventory (LASSI) is a diagnostic measure to help students discover the areas in which they need help. This assessment measures everything from attitude and motivation to test anxiety and information processing. The college's Academic Support Services includes independent tutoring and group sessions, as well as learning skills workshops, academic advising and access to a series of helpful hand-outs.

Luther College dedicated guidance for: academic · career · personal · psychological · minority students · non-traditional students · family planning · religious. The average freshman year GPA is 3.1, and 87 percent of freshmen students return for their sophomore year. Approximately 20 percent of students return for a graduate degree right after graduation. About 78 percent of students who are employed enter a field related to their major within six months of graduation. Companies that most frequently hire graduates from Luther College include: Mayo Clinic · Wells Fargo · Thrivent · Gunderson Lutheran · Fastenal Company · Target · Jeld Wenn · IBM · Epic Systems · Accenture · Hormel · University of Iowa Hospital & Research Center · Securian Financial Group · Best Buy · Weber Shandwick.

Support for Students with Learning Disabilities

Luther College grants additional time to students with learning disabilities to complete their degree. Credit is given for remedial courses taken. High school foreign language and math waivers are accepted. LD students may want to access: tutors · learning center · testing accommodations · extended time for tests · take-home exam · oral tests · typist/scribe · note-taking services · tape recorders · waiver of math degree requirement. Individual or small group tutorials are also available in: time management · organizational skills · learning strategies · specific subject areas · writing labs · math labs · study skills. An advisor/advocate from the Student Academic Support Center is available to students.

How to Get Admitted

For admissions decisions, non-academic factors considered: interview · extracurricular activities · special talents, interests and abilities · character/personal qualities · volunteer work · state of residency · minority affiliation · alumni relationship. A high school diploma is required, although a GED is also accepted for admissions consideration. SAT or ACT test scores are required of all applicants.

Academic units recommended: 4 English, 3 Math, 2 Science, 3 Social Studies, 2 Foreign Language.

How to Pay for College

To apply for financial aid, students should submit the following: Free Application for Federal Student Aid (FAFSA) · institution's own financial aid forms. Luther College participates in the Federal Work Study program. *Need-based aid programs include:* scholarships and grants · general need-based awards · Federal Pell grants · state scholarships and grants · college-based scholarships and grants · private scholarships and grants. *Non-need-based aid programs include:* scholarships and grants · state scholarships and grants · creative arts and performance awards.

LUTHER COLLEGE

Highlights

Admissions
Applicants: 3,490
Accepted: 2,517
Acceptance rate: 72.1%
Average GPA: 3.7
ACT range: 23-29
SAT Math range: 500-620
SAT Reading range: 450-605
SAT Writing range: 5-16
Top 10% of class: 32%
Top 25% of class: 56%
Top 50% of class: 87%

Deadlines
Early Action: No
Early Decision: No
Regular Action: Rolling admissions
Common Application: Accepted

Financial Aid
In-state tuition: $38,170
Out-of-state tuition: $38,170
Room: $3,140
Board: $3,950
Books: $1,040
Freshmen receiving need-based aid: 73%
Undergrads rec. need-based aid: 71%
Avg. % of need met by financial aid: 85%
Avg. aid package (freshmen): $31,153
Avg. aid package (undergrads): $28,581
Avg. debt upon graduation: $34,395

Prominent Alumni
Arne Sorenson, president and CEO, Marriott International Inc.; Brian Andreas, creator, StoryPeople.

School Spirit
Mascot: Norse
Colors: Blue and white

273

LYCOMING COLLEGE

700 College Place, Williamsport, PA 17701
Admissions: 570-321-4026 · Financial Aid: 570-321-4040
Email: admissions@lycoming.edu · Website: http://www.lycoming.edu

From the College

"The mission of Lycoming College is to offer students a distinguished education in the traditional liberal arts and sciences. The college has sought to accomplish that goal by gathering a strong faculty with a primary focus on teaching and a strong secondary focus on research. The college has established a teaching effectiveness program to focus on new strategies for the classroom including those involving the most recent technology. Lycoming features an extensive writing program for students in which they are expected to have a specific writing component in all their general education courses and to take an additional three courses designated as writing intensive. The college has encouraged student research across the curriculum with a particular focus in the sciences. Lycoming has also introduced capstone courses in most departments featuring an opportunity for students to bring their academic work together in some form of major research project or artistic presentation. In order to accomplish the close work between faculty and students required by our mission, the college has sustained a full-time faculty of approximately 90 percent of the total."

Campus Setting

Lycoming is a private, four-year, coeducational, liberal arts college. Founded in 1812, it is one of the fifty oldest colleges in the United States. There are 1,365 undergraduate students from 28 states and 12 foreign countries that call Lycoming home. Eighty-five percent of Lycoming's students live on campus and are guaranteed housing all four years. According to the college, it is a "community with new vitality, ongoing momentum and a nationally recognized commitment to quality education." In the past few years, Lycoming has seen a new Recreation Center built and the restoration of a building that is now called Honors Hall. Also, the college recently opened a new residence hall, the first one with air conditioning. In addition to a large, well-stocked library, the campus also has an art gallery. Lycoming College provides on-campus housing able to accommodate 1,246 students. Housing options: coed dorms · women's dorms · sorority housing · fraternity housing · single-student apartments · special housing for disabled students. Recreation and sports facilities include: athletic complex · intramural fields · recreation center.

Student Life and Activities

The majority (85 percent) of students live on campus. Popular gathering spots include Wertz Student Center, residence halls, Pennington Lounge, The Pub and The Coffee and Tea Room. Popular campus events include Homecoming Weekend, Little Sibs Weekend, Carnival and concerts. Lycoming College has 81 official student organizations. The most popular are: Amnesty International · Creative Arts Society · equestrian club · FLOAT Tutoring Program · Gays, Lesbians Or BiSexuals and Allies at Lycoming (GLOBAL) · Habitat for Humanity · juggling club · Leadership Education Advancement Project (LEAP) · dance program · College Democrats · fly fishing club (FLYCO) · College Republicans · Environmental Awareness Foundation · Raging Stitches · Recreation Board · Student Senate (SSLC) · Best Buddies · Youth Leaders for Lyco · Big Brothers/Big Sisters · Campus Activities Board · Circle K · Colleges Against Cancer · Commuter Student Organization · Fencing Club and Guild of Swordsmen. For those interested in sports, there are intramural teams such as: basketball · dodgeball · flag football · fly fishing · soccer · volleyball · Wiffle ball.

Lycoming College is a member of the Commonwealth Conference (Division III) and the Middle Atlantic States Collegiate Athletic Conference (Division III).

Academics and Learning Environment

Lycoming College has 81 full-time and 38 part-time faculty members, offering a student-to-faculty ratio of 14:1. The most common course size is 10 to 19 students. Lycoming College offers 31 majors. The top choices are business administration, psychology and biology. The school has a general core requirement. Cooperative education is not offered. All first-year students must maintain a 1.8 GPA or higher to avoid academic probation, and a minimum overall GPA of 3.0 is required to graduate. Additional academic programs include: self-designed majors · pass/fail grading option · independent study · double majors · dual degrees · accelerated study · honors program · internships.

B Student Support and Success

Lycoming has an Academic Resource Center that offers subject tutors, writing consultants, study groups, study skills workshops and support services for learning disabilities. In addition, the school provides a program called Writing across the Curriculum, which helps students develop their ability to communicate clearly.

Lycoming College provides dedicated guidance for: academic · career · personal · psychological · minority students · non-traditional students · family planning · religious. The average freshman year GPA is 2.8, and 81 percent of freshmen students return for their sophomore year. About 20 percent of students return for a graduate degree following graduation. Of those who are employed, approximately 72 percent enter a field related to their major within six months of graduation. Companies that most frequently hire graduates from Lycoming College include: Merck · Kimberly Clark · Merrill Lynch · American Express · Vanguard Group · Marsh-McLennan.

Support for Students with Learning Disabilities

Lycoming College allows learning disabled students to take a less demanding course load, and more time to complete their degrees. Credit is given for remedial courses taken. LD students with learning disabilities may also want to investigate: remedial math · special classes · tutors · learning center · testing accommodations · untimed tests · extended time for tests · oral tests · readers · note-taking services · reading machines · tape recorders · videotaped classes · priority seating. Individual or small group tutorials are also available in: time management · organizational skills · learning strategies · specific subject areas · writing labs · math labs · study skills. An advisor/advocate from the Academic Resource Center is available to students.

How to Get Admitted

For admissions decisions, non-academic factors considered: interview · extracurricular activities · special talents, interests and abilities · character/personal qualities · volunteer work · work experience · state of residency · geographical location · minority affiliation · alumni relationship. A high school diploma is required, although a GED

LYCOMING COLLEGE

Highlights

Lycoming College
Williamsport (Pop. 29,534)
Location: Medium city
Four-year private
Founded: 1812
Website: http://www.lycoming.edu

Students
Total enrollment: 1,365
Undergrads: 1,365
Part-time students: 2%
From out-of-state: 32%
Male/Female: 44%/56%
Live on-campus: 85%
In fraternities: 15%
In sororities: 21%
Off-campus employment rating: Good
Caucasian: 78%
African American: 5%
Hispanic: 3%
Asian: 1%
Native American: <1%
Mixed (2+ ethnicities): 2%
International: 3%

Academics
Calendar: Semester
Student/faculty ratio: 14:1
Class size 9 or fewer: 22%
Class size 10-29: 63%
Class size 30-49: 14%
Class size 50-99: 1%
Class size 100 or more: 1%
Returning freshmen: 81%
Six-year graduation rate: 65%

Most Popular Majors
Business administration
Psychology
Biology

275

College Profiles

LYCOMING COLLEGE

Admissions
Applicants: 1,723
Accepted: 1,233
Acceptance rate: 71.6%
Average GPA: 3.4
ACT range: 20-26
SAT Math range: 470-590
SAT Reading range: 450-570
SAT Writing range: 1-12
Top 10% of class: 20%
Top 25% of class: 46%
Top 50% of class: 78%

Deadlines
Early Action: No
Early Decision: No
Regular Action: 12/1 (priority)
3/1 (final)
Notification of admission by: 12/15
Common Application: Accepted

Financial Aid
In-state tuition: $34,016
Out-of-state tuition: $34,016
Room: $5,294
Board: $5,082
Books: $1,000
Freshmen receiving need-based aid: 82%
Undergrads rec. need-based aid: 84%
Avg. % of need met by financial aid: 77%
Avg. aid package (freshmen): $27,893
Avg. aid package (undergrads): $27,007
Avg. debt upon graduation: $35,990

Prominent Alumni
Deidre Connelly, CEO of Lilly USA; Tom
Woodruff Jr., Oscar-winning special-
effects artist and actor.

School Spirit
Mascot: Warriors
Colors: Blue and gold

is also accepted for admissions consideration. SAT or ACT test scores are recommended but not required. SAT Subject Test scores are recommended but not required. *Academic units recommended:* 4 English, 4 Math, 3 Science, 4 Social Studies, 3 Foreign Language.

How to Pay for College

To apply for financial aid, students should submit the following: Free Application for Federal Student Aid (FAFSA) · institution's own financial aid forms · state aid form. Lycoming College participates in the Federal Work Study program. *Need-based aid programs include:* scholarships and grants · general need-based awards · Federal Pell grants · state scholarships and grants · college-based scholarships and grants · private scholarships and grants. *Non-need-based aid programs include:* scholarships and grants · state scholarships and grants · creative arts and performance awards · special achievements and activities awards · ROTC scholarships.

LYNN UNIVERSITY

3601 North Military Trail, Boca Raton, FL 33431
Admissions: 800-888-5966 · Financial Aid: 800-578-9737
Email: admission@lynn.edu · Website: http://www.lynn.edu

From the College

"Lynn University is an independent, innovative college based in Boca Raton, Florida. Lynn's NCAA Division II Fighting Knights have won 21 national titles, its Conservatory of Music features a world-renowned faculty of performers and scholars and its nationally recognized Institute for Achievement and Learning empowers students with learning differences to become independent learners. The school's Dialogues of Learning curriculum, award-winning iPad program and international student base help Lynn graduates gain the intellectual flexibility and global experience to fulfill their potential in an ever-changing world."

Campus Setting

Lynn University, founded in 1962, is a private liberal arts university. Its 123-acre campus is located in Boca Raton, 23 miles from Fort Lauderdale and Palm Beach and 50 miles from Miami. A four-year institution, Lynn University has an enrollment of 2,297 students, and has been co-ed since 1971. Lynn University provides on-campus housing with seven units that can accommodate 943 students. Housing options: coed dorms · women's dorms · special housing for disabled students. Recreation and sports facilities include: basketball court · fields · fitness and sports center · tennis complex.

Student Life and Activities

Just over half of the students (53 percent) live on campus. As reported by a school representative, "The campus is diverse with a strong international student population and a commitment to showcasing the global aspect of community living. With a number of on-campus and off-campus opportunities to engage as a learner, students are challenged to become active citizens and contribute to their holistic development." Popular gathering spots include beaches, parks, restaurants, shopping areas and Walt Disney World. Lynn University has 25 official student organizations. The most popular are: Music of the Knights · theatre improv group · Knights of the Roundtable · hospitality club · Students in Free Enterprise · Best Buddies · environmental club · Residence Hall Council. For those interested in sports, there are intramural teams such as: basketball · equestrian sports · flag football · golf · tennis. Lynn University is a member of the Sunshine State Conference (Division II).

Academics and Learning Environment

Lynn University has 89 full-time and 102 part-time faculty members, offering a student-to-faculty ratio of 17:1. The most common course size is 20 to 29 students. Lynn University offers 39 majors. The top choices are business administration, hospitality management and psychology. The school has a general core requirement. Cooperative education is available. All first-year students must maintain a 2.0 GPA or higher to avoid academic probation. Other special academic programs that would appeal to a B student include: independent study · double majors · dual degrees · accelerated study · honors program · internships · distance learning.

B Student Support and Success

Lynn's Institute for Achievement and Learning focuses on personalized education. The college states that the institute "embraces, empowers and engages its students to

LYNN UNIVERSITY

Lynn University
Boca Raton, FL (Pop. 87,836)
Location: Medium city
Four-year private
Founded: 1962
Website: http://www.lynn.edu

Students
Total enrollment: 2,297
Undergrads: 1,785
Part-time students: 8%
From out-of-state: 62%
Male/Female: 53%/47%
Live on-campus: 53%
In fraternities: 5%
In sororities: 8%
Off-campus employment rating: Good
Caucasian: 38%
African American: 10%
Hispanic: 12%
Asian: 2%
Hawaiian or Pacific Islander: <1%
Native American: 1%
International: 23%

Academics
Calendar: Semester
Student/faculty ratio: 17:1
Class size 9 or fewer: 10%
Class size 10-29: 80%
Class size 30-49: 9%
Class size 50-99: -
Class size 100 or more: -
Returning freshmen: 69%
Six-year graduation rate: 41%

Most Popular Majors
Business administration
Hospitality management
Psychology

offer opportunities for greater accomplishments in higher education and career realization."

Programs include First Year Experience, the Tutoring Center, Discovery Writing Center, Metamorphosis Coaching, Probationary Support and Academic Status Support. First Year Experience is required of all freshmen. This two-semester academic program connects new students with peers, campus resources and faculty. In the first class (FYE-1), students focus on the nature of education, including units on time management, test taking, communication skills, study techniques, university policies and procedures, resources and services, health and wellness issues and personal issues. FYE-1 also includes a pre-orientation to Academic Adventure, a faculty-led program in which the entire freshman class spends five days in the Caribbean on a ship studying the region's cultures and people. In FYE-2, students explore multicultural and diversity awareness, educational planning, career development, leadership, community service and learning potential—plus reflect upon their Academic Adventure. The Discovery Writing Center offers one-on-one tutoring for all levels of writing skills. The Hannifan Center for Career Development and Internships provides personalized career counseling, group career workshops, internships and job-placement assistance. Academic Status Support assists students who are on academic probation. This no-cost program includes advising and learning strategy suggestions to help students improve their grades. Probationary Support is similar and offers free advising, group tutoring, social activities, counseling sessions and workshops. Metamorphosis Coaching is geared to students who learn best from hands-on experience rather than traditional classroom methods. It takes students out of the classroom and into such settings as the campus butterfly garden or a local nature center as they learn observation skills logged into journals. According to the college, this program is not just about studying nature, but it also is "a study of life and the nature of our own selves. The 'lessons' learned through this reflective process will provide valuable insights about the way you learn best—and yourself." The program also includes group dinners and guest lecturers as well as private tutoring and field trips. (There is a charge for this program.)

Lynn University provides dedicated guidance for: academic · career · personal. The average freshman year GPA is 2.6, and 69 percent of freshmen students return for their sophomore year. Among students who enter the workforce, approximately 83 percent enter a field related to their major within six months of graduation. Companies that most frequently hire graduates from Lynn University include: Applied Card Systems · Boca Raton Resort and Club · Enterprise Rent-A-Car · Five-Star Productions · Four Seasons Resort · Lynn University · Nickelodeon · Palm Beach School System · Target Stores.

Support for Students with Learning Disabilities

Lynn University grants learning disabled students additional time to complete their degree. These students may also want to investigate: special classes · tutors · learning center · testing accommodations · untimed tests · extended time for tests · take-home exam · oral tests

· readers · note-taking services · reading machines · tape recorders · texts on tape · videotaped classes · early syllabus · diagnostic testing service · waiver of foreign language degree requirement. Individual or small group tutorials are also available in: time management · organizational skills · learning strategies · specific subject areas · writing labs · math labs · study skills. An advisor/advocate from the Institute for Achievement and Learning is available to students. This member also sits on the admissions committee.

How to Get Admitted

For admissions decisions, non-academic factors considered: interview · extracurricular activities · character/personal qualities · volunteer work · work experience · state of residency. A high school diploma is required, although a GED is also accepted for admissions consideration. SAT or ACT test scores are required of all applicants. *Academic units recommended:* 4 English, 4 Math, 4 Science, 2 Social Studies.

How to Pay for College

To apply for financial aid, students should submit the following: Free Application for Federal Student Aid (FAFSA) · institution's own financial aid forms. Lynn University participates in the Federal Work Study program. *Need-based aid programs include:* scholarships and grants · general need-based awards · Federal Pell grants · state scholarships and grants · college-based scholarships and grants · private scholarships and grants. *Non-need-based aid programs include:* scholarships and grants · general need-based awards · state scholarships and grants · creative arts and performance awards · special achievements and activities awards · special characteristics awards · athletic scholarships.

LYNN UNIVERSITY

Highlights

Admissions
Applicants: 2,698
Accepted: 2,094
Acceptance rate: 77.6%
Average GPA: 2.8
ACT range: 18-22
SAT Math range: 410-530
SAT Reading range: 410-520
SAT Writing range: 1-5
Top 10% of class: 1%
Top 25% of class: 9%
Top 50% of class: 41%

Deadlines
Early Action: No
Early Decision: No
Regular Action: Rolling admissions
Common Application: Accepted

Financial Aid
In-state tuition: $32,800
Out-of-state tuition: $32,800
Room: Varies
Board: Varies
Books: $800
Freshmen receiving need-based aid: 46%
Undergrads rec. need-based aid: 43%
Avg. % of need met by financial aid: 56%
Avg. aid package (freshmen): $19,743
Avg. aid package (undergrads): $20,042
Avg. debt upon graduation: $31,634

Prominent Alumni
Jean Alexandre, San Jose Earthquakes; John McCormack, college basketball coach at Florida Atlantic.

School Spirit
Mascot: Fighting Knights
Colors: Blue and white
Song: *Lynn University Fight Song*

MANHATTANVILLE COLLEGE

2900 Purchase Street, Purchase, NY 10577
Admissions: 800-32-VILLE · Financial Aid: 914-323-5357
Email: admissions@mville.edu · Website: http://www.mville.edu

From the College

"Manhattanville College is a vibrant global community of learners and educators dedicated to providing a nurturing environment for intellectual growth. The college is located on a beautiful 100-acre suburban campus just 30 miles from New York City. We have an amazingly international and national diverse mix of students from 36 states and 51 countries. Our Manhattanville Curriculum focuses on integrated learning, which ensures that students graduate with competencies in key areas such as critical reasoning, technology and global and intercultural awareness though both coursework and our groundbreaking Portfolio system. We offer 45 undergraduate courses of study, ranging from traditional Bachelor's to accelerated programs geared to adult learners."

Campus Setting

Manhattanville is a private, liberal arts college. Founded as an academy for girls in 1841, it adopted coeducation in 1971. Its 100-acre campus is located in Purchase, 25 miles from New York City. A four-year institution, Manhattanville College has an enrollment of 2,796 students. Manhattanville College provides on-campus housing with 744 units that can accommodate 1,263 students. Housing options: coed dorms.

Student Life and Activities

The majority (79 percent) of students live on campus. According to the editor of the school newspaper, "Social life has traditionally been slow and people usually went off-campus for activities, but recently there have been improvements aimed at keeping students on campus for the weekend. It's worth staying now." Popular on-campus hangouts include Reid Castle, Manhattanville Cafe, the quad and the commuter lounge. Off campus, students frequent Ivy, O'Henry's and 7 Willow Street. Popular events include Shakespeare Events, Community Service Trips, The Living Theatre, Fair Trade Week, Vagina Monologues, Cymbeline, Quad Jam, The Global Pot, Dance Concerts, Shabbat Dinners, Latin Bash, India Art Exhibit, Hispanic Summit and Kwanzaa Celebration. Manhattanville College has 57 official student organizations. The Student Programming Board, Quad Jam Committees, Student Government, and the Clubs' Council are influential on-campus groups. Manhattanville College is a member of the Eastern Collegiate Athletic Conference (Men's Hockey West, Women's Hockey East) and the MAC Freedom Conference (Division III).

Academics and Learning Environment

Manhattanville College has 102 full-time and 276 part-time faculty members, offering a student-to-faculty ratio of 11:1. The most common course size is 10 to 19 students. Manhattanville College's 45 majors and minors include the popular finance/management, visual/performing arts and psychology, and the less popular philosophy, world religions and computer science. The school has a general core requirement. Cooperative education is not offered. All first-year students must maintain a 2.0 GPA or higher to avoid academic probation, and a minimum overall GPA of 2.0 is required to graduate. Other special academic programs that would appeal to a B student include: self-designed majors · pass/fail grading option · independent study · double majors · dual degrees · accelerated study · honors program · internships · weekend college · distance learning certificate programs.

B Student Support and Success

Manhattanville's Academic Resource Center offers individual tutoring, group supplemental instruction and a variety of workshops. ARC has full-time professional instructors in writing, math and study strategies and part-time tutors in subjects that include accounting, foreign languages, math, music theory, statistics for social sciences and economic statistics. Special credit-bearing courses are offered to help students learn science, math and the humanities. According to the college, the philosophy of the ARC is one of "fostering independence in the students who seek help. We are equipped to deal with many types of academic difficulties and to offer personal assistance in a relaxed and supportive atmosphere."

Manhattanville College provides dedicated guidance for: academic · career · personal · psychological · minority students · veterans · family planning · religious. Manhattanville College offers remedial and refresher courses in: reading · writing · math · study skills. The average freshman year GPA is 3.2, and 69 percent of freshmen students return for their sophomore year. Approximately 22 percent return for a graduate degree soon after graduation. One year after graduation, the school reports that 22 percent of graduates have entered graduate school. Of those who are employed, 35 percent enter a field related to their major within six months of graduation. Companies that most frequently hire graduates from Manhattanville College include: PepsiCo · MasterCard International · MBIA · Salomon Smith Barney · Diversified Investment Advisors · NYC Board of Education · Bank of New York · Goldman Sachs · New York Rangers · New York Jets · Sesame Street Trips · Lincoln Center · Teach for America · Greenwich Hospital · MCI.

Support for Students with Learning Disabilities

Manhattanville College grants additional time to students with learning disabilities to complete their degree, as well as a lightened course load. Students with learning disabilities will find the following programs at Manhattanville College useful: remedial math · remedial English · tutors · learning center · testing accommodations · untimed tests · extended time for tests · take-home exam · oral tests · readers · note-taking services · reading machines · tape recorders · texts on tape · early syllabus · priority registration · waiver of foreign language and math degree requirement. Individual or small group tutorials are also available in: time management · organizational skills · learning strategies · specific subject areas · writing labs · math labs · study skills. An advisor/advocate from the Office of Disability Services, HELP Center is available to students.

How to Get Admitted

For admissions decisions, non-academic factors considered: interview · extracurricular activities · special talents, interests and abilities · character/personal qualities · volunteer work · work experience · state of residency · geographical location · alumni relationship. A high school diploma is required, although a GED is also accepted for admissions consideration. SAT or ACT test scores are considered, if submitted, but are not required. SAT Subject Test scores are considered, if submitted, but are not required. *According to the admissions office:* Minimum grade average of 'B' required. *Academic units recommended:* 4 English, 3 Math, 2 Science, 2 Social Studies.

MANHATTANVILLE COLLEGE

Highlights

Manhattanville College
Purchase (Pop. 8,000)
Location: Large town
Four-year private
Founded: 1841
Website: http://www.mville.edu

Students
Total enrollment: 2,750
From out-of-state: 34%
Male/Female: 36%/64%
Live on-campus: 79%
Off-campus employment rating: Excellent
Caucasian: 23%
African American: 7%
Hispanic: 12%
Asian: 1%
Hawaiian or Pacific Islander: <1%
Native American: <1%
Mixed (2+ ethnicities): 1%
International: 9%

Academics
Calendar: Semester
Student/faculty ratio: 11:1
Class size 9 or fewer: 31%
Class size 10-29: 64%
Class size 30-49: 6%
Class size 50-99: -
Class size 100 or more: -
Returning freshmen: 69%
Six-year graduation rate: 56%

Most Popular Majors
Finance/management
Visual/performing arts
Psychology

281

College Profiles

MANHATTANVILLE COLLEGE

Highlights

Admissions
Applicants: 3,930
Accepted: 3,026
Acceptance rate: 77%
Average GPA: 3.0
ACT range: 22-26
SAT Math range: 490-590
SAT Reading range: 480-590
SAT Writing range: 470-580
Top 10% of class: 21%
Top 25% of class: 47%
Top 50% of class: 80%

Deadlines
Early Action: No
Early Decision: 12/1
Regular Action: Rolling admissions
Notification of admission by: 12/1
Common Application: Accepted

Financial Aid
In-state tuition: $34,870
Out-of-state tuition: $34,870
Room: $8,680
Board: $5,840
Books: $800
Freshmen receiving need-based aid: 76%
Undergrads rec. need-based aid: 72%
Avg. % of need met by financial aid: 84%
Avg. aid package (freshmen): Not reported
Avg. aid package (undergrads): Not reported

Prominent Alumni
Josie Natori, Fashion Designer; Trudy Sullivan, CEO, Talbots; Beatrice Wilkinson Welters, U.S. Ambassador to Trinidad and Tobago.

School Spirit
Mascot: Valiants
Colors: Red and white

How to Pay for College
To apply for financial aid, students should submit the following: Free Application for Federal Student Aid (FAFSA) · state aid form. Manhattanville College participates in the Federal Work Study program. *Need-based aid programs include:* scholarships and grants · general need-based awards · Federal Pell grants · state scholarships and grants · college-based scholarships and grants · private scholarships and grants. *Non-need-based aid programs include:* scholarships and grants · state scholarships and grants · creative arts and performance awards.

MARIETTA COLLEGE

215 Fifth Street, Marietta, OH 45750
Admissions: 800-331-7896 · Financial Aid: 800-331-2709
Email: admit@marietta.edu · Website: http://www.marietta.edu

From the College

"Marietta College's mission revolves around nine core values. The central value reflects our belief that 'the liberal arts are the best preparation for any career' and expresses our 'equal commitment to practical experience as a necessary prerequisite for the world of work.' Every Marietta student receives a liberal arts foundation and in-depth study in their major, and each of our graduates is 'prepared to succeed in a technological society…and to thrive in a diverse, global society.' In addition, all graduates understand 'the role of the citizen-leader…in a livable, sustainable, ethical future. Marietta has been recognized as one of America's 37 'Revolutionary Colleges.'"

Campus Setting

Marietta's 90-acre campus is located in Marietta, 115 miles southwest of Columbus. The campus's oldest building, of Greek Revival design, is listed in the National Register of Historic Places. A four-year private institution, Marietta College has an enrollment of 1,542 students, and has been co-ed since 1897. Campus facilities include: dinosaur exhibit · Planetarium. Marietta College provides on-campus housing with 15 units that can accommodate 1,199 students. Housing options: coed dorms · women's dorms · men's dorms · sorority housing · fraternity housing · single-student apartments · special housing for disabled students. Recreation and sports facilities include: athletic fields · recreation center · stadium · tennis courts.

Student Life and Activities

The majority (74 percent) of students live on campus. Popular events include Homecoming, Family Weekend, Little Sibs Weekend, Community Service Day and Make a Difference Day. Marietta College has 85 official student organizations. The most popular are: Concert choir · concert, jazz and pep bands. Jazz/rock ensemble · dance team · theatrical group · forensics team · team managers · environmental awareness group · computer club · Circle K · tournaments · Great Outdoors Club · Rainbow Alliance · Young Democrats · Young Republicans · Model UN · Philanthropy Connection · teacher education association · Society of Petroleum Engineers · marketing club · service and special-interest groups. Intramural teams include: basketball · football · handball · racquetball · soccer · softball · table tennis · volleyball. Marietta College is a member of the Ohio Athletic Conference (Division III).

Academics and Learning Environment

Marietta College has 114 full-time and 64 part-time faculty members, offering a student-to-faculty ratio of 11:1. The most common course size is 10 to 19 students. Marietta College offers 46 majors. The top choices are business/marketing, petroleum engineering and communication/journalism and less popular are philosophy/religious studies, liberal arts and foreign languages/literatures/linguistics. The school has a general core requirement. Cooperative education is available. All first-year students must maintain a 2.0 GPA or higher to avoid academic probation. Other special academic programs that would appeal to a B student include: self-designed majors · pass/fail grading option · independent study · double majors · dual degrees · honors program · Phi Beta Kappa · internships · certificate programs.

283

MARIETTA COLLEGE

Marietta College
Marietta, OH (Pop. 14,027)
Location: Medium city
Four-year private
Founded: 1835
Website: http://www.marietta.edu

Students
Total enrollment: 1,542
Undergrads: 1,416
Freshmen: 425
Part-time students: 5%
From out-of-state: 40%
Male/Female: 58%/42%
Live on-campus: 74%
In fraternities: 15%
In sororities: 30%
Off-campus employment rating: Excellent
Caucasian: 70%
African American: 6%
Hispanic: 3%
Asian: 1%
Native American: <1%
Mixed (2+ ethnicities): 2%
International: 12%

Academics
Calendar: Semester
Student/faculty ratio: 11:1
Class size 9 or fewer: 39%
Class size 10-29: 56%
Class size 30-49: 5%
Class size 50-99: -
Class size 100 or more: -
Returning freshmen: 71%
Six-year graduation rate: 55%

Most Popular Majors
Petroleum engineering
Business/marketing
Communication/journalism

B Student Support and Success

At Marietta, the Academic Resource Center offers individualized academic support for students by means of several different avenues. Students are advised early on when their performance assessment may be dangerously low through the use of the college's early warning system. Help is available to struggling students through individual and small group tutoring and study skills assistance. Additionally, students have access to computers and educational technology, personal development workshops on topics like study skills and time management, a resource library and referral to additional resources.

Marietta College provides support programs for: academic · career · personal · psychological · minority students · family planning. Marietta College offers remedial and refresher courses in: reading · writing · math · study skills. The average freshman year GPA is 3.1 and 71 percent of freshmen students return for their sophomore year. Approximately 12 percent of students return right after graduation to earn a graduate degree. A year after graduation, 19 percent of graduates have entered graduate school. Of those students who are employed, 95 percent are in a field related to their major within six months of graduation. Companies that most frequently hire graduates from Marietta College include: Chevron · Unocal · Marathon · Anadarko · Exxon-Mobil · Deloitte.

Support for Students with Learning Disabilities

Marietta College provides extra time to students with learning disabilities to complete their degree. High school foreign language and math waivers are accepted. According to the school, recent documentation, guidelines and criteria requirements are available for specific disabilities, and services are individualized based on disability, while progress is monitored. Students with learning disabilities will find the following programs at Marietta College useful: remedial math · remedial English · tutors · learning center · testing accommodations · untimed tests · extended time for tests · take-home exam · oral tests · readers · note-taking services · reading machines · tape recorders · texts on tape · early syllabus · priority registration · waiver of math degree requirement. Individual or small group tutorials are also available in: time management · organizational skills · learning strategies · specific subject areas · writing labs · math labs · study skills. An advisor/advocate from the Academic Resource Center is available to students.

How to Get Admitted

For admissions decisions, non-academic factors considered: interview · extracurricular activities · special talents, interests and abilities · character/personal qualities · volunteer work · work experience · geographical location · minority affiliation · alumni relationship. A high school diploma is required, although a GED is also accepted for admissions consideration. SAT or ACT test scores are required of all applicants. SAT Subject Test scores are considered, if submitted, but are not required. *Academic units recommended:* 4 English, 4 Math, 4 Science, 2 Social Studies, 4 Foreign Language.

How to Pay for College

To apply for financial aid, students should submit the following: Free Application for Federal Student Aid (FAFSA) · institution's own financial aid forms. Marietta College participates in the Federal Work Study program. *Need-based aid programs include:* scholarships and grants · general need-based awards · Federal Pell grants · state scholarships and grants · college-based scholarships and grants · private scholarships and grants. *Non-need-based aid programs include:* scholarships and grants · general need-based awards · state scholarships and grants · creative arts and performance awards · special achievements and activities awards.

MARIETTA COLLEGE

Highlights

Admissions
Applicants: 4,053
Accepted: 2,579
Acceptance rate: 63.6%
Average GPA: 3.5
ACT range: 21-27
SAT Math range: 500-630
SAT Reading range: 470-590
SAT Writing range: Not reported
Top 10% of class: 32%
Top 25% of class: 59%
Top 50% of class: 85%

Deadlines
Early Action: No
Early Decision: No
Regular Action: Rolling admissions
Common Application: Accepted

Financial Aid
In-state tuition: $32,216
Out-of-state tuition: $32,216
Room: $5,994
Board: $4,400
Books: $1,184
Freshmen receiving need-based aid: 86%
Undergrads rec. need-based aid: 68%
Avg. % of need met by financial aid: 87%
Avg. aid package (freshmen): $26,741
Avg. aid package (undergrads): $24,569
Avg. debt upon graduation: $36,241

Prominent Alumni
Charles Gates Dawes, U.S. Vice President, Nobel Prize Winner; Story Musgrave, scientist, physician, astronaut; Jim Tracy, manager, Pittsburgh Pirates.

School Spirit
Mascot: Pioneers
Colors: Navy blue and white

285

Highlights

Marymount Manhattan College
New York (Pop. 8,244,910)
Location: Major city
Four-year private
Founded: 1936
Website: http://www.mmm.edu

Students
Total enrollment: 2,095
From out-of-state: 68%
Male/Female: 23%/77%
Live on-campus: 36%
Off-campus employment rating: Fair
Caucasian: 58%
African American: 10%
Hispanic: 16%
Asian: 4%
Hawaiian or Pacific Islander: <1%
Native American: 1%
Mixed (2+ ethnicities): 1%
International: 5%

Academics
Calendar: Semester
Student/faculty ratio: 11:1
Class size 9 or fewer: 9%
Class size 10-29: 90%
Class size 30-49: 1%
Class size 50-99: -
Class size 100 or more: -
Returning freshmen: 63%
Six-year graduation rate: 49%

Most Popular Majors
Communication/rhetoric
Drama/dramatic arts
Psychology

286

America's
Best Colleges for
B Students

MARYMOUNT MANHATTAN COLLEGE

221 East 71st Street, New York, NY 10021
Admissions: 800-MARYMOU · Financial Aid: 212-517-0480
Email: admissions@mmm.edu
Website: http://www.mmm.edu

From the College

The college offers a "commitment to intercultural dialogue; commitment to complementary career preparation courses and liberal arts courses; strong programs in biology, English, psychology, international studies, communication arts, business, theatre and dance."

Campus Setting

Marymount Manhattan, founded in 1936, is a private, liberal arts college. Founded as a branch of Marymount College of Tarrytown, N.Y., it became an independent institution in 1961. Its one-acre campus is located in midtown Manhattan. A four-year institution, Marymount Manhattan College has an enrollment of 2,095 students, and has been co-ed since 1989. Marymount Manhattan College provides on-campus housing with three units that can accommodate 675 students. Housing options: coed dorms.

Student Life and Activities

Most students (64 percent) live off campus. Students enjoy various events including Snow Ball, 100 Nights Celebration, Earth Day, Leadership Awards Reception, Charter Day and Strawberry Festival. Marymount Manhattan College has 43 official student organizations. The most popular are: Advocates for Animals · Amnesty International · Art Fusion · Campus Activities Board · dance club · Expressions of Grace · Feminist Majority Leadership Alliance · French club · international studies club · literary society · Marymount Outreach · Nutz and Boltz of Comedy · philosophy club · Poptards 101 · psychology club · reading society · science society · Soldiers of Hip Hop · speech club · Student Political Association · Students against Violence · finance and accounting team.

Academics and Learning Environment

Marymount Manhattan College has 101 full-time and 229 part-time faculty members, offering a student-to-faculty ratio of 11:1. It offers 18 majors with the most popular being communication/rhetoric, drama/dramatic arts and psychology. The least popular choices include liberal arts, philosophy/religion and biology. The school has a general core requirement. Cooperative education is not offered. Other special academic programs include: pass/fail grading option · independent study · double majors · accelerated study · honors program · internships · distance learning certificate programs.

B Student Support and Success

Marymount's students may find assistance with coursework at a tutoring center that provides full support to walk-ins through student tutors as well as trained staff. The Center for Academic Advancement (formerly known as College Skills) has courses for students who need to reinforce their skills in reading comprehension, vocabulary, grammar and basic writing. According to the college, "It is our mission to provide these services in any reasonable manner in order to secure student futures. Our main objective is to assure each student who passes through our doors that they can and will succeed in college."

Marymount Manhattan College provides a variety of support programs including academic · career · personal · psychological · minority students · non-traditional students. Recognizing that some students may need extra preparation, Marymount Manhattan College offers remedial and refresher courses in: reading · writing · math · study skills. The average freshman year GPA is 3.0, and 63 percent of freshmen students return for their sophomore year. Approximately 31 percent pursue a graduate degree soon after graduation. One year after graduation, the school reports that 40 percent of graduates have entered graduate school.

Support for Students with Learning Disabilities

Marymount Manhattan College accepts both high school foreign language and math waivers. Students with learning disabilities will find the following programs quite useful: remedial math · remedial English · remedial reading · tutors · extended time for tests · tape recorders · diagnostic testing service. Individual or small group tutorials are also available in: time management · organizational skills · learning strategies · specific subject areas · writing labs · math labs · study skills. An advisor/advocate from the Access Program is available to students. This member also sits on the admissions committee.

How to Get Admitted

For admissions decisions, non-academic factors considered: interview · extracurricular activities · special talents, interests and abilities · character/personal qualities · volunteer work · work experience · state of residency · alumni relationship. A high school diploma is required, although a GED is also accepted for admissions consideration. SAT or ACT test scores are required for some applicants. SAT Subject Test scores are considered, if submitted, but are not required. *According to the admissions office:* Minimum SAT Reasoning scores of 450 in both critical reading and math and minimum 2.0 GPA recommended. *Academic units recommended:* 4 English, 3 Math, 3 Science, 3 Social Studies, 2 Foreign Language.

How to Pay for College

To apply for financial aid, students should submit the following: Free Application for Federal Student Aid (FAFSA). Marymount Manhattan College participates in the Federal Work Study program. *Need-based aid programs include:* scholarships and grants · general need-based awards · Federal Pell grants · state scholarships and grants · college-based scholarships and grants · private scholarships and grants. *Non-need-based aid programs include:* scholarships and grants · state scholarships and grants · creative arts and performance awards · special achievements and activities awards.

MARYMOUNT MANHATTAN COLLEGE

Highlights

Admissions
Applicants: 4,147
Accepted: 3,110
Acceptance rate: 75%
Average GPA: 3.2
ACT range: 21-26
SAT Math range: 450-560
SAT Reading range: 480-590
SAT Writing range: 470-590

Deadlines
Early Action: No
Early Decision: No
Regular Action: 3/15 (priority)
Common Application: Accepted

Financial Aid
In-state tuition: $26,352
Out-of-state tuition: $26,352
Room: Varies
Board: Varies
Books: $1,000
Freshmen receiving need-based or merit-based aid: 92%
Avg. aid package (freshmen): Not reported
Avg. aid package (undergrads): Not reported

Prominent Alumni
Annaleigh Ashford, Tony-nominated actress; Geraldine Ferraro, United States candidate for vice president; Erik Palladino, actor.

School Spirit
Mascot: Griffin
Colors: Blue and white

MCDANIEL COLLEGE

2 College Hill, Westminster, MD 21157
Admissions: 800-638-5005 · Financial Aid: 800-638-5005
Email: admissions@mcdaniel.edu · Website: http://www.mcdaniel.edu

From the College

"McDaniel College students become involved, connected and confident. First-year seminars, a January mini-mester of uncommon courses and options for self-designed majors provide learning opportunities. Less than an hour's drive from Washington, DC, students take advantage of all the career and cultural possibilities of the nation's capital while honing leadership skills on campus as faculty-research assistants across all majors, as volunteers directing over 100 student clubs or as teammates on the playing fields of 24 intercollegiate sports. A nine-hole golf course doubles as both a place to practice your swing or snowboard downhill in winter."

Campus Setting

McDaniel, founded in 1867, is a private, liberal arts college. Its 160-acre campus is located in Westminster, 35 miles northwest of Baltimore. A four-year institution, McDaniel College has an enrollment of 3,256 students. McDaniel College provides on-campus housing with 618 units that can accommodate 1,398 students. Housing options: coed dorms · women's dorms · men's dorms · sorority housing · fraternity housing · single-student apartments. Recreation and sports facilities include: baseball, football, lacrosse and softball fields · fitness center · gymnasium · golf course · tennis courts · outdoor track.

Student Life and Activities

The majority of students (82 percent) live on campus. The editor of the student newspaper observes, that, "Because the campus is small, it is possible to get to know just about everyone—and the campus is beautiful, with beautiful sunsets over the hill." On campus, students gather at Gazebo, Harvey Stone Park, Upper Decker and the Game Room. Popular off-campus haunts include Johannsons, O'Lourdans, Harry's and Maggie's. Popular social events include Spring Fling, Homecoming, Jazz Night, Performance Concerts, BSU Fashion Show, International Student Dinner, Soul Food Dinner and Unity Week. McDaniel College has 90 official student organizations. Influential groups on campus include Greeks, Christian Fellowship, CAPBoard, the football team, BACCHUS, SEAC, Residence Life and the International Club. For those interested in sports, there are intramural teams such as: badminton · basketball · flag football · floor hockey · soccer · tennis · volleyball · cheerleading · rugby · Ultimate Frisbee. McDaniel College is a member of the Centennial Conference (Division III) and Eastern College Athletic Conference.

Academics and Learning Environment

McDaniel College has 107 full-time and 266 part-time faculty members, offering a student-to-faculty ratio of 11:1. The most common course size is 10 to 19 students. McDaniel College offers 49 majors with the most popular being psychology, exercise science/physical education, and business administration/economics and least popular being theater, German and religious studies. The school has a general core requirement. Cooperative education is not offered. All first-year students must maintain a 1.5 GPA or higher to avoid academic probation, and a minimum overall GPA of 2.0 is required to graduate. Other special academic programs that would appeal to a B student include: self-designed majors · pass/fail grading option · independent study · double majors · dual degrees · accelerated study · honors program · Phi Beta Kappa · internships · distance learning certificate programs.

B Student Support and Success

McDaniel offers a variety of academic support for students. It has tutoring services, as well as faculty advising for choosing courses. The Writing Center works one on one with students to become "better, more confident writers" through peer tutoring. Students can get assistance with ideas, notes, rough drafts and final drafts. Computer resources are available and the college also has a range of services for any students with disabilities.

McDaniel College provides dedicated guidance for: academic · career · personal · minority students · family planning. The average freshman year GPA is 2.9, and 84 percent of freshmen students return for their sophomore year. Companies that most frequently hire graduates from McDaniel College include: Allstate · Carroll County Public Schools · Catholic Charities · Department of Defense · Rowe Price.

Support for Students with Learning Disabilities

McDaniel College accepts high school foreign language waivers. Students with learning disabilities will find the following programs at McDaniel College useful: remedial math · remedial English · tutors · learning center · extended time for tests · take-home exam · readers · note-taking services · reading machines · tape recorders. Individual or small group tutorials are also available in: time management · organizational skills · learning strategies · writing labs · study skills. An advisor/advocate from the Academic Skills Program is available to students.

How to Get Admitted

For admissions decisions, non-academic factors considered: interview · extracurricular activities · special talents, interests and abilities · character/personal qualities · volunteer work · work experience · state of residency · alumni relationship. A high school diploma is required, although a GED is also accepted for admissions consideration. SAT or ACT test scores are required of all applicants. SAT Subject Test scores are considered, if submitted, but are not required. *According to the admissions office:* Minimum score of 500 in both SAT Reasoning critical reading and math recommended. *Academic units recommended:* 4 English, 4 Math, 4 Science, 3 Social Studies, 4 Foreign Language.

How to Pay for College

To apply for financial aid, students should submit the following: Free Application for Federal Student Aid (FAFSA) · institution's own financial aid forms · state aid form. McDaniel College participates in the Federal Work Study program. *Need-based aid programs include:* scholarships and grants · general need-based awards · Federal Pell grants · state scholarships and grants · college-based scholarships and grants · private scholarships and grants. *Non-need-based aid programs include:* scholarships and grants · general need-based awards · state

MCDANIEL COLLEGE

McDaniel College
Westminster, MD (Pop. 18,628)
Location: Small town
Four-year private
Founded: 1867
Website: http://www.mcdaniel.edu

Students
Total enrollment: 3,256
Undergrads: 1,692
Freshmen: 455
Part-time students: 2%
From out-of-state: 39%
From public schools: 73%
Male/Female: 47%/53%
Live on-campus: 82%
In fraternities: 16%
In sororities: 18%
Off-campus employment rating: Fair
Caucasian: 74%
African American: 13%
Hispanic: 6%
Asian: 4%
Hawaiian or Pacific Islander: <1%
Native American: 1%
International: 1%

Academics
Calendar: 4-1-4 system
Student/faculty ratio: 11:1
Class size 9 or fewer: 15%
Class size 10-29: 84%
Class size 30-49: 2%
Class size 50-99: -
Class size 100 or more: -
Returning freshmen: 84%
Six-year graduation rate: 72%

Most Popular Majors
Psychology
Exercise science/physical education
Business administration/economics

289

College Profiles

MCDANIEL COLLEGE

scholarships and grants · special achievements and activities awards · ROTC scholarships.

Admissions
Applicants: 2,942
Accepted: 2,232
Acceptance rate: 75.9%
Placed on wait list: 49
Enrolled from wait list: 7
Average GPA: 3.5
ACT range: 21-27
SAT Math range: 500-610
SAT Reading range: 500-600
SAT Writing range: Not reported
Top 10% of class: 26%
Top 25% of class: 52%
Top 50% of class: 86%

Deadlines
Early Action: 12/1
Early Decision: No
Regular Action: 2/15 (priority)
Common Application: Accepted

Financial Aid
In-state tuition: $38,350
Out-of-state tuition: $38,350
Room: Varies
Board: Varies
Books: $1,200
Freshmen receiving need-based aid: 76%
Undergrads rec. need-based aid: 74%
Avg. % of need met by financial aid: 86%
Avg. aid package (freshmen): $30,159
Avg. aid package (undergrads): $31,352
Avg. debt upon graduation: $29,554

Prominent Alumni
Alan Rabinowitz, zoologist, world's foremost authority on jaguars and other big cats; Wendy Ruderman, Pulitzer-Prize winning journalist and author; Michelle Shearer, 2011 National Teacher of the Year; Greg Street, video game designer (League of Legends and World of Warcraft), former marine biologist; Victor McTeer, civil rights lawyer; F. Mason Sones, Jr., cardiologist.

School Spirit
Mascot: Green Terror
Colors: Green and gold

MCKENDREE UNIVERSITY

701 College Road, Lebanon, IL 62254
Admissions: 800-BEAR-CAT, extension 6400
Financial Aid: 800-BEAR-CAT, extension 6828
Email: inquiry@mckendree.edu · Website: http://www.mckendree.edu

From the College

"McKendree College provides students with a peaceful, residential campus in a small, friendly town, yet is just minutes away from St. Louis. McKendree students receive a broad-based, liberal arts-oriented education while also developing skills in preparation for a career or graduate studies. The college's philosophy reflects concern for individual development of its students and its commitment to personalized education. Co-curricular programs are also of importance, as McKendree students participate in community service, voluntary spiritual development, athletics and a wide variety of clubs and organizations meeting student needs and interests."

Campus Setting

McKendree, founded in 1828, is a liberal arts university. Its 237-acre campus is located in Lebanon, 23 miles east of St. Louis. A four-year private institution, McKendree University has an enrollment of 3,027 students. The school is also affiliated with the United Methodist Church. The school has a library with 110,000 books. McKendree University provides on-campus housing which can accommodate 1,017 students. Housing options: coed dorms · single-student apartments.

Student Life and Activities

Sixty percent of students live on campus. "Off-campus is more popular for the small campus community," reports the student newspaper. "Visiting area malls and trips into St. Louis are frequent. Most students go home on weekends, so weekly social activities are better attended." Hot spots on- and off-campus include Deneen center, Ron's, Olive Garden, Hideout, Schiappa's Pizza, Applebee's, St. Clair Square, the dorm and commuter's lounge. Favorite events include Technos International Week, McKendree Idol and The George E. McCammon Memorial Distinguished Speaker Series. McKendree University has 60 official student organizations. Campus Activities Board, Student Government Association, Greeks, Students Against Social Injustice and athletic teams have a strong presence on student social life. There are intramural teams available: basketball · football · softball · table tennis · Ultimate Frisbee · volleyball. McKendree University is a member of the NCAA and Great Lakes Valley Conference.

Academics and Learning Environment

McKendree University has 98 full-time and 187 part-time faculty members, offering a student-to-faculty ratio of 14:1. McKendree University offers 61 majors with the most popular being business administration, nursing and education and least popular being religious studies, art and philosophy. The school has a general core requirement. Cooperative education is available. All first-year students must maintain a 1.8 GPA or higher to avoid academic probation, and a minimum overall GPA of 2.0 is required to graduate. Other programs available: self-designed majors · pass/fail grading option · independent study · double majors · dual degrees · honors program · internships · distance learning.

291

College Profiles

MCKENDREE UNIVERSITY

McKendree University
Lebanon, IL (Pop. 4,466)
Location: Large town
Four-year private
Founded: 1828
Website: http://www.mckendree.edu

Students
Total enrollment: 3,027
Undergrads: 2,358
Freshmen: 390
Part-time students: 25%
From out-of-state: 25%
From public schools: 85%
Male/Female: 44%/56%
Live on-campus: 60%
In fraternities: 2%
In sororities: 6%
Off-campus employment rating: Excellent
Caucasian: 70%
African American: 15%
Hispanic: 4%
Asian: 1%
Hawaiian or Pacific Islander: <1%
Native American: 1%
Mixed (2+ ethnicities): 1%
International: 1%

Academics
Calendar: Semester
Student/faculty ratio: 14:1
Class size 9 or fewer: 29%
Class size 10-29: 66%
Class size 30-49: 5%
Class size 50-99: -
Class size 100 or more: -
Returning freshmen: 73%
Six-year graduation rate: 48%

Most Popular Majors
Business administration
Nursing
Education

B Student Support and Success

The college features small classes, is eager to accept students who are really trying and is dedicated to not letting any of them "slip through the cracks."

McKendree University provides dedicated guidance for: academic · career · personal · psychological · minority students · veterans · religious. McKendree University offers remedial and refresher courses in: reading · writing · math · study skills. The average freshman year GPA is 3.0, and 73 percent of freshmen students return for their sophomore year. Some students enter into the workforce, and approximately 23 percent pursue a graduate degree immediately after graduation. One year after graduation, the school reports that 24 percent of their graduates have entered graduate school. Among students who do decide to enter the workforce, approximately 79 percent enter a field related to their major within six months of graduation. Here's a compiled list of companies that most frequently hire graduates from McKendree University: Catholic Charities · Scott Air Force Base · Clinton County Sheriff · Judevine Center for Autism · Better Business Bureau · Stifel · Nicolaus · Springfield Police Department · Boeing · Kerber · Eck · Braeckel · CPA · Evangelical Children's Home · CHASI · National Children's Cancer Society · May Department Stores · Attorney Generals Office · Standard Lab · Edward Jones · CitiFinancial · Jims Formal Wear · Gliks · SBC · St. Louis Children's Hospital · Behavioral Intervention · Fuehne & Fuehne CPA · Anders, Minkler and Diehl · University of Illinois Extension · Celsis Lab · Allsup · Campus Crusade for Christ · D.C. Lobbying Firm · US Bank · Big Brothers Big Sisters · First Community Credit · Tri-National Inc. · UHY Advisors · American Water.

Support for Students with Learning Disabilities

Students with learning disabilities have several options available to them at McKendree University, including a lightened course load and additional time to complete their degree. High school foreign language waivers are accepted. Students with learning disabilities will find the following programs at McKendree University intriguing: remedial math · remedial English · tutors · learning center · untimed tests · extended time for tests · take-home exam · oral tests · reading machines · tape recorders · priority registration. Individual or small group tutorials are also available in: time management · organizational skills · learning strategies · specific subject areas · writing labs · math labs · study skills.

How to Get Admitted

For admissions decisions, non-academic factors considered: interview · extracurricular activities · special talents, interests and abilities · character/personal qualities · volunteer work · work experience · state of residency · alumni relationship. A high school diploma is required, although a GED is also accepted for admissions consideration. SAT or ACT test scores are required of all applicants. *According to the admissions office:* Minimum composite ACT score of 20, rank in top half of secondary school class and minimum 2.5 GPA required. *Academic units recommended:* 4 English, 2 Math, 2 Science, 2 Social Studies.

Insight

McKendree is the only place in southern Illinois where you have an average class size of 15 and all classes are under 50 according to Mark Campbell, vice president for enrollment management. The more intimate classes help students to feel less anonymous. "We do not evaluate students with multiple-choice tests," he adds. "Instead, we want to see how they write. There is a real gray area between students who are easy to admit and those who are easy to deny. The key is in the students' strength in English. How do they read, write and comprehend?" All students who are admitted must submit a writing sample before they are placed in an English class. All potential students are invited to write an essay for the university—even graded papers from school are allowed. "In the end, we are obligated to not admit students who will not do well. We simply focus on a student's determination to succeed," says Campbell.

How to Pay for College

To apply for financial aid, students should submit the following: Free Application for Federal Student Aid (FAFSA). McKendree University participates in the Federal Work Study program. *Need-based aid programs include:* scholarships and grants · general need-based awards · Federal Pell grants · state scholarships and grants · college-based scholarships and grants · private scholarships and grants *Non-need-based aid programs include:* scholarships and grants · state scholarships and grants · creative arts and performance awards · athletic scholarships · ROTC scholarships.

MCKENDREE UNIVERSITY

Highlights

Admissions
Applicants: 1,617
Accepted: 1,017
Acceptance rate: 62.9%
Average GPA: 3.4
ACT range: 20-25
SAT Math range: 490-530
SAT Reading range: 450-520
SAT Writing range: Not reported
Top 10% of class: 13%
Top 25% of class: 43%
Top 50% of class: 75%

Deadlines
Early Action: No
Early Decision: No
Regular Action: Rolling admissions
Common Application: Accepted

Financial Aid
In-state tuition: $25,900
Out-of-state tuition: $25,900
Room: $4,760
Board: $4,160
Books: $1,000
Freshmen receiving need-based aid: 82%
Undergrads rec. need-based aid: 86%
Avg. % of need met by financial aid: 76%
Avg. aid package (freshmen): $23,036
Avg. aid package (undergrads): $19,908
Avg. debt upon graduation: $26,485

Prominent Alumni
Harry Statham, men's basketball coach, McKendree College, all time wins leader in four year college basketball history; Andrew McChesney, editor, *Moscow Times.*

School Spirit
Mascot: Bearcats
Colors: Purple and white

MENLO COLLEGE

1000 El Camino Real, Atherton, CA 94027
Admissions: 800-556-3656 · Financial Aid: 800-556-3656
Email: admissions@menlo.edu · Website: http://www.menlo.edu

From the College

"Menlo College, located in the heart of the Silicon Valley, is a small, prestigious business school dedicated to providing students with a business education built on a foundation of liberal arts.

"Committed faculty and staff help students focus on their skills as leaders, communicators and team members, while preparing them for long-term success in the business world. Menlo works to give students a wide variety of opportunities to develop knowledge and personal relationships that will propel them into exciting careers. Menlo is a close community of motivated students who are driven to excel not only in business but in athletics, student organizations and off-campus activities that are available to them.

"Menlo has been named 'Best in the West' by Princeton Review for the past five years. In 2014 Menlo received AACSB (Association to Advance Collegiate Schools of Business) accreditation, a distinction earned by less than five percent of the world's business schools.

"Menlo College's location makes it uniquely suited to provide the nation's best in business education. Silicon Valley is one of the most entrepreneurial, innovative areas in the country, and its importance in the world of business and technology is well known. Menlo is situated midway between San Francisco and San Jose and gives students easy access to internships and work experience during their time at the college. The area also provides a multitude of career opportunities close at hand after graduation."

Campus Setting

Menlo, founded in 1927, is a private, business school. Its 62-acre campus is located in Atherton, 30 miles south of San Francisco. A four-year institution, Menlo College has an enrollment of 713 students and has been co-ed since 1971. The school also has a library with 60,600 books. Menlo College provides on-campus housing with 286 units that can accommodate 503 students. Housing options: coed dorms · men's dorms. Recreation and sports facilities include: pavilion · fields.

Student Life and Activities

Sixty-one percent of students live on campus. Popular gathering spots include the Student Union, Dutch Goose, The Oasis and the Stanford Mall. Popular campus events include The BSU's Apollo Night Talent Show, Powder Puff Football Game, Homecoming Football Game, Homecoming Dance, Women's Luncheon, International Week, Menlo Madness, Halloween Party, The BSU's Poetry Slam, The Oakies, The Rites of Spring, The Hawai'i Club Annual Luau, Women's Club Annual Women's Luncheon, Mystery Dance and The LSU's Latin Dance Classes and Competition. Menlo College has 35 official student organizations. The most popular are: The International Club · Old Oak Tavern · Hole in One Club · Mass Communication Club · Music Club · Newspaper Club · Outdoor Club · Psychology Club · Women's Club · Rize Hip Hop Dance · Student Athlete Leadership · Sixth Man Band · Video Game Appreciation · Video Production Club · Baywatch · Black Sunday Film Club · Menlo Cheerleaders · Disc-O-Fever · Gay Straight Alliance · Business Club · Contender's Club. Intramural basketball is offered. Menlo College is a member of the Northwest Conference (Division III, football) and California Pacific Conference (NAIA).

Academics and Learning Environment

Menlo College has 32 full-time and 56 part-time faculty members, offering a student-to-faculty ratio of 14:1. The most common course size is 10 to 19 students. Menlo College offers 11 majors with the most popular ones being management, marketing and accounting. The school has a general core requirement. Cooperative education is not offered. All first-year students must maintain a 2.0 GPA or higher to avoid academic probation. Other special academic programs that would appeal to a B student include: self-designed majors · independent study · double majors · internships.

B Student Support and Success

Menlo offers an Academic Success Center, which includes a great deal of information and support on changing careers, and advising on what courses to take to fulfill a degree. The Writing Center is available to all students on both a drop-in and appointment basis and helps them with any writing assignment at any stage of the writing process.

Menlo College provides its students with dedicated guidance for: academic · career · psychological. The average freshman year GPA is 3.0, and 82 percent of freshmen students return for their sophomore year. Many B students enter the workforce and approximately five percent pursue a graduate degree immediately after their graduation. One year after graduation, the school reports that nine percent of graduates have entered graduate school. Among those students who did enter the workforce, approximately 87 percent enter a field related to their major within six months of graduation. Companies that most frequently take on graduates from Menlo College include: Accenture · Alain Pinel Realtors · Apex Systems · CB Richard Ellis Realtors · Champion Development · ClearChannel Communications · Coldwell Banker Real Estate · Collier's International · ComGlobal Systems · Electronic Arts · Enterprise Rent-a-Car · Fathom Online · Intuit · Merrill Lynch Financial Services · Morgan Stanley Investments · MSNBC · Oracle Corporation · San Francisco Giants · San Jose State University · Siebel Systems · Stanford University.

Support for Students with Learning Disabilities

Students with learning disabilities have the options of additional time to complete their degree or a lightened course load. LD students should research these program options: remedial math · remedial English · special classes · tutors · learning center · testing accommodations · extended time for tests · exam on tape or computer · note-taking services · reading machines · tape recorders · early syllabus · waiver of math degree requirement. Individual or small group tutorials are also available in: time management · organizational skills · learning strategies · specific subject areas · writing labs · study skills. An advisor/advocate from the LD program is available to students.

MENLO COLLEGE

MENLO COLLEGE

Admissions
Applicants: 3,752
Accepted: 1,519
Acceptance rate: 40.5%
Average GPA: 3.2
ACT range: 19-25
SAT Math range: 450-565
SAT Reading range: 432-532
SAT Writing range: Not reported

Deadlines
Early Action: 11/15
Early Decision: No
Regular Action: 2/1 (priority)
4/1 (final)
Notification of admission by: 3/15
Common Application: Accepted

Financial Aid
In-state tuition: $36,900
Out-of-state tuition: $36,900
Room: Varies
Board: Varies
Books: $1,746
Freshmen receiving need-based aid: 64%
Undergrads rec. need-based aid: 64%
Avg. % of need met by financial aid: 67%
Avg. aid package (freshmen): $27,172
Avg. aid package (undergrads): $28,264
Avg. debt upon graduation: $28,972

Prominent Alumni
George Gund, owner San Jose Sharks;
Bud Adams, owner; Tennessee Titans;
Daniel Crown, real estate, Crown Theatres.

School Spirit
Mascot: Oaks
Colors: Navy and white

How to Get Admitted

For admissions decisions, non-academic factors considered: interview · extracurricular activities · special talents, interests and abilities · character/personal qualities · volunteer work · work experience · state of residency · alumni relationship. A high school diploma is required, although a GED is also accepted for admissions consideration. SAT or ACT test scores are required of all applicants. SAT Subject Test scores are considered, if submitted, but are not required. *Academic units recommended:* 4 English, 3 Math, 3 Science, 3 Social Studies, 2 Foreign Language.

How to Pay for College

To apply for financial aid, students should submit the following: Free Application for Federal Student Aid (FAFSA). Menlo College participates in the Federal Work Study program. *Need-based aid programs include:* scholarships and grants · general need-based awards · Federal Pell grants · state scholarships and grants · college-based scholarships and grants. *Non-need-based aid programs include:* scholarships and grants · state scholarships and grants.

MICHIGAN STATE UNIVERSITY

Administration Building, East Lansing, MI 48824
Admissions: 517-355-8332 · Financial Aid: 517-353-5940
Email: admis@msu.edu · Website: http://www.msu.edu

From the College

"Michigan State University has been advancing knowledge and transforming lives through innovative teaching, research and outreach for 150 years, and is known worldwide as a major public university with global reach and impact. MSU's degree-granting colleges and affiliated law college offer top-ranked academic programs in a park-like Big Ten campus and community setting. Undergraduate students can choose from more than 150 programs of study and have the opportunity to work with faculty on research projects. MSU distinctions include one of the largest study abroad programs, one of the leading residence hall systems, one of the oldest and most prestigious honors colleges and one of the largest and best career placement services in the nation. Programs are offered through the Colleges of Agriculture and Natural Resources, Arts and Letters, Eli Broad College of Business, Communication Arts and Sciences, Education, Engineering, Human Medicine, Music, Natural Science, Nursing, Osteopathic Medicine, Social Science, Veterinary Medicine, James Madison College, Lyman Briggs College and the Residential College in Arts/Humanities.

Campus Setting

Michigan State, founded in 1855, is a comprehensive, land-grant, public university. Its 5,315-acre campus is located in East Lansing, 80 miles northwest of Detroit. A four-year institution, Michigan State University has an enrollment of 49,343 students. The campus facilities include: library · museums · art center · center for performing arts · superconducting cyclotron · hotel · planetarium · chapel · magnetic resonance imaging center · veterinary medical center · clinical center · athletic academic center. Michigan State University provides on-campus housing with 11,000 units that can accommodate 22,200 students. Housing options: coed dorms · women's dorms · sorority housing · fraternity housing · single-student apartments · married-student apartments · special housing for disabled students · special housing for international students · cooperative housing.

Student Life and Activities

Sixty percent of students live off campus. Students enjoy gathering at football games, basketball games, concerts and bars. Popular campus events include home football and basketball games (particularly against University of Michigan), Homecoming Parade and concerts. Michigan State University has 600 official student organizations. Greek organizations are influential on campus. There are intramural teams available: baseball · basketball · billiards · cross-country · cycling · fencing · football · golf · ice hockey · lacrosse · martial arts · racquetball · rugby · sailing · scuba diving · skiing · soccer · softball · swimming · tennis · track and field · volleyball · water polo. Michigan State University is a member of the Big Ten Conference (NCAA Division I-FBS).

Academics and Learning Environment

Michigan State University has 2,365 full-time and 391 part-time faculty members, offering a student-to-faculty ratio of 17:1. The most common course size is 20 to 29 students. Michigan State University offers 446 majors with the most popular being psychology, accounting and finance. The school has a general core requirement. Cooperative education is available. All first-year students must maintain a 2.0 GPA or higher to avoid academic probation. Other programs include: self-designed majors

MICHIGAN STATE UNIVERSITY

Michigan State University
East Lansing, MI (Pop. 48,518)
Location: Medium city
Four-year public
Founded: 1855
Website: http://www.msu.edu

Students
Total enrollment: 49,343
Undergrads: 37,988
Part-time students: 8%
From out-of-state: 14%
Male/Female: 50%/50%
Live on-campus: 40%
In fraternities: 8%
In sororities: 7%
Off-campus employment rating: Excellent
Caucasian: 69%
African American: 7%
Hispanic: 4%
Asian: 4%
Hawaiian or Pacific Islander: <1%
Native American: <1%
Mixed (2+ ethnicities): 2%
International: 13%

Academics
Calendar: Semester
Student/faculty ratio: 17:1
Class size 9 or fewer: 6%
Class size 10-29: 52%
Class size 30-49: 20%
Class size 50-99: 10%
Class size 100 or more: 12%
Returning freshmen: 91%
Six-year graduation rate: 79%

Most Popular Majors
Accounting
Finance
Psychology

· pass/fail grading option · independent study · double majors · dual degrees · accelerated study · honors program · Phi Beta Kappa · internships · weekend college · distance learning certificate programs.

B Student Support and Success

MSU's Learning Resource Center offers help to students who are looking to improve their grades, to develop study strategies and to boost their overall scholastic performance. The center features a professional staff, interactive learning lab and tutoring services in the residence halls. Daytime tutoring is offered in one-hour individual sessions at no cost, and evening tutoring is available for math groups twice a week. Seminars and workshops are also offered on topics such as test taking and preparing for finals. Insight from the school includes this advice: "Great, dynamic learning environment is highlighted by extremely helpful and accessible professors and great on campus resources, including the Learning Resource Center, the English Language Center and the Office of Supportive Services.

"Apply before November 1. Complete a challenging curriculum in high school. Complete a well-written personal statement, required as part of the application. Use it to show how well rounded you are as a student and person. Be involved in activities."

Michigan State University provides several support programs, including: academic · career · personal · psychological · minority students · military · veterans · non-traditional students · family planning · religious. Michigan State University offers remedial and refresher courses in: reading · writing · math · study skills. Annually, 91 percent of freshmen students return for their sophomore year. Among students who enter the workforce, approximately 91 percent of them enter a field related to their major within six months of graduation. Other programs that commonly hire on these graduates include: 3M · Abbott Labs · ABC Group · ABN Amro · Accenture.

Support for Students with Learning Disabilities

Students with learning disabilities will be interested by the support programs offered by Michigan State University and should research the following programs further: remedial math · remedial English · tutors · learning center · testing accommodations · untimed tests · extended time for tests · take-home exam · readers · typist/scribe · reading machines · tape recorders · texts on tape · early syllabus · priority registration · waiver of math degree requirement. Individual or small group tutorials are also available in: time management · organizational skills · learning strategies · specific subject areas · writing labs · math labs · study skills. An advisor/advocate from the Resource Center for Persons with Disabilities is available to students.

How to Get Admitted

For admissions decisions, non-academic factors considered: interview · extracurricular activities · special talents, interests and abilities · character/personal qualities · volunteer work · work experience · state of residency · geographical location. A high school diploma is required, although a GED is also accepted for admissions consideration. SAT or ACT test scores are required of all applicants. SAT

Subject Test scores are not required. *Academic units recommended:* 4 English, 4 Math, 3 Science, 3 Social Studies, 2 Foreign Language.

How to Pay for College

To apply for financial aid, students should submit the following: Free Application for Federal Student Aid (FAFSA). Michigan State University participates in the Federal Work Study program. *Need-based aid programs include:* scholarships and grants · general need-based awards · Federal Pell grants · state scholarships and grants · college-based scholarships and grants · private scholarships and grants · United Negro College Fund. *Non-need-based aid programs include:* scholarships and grants · general need-based awards · state scholarships and grants · creative arts and performance awards · special achievements and activities awards · special characteristics awards · athletic scholarships · ROTC scholarships.

MICHIGAN STATE UNIVERSITY

Highlights

Admissions
Applicants: 31,479
Accepted: 21,610
Acceptance rate: 68.6%
Average GPA: 3.6
ACT range: 23-28
SAT Math range: 550-690
SAT Reading range: 420-580
SAT Writing range: 4-15
Top 10% of class: 28%
Top 25% of class: 66%
Top 50% of class: 94%

Deadlines
Early Action: 10/16
Early Decision: No
Regular Action: Rolling admissions
Common Application: Accepted

Financial Aid
In-state tuition: $13,246
Out-of-state tuition: $35,026
Room: Varies
Board: Varies
Books: $1,044
Freshmen receiving need-based aid: 47%
Undergrads rec. need-based aid: 48%
Avg. % of need met by financial aid: 61%
Avg. aid package (freshmen): $12,406
Avg. aid package (undergrads): $12,041
Avg. debt upon graduation: $25,821

Prominent Alumni
Richard Ford, author and Pulitzer Prize winner; Kay Koplovitz, founder of the USA Network; Earvin 'Magic' Johnson, Basketball Hall of Fame and Olympic Gold Medalist.

School Spirit
Mascot: Spartans
Colors: Green and white
Song: *MSU Fight Song*

MILLS COLLEGE

5000 MacArthur Boulevard, Oakland, CA 94613
Admissions: 800-87-MILLS · Financial Aid: 510-430-2000
Email: admission@mills.edu · Website: http://www.mills.edu

From the College

"Mills College offers women the opportunity to study and grow in a dynamic environment that supports intellectual exploration and a thoughtful approach to life. Working closely with faculty members and diverse students in intimate, collaborative classes, Mills women explore, debate and challenge conventional thinking both inside and outside the classroom. Students work with faculty members on meaningful real-world projects and engage with distinguished professors, thinkers, writers and artists. Set on a park-like campus, Mills provides a home with convenient access to the thriving cultural, artistic, social and professional worlds of the metropolitan San Francisco Bay Area."

Campus Setting

Mills, founded in 1852, is a private, liberal arts college for women with 1,595 students. Its 135-acre campus is located in Oakland, 18 miles east of San Francisco. Campus facilities include: art museum · theatres · contemporary music center · studios. Mills College provides on-campus housing with 593 units that can accommodate 733 students. Housing options: coed dorms · women's dorms · single-student apartments · married-student apartments · special housing for disabled students · cooperative housing. Recreation and sports facilities include: activity room · aquatic center with therapy spa · fitness center · fitness trail · gymnasium · jogging track · tennis courts · soccer field · boat house for rowing team.

Student Life and Activities

A little over half (58 percent) of students live on campus. According to a school representative, "The Mills experience extends beyond the classroom into extracurricular activities that challenge you to discover more about yourself, your peers and the world. With students of different backgrounds, ethnicities, cultures, ages and mind sets, the shared experiences of the close-knit Mills community ensure that the learning process continues both inside and outside of the classroom. Student- and college-run activities on campus encompass environmental activism, social justice issues, academic subjects and just plain fun, ensuring that there's never a shortage of engaging opportunities at Mills." Popular gathering spots include San Francisco, Berkeley, Oakland, Peet's Coffee, cafes, clubs, bookstores, clothes shops, movies and restaurants. On campus, students gather in the Tea Shop for a snack, Adam's Plaza, in the parenting lounge with their children and in the Solidarity or Mary Atkins lounges. Popular campus events include Black & White Ball, Literary Salon Series, Fetish Ball, Midnight Breakfast, Spring Fling, Movie on the Meadow, speakers, volleyball games, swim meets, the Sex Positive Fair, dorm parties, Second Saturdays and Final Fridays. Mills College has 63 official student organizations. Influential groups include Student Government, Black Women's Collective, Earth C.O.R.P.S., Asian Pacific Islander Sisterhood Alliance, Mujeres Unidas, Muslim Student Association, Mouthing Off!, Women's Health Resource Center, Fem Democrats, Phi Alpha Delta Pre-Law fraternity and the Campanil. Mills College is a member of the NCAA (Division III Independents).

Academics and Learning Environment

Mills College has 107 full-time and 104 part-time faculty members, offering a student-to-faculty ratio of 10:1. The most common course size is 10 to 19 students. Mills College offers 55 majors with the most popular being English, psychology and political/legal/economic analysis and least popular being American studies, Spanish/Spanish-American studies and dance. The school has a general core requirement. Cooperative education is not offered. All first-year students must maintain a 2.0 GPA or higher to avoid academic probation, and a minimum overall GPA of 2.0 is required to graduate. Other special academic programs include: self-designed majors · independent study · double majors · Phi Beta Kappa · internships · certificate programs.

B Student Support and Success

The Writing Center at Mills College provides assistance for students who need help in developing communication skills. It is staffed by graduate students from the English Department, and one-on-one tutoring is available. In addition, workshops on writing are offered throughout the entire school year. Classes are commonly 20 students or less, and the student-to-faculty ratio is 11:1.

Mills College provides a variety of support programs for: academic · career · personal · psychological · minority students · non-traditional students · family planning · religious. Additional counseling services include: Alcohol/substance abuse. The average freshman year GPA is 3.3, and 81 percent of freshmen students return for their sophomore year. While many enter the workforce, approximately 30 percent pursue a graduate degree right after graduation. A year later, 10 percent of graduates have entered graduate school. Companies that most frequently hire graduates from Mills College include: Cultural organizations · Enterprise · school districts · State of California · United States Government · Wells Fargo · media organization (Electronic media · TV · film · publishers) · arts organizations · finance (banking · insurance · investment).

Support for Students with Learning Disabilities

Mills College allows learning disabled students to take extra time to complete a degree, as well as carry a lighter course load. High school foreign language waivers are accepted. LD students will find the following programs quite useful: tutors · extended time for tests · take-home exam · oral tests · substitution of courses · readers · note-taking services · proofreading services · reading machines · tape recorders · texts on tape · early syllabus · priority registration · waiver of foreign language degree requirement. Individual or small group tutorials are also available in: time management · organizational skills · learning strategies · specific subject areas · writing labs · math labs · study skills. An advisor/advocate from the Services for Students with Disabilities is available to students.

How to Get Admitted

For admissions decisions, non-academic factors considered: interview · extracurricular activities · special talents, interests and abilities · character/personal qualities · volunteer work · work experience · geographical location · alumni relationship. A high school diploma is required, although a GED is also accepted for admissions consid-

MILLS COLLEGE

Highlights

Mills College
Oakland, CA (Pop. 400,740)
Location: Major city
Four-year private women's college
Founded: 1852
Website: http://www.mills.edu

Students
Total enrollment: 1,595
Undergrads: 985
Freshmen: 334
Part-time students: 6%
From out-of-state: 28%
From public schools: 78%
Male/Female: 0%/100%
Live on-campus: 58%
Off-campus employment rating: Good
Caucasian: 47%
African American: 6%
Hispanic: 22%
Asian: 12%
Hawaiian or Pacific Islander: 1%
Native American: 1%
Mixed (2+ ethnicities): 9%
International: 1%

Academics
Calendar: Semester
Student/faculty ratio: 10:1
Class size 9 or fewer: 30%
Class size 10-29: 59%
Class size 30-49: 11%
Class size 50-99: -
Class size 100 or more: -
Returning freshmen: 81%
Six-year graduation rate: 62%

Most Popular Majors
English
Psychology
Political/legal/economic analysis

MILLS COLLEGE

Admissions
Applicants: 1,827
Accepted: 1,242
Acceptance rate: 68.0%
Average GPA: 3.6
ACT range: 23-28
SAT Math range: 500-610
SAT Reading range: 540-640
SAT Writing range: 5-37
Top 10% of class: 41%
Top 25% of class: 71%
Top 50% of class: 97%

Deadlines
Early Action: 11/15
Early Decision: No
Regular Action: 1/15 (final)
Notification of admission by: 4/1
Common Application: Accepted

Financial Aid
In-state tuition: $41,618
Out-of-state tuition: $41,618
Room: $5,864
Board: $5,478
Books: $1,490
Freshmen receiving need-based aid: 88%
Undergrads rec. need-based aid: 85%
Avg. % of need met by financial aid: 78%
Avg. aid package (freshmen): $41,124
Avg. aid package (undergrads): $37,766
Avg. debt upon graduation: $24,861

Prominent Alumni
Barbara Lee, congresswoman; Thoraya Ahmed Obaid, Undersecretary General of UN Population Fund; April Glaspie, First Woman Ambassador to the Middle East.

School Spirit
Mascot: Cyclones
Colors: Yellow, white, and blue
Song: *Fires of Wisdom*

eration. SAT or ACT test scores are required of all applicants. SAT Subject Test scores are recommended but not required. *Academic units recommended:* 4 English, 4 Math, 4 Science, 4 Social Studies, 4 Foreign Language.

How to Pay for College

To apply for financial aid, students should submit the following: Free Application for Federal Student Aid (FAFSA) · institution's own financial aid forms · state aid form · Non-custodian (Divorced/Separated) Parent's Statement. Mills College participates in the Federal Work Study program. *Need-based aid programs include:* scholarships and grants · general need-based awards · Federal Pell grants · state scholarships and grants · college-based scholarships and grants · private scholarships and grants. *Non-need-based aid programs include:* scholarships and grants · state scholarships and grants · creative arts and performance awards · special achievements and activities awards · special characteristics awards.

MITCHELL COLLEGE

437 Pequot Avenue, New London, CT 06320
Admissions: 800-443-2811 · Financial Aid: 800-443-2811
Email: admissions@mitchell.edu · Website: http://www.mitchell.edu

From the College

"Mitchell College is a private institution, providing a transforming educational experience culminating in a bachelor's or associate's degree. Within a diverse and student-centered community and with an emphasis on holistic student development, Mitchell College supports individual learning differences, nurtures untapped academic potential and instills the professional knowledge and skills needed for students to contribute to an ever-changing world. Mitchell offers premier programs for students with diagnosed learning disabilities or ADHD within a mainstream college. A one-year pre-college experience allows students to earn up to 18 credits while strengthening academic preparedness. Each academic major provides students with internships tailored to their interests and career goals. Mitchell is located half-way between New York and Boston on a 68-acre waterfront campus with two private beaches, pond and nature preserve."

Campus Setting

Mitchell College, founded in 1938, is a private, co-educational college. Its 65-acre campus is located in New London. It provides a transforming educational experience. A four-year institution, Mitchell College has an enrollment of 858 students. The school also has a library with 73,590 books. Mitchell College provides on-campus housing, including these options: coed dorms · women's dorms · men's dorms.

Student Life and Activities

Sixty-two percent of students live on campus. Popular campus events include Applefest, Strawberryfest, Evening of International Song and Dance, Lighthouse Idol, Campus Luau, Late Night Breakfast and Mitchell Idol. Mitchell College has 30 official student organizations. The most popular are: Campus Activities Board · Class Officers · Commuter Students Association · early childhood education club · dance club · choir · drama society · gaming club · recreation club · behavior science club · business club · Thames Log. Mitchell College is a member of the Independents (Division III), NECC and ECAC.

Academics and Learning Environment

Mitchell College has 35 full-time and 52 part-time faculty members, offering a student-to-faculty ratio of 14:1. The most common course size is 10 to 19 students. Mitchell College offers 15 majors with the most popular being business administration, criminal justice and liberal/professional studies. The school has a general core requirement. Cooperative education is not offered. All first-year students must maintain a 1.7 GPA or higher to avoid academic probation, and a minimum overall GPA of 2.0 is required to graduate. Other programs include: self-designed majors · independent study · Phi Beta Kappa · internships · certificate programs.

B Student Support and Success

This statement from Mitchell College gives insight into its facilities and programs: "Mitchell College prides itself on the fact that its greatest success and satisfaction comes from working with students who have yet to realize their full academic potential." The college embraces student differences and provides the following resources and strategies that can help B students achieve success: free professional content

MITCHELL COLLEGE

Mitchell College
New London, CT (Pop. 27,569)
Location: Large town
Four-year private
Founded: 1938
Website: http://www.mitchell.edu

Students
Total enrollment: 858
Undergrads: 858
Freshmen: 240
Part-time students: 15%
From out-of-state: 44%
Male/Female: 53%/47%
Live on-campus: 62%
Off-campus employment rating: Good
Caucasian: 68%
African American: 13%
Hispanic: 7%
Asian: 2%
Hawaiian or Pacific Islander: <1%
Native American: 1%
Mixed (2+ ethnicities): 5%
International: 1%

Academics
Calendar: Semester
Student/faculty ratio: 14:1
Class size 9 or fewer: 20%
Class size 10-29: 78%
Class size 30-49: 2%
Class size 50-99: -
Class size 100 or more: -
Returning freshmen: 57%
Six-year graduation rate: 47%

Most Popular Majors
Liberal/professional studies
Business administration
Criminal justice

America's
Best Colleges for
B Students

tutoring, learning and writing specialists, LD support program, five-week summer transition enrichment program, post-grad transitional year certificate, Freshman Interest Groups mentoring program and Discovery program for undecided students.

Mitchell College provides a variety of programs, such as dedicated guidance for: academic · career · personal · minority students · veterans · family planning. Annually, 57 percent of freshmen students return for their sophomore year.

Support for Students with Learning Disabilities

Students with learning disabilities, also called LD students, may take advantage of specific support programs offered by Mitchell College. If its deemed necessary, the college will grant additional time to students with learning disabilities to complete their degree or a lightened course load may be granted. High school foreign language waivers are accepted. Students with learning disabilities will find the following programs of interest: tutors · learning center · testing accommodations · extended time for tests · take-home exam · oral tests · readers · note-taking services · reading machines · tape recorders · texts on tape · videotaped classes · early syllabus · priority registration. Individual or small group tutorials are also available in: time management · organizational skills · learning strategies · specific subject areas · writing labs · math labs · study skills. An advisor/advocate from the Learning Resource Center is available to students.

How to Get Admitted

For admissions decisions, non-academic factors considered: extracurricular activities · special talents, interests and abilities · character/personal qualities · volunteer work · work experience · state of residency · alumni relationship. A high school diploma is required, although a GED is also accepted for admissions consideration. SAT or ACT test scores are not considered or required. SAT Subject Test scores are not required. *Academic units recommended:* 4 English, 3 Math, 2 Science, 2 Social Studies.

Insight

"You are more than just your grade point average. While admission to Mitchell College is based on a comprehensive appraisal of your entire academic record, a huge part of that is also your personal character, aptitude, motivation and above all, your potential for academic success. We welcome the B student who recognizes his/her strengths and weaknesses and wants to be in an environment that will challenge him/her to improve and succeed.

"We would encourage B students to showcase their talents—those within the classroom and outside the classroom. Community and club involvement, volunteer and work experience, as well as hobbies and leadership opportunities, are a great way to show that a student has more to offer than just grades alone.

"Mitchell College has always been a college that focuses on asset development rather than deficit management. Our mission says it well when it states that we 'support individual learning differences and nurture untapped academic potential.' We welcome B and C students and find it very rewarding to have the privilege to be able to work with them to realize their full potential.

"Mitchell College's educational philosophy is one that is based on five distinctive values called C.A.R.E.S.—Character, Achievement, Respect, Engagement and Self-Discovery. It is a learning experience that provides students with the foundation and knowledge base they need for the education and life they wish to pursue. This partnership enables students to take their classroom instruction and apply it directly to the real world through a variety of unique internship and service learning opportunities—experiences that enable students to make a difference locally, nationally and globally."

How to Pay for College

To apply for financial aid, students should submit the following: Free Application for Federal Student Aid (FAFSA) · institution's own financial aid forms. Mitchell College participates in the Federal Work Study program. *Need-based aid programs include:* scholarships and grants · general need-based awards · Federal Pell grants · state scholarships and grants · college-based scholarships and grants · private scholarships and grants. *Non-need-based aid programs include:* scholarships and grants · general need-based awards · state scholarships and grants · creative arts and performance awards · special achievements and activities awards · leadership scholarships.

MITCHELL COLLEGE

Highlights

Admissions
Applicants: 1,041
Accepted: 621
Acceptance rate: 59.7%
Average GPA: 2.7
ACT range: Not reported
SAT Math range: Not reported
SAT Reading range: Not reported
SAT Writing range: Not reported

Deadlines
Early Action: No
Early Decision: 11/15
Regular Action: Rolling admissions
Common Application: Accepted

Financial Aid
In-state tuition: $28,272
Out-of-state tuition: $28,272
Room: $6,496
Board: $5,996
Books: $1,500
Freshmen receiving need-based aid: 83%
Undergrads rec. need-based aid: 73%
Avg. % of need met by financial aid: 59%
Avg. aid package (freshmen): $20,235
Avg. aid package (undergrads): $21,437
Avg. debt upon graduation: $28,182

School Spirit
Mascot: Mariner
Colors: Red and white
Song: *Mitchell College Alma Mater*

MONTANA TECH OF THE UNIVERSITY OF MONTANA

1300 West Park Street, Butte, MT 59701
Admissions: 800-445-TECH · Financial Aid: 800-445-TECH
Email: enrollment@mtech.edu · Website: http://www.mtech.edu

From the College

"Originally chartered as the Montana State School of Mines, Montana Tech has evolved into a dynamic institution offering 10 certificate programs, 17 associate degrees, 23 bachelors and 10 masters programs. With over 2,900 students, Montana Tech provides graduates with the knowledge and skills necessary to be successful, conduct basic and applied research and provide related services to the citizens of Montana and beyond.

"Montana Tech takes pride in quality instruction provided by highly qualified faculty members. A 15:1 student-to-faculty ratio and an average class size of 20 facilitate the relationships that lead to student success. Students learn from professors, most with current industry experience. Over $1.4 million in new student scholarships are awarded to new students each year. The low cost of living and affordable housing in Butte is a huge benefit to Tech students. Montana Tech has had a ten-year annual average placement rate of 93 percent including acceptance into professional and graduate programs. Tech is located in beautiful southwestern Montana with abundant opportunities for outdoor recreation. Campus life is full of activities ranging from hikes to the M to live bands to various fun events in the residence halls. Life here is laid back and personal where you will be on a first-name basis with your professors. Classes are challenging with an emphasis on teamwork and collaboration. Outdoor recreation provides a great balance to the rigors of the course work at Montana Tech.

"Overlooking the city from the shoulder of Big Butte, Montana Tech's north campus can be seen for miles. Its tree-shaded perimeter encloses both the stately buildings of the institution's past and the modern facilities reflecting its present and its future. Since its inception, Montana Tech has come a long way. The exceptional job placement rate of graduates and the success stories of alumni, combined with the low cost of attendance in a highly personalized environment, attest to both quality and value."

Campus Setting

Montana Tech, founded in 1896 as Montana College of Mineral Science and Technology, is a multipurpose institution. Its 56-acre campus is located in Butte. A four-year public institution, Montana Tech has an enrollment of 2,923 students. The campus offers its students mining and mineral museums, as well as a library. Montana Tech provides on-campus housing with five units that can accommodate 400 students. Housing options: coed dorms · single-student apartments · married-student apartments · special housing for disabled students. Recreation and sports facilities include: cardio room · gymnasium · racquetball and tennis courts · trails.

Student Life and Activities

Eighty-nine percent of students live off campus. Orientation, Homecoming (Parade, Bed Races, Games), M-Days, Holiday Stroll, Talent Show, Digger Hunt, Mulletfest, Career Fair, Late Night Breakfast, Montana Tech Ski Day and Mining and Mucking Contest are popular events. Montana Tech of the University of Montana has 47 official student organizations. The most popular are: Society Of Petroleum Engineers · Biology Club · Business Activities Club · Chemistry Club · Chess Club of Montana Tech · Circle K · Club Met · Copper Guard · Dance Club · American Association of

America's
Best Colleges for
B Students

Drilling Engineers · Environmental Engineers of Montana Tech · Fly Fishing Club · Geology Club · Health care Informatics Club · Inst. of Electrical and Electronic Engineers · Liberal Studies Club · Marcus Daly Mining Club · Math Club · Anime Club · Peace Seekers of Montana Tech · Pre-Professional Health Club · Residence Hall Association · Runners of Montana Tech · Saudi Club · Society of Exploration Geophysicists · Society of Mining Engineers · Society of Women Engineers · Student Nurses Association · Entertainment Committee · Unmanned Aerial Vehicles · American Society of Civil Engineers · American Society of Mechanical Engineers · American Society of Safety Engineers · American Welding Society. There are intramural teams available: basketball · biking · fishing · football · hiking · racquetball · rugby · skiing · snowboarding · softball · swimming · volleyball. Montana Tech of the University of Montana is a member of the Member of Frontier Conference (NAIA).

Academics and Learning Environment

Montana Tech of the University of Montana has 138 full-time and 78 part-time faculty members, offering a student-to-faculty ratio of 15:1. The most common course size is 10 to 19 students. Montana Tech of the University of Montana offers 50 majors with the most popular being petroleum engineering, general engineering and business information technology and least popular being geophysical engineering, general science and general studies. The school has a general core requirement. Cooperative education is available. All first-year students must maintain a 2.0 GPA or higher to avoid academic probation. Other programs include: pass/fail grading option · independent study · double majors · dual degrees · honors program · internships · distance learning certificate programs.

B Student Support and Success

A quote about Montana Tech explains the services that the college provides to its students: "Montana Tech has a great learning center. This is a place where all students can get help with any of their courses. Tech also has very attentive professors that are always available for personal help. "Montana Tech admits students who are in the top half of their graduating class or who have a 2.5 or higher. You do not need to have straight A's to get admitted or to get scholarships here. All B students are accepted to Montana Tech! Any student above a 2.5 is accepted in good academic standing. Students with lower GPAs than 2.5 are accepted on academic probation. They will be in college success courses and monitored carefully."

Montana Tech of the University of Montana provides a variety of support programs, among them, dedicated guidance for: academic · career · personal · minority students · military · veterans · non-traditional students. Annually, 69 percent of freshmen students return for their sophomore year. While many students do dedicate themselves to the workforce, approximately 11 percent pursue a graduate degree immediately after graduation. One year after graduation, the school reports that a full 19 percent of graduates have entered graduate school. Among students who enter the workforce, approximately 24 percent enter a field related to their major within six months of their actual graduation. Companies that most frequently employ graduates from Montana Tech of the University

MONTANA TECH OF THE UNIVERSITY OF MONTANA

Montana Tech of the University of Montana
Butte, MT (Pop. 33,730)
Location: Large town
Four-year public
Founded: 1896
Website: http://www.mtech.edu

Students
Total enrollment: 2,923
Undergrads: 2,757
Freshmen: 1,229
Part-time students: 21%
From out-of-state: 13%
From public schools: 90%
Male/Female: 60%/40%
Live on-campus: 11%
Off-campus employment rating: Good
Caucasian: 83%
African American: 1%
Hispanic: 2%
Asian: 1%
Native American: 2%
Mixed (2+ ethnicities): <1%
International: 7%

Academics
Calendar: Semester
Student/faculty ratio: 15:1
Class size 9 or fewer: 25%
Class size 10-29: 51%
Class size 30-49: 15%
Class size 50-99: 8%
Class size 100 or more: 1%
Returning freshmen: 69%
Six-year graduation rate: 48%

Most Popular Majors
Petroleum engineering
General engineering
Business information technology

307

MONTANA TECH OF THE UNIVERSITY OF MONTANA

Admissions

Applicants: 877
Accepted: 773
Acceptance rate: 88.1%
Average GPA: 3.5
ACT range: 22-26
SAT Math range: 565-640
SAT Reading range: 495-635
SAT Writing range: 3-24
Top 10% of class: 26%
Top 25% of class: 57%
Top 50% of class: 86%

Deadlines

Early Action: No
Early Decision: No
Regular Action: Rolling admissions
Common Application: Not accepted

Financial Aid

In-state tuition: $6,464
Out-of-state tuition: $18,606
Room: $3,524
Board: $4,404
Books: $1,000
Freshmen receiving need-based aid: 63%
Undergrads rec. need-based aid: 62%
Avg. % of need met by financial aid: 62%
Avg. aid package (freshmen): $9,725
Avg. aid package (undergrads): $10,848
Avg. debt upon graduation: $26,115

Prominent Alumni

Ryan Lance, Chairman and CEO, ConocoPhillips; Keith MacPhail, President and CEO, Bonavista Energy Trust; Gary Kolstad, President and CEO, Carbo.

School Spirit

Mascot: Orediggers
Colors: Green and copper
Song: *Forward Tech*

of Montana are: Arch Coal Inc. · Baker Hughes · BJ Services CCCS · Chevron · EnCana Oil & Gas · Granite Construction Company · Holy Rosary Healthcare · MSE · Pioneer Technical Services · Saudi Aramco · St. James HealthCare.

Support for Students with Learning Disabilities

Students handling learning disabilities may find themselves interested in the various support programs offered at Montana Tech of the University of Montana. The college will grant, if necessary, additional time to students with learning disabilities to complete their degree or a lightened course load may be offered. LD students will want to investigate these programs: remedial math · remedial English · tutors · learning center · testing accommodations · extended time for tests · oral tests · typist/scribe · note-taking services · priority registration · waiver of foreign language degree requirement. Individual or small group tutorials are also available in: time management · organizational skills · learning strategies · specific subject areas · writing labs · math labs · study skills. An advisor/advocate from the Disability Services is available to students.

How to Get Admitted

For admissions decisions, non-academic factors considered: state of residency. A high school diploma is required, although a GED is also accepted for admissions consideration. SAT or ACT test scores are required for some applicants. *According to the admissions office:* Minimum composite ACT score of 22 (combined SAT score of 1540), rank in top half of secondary school class or minimum 2.5 GPA required. *Academic units recommended:* 4 English, 4 Math, 2 Science, 3 Social Studies.

How to Pay for College

To apply for financial aid, students should submit the following: Free Application for Federal Student Aid (FAFSA) · Scholarship application. Montana Tech of the University of Montana participates in the Federal Work Study program. *Need-based aid programs include:* scholarships and grants · general need-based awards · Federal Pell grants · state scholarships and grants · college-based scholarships and grants · private scholarships and grants. *Non-need-based aid programs include:* scholarships and grants · general need-based awards · state scholarships and grants · athletic scholarships.

MOREHOUSE COLLEGE

830 Westview Drive, SW, Atlanta, GA 30314
Admissions: 800-851-1254 · Financial Aid: 800-873-9041
Email: admissions@morehouse.edu · Website: http://www.morehouse.edu

From the College

"Morehouse, a historically black liberal arts college for men, assumes a special responsibility for teaching students about the history and culture of black people. The college seeks to develop men with disciplined minds, emphasizing the continuing search for truth as a liberating force. Morehouse prepares its students for leadership and service through instructional programs and extracurricular activities that: develop skills in oral and written communications, analytical and critical thinking and interpersonal relationships; foster an understanding and appreciation of the elements and evolution of various cultures and the nature of the physical universe; foster an understanding and appreciation of the specific knowledge and skills needed for the pursuit of professional careers and/or graduate study; cultivate the personal attributes of self-confidence, tolerance, morality, ethical behavior, humility, a global perspective and a commitment to a social justice."

Campus Setting

Morehouse, founded in 1867, is a private, liberal arts men's college. Its 61-acre campus is located in downtown Atlanta. A four-year institution, Morehouse College is a historically black university with 2,187 students. The campus facilities include: library · leadership center · technology tower. Morehouse College provides on-campus housing with 1,500 units that can accommodate 1,500 students. Housing options: men's dorms · single-student apartments · special housing for international students.

Student Life and Activities

Sixty-five percent of students live on campus. As reported by a school official, "The campus offers a nice social environment with numerous diversities of individuals. It has a good cultural life that brings people together, regardless of backgrounds." Popular gathering spots include Lenox Mall and Jazzmans. Popular campus events include the New Student Orientation, Homecoming, Martin Luther King Celebration, Founder's Day, Prospective Student Seminar, Africa Awareness Week, Public Health Awareness Conference, Science and Spiritual Awareness Week and Annual Family Institute. Morehouse College has 50 official student organizations. There are intramural teams available: basketball · golf · indoor soccer · tennis · volleyball. Morehouse College is a member of the Southern Intercollegiate Athletic Conference (Division II).

Academics and Learning Environment

Morehouse College has 164 full-time and 59 part-time faculty members, offering a student-to-faculty ratio of 12:1. The most common course size is 20 to 29. Morehouse College offers 28 majors with the most popular being business administration, political science and biology and least popular being French, urban studies and child development. The school has a general core requirement. Cooperative education is available. All first-year students must maintain a 2.0 GPA or higher to avoid academic probation, and a minimum overall GPA of 2.0 is required to graduate. Other programs include: double majors · dual degrees · honors program · Phi Beta Kappa · internships.

MOREHOUSE COLLEGE

Morehouse College
Atlanta (Pop. 443,775)
Location: Major city
Four-year private men's college
Founded: 1867
Website: http://www.morehouse.edu

Students
Total enrollment: 2,187
Undergrads: 2,187
Freshmen: 530
Part-time students: 8%
From out-of-state: 74%
From public schools: 76%
Male/Female: 100%/ 0%
Live on-campus: 65%
In fraternities: 19%
Off-campus employment rating: Good
Caucasian: <1%
African American: 96%
Hispanic: <1%
Mixed (2+ ethnicities): <1%
International: 2%

Academics
Calendar: Semester
Student/faculty ratio: 12:1
Class size 9 or fewer: 21%
Class size 10-29: 66%
Class size 30-49: 13%
Class size 50-99: 1%
Class size 100 or more: -
Returning freshmen: 80%
Six-year graduation rate: 54%

Most Popular Majors
Business administration
Biology
Political science

B Student Support and Success

The Wellness Resource Center offers personal counseling to help students "resolve personal difficulties and acquire the skills, attitudes and knowledge that will enable them to take full advantage of their experiences at Morehouse College."

Morehouse College provides a variety of support programs including: academic · career · personal · psychological · non-traditional students · family planning. The average freshman year GPA is 2.7, and 80 percent of freshmen students return for their sophomore year. Some students commit themselves to the workforce, while approximately 25 percent pursue a graduate degree immediately after graduation. One year after graduation has passed, the school reports that 30 percent of graduates have entered into graduate school. Among those students that enter the workforce, approximately 68 percent enter a field related to their major within six months of graduation. Here's a compiled list of companies that most frequently hire graduates from Morehouse College: Bank of America · Deloitte · Goldman Sachs · JP Morgan Chase · Lehman Brothers · Merrill Lynch · McKinsey & Company · Morgan Stanley · PricewaterhouseCoopers · UBS · Wachovia.

Support for Students with Learning Disabilities

B students with learning disabilities may be interested in the support programs offered by Morehouse College. When necessary, the college will grant additional time to students with learning disabilities so that they can complete their degree. Also, a lightened course load may be offered. High school foreign language and math waivers are accepted. B students with learning disabilities will find the following programs at Morehouse College extremely helpful: remedial math · remedial English · remedial reading · tutors · learning center · testing accommodations · untimed tests · extended time for tests · take-home exam · oral tests · exam on tape or computer · readers · typist/scribe · note-taking services · proofreading services · reading machines · tape recorders · texts on tape · early syllabus · diagnostic testing service · special bookstore section · priority registration · priority seating · waiver of foreign language and math degree requirement. Individual or small group tutorials are also available in: time management · organizational skills · learning strategies · specific subject areas · writing labs · math labs · study skills. An advisor/advocate from the Disability Service Office is available to students.

How to Get Admitted

For admissions decisions, non-academic factors considered: interview · extracurricular activities · special talents, interests and abilities · character/personal qualities · volunteer work · state of residency · geographical location · minority affiliation · alumni relationship. A high school diploma is required, although a GED is also accepted for admissions consideration. SAT or ACT test scores are required of all applicants. *According to the admissions office:* Minimum combined SAT Reasoning score of 1500 (composite ACT score of 22), rank in top half of secondary school class and minimum 2.8 GPA required. *Academic units recommended:* 4 English, 3 Math, 2 Science, 2 Social Studies, 2 Foreign Language.

How to Pay for College

To apply for financial aid, students should submit the following: Free Application for Federal Student Aid (FAFSA) · institution's own financial aid forms · CSS/Financial Aid PROFILE · state aid form. Morehouse College participates in the Federal Work Study program. *Need-based aid programs include:* scholarships and grants · general need-based awards · Federal Pell grants · state scholarships and grants · college-based scholarships and grants · private scholarships and grants · United Negro College Fund. *Non-need-based aid programs include:* scholarships and grants · general need-based awards · state scholarships and grants · special achievements and activities awards · athletic scholarships · ROTC scholarships.

MOREHOUSE COLLEGE

Highlights

Admissions
Applicants: 2,697
Accepted: 1,802
Acceptance rate: 66.8%
Average GPA: 3.2
ACT range: 18-24
SAT Math range: 448-560
SAT Reading range: 450-550
SAT Writing range: 1-9
Top 10% of class: 22%
Top 25% of class: 41%
Top 50% of class: 73%

Deadlines
Early Action: 12/15
Early Decision: 11/1
Regular Action: 11/1 (priority)
2/15 (final)
Notification of admission by: 4/1
Common Application: Accepted

Financial Aid
In-state tuition: $23,966
Out-of-state tuition: $23,966
Room: $7,510
Board: $5,812
Books: $2,088
Freshmen receiving need-based aid: 93%
Undergrads rec. need-based aid: 93%
Avg. % of need met by financial aid: 48%
Avg. aid package (freshmen): $18,802
Avg. aid package (undergrads): $18,567
Avg. debt upon graduation: $37,559

Prominent Alumni
Reverend Dr. Martin Luther King, Jr., Nobel Peace Prize laureate and civil rights leader; Dr. David Satcher, former U.S. Surgeon General; Shelton 'Spike' Lee, filmmaker, president of 40 Acres & A Mule.

School Spirit
Mascot: Maroon Tigers
Colors: Maroon and white
Song: *Dear Old Morehouse*

311

MUSKINGUM UNIVERSITY

163 Stormont Street, New Concord, OH 43762
Admissions: 800-752-6082 · Financial Aid: 740-826-8139
Email: adminfo@muskingum.edu · Website: http://www.muskingum.edu

From the College

"At a recent Muskingum College commencement, the graduating class student representative talked about Muskingum this way: Muskingum has always been a small liberal arts school in rural Ohio with about 1,000 students at any given time (until the past ten years). Despite this amount of former graduates, compared to larger universities, Muskingum has produced a senator and astronaut, John Glenn, as many people know us for. But Muskingum has also provided the United States with an ambassador to Mexico and an editor of the Wall Street Journal. Muskingum has produced a vice president or president of the three largest corporations in the world: a former chairman and CEO of Ford Motor Co.; an executive vice president of AT&T, and a vice president for General Motors. The list could go on and on. We have already seen major impacts by our fellow graduates. One of today's graduates is at the forefront of city management with a job he has held several months before his actual graduation. Another graduate helped with a wildlife population project in Kenya. What mark will we have put on Ohio, the United States and the world? It is the same challenge that previous Muskingum graduates have had and they have gone beyond all expectations."

Campus Setting

Muskingum, founded in 1837, is a private, church-affiliated, liberal arts college. Its 245-acre campus is located in New Concord, 70 miles east of Columbus. A four-year institution, Muskingum University has an enrollment of 2,154 students and has been co-ed since 1854. The school is also affiliated with the Presbyterian Church. Besides a sizable library, the campus also offers its students a historic Site and Exploration Center. Muskingum University provides on-campus housing with 677 units that can accommodate 1,052 students. Housing options: coed dorms · women's dorms · men's dorms · sorority housing · fraternity housing · single-student apartments. Recreation and sports facilities include: artificial turf football field · baseball, soccer and softball fields · cross-country trail · recreation center · tennis courts.

Student Life and Activities

Seventy-one percent of students live on campus. Students create and manage most of their social life. A large part of their development is being at the core of making things happen. Popular places to spend time include Winn Cafe, Chess Center, Rec Center, BOC and Uppity's (coffee shop in town). Students enjoy events such as Muskiepalooza, Casino Night, Relay for Life, Coffee house events, comedians and musical artists. Muskingum University has 85 official student organizations. The most popular are: AGORA · GLASS · Residence Hall Advisors · Habitat for Humanity · Student Senate · Spirit Band · Bacchus · Circle K · Muskie Greens · Centerboard · Council for Exceptional Children · Peer Educators · Dance Team · Forensics · Democrat Students · Republican Students · CARE (vegetarian club) · MESA (environmental student activists) · Wellness club · Women's Resource Center · outdoor club · Magna Anime and gaming club. There are intramural teams available: basketball · bowling · flag football · golf · racquetball · softball · volleyball · walleyball. Muskingum University is a member of the Ohio Athletic Conference (Division III).

Academics and Learning Environment

Muskingum University has 96 full-time and 65 part-time faculty members, offering a student-to-faculty ratio of 14:1. The most common course size is 2 to 9. Muskingum University offers 55 majors with the most popular being business, nursing/health studies and education and least popular being philosophy and religion. The school has a general core requirement as well as a religion requirement. Cooperative education is not offered. All first-year students must maintain a 2.0 GPA or higher to avoid academic probation. Other programs include: self-designed majors · pass/fail grading option · independent study · double majors · accelerated study · internships · distance learning certificate programs.

B Student Support and Success

The Center for Advancement of Learning at Muskingum provides assistance to students in a number of different ways. Their PLUS program is a complex system for students with significant learning disabilities. There is also a Learning Strategies and Resources Program that helps at-risk students through weekly workshops, weekly strategy sessions and more. In addition, their First Step Transition Program provides an intensive and comprehensive summer orientation for students before they begin their undergraduate studies.

Muskingum University provides a variety of support programs including: academic · career · personal · psychological · minority students · veterans · family planning · religious. The average freshman year GPA is 2.8, and 69 percent of freshmen students return for their sophomore year. After college, a majority of students enter the workforce, while approximately 19 percent pursue a graduate degree immediately after graduation. One year after graduation, the school reports that eight percent of graduates have entered into graduate school. Among students who enter the workforce, approximately 87 percent of them enter into a field related to their actual major within six months of their graduation. Some companies that most frequently hire graduates from Muskingum University include: CED · Groveport Madison Schools · Nationwide Insurance · National City Bank · Resource Systems · State of Ohio Auditor's Office · Wal-Mart · Southeastern Equipment · Sherwin Williams · State Farm Insurance · The Longaberger Company · Verizon Wireless · Wells Fargo · Zanesville · Upper Arlington Schools · Fastenal · Mason Schools.

Support for Students with Learning Disabilities

Students coping with learning disabilities may want to take advantage of specific support programs offered by Muskingum University. If deemed appropriate by the college, LD students may be granted additional time to complete their degree. Another option is a lightened course load. High school foreign language and math waivers are accepted. Students with learning disabilities will find the following programs at Muskingum University rather beneficial: tutors · learning center · testing accommodations · untimed tests · extended time for tests · take-home exam · oral tests · readers · note-taking services · reading machines · tape recorders · texts on tape · waiver of foreign language degree requirement. Individual or small group tutorials are also available in: time management · organizational skills · learning strategies · specific subject areas · writing labs · study

MUSKINGUM UNIVERSITY

Highlights

Muskingum University
New Concord, OH (Pop. 2,490)
Location: Rural
Four-year private
Founded: 1837
Website: http://www.muskingum.edu

Students
Total enrollment: 2,154
Undergrads: 1,728
Freshmen: 508
Part-time students: 17%
From out-of-state: 9%
From public schools: 93%
Male/Female: 45%/55%
Live on-campus: 71%
In fraternities: 25%
In sororities: 34%
Off-campus employment rating: Fair
Caucasian: 79%
African American: 6%
Hispanic: 2%
Asian: <1%
Native American: <1%
Mixed (2+ ethnicities): 3%
International: 5%

Academics
Calendar: Semester
Student/faculty ratio: 14:1
Class size 9 or fewer: 39%
Class size 10-29: 55%
Class size 30-49: 5%
Class size 50-99: 1%
Class size 100 or more: -
Returning freshmen: 69%
Six-year graduation rate: 48%

Most Popular Majors
Business
Education
Nursing/health studies

313

MUSKINGUM UNIVERSITY

Highlights

Admissions
Applicants: 2,001
Accepted: 1,520
Acceptance rate: 76.0%
Average GPA: 3.1
ACT range: 18-24
SAT Math range: 420-540
SAT Reading range: 400-520
SAT Writing range: 2-7
Top 10% of class: 28%
Top 25% of class: 43%
Top 50% of class: 70%

Deadlines
Early Action: No
Early Decision: No
Regular Action: Rolling admissions
Common Application: Accepted

Financial Aid
In-state tuition: $24,000
Out-of-state tuition: $24,000
Room: $5,000
Board: $4,760
Books: $1,100
Freshmen receiving need-based aid: 89%
Undergrads rec. need-based aid: 84%
Avg. % of need met by financial aid: 75%
Avg. aid package (freshmen): $21,588
Avg. aid package (undergrads): $20,803
Avg. debt upon graduation: $33,976

Prominent Alumni
John Glenn, former U.S. Senator and astronaut; Jack Hanna, zoologist; Philip Caldwell, former CEO of Ford Motor Company.

School Spirit
Mascot: Fighting Muskies
Colors: Black and magenta

skills. An advisor/advocate from the PLUS Program is available to students. This member also sits on the admissions committee.

How to Get Admitted

For admissions decisions, non-academic factors considered: interview · extracurricular activities · special talents, interests and abilities · character/personal qualities · work experience · state of residency · geographical location · minority affiliation · alumni relationship. A high school diploma is required, although a GED is also accepted for admissions consideration. SAT or ACT test scores are required of all applicants. SAT Subject Test scores are considered, if submitted, but are not required. *According to the admissions office:* Minimum 2.5 GPA in college-preparatory courses required. *Academic units recommended:* 4 English, 3 Math, 3 Science, 1 Social Studies, 2 Foreign Language.

How to Pay for College

To apply for financial aid, students should submit the following: Free Application for Federal Student Aid (FAFSA) · state aid form. Muskingum University participates in the Federal Work Study program. *Need-based aid programs include:* scholarships and grants · general need-based awards · Federal Pell grants · state scholarships and grants · college-based scholarships and grants · private scholarships and grants. *Non-need-based aid programs include:* scholarships and grants · general need-based awards · state scholarships and grants · creative arts and performance awards · special achievements and activities awards · special characteristics awards.

NORWICH UNIVERSITY

158 Harmon Drive, Northfield, VT 05663
Admissions: 800-468-6679 · Financial Aid: 800-468-6679
Email: nuadm@norwich.edu
Website: http://www.norwich.edu

From the College

"Vision: Norwich University will be a learning community, American in character yet global in perspective, engaged in personal and intellectual transformation and dedicated to knowledge, mutual respect, creativity and service. Mission: To give our youth an education that shall be American in character- to enable them to act as well as to think-to execute as well as to conceive- to tolerate all opinions when reason is left free to combat them- to make moral, patriotic, efficient and useful citizens and to qualify them for all those high responsibilities resting upon a citizen of this free republic."

Campus Setting

Norwich University, founded in 1819, is a private co-educational university. For 20 years, Cadets and traditional students have shared the same campus at Norwich University, creating one of the most unique college cultures in the nation. A four-year institution, Norwich University has an enrollment of 3,111 students and has been co-ed since 1972. The campus provides students with a large library as well as a museum. Norwich University provides on-campus housing with 10 units that can accommodate 1,593 students. Housing options: coed dorms. Recreation and sports facilities include: arena · armory · field house.

Student Life and Activities

Many students live off campus. Norwich University has 80 official student organizations. The most popular are: regimental, stage, symphonic, marching and pep bands · choir · music ensembles · orchestra · drill team · artillery platoon · cavalry troop · drill team · military police · mountain rescue team · parachute club · team managers · departmental, service and special-interest groups. There are intramural teams available: basketball · dodgeball · football · hockey · softball · Wiffle ball. Norwich University is a member of the ECAC Hockey (Division III), Freedom Football Conference (Division III), Great Northeast Athletic Conference (Division III), New England College Wrestling Association (Division III) and Pilgrim League (Division III).

Academics and Learning Environment

Norwich University has 154 full-time and 174 part-time faculty members, offering a student-to-faculty ratio of 13:1. The most common course size is 10 to 19 students. Norwich University offers 39 majors. The school has a general core requirement. Cooperative education is not offered. All first-year students must maintain a 1.5 GPA or higher to avoid academic probation. Other programs include: pass/fail grading option · independent study · double majors · dual degrees · internships · distance learning.

Highlights

Norwich University
Northfield, VT (Pop. 2,086)
Location: Rural
Four-year private
Founded: 1819
Website: http://www.norwich.edu

Students
Total enrollment: 3,111
Undergrads: 2,256
Freshmen: 676
Part-time students: 3%
From out-of-state: 90%
Male/Female: 74%/26%
Live on-campus: Not reported
Off-campus employment rating: Good
Caucasian: 81%
African American: 3%
Hispanic: 6%
Asian: 3%
Hawaiian or Pacific Islander: <1%
Native American: 2%
Mixed (2+ ethnicities): 2%
International: 1%

Academics
Calendar: Semester
Student/faculty ratio: 13:1
Class size 9 or fewer: 16%
Class size 10-29: 76%
Class size 30-49: 6%
Class size 50-99: 1%
Class size 100 or more: -
Returning freshmen: 85%
Six-year graduation rate: 57%

315

College Profiles

NORWICH UNIVERSITY

Highlights

Admissions
Applicants: 3,081
Accepted: 1,955
Acceptance rate: 63.5%
Average GPA: 3.0
ACT range: 21-26
SAT Math range: 480-590
SAT Reading range: 470-570
SAT Writing range: Not reported
Top 10% of class: 11%
Top 25% of class: 33%
Top 50% of class: 70%

Deadlines
Early Action: No
Early Decision: No
Regular Action: 2/1 (priority)
Common Application: Not accepted

Financial Aid
In-state tuition: $32,812
Out-of-state tuition: $32,812
Room: Varies
Board: Varies
Books: $1,000
Freshmen receiving need-based aid: 88%
Undergrads rec. need-based aid: 79%
Avg. % of need met by financial aid: 74%
Avg. aid package (freshmen): $29,111
Avg. aid package (undergrads): $28,035
Avg. debt upon graduation: $34,318

Prominent Alumni
Ansel Briggs, first governor of Iowa; Harry Bates Thayer, former chairman of the board of AT&T; Emily Caruso, national air rifle champion.

School Spirit
Mascot: Cadets
Colors: Maroon and gold
Song: *Norwich Forever*

America's
Best Colleges for
B Students

B Student Support and Success

Norwich's Learning Support Services (LSC) offers assistance to those students who need it. LSC provides support for students who need help in planning, organizing and managing their responsibilities as well as assessing best ways of learning in different environments. Support services are also available in areas of reading, writing, note taking and exam-taking strategies. Additionally, students are afforded opportunities to receive tutoring and to participate in review sessions in selected course subject areas. Students may request counseling and coaching for specific academic problems such as probation status and learning disorders.

Norwich University offers dedicated guidance for: academic · career · personal · psychological · military · veterans · religious. Annually, 85 percent of freshmen students return for their sophomore year. Out of those students that enter the workforce, approximately 93 percent enter a field related to their major within six months of graduation. Here are companies that most frequently hire graduates from Norwich University: Army · Navy · Air Force (commissioned officers) · Bechtel · Cap World · Dartmouth-Hitchcock Medical Center · General Electric · Goodrich · Homeland Security · local hospitals · Metcalf & Eddy · state and local police departments.

Support for Students with Learning Disabilities

Students with learning disabilities, also referred to as LD students, may take advantage of specific support programs offered by Norwich University. If deemed necessary, the college will sometimes grant additional time to students with learning disabilities to complete their degree. Students with learning disabilities will find the following programs at Norwich University extremely helpful: remedial math · remedial English · tutors · learning center · testing accommodations · extended time for tests · take-home exam · oral tests · readers · typist/scribe. Individual or small group tutorials are also available in: time management · organizational skills · learning strategies · specific subject areas · math labs · study skills.

How to Get Admitted

For admissions decisions, non-academic factors considered: interview · extracurricular activities · special talents, interests and abilities · character/personal qualities · volunteer work · work experience · state of residency · minority affiliation · alumni relationship. A high school diploma is required, although a GED is also accepted for admissions consideration. SAT or ACT test scores are required of all applicants. *Academic units recommended:* 4 English, 4 Math, 4 Science, 3 Social Studies, 2 Foreign Language.

How to Pay for College

To apply for financial aid, students should submit the following: Free Application for Federal Student Aid (FAFSA) · institution's own financial aid forms · CSS/Financial Aid PROFILE. Norwich University participates in the Federal Work Study program. *Need-based aid programs include:* scholarships and grants · general need-based awards · Federal Pell grants · state scholarships and grants · college-based scholarships and grants · private scholarships and grants. *Non-need-based aid programs include:* scholarships and grants · state scholarships and grants · special achievements and activities awards · ROTC scholarships.

NOTRE DAME OF MARYLAND UNIVERSITY

4701 North Charles Street, Baltimore, MD 21210
Admissions: 800-435-0300 · Financial Aid: 410-532-5369
Email: admiss@ndm.edu · Website: http://www.ndm.edu

From the College

"Notre Dame of Maryland University educates women leaders to transform the world. Distinctive programs challenge women to strive for intellectual and professional excellence, to build inclusive communities, to engage in service to others and promote social responsibility."

Campus Setting

Notre Dame of Maryland University (formerly The College of Notre Dame of Maryland), founded in 1873, is a private, church-affiliated, liberal arts college for women. Its 58-acre campus is located inside city limits in northern Baltimore. A four-year college, Notre Dame Maryland University has an enrollment of 2,877 students. The school is also affiliated with the Roman Catholic Church. Notre Dame Maryland University provides on-campus housing accommodating 359 students. Housing options: women's dorms. Recreation and sports facilities include: athletic complex · fields · fitness center · gymnasium · track · racquetball and tennis courts.

Student Life and Activities

Most students (82 percent) live off campus. Gator Alley (an eatery) is a popular on-campus hangout and students often gather off-campus at other local college campuses. Popular campus events include the Advent Service, Tree Trim and Christmas Dinner, Family Weekend, Winter Ball, Notre Dame Day, 100 Nights, Lantern Chain, Winterfest, Spring Formal and Alternative Spring Break. Notre Dame of Maryland University has 40 official student organizations. Some groups with a strong social presence on campus include the Senate and the Interorganizational Council (IOC). Notre Dame of Maryland University is a member of the Colonial States Athletic Conference (Division III).

Academics and Learning Environment

Notre Dame of Maryland University has 125 full-time and nine part-time faculty members, offering a student-to-faculty ratio of 9:1. Notre Dame of Maryland University offers 36 majors with the most popular being business, nursing and education and least popular being economics, chemistry and music. The school has a general core requirement as well as a religion requirement. Cooperative education is not offered. All first-year students must maintain a 2.0 GPA or higher to avoid academic probation. Other special academic programs that would appeal to a B student: self-designed majors · pass/fail grading option · independent study · double majors · dual degrees · accelerated study · honors program · internships · weekend college.

NOTRE DAME OF MARYLAND UNIVERSITY

Highlights

Notre Dame of Maryland University
Baltimore (Pop. 621,342)
Location: Major city
Four-year private women's college
Founded: 1873
Website: http://www.ndm.edu

Students
Total enrollment: 2,877
Undergrads: 1,234
Freshmen: 137
Part-time students: 57%
From out-of-state: 20%
Male/Female: 5%/95%
Live on-campus: 18%
Off-campus employment rating: Fair
Caucasian: 57%
African American: 28%
Hispanic: 5%
Asian: 5%
Hawaiian or Pacific Islander: <1%
Native American: 1%
International: 1%

Academics
Calendar: Semester
Student/faculty ratio: 9:1
Class size 9 or fewer: 42%
Class size 10-29: 56%
Class size 30-49: 1%
Class size 50-99: -
Class size 100 or more: -
Returning freshmen: 71%
Six-year graduation rate: 53%

Most Popular Majors
Business
Nursing
Education

NOTRE DAME OF MARYLAND UNIVERSITY

Admissions
Applicants: 838
Accepted: 416
Acceptance rate: 49.6%
Average GPA: 3.7
ACT range: 20-23
SAT Math range: 460-560
SAT Reading range: 470-590
SAT Writing range: Not reported
Top 10% of class: 33%
Top 25% of class: 61%
Top 50% of class: 88%

Deadlines
Early Action: 12/1
Early Decision: No
Regular Action: Rolling admissions
Common Application: Accepted

Financial Aid
In-state tuition: $31,910
Out-of-state tuition: $31,910
Room: Varies
Board: Varies
Books: $1,200
Freshmen receiving need-based aid: 90%
Undergrads rec. need-based aid: 86%
Avg. % of need met by financial aid: 67%
Avg. aid package (freshmen): $24,726
Avg. aid package (undergrads): $21,973
Avg. debt upon graduation: $28,735

Prominent Alumni
Sister Cathy Arata, director of pastoral services for Solidarity with South Sudan; Sheri Booker, poet and spoken word artist; Leslie Simmons, president of Carroll Hospital Center.

School Spirit
Mascot: Gators
Colors: Royal blue and white

America's
Best Colleges for
B Students

B Student Support and Success

Notre Dame's campus-wide peer tutoring program is known as Each One, Teach One. It is designed to achieve "increases in the success rate of students in courses that have historically proved to be extremely challenging." A Writing Center is also available to all students either by appointment or on a drop-in basis.

Notre Dame of Maryland University provides a variety of support programs including dedicated guidance for: academic · career · personal · psychological · non-traditional students. Annually, 71 percent of freshmen students return for their sophomore year.

Support for Students with Learning Disabilities

Students with learning disabilities have the option of taking more time to complete a degree or take a less demanding course load. They also have the option to use: tutors · testing accommodations · untimed tests · extended time for tests · take-home exam · oral tests · exam on tape or computer · readers · typist/scribe · note-taking services · proofreading services · reading machines · tape recorders · texts on tape · early syllabus · priority registration · priority seating. Individual or small group tutorials are also available in: time management · organizational skills · learning strategies · specific subject areas · writing labs · math labs · study skills. An advisor/advocate from the LD program is available to students.

How to Get Admitted

For admissions decisions, non-academic factors considered: interview · extracurricular activities · special talents, interests and abilities · character/personal qualities · volunteer work · work experience · state of residency · alumni relationship. A high school diploma is required, although a GED is also accepted for admissions consideration. SAT or ACT test scores are required of all applicants. SAT Subject Test scores are not required. *According to the admissions office:* Minimum combined SAT Reasoning score of 950, minimum 2.5 GPA in college-preparatory courses and strong recommendations required; 3.0 GPA recommended. *Academic units recommended:* 4 English, 3 Math, 3 Science, 4 Foreign Language.

How to Pay for College

To apply for financial aid, students should submit the following: Free Application for Federal Student Aid (FAFSA) · institution's own financial aid forms. Notre Dame of Maryland University participates in the Federal Work Study program. *Need-based aid programs include:* scholarships and grants · general need-based awards · Federal Pell grants · state scholarships and grants · college-based scholarships and grants · private scholarships and grants. *Non-need-based aid programs include:* scholarships and grants · state scholarships and grants · creative arts and performance awards · special achievements and activities awards · special characteristics awards · ROTC scholarships · religious affiliation scholarships/grants.

OHIO NORTHERN UNIVERSITY

525 South Main Street, Ada, OH 45810
Admissions: 888-408-4668 · Financial Aid: 888-408-4668
Email: admissions-ug@onu.edu · Website: http://www.onu.edu

From the College

"Ohio Northern University seeks to educate and graduate students accomplished in scholastic achievement, prepared for a useful life and meaningful career, inspired with a desire to contribute to the good of mankind consistent with Judeo-Christian ideals and committed to a quality of life that will result in maximum personal and social worth. Ohio Northern University offers the heritage of a liberal arts tradition within the College of Arts and Sciences and the diversity of four professional colleges: the College of Business Administration, the College of Engineering, the College of Pharmacy and the College of Law."

Campus Setting

Ohio Northern University is a private, United Methodist-related institution of higher learning. ONU was founded in 1871 and is now organized into five colleges: arts and sciences, business administration, engineering, pharmacy and law. The 300-acre campus is located in Ada, a small rural village situated in northwestern Ohio. A four-year institution, Ohio Northern University has an enrollment of 3,557 students. The campus facilities include: library · art gallery · pharmacy museum. Ohio Northern University provides on-campus housing with 1,547 units that can accommodate 2,196 students. Housing options: coed dorms · women's dorms · men's dorms · sorority housing · fraternity housing · single-student apartments · married-student apartments · special housing for disabled students. Recreation and sports facilities include: baseball, soccer and softball fields · basketball, volleyball and tennis courts · stadium · swimming pool · track and field complex · wrestling center.

Student Life and Activities

Sixty-eight percent of students live on campus. Athletic events, performing arts events, the Regal Beagle (local tavern), comedians, concerts, performing arts programs and Homecoming are popular draws. Ohio Northern University has 170 official student organizations, including Greeks, athletes, Student Planning Committee and Student Senate. There are intramural teams available: basketball · roller hockey · ski club · soccer · Ultimate Frisbee · volleyball. Ohio Northern University is a member of the Ohio Athletic Conference (Division III).

Academics and Learning Environment

Ohio Northern University has 229 full-time and 76 part-time faculty members, offering a student-to-faculty ratio of 12:1. The most common course size is 10 to 19 students. Ohio Northern University offers 61 majors with the most popular being biology, mechanical engineering and pharmacy and least popular being philosophy, religion and health education. The school has a general core requirement as well as a religion requirement. Cooperative education is available. All first-year students must maintain a 2.0 GPA or higher to avoid academic probation. Other programs include: independent study · double majors · dual degrees · honors program · internships · distance learning certificate programs.

B Student Support and Success

Admission to Ohio Northern is based on class rank and SAT or ACT scores, but there is a strong willingness to look beyond the numbers. Letters of recommendation are

OHIO NORTHERN UNIVERSITY

Ohio Northern University
Ada, OH (Pop. 5,804)
Location: Rural
Four-year private
Founded: 1871
Website: http://www.onu.edu

Students
Total enrollment: 3,557
Undergrads: 2,629
Part-time students: 15%
From out-of-state: 22%
Male/Female: 54%/46%
Live on-campus: 68%
In fraternities: 15%
In sororities: 21%
Off-campus employment rating: Good
Caucasian: 83%
African American: 3%
Hispanic: 2%
Asian: 1%
Hawaiian or Pacific Islander: <1%
Native American: <1%
Mixed (2+ ethnicities): 3%
International: 7%

Academics
Calendar: Semester
Student/faculty ratio: 12:1
Class size 9 or fewer: 29%
Class size 10-29: 59%
Class size 30-49: 11%
Class size 50-99: 1%
Class size 100 or more: -
Returning freshmen: 86%
Six-year graduation rate: 67%

Most Popular Majors
Pharmacy
Mechanical engineering
Biology

not required but will be read if submitted. Extracurricular activities are considered, as well as recent academic trends. A special program helps with college transition.

Ohio Northern University provides dedicated guidance for: academic · career · personal · psychological · minority students · family planning · religious. Ohio Northern University offers remedial and refresher courses in: reading · writing · math · study skills. Annually, 86 percent of freshmen students return for their sophomore year. One year after graduation, the school reports that 24 percent of graduates have entered graduate school. Out of those students who enter the workforce, approximately 92 percent enter a field related to their actual major within six months of graduation. Here is a list of some companies that most frequently hire graduates from Ohio Northern University: Marathon Petroleum Company · Ashland Chemical Company · AEP · Deloitte · Walmart · CVS Pharmacy · Walgreen's · Kroger · School Systems of VA · Med Centers and Hospitals · ESPN · First Federal Bank · General Dynamics Land Systems · Indiana University Hospital.

Support for Students with Learning Disabilities

Students with learning disabilities will want to research the support programs provided by Ohio Northern University. If deemed necessary, the college will grant additional time to those students with learning disabilities so that they can complete their degree. Also, a lightened course load may be offered to LD students. According to the school, each undergraduate college has a representative that works with disability resources. LD students will want to investigate the following list of programs: remedial math · remedial English · remedial reading · special classes · tutors · untimed tests · extended time for tests · oral tests · readers · typist/scribe · note-taking services · tape recorders · waiver of math degree requirement. Individual or small group tutorials are also available in: time management · organizational skills · learning strategies · specific subject areas · writing labs · math labs · study skills.

How to Get Admitted

For admissions decisions, non-academic factors considered: interview · extracurricular activities · special talents, interests and abilities · character/personal qualities · volunteer work · state of residency · alumni relationship. A high school diploma is required, although a GED is also accepted for admissions consideration. SAT or ACT test scores are required of all applicants. *According to the admissions office:* Minimum composite ACT score of 20, rank in top half of secondary school class and minimum 2.8 GPA preferred. *Academic units recommended:* 4 English, 4 Math, 3 Science, 3 Social Studies, 2 Foreign Language.

Insight

According to Karen Condeni, vice president and dean of enrollment, the school makes a real effort to look past the standard statistics to the student behind them. "A strong number of students show potential but not number-wise," she says. "We look at their high school records overall as a whole picture and we look at trends."

The school also considers personal information that might affect grades. "We look to see if students were working while going to school or if they had a single parent they had to help. We are looking for students who show determination," she says. Ohio Northern University has a support program called College Transition that is not remedial work but helps students who need extra attention. For example, students in this program do not take a full load of classes (17 to 18 hours) but average 12 to 14 hours or three classes. The students are monitored more closely and meet regularly with an advisor. Tutors are also available.

How to Pay for College

To apply for financial aid, students should submit the following: Free Application for Federal Student Aid (FAFSA). Ohio Northern University participates in the Federal Work Study program. *Need-based aid programs include:* scholarships and grants · general need-based awards · Federal Pell grants · state scholarships and grants · college-based scholarships and grants · private scholarships and grants. *Non-need-based aid programs include:* scholarships and grants · general need-based awards · state scholarships and grants · creative arts and performance awards · special achievements and activities awards · special characteristics awards · ROTC scholarships.

OHIO NORTHERN UNIVERSITY

Highlights

Admissions
Applicants: 2,922
Accepted: 2,353
Acceptance rate: 80.5%
Average GPA: 3.7
ACT range: 23-28
SAT Math range: 540-660
SAT Reading range: 510-620
SAT Writing range: 8-31
Top 10% of class: 35%
Top 25% of class: 65%
Top 50% of class: 87%

Deadlines
Early Action: No
Early Decision: No
Regular Action: Rolling admissions
Common Application: Not accepted

Financial Aid
In-state tuition: $28,050
Out-of-state tuition: $28,050
Room: Varies
Board: Varies
Books: $1,800
Freshmen receiving need-based or merit-based aid: 99%
Avg. aid package (freshmen): Not reported
Avg. aid package (undergrads): Not reported

Prominent Alumni
Clayton Mathile, Chairman and CEO of the Mathile Institute; Mike DeWine, Ohio Attorney General; Bob Peterson, Co-Director and writer of movie 'Up'.

School Spirit
Mascot: Polar Bears
Colors: Burnt orange and black
Song: *Sons of Dear Old ONU*

321

College Profiles

OHIO UNIVERSITY

1 Ohio University, Athens, OH 45701
Admissions: 740-593-4100 · Financial Aid: 740-593-4141
Email: admissions@ohio.edu · Website: http://www.ohio.edu

From the College

"Ohio University holds as its central purpose the intellectual and personal development of its students. Distinguished by its rich history, diverse campus, international community and beautiful Appalachian setting, Ohio University is known as well for its outstanding faculty of accomplished teachers whose research and creative activity advance knowledge across many disciplines.

"The Vision Statement: Ohio University will be the nation's best transformative learning community where students realize their promise, faculty advance knowledge, staff achieve excellence and alumni become global leaders."

Campus Setting

Ohio University, founded in 1804, is a public, comprehensive institution. The 1,774-acre campus is located in Athens, 75 miles southeast of Columbus. A four-year institution, Ohio University has an enrollment of 28,786 students and has been co-ed since 1870. The campus possesses a sizable library and an art museum. Ohio University provides on-campus housing with 42 units that can accommodate 8,103 students. Housing options: coed dorms · women's dorms · sorority housing · fraternity housing · married-student apartments. Recreation and sports facilities include: centers · fields · track · courts · ice rink · golf course · stadiums.

Student Life and Activities

Sixty percent of students live off campus. Ohio University has 480 official student organizations. The most popular are: comedy for the masses · hip-hop congress · jitterbug club · stand up comedian club. There are intramural teams available: badminton · basketball · broomball · dodgeball · flag football · floor hockey · golf · racquetball · soccer · softball · table tennis · tennis · volleyball · wrestling. Ohio University is a member of the Mid-America Conference (Division I, Football I FBS).

Academics and Learning Environment

Ohio University has 889 full-time and 437 part-time faculty members, offering a student-to-faculty ratio of 18:1. The most common course size is 20 to 29 students. Ohio University offers 177 majors with the most popular being nursing, communication studies and health administration and least popular being African-American studies, comparative arts and women/gender studies. The school has a general core requirement. Cooperative education is available. All first-year students must maintain a 2.0 GPA or higher to avoid academic probation. Other programs include: self-designed majors · pass/fail grading option · independent study · double majors · dual degrees · accelerated study · honors program · internships · distance learning certificate programs.

B Student Support and Success

Ohio University's Academic Advancement Center helps prepare students for college-level work through a variety of student services that focus on computer, writing, reading and study skills. A brief overview of areas in which help is offered follows: Computer Skills: The computer lab offers equipment such as digital cameras, zip drives, scanners and more. A one-credit hour course for freshmen is available that provides detailed instruction in basic computer skills needed for college work. Writing

Support: The Writing Center gives free assistance to all undergrad and graduate students through peer tutoring. Help is given at all steps of the process from writing an outline to final revisions. Tutoring is available on a walk-in and appointment basis. Reading Skills: Reading instructors help students develop comprehension and vocabulary skills. They also explain how to draw conclusions, make inferences and recognize tone. A two-credit course called College Reading Skills is offered. Study Skills: A two-credit course called Learning Strategies teaches note taking, time management, exam preparation and other study habits. Private tutoring is available (at a cost) for students, and the college has a referral service to match tutors with students. Supplemental Instruction: Extra sessions in which students review lecture notes outside of class, clarify text materials, discuss ideas, organize material, evaluate and improve study skills are available for certain courses. These are free and led by students who have already completed the course. College Adjustment Program: Ohio University also offers assistance to students who are struggling with the adjustment to college life. Services include free tutoring, academic advising and study skills instruction.

Ohio University provides a variety of support programs including: academic · career · personal · psychological · minority students · military · veterans · family planning. Ohio University offers remedial and refresher courses in: reading · writing · math · study skills. The average freshman year GPA is 2.9, and 79 percent of freshmen students return for their sophomore year. Out of those students who do enter into the workforce, approximately 74 percent enter a field related to their initial major within six months of graduation. The following is a list of companies that most frequently hire graduates from Ohio University: PricewaterhouseCoopers · Progressive Insurance · Deloitte · JP Morgan Chase · Kroger · National City Bank.

Support for Students with Learning Disabilities

Students with learning disabilities may want to get involved with the support programs offered by Ohio University. The college might grant additional time to students with learning disabilities in order to complete their degree or a lightened course load might be granted. LD students will want to investigate the following programs at Ohio University: remedial math · remedial English · remedial reading · tutors · learning center · testing accommodations · extended time for tests · take-home exam · oral tests · readers · typist/scribe · note-taking services · reading machines · tape recorders · texts on tape · diagnostic testing service · priority registration. Individual or small group tutorials are also available in: time management · organizational skills · learning strategies · specific subject areas · writing labs · math labs · study skills. An advisor/advocate from the Access Ohio: Summer Bridge Program is available to students.

How to Get Admitted

For admissions decisions, non-academic factors considered: extracurricular activities · special talents, interests and abilities · character/personal qualities · volunteer work · work experience · geographical location · alumni relationship. A high school diploma is required, although a GED is also accepted for admissions consideration. SAT or ACT test scores are required of all applicants. *According to the admissions office:* Rank in top half of secondary school class recommended.

OHIO UNIVERSITY

Highlights

Ohio University
Athens, OH (Pop. 23,755)
Location: Small town
Four-year public
Founded: 1804
Website: http://www.ohio.edu

Students
Total enrollment: 28,786
Undergrads: 23,505
Freshmen: 4,244
Part-time students: 29%
From out-of-state: 13%
From public schools: 82%
Male/Female: 40%/60%
Live on-campus: 40%
In fraternities: 8%
In sororities: 8%
Off-campus employment rating: Good
Caucasian: 83%
African American: 5%
Hispanic: 2%
Asian: 1%
Hawaiian or Pacific Islander: <1%
Native American: <1%
Mixed (2+ ethnicities): 3%
International: 4%

Academics
Calendar: Semester
Student/faculty ratio: 18:1
Class size 9 or fewer: 9%
Class size 10-29: 52%
Class size 30-49: 23%
Class size 50-99: 10%
Class size 100 or more: 6%
Returning freshmen: 79%
Six-year graduation rate: 67%

Most Popular Majors
Nursing
Health administration
Communication studies

323

College Profiles

OHIO UNIVERSITY

Highlights

Admissions
Applicants: 20,765
Accepted: 15,149
Acceptance rate: 73.0%
Average GPA: 3.4
ACT range: 22-26
SAT Math range: 490-600
SAT Reading range: 480-600
SAT Writing range: 2-18
Top 10% of class: 17%
Top 25% of class: 42%
Top 50% of class: 82%

Deadlines
Early Action: No
Early Decision: No
Regular Action: 2/1 (priority)
Notification of admission by: 9/15
Common Application: Not accepted

Financial Aid
In-state tuition: $10,602
Out-of-state tuition: $19,566
Room: $6,050
Board: $4,428
Books: $916
Freshmen receiving need-based aid: 61%
Undergrads rec. need-based aid: 60%
Avg. % of need met by financial aid: 52%
Avg. aid package (freshmen): $9,239
Avg. aid package (undergrads): $8,800
Avg. debt upon graduation: $26,928

Prominent Alumni
George Voinovich; Roger Ailes; Matt Lauer.

School Spirit
Mascot: Bobcats
Colors: Hunter green and white
Song: *Stand Up and Cheer*

Academic units recommended: 4 English, 4 Math, 3 Science, 3 Social Studies, 2 Foreign Language.

How to Pay for College

To apply for financial aid, students should submit the following: Free Application for Federal Student Aid (FAFSA). Ohio University participates in the Federal Work Study program. *Need-based aid programs include:* scholarships and grants · general need-based awards · Federal Pell grants · state scholarships and grants · college-based scholarships and grants · private scholarships and grants. *Non-need-based aid programs include:* scholarships and grants · state scholarships and grants · athletic scholarships · ROTC scholarships.

America's
Best Colleges for
B Students

OHIO WESLEYAN UNIVERSITY

61 South Sandusky Street, Delaware, OH 43015
Admissions: 800-922-8953 · Financial Aid: 800-922-8953
Email: owuadmit@owu.edu · Website: http://www.owu.edu

From the College

"Founded in 1842 and located in Delaware, Ohio, on a beautiful 200-acre campus just 20 miles north of Columbus, the state capital and the nation's 16th-largest city, Ohio Wesleyan is remarkable for the broad range of its academic and pre-professional programs, the international dimensions of its curriculum, its historic emphasis on community through leadership and service and an unwavering commitment to linking theory and practice in every field of study. Its 1,850 students come from almost every state and 41 countries.

"A unique Honors Program offers unusual opportunities, including special housing and an extensive number of tutorials and courses, to talented students, while internships and research are encouraged of all students. The Economics Management Fellows Programs, for entering first-year students interested in business, selects approximately 15 students each year for exclusive programming, a generous book allowance, networking opportunities and a faculty-escorted trip to New York City's financial district. Students come to OWU from nearly every state and 41 countries. Housing options include six large residence halls; a number of Small Living Units, which are special interest houses ranging from the House of Black Culture to the Peace and Justice House and seven national fraternity houses. An eighth national fraternity has re-colonized, but is, as yet, nonresidential. The five national sorority houses are nonresidential.

"Students can participate in approximately 100 campus organizations as well as 23 NCAA Division III men's and women's athletic teams. The university boasts the largest number of both conference titles and Academic All America selections in the North Coast Athletic Conference. In 2011, men's soccer took its second Division III national championship, and in the process, the team's coach, Jay Martin, became the nation's all-time winningest men's soccer coach in all NCAA divisions. OWU also owns two women's national championships in soccer and one in men's basketball. A number of OWU athletes have won individual national championships in track and field and golf.

"The university's new and distinctive OWU Plan includes abundant opportunities for international experience through Travel-Learning Courses and university-funded competitive Theory-to-Practice Grants for independent research, internships, volunteering and cultural immersion throughout the world. Domestically, Ohio Wesleyan students participate in the New York Arts Program, Wesleyan in Washington and the Philadelphia Center, all of which provide independent living and work in some of the country's most vibrant cities. OWU's Course Connections allows students to study a topic of interest in depth and over time, taking specified courses throughout disciplines and university divisions for several semesters. Ohio Wesleyan's commitment to community services has been recognized by its inclusion on the President's Honor Roll for Community Service, with distinction, for the past five consecutive years. In 2010, OWU was one of only three schools in the nation granted the President's Award for Excellence in General Community Service."

Campus Setting

Ohio Wesleyan, founded in 1842, is a church-affiliated, liberal arts university. Its 200-acre campus is located in Delaware, 20 miles north of Columbus. A four-year private institution, Ohio Wesleyan University has an enrollment of 1,830 students,

OHIO WESLEYAN UNIVERSITY

Highlights

Ohio Wesleyan University
Delaware, OH (Pop. 35,541)
Location: Large town
Four-year private
Founded: 1842
Website: http://www.owu.edu

Students
Total enrollment: 1,830
Undergrads: 1,830
Freshmen: 560
Part-time students: 1%
From out-of-state: 48%
Male/Female: 46%/54%
Live on-campus: 94%
In fraternities: 44%
In sororities: 33%
Off-campus employment rating: Excellent
Caucasian: 72%
African American: 6%
Hispanic: 5%
Asian: 3%
Hawaiian or Pacific Islander: <1%
Native American: <1%
Mixed (2+ ethnicities): 4%
International: 7%

Academics
Calendar: Semester
Student/faculty ratio: 11:1
Class size 9 or fewer: 29%
Class size 10-29: 61%
Class size 30-49: 11%
Class size 50-99: -
Class size 100 or more: -
Returning freshmen: 80%
Six-year graduation rate: 69%

Most Popular Majors
Psychology
Economics/management
Politics/government

and has been co-ed since 1877. The school is also affiliated with the Methodist Church. Campus facilities include: art museum · observatories · scanning electron microscope · nine-inch refractor telescope · science center · nature preserve · Center for Economics, Business and Entrepreneurship. Ohio Wesleyan University provides on-campus housing with 26 units that can accommodate 1,695 students. Housing options: coed dorms · women's dorms · sorority housing · fraternity housing · single-student apartments · special housing for international students.

Student Life and Activities

Most of the students (94 percent) live on campus. Students gather at fraternities on campus and at local bars and theatres off campus. Favorite events include Homecoming Weekend, Performing Arts Series, Spring Fest, Unity Through Music and Sagan National Colloquium. Ohio Wesleyan University has 95 official student organizations. According to the student newspaper, Greeks are the most influential group on campus. Ohio Wesleyan University is a member of the North Coast Athletic Conference (Division III).

Academics and Learning Environment

Ohio Wesleyan University has 140 full-time and 81 part-time faculty members, offering a student-to-faculty ratio of 11:1. The most common course size is 10 to 19 students. Out of Ohio Wesleyan University's 66 majors, the most popular choices are psychology, economics/management and politics/government. The school has a general core requirement. Cooperative education is not offered. All first-year students must maintain a 2.0 GPA or higher to avoid academic probation, and a minimum overall GPA of 2.0 is required to graduate. Other special academic programs include: self-designed majors · pass/fail grading option · independent study · double majors · dual degrees · honors program · Phi Beta Kappa · internships · certificate programs.

B Student Support and Success

Students who need additional attention or academic help at Ohio Wesleyan will find the assistance they need at the Academic Skills Center where the motto is "Improving the Student Inside You." The center offers individual counseling that helps students assess their strengths and weaknesses and gives support in areas like time management, note taking, reading from texts, test taking and overcoming procrastination and anxiety. Group presentations are available on the same topics and may be given in fraternity houses, residence halls and other spots across the campus. A Lending Library gives students access to books on a variety of topics, including coping with learning disabilities and developing study skills. Computerized assessments help identify individual specific study skill deficits. In addition, the college offers a Quantitative Skills Center that helps students gain confidence in their ability to do math and related subjects like astronomy, chemistry and economics.

Ohio Wesleyan University provides dedicated guidance for: academic · career · personal · psychological · minority students · family planning · religious. The average freshman year GPA is 2.9, and 80 percent of freshmen students return for their sophomore year. Approximately 32 percent of students pursue a graduate degree soon after graduation. A year after graduation, 32 percent of graduates are in graduate school. Among students who enter the workforce, approximately 80 percent enter a field related to their major within six months of graduation. Companies that most frequently hire graduates from Ohio Wesleyan University include: MBNA America · Fifth Third Bank · US Air Force · James Cancer Hospital · National Science Foundation · World Bank · Cardinal Health · Batelle Laboratories · Ross Laboratories · Ernst & Young · CSI International · Prudential Financial · Deloitte · Ohio State University Medical Center · Towne Square Animal Clinic · AC Nielson · Nexus Technology Group · Ohio Department of Health Laboratory · US Forest Service · Ohio House of Representatives · Merrill Lynch · JP Morgan Chase · US Peace Corps · AmeriCorps · Columbus Public Schools · Citigroup Global Markets Inc.

Support for Students with Learning Disabilities

Ohio Wesleyan University permits extra time to complete their degrees, as well as lighter course loads to students with learning disabilities. These students may also find the following programs useful: remedial math · remedial English · special classes · tutors · learning center · extended time for tests · take-home exam · oral tests · note-taking services · tape recorders · waiver of math degree requirement. Individual or small group tutorials are also available in: time management · organizational skills · learning strategies · writing labs · math labs · study skills. An advisor/advocate from the Sagan Academic Resource Center is available to students.

How to Get Admitted

For admissions decisions, non-academic factors considered: interview · extracurricular activities · special talents, interests and abilities · character/personal qualities · volunteer work · work experience · state of residency · geographical location · minority affiliation · alumni relationship. A high school diploma is required, although a GED is also accepted for admissions consideration. SAT or ACT test scores are required for some applicants. *Academic units recommended:* 4 Math, 4 Science, 4 Social Studies, 3 Foreign Language.

How to Pay for College

To apply for financial aid, students should submit the following: Free Application for Federal Student Aid (FAFSA) · institution's own financial aid forms. Ohio Wesleyan University participates in the Federal Work Study program. *Need-based aid programs include:* scholarships and grants · general need-based awards · Federal Pell grants · state scholarships and grants · college-based scholarships and grants · private scholarships and grants. *Non-need-based aid programs include:* scholarships and grants · general need-based awards · state scholarships and grants · creative arts and performance awards · special achievements and activities awards · special characteristics awards.

OHIO WESLEYAN UNIVERSITY

Highlights

Admissions
Applicants: 4,029
Accepted: 3,035
Acceptance rate: 75.3%
Placed on wait list: 182
Enrolled from wait list: 77
Average GPA: 3.4
ACT range: 22-27
SAT Math range: 500-630
SAT Reading range: 490-620
SAT Writing range: 5-24
Top 10% of class: 32%
Top 25% of class: 55%
Top 50% of class: 82%

Deadlines
Early Action: 1/15
Early Decision: 11/15
Regular Action: Rolling admissions
Common Application: Accepted

Financial Aid
In-state tuition: $41,660
Out-of-state tuition: $41,660
Room: $6,050
Board: $5,160
Books: $1,100
Freshmen receiving need-based aid: 73%
Undergrads rec. need-based aid: 67%
Avg. % of need met by financial aid: 80%
Avg. aid package (freshmen): $32,580
Avg. aid package (undergrads): $32,150
Avg. debt upon graduation: $31,489

Prominent Alumni
Byron Pitts, CBS National News Correspondent; Branch Rickey, Hall of Fame baseball executive that broke the major league color barrier in professional baseball.

School Spirit
Mascot: Battling Bishops
Colors: Red and black

327

OLD DOMINION UNIVERSITY

5115 Hampton Boulevard, Norfolk, VA 23529
Admissions: 800-348-7926 · Financial Aid: 757-683-3683
Email: admissions@odu.edu · Website: http://www.odu.edu

From the College

"Old Dominion University is Virginia's forward-focused, public doctoral research university for high-performing students from around the world who want a rigorous academic experience in a fast-paced multi-cultural community. With an enrollment of more than 24,000 students, the university offers 69 bachelor's, 56 master's and 41 doctoral degree programs and two educational specialists degrees. A determined entrepreneurial approach to problem-solving drives cutting-edge research and strategic partnerships with government, business, industry, organizations and the arts."

Campus Setting

Old Dominion is a public university. Founded in 1930 as a division of the College of William and Mary, it became an independent state university in 1962. Programs are offered through the Colleges of Arts and Letters, Business and Public Administration, Education, Engineering and Technology, Health Sciences and Sciences. Its 188-acre campus in Norfolk reflects a Georgian architectural style. A four-year institution, Old Dominion University has an enrollment of 24,828 students. The campus facilities include: library · art gallery · planetarium · sub-/super-sonic wind tunnels · marine science research vessel · random wave pool · laser optics and robotics labs · orchid conservatory. Old Dominion University provides on-campus housing with 1,760 units that can accommodate 4,678 students. Housing options: coed dorms · single-student apartments · special housing for disabled students · special housing for international students. Recreation and sports facilities include: basketball arena · fitness center · golf course · gymnasium · sand volleyball courts · soccer varsity and practice fields · tennis courts · baseball stadium · wrestling practice room · turf field stadium for field hockey and lacrosse · practice football fields · golf course · sailing center · water area.

Student Life and Activities

Seventy-six percent of students live off campus. Popular on-campus gathering spots include the Webb Student Center, University Village and Ted Constant Center. Popular campus events include men's and women's basketball games, Homecoming, concerts, Cultural Explosion, Exam Jam, Campus Chaos, fashion shows/pageants, Main Street, Community Care Day, PAW events and movies. Old Dominion University has 285 official student organizations. Popular groups on campus include the Student Activities Council, F.O.R.E.I.G.N.E.R.S., Military Student Union, Anime Club and Ebony Impact Gospel Choir. There are intramural teams available: aikido · badminton · basketball · bowling · cheerleading/dance · cricket · cross-country · fencing · field hockey · golf · ice hockey · karate · lacrosse · martial arts · non-tackle football · officiating · pocket billiards · racquetball · rock climbing · rowing · rugby · sailing · soccer · softball · table tennis · tennis · triathlon · Ultimate Frisbee · volleyball. Old Dominion University is a member of the Conference USA (Division I).

Academics and Learning Environment

Old Dominion University has 787 full-time and 554 part-time faculty members, offering a student-to-faculty ratio of 20:1. The most common course size is 30 to 39 students. Old Dominion University offers 143 majors with the most popular being interdisciplinary studies, psychology and criminal justice and least popular being music performance, music and human services counseling. The school has a general core requirement. Cooperative education is available. All first-year students must maintain a 2.0 GPA or higher to avoid academic probation. Other programs include: self-designed majors · pass/fail grading option · independent study · double majors · dual degrees · accelerated study · honors program · internships · weekend college · distance learning.

B Student Support and Success

Old Dominion's Student Support Services provides academic support to increase the retention and graduation rates of eligible students. It includes tutorials, academic skills workshops, career exploration, advising services and cultural enrichment. At the end of each semester, the Office of Continuance reviews the records of all students who do not maintain a 2.0 GPA. They are placed on academic warning and have one semester to bring their grades up or to be placed on suspension.

There are a variety of support programs available through Old Dominion University, including dedicated guidance for: academic · career · personal · psychological · minority students · military · veterans · non-traditional students · family planning · religious. Additional counseling services include: alcohol/substance abuse, financial aid. The average freshman year GPA is 2.7, and 80 percent of freshmen students return for their sophomore year. The following is a list of companies that most frequently hire graduates of Old Dominion University: Bank of America · Cox Communications · Dominion Virginia Power · Ecolochem · Enterprise Rent-a-Car · Langley · local school districts · Naptheon · NASA · NAVSEA · Norfolk Southern · Northrop Grumman · Newport News Shipbuilding · Siemens Automotive · SPAWAR · Towers Perrin · Trader Publications/Landmark Communications · USAA · UPS · Verizon.

Support for Students with Learning Disabilities

Students with learning disabilities may take advantage of specific support programs offered by Old Dominion University, including additional time to complete degrees or a lightened course load. According to the school, Disability Services "strives to coordinate services using a developmental model that will enable students with disabilities to act as independently as possible in a supportive atmosphere that promotes self-reliance." Students with learning disabilities will find the following intriguing options: special classes · testing accommodations · extended time for tests · take-home exam · exam on tape or computer · readers · typist/scribe · note-taking services · tape recorders · texts on tape · early syllabus · priority registration · waiver of math degree requirement. Individual or small group tutorials are also available in: time management · organizational skills · learning strategies · specific subject areas · writing labs · study skills. An advisor/advocate from the Disability Services is available to students.

How to Get Admitted

For admissions decisions, non-academic factors considered: extracurricular activities · special talents, interests and abilities · character/personal qualities · volunteer work · work experience · state of residency · alumni relationship. A high school diploma is required, although a GED is also accepted for admissions consideration. SAT or ACT

OLD DOMINION UNIVERSITY

Old Dominion University
Norfolk, VA (Pop. 245,782)
Location: Medium city
Four-year public
Founded: 1930
Website: http://www.odu.edu

Students
Total enrollment: 24,828
Undergrads: 19,819
Freshmen: 4,550
Part-time students: 24%
From out-of-state: 10%
From public schools: 90%
Male/Female: 46%/54%
Live on-campus: 24%
In fraternities: 6%
In sororities: 5%
Off-campus employment rating: Excellent
Caucasian: 52%
African American: 26%
Hispanic: 7%
Asian: 4%
Hawaiian or Pacific Islander: <1%
Native American: <1%
Mixed (2+ ethnicities): 5%
International: 1%

Academics
Calendar: Semester
Student/faculty ratio: 20:1
Class size 9 or fewer: 10%
Class size 10-29: 46%
Class size 30-49: 32%
Class size 50-99: 8%
Class size 100 or more: 3%
Returning freshmen: 80%
Six-year graduation rate: 51%

Most Popular Majors
Psychology
Interdisciplinary studies
Criminal justice

OLD DOMINION UNIVERSITY

Highlights

Admissions
Applicants: 10,202
Accepted: 7,834
Acceptance rate: 76.8%
Average GPA: 3.3
ACT range: 18-23
SAT Math range: 470-570
SAT Reading range: 460-560
SAT Writing range: Not reported
Top 10% of class: 10%
Top 25% of class: 33%
Top 50% of class: 75%

Deadlines
Early Action: 12/1
Early Decision: No
Regular Action: Rolling admissions
Common Application: Not accepted

Financial Aid
In-state tuition: $8,970
Out-of-state tuition: $25,140
Room: $4,484
Board: $4,286
Books: Varies
Freshmen receiving need-based aid: 62%
Undergrads rec. need-based aid: 61%
Avg. % of need met by financial aid: 50%
Avg. aid package (freshmen): $10,129
Avg. aid package (undergrads): $9,677
Avg. debt upon graduation: $27,847

Prominent Alumni
Mills Godwin, former governor of Virginia;
William E. Lobeck, CEO, National Car
Rental System; Kenny Gattison, coach,
New Jersey Nets.

School Spirit
Mascot: Big Blue
Colors: Silver and navy blue

test scores are required of all applicants. *According to the admissions office:* Admission based on eligibility index of standardized test scores and minimum 2.7 GPA. *Academic units recommended:* 4 English, 4 Math, 3 Science, 3 Social Studies, 3 Foreign Language.

How to Pay for College

To apply for financial aid, students should submit the following: Free Application for Federal Student Aid (FAFSA). Old Dominion University participates in the Federal Work Study program. *Need-based aid programs include:* scholarships and grants · general need-based awards · Federal Pell grants · state scholarships and grants · college-based scholarships and grants · private scholarships and grants · Federal Nursing scholarships · United Negro College Fund. *Non-need-based aid programs include:* scholarships and grants · general need-based awards · state scholarships and grants · creative arts and performance awards · special achievements and activities awards · special characteristics awards · athletic scholarships · ROTC scholarships.

OREGON STATE UNIVERSITY

104 Kerr Administration Building, Corvallis, OR 97331
Admissions: 800-291-4192 · Financial Aid: 541-737-2241
Email: osuadmit@oregonstate.edu · Website: http://www.oregonstate.edu

From the College

"Founded in 1868, Oregon State is the state's Land Grant university and is one of only two universities in the U.S. to have Sea Grant, Space Grant and Sun Grant designations. Oregon State is also the only university in Oregon to hold both the Carnegie Foundation's top designation for research institutions and its prestigious Community Engagement classification.

"As Oregon's leading public research university, with $261.7 million in external funding in the 2011 fiscal year, Oregon State's impact reaches across the state and beyond. With 12 colleges, 15 Agricultural Experiment Stations, 35 county Extension offices, the Hatfield Marine Sciences Center in Newport and OSU-Cascades in Bend, Oregon State has a presence in every one of Oregon's 36 counties, with a statewide economic footprint of $2.06 billion.

"Oregon State welcomes a diverse student body of over 26,000 students from across Oregon, all 50 states and more than 100 countries. They can choose from more than 200 undergraduate and more than 80 graduate degree programs, including over 30 degrees online offered through Oregon State Ecampus. Oregon State increasingly attracts high-achieving students, with nationally recognized programs in areas such as conservation biology, agricultural sciences, nuclear engineering, forestry, fisheries and wildlife management, community health, pharmacy and zoology.

"Oregon State also ranks high in sustainability, fourth among universities nationwide for using renewable energy and first in the Pac-12 Conference. And our students literally help power the university: 22 exercise machines at Dixon Recreation Center are connected to the grid.

"Oregon State is located in Corvallis, a vibrant college town of 55,000 in the heart of Western Oregon's Willamette Valley. Corvallis consistently ranks among the best and safest cities to live in the U.S., as well as among the most environmentally responsible."

Campus Setting

Oregon State, founded in 1868, is a public, liberal arts university. Programs are offered through the Colleges of Agricultural Sciences, Business, Engineering, Forestry, Health and Human Performance, Home Economics and Education, Liberal Arts, Pharmacy and Science. Its 422-acre campus is in Corvallis, 85 miles south of Portland. A four-year institution, Oregon State University has an enrollment of 27,925 students. The campus facilities include: library · art gallery · herbarium. Oregon State University provides on-campus housing with 2,430 units that can accommodate 4,307 students. Housing options: coed dorms · sorority housing · fraternity housing · single-student apartments · married-student apartments · special housing for disabled students · special housing for international students · cooperative housing. Recreation and sports facilities include: baseball, football and soccer stadiums · basketball, volleyball, gymnastics and wrestling coliseum · boathouse and docks · golf club · gymnastics and football centers · softball complex · swimming pool · weight room.

Student Life and Activities

Eighty-one percent of students live off campus. "There are some plays and concerts available to students, but to see anything good, a student has to go to Eugene or

Portland," according to the editor of the student newspaper. Since all Greek parties are closed, "if you're not in a fraternity or a sorority, the party scene is dismal." Memorial Union Commons, the Beanery, American Dream Pizza and Top of the Peacock are favorite hangouts. Hawaii Night, Commencement, University Day, Pow-Wow, Japan Night, China Night, India Night, Mom's Weekend, Dad's Weekend, Martin Luther King Jr. Breakfast, Homecoming and Civil War Football Weekend are popular events on campus. Oregon State University has 400 official student organizations. Greeks have widespread influence on student social life. Oregon State University is a member of the Pacific-12 Conference (Division I, Football I-A).

Academics and Learning Environment

Oregon State University has 982 full-time and 434 part-time faculty members, offering a student-to-faculty ratio of 21:1. The most common course size is 20 to 29 students. Oregon State University offers 232 majors with the most popular being public health, liberal studies and human development/family sciences and least popular being health promotion/health behavior, mathematical sciences and wood science/technology. The school has a general core requirement. Cooperative education is available. All first-year students must maintain a 2.0 GPA or higher to avoid academic probation. Other programs include: self-designed majors · pass/fail grading option · independent study · double majors · dual degrees · accelerated study · honors program · internships · distance learning certificate programs.

B Student Support and Success

OSU's College of Business Beta Alpha Psi is a co-ed professional accounting fraternity that sponsors an accounting library, provides resource materials and whose members tutor accounting students. The Center for Writing and Learning gives instructions and advice to students and provides a study skills program. Basic writing skills such as organizing and revising are offered, and short grammar questions can be emailed for assistance. A student chapter offers tutoring in chemical engineering, and the chemistry department has a tutor list for an hourly fee. A general chemistry tutorial room known as the Mole Hole is available during certain weeks of each term. Free tutoring is available for undergrads in lower division core economics courses and for students of electrical engineering and computer science. Other departments offer assistance as well. The department of ethnic studies offers mentoring for students of color or anyone else interested in changing social patterns of race, gender, ethnic, class and other issues. Students taking French, German and Spanish can find tutorial support through the Department of Foreign Languages and Literatures. The College of Forestry offers tutoring to students in forestry or related classes. The Math Learning Center is available for drop-in tutoring from undergrads and volunteers and multiple resources, while the Microbiology Student Association tutors students in that subject, and physics grad students offer help to students in introductory physics courses. For students who have not yet declared a major, Exploratory Studies gives information, resources and other important materials to help.

Oregon State University provides dedicated guidance for: academic · career · personal · psychological · minority students · military · veterans · non-traditional students · family planning. Annually, 84 percent of freshmen students return for their sophomore year. This is a list of companies that most often hire graduates from Oregon State University: Abercrombie and Fitch · Acumed · Aerotek · Aflac · American Business Software · American Fidelity · Biotronik · Brass Media · CampusPoint · Cintas · College Pro · Devine Tarbull · Eaton · Enterprise Rent a Car · ESCO · Ethos Group · Evergreen Healthcare · Fisher Investments · FM Global · Frito Lay · Google · Gunderson · Harder Mechanical Contractors · Heinz · Hertz · Infosys · Intel · Invitrogen · Ironwood Communications · J&L Marketing · Liberty Northwest Insurance · Lithia Motors · Mass Mutual · Masterbrand Cabinets · Mountain Cascade · Mowat Construction · National Photocopy Corp. · Nautilus · Netflix · New England Financial Northwest · New York Life · Ocean Beauty Seafoods · State of Oregon · Pacific Office Automation · Peace Corps · Portland General Electric · City of Portland · Rainsweet · Regence · Rite Aid · State Farm Insurance · Stockamp and Associates · Stryker Endoscopy · Target · The Buckle · Sherwin Williams · US Government · Viewplus · Volt Technical · VTM · Wafertech · Walgreens · Web MD · Wells Fargo · Weyerhaeuser · ZONES.

Support for Students with Learning Disabilities

Students with learning disabilities will want to research support programs offered by Oregon State University. If necessary, the college will consider granting additional time to students with learning disabilities to complete their degree. A lightened course load might also be offered to the LD student. Students with learning disabilities will want to survey these options: remedial math · remedial English · remedial reading · learning center · extended time for tests · oral tests · note-taking services · reading machines. Individual or small group tutorials are also available in: time management · organizational skills · learning strategies · specific subject areas · writing labs · math labs · study skills. An advisor/advocate from the Office of Services for Students with Disabilities is available to students.

How to Get Admitted

For admissions decisions, non-academic factors considered: extracurricular activities · special talents, interests and abilities · character/personal qualities · volunteer work · work experience · state of residency. A high school diploma is required, although a GED is also accepted for admissions consideration. SAT or ACT test scores are required of all applicants. SAT Subject Test scores are required for some applicants. *According to the admissions office:* Minimum cumulative grade point average of 3.0. Class rank taken in context with academic rigor and class size of high school attended. *Academic units recommended:* 4 English, 3 Math, 3 Science, 3 Social Studies, 2 Foreign Language.

How to Pay for College

To apply for financial aid, students should submit the following: Free Application for Federal Student Aid (FAFSA) · AFSA · USAF · SAAC · CSX. Oregon State University participates in the Federal

OREGON STATE UNIVERSITY

Highlights

Oregon State University
Corvallis, OR (Pop. 54,998)
Location: Large town
Four-year public
Founded: 1868
Website: http://www.oregonstate.edu

Students
Total enrollment: 27,925
Undergrads: 23,161
Freshmen: 5,244
Part-time students: 20%
From out-of-state: 25%
Male/Female: 54%/46%
Live on-campus: 19%
In fraternities: 13%
In sororities: 18%
Off-campus employment rating: Excellent
Caucasian: 68%
African American: 1%
Hispanic: 7%
Asian: 7%
Hawaiian or Pacific Islander: <1%
Native American: 1%
Mixed (2+ ethnicities): 6%
International: 7%

Academics
Calendar: Quarter
Student/faculty ratio: 21:1
Class size 9 or fewer: 8%
Class size 10-29: 51%
Class size 30-49: 19%
Class size 50-99: 14%
Class size 100 or more: 9%
Returning freshmen: 84%
Six-year graduation rate: 62%

Most Popular Majors
Human development/family sciences
Liberal studies
Public health

College Profiles

OREGON STATE UNIVERSITY

Admissions
Applicants: 14,239
Accepted: 11,303
Acceptance rate: 79.4%
Average GPA: 3.6
ACT range: 21-27
SAT Math range: 490-620
SAT Reading range: 480-600
SAT Writing range: 3-19
Top 10% of class: 25%
Top 25% of class: 53%
Top 50% of class: 88%

Deadlines
Early Action: 11/1
Early Decision: No
Regular Action: Rolling admissions
Common Application: Not accepted

Financial Aid
In-state tuition: $6,804
Out-of-state tuition: $22,068
Room: $7,650
Board: $3,501
Books: $1,965
Freshmen receiving need-based aid: 60%
Undergrads rec. need-based aid: 58%
Avg. % of need met by financial aid: 69%
Avg. aid package (freshmen): $10,974
Avg. aid package (undergrads): $12,973
Avg. debt upon graduation: $22,831

Prominent Alumni
Linus Pauling, American chemist; Doug Englebart, inventor and computer pioneer; Mercedes Bates, 1966 Vice President General Mills Betty Crocker division.

School Spirit
Mascot: Benny the Beaver
Colors: Orange and black
Song: *OSU Fight Song*

Work Study program. *Need-based aid programs include:* scholarships and grants · general need-based awards · Federal Pell grants · state scholarships and grants · college-based scholarships and grants · private scholarships and grants. *Non-need-based aid programs include:* scholarships and grants · general need-based awards · state scholarships and grants · athletic scholarships · ROTC scholarships.

PACE UNIVERSITY

1 Pace Plaza, New York, NY 10038
Admissions: 800-874-7223 · Financial Aid: 877-672-1830
Email: infoctr@pace.edu · Website: http://www.pace.edu

From the College

"Pace University offers a comprehensive education combining exceptional academics, professional experience and the New York edge. Diverse students take advantage of Pace's over 100 majors in the liberal arts and sciences, business, law, nursing, education and computer science. Located in lower Manhattan and Westchester County near centers of finance, accounting, media, healthcare, performing arts and technology, Pace enhances the student experience with one of the metropolitan area's largest cooperative education and internship programs. Pace University draws strength from campuses in three locations, offering students choices of living and learning experiences, especially professional experiences that lead to careers and opportunities for students to improve their lives and the lives of others. Locations include our urban campus in New York City, blocks from Wall Street and South Street Seaport; our traditional suburban collegiate setting in the heart of Westchester County and our White Plains campus with a 13-acre Law School campus and a Graduate Center directly across the street from the train station. Pace combines the benefits and resources of a large university with the warmth and personal attention usually associated with a small college, with class sizes averaging 28 students. Campus housing is available on each campus."

Campus Setting

Pace, founded in 1906, is a private university. Pace University offers a comprehensive education combining exceptional academics, professional experience and the New York advantage. Pace enrolls 12,624 students in: Dyson College of Arts & Sciences, Lienhard School of Nursing, Lubin School of Business, School of Education and Seidenberg School of Computer Science & Information Systems. With campuses in Manhattan and Westchester County, near thousands of companies, Pace enhances the student experience with the metropolitan area's largest undergraduate cooperative education/internship program. Campus facilities include: actor's studio · theatre · environmental center · fitness center. Pace University provides on-campus housing that can accommodate 3,307 students. Housing options: coed dorms · single-student apartments. Recreation and sports facilities include: aerobics facility · weight rooms · arena · fitness and recreation centers.

Student Life and Activities

Most students (62 percent) live off campus. According to the student newspaper, on-campus activity is low on weekends, when most students go home. There are special dorm activities a couple of times each semester. Off-campus life all depends on whether students are involved in clubs, Greek life, etc. The campus student center and the gym/auditorium are popular gathering spots. New York City offers many attractions. Students in Westchester have options for activities in the Hudson Valley and also in NYC. Popular campus events include University Fest (combination of Homecoming, Alumni weekend, family weekend), Alternative Spring Break, Cariculture, Inside the Actor's Studio, Amateur Night, Spring Fest, Weekend in Montreal, Relay for Life, Townhouse Day, Ski Trips, Black Student Union Trip to Washington, DC, Community Service, and RHA: Come out and Play. Pace University has 110 official student organizations. Greeks are influential on student life for parties, and sports

PACE UNIVERSITY

Pace University
New York City (Pop. 8,405,837)
Location: Major city
Four-year private
Founded: 1906
Website: http://www.pace.edu

Students
Total enrollment: 12,624
Undergrads: 8,289
Freshmen: 3,189
Part-time students: 14%
From out-of-state: 51%
From public schools: 75%
Male/Female: 41%/59%
Live on-campus: 38%
In fraternities: 6%
In sororities: 9%
Off-campus employment rating: Excellent
Caucasian: 47%
African American: 11%
Hispanic: 16%
Asian: 9%
Hawaiian or Pacific Islander: <1%
Native American: <1%
Mixed (2+ ethnicities): 3%
International: 8%

Academics
Calendar: Semester
Student/faculty ratio: 14:1
Class size 9 or fewer: 10%
Class size 10-29: 75%
Class size 30-49: 12%
Class size 50-99: 2%
Class size 100 or more: -
Returning freshmen: 76%
Six-year graduation rate: 54%

Most Popular Majors
Finance
Communication studies
Criminal justice

teams to a lesser extent. For those interested in sports, there are intramural teams such as: basketball · dodgeball · flag football · soccer · volleyball. Pace University is a member of the Northeast-10 Conference (Division II).

Academics and Learning Environment

Pace University has 465 full-time and 861 part-time faculty members, offering a student-to-faculty ratio of 14:1. The most common course size is 10 to 19 students. Pace University's 116 majors include the very popular finance, communication studies and criminal justice and the less popular chemical engineering, Internet technology for e-commerce and math/adolescent education. The school has a general core requirement. Cooperative education is available. All first-year students must maintain a 2.0 GPA or higher to avoid academic probation, and a minimum overall GPA of 2.0 is required to graduate. Other special academic programs include: pass/fail grading option · independent study · dual degrees · accelerated study · honors program · internships · distance learning.

B Student Support and Success

Pace's Center for Academic Excellence is a comprehensive academic support network that helps students find their ideal path and make the transition from home to college life. It offers the following programs: The Office of First Year Programs: This one-credit, pass/fail course helps all freshmen with the transition through academic advisement, and the UNV 101 program. It provides students with an in-depth look at the university's academic and cultural life, its support network and the services it provides for students. It meets for 13 weeks during fall semester and covers topics such as time management, study skills, critical thinking, health and wellness and campus diversity. Academic Resources: The services of this program include meeting with an advisor, learning about different major and minors and choosing a course of study. The Tutoring Center: Students can find assistance with classes that they find difficult by calling the Tutoring Center. It offers individualized and small group tutoring in upper and lower division courses.

Pace University provides a variety of support programs including: academic · career · psychological · minority students. The average freshman year GPA is 3.2, and 76 percent of freshmen students return for their sophomore year. Among students who enter the workforce, approximately 74 percent enter a field related to their major within six months of graduation. Companies that most frequently hire graduates from Pace University include: Ernst & Young LLP · Friedman LLP · Protiviti, Rothstein, Kass & Co. · IBM · Verizon · Lehman Brothers · KPMG LLP · NY Presbyterian · New York City Department of Education · Westchester County School Districts · USB Financial Services Inc. · Merrill Lynch · AXA Advisors LLC · PricewaterhouseCoopers LLP · Deloitte · JPMorgan Chase & Co. · Goldman Sachs · Bank of New York · Morgan Stanley · RSM McGladrey & Pullen · Pace University · Pepsi Bottling Group · Citigroup · Westchester Medical Center.

Support for Students with Learning Disabilities

According to the school, learning disabled students must self-identify to receive services. High school foreign language and math waivers are accepted. They may also find the following programs quite helpful: remedial math · remedial English · remedial reading · tutors · learning center · testing accommodations · untimed tests · extended time for tests · take-home exam · oral tests · exam on tape or computer · substitution of courses · readers · typist/scribe · note-taking services · proofreading services · reading machines · tape recorders · texts on tape · early syllabus · priority registration · priority seating · waiver of math degree requirement. Individual or small group tutorials are also available in: time management · organizational skills · writing labs · math labs · study skills. An advisor/advocate from the LD program is available to students.

How to Get Admitted

For admissions decisions, non-academic factors considered: interview · extracurricular activities · special talents, interests and abilities · character/personal qualities · volunteer work · work experience · state of residency · alumni relationship. A high school diploma is required, although a GED is also accepted for admissions consideration. SAT or ACT test scores are required of all applicants. *According to the admissions office:* Minimum combined SAT Reasoning score of 1050 and minimum grade average of B required. *Academic units recommended:* 4 English, 4 Math, 2 Science, 2 Foreign Language.

How to Pay for College

To apply for financial aid, students should submit the following: Free Application for Federal Student Aid (FAFSA) · state aid form. Pace University participates in the Federal Work Study program. *Need-based aid programs include:* scholarships and grants · general need-based awards · Federal Pell grants · state scholarships and grants · college-based scholarships and grants · private scholarships and grants · Federal Nursing scholarships · Endowed and Restricted Scholarships and Grants. *Non-need-based aid programs include:* scholarships and grants · state scholarships and grants · creative arts and performance awards · athletic scholarships.

PACE UNIVERSITY

Admissions
Applicants: 14,590
Accepted: 11,853
Acceptance rate: 81.2%
Average GPA: 3.3
ACT range: 22-26
SAT Math range: 500-590
SAT Reading range: 500-590
SAT Writing range: Not reported
Top 10% of class: 16%
Top 25% of class: 48%
Top 50% of class: 85%

Deadlines
Early Action: 12/1
Early Decision: No
Regular Action: Rolling admissions
Common Application: Accepted

Financial Aid
In-state tuition: $38,200
Out-of-state tuition: $38,200
Room: Varies
Board: Varies
Books: $800
Freshmen receiving need-based aid: 77%
Undergrads rec. need-based aid: 75%
Avg. % of need met by financial aid: 70%
Avg. aid package (freshmen): $30,232
Avg. aid package (undergrads): $28,893
Avg. debt upon graduation: $36,558

Prominent Alumni
James N. Fernandez, CPA, Executive Vice President and Chief Operating and Financial Officer, Tiffany & Co.; Joseph Ianniello, Chief Operating Officer, CBS Corporation; Mark M. Besca, New York City Office Managing Partner, EY

School Spirit
Mascot: Setter
Colors: Navy and gold

PACIFIC LUTHERAN UNIVERSITY

1010 122nd Street, Tacoma, WA 98447
Admissions: 800-274-6758 · Financial Aid: 800-678-3243
Email: admissions@plu.edu · Website: http://www.plu.edu

From the College

"PLU consistently ranks among the top 15 in *U.S. News & World Report's* Best Universities in the West and was recently named second in the West for Best Colleges for Veterans. It also ranks in the top four percent of Master's Universities nationwide by *Washington Monthly* College Guide. The university has produced 94 Fulbright Scholars since 1975, and ranks third in the nation among small colleges and universities for the number of Peace Corps volunteers it produces. PLU combines a strong commitment to teaching in a highly personalized liberal arts residential environment with a diverse array of professional and graduate programs. Faculty and professional staff at PLU share a vision that links scholarship, teaching and service in fulfilling its mission. We seek to blend the classroom and community, coordinating theoretical and experiential learning through undergraduate and graduate research, professional practice and internships and community economic and social development projects in the local region.

"The first American university to have study away classes on all seven continents simultaneously, PLU is also the first private university on the west coast to receive the prestigious Senator Paul Simon Award for Campus Internationalization. An honoree on President Obama's Higher Education Community Service Honor Roll, PLU hosts an Emmy Award-winning Media Lab, a MacArthur Award-winning detachment of Army ROTC, an Edward R. Murrow Award-winning public radio station, KPLU and more than 100 clubs and activities, including 20 varsity athletic teams in the Northwest Conference of NCAA Division III.

"PLU is noted for its commitment to diversity, justice and sustainability. For its record on sustainability, the university was recognized with a Gold Award from the Association for the Advancement of Sustainability in Higher Education (AASHE). And for more than 30 years, PLU has been internationally known for its Holocaust studies program, which now includes the endowed Kurt Mayer Professorship in Holocaust Studies and the annual Powell-Heller Holocaust Education Conference. PLU is one of only a handful of universities nationwide that offer a minor in Holocaust Studies. Another of the hallmarks of PLU is its nationally acclaimed School of Arts & Communication. Recent alumni are performing and creating on Broadway (*Next to Normal*), TV (*Glee, The Mentalist, NCIS:LA*), film (*The Lord of the Rings*), as well as on stages and concert halls around the world (Metropolitan Opera) and at news and media organizations throughout the region. The recently renovated, $20-million Karen Hille Phillips Center for the Performing Arts is the premier performing arts center in the South Puget Sound region. The university offers 44 majors and 54 minors as well as graduate and professional programs in business administration, creative writing, education, finance, marriage and family therapy and nursing."

Campus Setting

Pacific Lutheran University, founded in 1890, is a church-affiliated university. Its 126-acre campus is located in Tacoma, Washington. A four-year private institution, Pacific Lutheran University has an enrollment of 3,462 students. The school is also affiliated with the Lutheran Church. The campus facilities include: library · music center · art gallery · observatory · science center · Scandinavian cultural center · Center for Learning and Technology. Pacific Lutheran University provides

America's
Best Colleges for
B Students

on-campus housing with 947 units that can accommodate 1,725 students. Housing options: coed dorms · women's dorms · single-student apartments · married-student apartments · special housing for disabled students. Recreation and sports facilities include: field house · fitness center · golf course · gymnasiums · swimming pool · tennis courts · track field.

Student Life and Activities

Fifty-seven percent of students live off campus. Students gather at The Cave and the University Commons while on campus and at Marzanos, Farelli's Pizza and Northern Pacific Coffee company while off campus. On the Road, Homecoming Dance, EXPLORE! Retreat, PLU Idol, Spring Break Service Trips, Dance Ensemble, Relay for Life, Hawaii Luau, Spring Formal, Tunnel of Oppression, Lute Loop 5k Run and Walk, Outdoor Recreation Trips, Global Get Down, University Congregation Mt. Rainier Hike, Sound Off, Songfest, Intramural Sports and Meant To Live Conference are popular events. Pacific Lutheran University has 83 official student organizations. The football team, Younglife, ASPLU (student government), Relay for Life, the Frisbee team and the Diversity Center hold a strong presence on the PLU Campus. There are intramural teams available: baseball · basketball · cycling club · field hockey · flag football · golf · soccer · softball · volleyball. Pacific Lutheran University is a member of the Northwest Conference (Division III).

Academics and Learning Environment

Pacific Lutheran University has 218 full-time and 59 part-time faculty members, offering a student-to-faculty ratio of 14:1. The most common course size is 10 to 19 students. Pacific Lutheran University offers 57 majors with the most popular being business administration, nursing and biology. The school has a general core requirement as well as a religion requirement. Cooperative education is available. All first-year students must maintain a 2.0 GPA or higher to avoid academic probation. Other programs include: self-designed majors · pass/fail grading option · independent study · double majors · dual degrees · honors program · internships.

B Student Support and Success

PLU's Academic Assistance Center offers tutors, foreign language conversation groups, independent study strategies, group review sessions and even free flashcards—and a bonus: hand-outs on issues like critical reading, time management, note taking and test taking. There is a math lab, a computer science lab, a biology/chemistry lab and a geo-science lab. All services are free of charge.

Pacific Lutheran University provides dedicated guidance for: academic · career · personal · psychological · minority students · military · veterans · family planning · religious. Annually, 82 percent of freshmen students return for their sophomore year. After college, many students enter into the workforce, and approximately 81 percent enter a field related to their major within six months of graduation. Some companies that most frequently employ graduates from Pacific Lutheran University include: AmeriCorps · regional health care providers · regional school systems.

PACIFIC LUTHERAN UNIVERSITY

Pacific Lutheran University
Tacoma (Pop. 202,010)
Location: Medium city
Four-year private
Founded: 1890
Website: http://www.plu.edu

Students
Total enrollment: 3,462
Undergrads: 3,142
Part-time students: 4%
From out-of-state: 26%
Male/Female: 38%/62%
Live on-campus: 43%
Off-campus employment rating: Good
Caucasian: 70%
African American: 3%
Hispanic: 7%
Asian: 6%
Hawaiian or Pacific Islander: 1%
Native American: 1%
Mixed (2+ ethnicities): 7%
International: 5%

Academics
Calendar: 4-1-4 system
Student/faculty ratio: 14:1
Class size 9 or fewer: 12%
Class size 10-29: 67%
Class size 30-49: 18%
Class size 50-99: 3%
Class size 100 or more: -
Returning freshmen: 82%
Six-year graduation rate: 70%

Most Popular Majors
Business administration
Nursing
Biology

PACIFIC LUTHERAN UNIVERSITY

Admissions
Applicants: 3,443
Accepted: 2,643
Acceptance rate: 76.8%
Average GPA: 3.7
ACT range: 22-28
SAT Math range: 490-610
SAT Reading range: 490-610
SAT Writing range: 3-20
Top 10% of class: 35%
Top 25% of class: 70%
Top 50% of class: 92%

Deadlines
Early Action: No
Early Decision: No
Regular Action: Rolling admissions
Common Application: Accepted

Financial Aid
In-state tuition: $36,180
Out-of-state tuition: $36,180
Room: Varies
Board: Varies
Books: $1,030
Freshmen receiving need-based aid: 81%
Undergrads rec. need-based aid: 76%
Avg. % of need met by financial aid: 83%
Avg. aid package (freshmen): $34,107
Avg. aid package (undergrads): $32,765
Avg. debt upon graduation: $31,639

Prominent Alumni
Sean Parnell, governor of Alaska; Lois Capps, member of the United States House of Representatives since 1998, representing California's 23rd congressional district; Brad Tilden, president, Alaska Airlines.

School Spirit
Mascot: Lutes
Colors: Black and gold

Support for Students with Learning Disabilities

Students with learning disabilities may want to research some of the support programs offered by Pacific Lutheran University. If deemed necessary by the college, the LD student may be granted additional time to finish their degree. High school foreign language waivers are accepted. Students with learning disabilities will want to survey the following list of programs: special classes · tutors · learning center · untimed tests · extended time for tests · take-home exam · oral tests · readers · typist/scribe · note-taking services · reading machines · tape recorders · videotaped classes · early syllabus · priority registration · priority seating · waiver of math degree requirement. Individual or small group tutorials are also available in: time management · organizational skills · learning strategies · specific subject areas · writing labs · math labs · study skills. An advisor/advocate from the Disability Support Services is available to students.

How to Get Admitted

For admissions decisions, non-academic factors considered: interview · extracurricular activities · special talents, interests and abilities · character/personal qualities · volunteer work · work experience · geographical location · religious affiliation/commitment · minority affiliation · alumni relationship. A high school diploma is required, although a GED is also accepted for admissions consideration. SAT or ACT test scores are required of all applicants. *Academic units recommended:* 4 English, 3 Math, 2 Science, 2 Social Studies, 2 Foreign Language.

How to Pay for College

To apply for financial aid, students should submit the following: Free Application for Federal Student Aid (FAFSA). Pacific Lutheran University participates in the Federal Work Study program. *Need-based aid programs include:* scholarships and grants · general need-based awards · Federal Pell grants · state scholarships and grants · college-based scholarships and grants · private scholarships and grants · Federal Nursing scholarships. *Non-need-based aid programs include:* scholarships and grants · general need-based awards · state scholarships and grants · creative arts and performance awards · ROTC scholarships.

PAUL SMITH'S COLLEGE

Route 86 & 30, P.O. Box 265, Paul Smiths, NY 12970-0265
Admissions: 518-327-6000 · Financial Aid: 800-421-2605
Email: admissions@paulsmiths.edu
Website: http://www.paulsmiths.edu

From the College

Paul Smith's College, founded in 1946, is a private, specialized institution located on 14,200 acres of beautiful wilderness.

Campus Setting

A four-year private institution, the only one located inside the Adirondack Park, Paul Smith's College has an enrollment of almost 1,000 students. The college has two schools: the School of Natural Resource Management and Ecology (NRME), which houses environmental studies, biology, forestry, fish and wildlife sciences and natural resources management and the School of Commercial, Applied and Liberal Arts (CALA), which offers majors including culinary arts and hotel and tourism.

Student Life and Activities

Paul Smith's College has 16 residence halls, and nearly all students live on campus. Some halls have a 24-hour quiet policy and are tobacco- and alcohol-free. On-campus organizations include the Adirondack Mycology Club, Baking and Pastry Arts, Birding Club, Fish and Game Club and Hospitality Sales and Marketing Association International. One of the most prominent events is the Winter Carnival, the oldest on the East Coast.

Academics and Learning Environment

Paul Smith's College offers a student-to-faculty ratio of 15:1. Paul Smith's College offers 20 majors with the most popular being natural resources, hotel/resort/tourism management and culinary arts/service management. The college offers hands-on opportunities such as helping with sustainable management of the college's property as a forestry major or writing a business plan for a local business as a business and entrepreneurship major. The school does not have a general core requirement. Cooperative education is not offered. All first-year students must maintain a 2.0 GPA or higher to avoid academic probation. Other programs: certificate programs.

B Student Support and Success

The theme at Paul Smith's Academic Center is "Helping Students Achieve their Goals for Academic Success." Here they offer peer tutoring, supplemental instruction, study groups and a Writing Center where experts strive to help students understand the assignment, build confidence, organize ideas, listen carefully, formulate comments and more.

Paul Smith's College provides a series of support programs. The average freshman year GPA is 2.8, and 64 percent of freshmen students return for their sophomore year.

PAUL SMITH'S COLLEGE

Highlights

Paul Smith's College

Location: Rural
Four-year private
Founded: 1946
Website: http://www.paulsmiths.edu

Students
Total enrollment: 981
From out-of-state: 34%
Male/Female: 66%/34%
Live on-campus: Not reported
Caucasian: 68%
African American: 1%
Hispanic: 3%
Asian: <1%
Hawaiian or Pacific Islander: <1%
Native American: <1%
Mixed (2+ ethnicities): 1%
International: <1%

Academics
Calendar: Semester
Student/faculty ratio: 15:1
Class size 9 or fewer: 11%
Class size 10-29: 67%
Class size 30-49: 20%
Class size 50-99: 1%
Class size 100 or more: 1%
Returning freshmen: 62%
Six-year graduation rate: 45%

Most Popular Majors
Natural resources
Hotel/resort/tourism management
Culinary arts/service management

341

PAUL SMITH'S COLLEGE

Highlights

Admissions
Applicants: 970
Accepted: 728
Acceptance rate: 75%
Average GPA: Not reported
ACT range: 20-25
SAT Math range: 430-530
SAT Reading range: 450-530
SAT Writing range: Not reported

Deadlines
Early Action: No
Early Decision: No
Regular Action: Rolling admissions
Common Application: Not accepted

Financial Aid
In-state tuition: $21,188
Out-of-state tuition: $21,188
Room: $5,304
Board: $4,645
Books: $1,000
Freshmen receiving need-based or merit-based aid: 99%
Avg. aid package (freshmen): Not reported
Avg. aid package (undergrads): Not reported

Prominent Alumni
Jon L. Luther, CEO of Dunkin' Donuts; Steve Ross, CEO of Time Warner.

School Spirit
Mascot: Bobcat
Colors: Green and white

Support for Students with Learning Disabilities

Students with learning disabilities will benefit from the specific support programs offered by Paul Smith's College. LD students will find the following programs at Paul Smith's College extremely helpful: tutors · waiver of math degree requirement.

How to Get Admitted

For admissions decisions, non-academic factors considered: state of residency. A high school diploma is required, although a GED is also accepted for admissions consideration. SAT or ACT test scores are required for some applicants. SAT Subject Test scores are recommended but not required. *According to the admissions office:* Minimum combined SAT Reasoning score of 800 (composite ACT score of 17) and rank in top half of secondary school class required.

How to Pay for College

To apply for financial aid, students should submit the following: Free Application for Federal Student Aid (FAFSA). Paul Smith's College participates in the Federal Work Study program. *Need-based aid programs include:* scholarships and grants · general need-based awards · Federal Pell grants · state scholarships and grants · college-based scholarships and grants · private scholarships and grants. *Non-need-based aid programs include:* scholarships and grants · state scholarships and grants.

America's
Best Colleges for
B Students

PINE MANOR COLLEGE

400 Heath Street, Chestnut Hill, MA 02467
Admissions: 800-762-1357 · Financial Aid: 800-762-1357
Email: admission@pmc.edu · Website: http://www.pmc.edu

From the College

"Pine Manor College prepares women for inclusive leadership and social responsibility in their workplaces, families and communities. We pursue this goal through: integration of an outcomes-based curriculum and co-curriculum demonstrated by portfolio presentations; active, collaborative, applied liberal arts learning and college-wide mentoring teams and community partnerships-in an environment that celebrates diversity and respects the common good."

Campus Setting

Pine Manor, founded in 1911, is a private, liberal arts college for women. Its 65-acre campus is located in Chestnut Hill, five miles from downtown Boston. The campus facilities include: library · art gallery · communication center · child study center. Pine Manor College provides on-campus housing that can accommodate 481 students. Housing options: women's dorms · special housing for disabled students. Recreation and sports facilities include: aerobics room · gymnasium · dance studio · soccer and lacrosse field · softball field · weight room.

Student Life and Activities

Seventy-seven percent of students live on campus. Pine Manor College has 23 official student organizations. The most popular are: anime club · Camerata Singers · dance ensemble · Campus Activities Board · The F-Group · psychology club · Bisexuals, Gays, Lesbians and Allies in Diversity. Pine Manor College is a member of the Great Northeast Athletic Conference (Division III).

Academics and Learning Environment

Pine Manor College offers 16 majors with the most popular being business administration, psychology and biology and least popular being social/political systems. The school has a general core requirement. Cooperative education is not offered. All first-year students must maintain a 2.0 GPA or higher to avoid academic probation, and a minimum overall GPA of 2.0 is required to graduate. Other programs include: self-designed majors · pass/fail grading option · independent study · double majors · internships.

B Student Support and Success

Freshmen at Pine Manor are required to take a First Year Experience Seminar that is led by faculty members, student life professionals and peer mentors. During their second year, they take a Portfolio Learning Seminar. Its purpose is to "encourage students to become reflective, self-directed learners, as well as to help them understand and fulfill degree requirements through development of a personalized learning portfolio." Presentation of this portfolio is one of the requirements for graduation. Many students use the Brown Learning Resource Center, staffed by professional, full-time tutors. Assistance is offered in writing, math, reading, study skills and time management. According to the college, students who use the Resource Center are "able to discover previously untapped strengths, adjust to new demands of the college environment, fill gaps in prior learning and most of all, learn how to take charge of their own learning." Other advice from the college includes these statements: "Students can tell us about themselves and their accomplishments and their goals in their

PINE MANOR COLLEGE

Pine Manor College
Chestnut Hill, MA
Location: Major city
Four-year private women's college
Founded: 1911
Website: http://www.pmc.edu

Students
Total enrollment: 346
Undergrads: 313
From out-of-state: 50%
Male/Female: 15%/85%
Live on-campus: 77%
Off-campus employment rating: Excellent
Caucasian: 8%
African American: 20%
Hispanic: 15%
Asian: 5%
Hawaiian or Pacific Islander: <1%
Native American: <1%
Mixed (2+ ethnicities): 12%
International: 29%

Academics
Calendar: Semester
Student/faculty ratio: 10:1
Class size 9 or fewer: 31%
Class size 10-29: 69%
Class size 30-49: -
Class size 50-99: -
Class size 100 or more: -
Returning freshmen: 65%
Six-year graduation rate: 39%

Most Popular Majors
Business administration
Psychology
Biology

personal essay. Recommendation letters and personal interviews also give us great insights to the young women we counsel. There are many talented and deserving young women with B and C level grades that would grow and be successful at Pine Manor. "Young women who attend PMC develop self confidence and leadership skills. You can really see these women transform themselves over the years."

Pine Manor College prides itself on its dedicated guidance for: academic · career · personal · psychological · minority students · family planning · religious. Pine Manor College offers remedial and refresher courses in: reading · writing · math · study skills. What about when college is over? Some students enter the workforce, and approximately five percent pursue a graduate degree immediately after graduation. One year after graduation, the school reports that 20 percent of graduates have entered graduate school. Out of those students that enter the workforce, approximately 20 percent enter a field related to their major within six months of graduation. Here is a compilation of companies that most frequently hire graduates from Pine Manor College: Fidelity · Smith Barney · Bank of America · Sovereign Bank · Commonwealth of Massachusetts · Boston Financial · Jasmine Sola · Century Bank · The Second Step · Crayon College · Salem Hospital · Youth Build · Harbor Side Healthcare · Harvard Vanguard · Massachusetts Housing Partnership.

Support for Students with Learning Disabilities

B students with learning disabilities may want to investigate specific support programs offered by Pine Manor College. Two options available for LD students include a lightened course load and additional time to conclude their degree. Credit is given for remedial courses taken. According to the school, The Brown Learning Resource Center is open to all students and offers individual tutoring in writing, mathematics, reading, study skills and time management. LD students will be intrigued by these program options: tutors · learning center · testing accommodations · untimed tests · extended time for tests · take-home exam · oral tests · readers · note-taking services · priority registration. Individual or small group tutorials are also available in: time management · organizational skills · learning strategies · writing labs · math labs · study skills. An advisor/advocate from the LD program is available to students. This member also sits on the admissions committee.

How to Get Admitted

For admissions decisions, non-academic factors considered: interview · extracurricular activities · special talents, interests and abilities · character/personal qualities · volunteer work · work experience · state of residency. A high school diploma is required, although a GED is also accepted for admissions consideration. SAT or ACT test scores are required of all applicants. SAT Subject Test scores are recommended but not required. *Academic units recommended:* 4 English, 3 Math, 3 Science, 2 Social Studies, 2 Foreign Language.

How to Pay for College

To apply for financial aid, students should submit the following: Free Application for Federal Student Aid (FAFSA). Pine Manor College participates in the Federal Work Study program. *Need-based* aid programs include: scholarships and grants · general need-based awards · Federal Pell grants · state scholarships and grants · college-based scholarships and grants · private scholarships and grants. *Non-need-based aid programs include:* scholarships and grants · state scholarships and grants.

PINE MANOR COLLEGE

Admissions
Applicants: 535
Accepted: 342
Acceptance rate: 64%
Average GPA: 2.5
ACT range: Not reported
SAT Math range: 340-420
SAT Reading range: 320-440
SAT Writing range: 330-440

Deadlines
Early Action: No
Early Decision: No
Regular Action: Rolling admissions
Common Application: Accepted

Financial Aid
In-state tuition: $25,516
Out-of-state tuition: $25,516
Room: Varies
Board: Varies
Books: $800
Freshmen receiving need-based aid: 85%
Undergrads rec. need-based aid: 94%
Avg. % of need met by financial aid: 77%
Avg. aid package (freshmen): $17,425
Avg. aid package (undergrads): $15,768
Avg. debt upon graduation: $18,000

Prominent Alumni
Pauline Tompkins, first female president of Cedar Crest College; Dorothy McGuire, Academy Award-nominated actress.

School Spirit
Mascot: Gators
Colors: Green and white

PRESCOTT COLLEGE

220 Grove Avenue, Prescott, AZ 86301
Admissions: 877-350-2100 · Financial Aid: 877-350-2100, extension 1111
Email: admissions@prescott.edu · Website: http://www.prescott.edu

From the College

"Prescott College subscribes to the philosophy of experiential education or 'learning by doing.' We believe that doing is as important as reading and discussing. In cooperation with faculty, Prescott College students are able to work in such interdisciplinary fields as human development, ecopsychology, abstract art, environmental education and interpretation, teacher education, human ecology, agroecology, creative writing, outdoor adventure education, management, counseling and wilderness leadership. Our faculty recognize that some of the most important lessons are learned in situations that require action. Many courses have strong field components and some are conducted entirely in the field. Internships, apprenticeships, independent studies, community service and study abroad are encouraged so that students may study and live in cultural contexts outside their normal experience.

"Students are taught by full-time faculty members, not graduate assistants. Faculty members are role models and mentors and often become life-long friends and colleagues. Prescott College has a mission to educate students of diverse ages and backgrounds to understand, thrive in and enhance our world community and environment. Students are encouraged to think critically and act ethically with sensitivity to both the human community and the biosphere.

"Prescott College has a block and semester academic calendar. Blocks are approximately four weeks in length and take place during September, January and March-May. An 11-week semester follows each block. During the block, students enroll in only one course and learn through deep involvement in the subject. Many block courses are conducted partially or entirely in the field and can take students to the Grand Canyon, the Sea of Cortez, Eastern Europe, Latin America and throughout the Southwest and the world.

"We encourage students to tailor their curriculum to suit their needs and to include off-campus internships, work study, faculty-student research projects, group and independent study, community service and study abroad. Prescott and the college are surrounded by 1,408,000 acres of National Forest, with more than 796 miles of trails. Prescott offers a diversity of outdoor activities, including rock climbing, hiking, mountain biking and nearby canoeing, rafting, kayaking and snow skiing. The old mining town of Jerome, the red rocks of Sedona, shopping in Phoenix and the Grand Canyon are all within a day's trip."

Campus Setting

Prescott College is a private college founded in 1966. The campus is located on six acres in Prescott, AZ, approximately 100 miles north of Phoenix. Prescott College is an independent, liberal arts college offering bachelor's, master's and doctoral degrees, as well as teacher certification. A four-year institution, Prescott College has an enrollment of 943 students. Campus facilities include: performing arts center · visual arts building · farm · GIS laboratory. Prescott College provides on-campus housing with seven units that can accommodate 120 students. Housing options: coed dorms.

Student Life and Activities

Most students (84 percent) live off campus. According to a school official, "College-sponsored activities, student groups and individuals throughout the College provide opportunities to meet, and enjoy yourself outside of classes. Music and dance performances, photography exhibits, slide shows, poetry and fiction reading, yoga, lectures, panel discussions, plays and talent shows bring students together. Students frequently go hiking, camping, rock climbing, canoeing, mountain biking and horseback riding." Popular on- and off-campus gathering spots include the Crossroads Cafe, Raven Cafe, Prescott Coffee Roasters and Coyote Joe's Bar and Grill. Popular campus events include the Ripple Showcase, Vagina Monologues and the Drag Show. Prescott College has 16 official student organizations. Popular groups on campus include the Student Advisory Council, Aztlan Center, HUB (Helping Understand Bikes), WEB (Women's Empowerment Breakthrough) and Ripple Project.

Academics and Learning Environment

Prescott College has 62 full-time and 42 part-time faculty members, offering a student-to-faculty ratio of 8:1. The most common course size is 10 to 19 students. Prescott College offers 23 majors with the most popular being education, environmental studies and psychology and least popular being English, social sciences and human services. The school has a general core requirement. Cooperative education is available. Other special academic programs include: self-designed majors · pass/fail grading option · independent study · double majors · internships · certificate programs.

B Student Support and Success

According to the college, "Prescott is an ideal environment for both A and B students. Our programs are academically rigorous and experientially based. We are able to accommodate a variety of learning styles. Qualified applicants demonstrate solid, consistent academic performance, well-written college essays and a high level of personal motivation. We use holistic evaluation that looks at our applicant's overall prospects for success in the college."

Prescott College provides a variety of support programs including dedicated guidance for: academic · career · personal · psychological. Prescott College offers remedial and refresher courses in: reading · writing · math · study skills. Annually, 71 percent of freshmen students return for the second year.

Support for Students with Learning Disabilities

Prescott gives students with learning disabilities additional time to students to complete their degree. LD students may also find these programs quite useful: tutors · testing accommodations · untimed tests · extended time for tests · take-home exam · readers · note-taking services · tape recorders · texts on tape · early syllabus · priority registration · waiver of math degree requirement. Individual or small group tutorials are also available in: time management · organizational skills · learning strategies · specific subject areas · writing labs · math labs · study skills. An advisor/advocate from the LD program is available to students.

How to Get Admitted

For admissions decisions, non-academic factors considered: interview · extracurricular activities · special talents, interests and abilities · character/personal qualities · volunteer work · work experience · state of residency. A high school diploma is required, although a

PRESCOTT COLLEGE

Highlights

Prescott College
Prescott, AZ (Pop. 40,308)
Location: Large town
Four-year private
Founded: 1966
Website: http://www.prescott.edu

Students
Total enrollment: 943
Undergrads: 545
Part-time students: 19%
From out-of-state: 98%
Male/Female: 45%/55%
Live on-campus: 16%
Off-campus employment rating: Fair
Caucasian: 73%
African American: 1%
Hispanic: 6%
Asian: 1%
Native American: 2%
Mixed (2+ ethnicities): 4%
International: 1%

Academics
Calendar: Semester
Student/faculty ratio: 8:1
Class size 9 or fewer: 46%
Class size 10-29: 53%
Class size 30-49: -
Class size 50-99: 1%
Class size 100 or more: -
Returning freshmen: 71%
Six-year graduation rate: 37%

Most Popular Majors
Education
Environmental studies
Psychology

PRESCOTT COLLEGE

Highlights

Admissions
Applicants: 399
Accepted: 291
Acceptance rate: 72.9%
Average GPA: 3.1
ACT range: 20-26
SAT Math range: 430-610
SAT Reading range: 480-650
SAT Writing range: 6-11
Top 10% of class: 14%
Top 25% of class: 28%
Top 50% of class: 86%

Deadlines
Early Action: No
Early Decision: 12/1
Regular Action: Rolling admissions
Common Application: Accepted

Financial Aid
In-state tuition: $24,960
Out-of-state tuition: $24,960
Room: Varies
Board: Varies
Books: $796
Freshmen receiving need-based aid: 73%
Undergrads rec. need-based aid: 67%
Avg. % of need met by financial aid: 60%
Avg. aid package (freshmen): $21,357
Avg. aid package (undergrads): $19,706
Avg. debt upon graduation: $27,213

Prominent Alumni
Cody Lundin, author, survivalist, instructor, consultant; Craig Childs, author, adventurer, naturalist, desert ecologist; Thomas Udall, New Mexico Representative to the US House of Representatives.

GED is also accepted for admissions consideration. SAT or ACT test scores are required of all applicants. SAT Subject Test scores are considered, if submitted, but are not required. *Academic units recommended:* 4 English, 3 Math, 2 Science, 3 Social Studies, 1 Foreign Language.

Insight

"We welcome students from a variety of backgrounds," says Natalie Canfield, admissions counselor. "We look at each person as a whole, not just numbers and essays. We look at bad grades and try to see how we can fix them." At Prescott, the essay is particularly evaluative for both writing level and content. The school requires two kinds of essays: one that is autobiographical ("To get to know the student") and one that is an academic autobiography ("To learn the student's writing style"). "Interviews are optional," continues Canfield. "They are relaxed and we talk about past education and different situations. We also give students a chance to ask us questions to see if we are a fit." Prescott College focuses on degrees having to do with the environment. According to Canfield, it has more 15-passenger vans for field trips than it does buildings on campus. "Many courses are field-based and most courses involve weekend-long trips," she explains.

How to Pay for College

To apply for financial aid, students should submit the following: Free Application for Federal Student Aid (FAFSA). Prescott College participates in the Federal Work Study program. *Need-based aid programs include:* scholarships and grants · general need-based awards · Federal Pell grants · state scholarships and grants · college-based scholarships and grants · private scholarships and grants. *Non-need-based aid programs include:* scholarships and grants · general need-based awards · state scholarships and grants.

348

PRINCIPIA COLLEGE

1 Maybeck Place, Elsah, IL 62028
Admissions: 800-277-4648, extension 2802
Financial Aid: 800-277-4648, extension 2813
Email: collegeadmissions@principia.edu
Website: http://www.principiacollege.edu

From the College

"Principia College is a unique college in that it is the only college in the world whose educational mission is to educate students who are Christian Scientists. Its purpose is to 'serve the Cause of Christian Science,' as stated by its founder Mary Kimball Morgan. The mission of the college is to provide students who are Christian Scientists with a comprehensive, co-educational academic program of liberal arts and sciences, leading to a Bachelor of Arts or a Bachelor of Science degree. The college is also committed to academic excellence and development of the spiritual, intellectual, moral, social and physical development of each student. In this context, Principia offers its students an international perspective and challenges them to be ethically strong in service to the world community. The college campus contains and is surrounded by vast and diverse natural habitat, including forests, prairies and the Mississippi River. Situated on limestone bluffs 200 feet above the river, Principia has developed in its many years on the 2,600-acre site a harmonious blend of landscaped ground anchoring a variety of English Tudor buildings designed by renowned California architect Bernard Maybeck that provide functional support to the campus community."

Campus Setting

Principia, founded in 1912, is a private, church-affiliated, liberal arts college. Its 2,600-acre campus is located in Elsah, 40 miles north of St. Louis. The campus facilities include: library · carillon · chapel · school of nations museum · science center · planetarium · natatorium. Principia College provides on-campus housing with 11 units that can accommodate 600 students. Housing options: coed dorms · women's dorms · men's dorms · married-student apartments. Recreation and sports facilities include: baseball, football, rugby, soccer and softball fields · basketball, tennis and volleyball courts · field house · swimming pool · outdoor and indoor track.

Student Life and Activities

Ninety-nine percent of students live on campus. Popular gathering sports include Principia Pub, St. Louis, nearby small towns and restaurants and movie theaters. The most popular student organizations are: Chorus · orchestra · instrumental groups · drama group · concert and lecture series · amateur radio and camera clubs · departmental, service and special-interest groups. There are intramural teams available: basketball · soccer · Ultimate Frisbee · sand volleyball · rugby. Principia College is a member of the St. Louis Intercollegiate Athletic Conference (Division III).

Academics and Learning Environment

Principia College has 61 full-time and nine part-time faculty mem-

PRINCIPIA COLLEGE

Highlights

Principia College
Elsah, IL (Pop. 670)
Location: Rural
Four-year private
Founded: 1912
Website: http://www.principiacollege.edu

Students
Total enrollment: 508
From out-of-state: 93%
Male/Female: 46%/54%
Live on-campus: 99%
Off-campus employment rating: Poor
Caucasian: 69%
African American: 1%
Hispanic: 3%
Asian: <1%
Hawaiian or Pacific Islander: <1%
Native American: <1%
Mixed (2+ ethnicities): 3%
International: 18%

Academics
Calendar: Semester
Student/faculty ratio: 7:1
Class size 9 or fewer: 46%
Class size 10-29: 53%
Class size 30-49: -
Class size 50-99: 1%
Class size 100 or more: -
Returning freshmen: 81%
Six-year graduation rate: 82%

Most Popular Majors
Mass communication
Business administration
Political science/sociology

PRINCIPIA COLLEGE

Admissions
Applicants: 189
Accepted: 159
Acceptance rate: 84.1%
Average GPA: 3.4
ACT range: 20-29
SAT Math range: 458-600
SAT Reading range: 460-623
SAT Writing range: 4-23
Top 10% of class: 26%
Top 25% of class: 50%
Top 50% of class: 83%

Deadlines
Early Action: No
Early Decision: No
Regular Action: Rolling admissions
Common Application: Not accepted

Financial Aid
In-state tuition: $26,350
Out-of-state tuition: $26,350
Room: $5,050
Board: $5,600
Books: $1,000
Freshmen receiving need-based aid: 74%
Undergrads rec. need-based aid: 70%
Avg. % of need met by financial aid: 74%
Avg. aid package (freshmen): $28,363
Avg. aid package (undergrads): $28,246

Prominent Alumni
Robert Duvall, Academy-Award winning actor; John H. Rousselot, United States Congressman from California; Ketti Frings, Pulitzer Prize-winning author.

School Spirit
Mascot: panther
Colors: Navy blue and gold
Song: *The Gold and Blue*

America's
Best Colleges for
B Students

bers, offering a student-to-faculty ratio of 7:1. The college offers 24 majors with the most popular being mass communication, business administration and political science/sociology and least popular being engineering science, philosophy/math and Spanish. The school has a general core requirement as well as a religion requirement. Cooperative education is not offered. All first-year students must maintain a 1.6 GPA or higher to avoid academic probation, and a minimum overall GPA of 2.0 is required to graduate. Other programs include: self-designed majors · independent study · double majors · internships.

B Student Support and Success

At Principia College's Academic and Career Advising Office, experts will help you "explore majors, plan internships, research graduate schools, prepare resumes and investigate career opportunities." They also give students guidance on subjects such as setting practical goals, time management and balancing academics and student life. New students are assigned a faculty or staff advisor to help make informed academic choices. The Writing Center sponsors a two week seminar that offers a wide range of reading and writing experiences, and tutors are available every evening for free assistance.

Principia College provides a variety of support programs, including: academic · career · personal. Additional counseling services include: Resident Counselors reside in each dorm, available to counsel students at their request. The average freshman year GPA is 3.2, and 81 percent of freshmen students return for their sophomore year. A large majority of graduates enter the workforce, and approximately 14 percent pursue a graduate degree immediately after graduation. Among students who enter the workforce, approximately 62 percent total enter a field related to their initial major within six months of graduation.

How to Get Admitted

For admissions decisions, non-academic factors considered: interview · extracurricular activities · special talents, interests and abilities · character/personal qualities · volunteer work · work experience · state of residency · religious affiliation/commitment · minority affiliation · alumni relationship. A high school diploma is required, although a GED is also accepted for admissions consideration. SAT or ACT test scores are required of all applicants. SAT Subject Test scores are considered, if submitted, but are not required. *According to the admissions office:* Applicants must be Christian Scientists. Minimum combined SAT Reasoning score of 1380 (composite ACT score of 19) and minimum 2.3 GPA required. *Academic units recommended:* 4 English, 4 Math, 4 Science, 2 Social Studies, 3 Foreign Language.

How to Pay for College

To apply for financial aid, students should submit the following: · institution's own financial aid forms · CSS/Financial Aid PROFILE · Non-custodian (Divorced/Separated) Parent's Statement · current tax returns · schedules and W-2's. Principia College does not participate in the Federal Work Study program. *Need-based aid programs include:* scholarships and grants · college-based scholarships and grants · private scholarships and grants. *Non-need-based aid programs include:* scholarships and grants · state scholarships and grants · special achievements and activities awards.

PURDUE UNIVERSITY – WEST LAFAYETTE

475 Stadium Mall Drive, West Lafayette, IN 47907-2050
Admissions: 765-494-1776 · Financial Aid: 765-494-0998
Email: admissions@purdue.edu · Website: http://www.purdue.edu

From the College

"Founded in 1869, Purdue is Indiana's land-grant university. It is one of the nation's premier institutions with more than 200 areas of undergraduate study and renowned research initiatives. Purdue's programs in a wide variety of undergraduate and graduate disciplines consistently rank among the best in the country. Twenty-two of America's astronauts hold Purdue degrees. Students from all 50 states and more than 124 countries attend the main campus in West Lafayette. Although a large university, Purdue maintains an intimate atmosphere that highly values individual needs and achievements."

Campus Setting

Purdue University is a public, comprehensive institution. Founded in 1869, its 2,559-acre campus is located in West Lafayette, 65 miles northwest of Indianapolis, Indiana. A four-year institution, Purdue has an enrollment of 38,788 students and has been co-ed since 1874. Besides a sizable library, Purdue University provides its students with an archive and special collections unit of the Purdue University Libraries. Purdue provides on-campus housing with 15 units that can accommodate 11,779 students. Housing options: coed dorms · women's dorms · men's dorms · sorority housing · fraternity housing · single-student apartments · married-student apartments · special housing for disabled students · cooperative housing. Recreation and sports facilities include: basketball courts · co-ed recreational center · diving pool · football fields · handball courts · soccer fields · softball field · swimming pool · tennis courts.

Student Life and Activities

Sixty-four percent of students live off campus. Popular events include Boiler Volunteer Network, Diversity Groups Activities Carnival, International Awareness Week, PMO Christmas Show, Senior Send-Off, Spring Fest/Bug Bowl, Step Shows, Athletic Events, Boiler Gold Rush, Concerts, Film Series, Grand Prix Race, Greek Week, Homecoming and Industrial Roundtable. Purdue University - West Lafayette has 948 official student organizations, including Greeks, Athletes, Christian groups, Black Cultural Center and Hispanic Group. There are intramural teams available: badminton · basketball · football · golf · racquetball · soccer · softball · swimming and diving · tennis · track and field · Ultimate Frisbee · volleyball. Purdue University - West Lafayette is a member of the Big Ten Conference (Division I, Football I-A).

Academics and Learning Environment

Purdue University - West Lafayette has 2,063 full-time and 313 part-time faculty members, offering a student-to-faculty ratio of 13:1. The most common course size is 10 to 19 students. Purdue University - West Lafayette offers 348 majors with the most popular being mechanical engineering, computer science and management. The school has a general core requirement. Cooperative education is available. All first-year students must maintain a 1.5 GPA or higher to avoid academic probation, and a minimum overall GPA of 2.0 is required to graduate. Other programs include: pass/fail grading option · independent study · double majors · accelerated study · honors program · Phi Beta Kappa · internships · weekend college · distance learning certificate programs.

351

College Profiles

PURDUE UNIVERSITY – WEST LAFAYETTE

Purdue University – West Lafayette
West Lafayette, IN (Pop. 30,419)
Location: Medium city
Four-year public
Founded: 1869
Website: http://www.purdue.edu

Students

Total enrollment: 38,788
Undergrads: 29,440
Freshmen: 6,283
Part-time students: 4%
From out-of-state: 35%
Male/Female: 57%/43%
Live on-campus: 36%
In fraternities: 10%
In sororities: 8%
Off-campus employment rating: Good
Caucasian: 67%
African American: 3%
Hispanic: 4%
Asian: 5%
Hawaiian or Pacific Islander: <1%
Native American: <1%
Mixed (2+ ethnicities): 2%
International: 17%

Academics

Calendar: Semester
Student/faculty ratio: 13:1
Class size 9 or fewer: 14%
Class size 10-29: 47%
Class size 30-49: 21%
Class size 50-99: 12%
Class size 100 or more: 6%
Returning freshmen: 91%
Six-year graduation rate: 70%

Most Popular Majors

Mechanical engineering
Computer science
Management

America's
Best Colleges for
B Students

B Student Support and Success

In order to "get the hang of college life quickly," Purdue offers a system called a "learning community." It consists of either a group of 20 to 30 first-year students who take two or three of the same courses together, a group of first-year students who share a common academic interest and live in the same residence hall or a group of first-year students who take part in both of these activities.

Purdue offers dedicated guidance for: academic · career · personal · psychological · minority students · military · veterans · nontraditional students · family planning. Purdue offers remedial and refresher courses in: reading · writing · math · study skills. The average freshman year GPA is 3.0, and 91 percent of freshmen students return for their sophomore year. Among students who enter the workforce, approximately 66 percent of them dedicate themselves to a field related to their major within six months of graduation. Firms that most frequently hire graduates include: Caterpillar · Eli Lilly · Boeing · Butler International · Cisco Systems · Cummins Engine · CVS Pharmacy · EDS · Exxon Mobil · Lockheed Martin · Procter and Gamble · Raytheon.

Support for Students with Learning Disabilities

Students with learning disabilities may find themselves impressed with the support programs available through Purdue. A lightened course load is available to LD students. According to the school, documentation must be provided before eligibility for classroom accommodations can be determined. Students with learning disabilities will find the following very intriguing: remedial math · special classes · learning center · testing accommodations · extended time for tests · take-home exam · oral tests · exam on tape or computer · readers · typist/scribe · note-taking services · reading machines · tape recorders · texts on tape · early syllabus · diagnostic testing service · priority registration · waiver of math degree requirement. Individual or small group tutorials are also available in: time management · organizational skills · learning strategies · specific subject areas · writing labs · math labs · study skills. An advisor/advocate from the Adaptive Programs is available to students.

How to Get Admitted

For admissions decisions, non-academic factors considered: extracurricular activities · special talents, interests and abilities · character/personal qualities · volunteer work · work experience · geographical location · minority affiliation · alumni relationship. A high school diploma is required, although a GED is also accepted for admissions consideration. SAT or ACT test scores are required of all applicants. *Academic units recommended:* 4 English, 4 Math, 3 Science, 3 Social Studies, 2 Foreign Language.

How to Pay for College

To apply for financial aid, students should submit the following: Free Application for Federal Student Aid (FAFSA). Purdue participates in the Federal Work Study program. *Need-based aid programs include:* scholarships and grants · general need-based awards · Federal Pell grants · state scholarships and grants · college-based scholarships and grants · private scholarships and grants · Academic Competitiveness Grant (ACG) and National Smart Grant Program. *Non-need-based aid programs include:* scholarships and grants · general need-based awards · state scholarships and grants · athletic scholarships · ROTC scholarships · leadership · music · drama.

PURDUE UNIVERSITY – WEST LAFAYETTE

Highlights

Admissions
Applicants: 30,955
Accepted: 18,684
Acceptance rate: 60.4%
Placed on wait list: 342
Enrolled from wait list: 31
Average GPA: 3.7
ACT range: 24-30
SAT Math range: 560-690
SAT Reading range: 520-630
SAT Writing range: 7-32
Top 10% of class: 47%
Top 25% of class: 80%
Top 50% of class: 98%

Deadlines
Early Action: 11/1
Early Decision: No
Regular Action: 3/1 (priority)
Notification of admission by: 12/13
Common Application: Accepted

Financial Aid
In-state tuition: $9,208
Out-of-state tuition: $28,010
Room: Varies
Board: Varies
Books: Varies
Freshmen receiving need-based aid: 50%
Undergrads rec. need-based aid: 46%
Avg. % of need met by financial aid: 86%
Avg. aid package (freshmen): $14,120
Avg. aid package (undergrads): $13,081
Avg. debt upon graduation: $29,121

Prominent Alumni
Neil Armstrong, astronaut, first man to walk on the moon; Drew Brees, NFL Quarterback; Brian Lamb, C-SPAN Founder.

School Spirit
Mascot: Boilermaker Special
Colors: Old gold and black
Song: *Hail Purdue*

353

College Profiles

QUINNIPIAC UNIVERSITY

275 Mount Carmel Avenue, Hamden, CT 06518
Admissions: 800-462-1944 · Financial Aid: 800-462-1944
Email: admissions@quinnipiac.edu · Website: http://www.quinnipiac.edu

From the College

"Quinnipiac University is committed to providing high-quality academic programs in a student-oriented environment, on a campus with a strong sense of community. The 600-acre campus (250-acre Mt. Carmel campus, plus nearby 250-acre York Hill campus plus 100-acre North Haven campus) is located minutes from New Haven, midway between New York City and Boston, and offers a variety of majors along with internship and clinical experiences in business, communications, health sciences, education, liberal arts and sciences and law to the 6,000 undergraduate and 2,000 graduate and part-time students.

"Students benefit from extensive opportunities for internships, community service, 'alternative' spring break service trips, clinical practice sites, and they live and study in a safe suburban setting. Excellent facilities on the Mount Carmel campus include the fully digital high-definition production study, audio production studio and the news technology center in the Ed McMahon center for Communications, the Arnold Bernhard Library (open 24-7), the Financial Technology Center (trading room) in the Lender School of Business building. On the North Haven campus, home to the professional programs in the Schools of Health Sciences, nursing and education, labs include the movement study, motion analysis and biomechanics labs, a radiography suite including: CT scan, MRI, mammography and ultrasound labs; for nursing - clinical simulation labs, pediatric/neonatal, intensive care units, and for all programs - physical diagnosis and exam suites, and health assessment labs. A School of Medicine opened in 2013. Twenty-one athletic teams (nickname, the 'Bobcats') compete in Division I sports (men's and women's ice hockey is a member of the ECAC, other teams are in the NEC (Northeast Conference). The TD Bank 3300 seat 'twin' arenas for basketball and ice hockey opened January 2007 on the nearby 'York Hill' campus of 250 acres - with residence facilities, a student center and parking garage.

"Quinnipiac is adjacent to the 1,700-acre Sleeping Giant State Park with trails for hiking and scenic views. Seventy-five percent of the entering class comes from out of state and 96 percent of the freshmen live on campus. Construction of new residence halls added 1,500 beds on the York Hill campus, along with a lodge-like student center, and the views are spectacular. Although resident freshmen may not bring a car to campus, the university maintains an extensive campus shuttle system which brings students to nearby shopping, restaurants, museums and the New Haven train station with access to Metro- North, and Amtrak."

Campus Setting

Quinnipiac, founded in 1929, is a private university offering 51 undergraduate and 17 graduate majors on a picturesque 600-acre campus located in Hamden, Connecticut which is eight miles from New Haven and mid-way between New York City and Boston. The 6,000 undergraduate and 2,000 graduate students choose from majors in the College of Arts and Sciences, Schools of Business, Communications, Health Sciences, Nursing, Education and Law. Small classes, excellent facilities and opportunities for clinical experience, internships and study abroad highlight the academic life on campus. Division I athletics, extensive intramurals, recreation, clubs, organizations, leadership development, community involvement and student government provides a student focus and sense of community. Housing is guaranteed for three years to incoming freshmen and most seniors opt to live in university housing as well. The nearby York Hill campus houses the TD Bank Sports Center, a student center and four-story parking garage. A four-year institution, Quinnipiac University has an enrollment of 8,803 students. Quinnipiac University has campus facilities including: library · museum · labs · financial trading room · production studio · news technology center · intensive care unit · CT scan lab · MRI · radiography · ultrasound · movement study · motion analysis · biomechanics · ergonomics and assistive technology · orthopedics · rehabilitative sciences · clinical simulation · pediatric/neonatal · clinical skills · physical diagnosis · health assessment labs. Quinnipiac University provides on-campus housing with 60 units that can accommodate 5,100 students. Housing options: coed dorms · single-student apartments. Recreation and sports facilities include: baseball, field hockey, soccer and softball fields · basketball arena · tennis courts · ice hockey arena · indoor track · recreation center.

Student Life and Activities

Eighty percent of students live on campus. As reported by a school official, "Quinnipiac students have access to both on campus and near campus social and cultural activities throughout the year. A student life 'activity fair' starts the fall semester where each club and organization displays materials to attract new members. Student government supports the undergraduate clubs with budget assistance. Major weekend events are hosted several times during the year, as well as speakers, 'alternative spring break' trips and community service. Many groups fund raise for national and local charities through activities and awareness."

Popular on campus gathering spots include the recreation center, the new 'Rocky Top' lodge-like student center, and the Mount Carmel library. Popular off-campus gathering spots include Sleeping Giant State Park for hiking, and various locations in Hamden and New Haven. Popular campus events include the December Holiday Party, Parents and Family Weekend, Little Siblings Weekend, Midnight madness and the Fall and Spring concert weekends. Quinnipiac University has 110 official student organizations. Popular groups on campus include the Student Government, Resident Assistants and Intramural Athletics. Students support particularly the basketball and hockey teams at the TD Bank Sports Center. There are intramural teams available: basketball · beach volleyball · bowling · flag football · indoor soccer · kickball · softball · tennis · Ultimate Frisbee · volleyball. Quinnipiac University is a member of the NCAA, MAAC Conference and ECAC Hockey.

Academics and Learning Environment

Quinnipiac University has 422 full-time and 599 part-time faculty members, offering a student-to-faculty ratio of 12:1. The most common course size is 10 to 19 students. Quinnipiac University offers 67 majors with the most popular being management, nursing and communications and least popular being microbiology/immunology and gerontology. The school has a general core requirement. Cooperative education is not offered. All first-year students must maintain a 1.8 GPA or higher to avoid academic probation, and a minimum overall GPA of 2.0 is required to graduate. Other programs include: self-designed majors · double majors · dual degrees · honors program · internships · distance learning.

QUINNIPIAC UNIVERSITY

Highlights

Quinnipiac University
Hamden, CT (Pop. 56,913)
Location: Large town
Four-year private
Founded: 1929
Website: http://www.quinnipiac.edu

Students
Total enrollment: 8,803
Undergrads: 6,542
Freshmen: 1,804
Part-time students: 4%
From out-of-state: 77%
From public schools: 65%
Male/Female: 38%/62%
Live on-campus: 80%
In fraternities: 14%
In sororities: 15%
Off-campus employment rating: Excellent
Caucasian: 78%
African American: 4%
Hispanic: 8%
Asian: 2%
Hawaiian or Pacific Islander: <1%
Native American: <1%
Mixed (2+ ethnicities): 2%
International: 2%

Academics
Calendar: 4-1-4 system
Student/faculty ratio: 12:1
Class size 9 or fewer: 12%
Class size 10-29: 63%
Class size 30-49: 24%
Class size 50-99: 1%
Class size 100 or more: -
Returning freshmen: 87%
Six-year graduation rate: 76%

Most Popular Majors
Management
Nursing
Communications

355

College Profiles

QUINNIPIAC UNIVERSITY

Admissions
Applicants: 20,695
Accepted: 13,912
Acceptance rate: 67.2%
Placed on wait list: 1,640
Enrolled from wait list: 180
Average GPA: 3.4
ACT range: 22-26
SAT Math range: 510-610
SAT Reading range: 490-580
SAT Writing range: 2-19
Top 10% of class: 25%
Top 25% of class: 66%
Top 50% of class: 93%

Deadlines
Early Action: No
Early Decision: 11/1
Regular Action: Rolling admissions
Common Application: Accepted

Financial Aid
In-state tuition: $39,170
Out-of-state tuition: $39,170
Room: $11,690
Board: $2,800
Books: $800
Freshmen receiving need-based aid: 65%
Undergrads rec. need-based aid: 63%
Avg. % of need met by financial aid: 64%
Avg. aid package (freshmen): $24,923
Avg. aid package (undergrads): $24,214
Avg. debt upon graduation: $44,552

Prominent Alumni
Murray Lender, Lender's Bagels; Bill Weldon, Johnson & Johnson.

School Spirit
Mascot: Bobcats
Colors: Navy and gold

America's
Best Colleges for
B Students

B Student Support and Success

Quinnipiac students have three special courses open to them to help introduce them to major topics in university life: QU 101, 201 and 301. The first course is QU 101, "The Individual in the Community." It explores the relationship between individual and community identities, the rights and responsibilities of citizenship, and the ethics of community life. In QU 201, "National Community," students explore the structure of the pluralistic American community and in QU 301, "Global Community," students find out about the political, social, cultural, ecological and economic systems that shape global communities. The college also offers a program called Writing across the Curriculum where students are engaged in hands-on learning experiences to become better writers, strong critical thinkers and innovative scholars.

Quinnipiac University provides a variety of support programs, including: academic · career · personal · psychological · veterans · non-traditional students · religious. The average freshman year GPA is 2.9, and 87 percent of freshmen students return for their sophomore year. Once they're done with college, many students enter into the workforce, and approximately 34 percent pursue a graduate degree immediately after graduation. One year after graduation, the school reports that only six percent of graduates have entered graduate school. Out of those students that do enter the workforce, approximately 82 percent enter a field related to their major within six months of their initial graduation. Here are some companies that most frequently take on graduates from Quinnipiac University: ABC stations and affiliates · AmeriCorps · Bristol-Myers Squibb Medical Imaging · CBS · CNN · elementary and high schools in several states · ESPN · Deloitte · MTV · NBC · The Travelers.

Support for Students with Learning Disabilities

Students with learning disabilities, commonly referred to as LD students, may take advantage of specific support programs offered by Quinnipiac University. According to the school, students are encouraged to self-advocate for services needed and can self-disclose at any point following their admissions decision. LD students will want to investigate the following: tutors · learning center. Individual or small group tutorials are also available in: time management · organizational skills · learning strategies · specific subject areas · writing labs · math labs · study skills.

How to Get Admitted

For admissions decisions, non-academic factors considered: interview · extracurricular activities · character/personal qualities · volunteer work · work experience · state of residency · minority affiliation · alumni relationship. A high school diploma is required, although a GED is also accepted for admissions consideration. SAT or ACT test scores are required of all applicants. *According to the admissions office:* Minimum combined SAT Reasoning score (reading and math) of 1050, rank in top two-fifths of secondary school class and minimum 3.0 GPA recommended. Minimum academic requirements may be higher for some majors. *Academic units recommended:* 4 English, 3 Math, 3 Science, 3 Social Studies, 2 Foreign Language.

How to Pay for College

To apply for financial aid, students should submit the following: Free Application for Federal Student Aid (FAFSA) · CSS/Financial Aid PROFILE. Quinnipiac University participates in the Federal Work Study program. *Need-based aid programs include:* scholarships and grants · general need-based awards · Federal Pell grants · state scholarships and grants · college-based scholarships and grants · private scholarships and grants. *Non-need-based aid programs include:* scholarships and grants · state scholarships and grants · athletic scholarships · ROTC scholarships · international scholarships/grants.

RADFORD UNIVERSITY

P.O. Box 6890, Radford, VA 24142
Admissions: 540-831-5371 · Financial Aid: 540-831-5408
Email: admissions@radford.edu · Website: http://www.radford.edu

From the College

Located in the heart of Virginia's New River Valley, Radford University is home to more than 9,000 students. The institution's seven colleges—Science and Technology, Humanities and Behavioral Sciences, Business and Economics, Health and Human Services, Education and Human Development, Visual and Performing Arts and Graduate and Professional Studies—provide a comprehensive and dynamic academic experience known for close student-faculty collaboration. Nationally recognized professors teach in classroom settings that are pleasant and technologically advanced. In all, RU offers more than 150 programs at the bachelor's, master's and doctoral levels. Within the last few years, the university has added a master's degree in occupational therapy and doctorates in nursing practice, counseling psychology and physical therapy. Progress continues on a $212 million building and renovation program designed to transform its American classic campus with 21st century opportunities. A 2009 renovation of Young Hall created one of the most technologically advanced academic buildings in the United States. Upon completion of a $44 million signature building for the College of Business and Economics in fall 2012, construction on a new Center for the Sciences began. A highly energized student center, which is home to all types of programs, organizations, recreation and food, offers RU students a diversity of opportunities outside the classroom. In addition, the university's NCAA Division I sports teams, nicknamed the Highlanders, provide entertainment and promote school spirit. The public university is not only recognized for its picturesque and well-maintained green space, but is also considered a national leader in environmental sustainability."

Campus Setting

Radford is a comprehensive, mid-sized university located in the Blue Ridge Mountains of Southwest Virginia. Founded as a teachers college for women in 1910, it became co-educational in 1972. Programs are offered through the Colleges of Business and Economics, Education and Human Development, Health and Human Services, Humanities and Behavioral Sciences, Science and Technology, Visual and Performing Arts and Graduate and Professional Studies. Its 191-acre campus is located in Radford, 45 miles west of Roanoke. A four-year public institution, Radford University has an enrollment of 9,928 students. The campus facilities include: library · gallery · museum · planetarium · nursing simulation lab · speech and hearing clinic · observatory · conservatory · athletic trainer lab · recital hall · forensics institute · advanced GIS and GPS capabilities · center for visual and performing arts. Radford University provides on-campus housing with 21 units that can accommodate 3,185 students. Housing options: coed dorms · single-student apartments · special housing for disabled students. Recreation and sports facilities include: arena · baseball park · field hockey · gymnasium · practice field · soccer and track stadiums · softball complex · swimming pool · tennis court · weight rooms.

Student Life and Activities

Sixty-four percent of students live off campus. A popular on-campus gathering spot is the Bonnie Hurlburt Student Center. Popular campus events include Up All Night at the Bonnie, spring concert/major visiting performer(s), Bonnie Days of Spring, Homecoming, Family Weekend, Winter and Spring Commencement, movie series and Highlander Picnic. Radford University has 235 official student organizations. Popular groups on campus include the Student Government Association and fraternities and sororities. There are intramural teams available: aerobics · basketball · bowling · climbing wall · disc golf · football · racquetball · soccer · softball · table tennis · tennis · volleyball · water polo. Radford University is a member of the Big South Conference (Division I).

Academics and Learning Environment

Radford University has 433 full-time and 264 part-time faculty members, offering a student-to-faculty ratio of 18:1. The most common course size is 20 to 29 students. Radford University offers 59 majors with the most popular being interdisciplinary studies, criminal justice and exercise/sport/health education and least popular being anthropological sciences, philosophy/religious studies and geography. The school has a general core requirement. Cooperative education is not offered. All first-year students must maintain a 2.0 GPA or higher to avoid academic probation. Other programs include: self-designed majors · pass/fail grading option · independent study · double majors · dual degrees · accelerated study · honors program · internships · distance learning certificate programs.

B Student Support and Success

Radford's Learning Assistance and Resource Center "strives to help all Radford University students achieve academic success in all disciplines." Through both individual and group tutoring sessions, students can get help from tutors who are certified by the College Reading and Learning Association. Writing tutors help with any writing assignments and math and science tutors helps with everything from grasping abstract concepts to reinforcing problem solving skills. Workshops and one-on-one consultations offer guidance in learning skills, reading comprehension and test taking strategies. Students with special needs, with language assistance, physical disabilities or learning challenges can get additional help.

Radford University provides a variety of support programs including dedicated guidance for: military · veterans · non-traditional students · family planning. Additional counseling services include: learning skills workshop. Radford University offers remedial and refresher courses in: reading · writing · math · study skills. Other remedial services include sciences and statistics, ESL. The average freshman year GPA is 2.7, and 78 percent of freshmen students return for their sophomore year. While many students do enter the workforce after college, approximately 13 percent pursue a graduate degree immediately after graduation. One year after graduation, the school reports that a total of 19 percent of graduates have entered graduate school. Some companies that most frequently hire graduates from Radford University are: Advance Auto Parts · Blue Ridge Behavioral Healthcare · Carilion Clinic · Carter Machinery Company · CGI · Cvent · Department of Veterans Affairs · DLT Solutions · Fasternal · Kearney & Company · Mutual of Omaha · Peace Corps · Target Corporation · Wells Fargo Financial · Wolseley's North American Division · Virginia Asset Management · VTLS.

RADFORD UNIVERSITY

Highlights

Radford University
Radford, VA (Pop. 16,685)
Location: Small town
Four-year public
Founded: 1910
Website: http://www.radford.edu

Students
Total enrollment: 9,928
Undergrads: 8,913
Freshmen: 2,370
Part-time students: 4%
From out-of-state: 7%
From public schools: 92%
Male/Female: 44%/56%
Live on-campus: 36%
In fraternities: 10%
In sororities: 13%
Off-campus employment rating: Good
Caucasian: 78%
African American: 10%
Hispanic: 5%
Asian: 1%
Hawaiian or Pacific Islander: <1%
Native American: <1%
Mixed (2+ ethnicities): 4%
International: 1%

Academics
Calendar: Semester
Student/faculty ratio: 18:1
Class size 9 or fewer: 8%
Class size 10-29: 62%
Class size 30-49: 23%
Class size 50-99: 7%
Class size 100 or more: 1%
Returning freshmen: 78%
Six-year graduation rate: 59%

Most Popular Majors
Interdisciplinary studies
Criminal justice
Exercise/sport/health education

RADFORD UNIVERSITY

Highlights

Admissions
Applicants: 7,774
Accepted: 6,088
Acceptance rate: 78.3%
Placed on wait list: 1,102
Enrolled from wait list: 132
Average GPA: 3.2
ACT range: 18-22
SAT Math range: 450-540
SAT Reading range: 450-540
SAT Writing range: Not reported
Top 10% of class: 6%
Top 25% of class: 22%
Top 50% of class: 61%

Deadlines
Early Action: 12/1
Early Decision: No
Regular Action: Rolling admissions
Common Application: Not accepted

Financial Aid
In-state tuition: $6,386
Out-of-state tuition: $18,626
Room: $4,632
Board: $3,774
Books: $1,100
Freshmen receiving need-based aid: 56%
Undergrads rec. need-based aid: 53%
Avg. % of need met by financial aid: 81%
Avg. aid package (freshmen): $8,575
Avg. aid package (undergrads): $9,316
Avg. debt upon graduation: $25,895

Prominent Alumni
R.J. Kirk, managing director and CEO, Third Security, LLC; Jayma Mays, actress, *Glee*; C. Novel Martin III, CFO, Medical Facilities of America.

School Spirit
Mascot: Highlander
Colors: Red and white

Support for Students with Learning Disabilities

Students with learning disabilities may want to take advantage of some specific support programs offered at Radford University. Sometimes, the college will grant additional time to students with learning disabilities in order to complete their degree. LD students will find the following programs at Radford University rather beneficial: tutors · learning center · testing accommodations · extended time for tests · take-home exam · oral tests · readers · typist/scribe · note-taking services · reading machines · tape recorders · texts on tape · early syllabus · priority registration · waiver of math degree requirement. Individual or small group tutorials are also available in: time management · organizational skills · learning strategies · specific subject areas · study skills. An advisor/advocate from the Disability Resource Office is available to students.

How to Get Admitted

For admissions decisions, non-academic factors considered: interview · extracurricular activities · special talents, interests and abilities · character/personal qualities · volunteer work · work experience · geographical location · alumni relationship. A high school diploma is required, although a GED is also accepted for admissions consideration. SAT or ACT test scores are required of all applicants. SAT Subject Test scores are not required. *Academic units recommended:* 4 English, 4 Math, 4 Science, 2 Social Studies, 4 Foreign Language.

How to Pay for College

To apply for financial aid, students should submit the following: Free Application for Federal Student Aid (FAFSA). Radford University participates in the Federal Work Study program. *Need-based aid programs include:* scholarships and grants · general need-based awards · Federal Pell grants · state scholarships and grants · college-based scholarships and grants · private scholarships and grants. *Non-need-based aid programs include:* scholarships and grants · general need-based awards · state scholarships and grants · creative arts and performance awards · special achievements and activities awards · athletic scholarships · ROTC scholarships · alumni affiliation · leadership scholarships.

America's
Best Colleges for
B Students

RANDOLPH-MACON COLLEGE

P.O. Box 5005, Ashland, VA 23005-5505
Admissions: 800-888-1762 · Financial Aid: 804-752-7259
Email: admissions@rmc.edu · Website: http://www.rmc.edu

From the College

"Randolph-Macon College is located in Ashland just north of Richmond and is a co-educational, liberal arts and sciences college with a mission of developing the minds and character of its students. The college achieves this mission through a combination of personal interaction and academic rigor. Enrollment is kept near 1,200 to maintain an intimate atmosphere. It states that it achieves its mission of developing the minds and character of its students by keeping class size low. Randolph-Macon College has a national reputation for its internships, study abroad and undergraduate research and offers a wealth of social and athletic programs. Founded in 1830, Randolph-Macon College is the oldest United Methodist Church- affiliated college in the nation, a Phi Beta Kappa college and ranked as a Baccalaureate I college by the Carnegie Foundation."

Campus Setting

Randolph-Macon, founded in 1830, is a church-affiliated, liberal arts college. Its 110-acre campus, located in Ashland, includes three buildings on the National Register of Historic Buildings and designated a National Historic Landmark. A four-year private institution, Randolph Macon College has an enrollment of 1,315 students, and has been co-ed since 1971. The school is also affiliated with the United Methodist Church. Campus facilities include: art gallery · observatory · greenhouse · historic buildings. Randolph Macon College provides on-campus housing with 43 units that can accommodate 1,005 students. Housing options: coed dorms · women's dorms · men's dorms · sorority housing · fraternity housing · single-student apartments · special housing for disabled students · special housing for international students. Recreation and sports facilities include a recreational center.

Student Life and Activities

Just over three-quarters (78 percent) of students live on campus. Popular on-campus gathering spots include the Brown Campus Center and Brock Recreational Center. Popular campus events include the Dance Marathon, Springfest, Hampden-Sydney Week and Homecoming. Randolph-Macon College has 80 official student organizations. The most popular are: Chamber singers · concert choir · drama guild · jazz vocal · dance team · pep band · Anime Club · photography club (Vanishing Point) · Campus Activities Board · Student Education Association · Sociology and Anthropology Club · Amnesty International · Habitat for Humanity · Volunteers in Actions · philosophy club · Washington Literary Society · Society for Collegiate Journalists · French, German, Japanese and Spanish Clubs · Organization of Sexual Minorities and Allies · Students for Environmental Action · Society for the Advancement of Management · Mathematics Association of America · Pre-Law · Franklin Debating Society · Judicial Board · Model UN · College Republicans · Young Democrats · Macon Greens · Pre-Med · psychology club · Society for Physics Students · American Chemical Society Student Affiliates · Association of Computing Machinery. For those interested in sports, there are intramural teams such as: basketball · flag football · racquetball · running · soccer · softball · Ultimate Frisbee · volleyball. Randolph-Macon College is a member of the Old Dominion Athletic Conference (Division III).

RANDOLPH-MACON COLLEGE

Randolph-Macon College
Ashland, VA (Pop. 7,289)
Location: Small town
Four-year private
Founded: 1830
Website: http://www.rmc.edu

Students

Total enrollment: 1,315
Undergrads: 1,315
Freshmen: 425
Part-time students: 2%
From out-of-state: 23%
From public schools: 77%
Male/Female: 47%/53%
Live on-campus: 78%
In fraternities: 26%
In sororities: 27%
Off-campus employment rating: Good
Caucasian: 76%
African American: 10%
Hispanic: 4%
Asian: 2%
Hawaiian or Pacific Islander: <1%
Native American: <1%
Mixed (2+ ethnicities): 3%
International: 3%

Academics

Calendar: 4-1-4 system
Student/faculty ratio: 12:1
Class size 9 or fewer: 26%
Class size 10-29: 73%
Class size 30-49: 1%
Class size 50-99: -
Class size 100 or more: -
Returning freshmen: 77%
Six-year graduation rate: 61%

Most Popular Majors

Biology
Psychology
Economics/business

America's
Best Colleges for
B Students

Academics and Learning Environment

Randolph-Macon College has 94 full-time and 55 part-time faculty members, offering a student-to-faculty ratio of 12:1. The most common course size is 10 to 19 students. Of Randolph-Macon College's 34 majors, the most popular are biology, psychology and economics/business. Least popular are French, philosophy and Latin. The school has a general core requirement as well as a religion requirement. Cooperative education is offered. All first-year students must maintain a 2.0 GPA or higher to avoid academic probation, and a minimum overall GPA of 2.0 is required to graduate. Other special academic programs that would appeal to a B student include: independent study · double majors · dual degrees · accelerated study · honors program · Phi Beta Kappa · internships.

B Student Support and Success

Randolph College offers a number of academic services to students. First-year students are assigned faculty advisors to help guide them in making course selections and career decisions. A Career Development Center focuses on helping students to "develop self knowledge related to their career choice and work performance by identifying, assessing and understanding competencies, interests, values and personal characteristics." The Ethyl Science and Mathematics Center provides tutoring to science and math students. The Learning Resources Center has interactive workshops, a Learning Strategies Program to help develop study strategies and clarify academic goals, tutors for every subject and printed and computerized materials.

Randolph-Macon College provides a variety of support programs including: academic · career · personal · psychological · minority students · religious. Randolph-Macon College offers remedial and refresher courses in: reading · writing · math · study skills. The average freshman year GPA is 2.6, and 77 percent of freshmen students return for their sophomore year. Approximately 11 percent of students return for a graduate degree immediately after graduation. A year after graduation, 35 percent of graduates have entered graduate school. Among students who enter the workforce, approximately 34 percent enter a field related to their major within six months of graduation. Companies that most frequently hire graduates from Randolph-Macon College include: Altria · BB&T · Hanover and Henrico County (VA) School System · Phillip Morris · U.S. Government · Virginia State Government.

Support for Students with Learning Disabilities

Randolph-Macon College grants additional time to students with learning disabilities to complete their degree. High school foreign language waivers are accepted. Students with learning disabilities may find these programs quite useful: tutors · learning center · testing accommodations · untimed tests · extended time for tests · take-home exam · exam on tape or computer · note-taking services · reading machines · tape recorders · early syllabus. Individual or small group tutorials are also available in: time management · organizational skills · learning strategies · specific subject areas · writing labs · math labs · study skills. An advisor/advocate from the LD program is available to students. This member also sits on the admissions committee.

How to Get Admitted

For admissions decisions, non-academic factors considered: interview · extracurricular activities · special talents, interests and abilities · character/personal qualities · volunteer work · work experience · state of residency · minority affiliation · alumni relationship. A high school diploma is required, although a GED is also accepted for admissions consideration. SAT or ACT test scores are required of all applicants. SAT Subject Test scores are considered, if submitted, but are not required. *Academic units recommended:* 4 English, 4 Math, 4 Science, 3 Social Studies, 4 Foreign Language.

How to Pay for College

To apply for financial aid, students should submit the following: Free Application for Federal Student Aid (FAFSA) · state aid form. Randolph-Macon College participates in the Federal Work Study program. *Need-based aid programs include:* scholarships and grants · general need-based awards · Federal Pell grants · state scholarships and grants · college-based scholarships and grants · private scholarships and grants · ACG and SMART grants. *Non-need-based aid programs include:* scholarships and grants · general need-based awards · state scholarships and grants · ROTC scholarships.

RANDOLPH-MACON COLLEGE

Highlights

Admissions
Applicants: 2,997
Accepted: 1,909
Acceptance rate: 63.7%
Placed on wait list: 224
Enrolled from wait list: 37
Average GPA: 3.6
ACT range: 21-26
SAT Math range: 490-590
SAT Reading range: 490-590
SAT Writing range: 1-19
Top 10% of class: 14%
Top 25% of class: 48%
Top 50% of class: 83%

Deadlines
Early Action: 11/15
Early Decision: No
Regular Action: 2/1 (priority)
3/1 (final)
Notification of admission by: 4/1
Common Application: Accepted

Financial Aid
In-state tuition: $35,360
Out-of-state tuition: $35,360
Room: $4,950
Board: $4,650
Books: $1,100
Freshmen receiving need-based aid: 75%
Undergrads rec. need-based aid: 75%
Avg. % of need met by financial aid: 78%
Avg. aid package (freshmen): $25,716
Avg. aid package (undergrads): $25,779
Avg. debt upon graduation: $32,020

Prominent Alumni
John W. Craine, Jr., president of SUNY Maritime College; Beth Dunkenberger, former head coach of the Virginia Tech women's basketball team; George Preston Marshall, first owner of the NFL Washington Redskins

School Spirit
Mascot: Yellow Jackets
Colors: Yellow and black

363

College Profiles

RIDER UNIVERSITY

2083 Lawrenceville Road, Lawrenceville, NJ 08648-3099
Admissions: 800-257-9026 · Financial Aid: 609-896-5360
Email: admissions@rider.edu · Website: http://www.rider.edu

From the College

"Rider attracts and graduates talented and motivated students with diverse backgrounds from across the nation and around the world and puts them at the center of our learning and living community. As a learner-centered university dedicated to the education of the whole student, Rider provides students the intellectual resources and breadth of student life opportunities of a comprehensive university with the personal attention and close student-faculty interactions of a liberal arts college. Through a commitment to high quality teaching, scholarship and experiential opportunities, faculty on both campuses provide undergraduate and graduate students programs of study to expand their intellectual, cultural and personal horizons and develop their leadership skills. Our programs in the arts, social sciences, sciences, music, business and education challenge students to become active learners who can acquire, interpret, communicate and apply knowledge within and across disciplines to foster the integrative thinking required in a complex and rapidly changing world. Rider attracts faculty, staff and administrators with diverse backgrounds who create an environment which inspires intellectual and social engagement, stimulates innovation and service and encourages personal and professional development. As key members of our University's community, it is their commitment to our values, vision and mission that will ensure Rider's success."

Campus Setting

With roots dating back to 1865, Rider is a private, co-educational university located on 280 beautiful acres on two campuses in New Jersey, one in Lawrenceville and one in Princeton, both within easy driving distance to New York City and Philadelphia. A four-year institution, Rider University has an enrollment of 5,410 students and has been co-ed since 1866. The campus facilities include: library · art gallery · Holocaust/genocide center · language and journalism labs · multimedia and finance/accounting rooms · multicultural center · flow cytometer · PCR machines · autoclaves · scintillation spectrometer · gamma counter · induction-coupled plasma emission spectro-photometer · nuclear magnetic resonance spectrometer · solomat (submersible instrument for environmental monitoring). Rider University provides on-campus housing with 1,329 units that can accommodate 2,515 students. Housing options: coed dorms · women's dorms · sorority housing · fraternity housing · single-student apartments · special housing for disabled students.

Student Life and Activities

Fifty-seven percent of students live on campus. Rider University has 84 official student organizations. The most popular are: chorus · concert and jazz bands · dance group · debating · drama/theatre group · film society · inspirational choir · jazz ensemble · musical theatre · music ensembles · opera · symphony orchestra · departmental and special-interest groups. Rider University is a member of the Metro Atlantic Athletic Conference (Division I).

Academics and Learning Environment

Rider University has 256 full-time and 338 part-time faculty members, offering a student-to-faculty ratio of 12:1. The most common course size is 10 to 19 students. Rider University offers 82 majors with the most popular being speech/rhetorical studies, elementary education and psychology and least popular being environmental science, Russian language/literature and French language/literature. The school has a general core requirement. Cooperative education is not offered. All first-year students must maintain a 2.0 GPA or higher to avoid academic probation, and a minimum overall GPA of 2.0 is required to graduate. Other programs available: pass/fail grading option · independent study · double majors · dual degrees · honors program · internships · weekend college · distance learning certificate programs.

B Student Support and Success

Tutoring services are available through the Rider Learning Center. Students struggling with academics can meet with peer tutors who have received excellent grades in their courses and are recommended by professors. Tutors work on both a drop-in and appointment basis. The center also offers a math skills lab. In addition to peer tutoring, Rider offers supplemental instruction for the most difficult classes. Students meet together to review notes, go over readings and learn test-taking strategies. Rider has two core classes for first-year students who have not met the criteria for college-level reading. These are "Introduction to Academic Reading" and "College Reading." In the first class, which is required, reading and learning strategies are taught to help students increase their reading comprehension. This class earns two credits. In the second (elective) course, students may earn three credits by developing and improving reading comprehension skills and study strategies.

There is dedicated guidance available at Rider University, including: academic · career · personal · psychological · minority students · veterans · non-traditional students · family planning · religious. Rider University offers remedial and refresher courses in: reading · writing · math · study skills. The average freshman year GPA is 3.0, and 79 percent of freshmen students return for their sophomore year.

Support for Students with Learning Disabilities

Students with learning disabilities may want to research some of the support programs available through Rider University. If deemed necessary, the college will discuss with the LD student various options, such as additional time to complete their degree or a lightened course load. Students with learning disabilities will find the following programs of interest: remedial math · remedial reading · special classes · tutors · learning center · testing accommodations · extended time for tests · take-home exam · oral tests · readers · typist/scribe · note-taking services · reading machines · tape recorders · texts on tape · diagnostic testing service · priority registration · waiver of math degree requirement. Individual or small group tutorials are also available in: time management · organizational skills · learning strategies · specific subject areas · writing labs · math labs · study skills. An advisor/advocate from the LD program is available to students.

How to Get Admitted

For admissions decisions, non-academic factors considered: interview · extracurricular activities · special talents, interests and abilities · character/personal qualities · volunteer work · work experience ·

RIDER UNIVERSITY

Highlights

Rider University
Lawrenceville, NJ (Pop. 4,081)
Location: Large town
Four-year private
Founded: 1865
Website: http://www.rider.edu

Students
Total enrollment: 5,410
Undergrads: 4,419
Part-time students: 14%
From out-of-state: 27%
Male/Female: 41%/59%
Live on-campus: 57%
In fraternities: 5%
In sororities: 9%
Off-campus employment rating: Good
Caucasian: 64%
African American: 10%
Hispanic: 10%
Asian: 4%
Hawaiian or Pacific Islander: <1%
Native American: <1%
Mixed (2+ ethnicities): 2%
International: 4%

Academics
Calendar: Semester
Student/faculty ratio: 12:1
Class size 9 or fewer: 10%
Class size 10-29: 72%
Class size 30-49: 17%
Class size 50-99: 1%
Class size 100 or more: -
Returning freshmen: 79%
Six-year graduation rate: 63%

Most Popular Majors
Speech/rhetorical studies
Elementary education
Psychology

RIDER UNIVERSITY

Admissions

Applicants: 8,078
Accepted: 5,606
Acceptance rate: 69.4%
Placed on wait list: 94
Enrolled from wait list: 47
Average GPA: 3.3
ACT range: 19-25
SAT Math range: 470-580
SAT Reading range: 460-570
SAT Writing range: 2-13
Top 10% of class: 14%
Top 25% of class: 38%
Top 50% of class: 68%

Deadlines

Early Action: 11/15
Early Decision: No
Regular Action: Rolling admissions
Common Application: Accepted

Financial Aid

In-state tuition: $36,120
Out-of-state tuition: $36,120
Room: $8,240
Board: $4,660
Books: $1,500
Freshmen receiving need-based aid: 78%
Undergrads rec. need-based aid: 71%
Avg. % of need met by financial aid: 70%
Avg. aid package (freshmen): $25,177
Avg. aid package (undergrads): $22,352
Avg. debt upon graduation: $32,718

Prominent Alumni

Jennifer Larmore-Powers, international mezzo-soprano opera singer; Thomas J. Lynch, CEO of Tyco Electronics Corporation; Richard 'Digger' Phelps, college basketball analyst for ESPN.

School Spirit

Mascot: Broncos
Colors: Cranberry, white and gray

geographical location · alumni relationship. A high school diploma is required, although a GED is also accepted for admissions consideration. SAT or ACT test scores are required of all applicants. SAT Subject Test scores are not required. *According to the admissions office:* Minimum combined SAT Reasoning score of 900, rank in top half of secondary school class, minimum grade average of 'B', essay and two letters of recommendation recommended. *Academic units recommended:* 4 English, 4 Math, 4 Science, 2 Social Studies, 2 Foreign Language.

How to Pay for College

To apply for financial aid, students should submit the following: Free Application for Federal Student Aid (FAFSA). Rider University participates in the Federal Work Study program. *Need-based aid programs include:* scholarships and grants · general need-based awards · Federal Pell grants · state scholarships and grants · college-based scholarships and grants · private scholarships and grants. *Non-need-based aid programs include:* scholarships and grants · state scholarships and grants · creative arts and performance awards · athletic scholarships.

RIPON COLLEGE

300 Seward Street, Ripon, WI 54971-0248
Admissions: 800-94-RIPON · Financial Aid: 920-748-8101
Email: adminfo@ripon.edu · Website: http://www.ripon.edu

From the College

"Ripon College offers an intensely personal liberal arts education in a residential setting. Part of that education includes a one-on-one dynamic between the student and the faculty member. Communicating Plus emphasizes the development of written and oral communication, critical thinking and problem-solving skills. The curriculum focuses on exploring career choices, selecting opportunities to reach those goals and connecting with faculty and alumni through the classroom, internships and research. Student-faculty collaboration is paramount, which results in participation in state, regional and national conferences and published research articles in many disciplines. Among Ripon's distinctions are a nationally competitive forensics team which offers scholarships to members, three Rhodes Scholars (including a 2002 selection) and a chapter of Phi Beta Kappa."

Campus Setting

Ripon, founded in 1851, is a private liberal arts college. Its 250-acre campus is located in Ripon, 80 miles northwest of Milwaukee. Ripon's curriculum and residential campus create an intimate learning community in which students experience a richly personalized education. The campus facilities include: outdoor classroom and nature preserve · museum · planetarium. Ripon College provides on-campus housing with 496 units that can accommodate 944 students. Housing options: coed dorms · women's dorms · men's dorms · sorority housing · fraternity housing. Recreation and sports facilities include: gymnasium · racquetball · squash and tennis courts · swimming pool · weight rooms.

Student Life and Activities

Ninety-one percent of students live on campus. According to the editor of the school newspaper, "Due to the interests of many professors and the more mature students, Ripon College has a rich cultural life. There are always great plays, concerts, art exhibits and comedians." Students gather at the library, cafeteria, pub, gym and the art building. Popular events include Homecoming, Murder Mystery, Late Night Breakfast, Joyce to the World (holiday celebration), Springfest, Iron Chef Cooking Competition, Couch Potato Play-offs, Martin Luther King Week, Diversity Week, International Night, Soul Food Dinners and Extrava-game-za. Ripon College has 45 official student organizations. Groups with a strong presence include Greek organizations and the Student Media & Activities Committee. There are intramural teams available: basketball · bowling · flag football · floor hockey · indoor soccer · inner tube water polo · softball · tennis · volleyball. Ripon College is a member of the Midwest Conference (Division III).

Academics and Learning Environment

Ripon College offers a student-to-faculty ratio of 13:1. Ripon College offers 32 majors with the most popular being history and English and least popular being environmental studies and computer science. The school has a general core requirement. Cooperative education is not offered. All first-year students must maintain a 1.8 GPA or higher to avoid academic probation. Other programs: self-designed majors · pass/fail grading option · independent study · double majors · accelerated study · Phi Beta Kappa · internships.

RIPON COLLEGE

B Student Support and Success

Ripon offers new college students an extensive program called Communicating Plus that emphasizes the core basics of written and oral communication. The course focuses on communication, as well as critical thinking and problem solving skills. It involves student peer mentoring and outreach programming. Student Support Services offers a number of ways to help struggling students. Tutoring is available in a number of subject areas and serves as a supplement to faculty assistance. A group of peer contacts meet regularly with students to facilitate communication between participants and staff. The SSS also offers academic, life and career guidance. In addition, SSS offers cultural enrichment experiences on and off campus.

Ripon College offers its students a wide array of support programs, including: academic · career · personal · minority students · military · family planning. The average freshman year GPA is 3.0, and 81 percent of freshman students return for their sophomore year. When it comes to after college, however, many students dedicate themselves to the workforce. Approximately 21 percent decide to pursue a graduate degree immediately after graduation. The school reports that after one year, 28 percent of graduates have entered graduate school. Among students who enter the workforce, approximately 63 percent of them enter a field related to their original major within six months of graduation. This is a list of companies that most frequently hire these graduates: Abbott Laboratories · U.S. Cellular · TEK Systems · US Bank · Environmental Protection Agency · Accenture · AmeriCorps · Convance Labs · Hewitt Associates · M&I Bank · Peace Corps · Wells Fargo Financial · DNR.

Support for Students with Learning Disabilities

Students with learning disabilities will want to take full advantage of Ripon College's support programs. High school foreign language waivers are accepted. LD students will want to research the following: tutors · untimed tests · extended time for tests · take-home exam · oral tests · readers · note-taking services · tape recorders · early syllabus · waiver of math degree requirement. Individual or small group tutorials are also available in: time management · organizational skills · learning strategies · specific subject areas · writing labs · math labs · study skills. An advisor/advocate from the Student Support Services is available to students.

How to Get Admitted

For admissions decisions, non-academic factors considered: interview · extracurricular activities · special talents, interests and abilities · character/personal qualities · volunteer work · work experience · state of residency · minority affiliation · alumni relationship. A high school diploma is required, although a GED is also accepted for admissions consideration. SAT or ACT test scores are required of all applicants. *According to the admissions office:* Minimum SAT Reasoning score of 1149 (composite ACT score of 24), minimum 3.4 GPA and rank in top quarter of secondary school class recommended. *Academic units recommended:* 4 English, 4 Math, 4 Science, 4 Social Studies, 1 Foreign Language.

How to Pay for College

To apply for financial aid, students should submit the following: Free Application for Federal Student Aid (FAFSA). Ripon College participates in the Federal Work Study program. *Need-based aid programs include:* scholarships and grants · general need-based awards · Federal Pell grants · state scholarships and grants · college-based scholarships and grants · private scholarships and grants. *Non-need-based aid programs include:* scholarships and grants · general need-based awards · state scholarships and grants · creative arts and performance awards · special achievements and activities awards · special characteristics awards · ROTC scholarships.

RIPON COLLEGE

Highlights

Admissions
Applicants: 1,320
Accepted: 990
Acceptance rate: 75%
Average GPA: 3.4
ACT range: 21-28
SAT Math range: 510-680
SAT Reading range: 490-630
SAT Writing range: Not reported
Top 10% of class: 30%
Top 25% of class: 61%
Top 50% of class: 94%

Deadlines
Early Action: 12/1
Early Decision: No
Regular Action: Rolling admissions
Common Application: Accepted

Financial Aid
In-state tuition: $33,207
Out-of-state tuition: $33,207
Room: $4,665
Board: $4,420
Books: $800
Freshmen receiving need-based or merit-based aid: 100%
Avg. aid package (freshmen): Not reported
Avg. aid package (undergrads): Not reported

Prominent Alumni
Spencer Tracy, actor; Harrison Ford, actor.

School Spirit
Mascot: Red Hawks
Colors: Crimson and white

College Profiles

ROANOKE COLLEGE

221 College Lane, Salem, VA 24153-3794
Admissions: 800-388-2276 · Financial Aid: 800-200-9221
Email: admissions@roanoke.edu · Website: http://www.roanoke.edu

From the College

"Roanoke College prepares its 2,057 students for their futures through its commitment to providing a true classic college experience. With a focus on learning firsthand and close personal connections, students receive a strong liberal arts foundation that is applied in a unique way to modern and future issues. Depth of knowledge comes from strong majors and experiential learning through independent study research projects, internships and similar experiences. Breadth of knowledge comes from a series of unique core courses that span the four years of the undergraduate experience. In the Intellectual Inquiry core curriculum, students get to choose from a wide range of focused special topic courses.

"At Roanoke College, students learn directly from professors who are experts in their fields. Ninety-five percent of the college's tenure-track faculty members have the highest degrees possible in their fields, and do scholarly work in their academic disciplines. The close-knit academic environment allows strong mentoring of students by these experts. This relationship also leads students to excellent graduate school placements or directly into fulfilling careers. While at Roanoke College, students also benefit from involvements as leaders or participants in the college's 100+ clubs and organizations, and on nationally ranked athletic teams.

"With half of its students from Virginia and half from out of state, the college offers regional and national exposure. Alumni have attended a fine selection of graduate schools such as Johns Hopkins, Duke, Columbia, University of Pennsylvania and Yale. Medical and professional schools are common destinations for graduates - two recent Roanoke alumni were inducted into the national medical school honor society at the University of Virginia. Graduates have gone on to fascinating careers starting their own businesses, doing scientific research or pursuing careers from underwater archaeology and medicine to television production, humanitarianism and government. Roanoke College seeks to give each student a passion for lifelong learning, service and leadership, along with an in-depth area of expertise."

Campus Setting

Roanoke, founded in 1842, is a church-affiliated, liberal arts college. The 80-acre campus, including several buildings registered as National Historic Landmarks, is located in Salem, seven miles west of Roanoke. A four-year private institution, Roanoke College has an enrollment of 2,029 students and has been co-ed since 1930. The school is also affiliated with the Evangelical Lutheran Church. The school also has a library with 270,620 books. Roanoke College provides on-campus housing that can accommodate 1,572 students. Housing options: coed dorms · women's dorms · men's dorms · sorority housing · fraternity housing · single-student apartments. Recreation and sports facilities include: golf club · field · fitness center · stadium · YMCA located off-campus · gymnasium · track.

Student Life and Activities

Seventy-nine percent of students live on campus. Popular gathering spots for students include the Colket student center, the back quad and local restaurants such as Mac and Bob's and Macado's. Popular campus events include Fridays on the Quad, the President's Ball, Winterfest, Relay For Life and Alumni Weekend. Roanoke College has 100 official student organizations. Groups with a strong presence on campus include Greek fraternities and sororities and a co-ed service fraternity. The most popular student organizations are: Mainstreet (vocal) · Looking for an Echo (vocal) · Campus Activities Board · Outdoor Adventures · Earthbound · Habitat for Humanity. There are intramural teams available: basketball · beach volleyball · canoeing · disc golf · dodgeball · flag football · hiking · kickball · mountain biking · soccer · softball. Roanoke College is a member of the Old Dominion Athletic Conference (Division III).

Academics and Learning Environment

Roanoke College has 167 full-time and 49 part-time faculty members, offering a student-to-faculty ratio of 11:1. The most common course size is 10 to 19 students. Roanoke College offers 32 majors with the most popular being business administration, psychology and history and least popular being Christian studies, physics and health/physical education. The school has a general core requirement. Cooperative education is not offered. All first-year students must maintain a 1.7 GPA or higher to avoid academic probation, and a minimum overall GPA of 2.0 is required to graduate. Other programs: pass/fail grading option · independent study · double majors · dual degrees · accelerated study · honors program · Phi Beta Kappa · internships.

B Student Support and Success

Roanoke College's Center for Learning and Teaching offers a number of special services to help the B student. It is located in the Fintel Library, and all students are welcomed on a drop-in or appointment basis. A Writing Center provides students with assistance for creating papers for class, while peer mentoring is also available as is subject tutoring. A program called Success Skills Forum offers students access to workshops that deal with the transitional issues of college life. Workshop titles include these: "Getting Started, Getting Organized," "Time Management," "Reading Textbooks and Taking Notes," "Study Skills" and "Test Preparation."

Roanoke College provides dedicated guidance for: academic · career · personal · psychological · minority students · non-traditional students · family planning · religious. The average freshman year GPA is 2.8, and 81 percent of freshmen students return for their sophomore year. Out of the total amount of students who enter the workforce, approximately 86 percent of them enter a field related to their major within six months of graduation.

Support for Students with Learning Disabilities

Students with learning disabilities may wish take advantage of some specific support programs available at Roanoke College. LD students should research the following list: tutors · learning center · testing accommodations · untimed tests · extended time for tests · oral tests · note-taking services · tape recorders. Individual or small group tutorials are also available in: time management · organizational skills · learning strategies · specific subject areas · writing labs · study skills. An advisor/advocate from the LD program is available to students.

ROANOKE COLLEGE

ROANOKE COLLEGE

Highlights

Admissions
Applicants: 4,167
Accepted: 3,034
Acceptance rate: 72.8%
Placed on wait list: 112
Enrolled from wait list: 12
Average GPA: 3.4
ACT range: 21-26
SAT Math range: 490-590
SAT Reading range: 490-600
SAT Writing range: 3-18
Top 10% of class: 18%
Top 25% of class: 42%
Top 50% of class: 76%

Deadlines
Early Action: No
Early Decision: 11/1
Regular Action: Rolling admissions
Common Application: Accepted

Financial Aid
In-state tuition: $36,688
Out-of-state tuition: $36,688
Room: $5,524
Board: $6,400
Books: $1,000
Freshmen receiving need-based aid: 76%
Undergrads rec. need-based aid: 74%
Avg. % of need met by financial aid: 77%
Avg. aid package (freshmen): $29,320
Avg. aid package (undergrads): $27,864
Avg. debt upon graduation: $32,311

Prominent Alumni
Bettie Sue Masters, professor, University of Texas Health Science Center; Jay Piccola, president, PUMA North America; Phil Conserva, TV producer, *Crime Scene Investigation* series.

School Spirit
Mascot: Maroons
Colors: Maroon and grey
Song: *Roanoke College Alma Mater*

How to Get Admitted

For admissions decisions, non-academic factors considered: interview · extracurricular activities · special talents, interests and abilities · character/personal qualities · volunteer work · work experience · state of residency · minority affiliation · alumni relationship. A high school diploma is required, although a GED is also accepted for admissions consideration. SAT or ACT test scores are required of all applicants. SAT Subject Test scores are considered, if submitted, but are not required. *Academic units recommended:* 4 English, 3 Math, 2 Science, 2 Social Studies, 4 Foreign Language.

How to Pay for College

To apply for financial aid, students should submit the following: Free Application for Federal Student Aid (FAFSA) · state aid form. Roanoke College participates in the Federal Work Study program. *Need-based aid programs include:* scholarships and grants · general need-based awards · Federal Pell grants · state scholarships and grants · college-based scholarships and grants · private scholarships and grants. *Non-need-based aid programs include:* scholarships and grants · general need-based awards · state scholarships and grants · creative arts and performance awards.

372

ROGER WILLIAMS UNIVERSITY

1 Old Ferry Road, Bristol, RI 02809
Admissions: 800-458-7144, extension 3500
Financial Aid: 800-458-7144, extension 3100
Email: admit@rwu.edu · Website: http://www.rwu.edu

From the College

"Roger Williams University is a regional leader in the liberal arts strengthened by professional schools. The 140-acre coastal campus lies in Bristol, Rhode Island, and is easily accessible from Boston and New York. Accredited by the New England Association of Schools and Colleges, the university draws over 5,000 undergraduate, graduate and professional students. Nearly 40 undergraduate majors blend the traditional and innovative, cultivating multiple areas of expertise. The university also offers six graduate programs and the state's only law school. The campus includes modern facilities, recreation, athletics and social opportunities. Students gain the tools to succeed in careers and further study."

Campus Setting

Roger Williams University, founded in 1956, is a private independent university, located on a 140-acre campus on Mount Hope Bay in Bristol, RI. A four-year institution, Roger Williams University has an enrollment of 4,732 students. The campus facilities include: library · performing arts center · center for marine and natural sciences. Roger Williams University provides on-campus housing that can accommodate 2,995 students. Housing options: coed dorms · single-student apartments. Recreation and sports facilities include: aquatic center · athletic fields · fitness center · gymnasium · recreation center · tennis courts.

Student Life and Activities

Sixty-three percent of students live on campus. Roger Williams University has 92 official student organizations. The most popular are: animal rights/environmental club · art society · bagpipe and pep bands · chess club · chorus · Commuters in Action · creative writing club · dance club · Elizabethan society · faith choir · Habitat for Humanity · historic preservation club · lesbian/gay/bisexual/transgender alliance · political studies club · psychology club · stage company · Students Against Destructive Decisions · construction engineering society · aquaculture club · natural science club. For those interested in sports, there are intramural teams such as: basketball · indoor soccer · soccer · softball · water basketball. Roger Williams University is a member of the Commonwealth Coast Conference (Division III) and New England College Wrestling Association (Division III).

Academics and Learning Environment

Roger Williams University has 203 full-time and 268 part-time faculty members, offering a student-to-faculty ratio of 14:1. The most common course size is 20 to 29 students. Roger Williams University offers 75 majors with the most popular being criminal justice, business management and psychology and least popular being economics, American studies and environmental chemistry. The school has a general core requirement. Cooperative education is not offered. All first-year students must maintain a 1.8 GPA or higher to avoid academic probation, and a minimum overall GPA of 2.0 is required to graduate. Other programs available include: self-designed majors · pass/fail grading option · independent study · double majors · honors program · internships · distance learning.

373

College Profiles

ROGER WILLIAMS UNIVERSITY

Roger Williams University
Bristol (Pop. 22,954)
Location: Small town
Four-year private
Founded: 1956
Website: http://www.rwu.edu

Students
Total enrollment: 4,732
Undergrads: 4,411
Freshmen: 1,208
Part-time students: 12%
From out-of-state: 83%
Male/Female: 50%/50%
Live on-campus: 63%
Off-campus employment rating: Fair
Caucasian: 75%
African American: 2%
Hispanic: 5%
Asian: 1%
Hawaiian or Pacific Islander: <1%
Native American: <1%
Mixed (2+ ethnicities): 2%
International: 5%

Academics
Calendar: Semester
Student/faculty ratio: 14:1
Class size 9 or fewer: 12%
Class size 10-29: 77%
Class size 30-49: 11%
Class size 50-99: -
Class size 100 or more: -
Returning freshmen: 83%
Six-year graduation rate: 63%

Most Popular Majors
Criminal justice
Business management
Psychology

B Student Support and Success

Roger Williams University provides a number of helpful tools for the B student, including three university libraries on site. The school's Center for Academic Development offers workshops, seminars and individual tutorial sessions. Topics such as time management, organization, note taking, textbook strategies, test preparation, learning styles, classroom technology and academic success are all covered. A Writing Center helps with the development of papers from beginning to end, while a Math Center helps with homework in a number of math courses. Finally, a Core Tutoring Center provides peer tutors for the school's five-course interdisciplinary Core Curriculum.

Roger Williams University offers support programs to its students, including: academic · career · personal · psychological · minority students · military · veterans · non-traditional students · family planning. Roger Williams University offers remedial and refresher courses in: reading · writing · math · study skills. The average freshman year GPA is 3.0, and 83 percent of freshmen students return for their sophomore year. Some companies that most frequently employ graduates from Roger Williams University include: State Street Bank and Trust · MEDITECH · U.S. Army · Fidelity Investments · Kaestle Boos Associates Inc. · Perkins & Will · PricewaterhouseCoopers.

Support for Students with Learning Disabilities

Students with learning disabilities will be pleased when they discover the various support programs available to them through Roger Williams University. If deemed appropriate, the college will grant additional time to LD students so that they can complete their degree. The college might also provide LD students with a lightened course load. Students with learning disabilities might find this list potentially helpful: tutors · learning center · extended time for tests · readers · note-taking services. Individual or small group tutorials are also available in: time management · organizational skills · learning strategies · writing labs · math labs · study skills. An advisor/advocate from the LD program is available to students.

How to Get Admitted

For admissions decisions, non-academic factors considered: interview · extracurricular activities · special talents, interests and abilities · character/personal qualities · volunteer work · work experience · state of residency · alumni relationship. A high school diploma is required, although a GED is also accepted for admissions consideration. SAT or ACT test scores are required for some applicants. SAT Subject Test scores are considered, if submitted, but are not required. *According to the admissions office:* Additional units of humanities, math, science and social studies recommended. *Academic units recommended:* 4 Math, 4 Science, 3 Social Studies, 2 Foreign Language.

How to Pay for College

To apply for financial aid, students should submit the following: Free Application for Federal Student Aid (FAFSA) · CSS/Financial Aid PROFILE · Tax forms. Roger Williams University participates in the Federal Work Study program. *Need-based aid programs include:*

scholarships and grants · general need-based awards · Federal Pell grants · state scholarships and grants · college-based scholarships and grants · private scholarships and grants. *Non-need-based aid programs include:* scholarships and grants · state scholarships and grants.

ROGER WILLIAMS UNIVERSITY

Highlights

Admissions
Applicants: 9,021
Accepted: 7,305
Acceptance rate: 81.0%
Placed on wait list: 376
Enrolled from wait list: 5
Average GPA: 3.2
ACT range: Not reported
SAT Math range: 500-600
SAT Reading range: 480-580
SAT Writing range: 1-14
Top 10% of class: 14%
Top 25% of class: 37%
Top 50% of class: 75%

Deadlines
Early Action: 11/7
Early Decision: No
Regular Action: Rolling admissions
Common Application: Accepted

Financial Aid
In-state tuition: $29,976
Out-of-state tuition: $29,976
Room: $7,840
Board: $3,430
Books: $900
Freshmen receiving need-based aid: 66%
Undergrads rec. need-based aid: 61%
Avg. % of need met by financial aid: 83%
Avg. aid package (freshmen): $20,164
Avg. aid package (undergrads): $20,050
Avg. debt upon graduation: $23,965

Prominent Alumni
James W. Nuttall, United States Army Major General; Joe Polisena, former member of the Rhode Island State Senate.

School Spirit
Mascot: Hawk
Colors: Blue and gold

RUST COLLEGE

Highlights

Rust College
Holly Springs, MS (Pop. 7,549)
Location: Small town
Four-year private
Founded: 1866
Website: http://www.rustcollege.edu

Students
Total enrollment: 934
From out-of-state: 63%
Male/Female: 39%/61%
Live on-campus: 67%
Off-campus employment rating: Fair
Caucasian: <1%
African American: 95%
Hispanic: <1%
Asian: <1%
Hawaiian or Pacific Islander: <1%
Native American: <1%
Mixed (2+ ethnicities): <1%
International: 3%

Academics
Calendar: Semester
Student/faculty ratio: 18:1
Class size 9 or fewer: 26%
Class size 10-29: 56%
Class size 30-49: 18%
Class size 50-99: -
Class size 100 or more: -
Returning freshmen: 53%
Six-year graduation rate: 28%

Most Popular Majors
Biology
Broadcast journalism
Business administration

150 Rust Avenue, Holly Springs, MS 38635
Admissions: 662-252-8000, extension 4058
Financial Aid: 888-886-8492, extension 4061
Email: admissions@rustcollege.edu
Website: http://www.rustcollege.edu

From the College

"Rust College has graduated renowned artists in journalism, music and writing. The College Social Work Program is accredited by the Council on Social Work Education (CSWE). The college has collaborative agreements with major research universities for student internship opportunities in The Division of Science and Math as well as programs leading to professions in the medical fields at major university teaching institutions."

Campus Setting

Rust College, founded in 1866, is a private, church-affiliated college. Its 126-acre campus is located in Holly Springs, 45 miles southeast of Memphis. A four-year institution, Rust College is a historically black university with 934 students. The school is also affiliated with the United Methodist Church. Campus facilities include a large library and an African tribal art collection. Rust College provides on-campus housing that can accommodate 856 students. Housing options: women's dorms · men's dorms · married-student apartments. Recreation and sports facilities include: arena · multi-purpose athletic center · park.

Student Life and Activities

Sixty-seven percent of students live on campus. "The students interact well with each other, enjoying intelligent conversations and physical recreation," reports the student newspaper. "They are culturally aware and very proud of their African-American heritage."

Popular gathering spots include the student recreation center, gymnasium, library, laundry room, Doxey Fine Arts Building, KFC, Club Octagon and Victor's. Popular campus events include Founder's Weekend, Health Fair, SIAC Basketball Tournament, Religious Emphasis Week, Theatre Productions, dances, movies and commencement. Rust College has 31 official student organizations. Influential student groups include Omega Psi Phi, Zeta Phi Beta, the Baptist Student Union Choir and the Student Government Association. There are intramural teams available: archery · basketball · billiards · dance · flag football · soccer · softball · swimming · table tennis · tennis · track · volleyball.

Academics and Learning Environment

Rust College has 48 full-time and two part-time faculty members, offering a student-to-faculty ratio of 18:1. Rust College offers 18 majors with the most popular being biology, broadcast journalism and business administration and least popular being chemistry, music and social science. The school has a general core requirement as well as a religion requirement. Cooperative education is not offered. All first-year students must maintain a 1.5 GPA or higher to avoid academic probation. Other programs: independent study · double majors · honors program · internships · dual degrees · certificate programs.

B Student Support and Success

With its open admissions system, Rust College considers students whose "educational goals, career objectives and intellectual abilities match the institution's academic and non-academic programs." The Academic Counseling Program helps students plan their courses and careers based on needs and interests. Freshmen are assigned faculty advisors. After the first year, a major is declared, and each student is given an academic counselor from the faculty to help with any problems or questions that might follow.

Rust College is proud to offer dedicated guidance for: academic · career · minority students · religious. Rust College offers remedial and refresher courses in: reading · writing · math · study skills. Other remedial services include English. The average freshman year GPA is 2.7, and 53 percent of freshmen students return for their sophomore year.

Support for Students with Learning Disabilities

Students with learning disabilities will want to further investigate the support programs provided by Rust College. A lightened course load is one of the many options open to LD students. They will want to survey these options: remedial math · remedial English · tutors · diagnostic testing service. Individual or small group tutorials are also available in: time management · organizational skills · learning strategies · writing labs · math labs · study skills. An advisor/advocate from the LD program is available to students.

How to Get Admitted

For admissions decisions, non-academic factors considered: interview · extracurricular activities · special talents, interests and abilities · character/personal qualities · state of residency. A high school diploma is required, although a GED is also accepted for admissions consideration. SAT Subject Test scores are considered, if submitted, but are not required. *According to the admissions office:* Minimum 2.3 GPA required. *Academic units recommended:* 4 English, 3 Math, 3 Science, 3 Social Studies.

How to Pay for College

To apply for financial aid, students should submit the following: Free Application for Federal Student Aid (FAFSA) · institution's own financial aid forms · state aid form · Non-custodian (Divorced/Separated) Parent's Statement · Business/Farm Supplement. Rust College participates in the Federal Work Study program. *Need-based aid programs include:* scholarships and grants · general need-based awards · Federal Pell grants · state scholarships and grants · private scholarships and grants · United Negro College Fund. *Non-need-based aid programs include:* scholarships and grants · general need-based awards · state scholarships and grants.

RUST COLLEGE

Highlights

Admissions
Applicants: 3,152
Accepted: 441
Acceptance rate: 14.0%
Average GPA: 2.7
ACT range: 13-14
SAT Math range: 320-440
SAT Reading range: 310-360
SAT Writing range: Not reported

Deadlines
Early Action: No
Early Decision: No
Regular Action: Rolling admissions
Common Application: Not accepted

Financial Aid
In-state tuition: $9,286
Out-of-state tuition: $9,286
Room: Varies
Board: Varies
Books: Varies
Freshmen receiving need-based aid: 91%
Undergrads rec. need-based aid: 99%
Avg. % of need met by financial aid: 84%
Avg. aid package (freshmen): Not reported
Avg. aid package (undergrads): Not reported

Prominent Alumni
Zondra Hughes, author, editor, journalist; Cleveland Payne, author; Anita Ward, singer.

School Spirit
Mascot: Bearcats
Colors: Royal and white
Song: *Rust College Mine Mine Mine*

377

SALVE REGINA UNIVERSITY

100 Ochre Point Avenue, Newport, RI 02840-4192
Admissions: 888-GO-SALVE · Financial Aid: 888-GO-SALVE
Email: sruadmis@salve.edu · Website: http://www.salve.edu

From the College

"Salve Regina University is a small university with big opportunity. Salve Regina's oceanfront campus is a place where students feel at home. Students study and live in historic mansions, yet receive an education that prepares them for modern careers and a lifetime of serving their communities. Salve offers excellent professional and liberal arts programs (most popular are: business, education, administration of justice and biology). The classes are small and are all taught by professors (no grad assistants). Salve's small size also makes it easy for students to get involved on campus with clubs, activities, athletics or intramurals. At Salve, it is easy to become a leader, even in your first year. Newport offers the perfect location for students who love history, sailing and the outdoors. Students can surf, ocean kayak from First Beach or bike ride on Ocean Drive. Newport also hosts several festivals throughout the year. All students get a free statewide trolley/bus pass that takes them throughout Newport or to Providence 30 minutes away. Admission to Salve Regina is competitive. The Admissions Office looks at several factors in reviewing applications. Most important is your day-to-day academic work and the level of the courses you have taken. We also review recommendation letters and test scores. Leadership positions and community involvement are also considered in the review process."

Campus Setting

Salve Regina, founded in 1934, is a private, church-affiliated, liberal arts university. Its 65-acre campus, situated among turn-of-the-century summer estates listed with the National Register of Historic Places, is located in Newport, 35 miles from Providence. A four-year institution, Salve Regina University has an enrollment of 2,603 students and has been co-ed since 1973. The school is also affiliated with the Roman Catholic Church (Religious Sisters of Mercy). Campus facilities include a sizable library and a public service center. Salve Regina University provides on-campus housing that can accommodate 1,242 students. Housing options: coed dorms · women's dorms · men's dorms · single-student apartments · special housing for disabled students. Recreation and sports facilities include: fields · ice rink · fitness center · recreation center · tennis courts.

Student Life and Activities

Fifty-eight percent of students live on campus. Students gather on campus at O'Hare Academic Center, Wakehurst Campus Center and Miley Hall. Off campus, students often head to the Brick Alley Pub and Restaurant. Popular campus events include Spring Weekend, Wakehurst Day and the all-campus BBQ and Salve Dance Company shows. Salve Regina University has 42 official student organizations. Influential campus groups include Sigma Phi Sigma honor society, the Student Life Senate, the Campus Activities Board and the Activities Office. There are intramural teams available. Salve Regina University is a member of the Commonwealth Coast Conference (Division III), ECAC Hockey League (Division III), New England Football Conference (Division III) and New England Women's Lacrosse Alliance (Division III).

Academics and Learning Environment

Salve Regina University has 118 full-time and 150 part-time faculty members, offering a student-to-faculty ratio of 13:1. The most common course size is 20 to 29 students. Salve Regina University offers 59 majors with the most popular being business administration, education and nursing and least popular being women's studies, secondary education/biology and anthropology. The school has a general core requirement as well as a religion requirement. Cooperative education is not offered. All first-year students must maintain a 2.0 GPA or higher to avoid academic probation. Other programs: independent study · double majors · accelerated study · honors program · internships · distance learning certificate programs.

B Student Support and Success

Salve Regina looks at a student's high school transcript, and one of the first things admissions does is recalculate the GPA. All extracurricular classes are eliminated and the average is obtained from the core academic classes only. Students who need academic assistance will find a Writing Center and Student Tutorial Center on campus. Faculty and staff make an extra effort to help first-year students with the transition from high school to college.

There are a variety of support programs available at Salve Regina University, including dedicated guidance for: academic · career · personal · psychological · minority students · military · veterans · religious. The average freshman year GPA is 3.0, and 79 percent of freshmen students return for their sophomore year. After college, however, many students enter the workforce, and approximately 23 percent of them pursue a graduate degree immediately after graduation. One year after graduation, the school reports that 32 percent of the number of graduates have entered graduate school. Out of those students who enter the workforce, approximately 63 percent enter a field actually related to their major within six months of graduation. Companies that most frequently hire these graduates: Federal Bureau of Investigation · MTV · Pfizer · Ernst and Young · Mt. Sinai Hospital · Liberty Mutual Group · The Boeing Company · New York State Police · Child and Family Services · Sun Life Financial.

Support for Students with Learning Disabilities

Students with learning disabilities may want to research those support programs available through Salve Regina University. The college will consider offering LD students additional time to finish their degree and/or offer a lightened course load. Students with learning disabilities will want to research these: tutors · learning center · testing accommodations · untimed tests · extended time for tests · oral tests · readers · note-taking services · tape recorders · videotaped classes. Individual or small group tutorials are also available in: time management · organizational skills · learning strategies · specific subject areas · writing labs · math labs · study skills. An advisor/advocate from the Disability Services is available to students.

How to Get Admitted

For admissions decisions, non-academic factors considered: extracurricular activities · special talents, interests and abilities · character/personal qualities · volunteer work · work experience · state of residency · minority affiliation · alumni relationship. A high school diploma

SALVE REGINA UNIVERSITY

Highlights

Salve Regina University
Newport (Pop. 24,034)
Location: Large town
Four-year private
Founded: 1934
Website: http://www.salve.edu

Students
Total enrollment: 2,603
Undergrads: 2,026
Freshmen: 529
Part-time students: 8%
From out-of-state: 87%
From public schools: 77%
Male/Female: 30%/70%
Live on-campus: 58%
Off-campus employment rating: Good
Caucasian: 76%
African American: 2%
Hispanic: 6%
Asian: 1%
Hawaiian or Pacific Islander: <1%
Native American: <1%
Mixed (2+ ethnicities): 2%
International: 1%

Academics
Calendar: Semester
Student/faculty ratio: 13:1
Class size 9 or fewer: 39%
Class size 10-29: 42%
Class size 30-49: 19%
Class size 50-99: -
Class size 100 or more: -
Returning freshmen: 79%
Six-year graduation rate: 64%

Most Popular Majors
Business administration
Education
Nursing

379

SALVE REGINA UNIVERSITY

Highlights

Admissions
Applicants: 5,070
Accepted: 3,400
Acceptance rate: 67.1%
Placed on wait list: 324
Enrolled from wait list: 10
Average GPA: 3.2
ACT range: 19-31
SAT Math range: 510-600
SAT Reading range: 510-590
SAT Writing range: 1-25
Top 10% of class: 15%
Top 25% of class: 30%
Top 50% of class: 83%

Deadlines
Early Action: 11/1
Early Decision: No
Regular Action: Rolling admissions
Common Application: Accepted

Financial Aid
In-state tuition: $35,140
Out-of-state tuition: $35,140
Room: $7,530
Board: $2,370
Books: $900
Freshmen receiving need-based aid: 80%
Undergrads rec. need-based aid: 77%
Avg. % of need met by financial aid: 67%
Avg. aid package (freshmen): $25,023
Avg. aid package (undergrads): $23,401
Avg. debt upon graduation: $38,885

Prominent Alumni
Janet Robinson, President and CEO, *New York Times*; General Carol Mutter, U.S. Marine Corps (first female three-star general); Kevin Favreau, Special agent in charge/counter intelligence/Washington, DC FBI field office.

School Spirit
Mascot: Seahawks
Colors: Blue, white and green

is required, although a GED is also accepted for admissions consideration. SAT or ACT test scores are required of all applicants. SAT Subject Test scores are considered, if submitted, but are not required. *Academic units recommended:* 4 English, 3 Math, 2 Science, 1 Social Studies, 2 Foreign Language.

Insight

"There is a college for everyone," says Amanda Warhurst Webster, senior associate director of admissions. "Here we look at the profile of the high school itself. Does it offer an honors curriculum? How many academic classes will the student choose to take, including their senior year? Do the students take state tests?" According to Warhurst Webster, emphasis is also put on recommendations. "We want to see the third party perspective," she says. "And we can tell when a letter is a general one or a truly personal one." The essay is very important at Salve Regina. "It is the only part of the application process that is in the student's own voice," says Warhurst Webster. "The essays bring the kids to life. I always encourage students to think, 'How do I want to appear to the people in admissions?' The essay topics are open-ended, and officers look at the concepts presented in the essay along with grammar, mechanics and usage issues. One common essay question is 'Tell us something more about yourself that you want us to know.' We certainly give leeway to students who do not have a support system," explains Warhurst Webster.

How to Pay for College

To apply for financial aid, students should submit the following: Free Application for Federal Student Aid (FAFSA) · CSS/Financial Aid PROFILE · Non-custodian (Divorced/Separated) Parent's Statement · Business/Farm Supplement. Salve Regina University participates in the Federal Work Study program. *Need-based aid programs include:* scholarships and grants · general need-based awards · Federal Pell grants · state scholarships and grants · college-based scholarships and grants · private scholarships and grants. *Non-need-based aid programs include:* scholarships and grants · state scholarships and grants · ROTC scholarships · minority status.

SARAH LAWRENCE COLLEGE

1 Mead Way, Bronxville, NY 10708-5999
Admissions: 800-888-2858 · Financial Aid: 914-395-2570
Email: slcadmit@sarahlawrence.edu · Website: http://www.slc.edu

From the College

"Sarah Lawrence is a co-educational college of the liberal arts and sciences offering undergraduate and graduate degrees. The college is known for its rigorous academic standards, which are fostered by small seminars and individual student-faculty conferences, made possible by a low student-to-faculty ratio of 6-to-1. Students at SLC design their own course of study with the help of a faulty adviser or "don." Study abroad is a popular option for many juniors, and Sarah Lawrence has programs in Paris, Florence, Catania, Oxford, London and Havana. Students in all years frequently augment their classes and conferences with work in neighboring communities and New York City through service learning, volunteer opportunities and internships. Long respected in arts education, Sarah Lawrence recognizes the creative and performing arts as integral to a liberal arts education."

Campus Setting

Sarah Lawrence, a coeducational liberal arts college, offers undergraduate as well as graduate degrees. Located just north of New York City, the college is nationally renowned for its rigorous academic and creative programs. A four-year private institution, Sarah Lawrence College has been co-ed since 1968. The campus facilities include: library · art galleries · dance studios · music building · theatre · visual arts building · science center. Sarah Lawrence College provides on-campus housing with 716 units that can accommodate 1,000 students. Housing options: coed dorms · women's dorms · single-student apartments · cooperative housing. Recreation and sports facilities include: fitness center · gymnasium · softball field · swimming pool · tennis and squash courts.

Student Life and Activities

Eighty-five percent of students live on campus. Common Ground, The Pub and Westlands Lawn are popular gathering spots. Popular campus events include Poetry Festival, Fall and Spring Formals, Midnight Cabaret, May Fair and Student Auction. Sarah Lawrence College has 61 official student organizations. The most popular are: Amnesty International · a cappella group · chamber music groups · chorus · dance group · drama group · environmental awareness group · feminist alliance · film society · jazz band · Model UN · orchestra · Queer Coalition · theatre outreach · outdoor club. bike club · voices for Palestine · visual arts review · literary review · the Sadie Lou Standard (newspaper) · the Phoenix (newspaper) · solidarity club · SLC Stitch 'n' Bitch · SLC Chess Club · SLC Book Clubbers · The SLC Annual (yearbook) · Sarah Lawrence Spoken Word Collective · Sarah Lawrence Dueling Club · Sarah Lawrence Activities Council · Porcelain Baby Burlesque · PETA · Namaste Bollywood · Midnight Cabaret · The Melancholy Players · Kamikazes Anonymous · Improvalot · Cranked Up (bike club) · Call and Response (international publication) · Annual Rocky Horror Productions · American Sign Language. There are intramural teams available: badminton · basketball · bowling · fencing · martial arts · soccer · squash · tennis · Ultimate Frisbee · volleyball. Sarah Lawrence College is a member of the Hudson Valley Men's Athletic Conference.

381

SARAH LAWRENCE COLLEGE

Highlights

Sarah Lawrence College
Yonkers/Bronxville (Pop. 195,976)
Location: Medium city
Four-year private
Founded: 1926
Website: http://www.slc.edu

Students
Total enrollment: 1,782
Undergrads: 1,471
From out-of-state: 86%
Male/Female: 28%/72%
Live on-campus: 85%
Off-campus employment rating: Excellent
Caucasian: 55%
African American: 4%
Hispanic: 9%
Asian: 4%
Hawaiian or Pacific Islander: <1%
Native American: <1%
Mixed (2+ ethnicities): 5%
International: 11%

Academics
Calendar: Semester
Student/faculty ratio: 6:1
Class size 9 or fewer: 30%
Class size 10-29: 66%
Class size 30-49: 3%
Class size 50-99: 1%
Class size 100 or more: -
Returning freshmen: 89%
Six-year graduation rate: 70%

Academics and Learning Environment

Sarah Lawrence College has a student-to-faculty ratio of 6:1. Sarah Lawrence College offers 53 majors. The school does not have a general core requirement. Cooperative education is not offered. All first-year students must maintain a minimum GPA to avoid academic probation. Other programs available: self-designed majors · pass/fail grading option · independent study · dual degrees · internships.

B Student Support and Success

Sarah Lawrence College provides a variety of support programs, including: academic · career · personal · psychological · minority students · non-traditional students · family planning. Annually, 89 percent of freshmen students return for their sophomore year. The following are some companies that most frequently hire graduates of Sarah Lawrence College: Teach for America · NYC Dept. of Parks and Recreation · Phillips Exeter Academy · JET Program · NYC Board of Education · Bloomberg Financial Markets · AFL-CIO · ABC News · Penguin-Putnam Press · Guggenheim Museum · Carnegie Bank · Eastchester Child Development Center · National Council for the Arts · Ruder-Finn · Memorial Sloan-Kettering · CBS · Council on Foreign Relations · Spin Magazine · Assoc. to Benefit Children · United Steel Workers of America · MTV-Group · Merrill Lynch · Citizen Schools · Brealey School.

Support for Students with Learning Disabilities

Students with learning disabilities, commonly referred to as LD students, may take advantage of specific support programs offered by Sarah Lawrence College. If deemed necessary, the college will may additional time to students with learning disabilities in order to complete their degree. Other programs for LD students: extended time for tests · take-home exam · readers · note-taking services · tape recorders · texts on tape · priority registration. Individual or small group tutorials are also available in: time management · organizational skills · learning strategies · study skills. An advisor/advocate from the LD program is available to students.

How to Get Admitted

For admissions decisions, non-academic factors considered: interview · extracurricular activities · special talents, interests and abilities · character/personal qualities · volunteer work · work experience · state of residency · geographical location · minority affiliation · alumni relationship. A high school diploma is required, although a GED is also accepted for admissions consideration. SAT or ACT test scores are optional. *Academic units recommended:* 4 English, 4 Math, 4 Science, 4 Social Studies, 4 Foreign Language.

How to Pay for College

To apply for financial aid, students should submit the following: Free Application for Federal Student Aid (FAFSA) · CSS/Financial Aid PROFILE · state aid form · Non-custodian (Divorced/Separated) Parent's Statement. Sarah Lawrence College participates in the Federal Work Study program. *Need-based aid programs include:*

382

scholarships and grants · general need-based awards · Federal Pell grants · state scholarships and grants · college-based scholarships and grants · private scholarships and grants.

SARAH LAWRENCE COLLEGE

Admissions
Applicants: 2,165
Accepted: 1,342
Acceptance rate: 62%
Average GPA: 3.6
ACT range: Not reported
SAT Math range: Not reported
SAT Reading range: Not reported
SAT Writing range: Not reported
Top 10% of class: 37%
Top 25% of class: 59%
Top 50% of class: 91%

Deadlines
Early Action: No
Early Decision: 11/1
Regular Action: 1/1 (final)
Notification of admission by: 4/1
Common Application: Accepted

Financial Aid
In-state tuition: $49,680
Out-of-state tuition: $49,680
Room: $9,510
Board: $1,192
Books: Varies
Freshmen receiving need-based aid: 66%
Undergrads rec. need-based aid: 60%
Avg. % of need met by financial aid: 89%
Avg. aid package (freshmen): Not reported
Avg. aid package (undergrads): Not reported

Prominent Alumni
Barbara Walters, nationally-renowned journalist. W. Ian Lipkin, molecular neurobiologist who helped identify the West Nile Virus as the cause of the encephalitis outbreak in NY state in 1999; Vera Wang, fashion designer.

School Spirit
Mascot: Gryphons
Colors: Hunter green and white

SCHREINER UNIVERSITY

2100 Memorial Boulevard, Kerrville, TX 78028
Admissions: 800-343-4919 · Financial Aid: 800-343-4919
Email: admissions@schreiner.edu · Website: http://www.schreiner.edu

From the College

"Mission: Schreiner University, a liberal arts institution affiliated by choice and covenant with the Presbyterian Church (USA), is committed to educating students holistically. Primarily undergraduate, the university offers a personalized, integrated education that prepares its students for meaningful work and purposeful lives in a changing global society.

"Vision: Schreiner University will always hold student success as its first priority. The university will be known for its academic rigor; it will continue to be an institution of opportunity where students from a variety of backgrounds and experiences learn through educational programs equipping them to achieve, excel and lead. The university aspires to serve as a standard to others in programs and practices. Outstanding programs that include: Interdisciplinary Studies Program introduces students to the Academy first, and then progressively broadens their knowledge and understanding of their place in the world. Honors Program, challenging curriculum for aggressive learners. Center for Innovative Learning, a vibrant collection of academic experiences and lecture series, each with its own focus. Mountaineer Leadership Institute; at Schreiner, students are trained and encouraged to view themselves as leaders. Undergraduate Research; Schreiner supports research that at other schools is reserved for graduate students. Living History Weekend; an event through which students learn about the past by immersing themselves in its music, stories and recreation of everyday life. Texas Music Coffeehouse; a popular music venue with big-name performers and an open mic in the student center. Study Abroad; more than 40 recognized student organizations Active Campus Ministry program."

Campus Setting

Schreiner is a private, church-affiliated, liberal arts university. Founded in 1923, its 175-acre campus is located in Kerrville, 60 miles northwest of San Antonio. A four-year institution, Schreiner University has an enrollment of 1,136 students and has been co-ed since 1971. The school is also affiliated with the Presbyterian Church. The school also has a library with 82,000 books. Schreiner University provides on-campus housing. Housing options: coed dorms · single-student apartments · married-student apartments · special housing for disabled students. Recreation and sports facilities include: baseball, soccer and softball fields · golf course · gymnasium · tennis courts · fitness center · disc golf course · swimming pool · outdoor basketball court.

Student Life and Activities

Sixty-nine percent of students live on campus. Popular campus events include Late Night Breakfast, Monday Night Fiction, Mountaineer Leadership Conference, Chautauqua Lecture Series, Crate Lecture Series and Coffeehouse. Schreiner University has 38 official student organizations. The most popular are: AHG · Association of Texas Professional Educators · Asian Cultures Club · Rotaract · College Democrats · Non-Traditional & Commuter Student Association · Pre-Law Society · Unicycle Club · Schreiner Big · Schreiner Wellness Action Team · Trull Community Council · Delaney Community Council · Pecan Grove Community Council · The Oaks Community Council · Flato/LA Community Council · Spanish Club · Society of Accounting & Finance Students · French Club. There are intramural teams available: basketball · cycling · dodgeball · flag football · kickball · soccer · tennis · Ultimate

Frisbee · volleyball · water polo · racquetball. Schreiner University is a member of the Southern Collegiate Athletic Conference.

Academics and Learning Environment

Schreiner University has 57 full-time and 61 part-time faculty members, offering a student-to-faculty ratio of 14:1. The most common course size is 20 to 29 students. Schreiner University offers 39 majors. The school has a general core requirement. Cooperative education is not offered. All first-year students must maintain a 1.8 GPA or higher to avoid academic probation. Other programs include: self-designed majors · independent study · double majors · accelerated study · honors program · Phi Beta Kappa · internships · certificate programs.

B Student Support and Success

Because the student-to-faculty ratio at Schreiner is 14:1, students receive individual attention. In some instances, they can even help to design their own internships. There is also a strong honors program at Schreiner. Students with learning disabilities can find help through Schreiner's Learning Support Services Program. Tutoring for all classes is free.

Schreiner University provides dedicated guidance for: academic · career · personal · psychological · non-traditional students · family planning · religious. Annually, 71 percent of freshmen students return for their sophomore year.

Support for Students with Learning Disabilities

Students with learning disabilities will want to investigate available programs. If the situation is appropriate, the college may grant LD students additional time or even a lightened course load. High school foreign language waivers are accepted. According to the school, new freshmen in the program are enrolled in a special section of a required freshman studies class that is taught by the director and focuses on issues of special concern to the success of LD college students. The director is also available to work with students on course selection and registration. Students with learning disabilities will find these programs potentially beneficial: remedial math · remedial English · tutors · learning center · testing accommodations · extended time for tests · take-home exam · oral tests · readers · note-taking services · reading machines. Individual or small group tutorials are also available in: time management · organizational skills · learning strategies · specific subject areas · writing labs · study skills. An advisor/advocate from the Learning Support Services is available to students. This member also sits on the admissions committee.

How to Get Admitted

For admissions decisions, non-academic factors considered: interview · extracurricular activities · special talents, interests and abilities · character/personal qualities · volunteer work · work experience · state of residency. A high school diploma is required, although a GED is also accepted for admissions consideration. SAT or ACT test scores are required of all applicants. SAT Subject Test scores are not required. *Academic units recommended:* 4 English, 3 Math, 3 Science, 2 Social Studies, 2 Foreign Language.

SCHREINER UNIVERSITY

Highlights

Schreiner University
Kerrville, TX (Pop. 22,455)
Location: Small town
Four-year private
Founded: 1923
Website: http://www.schreiner.edu

Students
Total enrollment: 1,136
Undergrads: 1,065
Part-time students: 3%
From out-of-state: 3%
Male/Female: 43%/57%
Live on-campus: 69%
In fraternities: 3%
In sororities: 6%
Off-campus employment rating: Fair
Caucasian: 62%
African American: 3%
Hispanic: 29%
Asian: 1%
Hawaiian or Pacific Islander: <1%
Native American: <1%
Mixed (2+ ethnicities): 4%
International: <1%

Academics
Calendar: Semester
Student/faculty ratio: 14:1
Class size 9 or fewer: 18%
Class size 10-29: 74%
Class size 30-49: 9%
Class size 50-99: -
Class size 100 or more: -
Returning freshmen: 71%
Six-year graduation rate: 41%

SCHREINER UNIVERSITY

Highlights

Admissions
Applicants: 894
Accepted: 828
Acceptance rate: 92.6%
Average GPA: 3.5
ACT range: 19-24
SAT Math range: 450-550
SAT Reading range: 430-540
SAT Writing range: 1-5
Top 10% of class: 11%
Top 25% of class: 34%
Top 50% of class: 73%

Deadlines
Early Action: No
Early Decision: No
Regular Action: Rolling admissions
Common Application: Accepted

Financial Aid
In-state tuition: $22,760
Out-of-state tuition: $22,760
Room: Varies
Board: Varies
Books: $100
Freshmen receiving need-based aid: 78%
Undergrads rec. need-based aid: 82%
Avg. % of need met by financial aid: 67%
Avg. aid package (freshmen): $16,504
Avg. aid package (undergrads): $16,982
Avg. debt upon graduation: $24,539

Prominent Alumni
Richard Marrs, MD; Raymond Berry, member of the pro football Hall of Fame; Frank Ikard, judge, congressman from Texas, President of American Petroleum Institute.

School Spirit
Mascot: Mountaineers
Colors: Maroon and white

Insight

Sandra Speed, dean of admission and financial aid, has important information for anyone thinking about coming to Schreiner. "If you want to fall through the cracks, do not come here," she warns. "If you don't come to class, you will be missed, and someone will try to help you resolve the problem before it becomes a bigger issue. The faculty at Schreiner is very involved with each student's success. They have a real personal commitment to students and will even give you their home phone numbers. At Schreiner, counseling is consistent and ongoing." The school has a faith-based mission and a strong emphasis on extracurricular work within the community, school and church. A student, Jay Govan III, took time to explain why he chose Schreiner University. "What led me to Schreiner was the ratio of students to professors," he explains. "I knew that would be a great benefit to me because if I were to struggle, the teachers always have their doors open to help students." He says the strong tutoring offered at Schreiner also led him to the school.

How to Pay for College

To apply for financial aid, students should submit the following: Free Application for Federal Student Aid (FAFSA) · institution's own financial aid forms · TASFA. Schreiner University participates in the Federal Work Study program. *Need-based aid programs include:* scholarships and grants · general need-based awards · Federal Pell grants · state scholarships and grants · college-based scholarships and grants · private scholarships and grants. *Non-need-based aid programs include:* scholarships and grants · state scholarships and grants · creative arts and performance awards · special achievements and activities awards · special characteristics awards.

386

SETON HILL UNIVERSITY

Seton Hill Drive, Greensburg, PA 15601
Admissions: 800-826-6234 · Financial Aid: 724-838-4293
Email: admit@setonhill.edu · Website: http://www.setonhill.edu

From the College

"Seton Hill has been educating students since 1883, and has long been known for the academic strength of its liberal arts program, its leading stance on the use of mobile technology in higher education, its signature degree programs in the health sciences and the visual and performing arts, its dedicated faculty and personal attention to students and its charming campus in the Laurel Highlands of southwestern Pennsylvania. In 2010, the university received international attention for its new Griffin Technology Advantage Program, which provides an Apple iPad to all full-time students and a MacBook Pro to all full-time first year students. Students have complete access to these mobile technologies for classes as well as at all times for personal use.

"Exceptional offerings in the health sciences include a 'high school to med school' program that enables qualified pre-med students to earn an undergraduate degree and a medical degree in as little as seven years. The Lake Erie College of Osteopathic Medicine opened a new medical school site on Seton Hill's campus in 2009, and Seton Hill pre-med freshmen have the opportunity to reserve a seat in the new medical school as soon as they are accepted to Seton Hill's Pre-Med Program and to move from undergraduate work to medical school in as little as three years. In 2010 the university opened its new ultramodern Center for Orthodontics, which provides direct care to patients in Seton Hill's community while training resident dentists to become orthodontists. The university's Physician Assistant Program is also well known for its rigor; program graduates in the past 10 years have a 96 percent first-attempt pass rate on the Physician Assistant National Certifying Exam.

"The performing arts have been an integral part of the Seton Hill experience since the school awarded its first two degrees - both Bachelors of Music - in 1919. In 2009, the university opened its new Performing Arts Center in Greensburg's historic cultural district. The Performing Arts Center contains two professional performance venues, the Reichgut Concert Hall and Ryan Theatre, in addition to theatre, dance and music classrooms, rehearsal rooms and technical areas that include the best equipment for learning and performing from Steinway pianos to the latest in lighting, sound, video and acoustics. In 2010, Seton Hill became one of only 116 colleges and universities and music schools in the world to receive the prestigious All-Steinway designation.

"Seton Hill's 200-acre main campus, located on a wooded hilltop above Greensburg, Pennsylvania (35 miles from Pittsburgh), features a mix of new and turn-of-the-century buildings, all of which are equipped with modern features and technology. The university has recently expanded its campus into downtown Greensburg's cultural district, and this new downtown campus includes Seton Hill's new Performing Arts Center, Center for Family Therapy and Visual Arts Center. Seton Hill has a 90 percent job placement rate after graduation across all of its programs, and 36 percent of graduates pursue other educational options, including graduate and professional schools."

Campus Setting

Seton Hill University, founded by the Sisters of Charity in 1883, is a coeducational Catholic liberal arts university in Greensburg, Pennsylvania. Originally a women's college, Seton Hill became a coeducational university in 2002. Seton Hill currently enrolls 2,044 students and offers more than 30 undergraduate programs, 12 graduate programs, several advanced certifications, an Honors Program and an Adult Degree Program. Located 35 miles east of Pittsburgh in southwestern Pennsylvania's Laurel

SETON HILL UNIVERSITY

Highlights

Seton Hill University
Greensburg, PA (Pop. 14,736)
Location: Small town
Four-year private
Founded: 1883
Website: http://www.setonhill.edu

Students
Total enrollment: 2,044
Undergrads: 1,649
Freshmen: 386
Part-time students: 11%
From out-of-state: 32%
Male/Female: 36%/64%
Live on-campus: 43%
Off-campus employment rating: Good
Caucasian: 82%
African American: 9%
Hispanic: 2%
Asian: <1%
Native American: <1%
Mixed (2+ ethnicities): 2%
International: 2%

Academics
Calendar: Semester
Student/faculty ratio: 14:1
Class size 9 or fewer: 15%
Class size 10-29: 73%
Class size 30-49: 12%
Class size 50-99: -
Class size 100 or more: -
Returning freshmen: 79%
Six-year graduation rate: 62%

Most Popular Majors
Accounting
Psychology
Biology

Highlands, Seton Hill educates dedicated practitioners and leaders in the fields of health care, science, the arts, business, education, the social sciences and government. Seton Hill also partners with the local community in economic development initiatives and as a source of cultural events and enrichment opportunities. Throughout its history, Seton Hill has embraced students of all faiths, and has pursued its mission in the tradition of Saint Elizabeth Ann Seton. Campus facilities include: art gallery · theatre performing arts center · visual arts center. Seton Hill University provides on-campus housing with eight units that can accommodate 780 students. Housing options: coed dorms · women's dorms · men's dorms. Recreation and sports facilities include: baseball, football, soccer and softball fields · equestrian facilities · gymnasium · field house · tennis courts · fitness center · weight room.

Student Life and Activities

Just over half (57 percent) of students live off campus. "There is always something to do," reports the editor of the student newspaper. Hot spots for students include the Cove in Sullivan Hall, Griffin's Lounge, Rialto and Main Bowling. Popular campus events include Midnight Breakfast, Christmas on the Hill, Cosmic Bowling, Laser Tag, Comedian performances, Foam Dance, Jam sessions and Midnight Bingo. Seton Hill University has 44 official student organizations. Groups that have a strong presence in student social life include Student Government Association, Student Activities Council, SHU-A-THON, Gay-Straight Alliance, Theatre/Music Program Students, Athletic Program Students and Peer Ministry. For those interested in sports, there are intramural teams such as: basketball · flag football · volleyball. Seton Hill University is a member of the NCAA (Division II).

Academics and Learning Environment

Seton Hill University has 100 full-time and 93 part-time faculty members, offering a student-to-faculty ratio of 14:1. The most common course size is 10 to 19 students. Seton Hill University offers 58 majors with the most popular being accounting, psychology and biology. The school has a general core requirement as well as a religion requirement. Cooperative education is not offered. All first-year students must maintain a 2.0 GPA or higher to avoid academic probation, and a minimum overall GPA of 2.0 is required to graduate. Other special academic programs that would appeal to a B student include: self-designed majors · pass/fail grading option · independent study · double majors · dual degrees · accelerated study · honors program · internships · weekend college · distance learning certificate programs.

B Student Support and Success

Seton Hill's Academic Support program provides assistance to students through a tutoring center, which offers individual and small group tutoring. There is a Writing Center, which helps with prewriting skills, organizing, drafting, revising and editing. The college also offers an Opportunity Program, which is a summer experience designed to help students get a head start by living on campus, participating in workshops and mastering the skills they will need for college work. The students who qualify for this program either have low SAT or ACT scores, a low high school GPA, non-academic courses in high school or grades that simply don't truly reflect the student's potential. In addition to these services, Seton Hill also offers Academic Counseling on study skills such as taking notes, reading college textbooks and taking tests. Common topics include time management, test anxiety, critical thinking and identifying personal learning styles.

Seton Hill University provides a variety of support programs for: academic · career · personal · psychological · minority students · veterans · non-traditional students · religious. The average freshman year GPA is 3.0, and 79 percent of freshmen students return for their sophomore year. Among students who enter the workforce, approximately 57 percent enter a field related to their major within six months of graduation. Companies that most frequently hire graduates from Seton Hill University include: Allegheny Energy Systems · Sony · University of Pittsburgh · Mine Safety Applications · Excela Westmoreland Health Care System · UPS · Citizen's Bank · YWCA · Family Behavioral Resources.

Support for Students with Learning Disabilities

Seton Hill University allows learning disabled students to carry lighter course loads, as well as take extra time to complete their degrees. Learning disabled students may also want to investigate the options: tutors · testing accommodations · untimed tests · extended time for tests · take-home exam · oral tests · readers · note-taking services · reading machines · tape recorders · texts on tape · videotaped classes · early syllabus · priority registration. Individual or small group tutorials are also available in: time management · organizational skills · learning strategies · specific subject areas · writing labs · study skills. An advisor/advocate from the Office of Disability Services is available to students.

How to Get Admitted

For admissions decisions, non-academic factors considered: interview · extracurricular activities · special talents, interests and abilities · character/personal qualities · volunteer work · work experience · state of residency · alumni relationship. A high school diploma is required, although a GED is also accepted for admissions consideration. SAT or ACT test scores are recommended but not required. SAT Subject Test scores are not required. *Academic units recommended:* 4 English, 2 Math, 1 Science, 2 Social Studies, 2 Foreign Language.

How to Pay for College

To apply for financial aid, students should submit the following: Free Application for Federal Student Aid (FAFSA) · institution's own financial aid forms · state aid form. Seton Hill University participates in the Federal Work Study program. *Need-based aid programs include:* scholarships and grants · general need-based awards · Federal Pell grants · state scholarships and grants · college-based scholarships and grants · private scholarships and grants. *Non-need-based aid programs include:* scholarships and grants · state scholarships and grants · creative arts and performance awards · athletic scholarships.

SETON HILL UNIVERSITY

Highlights

Admissions
Applicants: 2,414
Accepted: 1,574
Acceptance rate: 65.2%
Average GPA: 3.5
ACT range: 19-26
SAT Math range: 450-580
SAT Reading range: 450-570
SAT Writing range: 1-17
Top 10% of class: 20%
Top 25% of class: 47%
Top 50% of class: 77%

Deadlines
Early Action: No
Early Decision: No
Regular Action: Rolling admissions
Common Application: Accepted

Financial Aid
In-state tuition: $30,280
Out-of-state tuition: $30,280
Room: Varies
Board: Varies
Books: Varies
Freshmen receiving need-based aid: 90%
Undergrads rec. need-based aid: 86%
Avg. % of need met by financial aid: 74%
Avg. aid package (freshmen): $25,988
Avg. aid package (undergrads): $24,161
Avg. debt upon graduation: $36,519

Prominent Alumni
Bibiana Boerio, retired Sr. Executive of Ford Motor Company and former Chief of Staff for Member of Congress; Ronne Froman, Rear Admiral U.S. Navy (retired); Maureen O'Connor, Chief Justice, Supreme Court of Ohio.

School Spirit
Mascot: Griffins
Colors: Crimson and gold

389

Highlights

Shaw University
Raleigh, NC (Pop. 423,179)
Location: Major city
Four-year private
Founded: 1865
Website: http://www.shawu.edu

Students

Total enrollment: 2,062
Undergrads: 1,923
Freshmen: 908
Part-time students: 7%
From out-of-state: 31%
Male/Female: 44%/56%
Live on-campus: 40%
In fraternities: 4%
In sororities: 5%
Off-campus employment rating: Excellent
Caucasian: 1%
African American: 69%
Hispanic: <1%
Hawaiian or Pacific Islander: 1%
Native American: <1%
Mixed (2+ ethnicities): <1%
International: 1%

Academics

Calendar: Semester
Student/faculty ratio: 15:1
Class size 9 or fewer: 34%
Class size 10-29: 52%
Class size 30-49: 13%
Class size 50-99: -
Class size 100 or more: -
Returning freshmen: 43%
Six-year graduation rate: 30%

Most Popular Majors

Business administration
Social work
Sociology

390

SHAW UNIVERSITY

118 East South Street, Raleigh, NC 27601
Admissions: 800-214-6683 · Financial Aid: 800-475-6190
Email: admissions@shawu.edu
Website: http://www.shawu.edu

From the College

"In order to meet the challenges of a global society, Shaw University endeavors to develop graduates who are broadly educated in the liberal arts and sciences, possessing the knowledge and skills required of all disciplines, and the competencies associated with their chosen fields of study. Students who successfully complete undergraduate degree programs at Shaw University will demonstrate proficiency in critical and creative thinking, an ability to communicate effectively, both orally and in writing; proficiency in mathematical reasoning skills, scientific inquiry, technological and information literacy, an awareness of and commitment to ethical judgment, awareness of global issues, knowledge of diverse human cultures and a commitment to personal and social responsibility."

Campus Setting

Shaw, founded in 1865, is a private, church-affiliated, liberal arts university and is the oldest historically black college in the South. Its 30-acre campus is located in downtown Raleigh. Shaw University is also affiliated with the Baptist Church. A four-year private institution, Shaw University has 2,062 students. The university provides on-campus housing that can accommodate 1,273 students. The school has a large library and women's and men's dorms.

Student Life and Activities

Most students (60 percent) live off campus. Shaw University has 50 official student organizations which include: bands · choir · choral society · music ensembles · Shaw Players · Unique Horizon Dancers · debating · Order of Eastern Star · academic groups. Shaw University is a member of the Central Intercollegiate Athletic Association (Division II).

Academics and Learning Environment

Shaw University has 105 full-time and 68 part-time faculty members, offering a student-to-faculty ratio of 15:1. The most common course size is 2 to 9 students. Shaw University offers 31 majors with the most popular being business administration, social work and sociology and least popular being music, birth-kindergarten education and English. The school has a general core requirement. Cooperative education is not offered. All first-year students must maintain a 1.5 GPA or higher to avoid academic probation. Other special academic programs that would appeal to a B student: self-designed majors · independent study · double majors · dual degrees · accelerated study · honors program · internships · distance learning.

B Student Support and Success

Shaw's Freshman Year Program is focused on providing the tools students need to reach their academic goals. It features a series of activities and events that help ease the transition as students become more familiar with college life. Every student must take this program as part of graduation requirements. It includes a number of classes, including a cultural and spiritual enrichment seminar. Note that the college has a dress code, and community worship is mandatory, as is attendance to college events such as Homecoming, Senior Appreciation Day and University Awards Day. A new, free program called Freshmen Academy earns credit hours. It is an intense summer academic program, and participants receive room, board, books and supplies. They attend workshops, seminars and presentations and go on field trips.

Shaw University provides dedicated guidance for: academic · career · personal · psychological · minority students · military · veterans · non-traditional students · family planning · religious. Annually, 43 percent of freshmen return the next year.

Support for Students with Learning Disabilities

Students with learning disabilities may take additional time to complete their degree or pursue a lightened course load. Students with learning disabilities can find additional support through: tutors · untimed tests · extended time for tests · take-home exam · oral tests · note-taking services · tape recorders · diagnostic testing service · priority registration. Individual or small group tutorials are also available in: time management · organizational skills · learning strategies · specific subject areas · writing labs · math labs · study skills. An advisor/advocate from the LD program is available to students. This member also sits on the admissions committee.

How to Get Admitted

For admissions decisions, non-academic factors considered: extracurricular activities · special talents, interests and abilities · character/personal qualities · volunteer work · work experience · geographical location · alumni relationship. A high school diploma is required, although a GED is also accepted for admissions consideration. SAT or ACT test scores are recommended but not required. *According to the admissions office:* Minimum 2.0 GPA required.

How to Pay for College

To apply for financial aid, students should submit the following: Free Application for Federal Student Aid (FAFSA) · institution's own financial aid forms · state aid form. Shaw University participates in the Federal Work Study program. *Need-based aid programs include:* scholarships and grants · general need-based awards · Federal Pell grants · state scholarships and grants · college-based scholarships and grants · private scholarships and grants · United Negro College Fund. *Non-need-based aid programs include:* scholarships and grants · state scholarships and grants · creative arts and performance awards · athletic scholarships · ROTC scholarships.

SHAW UNIVERSITY

Highlights

Admissions
Applicants: 6,387
Accepted: 3,883
Acceptance rate: 60.8%
Average GPA: 2.4
ACT range: 13-16
SAT Math range: 320-410
SAT Reading range: 330-410
SAT Writing range: Not reported
Top 10% of class: 1%
Top 25% of class: 4%
Top 50% of class: 23%

Deadlines
Early Action: No
Early Decision: No
Regular Action: 7/30 (final)
Notification of admission by: 8/1
Common Application: Accepted

Financial Aid
In-state tuition: $16,480
Out-of-state tuition: $16,480
Room: $3,842
Board: $4,316
Books: Varies
Freshmen receiving need-based or merit-based aid: 99%
Avg. aid package (freshmen): Not reported
Avg. aid package (undergrads): Not reported

Prominent Alumni
Willie E. Gary, attorney; Cleveland L. Sellers, Jr., president, Voorhees College; Shirley Caesar, minister and Grammy Award-winning singer.

School Spirit
Mascot: Bears
Colors: Maroon and white

SHENANDOAH UNIVERSITY

1460 University Drive, Winchester, VA 22601
Admissions: 800-432-2266 · Financial Aid: 800-432-2266
Email: admit@su.edu · Website: http://www.su.edu

From the College

"Our main campus is located in the City of Winchester, VA, in the historic Shenandoah Valley. Our Northern Virginia campus, located in Leesburg, VA, 45 miles to the east, specializes in graduate study in education and nursing. Shenandoah is comprised of seven academic schools, offering 42 undergraduate degrees and 24 graduate degrees, as well as a broad spectrum of minors and undergraduate, post-baccalaureate and post-doctoral certificates. The College of Arts & Sciences provides a classic, broad-based education to satisfy both intellectual curiosity and career goals. Offering small classes and individualized learning opportunities, we put students at the center of all our decisions and events.

"Shenandoah Conservatory is Virginia's, and one of the country's, premier conservatories with a faculty of professionals in music, theatre and dance and alumni that take center stage from Broadway to the concert halls of Europe. With 32 performing ensembles and more than 300 concerts, recitals, clinics, master classes, theatre and opera productions and dance concerts yearly, students have continual opportunities to perform and be evaluated by both professionals and peers.

"The Harry F. Byrd, Jr. School of Business is led by academically experienced professors with real world backgrounds in business, government and the military to provide the knowledge and skills to apply on the job or in the community in today's fast-paced, global business environment.

"The Alumni Mentorship Program, designed by faculty in cooperation with the Office of Alumni Affairs, fosters undergraduate student growth and professional development. The School of Education & Human Development educates practitioner-leaders by offering master's and doctoral programs unique in their emphasis on the application of theory to real-world problems and lived experiences, preparing caring, capable and reflective teachers, administrators, human services and public sectors practitioners.

"The Bernard J. Dunn School of Pharmacy uses a highly integrated, learner-centered curriculum and progressive instructional technology to educate and train students and pharmacists to become ethical and compassionate healthcare professionals who serve their patients and community with optimal pharmaceutical care and advance the pharmacy profession.

"The Eleanor Wade Custer School of Nursing provides learning opportunities within the classroom and a range of clinical environments including hospitals, medical practices and pharmacies. The nursing school houses the Division of Respiratory Care.

"The School of Health Professions, relying on the deep experiences of a future-focused faculty and hands-on experiences in clinical rotations, includes four divisions: Athletic Training, Occupational Therapy, Physical Therapy and Physician Assistant Studies."

Campus Setting

Shenandoah is a private, church-affiliated, comprehensive university. It was founded in 1875 and gained university status in 1991. Its 125-acre campus is located in Winchester, VA, 72 miles from Washington, DC. A four-year institution, Shenandoah University has an enrollment of 4,003 students. The school is also affiliated with the United Methodist Church. Shenandoah University provides on-campus housing with 512 units that can accommodate 914 students. Housing options: coed dorms ·

special housing for disabled students. Recreation and sports facilities include: baseball, lacrosse, soccer, volleyball, basketball and softball fields · golf and indoor tennis club · gymnasium · weight room.

Student Life and Activities

Most students (78 percent) live off campus, but a school representative states, "Shenandoah students find scores of activities on campus. Our location provides access to hiking, kayaking/canoeing, and breathtaking beauty for those who draw inspiration from the natural world." Popular campus events include the Sun Block Party, International Days, Home Coming, Family Weekend and Relay for Life. Shenandoah University has 77 official student organizations. Student theater/music groups and athletes are influential in student life. Intramural teams include: basketball · indoor soccer · indoor volleyball · sand volleyball · soccer · table tennis. Shenandoah University is a member of the Old Dominion Athletic Conference (Division III).

Academics and Learning Environment

Shenandoah University has 239 full-time and 166 part-time faculty members, offering a student-to-faculty ratio of 10:1. The most common course size is 10 to 19 students. Shenandoah University offers 64 majors with the most popular being nursing, business and kinesiology. Least popular are music theatre accompanying, jazz studies and theatre stage management. The school has a general core requirement as well as a religion requirement. Cooperative education is available. All first-year students must maintain a 1.6 GPA or higher to avoid academic probation, and a minimum overall GPA of 2.0 is required to graduate. Other special academic programs include: self-designed majors · independent study · double majors · dual degrees · accelerated study · internships · weekend college · distance learning certificate programs.

B Student Support and Success

Known as the "Yes, You Can" University, Shenandoah offers the Academic Enrichment Center. Its mission is "to enhance student success, student learning and to help students become more effective and successful learners." It offers peer tutoring programs, study skills development course and workshops, services for students with disabilities and academic counseling. The staff works one on one with students and discusses topics such as the productive use of study time, goal setting for improved academic success, reading and note taking strategies, overcoming test taking challenges and any other academic skill students want to develop.

Shenandoah University provides a variety of support programs including: academic · career · personal · psychological · minority students · military · veterans · non-traditional students · family planning · religious. Recognizing that some students may need extra preparation, Shenandoah University offers remedial and refresher courses in: reading · writing · math · study skills. The average freshman year GPA is 3.0, and 76 percent of freshmen students return for their sophomore year. Approximately 18 percent pursue a graduate degree immediately after graduation. Companies that most frequently hire graduates from Shenandoah University include: Bank of America · BB&T Banks · Broadway shows · clinics · FedEx

SHENANDOAH UNIVERSITY

Highlights

Shenandoah University
Winchester, VA (Pop. 26,881)
Location: Large town
Four-year private
Founded: 1875
Website: http://www.su.edu

Students
Total enrollment: 4,003
Undergrads: 2,150
Freshmen: 490
Part-time students: 17%
From out-of-state: 47%
Male/Female: 39%/61%
Live on-campus: 22%
Off-campus employment rating: Good
Caucasian: 66%
African American: 13%
Hispanic: 6%
Asian: 5%
Hawaiian or Pacific Islander: <1%
Native American: 2%
International: 4%

Academics
Calendar: Semester
Student/faculty ratio: 10:1
Class size 9 or fewer: 22%
Class size 10-29: 69%
Class size 30-49: 8%
Class size 50-99: 1%
Class size 100 or more: -
Returning freshmen: 76%
Six-year graduation rate: 45%

Most Popular Majors
Nursing
Business
Kinesiology

393

College Profiles

SHENANDOAH UNIVERSITY

Admissions

Applicants: 1,632
Accepted: 1,377
Acceptance rate: 84.4%
Average GPA: 3.4
ACT range: 18-24
SAT Math range: 430-550
SAT Reading range: 420-540
SAT Writing range: 2-8
Top 10% of class: 13%
Top 25% of class: 36%
Top 50% of class: 74%

Deadlines

Early Action: No
Early Decision: No
Regular Action: Rolling admissions
Common Application: Not accepted

Financial Aid

In-state tuition: $28,998
Out-of-state tuition: $28,998
Room: Varies
Board: Varies
Books: $1,500
Freshmen receiving need-based aid: 81%
Undergrads rec. need-based aid: 75%
Avg. % of need met by financial aid: 31%
Avg. aid package (freshmen): $28,411
Avg. aid package (undergrads): $28,336
Avg. debt upon graduation: $28,738

Prominent Alumni

Steve Gober, assistant athletic trainer, Washington Nationals; J. Robert Spencer, Tony Award nominated actor, independent film director, producer/writer; Harold Perrineau, actor, *Lost*, *The Matrix* films and *Zero Dark Thirty*.

School Spirit

Mascot: Hornets
Colors: Navy, red, and white
Song: *Shenandoah*

· Frederick County School System · hospitals · Metropolitan Opera · MSNBC · MTV · private medical practices · professional sports organizations · public and private schools · Shenandoah University · Shockey · Winchester Medical Center.

Support for Students with Learning Disabilities

At Shenandoah, learning disabled students may take a lighter course load and take longer to complete their degrees. They may also find the following programs helpful: remedial math · tutors · learning center · testing accommodations · extended time for tests · take-home exam · oral tests · exam on tape or computer · readers · typist/scribe · note-taking services · reading machines · tape recorders · texts on tape · early syllabus · priority registration · waiver of math degree requirement. Individual or small group tutorials are also available in: time management · organizational skills · learning strategies · writing labs · study skills. An advisor/advocate from the Academic Success Services is available to students.

How to Get Admitted

For admissions decisions, non-academic factors considered: interview · extracurricular activities · special talents, interests and abilities · character/personal qualities · volunteer work · work experience · state of residency. A high school diploma is required, although a GED is also accepted for admissions consideration. SAT or ACT test scores are required of all applicants. *According to the admissions office:* Minimum combined SAT Reasoning score of 900 and minimum 2.5 GPA required or subject to committee review. *Academic units recommended:* 2 Foreign Language.

How to Pay for College

To apply for financial aid, students should submit the following: Free Application for Federal Student Aid (FAFSA) · state aid form · Virginia United Methodist Scholarship application. Shenandoah University participates in the Federal Work Study program. *Need-based aid programs include:* scholarships and grants · general need-based awards · Federal Pell grants · state scholarships and grants · college-based scholarships and grants · private scholarships and grants · Federal Nursing scholarships. *Non-need-based aid programs include:* scholarships and grants · general need-based awards · state scholarships and grants · creative arts and performance awards.

SHEPHERD UNIVERSITY

P.O. Box 5000, Shepherdstown, WV 25443-5000
Admissions: 800-344-5231, extension 5212
Financial Aid: 800-344-5231, extension 5470
Email: admissions@shepherd.edu · Website: http://www.shepherd.edu

From the College

"Shepherd University is a public institution within the West Virginia system of higher education. Shepherd offers bachelor's and master's degrees in the liberal arts, business administration, teacher education, social and natural sciences and other career-oriented areas. Shepherd is dedicated to expanding its intellectual and cultural resources with the assistance of technological advances and its location 70 miles from the Baltimore/Washington metropolitan area. At the same time, the residential setting of the university creates an environment in which students are able to work closely with faculty, staff, administrators and industry."

Campus Setting

Shepherd University, founded in 1871, is a public liberal arts university. Programs are offered through the schools of Arts and Humanities, Business and Social Sciences, Education and Professional Studies and Natural Science and Mathematics. Its 320-acre campus is located in Shepherdstown, 65 miles from Washington, DC. A four-year institution, Shepherd University has an enrollment of 4,221 students. Campus facilities include a library, as well as a center for the study of the Civil War and legislative studies. Shepherd University provides on-campus housing with 14 units that can accommodate 1,301 students. Housing options: coed dorms · single-student apartments. Recreation and sports facilities include: baseball, practice and softball fields · athletic center · stadium · tennis courts.

Student Life and Activities

Sixty-eight percent of students live off campus. Popular on-campus gathering spots include the student center, wellness center, and the dining hall. Popular campus events include ShepFest, Midnight Breakfast and Relay for Life. Shepherd University has 86 official student organizations. The most popular are: Ram Marching Band · Music Educators National Conference · Swing Cats · Amateur Filmmakers · dance team · Allies · Interclass Council · Rude Mechanical Players · Liberal Women's Association · Progressive Action Committee · Education Student Association · Student Global Aids Council · Student Life Council · Program Board · 4-H · Student Community Services · Habitat for Humanity · Amnesty International · CLU · AIGA · Junior American Red Cross · One in Four · Operation Ark · Rotaract · Philosophy Association · psychology club · Social Work Association · sociology club · Sustainability Council · Environmental Association · University Democrats · University Republicans · debate and forensics. Shepherd University is a member of the Mountain East Conference (Division II, NCAA).

Academics and Learning Environment

Shepherd University has 143 full-time and 234 part-time faculty members, offering a student-to-faculty ratio of 17:1. The most common course size is 10 to 19 students. Shepherd University offers 30 majors with the most popular being Regents B.A., business administration and nursing and least popular being Spanish, computer information technology and mathematics. The school has a general core requirement. Cooperative education is available. All first-year students must maintain a 2.0 GPA or higher to avoid academic probation, and a minimum overall GPA of 2.0 is required to

395

College Profiles

SHEPHERD UNIVERSITY

Shepherd University

Shepherdstown, WV (Pop. 1,736)
Location: Rural
Four-year public
Founded: 1871
Website: http://www.shepherd.edu

Students

Total enrollment: 4,221
Undergrads: 3,990
Freshmen: 1,001
Part-time students: 18%
From out-of-state: 35%
From public schools: 83%
Male/Female: 43%/57%
Live on-campus: 32%
In fraternities: 3%
In sororities: 4%
Off-campus employment rating: Fair
Caucasian: 83%
African American: 8%
Hispanic: 3%
Asian: 2%
Hawaiian or Pacific Islander: <1%
Native American: 1%
Mixed (2+ ethnicities): <1%
International: <1%

Academics

Calendar: Semester
Student/faculty ratio: 17:1
Class size 9 or fewer: 13%
Class size 10-29: 74%
Class size 30-49: 12%
Class size 50-99: 1%
Class size 100 or more: -
Returning freshmen: 68%
Six-year graduation rate: 38%

Most Popular Majors

Regents B.A.
Business administration
Nursing

graduate. Other academic programs B students will want to peruse are: pass/fail grading option · independent study · double majors · dual degrees · honors program · internships · distance learning.

B Student Support and Success

Shepherd has quite a bit to offer the B student. First, it has "stretch" model courses, i.e. courses that can be stretched to two semesters. The Academic Support Center offers tutoring and academic counseling and the Writing Center provides help for papers and writing assignments. "We welcome students without straight A's. The mean incoming GPA for freshmen is 3.07. The mean freshman SAT composite is 1024, and the mean freshman ACT composite is 21.72. SU's admission requirements are 2.0 GPA and 920 SAT or 19 ACT for freshmen. Applicants with a B average are successful at Shepherd University if they are successful on the SAT or ACT."

Shepherd University offers dedicated guidance for: academic · career · personal · psychological · minority students · military · veterans · non-traditional students · family planning. Shepherd University offers remedial and refresher courses in: reading · writing · math · study skills. Other remedial services include critical thinking. The average freshman year GPA is 2.7, and 68 percent of freshmen students return for their sophomore year. Many graduates enter the workforce, and approximately 43 percent of them pursue a graduate degree immediately after their graduation. One year after graduation, 43 percent of graduates have entered graduate school, the school reports. Out of those students who enter the workforce, approximately 53 percent enter a field actually related to their major within six months of graduation. Companies that most frequently hire Shepherd University graduates include: Businesses · federal agencies · hospitals · public schools.

Support for Students with Learning Disabilities

Students with learning disabilities, also commonly referred to as LD students, may desire to take advantage of specific support programs. LD students will find the following programs at Shepherd University to be rather useful: remedial math · remedial English · tutors · learning center · extended time for tests · take-home exam · readers · typist/scribe · note-taking services · tape recorders · texts on tape · videotaped classes · priority registration · waiver of foreign language and math degree requirement. Individual or small group tutorials are also available in: time management · organizational skills · learning strategies · writing labs · math labs · study skills. An advisor/advocate from the Disability Support Services is available to students.

How to Get Admitted

For admissions decisions, non-academic factors considered: interview · extracurricular activities · special talents, interests and abilities · character/personal qualities · volunteer work · work experience · state of residency. A high school diploma is required, although a GED is also accepted for admissions consideration. SAT or ACT test scores are required of all applicants. *According to the admissions office:* Minimum composite ACT score of 19 (combined SAT Reasoning score of 910) and minimum grade average of "B" required.

Academic units recommended: 4 English, 4 Math, 3 Science, 2 Social Studies, 2 Foreign Language.

How to Pay for College

To apply for financial aid, students should submit the following: Free Application for Federal Student Aid (FAFSA) · state aid form. Shepherd University participates in the Federal Work Study program. *Need-based aid programs include:* scholarships and grants · general need-based awards · Federal Pell grants · state scholarships and grants · college-based scholarships and grants · private scholarships and grants. *Non-need-based aid programs include:* scholarships and grants · general need-based awards · state scholarships and grants · creative arts and performance awards · special achievements and activities awards · athletic scholarships.

SHEPHERD UNIVERSITY

Highlights

Admissions
Applicants: 1,746
Accepted: 1,647
Acceptance rate: 94.3%
Average GPA: 3.3
ACT range: 19-24
SAT Math range: 440-530
SAT Reading range: 460-550
SAT Writing range: Not reported

Deadlines
Early Action: 11/15
Early Decision: No
Regular Action: 2/1 (priority)
8/15 (final)
Common Application: Not accepted

Financial Aid
In-state tuition: $6,570
Out-of-state tuition: $16,628
Room: $4,890
Board: $3,998
Books: $1,070
Freshmen receiving need-based aid: 64%
Undergrads rec. need-based aid: 63%
Avg. % of need met by financial aid: 73%
Avg. aid package (freshmen): $10,801
Avg. aid package (undergrads): $11,094
Avg. debt upon graduation: $23,025

Prominent Alumni
Dr. Stanley Ikenberry, President Emeritus, University of Illinois; Gina Groh, judge, U.S. District Court, Northern District West Virginia; Carolyn Malachi, singer/musician, Grammy Nominee.

School Spirit
Mascot: Rams
Colors: Blue and gold
Song: *Fight On (and Win Again for Old SU)*

SIMMONS COLLEGE

300 The Fenway, Boston, MA 02115
Admissions: 800-345-8468 · Financial Aid: 617-521-2001
Email: ugadm@simmons.edu · Website: http://www.simmons.edu

From the College

"Simmons College was founded in 1899, and is a small university in the heart of Boston that upholds an educational 'contract' with students and helps them achieve successful careers. Simmons honors this contract by delivering a strong education and professional preparation in a welcoming, collaborative environment. Students value the small classes, exceptional internship opportunities and individual attention from faculty who are experts and practitioners. Simmons offers more than 40 majors and programs for undergraduate women, the nation's only MBA designed for women and co-ed graduate programs in health studies, education, communications management, liberal arts, social work and library and information science."

Campus Setting

Simmons, founded in 1899, is a small university with an undergraduate college for women. Its 12-acre campus, located in Boston, includes nine Georgian-style dormitories. The graduate programs are open to men and women. The School of Management offers the only MBA program designed specifically for women. A four-year private college, Simmons College has an enrollment of 4,655 students. Campus facilities include: art gallery · technology resource center · radio station. Simmons College provides on-campus housing accommodating 1,071 students. Housing options: women's dorms · special housing for disabled students. Recreation and sports facilities include: basketball, racquetball, squash and volleyball courts · dance studio · fitness rooms · indoor running area · rowing · swimming pool · sauna.

Student Life and Activities

More than half of the college's students (58 percent) live on campus. A school representative stated, "We're a small college in the biggest college town. You can enjoy the small-college feel—the ability to get to know everyone, a strong feeling of community and support. At the same time, you have resources and ways to meet even more college students through out Colleges of the Fenway Consortium and the greater Boston college community." Popular campus events include May Day Celebration, Honors Convocation, Culture Shock and Simmons Cup. Simmons College has 66 official student organizations. The most popular are: music, theatre, political, academic, service and special-interest groups. Simmons College is a member of the Great Northeast Athletic Conference (Division III), North Atlantic Conference (Division III) and Eastern Collegiate Athletic Conference.

Academics and Learning Environment

Simmons College has 215 full-time and 422 part-time faculty members, offering a student-to-faculty ratio of 10:1. The most common course size is 10 to 19 students. Simmons College offers 109 majors. The most popular choices are nursing, psychology and communications. The school has a general core requirement. Cooperative education is not offered. All first-year students must maintain a 2.0 GPA or higher to avoid academic probation, and a minimum overall GPA of 2.0 is required to graduate. Other special academic programs include: self-designed majors · pass/fail grading option · independent study · double majors · dual degrees · accelerated study · honors program · internships.

B Student Support and Success

Simmons' Academic Support Center is focused on providing high-quality assistance to help students succeed academically. According to the college, its goal is to "help students become independent learners and to encourage them to take an active part in their educational and intellectual pursuits." The center achieves this through various methods. Academic Advising and Counseling assigns advisors to students who are having academic struggles. Placement examinations are given that provide results for math, language and chemistry levels. Services for Students with Disabilities is a program for those with a documented disability, while Tutorial Services matches students with course tutors in such subjects as biology, chemistry, foreign languages, math and physics. There are also study groups with weekly reviews of course material. Specialists offer one-on-one help by appointment and give instruction on study skills. Writing Assistance provides coaches to help students organize and structure their writing and learn how to self-edit.

Simmons College provides dedicated guidance for: academic · career · personal · psychological · minority students · non-traditional students · family planning · religious. Annually, 86 percent of freshmen students return for their sophomore year. Approximately 21 percent pursue a graduate degree immediately after graduation. One year after graduation, 22 percent of graduates have entered graduate school. Approximately 50 percent of graduates enter a field related to their major within six months of graduation. Companies that most frequently hire graduates from Simmons College include: Brigham & Women's Hospital · Beth Israel Deaconess Medical Center · Children's Hospital Boston · Boston Public Schools · Duke University Hospital · Massachusetts General Hospital · Simmons College · Tufts Medical Center.

Support for Students with Learning Disabilities

Simmons College offers students with learning disabilities the opportunity to take lighter course loads, and to take longer to complete their degrees. LD students may also want to investigate: learning center · testing accommodations · extended time for tests · take-home exam · exam on tape or computer · readers · note-taking services · tape recorders · early syllabus · priority registration · priority seating. Individual or small group tutorials are also available in: time management · organizational skills · learning strategies · specific subject areas · writing labs · study skills. An advisor/advocate from the Disability Services is available to students.

How to Get Admitted

For admissions decisions, non-academic factors considered: interview · extracurricular activities · special talents, interests and abilities · character/personal qualities · volunteer work · work experience · state of residency · alumni relationship. A high school diploma is required, although a GED is also accepted for admissions consideration. SAT or ACT test scores are required of all applicants. *Academic units recommended:* 4 English, 4 Math, 3 Science, 4 Social Studies, 4 Foreign Language.

SIMMONS COLLEGE

Highlights

Simmons College
Boston (Pop. 636,479)
Location: Major city
Four-year private women's college
Founded: 1899
Website: http://www.simmons.edu

Students
Total enrollment: 4,655
Undergrads: 1,792
Part-time students: 8%
From out-of-state: 44%
Male/Female: 0%/100%
Live on-campus: 58%
Off-campus employment rating: Good
Caucasian: 67%
African American: 6%
Hispanic: 6%
Asian: 9%
Hawaiian or Pacific Islander: <1%
Native American: <1%
Mixed (2+ ethnicities): 3%
International: 3%

Academics
Calendar: Semester
Student/faculty ratio: 10:1
Class size 9 or fewer: 17%
Class size 10-29: 68%
Class size 30-49: 10%
Class size 50-99: 4%
Class size 100 or more: -
Returning freshmen: 86%
Six-year graduation rate: 71%

Most Popular Majors
Nursing
Psychology
Communications

399

SIMMONS COLLEGE

Admissions
Applicants: 4,239
Accepted: 2,076
Acceptance rate: 49.0%
Placed on wait list: 337
Average GPA: 3.4
ACT range: 23-28
SAT Math range: 520-620
SAT Reading range: 520-630
SAT Writing range: 6-37
Top 10% of class: 26%
Top 25% of class: 61%
Top 50% of class: 90%

Deadlines
Early Action: 11/1
Early Decision: No
Regular Action: 11/1 (priority)
2/1 (final)
Notification of admission by: 3/15
Common Application: Accepted

Financial Aid
In-state tuition: $35,200
Out-of-state tuition: $35,200
Room: Varies
Board: Varies
Books: $1,280
Freshmen receiving need-based aid: 83%
Undergrads rec. need-based aid: 77%
Avg. % of need met by financial aid: 69%
Avg. aid package (freshmen): $29,386
Avg. aid package (undergrads): $26,527

Prominent Alumni
Gwen Ifill, journalist; Allyson Y. Schwartz, congresswoman; Denise DiNovi, film producer.

School Spirit
Mascot: Sharks
Colors: Blue and gold

How to Pay for College

To apply for financial aid, students should submit the following: Free Application for Federal Student Aid (FAFSA) · institution's own financial aid forms · federal tax returns. Simmons College participates in the Federal Work Study program. *Need-based aid programs include:* scholarships and grants · general need-based awards · Federal Pell grants · state scholarships and grants · college-based scholarships and grants · private scholarships and grants. *Non-need-based aid programs include:* scholarships and grants · state scholarships and grants · special achievements and activities awards.

SONOMA STATE UNIVERSITY

1801 East Cotati Avenue, Rohnert Park, CA 94928
Admissions: 707-664-2778 · Financial Aid: 707-664-2389
Email: student.outreach@sonoma.edu · Website: http://www.sonoma.edu

From the College

"Sonoma State University is a relatively small (8,000 students), residential, public university committed to student retention, graduation and satisfaction. Its primary mission is to develop and maintain excellent programs of undergraduate instruction grounded in the liberal arts and sciences. Instructional programs are designed to challenge students not only to acquire knowledge but also to develop the skills of critical analysis, careful reasoning, creativity and self-expression.

"Within its 36 academic departments, SSU offers 41 bachelor's degree programs and 14 master's degree programs. In addition, the university offers a joint master's degree in mathematics with San Francisco State University and a joint doctorate in educational administration with California State University, Sacramento and the University of California - Davis. The University offers nine credential programs and eight undergraduate and graduate certificate programs. Basic teaching credential programs in education include multiple subject, multiple subject BCLAD, single subject, administrative services, reading/language arts (certificate or specialist), special education (mild/moderate or moderate/severe) and pupil personnel services (via the Counseling Department).

"The university is committed to creating a learning community in which people from diverse backgrounds and cultures are valued for the breadth of their perspectives and are encouraged in their intellectual pursuits. Sonoma's faculty maintain active scholarly lives and the university encourages faculty projects that involve students in research and other creative activities.

"Instead of dormitory-style housing, the SSU residential community offers a variety of accommodations from shared bedrooms in residential suites to private bedrooms and baths in apartments. A 58,000-square-foot student recreation center received the Outstanding Sports Facilities Award by the National Intramural Recreational Sports Association.

"The university was gifted the Fairfield Osborne Preserve, located within a mile of campus, which is dedicated to protecting and restoring natural communities and fostering ecological understanding through education and research. Additionally, the university accepted a 3,500-acre wilderness preserve in northern Sonoma County called the Galbreath Wildlands Preserve to promote environmental education and research, as well as to steward the diverse landscape of the preserve."

Campus Setting

Sonoma State, founded in 1960, is a public, comprehensive university. Its 269-acre campus is located in Rohnert Park, 45 miles north of San Francisco. A four-year institution, Sonoma State University has an enrollment of 9,120 students. Campus facilities include: performing art center · information/technology center · nature preserve · observatory · electron microscope · seismograph · environmental technology center · wildlands preserve. Sonoma State University provides on-campus housing with 865 units that can accommodate 3,054 students. Housing options: single-student apartments · special housing for disabled students. Recreation and sports facilities include: field · gymnasium · recreation center · track · tennis court.

SONOMA STATE UNIVERSITY

Highlights

Sonoma State University
Rohnert Park, CA (Pop. 41,232)
Location: Large town
Four-year public
Founded: 1960
Website: http://www.sonoma.edu

Students

Total enrollment: 9,120
Undergrads: 8,351
Part-time students: 8%
From out-of-state: 1%
Male/Female: 39%/61%
Live on-campus: 37%
In fraternities: 20%
In sororities: 13%
Off-campus employment rating: Good
Caucasian: 59%
African American: 3%
Hispanic: 19%
Asian: 5%
Hawaiian or Pacific Islander: 1%
Native American: 1%
Mixed (2+ ethnicities): 8%
International: 2%

Academics

Calendar: Semester
Student/faculty ratio: 25:1
Class size 9 or fewer: 17%
Class size 10-29: 53%
Class size 30-49: 21%
Class size 50-99: 6%
Class size 100 or more: 3%
Returning freshmen: 83%
Six-year graduation rate: 54%

Most Popular Majors

Business administration
Psychology
Liberal studies

Student Life and Activities

The majority of students (63 percent) live off campus but, a school representative states that SSU has many on-campus activities. The SSU "Seawolf Scene" calendar posts daily events. Favorite student hangouts include the Pub, Northlight Books, Friar Tucks and Cotati Yacht Club. Popular events include Holocaust Lecture Series, Big Cats, Green Music Festival, Center for Performing Arts: Theater & Music, ASU Productions (multiple concerts & lectures), SF Comedy Night, Heritage Lecture Series, Big Night, Lip Jam, and Gender Bender. Sonoma State University has 109 official student organizations. Groups with a strong presence in social life include Greeks (fraternities and sororities) Associates Students (sponsors many events, concerts, dances, lectures, films) and Outdoor Pursuits (coordinates outdoor activities and trips). Intramural teams include: basketball · bowling · flag football · indoor soccer · soccer · softball · Ultimate Frisbee · volleyball · group fitness · personal training · rock wall climbing. Sonoma State University is a member of the California Collegiate Athletic Conference (Division II) and Western Water Polo Association (Division I).

Academics and Learning Environment

Sonoma State University has 231 full-time and 293 part-time faculty members, offering a student-to-faculty ratio of 25:1. The most common course size is 20 to 29 students. Sonoma State University offers 57 majors. Business administration, psychology and liberal studies are the most popular, while philosophy, French and women/gender studies are the least. The school has a general core requirement. Cooperative education is not offered. All first-year students must maintain a 2.0 GPA or higher to avoid academic probation. Other special academic programs include: self-designed majors · independent study · double majors · dual degrees · accelerated study · honors program · Phi Beta Kappa · internships · distance learning.

B Student Support and Success

Sonoma's Educational Mentoring Team helps students transition to college life with a Freshman Seminar and a strong advising department. They feel students should be connected to a faculty member, a student services professional and a peer mentor. The Freshman Seminar is an optional class, but all new students are encouraged to take it. The course focuses on the skills needed to succeed in college classes. Information is provided that teaches students how to be involved in their own education and individualized advising is available as well. Another part of the Freshman Seminar is the study of the university culture. SOAR, or Sonoma Orientation, Advising and Registration, is held each summer for entering freshmen and their parents and is geared to help with the transition to college life. Free tutoring is available for all undergraduate courses. Students are allowed four hours a week, with a maximum of two hours per subject. Sonoma State University provides dedicated guidance for: academic · career · personal · psychological · minority students · military · veterans · non-traditional students · family planning. Sonoma State University offers remedial and refresher courses in: reading · writing · math · study skills. The average freshman year GPA is 3.0, and 83 percent of freshmen students return for their sophomore year.

Companies most frequently hiring Sonoma graduates include: Contra Costa County · Kaiser Permanente Hospital · KRCB Television & Radio · KQED TV · Sonoma County · US Geological Survey.

Support for Students with Learning Disabilities

Students with learning disabilities may take advantage of specific support programs offered by Sonoma State University, including: remedial math · remedial English · remedial reading · special classes · learning center · testing accommodations · extended time for tests · take-home exam · readers · typist/scribe · note-taking services · reading machines · tape recorders. Individual or small group tutorials are also available in: time management · organizational skills · learning strategies · specific subject areas · writing labs · math labs · study skills. An advisor/advocate from the Disabled Student Services is available to students.

How to Get Admitted

For admissions decisions, non-academic factors considered: geographical location. A high school diploma is required, although a GED is also accepted for admissions consideration. SAT or ACT test scores are required of all applicants. SAT Subject Test scores are not required. *According to the admissions office:* Electives should be taken from advanced math, agriculture, English, foreign language, history, lab science, social science and visual/performing arts. Minimum grade of C required in listed secondary school courses. Minimum eligibility index of 2800 for SAT Reasoning (694 for ACT) required of in-state applicants; minimum eligibility index of 3402 for SAT Reasoning (842 for ACT) required of out-of-state applicants. *Academic units recommended:* 4 English, 3 Math, 2 Science, 2 Foreign Language.

How to Pay for College

To apply for financial aid, students should submit the following: Free Application for Federal Student Aid (FAFSA) · state aid form. Sonoma State University participates in the Federal Work Study program. *Need-based aid programs include:* scholarships and grants · general need-based awards · Federal Pell grants · state scholarships and grants · college-based scholarships and grants · private scholarships and grants · ACG and SMART grants. *Non-need-based aid programs include:* scholarships and grants · state scholarships and grants · creative arts and performance awards · special achievements and activities awards · special characteristics awards · athletic scholarships.

SONOMA STATE UNIVERSITY

Highlights

Admissions
Applicants: 14,272
Accepted: 12,870
Acceptance rate: 90.2%
Average GPA: 3.2
ACT range: 18-23
SAT Math range: 440-540
SAT Reading range: 440-540
SAT Writing range: Not reported

Deadlines
Early Action: No
Early Decision: No
Regular Action: Rolling admissions
Common Application: Not accepted

Financial Aid
In-state tuition: $8,996
Out-of-state tuition: $17,824
Room: Varies
Board: Varies
Books: $1,788
Freshmen receiving need-based aid: 33%
Undergrads rec. need-based aid: 44%
Avg. % of need met by financial aid: 27%
Avg. aid package (freshmen): $9,520
Avg. aid package (undergrads): $10,275
Avg. debt upon graduation: $20,568

Prominent Alumni
Ed Sayres, president, American Society for the Prevention of Cruelty to Animals, New York City; Peter Rooney, deputy staff director of U.S. House of Representative Science Committee; Laurie MacDonald, co-head with Walter F. Parkes of DreamWorks Pictures, Motion Picture Division.

School Spirit
Mascot: Seawolves
Colors: Navy columbia and white

403

SOUTHERN OREGON UNIVERSITY

1250 Siskiyou Boulevard, Ashland, OR 97520
Admissions: 541-552-6411 · Financial Aid: 541-552-6754
Email: admissions@sou.edu · Website: http://www.sou.edu

From the College

"From modest beginnings in 1872 as an institution to prepare teachers, Southern Oregon University has changed dramatically. In recent decades, the campus has grown up. We extended our presence into Medford and online. We expanded undergraduate and graduate programs to meet the needs of students and employers. We deepened partnerships locally and internationally.

"But always, at the forefront of our mission, has been change itself, transforming the lives of students and the communities of our region.

"We are becoming well-known as the public liberal arts university of the West. As a public university, we are committed to affordability and access. But, as a liberal arts institution, we offer a personalized experience and a curriculum that prepares students to be productive citizens, creative thinkers and effective problem solvers. Our graduates thrive in a rapidly changing world. The university is recognized for fostering intellectual creativity. At SOU, we don't simply encourage students to be creative. We surround students with a culture based on creative expression and critical thinking. We expose them to different points of view. We challenge conventional thinking. And we provide an open, inclusive environment where students are free to speak their minds. Southern Oregon has a long tradition of doing things differently. Not following the established rules and traditions. Being open to innovative ideas and innovative ways of thinking. This rich environment of creative individuals spans all fields of study and provides a common ground for SOU students from around the world. The local arts community, including the internationally acclaimed Oregon Shakespeare Festival, inspires our creativity. But it's more than just the arts that tap into critical thinking. Our culture reflects a way of thinking that stretches boundaries. SOU embraces a creative spirit in the way we interact with students. The way we teach. The way we involve the community. The way we learn together. We push ourselves, our students and our community to find creative solutions to tomorrow's challenges. Together we're discovering new ways to think and finding new ways to make a difference.

"At SOU, it's not business as usual. Any university can teach theory. To learn, explore and discover what really matters, students need to make a connection. And that's exactly what happens at Southern Oregon University. For SOU students, learning goes far beyond the classroom. SOU professors encourage students to put into practice what they are learning, preparing them to learn more deeply and make immediate contributions when they enter the work force. Through connected learning experiences–including internships, mentor relationships, field study, capstone experiences, volunteerism, civic engagement–SOU students translate learning into meaning as they apply classroom theory to the world around them. Beyond their own learning, they can be leaders, a force for change in the community, bringing a fresh and informed perspective to real challenges. That doesn't happen just anywhere. But then, southern Oregon isn't just anywhere. Southern Oregonians do things differently.

"Finally, SOU is known for the educational benefits of its unique geographic location. Our mountains and rivers are more than just an impressive backdrop. They serve as laboratories and classrooms for outdoor leadership, environmental studies, science research and hospitality and tourism. Our students don't just read about grazing rights, land management, water quality and wine production; they are out learning firsthand. The wild and scenic Rogue River, the Cascade-Siskiyou National Monument, Crater Lake National Park, Redwood National Park and the Deer Creek Center offer learning laboratories within an hour or two of campus."

Campus Setting

Southern Oregon University, founded in 1926, is a public, multi-purpose university. Its 175-acre campus is located in Ashland, in southwestern Oregon. A four-year public institution, Southern Oregon University has an enrollment of 5,864 students. Southern Oregon University has campus facilities including: art museums · theatre complex · center of excellence for the performing arts · ecology center. Southern Oregon University provides 800 units of on-campus housing that can accommodate 1,100 students. Housing options: coed dorms · single-student apartments · married-student apartments · special housing for disabled students · special housing for international students. Recreation and sports facilities include: fitness center · gymnasiums · swimming pool · tennis courts.

Student Life and Activities

Seventy-eight percent of students live off campus. Southern Oregon University has 100 official student organizations, and the most popular are: brass and concert bands · swing choirs · chamber ensemble · symphony · vocal and instrumental jazz groups · opera workshop · photography club · debating · public radio network. Southern Oregon University is a member of the NAIA, Cascade Collegiate Conference and Frontier Conference.

Academics and Learning Environment

Southern Oregon University has 181 full-time and 151 part-time faculty members, creating a student-to-faculty ration of 19:1. The most common course size is 10 to 19 students. The university offers 43 majors. Business, psychology and criminology are top favorites. Least favorites include liberal arts/general studies, interdisciplinary studies and foreign languages. The school has a general core requirement. Cooperative education is available. All first-year students must maintain a 2.0 GPA or higher to avoid academic probation, and a minimum overall GPA of 2.0 is required to graduate. Other special academic programs include: self-designed majors · pass/fail grading option · independent study · double majors · dual degrees · accelerated study · honors program · internships · distance learning certificate programs.

B Student Support and Success

Southern Oregon University offers students help through its AC-CESS Center, an acronym for Academic Advising, Counseling, Career Services and Educational Support Services. Their programs include a Writing Center and math tutoring. Academic advisors help students understand and organize the University Studies Requirements, i.e. General Studies.

Southern Oregon University provides a variety of support programs including: academic · career · personal · psychological · minority students · military · veterans · non-traditional students · family planning. The average freshman year GPA is 3.0, and 68 percent of freshmen return for the sophomore year. The companies recently hiring SOU graduates include: Bear Creek Corp. ·

SOUTHERN OREGON UNIVERSITY

SOUTHERN OREGON UNIVERSITY

Highlights

Admissions
Applicants: 1,985
Accepted: 1,837
Acceptance rate: 92.5%
Average GPA: 3.3
ACT range: 19-25
SAT Math range: 440-550
SAT Reading range: 450-570
SAT Writing range: Not reported

Deadlines
Early Action: No
Early Decision: No
Regular Action: Rolling admissions
Common Application: Accepted

Financial Aid
In-state tuition: $6,504
Out-of-state tuition: $19,882
Room: Varies
Board: Varies
Books: $1,260
Freshmen receiving need-based aid: 66%
Undergrads rec. need-based aid: 79%
Avg. % of need met by financial aid: 53%
Avg. aid package (freshmen): $7,513
Avg. aid package (undergrads): $8,714
Avg. debt upon graduation: $25,194

Prominent Alumni
Ty Burrel, actor; Michael Geisen, national teacher of the year.

School Spirit
Mascot: Red-Tailed Hawk
Colors: Red and black

Lithia Automotive Group · Asante Health · Ashland Springs Hotel · GlaxoSmithKline Pharmaceuticals · Pacific Retirement Services.

Support for Students with Learning Disabilities

Taking extra time to complete a degree and/or carrying a lighter course load are both options for students with learning disabilities. High school foreign language and math waivers are accepted. According to the school, students with disabilities who do not meet university admission requirements are invited to participate in special admissions process, and to coordinate this with DSS. Support services are available from both DSS and TRIO programs. Students with learning disabilities may explore: remedial math · special classes · tutors · learning center · testing accommodations · extended time for tests · take-home exam · oral tests · readers · typist/scribe · note-taking services · reading machines · tape recorders. Individual or small group tutorials are also available in: time management · organizational skills · learning strategies · specific subject areas · writing labs · math labs · study skills. An advisor/advocate from the LD program is available to students.

How to Get Admitted

For admissions decisions, non-academic factors considered: interview · extracurricular activities · volunteer work · geographical location. A high school diploma is required, although a GED is also accepted for admissions consideration. SAT or ACT test scores are required of all applicants. SAT Subject Test scores are required for some applicants. *According to the admissions office:* Minimum 3.0 GPA required. *Academic units recommended:* 4 English, 3 Math, 2 Science, 3 Social Studies, 2 Foreign Language.

How to Pay for College

To apply for financial aid, students should submit the following: Free Application for Federal Student Aid (FAFSA). Southern Oregon University participates in the Federal Work Study program. *Need-based aid programs include:* scholarships and grants · general need-based awards · Federal Pell grants · state scholarships and grants · college-based scholarships and grants · private scholarships and grants. *Non-need-based aid programs include:* scholarships and grants · general need-based awards · state scholarships and grants · creative arts and performance awards · special characteristics awards · athletic scholarships · Army GOLD scholarships.

SPELMAN COLLEGE

350 Spelman Lane, SW, Atlanta, GA 30314-4399
Admissions: 800-982-2411 · Financial Aid: 404-270-5212
Email: admissions@spelman.edu · Website: http://www.spelman.edu

From the College

"Our signature offerings include The Spelman MILE (My Integrated Learning Experience); African Diaspora and the World Program; Gordon-Zeto Center for Global Education; the SpelBots Robotics Team; the Spelman College Glee Club and the Women's Research and Resource Center–the first such center and the first to offer a women's studies major at an HBCU. During the academic year, the College hosts Cosby Distinguished Chair Professors such as Tananarive Due and distinguished lecturers such as Angela Davis and Melissa Harris-Perry. Each of these prominent women exemplify the high intellect, creativity, independent thinking and courage of convictions that the college works to cultivate in our students.

"Each Spelman student develops an electronic portfolio to capture her journey through The Spelman MILE, our unique combination of curricular and co-curricular experiences. Each student is encouraged to study abroad during her college years, and all students complete internships or undergraduate research projects in the major. Specialized courses, such as First Year Experience, Sophomore Year Experience and the Major Capstone help to define the Spelman education as one that reflects a strong foundation in the liberal arts that runs through the entire curriculum; strength and depth within the discipline and interdisciplinary perspectives on Big Questions confronting our world.

"The programs of the College are created with the expectation that the community and society at large will benefit from a student educated in the liberal arts. We know that employers value that preparation: intellectual and skill flexibility; intercultural experiences and competencies; excellent writing and communication skills and quantitative and strong critical thinking skills."

Campus Setting

Spelman, founded in 1881, is a private, historically black, liberal arts college for women. Its 32-acre campus is located one mile from downtown Atlanta. A four-year college, Spelman College has 2,129 students. Campus facilities include: art museum · digital media lab. Spelman College provides on-campus housing that can accommodate 1,398 students. Housing options: women's dorms · single-student apartments. Recreation and sports facilities include a gymnasium.

Student Life and Activities

More than half of the students (69 percent) live on campus. "There is a lot to do," reports the editor of the student newspaper. "Although we are a small private college, we are part of a larger university system. We are within walking distance of three other colleges/universities. We are also five minutes from the downtown Atlanta area." Popular gathering spots include the Lower Manley Student Center Plaza and Friday Market. Popular campus events include Founders Day, Spelman College Reunion, Family Weekend and Senior Soiree. Spelman College has 114 official student organizations. Student Government Association, sororities and AST (African Sisterhood) have widespread influence on student life.

Academics and Learning Environment

Spelman College has 176 full-time and 74 part-time faculty members, offering a student-to-faculty ratio of 10:1. The most common course size is 10 to 19 students.

SPELMAN COLLEGE

Highlights

Spelman College
Atlanta (Pop. 443,775)
Location: Major city
Four-year private women's college
Founded: 1881
Website: http://www.spelman.edu

Students
Total enrollment: 2,129
Undergrads: 2,129
Freshmen: 637
Part-time students: 3%
From out-of-state: 77%
Male/Female: 0%/100%
Live on-campus: 69%
In sororities: 10%
Off-campus employment rating: Good
Caucasian: <1%
African American: 85%
Hispanic: <1%
Asian: <1%
Hawaiian or Pacific Islander: <1%
Native American: <1%
Mixed (2+ ethnicities): 3%
International: 1%

Academics
Calendar: Semester
Student/faculty ratio: 10:1
Class size 9 or fewer: 21%
Class size 10-29: 66%
Class size 30-49: 9%
Class size 50-99: 3%
Class size 100 or more: -
Returning freshmen: 88%
Six-year graduation rate: 73%

Most Popular Majors
Psychology
Biology
English

Spelman College offers 26 majors. Psychology, biology and English are the top favorites, while least pursued include human services, interdisciplinary studies and French. The school has a general core requirement. Cooperative education is offered. All first-year students must maintain a 1.8 GPA or higher to avoid academic probation. Other special academic programs that would appeal to a B student include: self-designed majors · independent study · double majors · dual degrees · honors program · Phi Beta Kappa · internships.

B Student Support and Success

Spelman's Learning Resources Center provides extra help to all students and offers services such as lab instruction, academic advisement, peer tutoring, workshops and instruction in study techniques and learning strategies. According to the college, the center's major objective is to "empower students who will become creative, independent learners and problem solvers capable of processing and handling volumes of information." Peer tutors are available on both a drop-in and appointment basis throughout the year. Students can get help in study techniques, reading, note taking, test-taking strategies, problem-solving and communication skills. Academic advising is also offered through the Learning Resources Center.

Spelman College provides a variety of support programs including: academic · career · personal · family planning. Annually, 88 percent of freshmen students return for their sophomore year. Approximately 30 percent of students pursue a graduate degree following graduation. Just under half of students (45 percent) who are employed enter a field related to their major within six months of graduation. Companies that most frequently hire graduates from Spelman College include: Deloitte Consulting · Freddie Mac · Goldman Sachs · JP Morgan Chase · Teach For America.

Support for Students with Learning Disabilities

Students with learning disabilities may find these services helpful tutors · learning center · testing accommodations · extended time for tests · take-home exam · oral tests · readers · typist/scribe · note-taking services · tape recorders · priority registration · waiver of math degree requirement. Individual or small group tutorials are also available in: time management · organizational skills · writing labs · math labs. An advisor/advocate from the Office of Disability Services is available to students.

How to Get Admitted

For admissions decisions, non-academic factors considered: extracurricular activities · special talents, interests and abilities · character/personal qualities · volunteer work · work experience · state of residency · geographical location · alumni relationship. A high school diploma is required, although a GED is also accepted for admissions consideration. SAT or ACT test scores are required of all applicants. SAT Subject Test scores are considered, if submitted, but are not required. *Academic units recommended:* 4 English, 4 Math, 3 Science, 2 Social Studies, 3 Foreign Language.

How to Pay for College

To apply for financial aid, students should submit the following: Free Application for Federal Student Aid (FAFSA) · institution's own financial aid forms. Spelman College participates in the Federal Work Study program. *Need-based aid programs include:* scholarships and grants · general need-based awards · Federal Pell grants · state scholarships and grants · college-based scholarships and grants · private scholarships and grants · United Negro College Fund. *Non-need-based aid programs include:* scholarships and grants · general need-based awards · state scholarships and grants · ROTC scholarships.

SPELMAN COLLEGE

Highlights

Admissions
Applicants: 5,701
Accepted: 2,325
Acceptance rate: 40.8%
Placed on wait list: 470
Enrolled from wait list: 32
Average GPA: 3.3
ACT range: 18-27
SAT Math range: 420-600
SAT Reading range: 430-615
SAT Writing range: Not reported
Top 10% of class: 31%
Top 25% of class: 66%
Top 50% of class: 89%

Deadlines
Early Action: 11/15
Early Decision: 11/1
Regular Action: 2/1 (final)
Notification of admission by: 4/1
Common Application: Accepted

Financial Aid
In-state tuition: $22,055
Out-of-state tuition: $22,055
Room: Varies
Board: Varies
Books: $2,000
Freshmen receiving need-based aid: 80%
Undergrads rec. need-based aid: 82%
Avg. % of need met by financial aid: 44%
Avg. aid package (freshmen): $15,611
Avg. aid package (undergrads): $18,184
Avg. debt upon graduation: $35,168

Prominent Alumni
Rosalind G. Brewer, CEO, Sams Club; Alia Jones Harvey, only current African-American Broadway producer; La'Shonda Holmes, first African-American female helicopter pilot in Coast Guard.

School Spirit
Mascot: Jaguar
Colors: Columbia blue
Song: *Spelman Hymn*

SPRINGFIELD COLLEGE

263 Alden Street, Springfield, MA 01109
Admissions: 800-343-1257 · Financial Aid: 413-748-3108
Email: admissions@springfieldcollege.edu
Website: http://www.springieldcollege.edu

From the College

"A flexible and people-oriented approach reflects the college's commitment to the philosophy of Humanics and to the unique development of the whole person–in spirit, mind and body. Interdisciplinary programs, challenging courses and a supportive environment enable students to grow as responsible, healthy and productive citizens in service to others. Courses of study are designed to prepare young men and women for success in human-helping fields that enhance society and improve quality of life, especially for those in need. In the classroom, the Humanics philosophy translates into a careful balance of theory and practice–the daily application of education that connects people to people.

"Degrees are offered in 40 undergraduate and 14 graduate major areas of study, including doctoral degrees in physical education and physical therapy. Major areas of study are in health sciences, human and social services, sport management and movement studies and the arts and sciences. The academic experience encompasses coursework, research, laboratory experience and targeted fieldwork enhanced by cocurricular and voluntary service activities on campus and in the community.

"The newly renovated Schoo-Bemis Science Center, which opened in January 2007, is a state-of-the-art classroom and laboratory facility for science education, which over 85 percent of undergraduates take to complete their academic major or minor, and for enhancement of scientific research and discovery, better preparing the nation's future scientific leaders.

"Outstanding athletics and recreation facilities promote the college's athletic heritage and a campus-wide wellness initiative that reflects the balance of spirit, mind and body. The facilities include a six-lane, 50-meter pool; a three-level, multi-purpose, 2,000-seat arena with indoor jogging track; two teaching gymnasiums with handball/racquetball courts; eight tennis courts; two new multi-purpose fields surfaced with state-of-the-art synthetic turf; football field with synthetic turf; baseball and softball fields; indoor batting cages; an eight-lane outdoor track; weight room; climbing wall; aerobics room and a wellness center offering personal training, assessment and record keeping.

"Community volunteerism is more than just an extracurricular activity for students. The college is committed to being part of, and not apart from, the surrounding communities, and this presents students and faculty with opportunities to combine academic training with efforts to give back to the community and address unmet needs. In 2006, the College received $3.62 million to more than quadruple its AmeriCorps volunteer program. As a result, greater numbers of student volunteers can serve as academic coaches for underperforming schoolchildren, and counselors and health case managers for uninsured and underinsured persons."

Campus Setting

Springfield, founded in 1885, is a private, multipurpose college. Its 167-acre campus is located in Springfield, 50 miles west of Worcester. A four-year institution, Springfield College has an enrollment of 3,284 students, and has been co-ed since 1949. Springfield College provides on-campus housing with 11 units that can accommodate 1,900 students. Housing options: coed dorms · men's dorms · single-student apartments · special housing for disabled students. Recreation and sports facilities include: arena · fields · gymnasium · tennis courts.

Student Life and Activities

The majority of students (88 percent) live on campus. Springfield has 50 official student organizations. The most popular are: Best Buddies · Best of Broadway · Habitat for Humanity · history club · rehab club · Sti-Yu-Ka · Premedical Scholars · athletic training club · sports management cub · outing club · YMCA club. Intramural teams include: baseball · basketball · field hockey · flag football · floor hockey · inner-tube water polo · kickball · polo · punt-pass-kick · soccer · softball · triathlon · Ultimate Frisbee · Wiffle ball. Springfield College is a member of the ECAC (Division III, Football I-AA), Eastern Intercollegiate Volleyball Association (Division III), Empire Eight (Division III), New England College Wrestling Association (Division III), New England Women's and Men's Athletic Conference (Division III) and the Pilgrim League (Division III).

Academics and Learning Environment

Springfield College has 211 full-time and 415 part-time faculty members. Springfield College offers 60 majors with the most popular being physical education, rehabilitation services and physical therapy and least popular being computer graphics, medical informatics and history. The school has a general core requirement as well as a religion requirement. Cooperative education is not offered. All first-year students must maintain a 1.7 GPA or higher to avoid academic probation. Other special academic programs that would appeal to a B student include: pass/fail grading option · independent study · double majors · internships.

B Student Support and Success

Springfield's Academic Support Services includes access to one-on-one academic coaching. Qualified tutors help students in areas that include a variety of topics, including the following: taking and using class notes, preparing for exams, managing time, testing taking and alleviating test anxiety, actively reading and learning from your textbooks, concentrating during study sessions, organizing and outlining papers, avoiding procrastination and organizing study groups.

Springfield College provides a variety of support programs including dedicated guidance for: academic · career · personal · psychological · minority students · family planning · religious. The average freshman year GPA is 2.8. Approximately 26 percent pursue a graduate degree immediately after graduation. One year after graduation, the school reports that 41 percent of graduates have entered graduate school. Among students who enter the workforce, approximately 55 percent enter a field related to their major within six months of graduation. Companies that most frequently hire graduates from Springfield College include: Baystate Health · New York Jets · Bank of America · Shriner's Hospital for Children · The May Institute · YMCAs Nationwide · Enterprise · Springfield Public Schools · ESPN Productions · MassMutual · Jewish Family Services · Easter Seals.

SPRINGFIELD COLLEGE

Highlights

Springfield College
Springfield, MA (Pop. 153,155)
Location: Medium city
Four-year private
Founded: 1885
Website: http://www.springfieldcollege.edu

Students
Total enrollment: 3,284
Undergrads: 2,267
Freshmen: 625
Part-time students: 3%
From out-of-state: 63%
Male/Female: 54%/46%
Live on-campus: 88%
Off-campus employment rating: Fair
Caucasian: 79%
African American: 4%
Hispanic: 5%
Asian: 2%
Hawaiian or Pacific Islander: <1%
Native American: 1%
Mixed (2+ ethnicities): 1%

Academics
Calendar: Semester
Student/faculty ratio: 14:1
Class size 9 or fewer: 16%
Class size 10-29: 71%
Class size 30-49: 12%
Class size 50-99: 1%
Class size 100 or more: -
Returning freshmen: 84%
Six-year graduation rate: 67%

Most Popular Majors
Physical education
Rehabilitation services
Physical therapy

411

College Profiles

SPRINGFIELD COLLEGE

Highlights

Admissions
Applicants: 2,372
Accepted: 1,584
Acceptance rate: 66.8%
Average GPA: 3.1
ACT range: 20-25
SAT Math range: 470-580
SAT Reading range: 450-550
SAT Writing range: Not reported
Top 10% of class: 13%
Top 25% of class: 38%
Top 50% of class: 71%

Deadlines
Early Action: No
Early Decision: 12/1
Regular Action: Rolling admissions
Common Application: Not accepted

Financial Aid
In-state tuition: $33,455
Out-of-state tuition: $33,455
Room: Varies
Board: Varies
Books: $1,000
Freshmen receiving need-based or merit-based aid: 99%
Avg. aid package (freshmen): Not reported
Avg. aid package (undergrads): Not reported

Prominent Alumni
Hunter Golden, Blue Sox GM; Don Ho, Hawaiian musician; Mike Woicik, former coach for New England Patriots.

School Spirit
Mascot: Pride
Colors: Maroon and white
Song: *Song For Springfield*

Support for Students with Learning Disabilities

Students with learning disabilities may take additional time to complete their degree, or carry a lightened course load. In addition, LD students may find the following programs useful: remedial math · tutors · untimed tests · extended time for tests · readers · note-taking services · reading machines · tape recorders. Individual or small group tutorials are also available in: time management · organizational skills · learning strategies · study skills. An advisor/advocate from the Student Support Services is available to students.

How to Get Admitted

For admissions decisions, non-academic factors considered: interview · extracurricular activities · special talents, interests and abilities · character/personal qualities · volunteer work · work experience · state of residency · geographical location · minority affiliation · alumni relationship. A high school diploma is required, although a GED is also accepted for admissions consideration. SAT or ACT test scores are required of all applicants. SAT Subject Test scores are recommended but not required. *Academic units recommended:* 4 English, 4 Math, 4 Science, 2 Social Studies, 3 Foreign Language.

How to Pay for College

To apply for financial aid, students should submit the following: Free Application for Federal Student Aid (FAFSA) · institution's own financial aid forms · state aid form. Springfield College participates in the Federal Work Study program. *Need-based aid programs include:* scholarships and grants · general need-based awards · Federal Pell grants · state scholarships and grants · college-based scholarships and grants · private scholarships and grants · Federal ACG and SMART Grants. *Non-need-based aid programs include:* scholarships and grants · general need-based awards · state scholarships and grants · creative arts and performance awards · ROTC scholarships.

SAINT JOHN'S UNIVERSITY

Saint John's University, Collegeville, MN 56321
Admissions: 800-544-1489 · Financial Aid: 800-544-1489
Email: admissions@csbsju.edu · Website: http://www.csbsju.edu

From the College

"The College of St. Benedict (CSB) and St. John's University (SJU) are liberal arts colleges whose partnership offers students the educational choices of a large university and the individual attention of a premier small college. Students attend classes and activities together and have access to the resources of both campuses. Ranked nationally among the top baccalaureate institutions for the number of students who study abroad, CSB/SJU are committed to preparing students for leadership and service in a global society. The colleges enroll students from around the world and integrate global citizenship into the curriculum. Nearly all students live on-campus or in the immediate neighborhood, providing them with opportunities for a highly engaged learning experience. The colleges are located on 3,300 acres of woods and lakes of Minnesota, an hour from Minneapolis/St. Paul and just west of Saint Cloud. A commitment to arts and culture creates an environment for creativity. The Hill Museum and Manuscript Library at SJU is home to the St. John's Bible and a collection of religious sculpture, paintings, prints and artifacts. The learning experience is enlivened by Catholic and Benedictine traditions of hospitality, stewardship, service and the lively engagement of faith and reason. The colleges' values have been shaped by a commitment to ecumenism and interfaith dialogue."

Campus Setting

Saint John's is a church-affiliated, liberal arts university. Founded in 1857, it coordinates with College of Saint Benedict, for women. Its 2,500-acre campus is located in Collegeville, 75 miles north of Minneapolis. A four-year private men's college, Saint John's University has an enrollment of 1,978 students. The school is also affiliated with the Roman Catholic Church (Benedictine). The campus facilities include: library · art gallery · arboretum · greenhouse · observatory · pottery studio · Sommers digital film studio on St John's campus · Benedicta Arts Center · St Benedict's Monastery Heritage Museum · labyrinth on College of St Benedict campus. Saint John's University provides on-campus housing that can accommodate 1,540 students. Housing options: men's dorms · single-student apartments · special housing for disabled students.

Student Life and Activities

Eighty-five percent of students live on campus. "Our college and the College of Saint Benedict are close-knit schools; everyone tries to help everyone else," reports the student newspaper. On campus, students gather at Willy's Pub, Sexton Commons, McKeown Activity Center, the Loft, Mary Commons, Claire Lynch Hall and Gorecki Dining Center. Popular events include Club Involvement Fair, Welcome Fest, Pinestock, Festival of Cultures, Battle of the Bands, Asian New Year, Little Sibs Weekend and Stella Maris Ball. St. John's University has 100 official student organizations. The most popular are: accounting club · international affairs club · Math Society · music club · nursing club · nutrition club · philosophy club · pre-dentistry club · Pre-Law Society · pre-med club · psychology club · art club · Pseudonym · social work club · Society for the Advancement of Management · American Sign Language · Amnesty International · Campus Groove Recordings · Campus Greens · College DFL/Democrats · College Republicans · Echo · biology club · investment club · smiles and frowns drama club · Students in Free Enterprise · Students for Life · People Representing the Sexual Minority · The Record · Studio One · chemistry

413

College Profiles

ST. JOHN'S UNIVERSITY

St. John's University
Collegeville (Pop. 3,343)
Location: Rural
Four-year private men's
Founded: 1857
Website: http://www.csbsju.edu

Students
Total enrollment: 1,978
Undergrads: 1,871
Freshmen: 541
Part-time students: 1%
From out-of-state: 23%
From public schools: 73%
Male/Female: 100%/ 0%
Live on-campus: 85%
Off-campus employment rating: Fair
Caucasian: 83%
African American: 3%
Hispanic: 4%
Asian: 3%
Hawaiian or Pacific Islander: <1%
Native American: 1%
Mixed (2+ ethnicities): 1%
International: 5%

Academics
Calendar: Semester
Student/faculty ratio: 12:1
Class size 9 or fewer: 20%
Class size 10-29: 67%
Class size 30-49: 12%
Class size 50-99: 1%
Class size 100 or more: -
Returning freshmen: 86%
Six-year graduation rate: 80%

Most Popular Majors
Business/management
Accounting
Biology

America's
Best Colleges for
B Students

club · ballroom dance club · communication club · Swing Catz · trapshooting club · Student Coalition for Global Solidarity · Up 'til Dawn · Advocates for Sexual Consent · Emergency Medical Technicians · Joint Events Council · computer gaming club · Outdoor Leadership Center · Peer Resource Program · Saint John's Senate · St. John's Health Initiative · Step Club · economics club · education club · history club. There are intramural teams such as: aikido · ballroom dancing · basketball · bowling · climbing · cycling · disc golf · football · ice hockey · racquetball · sand volleyball · soccer · softball · table tennis · tae kwon do · tennis · volleyball · water polo. St. John's University is a member of the Minnesota Intercollegiate Athletic Conference (Division III).

Academics and Learning Environment

St. John's University has 142 full-time and 24 part-time faculty members, offering a student-to-faculty ratio of 12:1. The most common course size is 10 to 19 students. St. John's University offers 86 majors with the most popular majors being business/management, accounting and biology and least popular being humanities, classics and sociology. The school has a general core requirement as well as a religion requirement. Cooperative education is not offered. All first-year students must maintain a 2.0 GPA or higher to avoid academic probation, and a minimum overall GPA of 2.5 is required to graduate. These other programs might intrigue B students: self-designed majors · pass/fail grading option · independent study · double majors · honors program · Phi Beta Kappa · internships.

B Student Support and Success

St. John's University offers help to its students through several programs and facilities. The Writing Center provides tutoring on both a drop-in and appointment basis. The Math Skills Center helps students with all 100-level math classes as well as preparation for the math proficiency exam. Tutors help students review algebra, geometry, trigonometry and pre-calculus as they work on assignments for math classes and prepare for the math portions of standardized tests. In addition, the college offers an Academic Skills Center Reading Lab.

St. John's University provides dedicated guidance for: academic · career · personal · psychological · minority students · religious. The average freshman year GPA is 2.9, and 86 percent of freshmen students return for their sophomore year. Here are some companies that most frequently hire graduates just out of St. John's University: Target Corporation · United Health Group · United States Army · IBM · Genesis 10, Securian · Larson Allen and Weishair LLP · Wells Fargo.

Support for Students with Learning Disabilities

Students with learning disabilities will be pleased to learn that there are specific support programs available to them at St. John's University. According to the school, LD services are coordinated through the Academic Advising Office. "While our disability services are limited, we are committed to providing academic accommodations on a case-by-case basis for enrolled students who provide adequate documentation of a disability," according to the college. Individual tutoring is available as needed. Academic and psychological counseling are available on an unlimited basis. LD students will find the following list beneficial: tutors · testing accommodations · extended time for tests · take-home exam · exam on tape or computer · typist/scribe · note-taking services · reading machines · texts on tape · early syllabus · priority registration · waiver of math degree requirement. Individual or small group tutorials are also available in: writing labs · math labs · study skills. An advisor/advocate from the LD program is available to students.

How to Get Admitted

For admissions decisions, non-academic factors considered: interview · extracurricular activities · special talents, interests and abilities · character/personal qualities · volunteer work · work experience · state of residency · geographical location · minority affiliation · alumni relationship. A high school diploma is required, although a GED is also accepted for admissions consideration. SAT or ACT test scores are required of all applicants. SAT Subject Test scores are not required. *According to the admissions office:* Minimum composite ACT score of 21 (combined SAT Reasoning score of 1000), rank in top half of secondary school class and minimum 3.0 GPA in college preparatory courses recommended. *Academic units recommended:* 4 English, 3 Math, 2 Science, 2 Social Studies, 2 Foreign Language.

How to Pay for College

To apply for financial aid, students should submit the following: Free Application for Federal Student Aid (FAFSA) · institution's own financial aid forms · tax forms. St. John's University participates in the Federal Work Study program. *Need-based aid programs include:* scholarships and grants · general need-based awards · Federal Pell grants · state scholarships and grants · college-based scholarships and grants · private scholarships and grants. *Non-need-based aid programs include:* scholarships and grants · state scholarships and grants · creative arts and performance awards · special achievements and activities awards · ROTC scholarships · leadership scholarships/grants.

ST. JOHN'S UNIVERSITY

Highlights

Admissions
Applicants: 1,747
Accepted: 1,313
Acceptance rate: 75.2%
Average GPA: 3.5
ACT range: 23-28
SAT Math range: 480-625
SAT Reading range: 475-610
SAT Writing range: 1-18
Top 10% of class: 22%
Top 25% of class: 52%
Top 50% of class: 83%

Deadlines
Early Action: November 15 and December 15
Early Decision: No
Regular Action: 11/15 (priority)
Common Application: Accepted

Financial Aid
In-state tuition: $38,024
Out-of-state tuition: $38,024
Room: $4,640
Board: $4,640
Books: $1,000
Freshmen receiving need-based aid: 72%
Undergrads rec. need-based aid: 66%
Avg. % of need met by financial aid: 88%
Avg. aid package (freshmen): $31,083
Avg. aid package (undergrads): $28,897
Avg. debt upon graduation: $35,349

Prominent Alumni
Michael Hayden, Broadway, London Theater and TV actor, nominee for Tony Award; Denis McDonough, White House Chief of Staff; Steven Sommers, Hollywood writer, movie director and producer.

School Spirit
Mascot: Johnnies
Colors: Cardinal and blue
Song: *Johnnie Fight Song*

415

ST. LAWRENCE UNIVERSITY

23 Romoda Drive, Canton, NY 13617
Admissions: 800-285-1856 · Financial Aid: 800-355-0863
Email: admissions@stlawu.edu · Website: http://www.stlawu.edu

From the College

"St. Lawrence University is a vibrant, collaborative community of learners who value thought and action. Students tap their full potential as they embrace the natural environment, engage with global challenges and experience the relevance and adventure of a liberal arts education in a complex and changing world.

"St. Lawrence enrolls approximately 2,450 undergraduate students from 40 states and 45 nations, and about 120 graduate students in a non-residential Master of Education program. Over 95 percent of our undergraduates reside on campus. About 11 percent of our students represent U.S. ethnic diversity.

"Located between the high peaks of the Adirondack Mountains and the national capital of Canada, the university provides unparalleled access to international government, cultural and social opportunities and outdoor recreation. Among the features of St. Lawrence's curriculum are international programs in 15 nations and three domestic off-campus programs (including an Adirondack Semester, Sustainability Semester and a New York City Semester); a nationally recognized, model interdisciplinary program for first-year students and 12 interdepartmental programs.

"A science complex, LEED certified at the GOLD level, opened fall 2007 and new arts technology center opened spring 2007. A new performance hall was dedicated in the fall of 2010. The university opened a new 155-bed residence hall in 2014."

Campus Setting

St. Lawrence, founded in 1856, is a private, liberal arts university. Its 1,000-acre campus is located in Canton, in northern New York. A four-year institution, Saint Lawrence University has an enrollment of 2,506 students. There is a sizable library on campus, as well as an art gallery. Saint Lawrence University provides on-campus housing with 30 units that can accommodate 2,220 students. Housing options: coed dorms · women's dorms · sorority housing · fraternity housing · single-student apartments · special housing for disabled students · special housing for international students. Recreation and sports facilities include: all-weather, baseball, football, practice and soccer fields · arena · fitness center · gymnasium · ice rink · stadium · swimming pool · tennis courts.

Student Life and Activities

Ninety-eight percent of students live on campus. Campus events are plentiful and varied, and students are encouraged to develop programming. Sullivan Student Center, Stafford Fitness Center, bookstore and ODY (library) are favorite student hangouts. Popular campus events include Moving-Up Day, 100th Night, Quad Experience, Winterfest, Peak Weekend, Festival of Science and Candlelight holiday service. St. Lawrence University has 125 official student organizations. Groups with an influence on campus social life include athletes, student government and ACE, which provides a wide array of social and cultural activities from movies to plays to art openings. There are intramural teams such as: basketball · broomball · flag football · ice hockey · Ultimate Frisbee · soccer · softball · volleyball. St. Lawrence University is a member of the Upstate Collegiate Athletic Association (Division III) and Eastern College Athletic Association.

Academics and Learning Environment

St. Lawrence University has 173 full-time and 34 part-time faculty members, offering a student-to-faculty ratio of 12:1. The most common course size is 10 to 19 students. St. Lawrence University offers 32 majors with the most popular being economics, psychology and biology. The school has a general core requirement. Cooperative education is not offered. All first-year students must maintain a 2.0 GPA or higher to avoid academic probation. B students might want to explore these alternative options: self-designed majors · pass/fail grading option · independent study · double majors · Phi Beta Kappa · internships.

B Student Support and Success

According to St. Lawrence, it "is a student-centered institution which focuses on active learning. With a student to faculty ratio of 12:1, students are expected to be fully engaged in their academic coursework. Small seminar courses are common at St. Lawrence, allowing students to interact easily with faculty and other students. Professors are very accessible to students who need/want extra assistance. Our Academic Resources Department also offers students peer tutors as needed. We have writing and quantitative labs available to students who seek extra assistance with their communication and mathematical skills."

There are a variety of support programs available at St. Lawrence University, including dedicated guidance for: academic · career · personal · psychological · family planning · religious. Annually, 90 percent of freshmen students return for their sophomore year. While many graduates dedicate themselves to the workforce, approximately 22 percent pursue a graduate degree immediately after graduation. Some companies that most frequently employ graduates from St. Lawrence University are: Goldman Sachs · Hartford Insurance · Amica Insurance · Morgan Stanley · Permal Asset Management.

Support for Students with Learning Disabilities

Those students with learning disabilities have the option of requesting a lightened course load or asking for additional time in order to complete their degree. High school foreign language waivers are accepted. High school math waivers are also accepted. According to the school, all requests for accommodations must be supported by appropriate documentation. LD students should research these: tutors · testing accommodations · untimed tests · extended time for tests · take-home exam · substitution of courses · readers · typist/scribe · note-taking services · reading machines · tape recorders · texts on tape · early syllabus · priority registration · waiver of math degree requirement. Individual or small group tutorials are also available in: time management · organizational skills · specific subject areas · writing labs · math labs · study skills. An advisor/advocate from the LD program is available to students.

How to Get Admitted

For admissions decisions, non-academic factors considered: interview · extracurricular activities · special talents, interests and abilities · character/personal qualities · volunteer work · work experience · state of residency · geographical location · minority affiliation ·

St. Lawrence University
Canton, NY (Pop. 6,669)
Location: Small town
Four-year private
Founded: 1856
Website: http://www.stlawu.edu

Students
Total enrollment: 2,506
Undergrads: 2,414
Freshmen: 631
Part-time students: 1%
From out-of-state: 53%
From public schools: 67%
Male/Female: 45%/55%
Live on-campus: 98%
In fraternities: 8%
In sororities: 18%
Off-campus employment rating: Fair
Caucasian: 80%
African American: 3%
Hispanic: 4%
Asian: 2%
Hawaiian or Pacific Islander: <1%
Native American: <1%
Mixed (2+ ethnicities): 2%
International: 8%

Academics
Calendar: Semester
Student/faculty ratio: 12:1
Class size 9 or fewer: 20%
Class size 10-29: 68%
Class size 30-49: 10%
Class size 50-99: 1%
Class size 100 or more: -
Returning freshmen: 90%
Six-year graduation rate: 80%

Most Popular Majors
Economics
Psychology
Biology

ST. LAWRENCE UNIVERSITY

Highlights

Admissions
Applicants: 4,424
Accepted: 2,054
Acceptance rate: 46.4%
Placed on wait list: 148
Enrolled from wait list: 8
Average GPA: 3.5
ACT range: 25-29
SAT Math range: 570-660
SAT Reading range: 550-650
SAT Writing range: 9-46
Top 10% of class: 34%
Top 25% of class: 70%
Top 50% of class: 95%

Deadlines
Early Action: No
Early Decision: 11/1
Regular Action: 2/1 (final)
Notification of admission by: late March
Common Application: Accepted

Financial Aid
In-state tuition: $47,350
Out-of-state tuition: $47,350
Room: $616
Board: $5,670
Books: $650
Freshmen receiving need-based aid: 62%
Undergrads rec. need-based aid: 60%
Avg. % of need met by financial aid: 88%
Avg. aid package (freshmen): $40,794
Avg. aid package (undergrads): $41,005
Avg. debt upon graduation: $26,832

Prominent Alumni
Maine Senator Susan Collins; Jeff Boyd, chair of the board, priceline.com; Viggo Mortensen, actor.

School Spirit
Mascot: Saints
Colors: Scarlet and brown
Song: *Alma Mater*

alumni relationship. A high school diploma is required, although a GED is also accepted for admissions consideration. SAT or ACT test scores are considered, if submitted, but are not required. SAT Subject Test scores are not required. *Academic units recommended:* 4 English, 4 Math, 4 Science, 2 Social Studies, 4 Foreign Language.

How to Pay for College

To apply for financial aid, students should submit the following: Free Application for Federal Student Aid (FAFSA) · Non-custodian (Divorced/Separated) Parent's Statement · Business/Farm Supplement · Institutional OR CSS. St. Lawrence University participates in the Federal Work Study program. *Need-based aid programs include:* scholarships and grants · general need-based awards · Federal Pell grants · state scholarships and grants · college-based scholarships and grants. *Non-need-based aid programs include:* scholarships and grants · general need-based awards · state scholarships and grants · special achievements and activities awards · athletic scholarships.

America's
Best Colleges for
B Students

ST. THOMAS UNIVERSITY

16401 Northwest 37th Avenue, Miami Gardens, FL 33054
Admissions: 800-367-9010 · Financial Aid: 800-367-9010
Email: signup@stu.edu · Website: http://www.stu.edu

From the College

"St. Thomas University is the only Catholic Archdiocesan-sponsored university in Florida and places an institutional emphasis on social justice and ethical behavior. Our School of Law ranks first among ABA- approved law schools in our proportion of Hispanic students, and sixth among African American students. We are one of the only law schools in the nation with a Human Rights Institute and offer a joint M.B.A./J.D. in accounting, international business, marriage and family counseling and sports administration in addition to our 25 undergraduate and 12 graduate degrees. Approximately 90 percent of the faculty hold the highest degrees in their fields. Rich in diversity and small in size, our community is one of cohesiveness and collegiality where faculty are accessible and approachable, sharing a commitment to respond to student needs."

Campus Setting

St. Thomas is a private, church-affiliated, liberal arts university. Founded in 1961, its 140-acre campus is located in Miami. A four-year institution, Saint Thomas University has an enrollment of 2,315 students. Although not originally a co-educational college, Saint Thomas University has been co-ed since 1975. The school is also affiliated with the Roman Catholic Church. The campus facilities include a library, an archives and a museum. Saint Thomas University provides on-campus housing with four units that can accommodate 300 students. Housing options: women's dorms · men's dorms. Recreation and sports facilities include: baseball, soccer and softball fields · gymnasium · tennis courts.

Student Life and Activities

Seventy percent of students live off campus. St. Thomas University has 17 official student organizations. The most popular are: Writers United · Lady Dimondettes · Men Achieving Leadership, Excellence and Success · Students Advocating and Valuing Earth · Global Leadship Pax Romana Student Society · political action club · psychology club · biology club. There are intramural teams available: basketball · flag football · softball · volleyball. St. Thomas University is a member of the NAIA Florida Sun Conference.

Academics and Learning Environment

St. Thomas University has 105 full-time and 117 part-time faculty members, offering a student-to-faculty ratio of 14:1. The most common course size is 10 to 19 students. St. Thomas University offers 51 majors with the most popular being criminal justice, communication arts and organizational leadership and least popular being economics, religious studies and liberal studies. The school has a general core requirement as well as a religion requirement. Cooperative education is not offered. All first-year students must

ST. THOMAS UNIVERSITY

Highlights

St. Thomas University
Miami Gardens (Pop. 110,754)
Location: Medium city
Four-year private
Founded: 1961
Website: http://www.stu.edu

Students
Total enrollment: 2,315
Undergrads: 1,035
Freshmen: 357
Part-time students: 7%
From out-of-state: 21%
From public schools: 60%
Male/Female: 45%/55%
Live on-campus: 30%
Off-campus employment rating: Good
Caucasian: 8%
African American: 24%
Hispanic: 43%
Asian: <1%
Hawaiian or Pacific Islander: <1%
Native American: <1%
Mixed (2+ ethnicities): 1%
International: 19%

Academics
Calendar: Semester
Student/faculty ratio: 14:1
Class size 9 or fewer: 16%
Class size 10-29: 75%
Class size 30-49: 9%
Class size 50-99: -
Class size 100 or more: -
Returning freshmen: 62%
Six-year graduation rate: 38%

Most Popular Majors
Criminal justice
Communication arts
Organizational leadership

419

College Profiles

ST. THOMAS UNIVERSITY

Highlights

Admissions
Applicants: 817
Accepted: 347
Acceptance rate: 42.5%
Average GPA: 3.0
ACT range: 17-21
SAT Math range: 395-510
SAT Reading range: 390-480
SAT Writing range: Not reported
Top 10% of class: 6%
Top 25% of class: 11%
Top 50% of class: 46%

Deadlines
Early Action: No
Early Decision: No
Regular Action: Rolling admissions
Common Application: Accepted

Financial Aid
In-state tuition: $27,150
Out-of-state tuition: $27,150
Room: Varies
Board: Varies
Books: $1,200
Freshmen receiving need-based aid: 76%
Undergrads rec. need-based aid: 72%
Avg. aid package (freshmen): Not reported
Avg. aid package (undergrads): Not reported

Prominent Alumni
Mike Fitzpatrick, U.S. representative; Stan Van Gundy, head coach of the Orlando Magic; Christina Fernandez, Chief Marshall for the Southern Region U.S. Marshals Service.

School Spirit
Mascot: Bobcats
Colors: Columbia navy and white

America's
Best Colleges for
B Students

maintain a 2.0 GPA or higher to avoid academic probation. Other programs include: pass/fail grading option · independent study · double majors · dual degrees · honors program · internships · distance learning certificate programs.

B Student Support and Success

The university's academic support program includes an ombudsman, or "a person who investigates and attempts to resolve complaints and problems between students and a university." At STU, the "ombud," as he/she is called, listens/evaluates/assists the student with academic concerns, clarifies any academic miscommunications and then helps with all aspect of solving the problem. In addition, the Writing Center offers help with all writing assignments in both one-on-one or group settings.

There are a variety of support programs available at St. Thomas University, including dedicated guidance for: academic · career · personal · psychological · religious. St. Thomas University offers remedial and refresher courses in: reading · writing · math · study skills. The average freshman year GPA is 2.9, and 62 percent of freshmen students return for their sophomore year.

Support for Students with Learning Disabilities

There are specific support programs available to students with learning disabilities. LD students will find the following programs at St. Thomas University very beneficial: remedial math · remedial English · remedial reading · tutors · learning center · untimed tests · extended time for tests. Individual or small group tutorials are also available in: writing labs · math labs · study skills. An advisor/advocate from the LD program is available to students.

How to Get Admitted

For admissions decisions, non-academic factors considered: extracurricular activities · special talents, interests and abilities · character/personal qualities · volunteer work · work experience · state of residency · alumni relationship. A high school diploma is required, although a GED is also accepted for admissions consideration. SAT or ACT test scores are required of all applicants. SAT Subject Test scores are not required. *According to the admissions office:* Rank in top three-fifths of secondary school class and minimum 2.5 GPA required.

How to Pay for College

To apply for financial aid, students should submit the following: Free Application for Federal Student Aid (FAFSA) · state aid form. St. Thomas University participates in the Federal Work Study program. *Need-based aid programs include:* scholarships and grants · general need-based awards · Federal Pell grants · state scholarships and grants · college-based scholarships and grants · private scholarships and grants. *Non-need-based aid programs include:* scholarships and grants · general need-based awards · state scholarships and grants · creative arts and performance awards · special achievements and activities awards · special characteristics awards · athletic scholarships · religious affiliation and alumni/ae affiliation scholarships/grants.

SUNY – PURCHASE COLLEGE

735 Anderson Hill Road, Purchase, NY 10577
Admissions: 914-251-6300 · Financial Aid: 914-251-6350
Email: admissions@purchase.edu
Website: http://www.purchase.edu

From the College

"SUNY - Purchase College combines conservatory programs in the arts with distinctive liberal arts programs. Its location in Westchester allows access to New York City 35 miles away but provides a safe self-contained 500-acre campus in a suburban location that contains facilities including a Performing Arts Center and the Neuberger Museum of Art. Its academic programs combine attention to general education with structured curricula; all programs culminate in a required senior project, and increasingly students enter learning communities that provide faculty and peer mentors, advisors and shared academic and co-curricular activities."

Campus Setting

Purchase College, SUNY, founded in 1967 as SUNY College at Purchase, is a public, multipurpose college and conservatory of liberal and fine arts. Programs are offered through Liberal Arts, Performing Arts and Visual Arts divisions. Its 550-acre campus is located in Purchase, three miles from White Plains. A four-year institution, SUNY - Purchase College has an enrollment of 4,379 students. The campus facilities include a sizable library and an art museum. SUNY - Purchase College provides on-campus housing that can accommodate 2,620 students. Housing options: coed dorms · single-student apartments · special housing for disabled students · special housing for international students. Recreation and sports facilities include: aerobics studio · baseball, softball and soccer fields · basketball and tennis courts · fitness center · gymnasium · weight room · Turf field with lights.

Student Life and Activities

Two-thirds of students live on campus. Popular campus events include Culture Shock and the Purchase Wide Open Festival. SUNY - Purchase College has 32 official student organizations. There are intramural teams such as: aerobics · basketball · bowling · dodgeball · flag football · floor hockey · golf · ice skating · Pilates · racquetball · rock climbing · soccer · softball · table tennis · tae kwon do · tennis · Ultimate Frisbee · volleyball · weight lifting · yoga · ski trips. SUNY - Purchase College is a member of the NCAA, Skyline Conference (Division III) and ECAC.

Academics and Learning Environment

SUNY - Purchase College has 163 full-time and 262 part-time faculty members, offering a student-to-faculty ratio of 16:1. The most common course size is 10 to 19 students. SUNY - Purchase College offers 47 majors with the most popular being visual/performing arts, liberal arts/general studies and social sciences. The school has a general core requirement. Cooperative education is not offered.

SUNY – PURCHASE COLLEGE

Highlights

SUNY – Purchase College
Purchase, NY (Pop. 23,000)
Location: Large town
Four-year public
Founded: 1967
Website: http://www.purchase.edu

Students
Total enrollment: 4,379
Undergrads: 4,265
Part-time students: 9%
From out-of-state: 20%
Male/Female: 44%/56%
Live on-campus: 66%
Off-campus employment rating: Fair
Caucasian: 56%
African American: 8%
Hispanic: 18%
Asian: 3%
Hawaiian or Pacific Islander: <1%
Native American: <1%
Mixed (2+ ethnicities): 4%
International: 2%

Academics
Calendar: Semester
Student/faculty ratio: 16:1
Class size 9 or fewer: 33%
Class size 10-29: 59%
Class size 30-49: 8%
Class size 50-99: 1%
Class size 100 or more: -
Returning freshmen: 82%
Six-year graduation rate: 60%

Most Popular Majors
Visual/performing arts
Liberal arts/general studies
Social sciences

421

College Profiles

SUNY – PURCHASE COLLEGE

Admissions
Applicants: 8,405
Accepted: 2,790
Acceptance rate: 33.2%
Average GPA: 3.2
ACT range: 21-26
SAT Math range: 480-580
SAT Reading range: 500-600
SAT Writing range: 5-21
Top 10% of class: 13%
Top 25% of class: 36%
Top 50% of class: 73%

Deadlines
Early Action: 11/15
Early Decision: No
Regular Action: Rolling admissions
Common Application: Accepted

Financial Aid
In-state tuition: $5,870
Out-of-state tuition: $15,320
Room: $8,518
Board: $4,190
Books: $1,200
Freshmen receiving need-based aid: 62%
Undergrads rec. need-based aid: 62%
Avg. % of need met by financial aid: 48%
Avg. aid package (freshmen): $9,541
Avg. aid package (undergrads): $10,456
Avg. debt upon graduation: $25,159

Prominent Alumni
Edie Falco, actress; Wesley Snipes, actor; Moby, musician.

School Spirit
Mascot: Panther
Colors: Royal blue and white

All first-year students must maintain a 2.0 GPA or higher to avoid academic probation. B students will no doubt find the following of particular interest: self-designed majors · pass/fail grading option · independent study · double majors · internships · distance learning.

B Student Support and Success

Struggling students at SUNY can go to the Learning Center for free tutoring services in writing, math and foreign languages. Sessions with tutors in additional subjects can be arranged. The center also offers students study skills help and printed materials in areas such as time management, making outlines, taking notes and studying. There are multimedia stations for computer assisted learning. Students interested in forming a study group can organize it through the Learning Center, and those with learning disabilities or other special needs can get help using a reading machine and other software.

SUNY - Purchase College offers its students dedicated guidance, including these: career · psychological. SUNY - Purchase College offers remedial and refresher courses in: reading · writing · math · study skills. Annually, 82 percent of freshmen students return for their sophomore year.

Support for Students with Learning Disabilities

Students with learning disabilities may take advantage of the Learning Center, which offers tutorials and help with writing skills, study skills and note taking as well as reading machines.

How to Get Admitted

For admissions decisions, non-academic factors considered: interview · extracurricular activities · special talents, interests and abilities · character/personal qualities · state of residency. A high school diploma is required, although a GED is also accepted for admissions consideration. SAT or ACT test scores are required of all applicants. SAT Subject Test scores are not required. *According to the admissions office:* Minimum combined SAT Reasoning score of 1100 or minimum grade average of 3.0 required. *Academic units recommended:* 4 English, 4 Math, 3 Science, 4 Social Studies, 3 Foreign Language.

How to Pay for College

To apply for financial aid, students should submit the following: Free Application for Federal Student Aid (FAFSA) · state aid form. SUNY - Purchase College participates in the Federal Work Study program. *Need-based aid programs include:* scholarships and grants · general need-based awards · Federal Pell grants · state scholarships and grants · college-based scholarships and grants · private scholarships and grants. *Non-need-based aid programs include:* scholarships and grants · state scholarships and grants · creative arts and performance awards.

STETSON UNIVERSITY

421 North Woodland Boulevard, Deland, FL 32723
Admissions: 800-688-0101 · Financial Aid: 800-688-7120
Email: admissions@stetson.edu
Website: http://www.stetson.edu

From the College

"Stetson University is a private, selective, comprehensive university comprised of a rich array of liberal arts and professional academic programs that integrate learning with personal and social responsibility. Stetson is dedicated to leading students from success to significance, whether that be in the world of work or graduate study.

"The university is located in Central Florida with two campuses and two satellite centers across the state. Its main campus in Deland includes the College of Arts & Sciences, the School of Business Administration and the School of Music. The Stetson University College of Law and Law Center are located in the greater St. Petersburg area, and the university's Celebration campus near Orlando. Graduate programs include business, teacher education and counselor education–and the College of Law offers the J.D. and Master of Law degrees as well as a joint J.D./M.B.A. degree. In all these programs, Stetson is committed to academic excellence, liberal learning and the integration of values in the teaching-learning process.

"Stetson, Florida's first Phi Beta Kappa institution, has programs that extend well beyond the physical boundaries of its four campuses into the community locally, nationally and globally. For five consecutive years, the university has been named to the President's Higher Education Community Service Honor Roll by the Corporation for National and Community Service. The university is affiliated with the Bonner Scholars program, which provides scholarships to approximately 60 undergraduate students who actively and consistently engage in community service. Using principles of green design for their construction, four of Stetson's buildings have received the Leadership in Energy and Environmental Design (LEED) Gold Certification.

"Integral to Stetson's mission is the value of an inclusive community, a place where all paths can be explored. The university has worked to foster social change by acknowledging and respecting differences that result from racial/ethnic background, gender, sexual orientation, religious heritage or other factors and celebrating their points of intersection. Through Stetson Undergraduate Research Experience (SURE) grants, students complete a summer research project in the field of their choice while receiving a stipend. All students in the College of Arts and Sciences are required to complete a research project prior to graduation. Students in the Roland George Investments Program assume full responsibility for active management of a portfolio valued at approximately $3 million. Stetson's Family Business Center offers the nation's first major devoted to family enterprises."

Campus Setting

Stetson, founded in 1883, is a private university. Programs are offered through the Colleges of Law and Liberal Arts and the Schools of Business Administration and Music. Its 140-acre campus is located in DeLand, 40 miles north of Orlando. A four-year institution, Stetson University has an enrollment of 4,044 students. Campus facilities include: art gallery · mineral museum · theatre. Stetson University provides on-campus housing with 989 units that can accommodate 1,900 students. Housing options: coed dorms · women's dorms · men's dorms · sorority housing · fraternity housing · single-student apartments. Recreation and sports facilities include Hollis Center, which houses a gym, field house and recreation center.

STETSON UNIVERSITY

Stetson University
DeLand, FL (Pop. 27,447)
Location: Large town
Four-year private
Founded: 1883
Website: http://www.stetson.edu

Students
Total enrollment: 4,044
Undergrads: 2,729
Freshmen: 941
Part-time students: 1%
From out-of-state: 35%
From public schools: 78%
Male/Female: 43%/57%
Live on-campus: 68%
In fraternities: 28%
In sororities: 27%
Off-campus employment rating: Good
Caucasian: 65%
African American: 8%
Hispanic: 14%
Asian: 2%
Hawaiian or Pacific Islander: <1%
Native American: <1%
Mixed (2+ ethnicities): 4%
International: 5%

Academics
Calendar: Semester
Student/faculty ratio: 12:1
Class size 9 or fewer: 12%
Class size 10-29: 81%
Class size 30-49: 6%
Class size 50-99: 1%
Class size 100 or more: -
Returning freshmen: 78%
Six-year graduation rate: 64%

Most Popular Majors
Business administration
Finance
Psychology

Student Life and Activities

Sixty-eight percent of students live on campus and, as reported by a school representative, "an abundance of opportunities exist." Popular gathering spots include the Commons on campus, around the fountain in the quad, the Abbey and beaches of the Atlantic Ocean. Popular campus events include Greenfeather, School of Music concerts, various lecture series and Spring homecoming. Stetson University has 120 official student organizations. Greeks, the Student Government Association and a wide variety of student-run clubs influence campus life. Intramural teams include: baseball · basketball · billiards · bowling · cross-country/track · darts · dodge-ball · flag football · floor ball/hockey · foosball · golf · inner-tube water polo · kickball · lacrosse · melonball · sand volleyball · soccer · softball · swimming · table tennis · tennis · Ultimate Frisbee · volleyball · Wiffle ball. Stetson University is a member of the Atlantic Sun Conference (Division I).

Academics and Learning Environment

Stetson University has 255 full-time and 165 part-time faculty members, offering a student-to-faculty ratio of 12:1. The most common course size is 10 to 19 students. Stetson University offers 64 majors. Business administration, finance and psychology are top of the list. The school has a general core requirement. Cooperative education is available. All first-year students must maintain a 2.0 GPA or higher to avoid academic probation. Other special academic programs that would appeal to a B student include: self-designed majors · pass/fail grading option · independent study · double majors · dual degrees · accelerated study · honors program · Phi Beta Kappa · internships · weekend college · distance learning.

B Student Support and Success

Stetson offers a first-year program designed specifically to help the new student transition to college life. It features a center with a computer lab and study room, and F.O.C.U.S., or "Friends on Campus Uniting Students." This five-day orientation program teaches students about all about the resources available at Stetson. First-year seminars are offered in order to help students learn to read critically, analyze and interpret ideas, develop arguments, write persuasive text and produce different academic work.

Stetson University provides a dedicated guidance for: academic · career · personal · psychological · minority students · family planning · religious. The average freshman year GPA is 2.8, and 78 percent of freshmen students return for their sophomore year. Twenty-two percent of students pursue a graduate degree right away. After one year of graduation, 24 percent of graduates have entered graduate school. Companies that most frequently hire graduates from Stetson University include: ABC News · American Express · AmeriCorps · AT&T · Ballet Hispanico of New York · Blockbuster · Bogdahn Consulting · Brighthouse · Carasoft Technology Corporation · CIGNA Foundation · Charles Schwab · Coach · CVS · Disney · Edward Jones · Florida Hospital · FBI · French Ministry of Education · Gap Clothing · Google · Morgan Stanley · New York State Council on the Arts · Northwestern Mutual Financial Network · Orlando Resorts Rental · Peace Corps · Pennsylvania Academy of the Fine Arts · Pershing · Princeton University Press

· Raymond James Financial · SEI Investments · Siemens Energy · Sherwin-Williams Company · Teach For America · The Dolphin Research Center · United Nations · United States Army · United States Marine Corps · Wells Fargo · Wyndham Vacation Resorts.

Support for Students with Learning Disabilities

Students with learning disabilities may take longer to complete a degree and/or carry a lighter course load. In addition, LD students might want to explore the options of: tutors · learning center · extended time for tests · take-home exam · oral tests · exam on tape or computer · readers · typist/scribe · note-taking services · tape recorders · texts on tape · early syllabus · priority registration · priority seating. Individual or small group tutorials are also available in: time management · organizational skills · learning strategies · specific subject areas · writing labs · math labs · study skills. An advisor/advocate from the Academic Resources Center is available to students.

How to Get Admitted

For admissions decisions, non-academic factors considered: interview · extracurricular activities · special talents, interests and abilities · character/personal qualities · volunteer work · work experience · geographical location · minority affiliation · alumni relationship. A high school diploma is required, although a GED is also accepted for admissions consideration. SAT or ACT test scores are required for some applicants. SAT Subject Test scores are not required.

How to Pay for College

To apply for financial aid, students should submit the following: Free Application for Federal Student Aid (FAFSA) · institution's own financial aid forms · state aid form. Stetson University participates in the Federal Work Study program. *Need-based aid programs include:* scholarships and grants · general need-based awards · Federal Pell grants · state scholarships and grants · college-based scholarships and grants · private scholarships and grants. *Non-need-based aid programs include:* scholarships and grants · general need-based awards · state scholarships and grants · creative arts and performance awards · special achievements and activities awards · special characteristics awards · athletic scholarships · ROTC scholarships.

STETSON UNIVERSITY

Highlights

Admissions
Applicants: 10,509
Accepted: 6,227
Acceptance rate: 59.3%
Average GPA: 3.9
ACT range: 23-28
SAT Math range: 530-630
SAT Reading range: 540-640
SAT Writing range: 3-31
Top 10% of class: 26%
Top 25% of class: 61%
Top 50% of class: 89%

Deadlines
Early Action: No
Early Decision: No
Regular Action: Rolling admissions
Common Application: Accepted

Financial Aid
In-state tuition: $39,690
Out-of-state tuition: $39,690
Room: $6,616
Board: $4,860
Books: $1,200
Freshmen receiving need-based aid: 79%
Undergrads rec. need-based aid: 75%
Avg. % of need met by financial aid: 77%
Avg. aid package (freshmen): $32,906
Avg. aid package (undergrads): $31,980
Avg. debt upon graduation: $33,278

Prominent Alumni
Max Cleland, former U.S. Senator; George Winston, recording artist; J. Craig Crawford, Congressional Quarterly columnist.

School Spirit
Mascot: Hatters
Colors: Hunter green and white

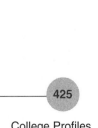

STEVENSON UNIVERSITY

1525 Greenspring Valley Road, Stevenson, MD 21153-0641
Admissions: 877-468-6852 · Financial Aid: 877-468-6852
Email: admissions@stevenson.edu · Website: http://www.stevenson.edu

From the College

"Stevenson University (formerly Villa Julie College) is the third-largest independent university in Maryland. Students pursue undergraduate, master's and adult accelerated degrees at locations in Greenspring and Owings Mills. Stevenson has grown rapidly in recent years, setting new records for enrollment every year while maintaining quality academic programs and affordable tuition. Career Architecture allows students to undergo self-discovery exercises as soon as they arrive on campus in order to help them align their career goals with their personal interests and values.

"The Owings Mills campus opened in 2004 with seven apartment buildings and a community center for student events. The 100-acre campus now has four additional residence halls, a dining hall and student activities building, School of Business and Leadership, athletic fields and wellness center (formerly the home of the football Baltimore Ravens) and office and classroom space. Stevenson has added four-year programs in medical technology, public history and middle school education as well as the master's degree program in forensic studies. The forensic studies program, which includes tracks in law, accounting, information technology, investigations and interdisciplinary studies, is also available online.

"In fall 2011, Stevenson also added a huge stadium to host various sporting events, as well as concerts and other performances.

"In addition to these new programs, Stevenson has expanded its offerings in the sciences and embraced distance-learning technology to bring its successful RN-to-BS nursing program to working nurses across the state. Since its founding in 1947 as a one-year school to train medical secretaries, Stevenson has focused on preparing its students to make positive contributions in the working world after graduation."

Campus Setting

Stevenson University is located in Stevenson, Maryland. A four-year private institution, Stevenson University has an enrollment of 4,290 students, and has been co-ed since 1972. Campus facilities include: art gallery · theatre · science center · labs · greenhouse. Stevenson University provides on-campus housing with 1,300 units that can accommodate 1,845 students. Housing options: single-student apartments. Recreation and sports facilities include: fitness centers · outdoor fields · training facilities · wellness center.

Student Life and Activities

Just over half of students (52 percent) live off campus and, as reported by a school representative, students meet friends on-campus and organize off-campus activities. Students gather on campus at the Student Center, Exchange, Rockland and the Quad. Off campus, students frequent area nightlife, Baltimore Orioles and Ravens games, Inner Harbor offerings, etc. Popular campus events include the Welcome Picnic, Villa Fest, Mr. and Ms. VJC, May Day and Founder's Day. Stevenson University has 45 official student organizations. Influential campus groups include the student government, athletes, the Black Student Union, the Accounting Association, the Student Nurses Association and political clubs. Intramural teams include: basketball · football · racquetball · soccer · tennis. Stevenson University is a member of the Capital Athletic Conference (Division III).

Academics and Learning Environment

Stevenson University has 130 full-time and 393 part-time faculty members, offering a student-to-faculty ratio of 13:1. The most common course size is 10 to 19 students. Stevenson University offers 36 majors with the most popular being nursing, business administration and computer science/information systems and least popular being junior high/intermediate/middle school education, applied mathematics and fashion merchandising. The school has a general core requirement. Cooperative education is available. All first-year students must maintain a 1.9 GPA or higher to avoid academic probation, and a minimum overall GPA of 2.0 is required to graduate. Other special academic programs include: self-designed majors · independent study · double majors · dual degrees · accelerated study · honors program · internships · distance learning.

B Student Support and Success

Stevenson University provides dedicated guidance for: academic · career · personal · psychological · minority students · military · veterans · non-traditional students · family planning. Recognizing that some students may need extra preparation, Stevenson University offers remedial and refresher courses in: reading · writing · math · study skills. Other remedial services include tutoring in all academic areas. The average freshman year GPA is 3.0, and 75 percent of freshmen students return for their sophomore year. Approximately 82 percent of graduates enter a field related to their major within six months of graduation. Companies that most frequently hire graduates from Stevenson University include: Baltimore County School System · Blue Cross & Blue Shield · Carroll County School System · Greater Baltimore Medical Center · Hartford County School System · Johns Hopkins Hospital · Sinai Hospital · St. Joseph Medical Center · T. Rowe Price · various accounting firms.

Support for Students with Learning Disabilities

As with the majority of colleges, students at Stevenson University who are coping with learning disabilities may take extra time to complete their degree or carry a lightened course load. High school foreign language and math waivers are accepted. Students with learning disabilities may want to investigate the options of: remedial math · remedial English · remedial reading · tutors · learning center · testing accommodations · untimed tests · extended time for tests · oral tests · readers · note-taking services · reading machines · tape recorders · texts on tape · early syllabus · priority registration. Individual or small group tutorials are also available in: time management · organizational skills · learning strategies · specific subject areas · writing labs · math labs · study skills. An advisor/advocate from the Academic Support Services is available to students.

How to Get Admitted

For admissions decisions, non-academic factors considered: interview · extracurricular activities · special talents, interests and abilities · character/personal qualities · volunteer work · work experience · state of residency · geographical location · alumni relationship. A high school diploma is required, although a GED is also accepted for admissions consideration. SAT or ACT test scores are required

STEVENSON UNIVERSITY

Highlights

Stevenson University
Baltimore (Pop. 621,342)
Location: Major city
Four-year private
Founded: 1947
Website: http://www.stevenson.edu

Students
Total enrollment: 4,290
Undergrads: 3,847
Freshmen: 759
Part-time students: 14%
From out-of-state: 25%
From public schools: 75%
Male/Female: 35%/65%
Live on-campus: 48%
In sororities: 2%
Off-campus employment rating: Excellent
Caucasian: 57%
African American: 28%
Hispanic: 4%
Asian: 3%
Hawaiian or Pacific Islander: <1%
Native American: <1%
Mixed (2+ ethnicities): 2%
International: <1%

Academics
Calendar: Semester
Student/faculty ratio: 13:1
Class size 9 or fewer: 13%
Class size 10-29: 83%
Class size 30-49: 4%
Class size 50-99: -
Class size 100 or more: -
Returning freshmen: 75%
Six-year graduation rate: 64%

Most Popular Majors
Nursing
Business administration
Computer science/information systems

STEVENSON UNIVERSITY

Admissions

Applicants: 5,318
Accepted: 3,169
Acceptance rate: 59.6%
Average GPA: 3.2
ACT range: 18-24
SAT Math range: 440-550
SAT Reading range: 440-540
SAT Writing range: Not reported
Top 10% of class: 11%
Top 25% of class: 31%
Top 50% of class: 58%

Deadlines

Early Action: No
Early Decision: No
Regular Action: Rolling admissions
Common Application: Accepted

Financial Aid

In-state tuition: $26,976
Out-of-state tuition: $26,976
Room: $8,284
Board: $1,894
Books: $1,250
Freshmen receiving need-based aid: 83%
Undergrads rec. need-based aid: 75%
Avg. % of need met by financial aid: 57%
Avg. aid package (freshmen): $16,803
Avg. aid package (undergrads): $15,500
Avg. debt upon graduation: $28,032

Prominent Alumni

Dr. P. Ann Cotten, director, Schaeffer Center for Public Policy, School of Public Affairs, University of Baltimore; Martha Kilma, former delegate, Maryland State Legislator.

School Spirit

Mascot: Mustangs
Colors: Green, black and white

of all applicants. *Academic units recommended:* 4 English, 3 Math, 3 Science, 2 Social Studies, 2 Foreign Language.

Insight

John Buettner, assistant vice president, says that Stevenson University is a former Catholic junior college (Villa Julie College before a name change in 2008) that has transitioned from a junior college for commuters to a four-year residential university over the last three decades, with the last 10 years being the university's time of greatest growth and acceleration.

How to Pay for College

To apply for financial aid, students should submit the following: Free Application for Federal Student Aid (FAFSA). Stevenson University participates in the Federal Work Study program. *Need-based aid programs include:* scholarships and grants · general need-based awards · Federal Pell grants · state scholarships and grants · college-based scholarships and grants · private scholarships and grants. *Non-need-based aid programs include:* scholarships and grants · state scholarships and grants · creative arts and performance awards · special achievements and activities awards · special characteristics awards · ROTC scholarships.

America's
Best Colleges for
B Students

SUFFOLK UNIVERSITY

8 Ashburton Place, Boston, MA 02108
Admissions: 617-573-8460 · Financial Aid: 617-573-8470
Email: admission@suffolk.edu · Website: http://www.suffolk.edu

From the College

"Suffolk University is a comprehensive university offering a wide range of under-graduate and graduate degrees in the College of Arts and Sciences, Sawyer Business School and Law School. The university's academic programs emphasize high-quality teaching, small class size and real-world career applications. Ninety-four percent of the faculty members hold Ph.D.'s, and many are practicing professionals in their fields. However, their first priority is teaching and mentoring. The undergraduate academic program offers more than 70 majors and 1,000 courses.

"Suffolk was selected to the first tier of "Best Universities Master's in the North" by *U.S. News & World Report*, as one of the "Best 361 Colleges" by the Princeton Review, to *Barron's* Best Buys in College Education and, most recently, as a College of Distinction by an independent committee of high school guidance counselors and college admissions professionals.

"Suffolk offers more than 75 student clubs and organizations, a nationally ranked debate team, three student-run publications, a strong performing arts program and numerous special events, dances, lectures and community service activities. Suffolk has three residence halls, a new state-of-the-art undergraduate library and a new theater. Modern dormitory facilities provide Internet, cable and telephone access and beautiful views of the city.

"The university has campuses in Boston; Madrid, Spain and Dakar, Senegal. Nearly 1,000 international students are enrolled at the Boston, Madrid and Dakar campuses. The university is committed to helping international students adjust to life in the United States. The Center for International Education assists students and advises them on immigration, administrative and cultural adjustment issues. Special social and cultural activities are offered to all international students. Courses in English as a second language, writing and tutoring are also offered."

Campus Setting

Suffolk University is located in the heart of Boston, a cosmopolitan city in the north-eastern United States. Boston is known worldwide as a premier center for academics, research and business. Suffolk's campus is in historic Beacon Hill, a secure residential neighborhood of brick homes and the grand state capitol building. The undergraduate academic program offers more than seventy majors and 1,000 courses. A four-year private institution, Suffolk University has an enrollment of 8,796 students. Suffolk University has campus facilities including: library · theatre · arts and design gallery · biology field station · law school gallery · audio, video and DVD equipment. Suffolk University provides on-campus housing with 550 units that can accommodate 1,249 students. Housing options: coed dorms · single-student apartments. Recreation and sports facilities include: fitness center · gymnasium · shared ice rink with Boston U · off-campus tennis courts and softball fields.

Student Life and Activities

Seventy-nine percent of students live off campus. Popular on-campus gathering spots include the Sawyer Library, local pubs, dance clubs and student lounges in the Sawyer and Donahue buildings. Popular campus events include the Commuter Fair, Spring Fling, Fall Fest, Various Performance Series, Winter Ball and Temple Street Fair. Suffolk University has 75 official student organizations. Popular groups on campus

SUFFOLK UNIVERSITY

Suffolk University
Boston (Pop. 636,479)
Location: Major city
Four-year private
Founded: 1906
Website: http://www.suffolk.edu

Students
Total enrollment: 8,796
Undergrads: 5,779
Freshmen: 1,355
Part-time students: 7%
From out-of-state: 34%
From public schools: 66%
Male/Female: 45%/55%
Live on-campus: 21%
Off-campus employment rating: Good
Caucasian: 40%
African American: 5%
Hispanic: 11%
Asian: 7%
Native American: <1%
Mixed (2+ ethnicities): 1%
International: 19%

Academics
Calendar: Semester
Student/faculty ratio: 11:1
Class size 9 or fewer: 8%
Class size 10-29: 72%
Class size 30-49: 18%
Class size 50-99: 1%
Class size 100 or more: -
Returning freshmen: 75%
Six-year graduation rate: 55%

Most Popular Majors
Sociology
Management
Marketing

include athletes, Student Government Association, Women in Business, Program Council, Council of Presidents, the Off-Campus Housing Office, Commuter Student Association, Suffolk University Hispanic Association (SUHA), and Black Student Union. There are intramural teams available: basketball · volleyball. Suffolk University is a member of the NCAA, ECAC (Division III) and GNAC Great Northeast Athletic Conference (Division III).

Academics and Learning Environment

Suffolk University has 360 full-time and 412 part-time faculty members, offering a student-to-faculty ratio of 11:1. The most common course size is 20 to 29 students. Suffolk University offers 80 majors with the most popular being sociology, management and marketing and least popular being philosophy, computer science and mathematics. The school has a general core requirement. Cooperative education is available. All first-year students must maintain a 1.8 GPA or higher to avoid academic probation, and a minimum overall GPA of 2.0 is required to graduate. Other programs for B students to research are: pass/fail grading option · independent study · double majors · dual degrees · accelerated study · honors program · internships · distance learning certificate programs.

B Student Support and Success

Suffolk has many different methods of helping students who are feeling a little lost or falling behind. At the Ballotti Learning Center, a Tutor Program matches students with peer tutors who can help students in two ways: 1) by providing extra support for students who are taking a course that is proving difficult for them or 2) through teaching general academic strategies like note taking, exam prep, time management, etc. The service is free, and tutors and students meet up to twice a week for one-hour sessions. In a survey done by the Learning Center, 97 percent of the students tutored reported that it helped them to become more independent learners. Study groups are also offered at the center. They focus on the traditionally high-risk courses and give students the time to review notes and prepare questions for class. Staff consultants at Ballotti are doctoral students in the field of psychology. Their job is to assist students with personal concerns and challenges. (Sessions are private and confidential.)

The AHANA (African Hispanic Asian Native American) International Program is an outreach program for students of color. Peer liaisons help with issues like second language, stereotypes and cultural differences that may occur. Suffolk recognizes that some students may face academic challenges that could result in low grades.

To help provide support for these struggling students, Suffolk has put two programs into place: High Profile and the Roster Project. The school's High Profile Program is for students who are in "academic jeopardy." A team of counselors and technicians connect these students with services that can provide academic support. The Roster Project identifies students who are heading for "academic risk" by mid-semester (at risk of failing because of missing class, poor study habits or communication skills, second language issues, etc.). Letters or calls are made as a warning and then students are encouraged to seek the help they need. Educational consultants are on campus to address issues that affect a student's academic life. This often includes matching student with tutor and then monitoring the relationship to make sure it is successful and effective.

Suffolk University is proud to present dedicated guidance for: academic · career · personal · psychological · minority students · veterans · non-traditional students · family planning. Suffolk University offers remedial and refresher courses in: reading · writing · math · study skills. Other services provided on an individual basis. The average freshman year GPA is 3.0, and 75 percent of freshmen students return for their sophomore year. Among those students who do decide to get involved with the workforce, approximately 70 percent enter a field related to their major within six months of graduation. This is a list of organizations that most frequently hire graduates: Bank of America · Commonwealth of Massachusetts · Ernst & Young · Fidelity Investments · KPMG · Mass General Hospital · PricewaterhouseCoopers.

Support for Students with Learning Disabilities

Students with learning disabilities have the option of involving themselves with specific support programs. If it fits the student's circumstances, the college will grant additional time to LD students to complete their degree. Also, a lightened course load may be granted if applicable. According to the school, LD program varies by student based on needs. Students with learning disabilities will find the following program options at Suffolk University very helpful: remedial math · remedial English · tutors · learning center · testing accommodations · untimed tests · extended time for tests · take-home exam · oral tests · readers · typist/scribe · note-taking services · reading machines · texts on tape · early syllabus · priority registration · waiver of math degree requirement. Individual or small group tutorials are also available in: organizational skills · learning strategies · specific subject areas · writing labs · math labs · study skills. An advisor from the LD program is available to students.

How to Get Admitted

For admissions decisions, non-academic factors considered: interview · extracurricular activities · special talents, interests and abilities · character/personal qualities · volunteer work · work experience · state of residency · alumni relationship. A high school diploma is required, although a GED is also accepted for admissions consideration. SAT or ACT test scores are required of all applicants. *According to the admissions office:* Minimum 2.5 GPA highly recommended. *Academic units recommended:* 4 English, 4 Math, 4 Science, 3 Foreign Language.

How to Pay for College

To apply for financial aid, students should submit the following: Free Application for Federal Student Aid (FAFSA) · institution's own financial aid forms. Suffolk University participates in the Federal Work Study program. *Need-based aid programs include:* scholarships and grants · general need-based awards · Federal Pell grants · state scholarships and grants · private scholarships and grants. *Non-need-based aid programs include:* scholarships and grants · state scholarships and grants.

SUFFOLK UNIVERSITY

Highlights

Admissions
Applicants: 9,275
Accepted: 7,652
Acceptance rate: 82.5%
Placed on wait list: 710
Enrolled from wait list: 181
Average GPA: 3.1
ACT range: 20-25
SAT Math range: 450-570
SAT Reading range: 440-560
SAT Writing range: 1-13
Top 10% of class: 13%
Top 25% of class: 42%
Top 50% of class: 79%

Deadlines
Early Action: 11/15
Early Decision: No
Regular Action: Rolling admissions
Notification of admission by: 3/15
Common Application: Accepted

Financial Aid
In-state tuition: $32,530
Out-of-state tuition: $32,530
Room: $11,582
Board: $2,506
Books: $1,200
Freshmen receiving need-based aid: 70%
Undergrads rec. need-based aid: 63%
Avg. % of need met by financial aid: 66%
Avg. aid package (freshmen): $23,784
Avg. aid package (undergrads): $23,254
Avg. debt upon graduation: $33,812

Prominent Alumni
Sharon Bryan, Chief Operating Officer, The Rockport Company; Dr. Karen DeSalvo, Commissioner of Health, Senior Health Policy Advisor to Mayor Landrieu, City of New Orleans; Trish Gannon, EVP and CFO of Finance and Planning, Boys & Girls Clubs of Boston.

School Spirit
Mascot: Rams
Colors: Blue and gold

SWEET BRIAR COLLEGE

134 Chapel Road, Sweet Briar, VA 24595
Admissions: 800-381-6142 · Financial Aid: 800-381-6156
Email: admissions@sbc.edu · Website: http://www.sbc.edu

From the College

"Sweet Briar College grants bachelor's of arts, science and fine arts and master of arts in teaching and master of education degrees. The College sits on 3,250 acres, which makes it the fourth largest campus for a private, liberal arts college in the country. Sweet Briar offers more than 40 programs of study, including areas of art, business, education, humanities and science, including environmental science. Students collaborate with an exceptional faculty, working in and outside the classroom. Learning is a two-way conversation with professors who are mentors and allies."

Campus Setting

Sweet Briar, founded in 1901, is a private, liberal arts college for women. The campus has retained the Georgian architectural style of the original campus buildings, designed by Ralph Adams Cram. Its 3,300-acre campus is located in Sweet Briar, VA, 12 miles from Lynchburg. A four-year college, Sweet Briar College has an enrollment of 710 students. The campus facilities include: library · museum · center for the creative arts. Sweet Briar College provides on-campus housing with 384 units that can accommodate 625 students. Housing options: women's dorms. Recreation and sports facilities include: field hockey, lacrosse, soccer and softball fields · fitness center · gymnasium · swimming pool · tennis court · trails · weight room.

Student Life and Activities

Ninety-six percent of students live on campus. Popular on-campus gathering spots include: Le Bistro and Vixen Den, Boat House, Bookstore Cafe, Prothro Dining Hall and Student Commons Courtyard. Popular campus events include: The Spring Fling, Quadrocks & Student Involvement Fair and Parents' Weekend. Sweet Briar College has 52 official student organizations. The most popular are: Chamber orchestra · Sweet Tones · Paints and Patches · Amnesty International · Gay-Straight Alliance · Student Union-Campus Events Organization · Red Clay · College Republicans · Young Democrats · Model UN · Sociological Society. There are intramural teams such as: hiking · kayaking · mountain biking · riding · rock climbing · running · tennis · touch football. Sweet Briar College is a member of the Old Dominion Athletic Conference (Division III).

Academics and Learning Environment

Sweet Briar College has 78 full-time and 19 part-time faculty members, offering a student-to-faculty ratio of 8:1. The most common course size is 10 to 19 students. Sweet Briar College offers 36 majors with the most popular being business, biology and English/creative writing. The school has a general core requirement. Cooperative education is not offered. All first-year students must maintain a 2.0 GPA or higher to avoid academic probation. Here is a list of other special academic programs that would appeal to a B student: self-designed majors · independent study · double majors · dual degrees · accelerated study · honors program · internships.

B Student Support and Success

The Academic Resource Center (ARC) at Sweet Briar College provides many different opportunities for student support, including ways to help make college life and courses easier. The center is available to all students and is staffed by trained student assistants. ARC offers information on time management, writing, reading, study skills, stress management, peer tutoring and mentoring. ARC staff also offers assistance for students with learning differences, intent on "encouraging a higher standard of academic performance." The writing tutoring service is ARC's main focus. The staff works with students on all stages of their papers' preparation, from forming a thesis to perfecting punctuation. Experienced student mentors help freshmen adjust to college academics. ARC also offers online and printed resources on topics like weekly time management and course preparation. In addition, it assists with the social aspects of college life and the potential stress this can bring.

Sweet Briar College is proud to offer dedicated guidance for: academic · career · personal · psychological · religious. Annually, 69 percent of freshmen students return for their sophomore year. Here is a compiled list of companies that most frequently hire graduates: Affinion Loyalty Group · Ann Taylor · Blue Competition Cycles · Books a Million · Center for Coastal Studies · Corporate Executive Board · Edelman Public Relations · Federal Bureau of Investigation (FBI) · Freddie Mac · Genworth Financial · On Site Insight · Liz Kos LLC · Merck Pharmaceuticals · National Association of Real Estate Executives · National Security Agency · NAVAIR · North Carolina State Forestry Department · Northwest Mutual financial Network · Otsuka America · Quimonda · Randolph College · Savannah Dance Theater · Senator Elizabeth Dole · Smith Barney · Snag-a-Job · SNL Financial · Sweet Briar College Athletics · Sweet Briar College Admissions · Sweet Briar College Development Office · Trax Services · Tyco · University of North Florida Career Services · various private schools · VISTA · VCU Department of History · Virginian's for Brian Moran · Washington Post · Yale University Cancer Center.

Support for Students with Learning Disabilities

Sweet Briar College caters to its learning disability students as much as it can. If necessary, the college may very well grant additional time to LD students so that they can complete their degree. High school foreign language waivers are accepted. High school math waivers are also accepted. Students with learning disabilities will want to further investigate these: tutors · learning center · extended time for tests. Individual or small group tutorials are also available in: time management · organizational skills · learning strategies · specific subject areas · writing labs · study skills. An advisor/advocate from the Academic Advising is available to students. This member also sits on the admissions committee.

How to Get Admitted

For admissions decisions, non-academic factors considered: interview · extracurricular activities · special talents, interests and abilities · character/personal qualities · volunteer work · work experience · state of residency · minority affiliation · alumni relationship. A high school diploma is required, although a GED is also accepted for admissions consideration. SAT or ACT test scores are required of all applicants. SAT Subject Test scores are considered, if submitted, but are not required. *According to the admissions office:* Mathematics preparation must be at least through Algebra II. Foreign language must include two consecutive years of same language. *Academic*

SWEET BRIAR COLLEGE

Highlights

Sweet Briar College
Amherst, VA (Pop. 2,225)
Location: Rural
Four-year private women's college
Founded: 1901
Website: http://www.sbc.edu

Students
Total enrollment: 710
Undergrads: 703
Freshmen: 208
Part-time students: 3%
From out-of-state: 60%
From public schools: 68%
Male/Female: 2%/98%
Live on-campus: 96%
Off-campus employment rating: Poor
Caucasian: 74%
African American: 9%
Hispanic: 7%
Asian: 2%
Hawaiian or Pacific Islander: <1%
Native American: 1%
Mixed (2+ ethnicities): 2%
International: 3%

Academics
Calendar: Semester
Student/faculty ratio: 8:1
Class size 9 or fewer: 39%
Class size 10-29: 59%
Class size 30-49: 2%
Class size 50-99: -
Class size 100 or more: -
Returning freshmen: 69%
Six-year graduation rate: 57%

Most Popular Majors
Business
Biology
English/creative writing

SWEET BRIAR COLLEGE

Highlights

Admissions
Applicants: 905
Accepted: 763
Acceptance rate: 84.3%
Average GPA: 3.5
ACT range: 21-27
SAT Math range: 458-590
SAT Reading range: 480-620
SAT Writing range: 4-19
Top 10% of class: 30%
Top 25% of class: 58%
Top 50% of class: 82%

Deadlines
Early Action: No
Early Decision: No
Regular Action: February 1 (priority deadline for scholarship consideration)
Common Application: Accepted

Financial Aid
In-state tuition: $34,460
Out-of-state tuition: $34,460
Room: Varies
Board: Varies
Books: $1,250
Freshmen receiving need-based aid: 83%
Undergrads rec. need-based aid: 73%
Avg. % of need met by financial aid: 76%
Avg. aid package (freshmen): $27,022
Avg. aid package (undergrads): $26,423
Avg. debt upon graduation: $23,265

Prominent Alumni
Sarah Porter Boehmler, first senior vice president, American Stock Exchange; Anne Litle Poulet, former director, Frick Collection; Leah Busque, creator, TaskRabbit.com.

School Spirit
Mascot: Vixen
Colors: Forest green and pink
Song: *Sweet Briar, Sweet Briar, Flower Fair*

units recommended: 4 English, 4 Math, 4 Science, 4 Social Studies, 4 Foreign Language.

How to Pay for College

To apply for financial aid, students should submit the following: Free Application for Federal Student Aid (FAFSA) · Non-custodian (Divorced/Separated) Parent's Statement. Sweet Briar College participates in the Federal Work Study program. *Need-based aid programs include:* scholarships and grants · general need-based awards · Federal Pell grants · state scholarships and grants · college-based scholarships and grants · private scholarships and grants. *Non-need-based aid programs include:* scholarships and grants · general need-based awards · state scholarships and grants · creative arts and performance awards · special achievements and activities awards · special characteristics awards.

TEMPLE UNIVERSITY

1801 North Broad Street, Philadelphia, PA 19122-6096
Admissions: 888-340-2222 · Financial Aid: 215-204-2244
Email: tuadm@temple.edu · Website: http://www.temple.edu

From the College

"Temple University is a public four-year research university and a national leader in education, research and health care. Founded by Dr. Russell H. Conwell in 1888, Temple's official motto, Perseverantia Vincit, 'Perseverance Conquers' reflects its students' drive to succeed and commitment to excellence. Temple is a vital institution in the Philadelphia region and Commonwealth of Pennsylvania, contributing more than $3 billion toward Pennsylvania's economy each year. The university also has a strong global reach, with long-standing and vibrant campuses in Tokyo and Rome, programs in London, Beijing and other locations worldwide and nearly 300,000 alumni living around the world."

Campus Setting

Temple, founded in 1888, is a public, high research university. Its 186-acre main campus is located in the center of Philadelphia. A four-year institution, it has an enrollment of 37,270 students. Campus facilities include: dentistry, pharmacy and podiatric museums · planetarium · observatory · art gallery · recording booths. Temple University provides on-campus housing with 5,718 units. Housing options: coed dorms · single-student apartments · special housing for disabled students. Recreation and sports facilities include: gymnastics, fencing and volleyball hall · baseball, football, soccer and softball fields · basketball center · recreation center · tennis pavilion.

Student Life and Activities

Most students (85 percent) live off campus. Temple has every type of person doing every type of thing. The Office of Student Activities is proud home to more than 300 student organizations with groups devoted to everything from fashion to the environment to community service. The sports enthusiast is well served at Temple. It is an NCAA Division IA school with 11 men's and 13 women's sports. Popular campus gathering spots include the Tech Center, Howard Gittis Student Center, Liacouras Center, The Shops at Liacouras Walk and Bell Tower. Off campus, students gather at Liberty Bell, Penn's Landing, Philadelphia Art Museum, Olde City, South Street, Fairmount Park & Kelly's Drive, Kimmel Center for the Performing Arts, Liberty Place Shopping Mall and the Gallery Shopping Mall. Temple University has 315 official student organizations. Popular campus events include Spring Fling, Homecoming, Ambler College Lecture Series, EarthFest, Free Friday, Welcome Week, Memorable Moments, Welcome Back Week and Film Series at the Reel. The most popular student organizations are: Accounting Professional Society · American Medical Student Association · American Society of Civil Engineers · American Society of Mechanical Engineers · Association for computing Machinery · Business Honors Student Association · Collegiate Music Educators Conference · Construction Management Student organization · Criminal Justice Society · Entrepreneurial Student Association · Financial Management Association · Institute of Electrical and Electronics Engineers · International Business Association · National Society of Black Engineers · Economic Society · Toastmasters · Tuners · The Movement · Common Ground · Exceptionalities Organization. Intramural teams include: basketball · dodge ball · flag football · floor hockey · soccer · softball · volleyball. Temple University is a member of the American Athletic Conference, Big East Conference and Eastern College Athletic Conference.

435

College Profiles

TEMPLE UNIVERSITY

Temple University
Philadelphia, PA (Pop. 1,547,607)
Location: Major city
Four-year public
Founded: 1888
Website: http://www.temple.edu

Students
Total enrollment: 37,270
Undergrads: 28,068
Freshmen: 6,418
Part-time students: 12%
From out-of-state: 23%
Male/Female: 49%/51%
Live on-campus: 15%
In fraternities: 4%
In sororities: 4%
Off-campus employment rating: Excellent
Caucasian: 60%
African American: 13%
Hispanic: 5%
Asian: 10%
Hawaiian or Pacific Islander: <1%
Native American: <1%
Mixed (2+ ethnicities): 2%
International: 4%

Academics
Calendar: Semester
Student/faculty ratio: 14:1
Class size 9 or fewer: 7%
Class size 10-29: 61%
Class size 30-49: 25%
Class size 50-99: 5%
Class size 100 or more: 2%
Returning freshmen: 89%
Six-year graduation rate: 66%

Most Popular Majors
Biology
Psychology
Kinesiology

436

Academics and Learning Environment

Temple University has 2,034 full-time and 1,514 part-time faculty members, offering a student-to-faculty ratio of 14:1. The most common course size is 20 to 29 students. Temple University offers 295 majors. Biology, psychology and kinesiology are the most popular. The least popular are civil/constructions engineering technology, piano pedagogy and Jewish studies. The school has a general core requirement. Cooperative education is available. All first-year students must maintain a 2.0 GPA or higher to avoid academic probation, and a minimum overall GPA of 2.0 is required to graduate. Other special academic programs that would appeal to a B student include: self-designed majors · pass/fail grading option · independent study · double majors · dual degrees · honors program · Phi Beta Kappa · internships · distance learning certificate programs.

B Student Support and Success

Temple University offers plenty of support for its students, including computer labs, counseling and tutoring. The school provides students with the choice of more than 30 computer labs plus a Student Computer Center. Advisors are available to aid students with choosing majors and resolving academic and/or curriculum issues. Counselors are eager to provide "academic counseling for students to develop a meaningful education plan compatible with life goals." In addition, the advising center offers a new student orientation. The Student Support Services Program is part of the Russell Conwell Educational Service Center. It gives students intensive academic support through free year-round counseling and tutoring activities. In addition, the college offers a required six-week intensive Summer Bridge Program that includes skill building courses in math, computer technology, library usage, reading, writing and study skills as well as workshops on personal development, art appreciation and career choices.

Temple University provides support programs for: academic · career · personal · psychological · veterans · non-traditional students · family planning. Additional counseling services include: nutritionist/nutritional counseling · eating disorder counseling and support groups. Temple University offers remedial and refresher courses in: reading · writing · math · study skills. Annually, 89 percent of freshmen students return for their sophomore year.

Support for Students with Learning Disabilities

At Temple University, learning disabled students are offered the option of a less demanding course load and extra time to finish a degree. LD students may want to investigate the options of: testing accommodations · extended time for tests · take-home exam · exam on tape or computer · note-taking services · reading machines · tape recorders · texts on tape · videotaped classes · early syllabus · waiver of math degree requirement. Individual or small group tutorials are also available in: time management · specific subject areas · writing labs · math labs · study skills. An advisor/advocate from the LD program is available to students.

How to Get Admitted

For admissions decisions, non-academic factors considered: extracurricular activities · special talents, interests and abilities · character/personal qualities · volunteer work · work experience · geographical location · minority affiliation · alumni relationship. A high school diploma is required, although a GED is also accepted for admissions consideration. SAT or ACT test scores are required of all applicants. *Academic units recommended:* 4 English, 4 Math, 3 Science, 2 Social Studies, 2 Foreign Language.

How to Pay for College

To apply for financial aid, students should submit the following: Free Application for Federal Student Aid (FAFSA) · institution's own financial aid forms. Temple University participates in the Federal Work Study program. *Need-based aid programs include:* scholarships and grants · general need-based awards · Federal Pell grants · state scholarships and grants · college-based scholarships and grants · private scholarships and grants · Federal Nursing scholarships. *Non-need-based aid programs include:* scholarships and grants · state scholarships and grants · creative arts and performance awards · athletic scholarships · ROTC scholarships · music and drama scholarships.

TEMPLE UNIVERSITY

Highlights

Admissions
Applicants: 18,813
Accepted: 12,016
Acceptance rate: 63.9%
Placed on wait list: 1,479
Enrolled from wait list: 264
Average GPA: 3.4
ACT range: 21-27
SAT Math range: 510-620
SAT Reading range: 500-610
SAT Writing range: 5-25
Top 10% of class: 20%
Top 25% of class: 52%
Top 50% of class: 88%

Deadlines
Early Action: No
Early Decision: No
Regular Action: Rolling admissions
Common Application: Accepted

Financial Aid
In-state tuition: $14,006
Out-of-state tuition: $24,032
Room: $6,886
Board: $638
Books: Varies
Freshmen receiving need-based aid: 70%
Undergrads rec. need-based aid: 69%
Avg. % of need met by financial aid: 68%
Avg. aid package (freshmen): $15,200
Avg. aid package (undergrads): $16,154
Avg. debt upon graduation: $34,382

Prominent Alumni
Shirley Tilghman, President, Princeton University; Dennis Alter, Advanta Co., Chairman/CEO; William (Bill) Cosby, T.V. personality and educator.

School Spirit
Mascot: Owl
Colors: Cherry and white
Song: *T for Temple U University*

437

TEXAS TECH UNIVERSITY

Box 45005, Lubbock, TX 79409
Admissions: 806-742-1480 · Financial Aid: 806-742-3681
Email: admissions@ttu.edu · Website: http://www.ttu.edu

From the College

"At Texas Tech University, graduate and undergraduate enrollments are at record levels. Total research expenditures continue to climb. Our faculty and students are winning international acclaim. We are recruiting and hiring top-flight faculty in a variety of disciplines. Texas Tech University is emerging as one of the nation's great research universities.

"In 2009, the Texas Legislature established the National Research University Fund (NRUF) to aid seven designated universities, including Texas Tech, in improving their presence as nationally recognized research universities. The universities were required to meet specific criteria to receive research funding from NRUF. Texas Tech met the criteria during each qualifying year and received the designation in 2012. A strong art and music program is balanced with growing research in a number of sustainable energy areas. New areas of research in solar and nuclear energies as well as smart grids and storage are supported by major endowed chairs for which national searches are currently underway. Texas Tech researchers are also known for their work in creative and technical writing, food safety, environmental toxicology and wind science. Texas Tech faculty members excel at 'integrative scholarship,' combining strengths in teaching, research and service. This excellence is demonstrated by nationally recognized awards and membership in professional academies. Texas Tech students reflect this excellence in their accomplishments. From prestigious nationally competitive scholarships, such as the William J. Fulbright, Gates-Cambridge and Barry M. Goldwater, to national championships in debate, chess, animal science and law, Texas Tech students are known nationwide for their successes. Texas Tech attracts top-quality students. That is evident in our Phi Beta Kappa chapter, which received the highest possible rating from the national Phi Beta Kappa Society.

"Community engagement plays an important role at Texas Tech. In 2006, the university was one of the first 62 institutions in the nation and the first in Texas to earn the Carnegie Foundation's classification for Community Engagement. Since 2007, the university has been annually recognized by the Corporation for National and Community Service President's Higher Education Community Service Honor Roll. Texas Tech is the leading employer in Lubbock, a university-friendly city which serves as the retail and medical center for West Texas and Eastern New Mexico. The city features major retailers, numerous restaurants and internationally recognized wineries. Recreational opportunities are abundant, with top-flight golf courses, city parks and swimming pools, recreational lakes and the Palo Duro Canyon in the region. The city is home to a symphony orchestra, the Lubbock Ballet and thriving community art and theater groups. Several airlines, including Southwest, American and United/Continental, serve the city."

Campus Setting

Texas Tech University, founded in 1923, is a major comprehensive research university. Its 1,839-acre campus is located in Lubbock, TX. A four-year public institution, Texas Tech University has an enrollment of 33,111 students. Campus facilities include: Vietnam Center and Archive · Texas Tech Museum · Ranching Heritage. Texas Tech University provides on-campus housing with 3,343 units that can accommodate 7,255 students. Housing options: coed dorms · women's dorms · men's dorms · single-student apartments · special housing for disabled students. Recreation

438

America's
Best Colleges for
B Students

and sports facilities include: aquatic center · arena · athletic training center · recreational fields · softball complex · tennis courts · track complex · leisure pool.

Student Life and Activities

Seventy-four percent of students live off campus. Popular gathering spots on campus include Tech Activities Board, activities, Student Union and athletic venues. Popular gathering spots off campus include Depot District, Greek Circle, Lone Star Pavilion, Student rec center and Leisure Pool. Popular campus events include Homecoming Week, Arbor Day, Athletic and Pre-Athletic Events (Raidergate), Speakers and Lectures, Hispanic Culture Week, Raider Welcome, Tech Activities Board activities, Intramural Sports, Relay for Life and community service. Texas Tech University has 450 official student organizations. Popular groups on campus include Greeks, community service organizations, multicultural and international student organizations, Student Government Association, Senate and Freshman Council and spirit groups. Intramural teams include: badminton · baseball · basketball · bowling · disc golf · dodgeball · flag football · golf · inner-tube water polo · miniature golf · racquetball · sand volleyball · soccer · softball · swimming · table tennis · tennis · Ultimate Frisbee · volleyball · water polo · weight lifting. Texas Tech University is a member of the Big 12 Conference (Division I, Football I-A).

Academics and Learning Environment

Texas Tech University has 1,412 full-time and 234 part-time faculty members, offering a student-to-faculty ratio of 20:1. The most common course size is 20 to 29 students. Texas Tech University offers 253 majors with the most popular being university studies, exercise/sport science and psychology and least popular being conservation law enforcement, engineering technology construction and health. The school has a general core requirement. Cooperative education is available. All first-year students must maintain a 2.0 GPA or higher to avoid academic probation. Other special academic programs that would appeal to a B student include: self-designed majors · pass/fail grading option · independent study · double majors · dual degrees · accelerated study · honors program · Phi Beta Kappa · internships · distance learning certificate programs.

B Student Support and Success

The Discovery! Program's primary goal is to help students determine their major by examining their skills, values, interests and abilities.

Texas Tech University provides support programs for: academic · career · personal · psychological · minority students · veterans. Additional counseling services include: individual and group therapy for many psychological disorders. Texas Tech University offers remedial and refresher courses in: reading · writing · math · study skills. Other remedial services include advisement in course selection. Annually, 82 percent of freshmen students return for their sophomore year. Approximately 28 percent pursue a graduate degree immediately after graduation. One year after graduation, the school reports that 42 percent of graduates have entered graduate school. Among students who enter the workforce, approximately 73 percent

TEXAS TECH UNIVERSITY

TEXAS TECH UNIVERSITY

Highlights

Admissions
Applicants: 19,170
Accepted: 12,709
Acceptance rate: 66.3%
Average GPA: Not reported
ACT range: 22-27
SAT Math range: 520-620
SAT Reading range: 490-590
SAT Writing range: 1-13
Top 10% of class: 22%
Top 25% of class: 55%
Top 50% of class: 86%

Deadlines
Early Action: No
Early Decision: No
Regular Action: Rolling admissions
Common Application: Not accepted

Financial Aid
In-state tuition: $8,942
Out-of-state tuition: $19,562
Room: $4,380
Board: $2,945
Books: $1,200
Freshmen receiving need-based aid: 50%
Undergrads rec. need-based aid: 51%
Avg. % of need met by financial aid: 70%
Avg. aid package (freshmen): $14,305
Avg. aid package (undergrads): $13,826
Avg. debt upon graduation: $23,838

Prominent Alumni
Angela Braly, CEO of Wellpoint; Ed Whitacre Jr., former CEO AT&T and General Motors; Wes Welker, Professional Athlete, Denver Broncos.

School Spirit
Mascot: Raider Red
Colors: Scarlet and black
Song: *Matador Song*

enter a field related to their major within six months of graduation. Companies that most frequently hire graduates from Texas Tech University include: 3M Company · BWXT Pantex · Carter & Burgess · Chevron Phillips Chemical · Cintas · ConocoPhillips · Ernst & Young · ExxonMobil · Ferguson Enterprises · Freese & Nichols · General Dynamics · Halff Associates · Halliburton KBR · Huitt-Zollars · Hurricane Text Lab · IBM · Jacobs Engineering · KSA Engineers · Lockheed Martin · Parkhill · PricewaterhouseCoopers · Raytheon · Smith & Cooper · Teague, Nall & Perkings · Texas Department of Transportation · US Gypsum · Walgreens · Weatherford International · Wells Fargo.

Support for Students with Learning Disabilities

Texas Tech offers students with learning disabilities the chance to take a less demanding course load, as well as access to: remedial math · remedial English · remedial reading · tutors · learning center · extended time for tests · take-home exam · readers · typist/scribe · note-taking services · tape recorders · priority registration. Individual or small group tutorials are also available in: time management · organizational skills · learning strategies · specific subject areas · writing labs · math labs · study skills. An advisor/advocate from the Student Disability Services is available to students.

How to Get Admitted

For admissions decisions, non-academic factors considered: extracurricular activities · special talents, interests and abilities · character/personal qualities · volunteer work · work experience · state of residency · geographical location. A high school diploma is required, although a GED is also accepted for admissions consideration. SAT or ACT test scores are required of all applicants. *According to the admissions office:* Applicants with rank in top tenth of secondary school class may be admitted regardless of standardized test scores. Minimum combined SAT Reasoning score of 1140 (composite ACT score of 25) and rank in top quarter of secondary school class; minimum combined SAT Reasoning score of 1230 (composite ACT score of 28) and rank in second quarter of secondary school class; or combined SAT Reasoning score of 1270 (composite ACT score of 29) and rank in third quarter of secondary school class required. *Academic units recommended:* 4 English, 4 Math, 4 Science, 3.5 Social Studies, 2 Foreign Language.

How to Pay for College

To apply for financial aid, students should submit the following: Free Application for Federal Student Aid (FAFSA) · institution's own financial aid forms. Texas Tech University participates in the Federal Work Study program. *Need-based aid programs include:* scholarships and grants · general need-based awards · Federal Pell grants · state scholarships and grants · college-based scholarships and grants · private scholarships and grants. *Non-need-based aid programs include:* scholarships and grants · state scholarships and grants · creative arts and performance awards · special achievements and activities awards · special characteristics awards · athletic scholarships · ROTC scholarships.

TUSKEGEE UNIVERSITY

1200 West Montgomery Road, Tuskegee, AL 36088
Admissions: 800-622-6531 · Financial Aid: 800-416-2831
Email: admissions@mytu.tuskegee.edu · Website: http://www.tuskegee.edu

From the College

"Imagine: Your assignment today involves more than reading a few pages from the textbook. Instead, you will measure forces at work inside a low turbulence wind tunnel, or you will be among the pioneer users of the most advanced surgical laser equipment. Perhaps you will work alongside professors studying nanocomposites - an emerging class of materials roughly 1,000 times smaller than a human hair. Welcome to Tuskegee University...where the future is now. Here, groundbreaking research and the quest for new knowledge are how we prepare our students-and the world-for the demands of tomorrow. If you think learning in such a high-tech, high-touch environment is exciting, wait until you see what this rigorous experience can do for your future employment opportunities. All of this doesn't just happen, of course. At Tuskegee, we have spent well over a century building this model of excellence in teaching and learning. A solid foundation, a promising future...Tuskegee. There is no better connection."

Campus Setting

Tuskegee, founded in 1881, is a private, state-related, comprehensive university. Programs are offered through the Colleges of Agriculture, Environmental, and Natural Sciences; Business and Information Science; Engineering, Architecture, and Physical Sciences; Liberal Arts and Sciences; and Veterinary Medicine, Nursing, and Health Professions. Its 5,000-acre campus, located in Tuskegee, has been designated a National Historic Landmark. A four-year institution, Tuskegee University is a historically black university with 3,118 students. The campus provides its students with a large library, as well as a George Washington Carver museum. Tuskegee University provides on-campus housing with 192 units that can accommodate 2,020 students. Housing options: women's dorms · men's dorms · single-student apartments · married-student apartments.

Student Life and Activities

Fifty-five percent of students live on campus. The most popular student organizations are: Chapel orchestra · choir · marching and concert bands · professional and special-interest groups. One tradition for the university is crowning a Miss Tuskegee University and Mr. Tuskegee University. Selection is based on criteria including a dance, oratorical skills, talent and appearance. Tuskegee University is a member of the Southern Intercollegiate Athletic Conference (Division II).

Academics and Learning Environment

Tuskegee University offers a student-to-faculty ratio of 12:1. The most common course size is 40 to 49 students. Tuskegee University offers 48 majors with the most popular being electrical engineering, biology and business administration and least popular being medical technology. The school has a general core requirement. Co-operative education is available. All first-year students must maintain a 2.0 GPA or higher to avoid academic probation. B students should learn more about: pass/fail grading option · independent study · double majors · dual degrees · honors program · internships.

441

TUSKEGEE UNIVERSITY

Tuskegee University
Tuskegee, AL (Pop. 9,477)
Location: Small town
Four-year private
Founded: 1881
Website: http://www.tuskegee.edu

Students

Total enrollment: 3,118
Undergrads: 2,866
Freshmen: 700
Part-time students: 4%
From out-of-state: 63%
Male/Female: 40%/60%
Live on-campus: 55%
In fraternities: 6%
In sororities: 5%
Off-campus employment rating: Good
Caucasian: <1%
African American: 78%
Hispanic: <1%
Asian: <1%
Hawaiian or Pacific Islander: <1%
Native American: <1%
Mixed (2+ ethnicities): <1%
International: <1%

Academics

Calendar: Semester
Student/faculty ratio: 12:1
Class size 9 or fewer: 4%
Class size 10-29: 71%
Class size 30-49: 18%
Class size 50-99: 10%
Class size 100 or more: -
Returning freshmen: 74%
Six-year graduation rate: 43%

Most Popular Majors

Electrical engineering
Biology
Business administration

America's
Best Colleges for
B Students

B Student Support and Success

Tuskegee offers a peer tutoring program for students who are taking first- or second-year courses in gross anatomy, microanatomy, neuroanatomy, physiology, microbiology, parasitology or clinical pathology, anatomic pathology and pharmacology. Peer tutors are available to help the needs of nursing, medical technology and occupational therapy students. These tutors give advice and guidance on information given in lectures; they also monitor more general study skills like questioning and answering and they help to establish study groups. An Academic Skills Guide discusses the importance of effective study skills. According to the college, the guide "addresses the how-to's of studying" and covers such elements as taking part in effective group study, developing thinking skills, taking tests and notes and managing time.

B students will benefit from the dedicated guidance available for the following: academic · career · personal · minority students · veterans · family planning · religious. Recognizing that some students may need extra preparation, Tuskegee University offers remedial and refresher courses in: reading · writing · math · study skills. The average freshman year GPA is 2.7. After students move on from college, a majority enter the workforce, and approximately 21 percent pursue a graduate degree immediately after graduation. After one year has passed since graduation, the school reports that 45 percent of graduates have entered graduate school. Among students who enter the workforce, approximately 21 percent get involved with a field related to their major within six months of graduation. Organizations that most often take graduates from Tuskegee University include: Amoco Oil · U.S. Department of Agriculture · General Electric · General Motors · IBM.

Support for Students with Learning Disabilities

Students with learning disabilities, also referred to as LD students, may want to get involved with specific support programs offered by Tuskegee University. These LD students will want to research these recommended programs: remedial math · remedial English · remedial reading · learning center · diagnostic testing service.

How to Get Admitted

For admissions decisions, non-academic factors considered: extracurricular activities · special talents, interests and abilities · character/personal qualities · volunteer work · work experience · geographical location · minority affiliation · alumni relationship. A high school diploma is required, although a GED is also accepted for admissions consideration. SAT or ACT test scores are required of all applicants. *According to the admissions office:* Minimum combined SAT Reasoning score of 1000 (composite ACT score of 21) and minimum 3.0 GPA recommended. *Academic units recommended:* 4 English, 3 Math, 2 Science, 3 Social Studies.

How to Pay for College

To apply for financial aid, students should submit the following: Free Application for Federal Student Aid (FAFSA) · institution's own financial aid forms · CSS/Financial Aid PROFILE · Non-custodian (Divorced/Separated) Parent's Statement. Tuskegee University participates in the Federal Work Study program. *Need-based aid* programs include: scholarships and grants · general need-based awards · Federal Pell grants · state scholarships and grants · college-based scholarships and grants · private scholarships and grants · Federal Nursing scholarships · United Negro College Fund. *Non-need-based aid programs include:* scholarships and grants · state scholarships and grants · athletic scholarships · ROTC scholarships.

TUSKEGEE UNIVERSITY

Admissions
Applicants: 8,665
Accepted: 3,310
Acceptance rate: 38.2%
Average GPA: 3.1
ACT range: 17-22
SAT Math range: 390-500
SAT Reading range: 400-490
SAT Writing range: 400-510

Deadlines
Early Action: No
Early Decision: No
Regular Action: Rolling admissions
Common Application: Accepted

Financial Aid
In-state tuition: $18,560
Out-of-state tuition: $18,560
Room: $2,150
Board: $2,402
Books: Varies
Freshmen receiving need-based aid: 75%
Undergrads rec. need-based aid: 87%
Avg. % of need met by financial aid: 85%
Avg. aid package (freshmen): Not reported
Avg. aid package (undergrads): Not reported

Prominent Alumni
Lionel Richie, singer and songwriter; Keenan Ivory Wayans, actor and producer; Alice Coachman, Olympics athlete.

School Spirit
Mascot: Golden Tigers/Tigerettes
Colors: Crimson and gold

UNIVERSITY OF ALABAMA

Box 870100, Tuscaloosa, AL 35487-0100
Admissions: 800-933-BAMA · Financial Aid: 855-469-2262
Email: admissions@ua.edu · Website: http://www.ua.edu

From the College

"The University of Alabama is a major, comprehensive, student-centered research university founded in 1831 as Alabama's first public college. We provide a creative, nurturing campus environment where our students can become the best individuals possible, learn from the best and brightest faculty and make a positive difference in the community, the state and the world. On a typical day on our campus, an undergraduate student works side by side with a top molecular biologist researching Parkinson's disease, students openly debate controversial topics at the Center for Ethics and Social Responsibility and volunteers tutor in local schools through the Community Service Center. Fall weekends are alive with the excitement of Alabama football—and "Roll Tide, Roll" echoes across the campus. Ranked sixth in the nation among public universities in the enrollment of National Merit scholars, UA's rising tide of academic excellence is attracting the best and brightest students from across the nation. Our 2011 freshman class was the largest and best qualified in UA history, with one in four freshmen enrolling in Honors College. UA's graduates and students include numerous Rhodes, Goldwater, Truman and Hollings Scholars. Participation in original research and creative activities is becoming a hallmark of the undergraduate experience at UA, with students working closely with faculty on a wide variety of challenging and innovative projects. In addition to equipping our students to succeed academically, The University of Alabama's programs set the bar high for character, service and citizenship. Students are encouraged to participate in one or more of hundreds of campus organizations. Campus ministries are thriving. At the University of Alabama, our students are members of a proud family that's more than 175 years old."

Campus Setting

The University of Alabama, founded in 1831, is a public, comprehensive doctoral and research institution. Its 1,000-acre campus is located in west central Alabama, approximately 50 miles southwest of Birmingham. A four-year institution, University of Alabama has an enrollment of 34,752 students. Although not originally a co-educational college, it has been co-ed since 1893. The campus facilities include: library · art gallery · natural history museum · concert hall · archaeologic site and museum · arboretum · observatory · simulated coal mine · robotics lab · wind tunnel · artificial intelligence lab · jet propulsion engine mini-lab · special collections building. University of Alabama provides on-campus housing with 3,297 units that can accommodate 9,198 students. Housing options: coed dorms · women's dorms · men's dorms · sorority housing · fraternity housing · single-student apartments · married-student apartments · special housing for disabled students. Recreation and sports facilities include: aquatic center · park · fields complex · golf course · lake · intramural fields · ice arena · regional rock climbing facilities · outdoor swimming pool · recreation center · tennis courts.

Student Life and Activities

Seventy-four percent of students live off campus. As reported by a school official, "A wide variety of events are offered surrounding the arts and culture: such as the Druid City Arts Fest, Tuscaloosa Symphony, Alabama Boys Choir, Kentuck Festival, Dickens Christmas Festival and Hilaritas Christmas concert." Popular gathering spots include The Landing at Manderson Park, Quadrangle, Riverside Commons, Ferguson Plaza and Ferguson Union. Popular campus events include Homecoming, A-Day Game, Bama Bound Orientation, Beat Auburn Beat Hunger, Capstone Creed Week, Iron Bowl, Kick-Off on the Quad, Get on Board Day, Realizing the Dream Concert, University Day, Sakura Festival, Earth Day, Honors Week, Bama Blast, University Concert, Week of Welcome, Riffle Effect Community Service Series and Family Weekend. The University of Alabama has 471 official student organizations. Popular groups on campus include Campus Ministers Association, Greek organizations, Black Student Union, International Student Association, Future Alumni for Tradition of Excellence and honor societies. There are intramural teams available: badminton · basketball · bowling · dodgeball · flag football · golf · horseshoes · inner-tube water polo · kickball · punt-pass-kick competition · racquetball · rock climbing · soccer · softball · swimming · table tennis · tennis · turkey trot · Ultimate Frisbee · volleyball · walleyball · Wiffle ball. The University of Alabama is a member of the Southeastern Conference (Division I, Football I-A).

Academics and Learning Environment

The University of Alabama has 1,211 full-time and 520 part-time faculty members, offering a student-to-faculty ratio of 21:1. The most common course size is 10 to 19 students. The University of Alabama offers 190 majors with the most popular being marketing, nursing and LD general business/management. The school has a general core requirement. Cooperative education is available. All first-year students must maintain a 2.0 GPA or higher to avoid academic probation, and a minimum overall GPA of 2.0 is required to graduate. B students might want to investigate this list of programs: self-designed majors · pass/fail grading option · independent study · double majors · dual degrees · accelerated study · honors program · Phi Beta Kappa · internships · weekend college · distance learning certificate programs.

B Student Support and Success

The University of Alabama has several programs in place to help the new college student who might be struggling. WOW, the Week of Welcome, helps students get familiar with all aspects of campus life before classes begin. The Tide Early Alert program allows faculty, staff, parents and students the chance to help any student who is having a tough time maintaining grades. The system identifies any students who have received a D or F on an assignment, test or paper. It also pinpoints students who have had excessive absences or has exhibited behavior that indicates a problem. This alert is transmitted to the staff and they, in turn, link the student to the most helpful campus resources. UA also offers Peer Mentoring from upper class students.

The University of Alabama provides its students with dedicated guidance for: academic · career · personal · psychological · minority students · military · veterans · non-traditional students · family planning · religious. Recognizing that some students may need extra preparation, the University of Alabama offers remedial and refresher courses in: reading · writing · math · study skills. Other remedial services include: Supplemental instruction · course review

UNIVERSITY OF ALABAMA

University of Alabama
Tuscaloosa, AL (Pop. 93,357)
Location: Medium city
Four-year public
Founded: 1831
Website: http://www.ua.edu

Students
Total enrollment: 34,752
Undergrads: 29,440
Freshmen: 8,668
Part-time students: 10%
From out-of-state: 56%
Male/Female: 46%/54%
Live on-campus: 26%
In fraternities: 24%
In sororities: 35%
Off-campus employment rating: Good
Caucasian: 78%
African American: 11%
Hispanic: 3%
Asian: 1%
Hawaiian or Pacific Islander: <1%
Native American: <1%
Mixed (2+ ethnicities): 2%
International: 4%

Academics
Calendar: Semester
Student/faculty ratio: 21:1
Class size 9 or fewer: 14%
Class size 10-29: 49%
Class size 30-49: 19%
Class size 50-99: 11%
Class size 100 or more: 7%
Returning freshmen: 87%
Six-year graduation rate: 67%

Most Popular Majors
Marketing
Nursing
LD general business/management

UNIVERSITY OF ALABAMA

Admissions
Applicants: 30,975
Accepted: 17,515
Acceptance rate: 56.5%
Average GPA: 3.6
ACT range: 22-30
SAT Math range: 500-640
SAT Reading range: 490-620
SAT Writing range: 6-22
Top 10% of class: 41%
Top 25% of class: 60%
Top 50% of class: 83%

Deadlines
Early Action: No
Early Decision: No
Regular Action: Rolling admissions
Common Application: Not accepted

Financial Aid
In-state tuition: $9,826
Out-of-state tuition: $24,950
Room: $5,600
Board: $3,266
Books: $1,200
Freshmen receiving need-based aid: 44%
Undergrads rec. need-based aid: 43%
Avg. % of need met by financial aid: 49%
Avg. aid package (freshmen): $12,431
Avg. aid package (undergrads): $11,122
Avg. debt upon graduation: $28,508

Prominent Alumni
Dr. E.O. Wilson, double Pulitzer Prize Winner; Harper Lee, author, 'To Kill a Mockingbird'; Hugo Black, former Supreme Court Justice.

School Spirit
Mascot: Elephant – Big Al
Colors: Crimson and white
Song: *Yea Alabama*

America's
Best Colleges for
B Students

· help sessions · professional entrance exam preparation. The average freshman year GPA is 3.1, and 87 percent of freshmen students return for their sophomore year. Among students who enter the work force, approximately 43 percent enter a field related to their major within six months of graduation. These companies are some of the ones that most frequently employ graduates: Alabama Power · DCH Regional Medical Center · Deloitte · Ernst & Young · Exxon Mobil Corp. · Hewitt Associates · KPMG · Southern Company · PricewaterhouseCoopers · Princeton Baptist Hospital · Southern Nuclear · University of Alabama - Birmingham Hospital · The University of Alabama · U.S. Air Force · U.S. Army · Walmart.

Support for Students with Learning Disabilities

Students with learning disabilities will find that there is a wide variety of programs available to them at the University of Alabama. If deemed necessary, the college will grant additional time to students with learning disabilities so that they might complete their degree. A lightened course load is another available option. According to the school, accommodations for students with learning disabilities are coordinated through the Office of Disability Services (ODS), which is the designated unit at the university serving all students with disabilities who have self-identified and requested disability-related assistance. Services such as tutoring and writing assistance are offered through the same channels as for students who do not have disabilities. ODS is not specific to students with learning disabilities, and the services available are not specifically designed just for students with LD. Students with learning disabilities will find the following programs worth further investigation: remedial math · tutors · learning center · testing accommodations · extended time for tests · take-home exam · oral tests · exam on tape or computer · typist/scribe · note-taking services · reading machines · texts on tape · early syllabus · priority registration · waiver of math degree requirement. Individual or small group tutorials are also available in: organizational skills · learning strategies · specific subject areas · writing labs · math labs · study skills. An advisor/advocate from the Office of Disability Services is available to students.

How to Get Admitted

For admissions decisions, non-academic factors considered: interview · extracurricular activities · special talents, interests and abilities · character/personal qualities · volunteer work · work experience · state of residency · alumni relationship. A high school diploma is required, although a GED is also accepted for admissions consideration. SAT or ACT test scores are required of all applicants. *According to the admissions office:* Minimum combined SAT Reasoning score of 1000 (composite ACT score of 21) and minimum cumulative 3.0 GPA required. *Academic units recommended:* 4 English, 3 Math, 3 Science, 4 Social Studies, 1 Foreign Language.

How to Pay for College

To apply for financial aid, students should submit the following: Free Application for Federal Student Aid (FAFSA). The University of Alabama participates in the Federal Work Study program. *Need-based aid programs include:* scholarships and grants · general need-based awards · Federal Pell grants · state scholarships and grants

· college-based scholarships and grants · private scholarships and grants · Federal Nursing scholarships. *Non-need-based aid programs include:* scholarships and grants · general need-based awards · state scholarships and grants · creative arts and performance awards · special achievements and activities awards · special characteristics awards · athletic scholarships · ROTC scholarships · alumni/ae affiliation scholarships/grants.

UNIVERSITY OF ARIZONA

P.O. Box 210040, Tucson, AZ 85721-0066
Admissions: 520-621-3237 · Financial Aid: 520-621-1858
Email: admissions@arizona.edu · Website: http://www.arizona.edu

From the College

"Surrounded by the scenic beauty of desert mountain ranges and basking in 350 days of sunshine per year, the University of Arizona offers a top-notch education in a resort-like setting. From day one students are part of Arizona's 100 percent engagement mission, which holds that every undergrad will gain real-world experience in the form of internships, research or community service by the time they graduate. The clear Arizona skies provide an ideal setting for one of the country's best astronomy programs and nationally rated programs including business (entrepreneurship), nursing, management information systems, computer and aerospace engineering, anthropology, sociology and creative writing. The UA balances its world-class research curriculum with a faculty that includes Nobel and Pulitzer Prize winners. A wealth of academic choices and support 417 majors, with numerous concentration options is supplemented by an active, cheerful and inviting campus atmosphere that includes more than 500 student clubs and organizations, conference-winning and national title-winning basketball, baseball, swimming, softball and football teams and countless recreational opportunities."

Campus Setting

The University of Arizona, founded in 1885, is a public institution. Programs are offered through the Colleges of Agriculture, Architecture, Business and Public Administration, Education, Engineering and Mines, Fine Arts, Humanities, Nursing, Pharmacy, Science and Social and Behavioral Sciences; the Schools of Family and Consumer Resources and Health-Related Professions and the University College and Arizona International College. Its 353-acre campus is located in a residential area of Tucson. A four-year public institution, University of Arizona has an enrollment of 40,621 students. The campus facilities include: library · art, minerals and pharmacy museums · herbarium · science center · planetarium. University of Arizona provides on-campus housing with 44 units that can accommodate 7,000 students. Housing options: coed dorms · women's dorms · sorority housing · fraternity housing · single-student apartments · special housing for disabled students · special housing for international students.

Student Life and Activities

Eighty percent of students live off campus. On campus, students gather at the Union Memorial Center. Off campus, students head to University Blvd and Fourth Ave, which are both home to great shops and restaurants. Wildcat Welcome, Spring Fling, Tucson Festival of Books, UA Football, UA Basketball, Homecoming and UA Presents are popular events on campus. The University of Arizona has 500 official student organizations. The most popular are: marching and pep bands · chess · baton twirling · team managers. Greeks, Social Justice Groups and Leadership Groups from CSIL have a strong influence on student life. There are intramural teams available to students with athletic interests: basketball · flag football · floor hockey · indoor soccer · inner tube water polo · kickball · sand volleyball · soccer · softball · tennis · Ultimate Frisbee · volleyball. The University of Arizona is a member of the Mountain Pacific Sports Federation and the Pacific-12 Conference (Football I-A).

Academics and Learning Environment

The University of Arizona has 1,561 full-time and 247 part-time faculty members, offering a student-to-faculty ratio of 22:1. The most common course size is 20 to 29 students. The University of Arizona offers 417 majors with the most popular being business, social sciences and biological/life sciences. The school has a general core requirement. Cooperative education is not offered. All first-year students must maintain a 2.0 GPA or higher to avoid academic probation. Some other special academic programs that might intrigue a B student are: pass/fail grading option · independent study · double majors · dual degrees · accelerated study · honors program · Phi Beta Kappa · internships · weekend college · distance learning.

B Student Support and Success

The University of Arizona offers an extensive Student Support Services designed to help students manage the demands of college life. Their programs include: Academic Career Advising, Peer Advising, a three-credit Connections Course that "explores and critically discusses a variety of topics to help students successfully transition into the UA" and the SSS Colloquia called "Leadership in Student Support Services." The course promotes career and academic related leadership skills, critical thinking and civic engagement projects. The University of Arizona is proud of its support programs and its dedicated guidance for: academic · career · personal · psychological · minority students · military · veterans · family planning. The average freshman year GPA is 2.6, and 82 percent of freshmen students return for their sophomore year.

Support for Students with Learning Disabilities

B students will be pleased to learn that the University of Arizona has programs specifically geared towards those with learning disabilities. The college will grant extra time to LD students wishing to finish up their degree, as well as sometimes offer a lightened course load. According to the school, The Strategic Alternative Learning Techniques (SALT) Center at the University of Arizona (UA) was founded during the 1980-1981 academic year, as a program within the Student Resource Center. SALT students receive individualized educational planning and monitoring, assistance from certified tutors with coursework and an array of workshops geared towards their individual academic needs. The SALT Center is an enhanced service program for LD students, and charges fees for some services. Students with learning disabilities will want to research these: remedial math · remedial English · tutors · learning center · testing accommodations · extended time for tests · take-home exam · readers · note-taking services · reading machines · tape recorders · texts on tape · early syllabus. Individual or small group tutorials are also available in: time management · organizational skills · learning strategies · specific subject areas · writing labs · math labs · study skills. An advisor/advocate from the Disability Resources is available to students. This member also sits on the admissions committee.

UNIVERSITY OF ARIZONA

Highlights

University of Arizona
Tucson, AZ (Pop. 524,295)
Location: Major city
Four-year public
Founded: 1885
Website: http://www.arizona.edu

Students
Total enrollment: 40,621
Undergrads: 31,670
Part-time students: 9%
From out-of-state: 35%
From public schools: 90%
Male/Female: 48%/52%
Live on-campus: 20%
In fraternities: 10%
In sororities: 11%
Off-campus employment rating: Excellent
Caucasian: 55%
African American: 3%
Hispanic: 24%
Asian: 6%
Hawaiian or Pacific Islander: <1%
Native American: 1%
Mixed (2+ ethnicities): 4%
International: 6%

Academics
Calendar: Semester
Student/faculty ratio: 22:1
Class size 9 or fewer: 13%
Class size 10-29: 54%
Class size 30-49: 17%
Class size 50-99: 8%
Class size 100 or more: 8%
Returning freshmen: 82%
Six-year graduation rate: 61%

Most Popular Majors
Business
Social sciences
Biological/life sciences

449

UNIVERSITY OF ARIZONA

Admissions
Applicants: 26,481
Accepted: 20,546
Acceptance rate: 77.6%
Average GPA: 3.4
ACT range: 21-27
SAT Math range: 490-620
SAT Reading range: 480-600
SAT Writing range: 4-20
Top 10% of class: 31%
Top 25% of class: 60%
Top 50% of class: 88%

Deadlines
Early Action: No
Early Decision: No
Regular Action: Rolling admissions
Common Application: Not accepted

Financial Aid
In-state tuition: $9,388
Out-of-state tuition: $26,070
Room: Varies
Board: Varies
Books: $1,000
Freshmen receiving need-based aid: 53%
Undergrads rec. need-based aid: 52%
Avg. % of need met by financial aid: 62%
Avg. aid package (freshmen): $12,526
Avg. aid package (undergrads): $12,621
Avg. debt upon graduation: $22,497

Prominent Alumni
Richard Russo, Pulitzer Prize winner;
Richard Carmona, U.S. Surgeon General;
Joan Ganz Cooney, creator of *Sesame Street*.

School Spirit
Mascot: Wildcats
Colors: Cardinal red and navy blue
Song: *Bear Down Fight Song*

How to Get Admitted

For admissions decisions, non-academic factors considered: extracurricular activities · special talents, interests and abilities · character/personal qualities · volunteer work · work experience · state of residency. A high school diploma is required, although a GED is also accepted for admissions consideration. SAT or ACT test scores are recommended but not required. SAT Subject Test scores are considered, if submitted, but are not required. *According to the admissions office:* Minimum combined SAT Reasoning score of 1040 (composite ACT score of 22), rank in top half of secondary school class or minimum 2.5 GPA required of in-state applicants; minimum combined SAT Reasoning score of 1110 (composite ACT score of 24), rank in top quarter of secondary school class or minimum 3.0 GPA required of out-of-state applicants. *Academic units recommended:* 4 English, 4 Math, 3 Science, 1 Social Studies, 2 Foreign Language.

How to Pay for College

To apply for financial aid, students should submit the following: Free Application for Federal Student Aid (FAFSA). University of Arizona participates in the Federal Work Study program. *Need-based aid programs include:* scholarships and grants · general need-based awards · Federal Pell grants · state scholarships and grants · college-based scholarships and grants · private scholarships and grants · Federal Nursing scholarships. *Non-need-based aid programs include:* scholarships and grants · state scholarships and grants · creative arts and performance awards · ROTC scholarships.

UNIVERSITY OF CALIFORNIA – DAVIS

One Shields Avenue, Davis, CA 95616
Admissions: 530-752-2971 · Financial Aid: 530-752-2390
Email: undergraduateadmissions@ucdavis.edu
Website: http://www.ucdavis.edu

From the College

"The University of California - Davis, makes a difference in the lives of people every day. Fueled by learning and energized by discovery, the UC Davis tradition of engagement with the local community, the nation and the world guides all that it does. The university's commitment to providing an attentive and research-enriched education creates a supportive learning environment for both students and faculty. UC Davis is a pioneer in interdisciplinary problem-solving, and its four colleges, five professional schools, more than 200 academic majors and 86 graduate programs make it the most comprehensive of all the University of California campuses. For more than 100 years, UC Davis has engaged in teaching, research and public service that matter to California and transform the world. Located close to the state capital, UC Davis has more than 31,000 students and offers interdisciplinary graduate study and more than 100 undergraduate majors in four colleges—Agricultural and Environmental Sciences, Biological Sciences, Engineering and Letters and Science. It also houses six professional schools—Education, Law, Management, Medicine, Veterinary Medicine and the Betty Irene Moore School of Nursing."

Campus Setting

UC Davis, founded in 1908, is a public, comprehensive university. Programs are offered through the Colleges of Agricultural and Environmental Science, Engineering, and Letters and Science and the Graduate School of Management. Its 5,200-acre campus is located in Davis, 15 miles from Sacramento. A four-year institution, UC Davis has an enrollment of 33,307 students. The campus facilities include: library · art galleries · arboretum · herbarium · entomology and design museums. UC Davis provides on-campus housing with 5,534 units. Housing options: coed dorms · women's dorms · single-student apartments · married-student apartments · special housing for disabled students · special housing for international students · cooperative housing. Recreation and sports facilities include: aquatic center · athletic and recreational fields · gymnasium · recreation center · stadium · swimming pool.

Student Life and Activities

Three-quarters of students live off campus. UC Davis has 452 official student organizations. The most popular are: AIDS education project · American Field Service · anime club · ballroom dance group · Block and Bridle · Coalition Against Genocide · comedy troupe · gospel choir · law society · marching and pep bands · Model UN · Parents Under Pressure · square dance group · modern dance group · wildlife society · visually-impaired persons group · International Association of Business Communicators · Vet Student Association · astronomy club · team managers. There are intramural teams available too, such as: basketball · flag football · floor hockey · golf · grass volleyball · indoor soccer · racquetball · roller hockey · soccer · softball · table tennis · tennis · Ultimate Frisbee · volleyball. UC Davis is a member of the Big West Conference, Mountain Pacific Sports Federation, Pacific-10 Conference, Great West Football Conference, Western Water Polo Association, Western Intercollegiate Rowing Association and NorPac Field Hockey Conference.

UNIVERSITY OF CALIFORNIA – DAVIS

University of California – Davis
Davis, CA (Pop. 65,993)
Location: Large town
Four-year public
Founded: 1908
Website: http://www.ucdavis.edu

Students
Total enrollment: 33,307
Undergrads: 26,663
Part-time students: 1%
From out-of-state: 5%
Male/Female: 44%/56%
Live on-campus: 25%
Off-campus employment rating: Good
Caucasian: 31%
African American: 2%
Hispanic: 17%
Asian: 35%
Hawaiian or Pacific Islander: <1%
Native American: <1%
Mixed (2+ ethnicities): 5%
International: 6%

Academics
Calendar: Quarter
Student/faculty ratio: 17:1
Class size 9 or fewer: 13%
Class size 10-29: 51%
Class size 30-49: 12%
Class size 50-99: 11%
Class size 100 or more: 12%
Returning freshmen: 93%
Six-year graduation rate: 81%

Most Popular Majors
Psychology
Economics
Biological sciences

America's
Best Colleges for
B Students

Academics and Learning Environment

UC Davis has 1,605 full-time and 187 part-time faculty members, offering a student-to-faculty ratio of 17:1. The most common course size is 10 to 19 students. UC Davis offers 235 majors with the most popular being psychology, economics and biological sciences. The school has a general core requirement. Cooperative education is not offered. All first-year students must maintain a 2.0 GPA or higher to avoid academic probation. B students might find these other program options worth further investigation: self-designed majors · pass/fail grading option · independent study · double majors · dual degrees · accelerated study · honors program · Phi Beta Kappa · internships.

B Student Support and Success

The Learning Skills Center offers courses in a number of helpful topics including General Study Skills, Time Scheduling, Top Ten Survival Tips, Developing a Growth Mind Set for Academic Success, Critical Reading, Lecture Note Taking Strategies, Annotating, Multiple Choice Exam Prep and Test Taking Skills and Essay Exam Strategies. In addition to these general courses, there are specific subject courses for writing skills (pre-writing techniques, term paper assistance, grammar, etc.), ESL, science and math. All workshops are free.

UC Davis boasts a variety of support programs, as well as dedicated guidance for: academic · career · personal · psychological · minority students · military · veterans · non-traditional students · family planning. Recognizing that some students may need extra preparation, UC Davis offers remedial and refresher courses in: reading · writing · math · study skills. Annually, 93 percent of freshmen students return for their sophomore year. Companies that most frequently end up employing graduates from UC Davis include: Calgene · California school districts · Genentech · Hewlett-Packard · government agencies · Intel · Kaiser Permanente · Oracle · Washington Mutual · Wells Fargo.

Support for Students with Learning Disabilities

Students with learning disabilities will want to pay special attention to UC Davis support programs. According to the school, UC Davis is committed to ensuring equal access to educational opportunities for students with disabilities. An integral component in the implementation of that commitment is the coordination of academic accommodations and support services through the Student Disability Center (SDC). Students requesting accommodations must first establish eligibility by providing documentation of an impairment that limits a major life activity. The university reserves the right to request supplemental information to verify a student's current functional limitations. Documentation must meet the following criteria: 1) Appropriate standardized testing measures that are adult-normed and reflect current abilities and achievement; 2) Comprehensive written report discussing student's medical, educational and learning history, including current presenting concerns; 3) Clear statement of the existence of an impairment, and a summary indicating the current functional limitations and their extent and 4) Report must be signed by a qualified diagnosing professional (e.g., licensed educational or clinical psychologist). Requests for accommodations are considered on an individual basis by taking into account institutional obligations to provide equal access to educational opportunities, documented current functional limitation and the student's course requirements. It is the student's responsibility to submit all requests for disability-based accommodations to the SDC each academic quarter. LD students will benefit from researching the following: waiver of math degree requirement. An advisor/advocate from the Advising Services - Student Disability Center is available to students.

How to Get Admitted

For admissions decisions, non-academic factors considered: extracurricular activities · special talents, interests and abilities · character/personal qualities · volunteer work · work experience. A high school diploma is required, although a GED is also accepted for admissions consideration. SAT or ACT test scores are required of all applicants. SAT Subject Test scores are considered, if submitted, but are not required. *According to the admissions office:* Minimum 3.3 GPA required of in-state applicants; minimum 3.4 GPA required of out-of-state applicants. Specific SAT Reasoning or ACT scores required of applicants with GPA between 2.82 and 3.29. *Academic units recommended:* 4 English, 4 Math, 3 Science, 1 Social Studies, 3 Foreign Language.

How to Pay for College

To apply for financial aid, students should submit the following: Free Application for Federal Student Aid (FAFSA) · state aid form. UC Davis participates in the Federal Work Study program. *Need-based aid programs include:* scholarships and grants · general need-based awards · Federal Pell grants · state scholarships and grants · college-based scholarships and grants · private scholarships and grants · Academic Competitiveness Grant · National SMART grant. *Non-need-based aid programs include:* scholarships and grants · ROTC scholarships.

UNIVERSITY OF CALIFORNIA – DAVIS

Highlights

Admissions
Applicants: 55,833
Accepted: 23,049
Acceptance rate: 41.3%
Placed on wait list: 6,604
Enrolled from wait list: 1071
Average GPA: 4.0
ACT range: 24-30
SAT Math range: 570-700
SAT Reading range: 510-640
SAT Writing range: Not reported

Deadlines
Early Action: No
Early Decision: No
Regular Action: 11/30 (final)
Notification of admission by: 3/31
Common Application: Not accepted

Financial Aid
In-state tuition: $13,902
Out-of-state tuition: $36,780
Room: Varies
Board: Varies
Books: $1,620
Freshmen receiving need-based aid: 63%
Undergrads rec. need-based aid: 64%
Avg. % of need met by financial aid: 78%
Avg. aid package (freshmen): $21,876
Avg. aid package (undergrads): $19,685
Avg. debt upon graduation: $19,970

Prominent Alumni
Tani Cantil-Sakauye, Chief Justice of the California State Supreme Court; John Watson, President and CEO, Chevron; Tracy Caldwell-Dyson, astronaut.

School Spirit
Mascot: Gunrock (Mustang)
Colors: Blue and gold
Song: *Aggie Fight*

453

UNIVERSITY OF CALIFORNIA – RIVERSIDE

900 University Avenue, Riverside, CA 92521
Admissions: 951-827-3411 · Financial Aid: 951-827-3878
Email: admissions@ucr.edu · Website: http://www.ucr.edu

From the College

"The University of California, Riverside (UCR) is a doctoral research university, a living laboratory for groundbreaking exploration of issues critical to Inland Southern California, the state and communities around the world. Reflecting California's diverse culture, UCR's enrollment has exceeded 21,000 students. The campus opened a medical school in 2013 and was recently named a "Next Generation University" (New American Foundation, 2013), thanks to our expanding enrollment and high graduation rates. UC Riverside puts a world-class education within every student's reach through strong core programs, new and emerging disciplines and faculty recognized for their dedication, high standards and accessibility to students. At UC Riverside, students can pursue their passion."

Campus Setting

UC Riverside, founded as an agricultural research center in 1907, is a public, comprehensive university. Programs are offered through the Colleges of Natural and Agricultural Sciences, Humanities, Arts and Social Sciences and Engineering. Its 1,200-acre campus is located 60 miles east of Los Angeles. A four-year institution, UC Riverside has an enrollment of 21,210 students. The campus facilities include: library · art gallery · museum · research centers · agricultural research institute · gardens · salinity laboratory. UC Riverside provides on-campus housing with 3,170 units that can accommodate 5,880 students. Housing options: coed dorms · single-student apartments · married-student apartments · special housing for disabled students · special housing for international students. Recreation and sports facilities include: baseball stadium · recreation center · softball fields · soccer fields · track · tennis courts.

Student Life and Activities

Sixty-nine percent of students live off campus. According to a school official, "Life at Riverside can be 'very calm', and the school's atmosphere in general is very quiet." One contributor to this sense of calm is the fact that many students commute to school. "We are not a huge party school," students admit, but "There is always a party to go to if that's what you're into." Although the city of Riverside has "very little to offer in the way of entertainment," students compensate by joining various clubs and student organizations, including sororities and fraternities, which have a noticeable presence on campus. The school also offers "countless events, including free movie screenings, concerts, academic discussion forums, plays and trips." Popular campus hangouts include "a great rec center," the student commons and "a campus movie theater, where some of our classes are held." Students seem to agree, however, that "intercollegiate sports need more student support." Those with cars leave campus relatively frequently on the weekends, finding plenty to do outside of town; one student explains, "Within an hour's drive you can ski in the mountains, go sunbathing at the beach, visit a major theme park or even hang out in Hollywood for a day."

Popular campus events include Block Party, Welcome Week, Homecoming, Spring Splash and Heat. UC Riverside has 350 official student organizations. The most popular are: Bagpipe and pep bands · jazz ensemble · drill team · performing arts program · film society · folk dance club · chess · team managers · service groups · human corps program · academic, environmental and recreational clubs. For athletic students, there are intramural teams such as: badminton · basketball · bowling · flag football · hockey · in-line skating · racquetball · soccer · softball · table tennis · tennis · volleyball. UC Riverside is a member of the Big West Conference.

Academics and Learning Environment

UC Riverside has 763 full-time and 152 part-time faculty members, offering a student-to-faculty ratio of 19:1. The most common course size is 20 to 29 students. UC Riverside offers 173 majors. The school has a general core requirement. Cooperative education is offered. All first-year students must maintain a 2.0 GPA or higher to avoid academic probation. B students should be made aware of the following program options: self-designed majors · pass/fail grading option · independent study · double majors · dual degrees · accelerated study · honors program · Phi Beta Kappa · internships.

B Student Support and Success

Educators, counselors and advanced students help with academic performance through services at the school's Learning Center. Any student who is not satisfied with the grade he/she is getting in a class is welcome, including freshmen and students on academic probation. Virtually all services are free.

Students of UC Riverside will be pleased to learn that there is dedicated guidance for: academic · career · personal · psychological · minority students · military · veterans · non-traditional students · family planning · religious. Recognizing that some students may need extra preparation, UC Riverside offers remedial and refresher courses in: reading · writing · math · study skills. The average freshman year GPA is 2.7, and 89 percent of freshmen students return for their sophomore year. Following college? Many students dedicate themselves to the workforce, while approximately 30 percent pursue a graduate degree immediately after graduation. A year following graduation, the school reports that 38 percent of graduates have entered graduate school. Among students who do dedicate themselves to the workforce, approximately 70 percent of them enter a field related to their major within six months of their graduation. This is an assortment of companies that most frequently hire these graduates: Abbott Vascular · Anheuser Busch Sales Co. · BDO Seidman · CIA · Cintas Corp. · Countrywide Financial · Deloitte · Eli Lilly & Co. · Enterprise Rent-a-Car · Ernst & Young · ESRI · FedEX Ground · GlaxoSmithKline · Grant Thornton · IRS · Jacobs Engineering · Kaiser Permanente · KPMG · Maxim Healthcare Services · Merck · Northrup Grumman · Novartis Pharmaceuticals · Pacific Life · Pepsi Bottling Group · Schlumberger Technology · Sherwin-Williams Company · Southern California Gas Co. · Target Corp. · Walt Disney · Washington Mutual · Wells Fargo · Wolseley North America-Fergusun · Verizon.

Support for Students with Learning Disabilities

Students with learning disabilities will want to be made aware of some specific support programs available to them at UC Riverside. According to the school, accommodations are individually tailored to meet each student's disability-related needs and are based on the student's current functional limitations and the requirements of the specific class in which the student is enrolled.

Highlights

University of California – Riverside
Riverside, CA (Pop. 313,673)
Location: Medium city
Four-year public
Founded: 1907
Website: http://www.ucr.edu

Students
Total enrollment: 21,210
Undergrads: 18,612
Freshmen: 4,969
Part-time students: 2%
From out-of-state: 3%
From public schools: 90%
Male/Female: 49%/51%
Live on-campus: 31%
In fraternities: 5%
In sororities: 8%
Off-campus employment rating: Excellent
Caucasian: 14%
African American: 5%
Hispanic: 36%
Asian: 36%
Hawaiian or Pacific Islander: <1%
Native American: <1%
Mixed (2+ ethnicities): 4%
International: 3%

Academics
Calendar: Quarter
Student/faculty ratio: 19:1
Class size 9 or fewer: 14%
Class size 10-29: 47%
Class size 30-49: 10%
Class size 50-99: 16%
Class size 100 or more: 13%
Returning freshmen: 89%
Six-year graduation rate: 69%

455

College Profiles

UNIVERSITY OF CALIFORNIA – RIVERSIDE

Admissions
Applicants: 34,816
Accepted: 20,973
Acceptance rate: 60.2%
Placed on wait list: 3,678
Enrolled from wait list: 509
Average GPA: 3.6
ACT range: 20-25
SAT Math range: 510-630
SAT Reading range: 480-580
SAT Writing range: 2-21
Top 10% of class: 94%
Top 25% of class: 100%
Top 50% of class: 100%

Deadlines
Early Action: No
Early Decision: No
Regular Action: Rolling admissions
Common Application: Not accepted

Financial Aid
In-state tuition: $11,220
Out-of-state tuition: $34,098
Room: Varies
Board: Varies
Books: $1,800
Freshmen receiving need-based aid: 77%
Undergrads rec. need-based aid: 79%
Avg. % of need met by financial aid: 83%
Avg. aid package (freshmen): $23,198
Avg. aid package (undergrads): $20,947
Avg. debt upon graduation: $21,300

Prominent Alumni
Stephen Breen, Pulitzer Prize-Editorial Cartoonist; Billy Collins, Poet Laureate; Richard Schrock, Nobel Prize recipient, chemistry.

School Spirit
Mascot: Highlanders
Colors: Blue and gold
Song: *Brave Scots/Sons of California*

How to Get Admitted

For admissions decisions, non-academic factors considered: state of residency. A high school diploma is required, although a GED is also accepted for admissions consideration. SAT or ACT test scores are required of all applicants. SAT Subject Test scores are considered, if submitted, but are not required. *According to the admissions office:* Minimum grade of 'C' in listed secondary school units required of in-state applicants; minimum 3.4 GPA required of out-of-state applicants. *Academic units recommended:* 4 English, 4 Math, 3 Science, 3 Foreign Language.

How to Pay for College

To apply for financial aid, students should submit the following: Free Application for Federal Student Aid (FAFSA) · state aid form. UC Riverside participates in the Federal Work Study program. *Need-based aid programs include:* scholarships and grants · general need-based awards · Federal Pell grants · state scholarships and grants · college-based scholarships and grants · private scholarships and grants. *Non-need-based aid programs include:* scholarships and grants · state scholarships and grants · creative arts and performance awards · athletic scholarships · ROTC scholarships.

UNIVERSITY OF CINCINNATI

P.O. Box 210063, Cincinnati, OH 45221-0063
Admissions: 800-827-8728 · Financial Aid: 513-556-1000
Email: admissions@uc.edu · Website: http://www.uc.edu

From the College

"As a research institution in a vibrant urban community, UC offers a rich and diverse collection of co-curricular experiences and support services in partnership with our academic programs. Students can choose to participate in 100s of organizations, work out in our state-of-the-art recreation center, play and/or watch intramural and collegiate sports, and assume leadership roles of all kinds. UC also provides key support services aimed at ensuring student success through graduation."

Campus Setting

The University of Cincinnati's 137-acre campus is located two miles from downtown Cincinnati. A four-year institution, University of Cincinnati has an enrollment of 34,379 students. The school has a library with 3,715,957 books. University of Cincinnati provides on-campus housing which can accommodate 4,716 students: coed dorms · women's dorms · men's dorms · sorority housing · fraternity housing · single-student apartments · married-student apartments. Recreation and sports facilities include: baseball, football, soccer and track stadium · basketball and volleyball arena · tennis courts.

Student Life and Activities

Seventy-nine percent of students live off campus. University of Cincinnati has 300 official student organizations. The most popular are: choral groups · concert, jazz, marching and pep bands · opera · musical theatre · drama · dance · film society · baton twirling · drill team · team managers · Showboat Majestic · special-interest groups. There are intramural teams available to those interested: basketball · flag football · soccer · softball · volleyball · walleyball. University of Cincinnati is a member of the Big East Conference (Division I, Football FBS).

Academics and Learning Environment

University of Cincinnati has 1,157 full-time and 26 part-time faculty members, offering a student-to-faculty ratio of 18:1. The most common course size is 20 to 29 students. University of Cincinnati offers 389 majors with the most popular being marketing, nursing and communications. The school has a general core requirement. Cooperative education is available. B students will want to learn more about the following programs: pass/fail grading option · independent study · double majors · accelerated study · honors program · Phi Beta Kappa · internships · weekend college · distance learning certificate programs.

B Student Support and Success

At the University of Cincinnati, helping new students with lower GPAs get up to speed is usually achieved through the Center for

UNIVERSITY OF CINCINNATI

University of Cincinnati
Cincinnati (Pop. 296,223)
Location: Major city
Four-year public
Founded: 1819
Website: http://www.uc.edu

Students
Total enrollment: 34,379
Undergrads: 23,706
Freshmen: 4,449
Part-time students: 14%
From out-of-state: 11%
Male/Female: 50%/50%
Live on-campus: 21%
In fraternities: 11%
In sororities: 11%
Off-campus employment rating: Good
Caucasian: 76%
African American: 8%
Hispanic: 3%
Asian: 3%
Hawaiian or Pacific Islander: <1%
Native American: <1%
Mixed (2+ ethnicities): 2%
International: 4%

Academics
Calendar: Semester
Student/faculty ratio: 18:1
Class size 9 or fewer: 20%
Class size 10-29: 52%
Class size 30-49: 16%
Class size 50-99: 10%
Class size 100 or more: 3%
Returning freshmen: 85%
Six-year graduation rate: 64%

Most Popular Majors
Marketing
Nursing
Communications

UNIVERSITY OF CINCINNATI

Admissions
Applicants: 16,069
Accepted: 11,680
Acceptance rate: 72.7%
Average GPA: 3.4
ACT range: 22-28
SAT Math range: 510-640
SAT Reading range: 490-620
SAT Writing range: 4-22
Top 10% of class: 22%
Top 25% of class: 50%
Top 50% of class: 81%

Deadlines
Early Action: No
Early Decision: No
Regular Action: Rolling admissions
Common Application: Accepted

Financial Aid
In-state tuition: $11,000
Out-of-state tuition: $26,334
Room: Varies
Board: Varies
Books: $1,480
Freshmen receiving need-based aid: 60%
Undergrads rec. need-based aid: 56%
Avg. % of need met by financial aid: 42%
Avg. aid package (freshmen): $9,167
Avg. aid package (undergrads): $8,330
Avg. debt upon graduation: $28,333

Prominent Alumni
Louise McCarren Herring, pioneering founder of credit unions; Tony Campana, Major League baseball player; Michael Graves, designer and architect.

School Spirit
Mascot: Bearcat
Colors: Red and black
Song: *Fight Cincinnati*

Access and Transition. CAT is geared to help students have the knowledge, skills and resources to earn their degree. This is accomplished through one-on-one advising and individually tailored academic plans. (For an example of this kind of plan, go to the website.) Services include free tutoring and academic skill-enhancing workshops designed to increase GPAs, to improve study skills and time management strategies and to increase classroom attendance. Each student who is assisted by CAT has an advisor to create the personalized learning agreement. This will show the student how to meet each requirement for his/her major and may include required homework, workshop attendance or use of various campus resources. The plan clearly outlines the student's responsibilities, which commonly include meeting with his/her academic advisor and regular progress reports from instructors. Tutoring at no charge is available to all UC students and the campus has a Writing Lab and a Math Resource Center for students as well.

B students will be pleased to learn that University of Cincinnati provides dedicated guidance for: career · personal · psychological. Recognizing that some students may need extra preparation, University of Cincinnati offers remedial and refresher courses in: reading · writing · math · study skills. The average freshman year GPA is 3.1, and 85 percent of freshmen students return for their sophomore year.

Support for Students with Learning Disabilities

LD students will want to investigate the following programs offered by the Learning Assistance Center: academic coaching · supplemental instruction · academic peer tutoring · accommodated testing. Individual or small group tutorials are also available.

How to Get Admitted

For admissions decisions, non-academic factors considered: extracurricular activities · special talents, interests and abilities · state of residency. A high school diploma is required, although a GED is also accepted for admissions consideration. SAT or ACT test scores are required of all applicants. SAT Subject Test scores are not required. *Academic units recommended:* 4 English, 4 Math, 3 Science, 2 Social Studies, 2 Foreign Language.

How to Pay for College

To apply for financial aid, students should submit the following: Free Application for Federal Student Aid (FAFSA). University of Cincinnati participates in the Federal Work Study program. *Need-based aid programs include:* scholarships and grants · general need-based awards · Federal Pell grants · state scholarships and grants · college-based scholarships and grants · private scholarships and grants · Federal Nursing scholarships · United Negro College Fund · ACG · SMART · TEACH. *Non-need-based aid programs include:* scholarships and grants · general need-based awards · state scholarships and grants · creative arts and performance awards · special achievements and activities awards · special characteristics awards · athletic scholarships · ROTC scholarships.

UNIVERSITY OF HARTFORD

200 Bloomfield Avenue, West Hartford, CT 06117-1599
Admissions: 800-947-4303 · Financial Aid: 860-768-4296
Email: admission@hartford.edu · Website: http://www.hartford.edu

From the College

"The University of Hartford provides a learning environment in which students may transform themselves intellectually, personally and socially. We provide students with educational experiences that blend the feel of a small residential college with an array of academic programs and opportunities characteristic of a large university. Through relationships with faculty and staff dedicated to teaching, scholarship, research, the arts and civic engagement, every student may prepare for a lifetime of learning and for personal and professional success."

Campus Setting

The University of Hartford, founded in 1877, is a private, comprehensive institution. Its 200-acre campus is located in West Hartford, two miles from downtown Hartford. A four-year institution, University of Hartford has an enrollment of 6,820 students. The campus facilities include: library · gallery · hall of fame. University of Hartford provides on-campus housing with 17 units that can accommodate 3,514 students. Housing options: coed dorms · women's dorms · men's dorms · single-student apartments · special housing for disabled students. Recreation and sports facilities include a sports arena.

Student Life and Activities

Sixty-eight percent of students live on campus. Popular on-campus gathering spots include the Hawks Nest and the Gengras Student Union. Popular campus events include Parents Weekend and Spring Fling. University of Hartford has 46 official student organizations. The most popular are: chorus · jazz ensemble · orchestra · university players · film series · art magazine · amateur radio club · residence hall association · student union board of governors · program council · commuter/transfer association · team managers. For athletics, B students should research these intramural teams: basketball · football · handball · racquetball · soccer · softball · tennis · volleyball. University of Hartford is a member of the American East Conference (Division I).

Academics and Learning Environment

University of Hartford has 343 full-time and part-time faculty members, offering a student-to-faculty ratio of 10:1. The most common course size is 10 to 19 students. University of Hartford offers 120 majors with the most popular being business/marketing, visual/performing arts and health professions and least popular being interdisciplinary studies, philosophy/religious studies and public administration/social services. The school has a general core requirement. Cooperative education is available. All first-year students must maintain a 1.8 GPA or higher to avoid academic probation. The following is an assortment of programs that might interest a B student: self-designed majors · pass/fail grading option · independent study · double majors · dual degrees · honors program · internships · weekend college · distance learning.

B Student Support and Success

The Center for Reading and Writing (CRW) at Hartford provides writing tutors that work one on one with students in all phases of writing, from start to finish. Hartford also has a math and physics tutoring lab, chemistry tutors, computer science tutoring labs and an on-campus tutoring service that matches new students with trained and

UNIVERSITY OF HARTFORD

University of Hartford
West Hartford, CT (Pop. 63,268)
Location: Large town
Four-year private
Founded: 1877
Website: http://www.hartford.edu

Students
Total enrollment: 6,820
Undergrads: 5,187
Freshmen: 1,634
Part-time students: 13%
From out-of-state: 62%
From public schools: 80%
Male/Female: 50%/50%
Live on-campus: 68%
Off-campus employment rating: Good
Caucasian: 58%
African American: 15%
Hispanic: 9%
Asian: 3%
Hawaiian or Pacific Islander: <1%
Native American: 1%
Mixed (2+ ethnicities): 2%
International: 5%

Academics
Calendar: Semester
Student/faculty ratio: 10:1
Class size 9 or fewer: 17%
Class size 10-29: 76%
Class size 30-49: 6%
Class size 50-99: 1%
Class size 100 or more: -
Returning freshmen: 73%
Six-year graduation rate: 58%

Most Popular Majors
Business/marketing
Visual/performing arts
Health professions

America's
Best Colleges for
B Students

experienced student tutors. The All University Curriculum covers 11 categories of learning, from arts and culture to responsibility for civic life and values identification. These classes are taught through a variety of methods including simulations, debates, field trips, interviews, surveys, discussions, oral reports and skits or dramatic scenes. Students are required to take at least four of these courses over a four-year period.

University of Hartford brings to its students dedicated guidance for: academic · career · personal · psychological · minority students · veterans · family planning · religious. Additional counseling services include: high school advanced enrollment program. Recognizing that some students may need extra preparation, University of Hartford offers remedial and refresher courses in: reading · writing · math · study skills. Annually, 73 percent of freshmen students return for their sophomore year. After college, however, many enter the workforce and approximately 26 percent pursue a graduate degree immediately after graduation. Out of the students that do enter the workforce, approximately 63 percent of them enter a field related to their major within six months of graduation. Below is a collection of companies that most frequently hire graduates from University of Hartford: Bank of America · Cigna · ESPN · Prudential Financial · St. Francis Hospital · United Technologies · University of Hartford · Yale University.

Support for Students with Learning Disabilities

University of Hartford is pleased to offer its learning disability students specific support programs. If the college deems it appropriate, they will sometimes offer an LD student a lightened course load or even provide additional time to complete their degree. The following list was specifically compiled with LD students in mind: learning center · extended time for tests · take-home exam · readers · typist/scribe · note-taking services · reading machines · tape recorders · texts on tape · waiver of math degree requirement. Individual or small group tutorials are also available in: time management · organizational skills · learning strategies · writing labs · study skills. An advisor/advocate from the LD program is available to students.

How to Get Admitted

For admissions decisions, non-academic factors considered: interview · extracurricular activities · special talents, interests and abilities · character/personal qualities · state of residency. A high school diploma is required, although a GED is also accepted for admissions consideration. SAT or ACT test scores are required of all applicants. SAT Subject Test scores are not required. *Academic units recommended:* 4 English, 3 Math, 3 Science, 3 Social Studies, 2 Foreign Language.

How to Pay for College

To apply for financial aid, students should submit the following: Free Application for Federal Student Aid (FAFSA) · institution's own financial aid forms. University of Hartford participates in the Federal Work Study program. *Need-based aid programs include:* scholarships and grants · general need-based awards · Federal Pell grants · state scholarships and grants · college-based scholarships and grants · private scholarships and grants. *Non-need-based aid programs include:*

scholarships and grants · state scholarships and grants · creative arts and performance awards · athletic scholarships.

UNIVERSITY OF HARTFORD

Highlights

Admissions
Applicants: 16,481
Accepted: 10,750
Acceptance rate: 65.2%
Average GPA: Not reported
ACT range: 20-26
SAT Math range: 480-580
SAT Reading range: 470-570
SAT Writing range: Not reported

Deadlines
Early Action: No
Early Decision: No
Regular Action: Rolling admissions
Notification of admission by: 10/1
Common Application: Accepted

Financial Aid
In-state tuition: $32,758
Out-of-state tuition: $32,758
Room: $7,548
Board: $3,970
Books: $1,118
Freshmen receiving need-based aid: 81%
Undergrads rec. need-based aid: 74%
Avg. % of need met by financial aid: 66%
Avg. aid package (freshmen): $24,161
Avg. aid package (undergrads): $23,772
Avg. debt upon graduation: $45,778

Prominent Alumni
John C. Shaw, investment banker and buyout specialist; Jerome P. Kelly, professional golfer.

School Spirit
Mascot: Hawks
Colors: Red and white

461

UNIVERSITY OF HAWAII AT MANOA

2500 Campus Road, Honolulu, HI 96822
Admissions: 800-823-9771 · Financial Aid: 808-956-7251
Email: uhmanoa.admissions@hawaii.edu
Website: http://www.manoa.hawaii.edu

From the College

"The University of Hawai`i at Manoa's special distinction is found in its Hawaiian, Asian and Pacific orientation and its unique location in the middle of the Pacific Ocean. Its setting and the diversity of its students and faculty foster unique advantages in the study of Asian and Pacific cultures, foreign languages, tropical agriculture, tropical medicine, ocean and marine sciences, astronomy, volcanology and international business.

"Our unique geographical, cultural and historical heritage suggests that Manoa values and the responsibilities inherent in embracing those values include the following:

"A focus on developing an awareness of and sensitivity to diversity and commonality. The Manoa campus is culturally rich and complex, providing a perfect social setting for frequent interactions with persons from cultures other than one's own. At Manoa we incorporate and celebrate intercultural experiences and understanding into our social and educational environments in a comprehensive fashion. Manoa is also a place where historic political, economic and social conflicts between Native Hawaiian people, settlers and working immigrants have contributed to the diverse perspectives, beliefs, values and even conceptual frameworks of our islands' people. Growing out of the core Hawaiian value of aloha, an essential component of the Manoa Experience, are insights that both bond us and simultaneously express the variations that collectively enrich us.

"A focus on global awareness and local responsibility. These values are consistent with a uniquely Hawaiian place of learning. Hawai`i is a place where the strength of identity is important to Native Hawaiian people struggling to maintain traditional connections while establishing new global relationships. Their struggle for cultural distinction forms a significant part of the story of human history and change. Hawai`i is also a place where the peoples from Asia, Europe and the Pacific regions gathered, formed communities and built lives together. The pluricultural children of Hawai`i are global citizens, a true pan-ethnic population. Hence, we attempt to infuse our pedagogical, social and cultural environments with a global perspective and with questions and issues of global significance. Moreover, engaging and acting upon local questions and issues during their educational experience at Manoa engenders in students a sense of responsibility toward future generations.

"A focus on sustainability and renewability. These values are also a reflection of our unique Hawaiian cultural history, as voiced in the Hawaiian core value of malama i ka aina, malama i ke kai (caring for the land and sea that sustain us). The Hawaiian culture teaches us to see Manoa as part of an ahupua`a extending from mountaintop to ocean, emphasizing an ecosystem understanding of our home. Hawai`i's unique geographical status as the most isolated, populated land mass on the planet makes it incumbent upon us to develop research, technologies, economy and a way of life based on sustainability and renewability, as Polynesians did over thousands of years of voyaging, discovery and settlement. Fostering a pedagogical, social and cultural environment that reflects these values and the knowledge developed by Native Hawaiians over millennia is central to our efforts. Cultivating, practicing and communicating these values are our university's gifts and obligation to the rest of the world."

462

Campus Setting

The UH Manoa, founded in 1907, is a public institution. Programs are offered through the Colleges of Arts and Sciences, Business Administration, Education, Engineering and Tropical Agriculture and the Schools of Accountancy, Architecture, Hawaiian, Asian, and Pacific Studies, Law, Medicine, Nursing, Ocean and Earth Science Technology, Public Health, Social Work and Travel Industry Management. Its 300-acre campus is located in Manoa Valley, a residential area near the center of metropolitan Honolulu. A four-year public institution, University of Hawaii at Manoa has an enrollment of 20,006 students. Campus facilities include: art museum · center for Hawaiian studies · Korean studies center · arboretum · aquarium · institute for astronomy · cancer research center · undersea research lab · institution of geophysics and planetology · institute of marine biology. UH Manoa provides on-campus housing with 1,298 units that can accommodate 3,900 students. Housing options: coed dorms · single-student apartments · married-student apartments · special housing for disabled students. Recreation and sports facilities include: aquatic complex · gymnasium · marine training facility · tennis courts · track · weight room.

Student Life and Activities

Three-quarters of the students (77 percent) live off campus. Students gather at the Campus Center, Manoa Gardens, Manoa Marketplace and Puck's Alley. Football games, orientation week, Manoa Arts and Minds and Friday concerts are popular events. UH Manoa has 150 official student organizations. The most popular are: music, theatre, political, service and special-interest groups. Intramural teams include: badminton · basketball · bench press · free-throw contest · golf · indoor soccer · table tennis · tennis · turkey trot · volleyball. UH Manoa is a member of the Mountain Pacific Sports Federation and Western Athletic Conference (Football I-A).

Academics and Learning Environment

For the B student, the learning environment of a college is just as important as the quality of its academic program. UH Manoa has 1,209 full-time and 62 part-time faculty members, offering a student-to-faculty ratio of 14:1. The most common course size is 10 to 19 students. UH Manoa offers 215 majors with the most popular being psychology, nursing and biology and least popular being Pacific Islands studies, plant and environmental biotechnology and classics. The school has a general core requirement. Cooperative education is available. All first-year students must maintain a 2.0 GPA or higher to avoid academic probation. Other special academic programs that would appeal to a B student include: self-designed majors · pass/fail grading option · independent study · double majors · dual degrees · honors program · Phi Beta Kappa · internships · distance learning certificate programs.

B Student Support and Success

The Learning Center at UH has a variety of services including testing, tutoring, study skills information and computer services. Practical skills are taught in areas like speed reading, test taking and time management. Tutoring in math, English, foreign language and other subjects is available by appointment or walk-in. The university

UNIVERSITY OF HAWAII AT MANOA

Highlights

University of Hawaii at Manoa
Honolulu (Pop. 374,658)
Location: Major city
Four-year public
Founded: 1907
Website: http://www.manoa.hawaii.edu

Students
Total enrollment: 20,006
Undergrads: 14,499
Part-time students: 17%
From out-of-state: 36%
From public schools: 66%
Male/Female: 45%/55%
Live on-campus: 23%
In fraternities: 1%
In sororities: 1%
Off-campus employment rating: Excellent
Caucasian: 21%
African American: 1%
Hispanic: 2%
Asian: 41%
Hawaiian or Pacific Islander: 17%
Native American: <1%
Mixed (2+ ethnicities): 15%
International: 3%

Academics
Calendar: Semester
Student/faculty ratio: 14:1
Class size 9 or fewer: 14%
Class size 10-29: 57%
Class size 30-49: 16%
Class size 50-99: 8%
Class size 100 or more: 5%
Returning freshmen: 78%
Six-year graduation rate: 57%

Most Popular Majors
Psychology
Nursing
Biology

College Profiles

UNIVERSITY OF HAWAII AT MANOA

Highlights

Admissions
Applicants: 7,361
Accepted: 5,869
Acceptance rate: 79.7%
Average GPA: 3.5
ACT range: 20-26
SAT Math range: 500-620610
SAT Reading range: 470-580
SAT Writing range: 2-16
Top 10% of class: 27%
Top 25% of class: 58%
Top 50% of class: 89%

Deadlines
Early Action: No
Early Decision: No
Regular Action: Rolling admissions
Common Application: Not accepted

Financial Aid
In-state tuition: $9,840
Out-of-state tuition: $28,632
Room: Varies
Board: Varies
Books: $1,246
Freshmen receiving need-based aid: 54%
Undergrads rec. need-based aid: 53%
Avg. % of need met by financial aid: 67%
Avg. aid package (freshmen): $12,137
Avg. aid package (undergrads): $11,611

Prominent Alumni
Daniel Akaka, U.S. senator; Daniel K. Inouye, U.S. senator; Jay H. Shidler, philanthropist.

School Spirit
Mascot: Warriors, Rainbow Warriors, Rainbow Wahine, Rainbows
Colors: Green, white, black and silver

also has two computer labs that provide extra assistance to students. UH Manoa provides a variety of support programs including dedicated guidance for: academic · career · personal · psychological · military · family planning. The average freshman year GPA is 2.8, and 78 percent of freshmen students return for their sophomore year. Approximately 10 percent of students pursue a graduate degree immediately after graduation. Among students who enter the workforce, approximately 86 percent enter a field related to their major within six months of graduation. Companies that most frequently hire graduates from UH Manoa include: Bank of Hawaii · Grant Thornton LLP · Hawaiian Airlines · Hawaiian Electric Industries · Hilton Hawaii · Japanese English Teaching (JET) Program · Kaiser Permanente · Kamehameha Schools · KPMG · Marriott International Hotels and Resorts · Pearl Harbor Naval Shipyard and Immediate Maintenance Facility · PricewaterhouseCoopers LLP · US Undersea Naval Warfare Center Detachment · Verizon Hawaii.

Support for Students with Learning Disabilities

Students with learning disabilities may take additional time to complete their degree and/or take a lightened course load. They may also access: tutors · extended time for tests · take-home exam · readers · typist/scribe · note-taking services · reading machines · tape recorders · texts on tape · early syllabus. An advisor/advocate from the KOKUA Program is available to students.

How to Get Admitted

For admissions decisions, non-academic factors considered: interview · extracurricular activities · special talents, interests and abilities · geographical location. A high school diploma is required, although a GED is also accepted for admissions consideration. SAT or ACT test scores are required of all applicants. SAT Subject Test scores are not required. *According to the admissions office:* Minimum combined SAT Reasoning score of 1530 (composite ACT score of 22), rank in top two-fifths of secondary school class and minimum 2.8 GPA required. *Academic units recommended:* 4 English, 3 Math, 3 Science, 3 Social Studies.

How to Pay for College

To apply for financial aid, students should submit the following: Free Application for Federal Student Aid (FAFSA). UH Manoa participates in the Federal Work Study program. *Need-based aid programs include:* scholarships and grants · general need-based awards · Federal Pell grants · state scholarships and grants · college-based scholarships and grants · private scholarships and grants · Federal Nursing scholarships. *Non-need-based aid programs include:* scholarships and grants · general need-based awards · state scholarships and grants · creative arts and performance awards · athletic scholarships · ROTC scholarship.

UNIVERSITY OF HOUSTON

4800 Calhoun Road, Houston, TX 77004
Admissions: 713-743-1010 · Financial Aid: 713-743-1010
Email: admissions@uh.edu · Website: http://www.uh.edu

From the College

"The University of Houston is a Carnegie-designated Tier-One public research university recognized throughout the world as a leader in energy research, law, business and environmental education. UH serves the globally competitive Houston and Gulf Coast region by providing world-class faculty, experiential learning, strategic industry partnerships and state-of-the-art facilities such as the interdisciplinary Energy Research Park and the Nanofabrication Facility. Located in America's fourth-largest city, UH is the most ethnically diverse metropolitan research university in the United States, serving more than 39,800 students in one of the most culturally diverse regions in the country. In addition to preparing its students to succeed in today's global economy, UH is a catalyst within its own community - changing lives through health, education and outreach projects that help build a future for children in Houston, in Texas and around the world. Other distinctive merits of UH include a strong student experience, a historic Division I athletics program, top-level arts programs and an internationally recognized faculty that includes a Nobel Laureate, National Medal of Science winners, Pulitzer and Tony awards winners and members of prestigious National Academies. The Princeton Review has chosen UH for inclusion in its guidebooks of the nation's best colleges and the nation's best value colleges for undergraduates. Nestled on a tree-lined street, UH campus is just minutes from Houston's bustling theater and museum districts, the University of Houston is home to world-class teaching, revolutionary research and nationally recognized students - all working together to create a globally competitive educational environment."

Campus Setting

University of Houston, founded in 1927, is a public research institution comprised of 12 academic colleges and an interdisciplinary Honors College. Programs are offered through the Colleges of Architecture, Business Administration, Education, Liberal Arts and Social Sciences, Natural Science and Mathematics, Optometry, Pharmacy and Technology; the Graduate School of Social Work; the Cullen College of Engineering; the Hilton College of Hotel and Restaurant Management and the Bates College of Law. Its 667-acre campus is located in a residential area, three miles from downtown Houston. A four-year institution, UH has an enrollment of 39,540 students. Campus facilities comprise of a large library, as well as a gallery. UH provides on-campus housing with 4,078 units that can accommodate 8,008 students. Housing options: coed dorms · sorority housing · fraternity housing · single-student apartments · married-student apartments · special housing for disabled students. Recreation and sports facilities include: field · pavilion · recreation center · stadium · softball complex · track · tennis courts.

Student Life and Activities

Eighty-two percent of students live off campus. University Center, Recreation Center and UC-Satellite are popular gathering places. Frontier Fiesta and Homecoming are popular events. University of Houston has 357 official student organizations. The most popular are: Frontier Fiesta Association · Homecoming · Cougar First Impression. For those wishing involvement in sports, there are a variety of intramural teams: badminton · basketball · bowling · cross-country · football (non-tackle) · golf · racquetball · soccer · softball · swimming · table tennis · tennis · track and field ·

465

College Profiles

UNIVERSITY OF HOUSTON

University of Houston
Houston, TX (Pop. 2,160,821)
Location: Major city
Four-year public
Founded: 1927
Website: http://www.uh.edu

Students
Total enrollment: 39,540
Undergrads: 31,587
Freshmen: 4,539
Part-time students: 28%
From out-of-state: 3%
From public schools: 93%
Male/Female: 50%/50%
Live on-campus: 18%
In fraternities: 4%
In sororities: 3%
Off-campus employment rating: Excellent
Caucasian: 29%
African American: 11%
Hispanic: 30%
Asian: 21%
Hawaiian or Pacific Islander: <1%
Native American: <1%
Mixed (2+ ethnicities): 3%
International: 5%

Academics
Calendar: Semester
Student/faculty ratio: 22:1
Class size 9 or fewer: 10%
Class size 10-29: 46%
Class size 30-49: 22%
Class size 50-99: 13%
Class size 100 or more: 9%
Returning freshmen: 85%
Six-year graduation rate: 48%

Most Popular Majors
Psychology
Accounting
Teaching/learning

volleyball. University of Houston is a member of the Member of the American Athletic Conference (Division I).

Academics and Learning Environment

University of Houston has 1,405 full-time and 582 part-time faculty members, offering a student-to-faculty ratio of 22:1. The most common course size is 20 to 29 students. University of Houston offers 227 majors with the most popular being psychology, accounting and teaching/learning and least popular being earth science, German and music theory. The school has a general core requirement. Cooperative education is available. All first-year students must maintain a 2.0 GPA or higher to avoid academic probation, and a minimum overall GPA of 2.0 is required to graduate. B students might want to further investigate these program options: pass/fail grading option · independent study · double majors · dual degrees · accelerated study · honors program · internships · weekend college · distance learning certificate programs.

B Student Support and Success

Learning and Assessment Services at UH offers workshops covering topics such as improving memory power, overcoming procrastination, reducing test anxiety, preparing for exams and time management. Tutoring is available for no cost on both a walk-in and appointment basis. Multimedia Resources can help students who learn best on the computer, and math, science and business majors can find supplemental instruction study groups that meet on a regular basis. The Texas Success Initiative Program provides non-course, non-credit developmental instruction in reading, writing, math and test preparation.

University of Houston is proud to give its students a variety of program options, including dedicated guidance for: academic · career · personal · psychological · minority students · military · veterans · non-traditional students · family planning · religious. Recognizing that some students may need extra preparation, University of Houston offers remedial and refresher courses in: reading · writing · math · study skills. The average freshman year GPA is 2.8, and 85 percent of freshmen students return for their sophomore year. Organizations that most often hire graduates from University of Houston are: ExxonMobil · Allstate Insurance · New York Life · Bank of America · Wal-Mart · Sam's Club · Baker and Associate · MD Anderson Hospital · Child Protective Services · UT Health Science Center · Texas Children's Hospital · Chevron · Social Services Administration · Realty USA · Foley's/Macy's · Neiman Marcus · Saks 5th Avenue · Target · Dillard's · Al-Formal Wear · Centerpoint Energy · Pulte Homes · Shell Oil Company · Welker Engineering Company · Methodist Hospital · Memorial Hermann Hospital · Heartland Home Health · Manhattan Construction · Electrical Reliability Services Inc. · Noble Energy · Marathon · Anadarko · Deloitte · Ernst & Young · El Paso Corporation · Blue Cross Blue Shield of Florida.

Support for Students with Learning Disabilities

University of Houston prides itself on catering its programs towards students coping with learning disabilities. The college has been known to offer its LD students additional time to finish their degrees or occasionally grant a lightened course load. The Center for Students with Disabilities (CSD) provides numerous academic support services to individuals with any type of learning disability, health impairment, physical limitation or psychiatric disorder. Our goal is to help ensure that qualified students with disabilities at the University of Houston are able to successfully compete with non-disabled students. CSD services are confidential. CSD student information is shared only with the student's written permission to do so. Students with learning disabilities should consider the potential benefits of the following: remedial math · remedial English · remedial reading · tutors · learning center · testing accommodations · extended time for tests · take-home exam · oral tests · readers · typist/scribe · note-taking services · reading machines · tape recorders · texts on tape · videotaped classes · early syllabus · diagnostic testing service · priority registration · priority seating · waiver of foreign language and math degree requirement. Individual or small group tutorials are also available in: time management · organizational skills · learning strategies · specific subject areas · writing labs · math labs · study skills. An advisor/advocate from the LD program is available to students.

How to Get Admitted

For admissions decisions, non-academic factors considered: extracurricular activities · special talents, interests and abilities · volunteer work · work experience · state of residency. A high school diploma is required, although a GED is also accepted for admissions consideration. SAT or ACT test scores are required of all applicants. *Academic units recommended:* 4 English, 4 Math, 4 Science, 4 Social Studies, 2 Foreign Language.

How to Pay for College

To apply for financial aid, students should submit the following: Free Application for Federal Student Aid (FAFSA). University of Houston participates in the Federal Work Study program. *Need-based aid programs include:* scholarships and grants · general need-based awards · Federal Pell grants · state scholarships and grants · college-based scholarships and grants · private scholarships and grants. *Non-need-based aid programs include:* scholarships and grants · general need-based awards · state scholarships and grants · creative arts and performance awards · athletic scholarships · ROTC scholarships.

UNIVERSITY OF HOUSTON

Highlights

Admissions
Applicants: 17,407
Accepted: 10,167
Acceptance rate: 58.4%
Average GPA: Not reported
ACT range: 22-27
SAT Math range: 540-640
SAT Reading range: 490-610
SAT Writing range: Not reported
Top 10% of class: 34%
Top 25% of class: 69%
Top 50% of class: 92%

Deadlines
Early Action: No
Early Decision: No
Regular Action: 12/1 (priority)
4/1 (final)
Notification of admission by: 4/15
Common Application: Accepted

Financial Aid
In-state tuition: $9,354
Out-of-state tuition: $19,974
Room: Varies
Board: Varies
Books: $1,200
Freshmen receiving need-based aid: 62%
Undergrads rec. need-based aid: 61%
Avg. % of need met by financial aid: 68%
Avg. aid package (freshmen): $13,491
Avg. aid package (undergrads): $12,977
Avg. debt upon graduation: $18,244

Prominent Alumni
David Williams; Carl Lewis; Clyde Drexler.

School Spirit
Mascot: Cougars
Colors: Red and white
Song: *University*

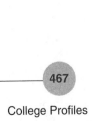

467

UNIVERSITY OF IDAHO

875 Perimeter Drive MS 2282, Moscow, ID 83844-2282
Admissions: 888-884-3246 · Financial Aid: 888-884-3246
Email: admissions@uidaho.edu · Website: http://www.uidaho.edu

From the College

"The University of Idaho offers a complete living and learning experience. It's a residential campus located in a small, friendly community. There are fresh air outdoor activities and surprising cultural gems, including the Lionel Hampton International Jazz Festival and Moscow's active art scene. Many students take advantage of an emphasis on undergraduate research opportunities in computer security, transportation innovations, environmental science, evolutionary biology and biomedical research. Our facilities create a dynamic and engaging learning environment. These facilities include: the stunning Student Recreation Center, Kibbie Dome, Idaho Commons, Student Union and Pritchard Art Gallery. The University of Idaho is nationally ranked as a best buy for the quality and value and ranked as one of the most wired college campuses in the United States."

Campus Setting

The University of Idaho, founded in 1889, is a public, comprehensive, land-grant institution. Its 1,354-acre campus and university farm are located in Moscow, 90 miles southeast of Spokane, Washington. A four-year institution, University of Idaho has an enrollment of 11,834 students. The campus is proud of its sizable library and its various art galleries. The university provides on-campus housing with 2,260 units. Housing options: coed dorms · women's dorms · men's dorms · sorority housing · fraternity housing · single-student apartments · married-student apartments · special housing for disabled students · special housing for international students · cooperative housing. Recreation and sports facilities include: fields · gymnasium · golf course · recreation center · track and field complex · weight rooms · swim center · activity center.

Student Life and Activities

Sixty-one percent of students live off campus. ASUI Productions is a forum for students to organize almost all entertainment each year including blockbuster film series, small concerts, coffeehouses, "open mic" nights, comedians, educational speakers and nationally touring bands. In the process, students gain experience with event planning and marketing. Idaho Commons and Student Union Programs feature weekly foreign and alternative films, noontime and summertime concerts and educational enrichment events. Students gather at Idaho Commons, Student Union, Kibbie Dome, Arboretum, Latah Trail, Kenworthy Performing Arts Center, Moscow downtown restaurants and coffee shops and Palouse Mall. Popular events include Lional Hampton International Jazz Festival, Cruise the World, Martini Forum, Dancers, Drummers and Dreamers, Tuxinmepu PowWow, Borah Symposium, Student Musical and Theatre productions, student and faculty recitals, Palousafest and Kibbie Dome athletic events. The university has 199 official student organizations. Associated Students University of Idaho (ASUI), Greeks, Lionel Hampton School of Music students, and international groups are influential in campus life. Intramural teams are bountiful at University of Idaho, among them: badminton · basketball · billiards · disc golf · dodgeball · flag football · floor hockey · foosball · horseshoes · kickball · power lifting · racquetball · roller hockey · soccer · softball · swimming · tennis · Ultimate Frisbee · volleyball · Wiffleball · wrestling. University of Idaho is a member of the Western Athletic Conference and Big Sky Conference.

Academics and Learning Environment

University of Idaho has 559 full-time and 155 part-time faculty members, offering a student-to-faculty ratio of 18:1. The most common course size is 20 to 29 students. The university offers 203 majors with the most popular being business, psychology/communication studies and curriculum/instruction and least popular being biological/agricultural engineering, environmental science and physics. The school has a general core requirement. Cooperative education is available. All first-year students must maintain a 2.0 GPA or higher to avoid academic probation, and a minimum overall GPA of 2.0 is required to graduate. B students might be interested to learn more about: self-designed majors · pass/fail grading option · independent study · double majors · dual degrees · accelerated study · honors program · Phi Beta Kappa · internships · distance learning certificate programs.

B Student Support and Success

The University of Idaho offers three academic assistance programs, each with its own focus. Tutoring and Learning Services provides one-on-one tutoring as well as a series of workshops called the College Success Series. These workshops cover such areas as note taking, active learning, college textbook reading and time management. Freshmen are also offered a one-credit study skills course, and there is an online learning center as well. Students in accounting, computer science and chemistry have their own learning labs and study groups, and there is a separate Math Lab. The English Writing Center helps with all facets of written communication. Student Support Services is designed to provide academic support and assistance to students who meet the TRIO eligibility standards: 1) neither parent has a college degree, 2) they come from a low-income family or 3) they are physically/learning disabled. The Disability Support Services is geared to assist students who are physically challenged as defined by the American Disabilities Act.

University of Idaho provides its students with a large variety of support programs, especially dedicated guidance for: academic · career · personal · psychological · minority students · military · veterans · non-traditional students · family planning. Recognizing that some students may need extra preparation, University of Idaho offers remedial and refresher courses in: reading · writing · math · study skills. The average freshman year GPA is 3.0, and 79 percent of freshmen students return for their sophomore year.

Support for Students with Learning Disabilities

Students with learning disabilities will be pleased to learn that the university offers a plethora of support programs. Sometimes the college will offer additional time in order to complete the LD students degree or a lightened course load may even be granted. Diagnostic Testing Service is offered through the Counseling and Testing Center. LD students will want to research these programs: tutors · learning center · extended time for tests · oral tests · readers · typist/scribe · note-taking services · reading machines · tape recorders · videotaped classes · waiver of math degree requirement. Individual or small group tutorials are also available in: time management · organizational skills · learning strategies · specific subject areas ·

Highlights

University of Idaho
Moscow, ID (Pop. 24,499)
Location: Large town
Four-year public
Founded: 1889
Website: http://www.uidaho.edu

Students
Total enrollment: 11,834
Undergrads: 9,456
Freshmen: 1,858
Part-time students: 16%
From out-of-state: 25%
From public schools: 95%
Male/Female: 53%/47%
Live on-campus: 39%
In fraternities: 20%
In sororities: 20%
Off-campus employment rating: Good
Caucasian: 79%
African American: 1%
Hispanic: 8%
Asian: 1%
Hawaiian or Pacific Islander: <1%
Native American: 1%
Mixed (2+ ethnicities): 3%
International: 3%

Academics
Calendar: Semester
Student/faculty ratio: 18:1
Class size 9 or fewer: 22%
Class size 10-29: 54%
Class size 30-49: 14%
Class size 50-99: 8%
Class size 100 or more: 3%
Returning freshmen: 79%
Six-year graduation rate: 54%

Most Popular Majors
Business
Psychology/communication studies
Curriculum/instruction

469

UNIVERSITY OF IDAHO

Highlights

Admissions
Applicants: 7,994
Accepted: 5,173
Acceptance rate: 64.7%
Average GPA: 3.4
ACT range: 20-26
SAT Math range: 460-590
SAT Reading range: 450-580
SAT Writing range: 3-13
Top 10% of class: 16%
Top 25% of class: 42%
Top 50% of class: 73%

Deadlines
Early Action: No
Early Decision: No
Regular Action: Rolling admissions
Common Application: Accepted

Financial Aid
In-state tuition: $6,784
Out-of-state tuition: $20,314
Room: Varies
Board: Varies
Books: $1,232
Freshmen receiving need-based aid: 66%
Undergrads rec. need-based aid: 65%
Avg. % of need met by financial aid: 73%
Avg. aid package (freshmen): $13,670
Avg. aid package (undergrads): $13,315
Avg. debt upon graduation: $25,961

Prominent Alumni
Jeffrey Ashby, astronaut; Kristin Armstrong, cyclist and Olympic gold medalist; General James F. Amos, 35th Commandant of the USMC.

School Spirit
Mascot: Joe Vandal
Colors: Silver and gold
Song: *Here We Have Idaho (alma mater)*

writing labs · math labs · study skills. An advisor/advocate from the LD program is available to students.

How to Get Admitted

For admissions decisions, non-academic factors considered: state of residency. A high school diploma is required, although a GED is also accepted for admissions consideration. SAT or ACT test scores are required of all applicants. SAT Subject Test scores are not required. *According to the admissions office:* 2.2 GPA recommended. *Academic units recommended:* 4 English, 3 Math, 3 Science, 2.5 Social Studies, 1 Foreign Language.

How to Pay for College

To apply for financial aid, students should submit the following: Free Application for Federal Student Aid (FAFSA). University of Idaho participates in the Federal Work Study program. *Need-based aid programs include:* scholarships and grants · general need-based awards · Federal Pell grants · state scholarships and grants · college-based scholarships and grants · private scholarships and grants. *Non-need-based aid programs include:* scholarships and grants · general need-based awards · state scholarships and grants · creative arts and performance awards · special achievements and activities awards · special characteristics awards · athletic scholarships · ROTC scholarships.

UNIVERSITY OF KENTUCKY

101 Main Building, Lexington, KY 40506
Admissions: 866-900-4685 · Financial Aid: 859-257-3172
Email: admissions@uky.edu · Website: http://www.uky.edu

From the College

"The University of Kentucky is a public land grant institution that prepares students for an increasingly diverse and technological world. As one of only seven universities in the nation with colleges of agriculture, engineering, medicine and pharmacy all on one campus, the University of Kentucky offers a broad array of undergraduate, graduate and professional degree programs, many with national prominence. The university strives to nurture a true learning community—one that inspires academic growth and learning among faculty, staff and students. Research, scholarship and creative activities support human and economic development through the expansion of knowledge and its applications in the sciences, social sciences, education, arts, humanities, business and the professions."

Campus Setting

University of Kentucky, founded in 1865, is located in Lexington, 75 miles from Cincinnati. A four-year public institution, University of Kentucky has an enrollment of 28,034 students. The campus facilities include: library · art galleries · center for American music · art and anthropology museums. University of Kentucky provides on-campus housing with 2,918 units that can accommodate 5,397 students. Housing options: coed dorms · women's dorms · men's dorms · sorority housing · fraternity housing · single-student apartments · married-student apartments · special housing for disabled students · special housing for international students. Recreation and sports facilities include: aquatics and tennis recreation center · basketball and volleyball courts · gymnasium · track.

Student Life and Activities

Almost three-quarters of students (74 percent) live off campus. University of Kentucky has 450 official student organizations. The most popular are: chorus · glee club · marching and pep bands · symphonic band and orchestra · opera workshop · drill team · modern dance club · theatre · debate club · team managers · other academic and special-interest groups. For students with athletic leanings, there are intramural teams such as: basketball · flag football · golf · inner-tube water polo · racquetball · soccer · softball · swimming · table tennis · tennis · team handball · track · tug-of-war · turkey trot · Ultimate Frisbee · volleyball. University of Kentucky is a member of the Southeastern Conference (Division I, Football I-A).

Academics and Learning Environment

University of Kentucky has 1,365 full-time and 317 part-time faculty members, offering a student-to-faculty ratio of 18:1. The most common course size is 20 to 29 students. University of Kentucky offers 202 majors with the most popular being accounting, biology and marketing and least popular being Latin American studies and Russian/East European studies. The school has a general core requirement. Co-operative education is available. All first-year students must maintain a 2.0 GPA or higher to avoid academic probation, and a minimum overall GPA of 2.0 is required to graduate. Other special academic programs that a B student might want to research would include: pass/fail grading option · independent study · double majors · dual degrees · accelerated study · honors program · Phi Beta Kappa · internships · weekend college · distance learning certificate programs.

471

College Profiles

UNIVERSITY OF KENTUCKY

University of Kentucky
Lexington, KY (Pop. 305,489)
Location: Major city
Four-year public
Founded: 1865
Website: http://www.uky.edu

Students
Total enrollment: 28,034
Undergrads: 20,827
Part-time students: 8%
From out-of-state: 32%
Male/Female: 50%/50%
Live on-campus: 26%
In fraternities: 16%
In sororities: 25%
Caucasian: 78%
African American: 8%
Hispanic: 3%
Asian: 3%
Native American: <1%
Mixed (2+ ethnicities): 3%
International: 3%

Academics
Calendar: Semester
Student/faculty ratio: 18:1
Class size 9 or fewer: 9%
Class size 10-29: 55%
Class size 30-49: 20%
Class size 50-99: 10%
Class size 100 or more: 6%
Returning freshmen: 81%
Six-year graduation rate: 59%

Most Popular Majors
Accounting
Biology
Marketing

America's
Best Colleges for
B Students

B Student Support and Success

The University of Kentucky has an Academic Enhancement Program which is typically referred to as "the Study." It is geared to help students reach their academic goals through study groups, tutoring or learning skills workshops. The Writing Center offers free individual or group consultations and helps with class assignments, creative writing, dissertations, reports, articles and more. The Math Resource Center (Mathskeller) has tutors for 100-level math courses, and the Counseling and Testing Center offers personal sessions as well as interactive workshops.

University of Kentucky prides itself on providing stellar support programs, including dedicated guidance for: academic · career · psychological · minority students · military. Annually, 81 percent of freshmen students return for their sophomore year.

Support for Students with Learning Disabilities

Students coping with learning disabilities may find University of Kentucky's support programs particularly beneficial. The college will sometimes grant an LD student additional time to finish their degree. According to the school, each student with learning disabilities receives accommodations that are specific to his/her needs and that are supported by documentation. All students with learning disabilities are not eligible for all accommodations. LD students might want to consider researching the following programs: remedial math · remedial English · remedial reading · testing accommodations · extended time for tests · take-home exam · oral tests · readers · typist/scribe · reading machines · texts on tape · early syllabus · diagnostic testing service. Individual or small group tutorials are also available in: time management · organizational skills · learning strategies · specific subject areas · writing labs · math labs · study skills. An advisor/advocate from the Disability Resource Center is available to students.

How to Get Admitted

For admissions decisions, non-academic factors considered: interview · extracurricular activities · special talents, interests and abilities · character/personal qualities · volunteer work · state of residency · geographical location · minority affiliation · alumni relationship. A high school diploma is required, although a GED is also accepted for admissions consideration. SAT or ACT test scores are required of all applicants. *According to the admissions office:* Minimum 2.0 GPA required. *Academic units recommended:* 4 English, 4 Math, 4 Science, 3 Social Studies, 2 Foreign Language.

How to Pay for College

To apply for financial aid, students should submit the following: Free Application for Federal Student Aid (FAFSA). University of Kentucky participates in the Federal Work Study program. *Need-based aid programs include:* scholarships and grants · general need-based awards · Federal Pell grants · state scholarships and grants · college-based scholarships and grants · private scholarships and grants. *Non-need-based aid programs include:* scholarships and grants · general need-based awards · state scholarships and grants · creative arts and performance awards · special achievements and activities awards

· athletic scholarships · ROTC scholarships · alumni affiliation · leadership, minority and music/drama scholarships/grants.

UNIVERSITY OF KENTUCKY

Highlights

Admissions
Applicants: 19,810
Accepted: 13,592
Acceptance rate: 68.6%
Average GPA: 3.5
ACT range: 23-28
SAT Math range: 510-630
SAT Reading range: 500-620
SAT Writing range: 6-24
Top 10% of class: 32%
Top 25% of class: 61%
Top 50% of class: 88%

Deadlines
Early Action: 12/1
Early Decision: No
Regular Action: Rolling admissions
Common Application: Accepted

Financial Aid
In-state tuition: $10,616
Out-of-state tuition: $22,888
Room: Varies
Board: Varies
Books: $1,000
Freshmen receiving need-based or merit-based aid: 93%
Avg. aid package (freshmen): Not reported
Avg. aid package (undergrads): Not reported

Prominent Alumni
Tom Hammond, sportscaster, NBC; Ashley Judd, philanthropist, activist, actress; Story Musgrave, retired NASA astronaut.

School Spirit
Mascot: Wildcats
Colors: Blue and white
Song: *On, On U of K*

473

UNIVERSITY OF LOUISIANA AT LAFAYETTE

P.O. Drawer 41008, Lafayette, LA 70504-1008
Admissions: 337-482-6473 · Financial Aid: 337-482-6506
Email: admissions@louisiana.edu · Website: http://www.louisiana.edu

From the College

"The University of Louisiana - Lafayette is a vibrant member of a culturally sophisticated community that has an intimate feel. On campus, students can view major art exhibits at the Paul and Lulu Hilliard University Art Museum, watch musical and theatrical performances, catch big name acts in the 12,000-seat Cajundome and support their favorite Ragin' Cajun sports teams. There are plenty of off-campus entertainment offerings, too. Downtown Lafayette, which is within walking distance of campus, features live music, art galleries and restaurants. Festivals abound in the area throughout the year; Mardi Gras reigns supreme. UL Lafayette students embody the spirit of the region's unique Cajun and Creole heritage. That means they work hard and play hard. They value family and respect each other's religious beliefs. They embrace diversity and treat strangers like family. Their compassion for others inspires public service. The seamless blend of campus and community creates a synergy that sets UL Lafayette apart from other universities.

"The university takes as its primary purpose the examination, transmission, preservation and extension of mankind's intellectual traditions. The university provides intellectual leadership for the educational, cultural and economic development of the region and state through its instructional, research and service activities. The university extends its resources to diverse constituency groups it serves through research centers, continuing education, public outreach programs cultural activities and access to campus facilities."

Campus Setting

University of Louisiana - Lafayette, founded in 1898, is a public, comprehensive university. Programs are offered through the Colleges of Applied Life Sciences, the Arts, Business Administration, Education, Engineering, General Studies, Liberal Arts, Nursing and Sciences, and through the Graduate School. Its 1,375-acre campus is located in Lafayette, 50 miles from Baton Rouge. A four-year institution, University of Louisiana - Lafayette has an enrollment of 16,688 students. The university is pleased to provide its students with all the benefits of a large library and an art museum. University of Louisiana - Lafayette provides on-campus housing with 20 units that can accommodate 2,154 students. Housing options: women's dorms · men's dorms · fraternity housing · single-student apartments · married-student apartments. The rec center offers indoor basketball and racquetball courts, an indoor track, weight and conditioning equipment and a two-story climbing wall.

Student Life and Activities

Eighty-six percent of students live off campus. University of Louisiana - Lafayette has 192 official student organizations. The most popular are: Accounting Society · Club for Academic Competition · College Democrats · College Republicans · Ducks Unlimited · Gospel Choir · Greek Council · Computer Society · Interfraternity Council · American Institute of Architecture Students · Law Club · MBA Association · National Panhellenic Conference · Outdoor Club · Pre-Vet Society · Pride Society · Residence Hall Association · American Institute of Chemical Engineers Student Chapter · American Society of Civil Engineers · Anime Club · ACM · Beacon Club ·

Best Buddies · Bowling Club. The intramural teams listed below are geared towards those interested in sports: basketball · flag football · racquetball · soccer · softball · tennis · triathlon · volleyball · water polo. University of Louisiana - Lafayette is a member of the Sun Belt Conference (Division I, Football I-A).

Academics and Learning Environment

University of Louisiana - Lafayette has 584 full-time and 159 part-time faculty members, offering a student-to-faculty ratio of 22:1. University of Louisiana - Lafayette offers 94 majors with the most popular being nursing, management and biology. The school has a general core requirement. Cooperative education is not offered. All first-year students must maintain a 2.0 GPA or higher to avoid academic probation. A B student should investigate: self-designed majors · independent study · double majors · dual degrees · accelerated study · honors program · internships · distance learning certificate programs.

B Student Support and Success

Students may be admitted through the University of Louisiana's Guaranteed Admission requirements: Completion of the Louisiana Board of Regents' high school core curriculum and a mathematics ACT score of at least 18 (430 math SAT) or an English ACT score of at least 18 (450 critical reading SAT) and one of the following: High school GPA of 2.5 or higher using an unweighted 4.0 scale, ACT composite score of at least 23 (SAT 1060) with at least a 2.0 GPA or rank in the top 25 percent of the high school graduating class and at least a 2.0 GPA. Students who don't meet the Guaranteed Admission requirements may apply for Admission by Committee by submitting a completed application. Once students are accepted and enrolled at the University of Louisiana, they can find help for succeeding in their studies. The Learning Center offers walk-in tutoring, although appointments are sometimes recommended. The Writing Center helps students with all stages of the writing process. Free online tutoring is offered through Smart Thinking. With it, students can access live tutorials in writing, math, accounting, statistics and economics. They can also consult writing manuals, sample problems, research tools and study skills manuals. Study groups are available on campus so that several students can get help on a weekly basis. They are student led, and sessions cover problems and questions from weekly class material. Study skills and time management helps are found on the college website, including information on reading, note taking, studying, test anxiety, test taking and general study skills. The college also offers a Career Counseling Center that can provide help to a student in deciding a major. A career counselor is there to guide students to resources and informational material. Along with this, a half-semester, one-credit course on career decision-making assists students who want an in-depth career analysis.

University of Louisiana - Lafayette provides an assortment of support programs. There is dedicated guidance for: academic · career · personal. Recognizing that some students may need extra preparation, University of Louisiana - Lafayette offers remedial and refresher courses in: reading · writing · math · study skills. The aver-

UNIVERSITY OF LOUISIANA – LAFAYETTE

Highlights

University of Louisiana – Lafayette
Lafayette, LA (Pop. 122,761)
Location: Medium city
Four-year public
Founded: 1898
Website: http://www.louisiana.edu

Students
Total enrollment: 16,688
Undergrads: 15,144
From out-of-state: 7%
Male/Female: 45%/55%
Live on-campus: 14%
In fraternities: 7%
In sororities: 7%
Off-campus employment rating: Good
Caucasian: 69%
African American: 21%
Hispanic: 3%
Asian: 2%
Hawaiian or Pacific Islander: <1%
Native American: <1%
Mixed (2+ ethnicities): 2%
International: 2%

Academics
Calendar: Semester
Student/faculty ratio: 22:1
Class size 9 or fewer: 12%
Class size 10-29: 52%
Class size 30-49: 28%
Class size 50-99: 6%
Class size 100 or more: -
Returning freshmen: 74%
Six-year graduation rate: 42%

Most Popular Majors
Nursing
Management
Biology

475

College Profiles

UNIVERSITY OF LOUISIANA – LAFAYETTE

Admissions
Applicants: 8,506
Accepted: 5,019
Acceptance rate: 59.0%
Average GPA: 3.2
ACT range: 21-25
SAT Math range: 490-600
SAT Reading range: Not reported
SAT Writing range: 450-590
Top 10% of class: 17%
Top 25% of class: 42%
Top 50% of class: 73%

Deadlines
Early Action: No
Early Decision: No
Regular Action: Rolling admissions
Common Application: Not accepted

Financial Aid
In-state tuition: $6,872
Out-of-state tuition: $19,272
Room: Varies
Board: Varies
Books: $1,200
Freshmen receiving need-based aid: 57%
Undergrads rec. need-based aid: 51%
Avg. % of need met by financial aid: 56%
Avg. aid package (freshmen): Not reported
Avg. aid package (undergrads): Not reported

Prominent Alumni
Jake Delhomme, professional football player; Kathleen Blanco, Governor of Louisiana.

School Spirit
Mascot: Ragin' Cajuns
Colors: Vermillion and white
Song: *UL Fight Song*

age freshman year GPA is 2.6, and 74 percent of freshman students return for their sophomore year.

Support for Students with Learning Disabilities

Students with learning disabilities are met with a wide variety of options when attending University of Louisiana - Lafayette. Support programs are available and if necessary, the college will grant additional time to students with learning disabilities to complete their degree. According to the school, math study groups, special 5-days a week math classes, videos in remedial math and college algebra classes, online tutoring and SMART THINKING are available through the university, plus a writing lab is available in the English Department. In addition, workshops in study skills, time management and individual counseling are offered. LD students will find the following list of programs of particular interest: remedial math · remedial English · remedial reading · special classes · tutors · learning center · untimed tests · extended time for tests · oral tests · readers · typist/scribe · note-taking services · reading machines · tape recorders · diagnostic testing service · priority registration · waiver of foreign language degree requirement. An advisor/advocate from the LD program is available to students.

How to Get Admitted

For admissions decisions, non-academic factors considered: A high school diploma is required, although a GED is also accepted for admissions consideration. SAT or ACT test scores are required of all applicants. SAT Subject Test scores are recommended but not required. *According to the admissions office:* Minimum 2.0 GPA required. Minimum composite ACT score of 17 required of out-of-state applicants. *Academic units recommended:* 4 English, 3 Math, 3 Science, 1 Social Studies, 1 Foreign Language.

How to Pay for College

To apply for financial aid, students should submit the following: Free Application for Federal Student Aid (FAFSA). University of Louisiana - Lafayette participates in the Federal Work Study program. *Need-based aid programs include:* scholarships and grants · general need-based awards · Federal Pell grants · state scholarships and grants · college-based scholarships and grants · private scholarships and grants · Federal Nursing scholarships · United Negro College Fund. *Non-need-based aid programs include:* scholarships and grants · state scholarships and grants · creative arts and performance awards · athletic scholarships.

UNIVERSITY OF MAINE

168 College Avenue, Orono, ME 04469
Admissions: 877-486-2364 · Financial Aid: 207-581-1324
Email: um-admit@maine.edu · Website: http://www.umaine.edu

From the College

"While the University of Maine embraces its tradition of providing high-quality education, research and service all relevant and important to Maine, it also recognizes that its work affects people far beyond the state's borders. Its nationally and internationally programs in areas like climate change provide outstanding learning opportunities for its students, while advancing knowledge in critical disciplines. UMaine is also a leader in developing teaching and research partnerships with other institutions—both educational and research—to maximize resources and share expertise, with the ultimate goal of producing high-quality results."

Campus Setting

The University of Maine, founded in 1862, is a public, land-grant institution. Programs are offered through the Colleges of Business, Public Policy; Health, Education and Human Development, Engineering, Liberal Arts and Sciences, Natural Resources, Forestry and Agriculture. Its 3,300-acre main campus is located in Orono, eight miles north of Bangor. A four-year institution, University of Maine has an enrollment of 11,247 students. Although not originally a co-educational college, the university has been co-ed since 1872. The campus facilities include: library · arts · Canadian-American and Franco-American centers · art museum · digital media lab · hall for performing arts · anthropology museum · aquatic production facility · farm museum · botanical gardens · environmental research facility · marine lab · woodland preserve · observatory · planetarium · woods composites building · advanced manufacturing center · lab for advanced surface science and technology · climbing wall. University of Maine provides on-campus housing with 18 units that can accommodate 3,517 students. Housing options: coed dorms · sorority housing · fraternity housing · single-student apartments · married-student apartments · special housing for disabled students · special housing for international students.

Student Life and Activities

Sixty-eight percent of students live off campus. The university has more than 234 student organizations, including honor and professional societies, fraternities and sororities. Eight women's and seven men's intercollegiate NCAA Division I athletic programs are part of the campus community. Numerous intramural and club sports give all students an opportunity to be physically active. Two gymnasiums, a field house, an indoor pool, a sports arena, a domed field and a 10,000-seat athletic stadium are used for NCAA Division I athletics. A 14,000-square-foot recreation center, which opened in fall 2007, and the Maine Bound Center, with a climbing wall, provides opportunities for recreational sports. For students' creative interests, there are two theaters, excellent music facilities, recital halls and studios for dance and the visual arts. Community services include a newspaper, a radio station, a police and safety department and a health facility. Popular gathering spots include Memorial Union, Student Recreation Center, Bear Brew Pub and Pat's Pizza. Maine Day and Homecoming are popular campus events. University of Maine has 228 official student organizations. The most popular are: concert, jazz, marching, symphonic, varsity and pep bands · orchestra · music ensembles · university singers · women's glee club · Oratorio Society · opera workshop · Maine Masque Theatre · musical theatre · dance club · debating · language clubs · Sophomore Eagles · Blade Society · Maine

UNIVERSITY OF MAINE

University of Maine
Orono, ME (Pop. 9,112)
Location: Rural
Four-year public
Founded: 1862
Website: http://www.umaine.edu

Students
Total enrollment: 11,247
Undergrads: 9,182
Freshmen: 2,461
Part-time students: 14%
From out-of-state: 30%
Male/Female: 52%/48%
Live on-campus: 32%
Off-campus employment rating: Fair
Caucasian: 79%
African American: 2%
Hispanic: 2%
Asian: 1%
Hawaiian or Pacific Islander: <1%
Native American: 1%
Mixed (2+ ethnicities): 2%
International: 3%

Academics
Calendar: Semester
Student/faculty ratio: 16:1
Class size 9 or fewer: 12%
Class size 10-29: 58%
Class size 30-49: 16%
Class size 50-99: 11%
Class size 100 or more: 4%
Returning freshmen: 81%
Six-year graduation rate: 56%

Most Popular Majors
Psychology
Elementary education
Nursing

America's
Best Colleges for
B Students

Bound · drill team. University of Maine is a member of the American East Conference (Division I), Atlantic 10 Conference (Division I, Football I-AA) and Hockey East Association (Division I).

Academics and Learning Environment

University of Maine has 483 full-time and 310 part-time faculty members, offering a student-to-faculty ratio of 16:1. The most common course size is 10 to 19 students. The university offers 175 majors with the most popular being psychology, elementary education and nursing and least popular being modern languages, forest ecosystem sciences/conservation and wood science/technology. The school has a general core requirement. Cooperative education is not offered. All first-year students must maintain a 1.6 GPA or higher to avoid academic probation. Special academic programs that a B student would find appealing: pass/fail grading option · independent study · double majors · accelerated study · honors program · Phi Beta Kappa · internships · distance learning certificate programs.

B Student Support and Success

The Tutor Program at the university is designed to meet with students in small group settings who need help in their 100- and 200-level, non-web-based courses. Peer tutors meet with students two or three times a week throughout the semester. One student is quoted on the website as saying, "I was not grasping the problems in lecture, and I was often confused on which technique to apply. Having students explain ideas and concepts to each other has been very helpful. I have had to be prepared for each session, which keeps me on task." This no-cost service is open to any student who has registered for at least six credit hours as well as students who need help in math classes. For those needing help with writing, the college's Writing Center staff is there to give advice as well.

There are a handful of support programs available at University of Maine, including dedicated guidance for: academic · career · personal · psychological · minority students · military · veterans · non-traditional students · family planning · religious. The average freshman year GPA is 2.8, and 81 percent of freshmen students return for their sophomore year. Here is a compiled list of companies that most frequently hire these graduates: Eastern Maine Medical Center · Portsmouth Naval Shipyard · Circuit City · MBNA America · Enterprise Rent-a-Car · Forum Financial · Community Health and Counseling · AmeriCorps · Dartmouth Medical School.

Support for Students with Learning Disabilities

University of Maine is proud to present its LD students, those students dealing with learning disabilities, a wide array of specific support programs. The college may offer LD students a lightened course load or just additional time in order for them to finish their degree. The following is a list of programs that would benefit an LD student: remedial math · remedial English · remedial reading · tutors · testing accommodations · extended time for tests · take-home exam · oral tests · readers · note-taking services · tape recorders · early syllabus. Individual or small group tutorials are also available in: learning strategies · study skills. An advisor/advocate from the LD program is available to students.

How to Get Admitted

For admissions decisions, non-academic factors considered: interview · extracurricular activities · special talents, interests and abilities · character/personal qualities · volunteer work · work experience · geographical location. A high school diploma is required, although a GED is also accepted for admissions consideration. SAT or ACT test scores are required of all applicants. SAT Subject Test scores are recommended but not required. *According to the admissions office:* Rank in top half of secondary school class and minimum 2.5 GPA recommended. *Academic units recommended:* 4 English, 4 Math, 4 Science, 3 Social Studies, 2 Foreign Language.

How to Pay for College

To apply for financial aid, students should submit the following: Free Application for Federal Student Aid (FAFSA). University of Maine participates in the Federal Work Study program. *Need-based aid programs include:* scholarships and grants · general need-based awards · Federal Pell grants · state scholarships and grants · college-based scholarships and grants · private scholarships and grants. *Non-need-based aid programs include:* scholarships and grants · general need-based awards · state scholarships and grants · creative arts and performance awards · athletic scholarships · ROTC scholarships.

UNIVERSITY OF MAINE

Highlights

Admissions
Applicants: 9,336
Accepted: 7,789
Acceptance rate: 83.4%
Average GPA: 3.2
ACT range: 21-27
SAT Math range: 480-600
SAT Reading range: 470-590
SAT Writing range: 1-16
Top 10% of class: 19%
Top 25% of class: 46%
Top 50% of class: 78%

Deadlines
Early Action: 12/15
Early Decision: No
Regular Action: Rolling admissions
Common Application: Accepted

Financial Aid
In-state tuition: $8,370
Out-of-state tuition: $26,250
Room: Varies
Board: Varies
Books: $1,000
Freshmen receiving need-based aid: 72%
Undergrads rec. need-based aid: 70%
Avg. % of need met by financial aid: 78%
Avg. aid package (freshmen): $16,749
Avg. aid package (undergrads): $15,176
Avg. debt upon graduation: $32,438

Prominent Alumni
Stephen King, author, Cindy Blodgett, former WNBA player; Maurice Goddard, former secretary of the Pennsylvania Department of Conservation and Natural Resources.

School Spirit
Mascot: Black Bears
Colors: Maine blue, navy blue and white
Song: *Stein Song*

479

UNIVERSITY OF MARYLAND – EASTERN SHORE

1 Backbone Road, Princess Anne, MD 21853
Admissions: 410-651-8410 · Financial Aid: 410-651-6172
Email: umesadmissions@umes.edu · Website: http://www.umes.edu

From the College

"The University of Maryland - Eastern Shore (UMES), the State Historically Black 1890 Land-Grant Institution, is a teaching, research and doctoral institution that nurtures and launches leaders in a student-centered environment. Its unique programs in the University System of Maryland include Aviation Science, Hotel and Restaurant Management, Professional Golf Management, Physician Assistant, Professional Practice Doctorate of Physical Therapy and Doctorate of Pharmacy degree. It is the first Historically Black Institution in the nation to offer a bachelor's degree in Professional Golf Management that is accredited by the Professional Golfers' Association of America."

Campus Setting

UMES is a public, multipurpose institution. It was founded in 1886, became a state college in 1948 and gained university status in 1970. Its 745-acre campus is located in Princess Anne, 15 miles from Salisbury. A four-year institution, UMES is a historically black university with 4,222 students. The school also has a library with 217,429 books. UMES provides on-campus housing with 49 units that can accommodate 2,206 students. Housing options: coed dorms · women's dorms · men's dorms. Recreation and sports facilities include: bowling alley · center · field · gymnasium · stadium.

Student Life and Activities

Sixty-two percent of students live off campus. Popular campus events include Homecoming, Mr. and Miss UMES and National Women's History Month. UMES has 79 official student organizations. The most popular are: Student Activity Advisory Group · Criminal Justice Society · National Student Business League · Social Work Student Association · Student Chapter of the Council for Exceptional Children · Rehabilitation Services Student Association · Physical Therapy Association · Biology Society · poultry science club · math and computer science club · Engineering Technology Society · human ecology club. The following is a list of intramural teams: basketball · billiards · bowling · flag football · soccer · table tennis · volleyball. UMES is a member of the Mid-Eastern Athletic Conference (Division I).

Academics and Learning Environment

UMES has 215 full-time and 150 part-time faculty members, offering a student-to-faculty ratio of 14:1. The most common course size is 2 to 9 students. UMES offers 50 majors with the most popular being business/marketing, criminal justice and health professions/related clinical sciences, other and least popular being engineering, mathematics and computer/information sciences. The school has a general core requirement. Cooperative education is available. All first-year students must maintain a 2.0 GPA or higher to avoid academic probation, and a minimum overall GPA of 2.0 is required to graduate. B students will benefit from reading the following: pass/fail grading option · independent study · dual degrees · honors program · internships · distance learning.

480

B Student Support and Success

UMES has an extensive Academic Support Center, which includes a tutorial program that helps students in all lower-level courses. Both individual and small group tutoring are available and all services are free. Through the school's Computer Assisted Instruction Program, students can use a system known as Accuplacer to obtain a comprehensive analysis of where they stand in reading, math and English. Developmental skills classes are offered by professional staff specialists. Students who need a stronger background in liberal arts may find help through the General Studies Program. Additionally, students who are 1) from families with low income, 2) first generation college enrollees or 3) disabled (learning or physical) can take part in the federally funded Student Support Services Program.

UMES provides a plethora of support programs, among them, dedicated guidance for: academic · career · personal · psychological · minority students · veterans · religious. Recognizing that some students may need extra preparation, UMES offers remedial and refresher courses in: reading · writing · math · study skills. Other remedial services include: Pre-admission summer program. Annually, 68 percent of freshmen students return for their sophomore year. What about after college though? While many students enrolled at UMES enter the workforce, approximately 27 percent pursue a graduate degree immediately after graduation. Approximately 21 percent of students who enter the workforce, enter a field related to their major within six months of their graduation.

Support for Students with Learning Disabilities

Students with learning disabilities will be pleased to learn that there are multiple support programs available to them at UMES. The college may grant LD students additional time to complete their degree. Those students dealing with learning disabilities will find the following programs at UMES very beneficial: remedial math · remedial English · remedial reading · tutors · untimed tests · extended time for tests · take-home exam · note-taking services · tape recorders · early syllabus · priority registration · waiver of math degree requirement. Individual or small group tutorials are also available in: time management · organizational skills · specific subject areas · writing labs. An advisor/advocate from the Office of Services for Students with Disabilities is available to students.

How to Get Admitted

For admissions decisions, non-academic factors considered: interview · extracurricular activities · special talents, interests and abilities · character/personal qualities. A high school diploma is required, although a GED is also accepted for admissions consideration. SAT or ACT test scores are required of all applicants. *According to the admissions office:* Minimum combined SAT Reasoning score of 850 and minimum 2.5 GPA recommended. In-state applicants with secondary school diploma and minimum 2.5 GPA may be admitted on basis of SAT Reasoning scores and GPA.

How to Pay for College

To apply for financial aid, students should submit the following: Free Application for Federal Student Aid (FAFSA) · institution's own financial aid forms. UMES participates in the Federal Work Study

UNIVERSITY OF MARYLAND – EASTERN SHORE

Highlights

University of Maryland – Eastern Shore
Princess Anne, MD (Pop. 3,308)
Location: Rural
Four-year public
Founded: 1886
Website: http://www.umes.edu

Students
Total enrollment: 4,222
Undergrads: 3,531
Freshmen: 1,193
Part-time students: 10%
From out-of-state: 18%
From public schools: 90%
Male/Female: 44%/56%
Live on-campus: 38%
In fraternities: 3%
In sororities: 1%
Off-campus employment rating: Fair
Caucasian: 12%
African American: 73%
Hispanic: 2%
Asian: 1%
Hawaiian or Pacific Islander: <1%
Native American: <1%
Mixed (2+ ethnicities): 8%
International: 3%

Academics
Calendar: Semester
Student/faculty ratio: 14:1
Class size 9 or fewer: 30%
Class size 10-29: 54%
Class size 30-49: 12%
Class size 50-99: 3%
Class size 100 or more: -
Returning freshmen: 68%
Six-year graduation rate: 32%

Most Popular Majors
Business/marketing
Criminal justice
Health professions/related clinical sciences, other

481

College Profiles

UNIVERSITY OF MARYLAND – EASTERN SHORE

Highlights

Admissions
Applicants: 4,073
Accepted: 2,241
Acceptance rate: 55.0%
Average GPA: 2.9
ACT range: 16-19
SAT Math range: 390-480
SAT Reading range: 400-480
SAT Writing range: Not reported

Deadlines
Early Action: No
Early Decision: No
Regular Action: Rolling admissions
Common Application: Accepted

Financial Aid
In-state tuition: $4,767
Out-of-state tuition: $13,791
Room: $4,994
Board: $3,100
Books: $2,000
Freshmen receiving need-based aid: 83%
Undergrads rec. need-based aid: 81%
Avg. % of need met by financial aid: 47%
Avg. aid package (freshmen): $9,562
Avg. aid package (undergrads): $9,274
Avg. debt upon graduation: $27,215

Prominent Alumni
Earl Richardson, retired president, Morgan State University; Art Shell, NFL coach; Dr. Thomas LaVeist, professor of health, Johns Hopkins University.

School Spirit
Mascot: Fighting Hawks/Lady Hawks
Colors: Maroon and grey

program. *Need-based aid programs include:* scholarships and grants · general need-based awards · Federal Pell grants · state scholarships and grants · college-based scholarships and grants · private scholarships and grants. *Non-need-based aid programs include:* scholarships and grants · state scholarships and grants · creative arts and performance awards · athletic scholarships.

UNIVERSITY OF MASSACHUSETTS AMHERST

37 Mather Drive, Amherst, MA 01003-9313
Admissions: 413-545-0222 · Financial Aid: 413-545-0801
Email: mail@admissions.umass.edu · Website: http://www.umass.edu

From the College

"The University of Massachusetts - Amherst is the flagship campus of the Commonwealth, combining the academic resources of a nationally ranked research university with the support and individualized attention usually reserved for a small college. Students come from every state and over 100 countries, making this New England campus a national and international center for intellectual and cultural activity. With over 110 associate's and bachelor's degree programs, UMass Amherst offers its students a wide array of academic disciplines and nationally known programs of study, including the Bachelor's Degree with Individual Concentration (BDIC), which allows students to create their own major. The outstanding full-time faculty of over 1,200 are the best in their fields and they take teaching seriously.

"Students complement their classroom work with internships, co-ops and research, working side-by-side with their faculty. Students take what they learn in the classroom, and apply it in the studio, the lab, the concert hall and the field. With this intersection of learning and doing, students find their intellectual voice and independence.

"The Commonwealth Honors College Residential Complex is a national model and welcomes students who seek additional academic challenge and meet the requirements for acceptance. The extensive library system is the largest at any public institution in the Northeast, and offers students a state-of-the-art learning environment through the Learning Commons, a place that fosters academic collaboration.

"The campus is undergoing a facilities renaissance, with new cutting edge academic buildings that emphasize team-based learning. UMass Amherst is also ranked one of the most sustainable "green" campuses in the country, with students recently invited to the White House to receive an award for their efforts. Through the Five College Interchange, students enroll in classes at nearby Amherst, Hampshire, Mount Holyoke and Smith Colleges at no extra charge. A free bus system connects these five campuses, allowing students to participate in a wide array of social and cultural events.

"Through the Residential First-Year Experience (RFYE), first-year students live with other peers who share common interests and experiences. Other opportunities for personal development are found through the Center for Student Development, which brings together more than 300 clubs and organizations; groups include community service organizations, student government, ethnic and cultural groups, religious and spiritual organizations, fraternity and sororities, student run businesses, media related groups, groups that grow from academic interests and groups dedicated to athletics and recreation, socializing, arts and entertainment and politics.

"UMass Amherst competes in NCAA Division I Intercollegiate Athletics. Students attend every home game free in regular season, and wear their Minutemen and Minutewomen maroon proudly. All students can work out at the immensely popular Recreation Center, and any student who enjoys athletic competition can participate in an extensive intramural sports program. UMass Dining Services is consistently ranked top in the country with students and families raving about the food. Just off campus, the picturesque town of Amherst offers scores of shops and restaurants from Mexican or Thai, to pizza, burgers and Indian. Appearing on 'the top ten' lists for college towns, Amherst has a truly unusual combination of New England charm and international sophistication. Boston is less than two hours away, and New York City

UNIVERSITY OF MASSACHUSETTS – AMHERST

University of Massachusetts – Amherst
Amherst, MA (Pop. 34,874)
Location: Large town
Four-year public
Founded: 1863
Website: http://www.umass.edu

Students
Total enrollment: 28,518
Undergrads: 22,134
Freshmen: 4,827
Part-time students: 7%
From out-of-state: 24%
Male/Female: 51%/49%
Live on-campus: 64%
In fraternities: 7%
In sororities: 6%
Off-campus employment rating: Excellent
Caucasian: 66%
African American: 4%
Hispanic: 5%
Asian: 8%
Hawaiian or Pacific Islander: <1%
Native American: <1%
Mixed (2+ ethnicities): 2%
International: 2%

Academics
Calendar: Semester
Student/faculty ratio: 18:1
Class size 9 or fewer: 13%
Class size 10-29: 54%
Class size 30-49: 14%
Class size 50-99: 9%
Class size 100 or more: 10%
Returning freshmen: 89%
Six-year graduation rate: 73%

Most Popular Majors
Psychology
Biology
Management

just three hours south. For outdoor enthusiasts, the mountains of Vermont are less than an hour away and offer skiing and hiking."

Campus Setting

The University of Massachusetts - Amherst is a nationally ranked public research university located in the beautiful, culturally rich New England town of Amherst. Undergraduates choose from almost 90 areas of academic study, and with its size, diversity and the richness of its academic and extracurricular offerings, UMass Amherst provides almost unlimited possibilities for personal growth and professional development. As a distinctive feature of UMass Amherst, undergraduates become directly involved in research, and get hands-on experience in numerous areas through internships or field experience. UMass Amherst also offers a wide range of service learning and volunteer opportunities. Academically talented students may participate in the Commonwealth Honors College that offers both the advantages of a small honors college and the wide-ranging opportunities of a nationally recognized research university. A four-year institution, UMass Amherst has an enrollment of 28,518 students. The campus has a large library, a recreation center, contemporary art museum, and an astronomical observatory. UMass Amherst provides on-campus housing with 51 units that can accommodate 13,318 students. Housing options: coed dorms · women's dorms · men's dorms · sorority housing · fraternity housing · single-student apartments · married-student apartments · special housing for disabled students · special housing for international students. Recreation and sports facilities include: arena · artificial turf · dance studio · recreation fitness center · gymnasium · handball, racquetball and squash courts · ice rinks · indoor track · playing fields · soccer and softball fields · stadium · swimming pools · weight training room · wrestling room.

Student Life and Activities

Sixty-four percent of students live on campus. Time has not tarnished the city's small town connectedness, and the downtown itself is still centered on a traditional New England town common, with shops, cafés and restaurants lining the streets around it. While UMass's 10,000-seat Mullins Center is a venue for sports events and pop concerts, the Fine Arts Center hosts internally acclaimed performing arts groups and houses a visual arts gallery. Popular gathering spots include the Learning Commons, the Campus Center/Student Union, downtown Amherst and nearby Northampton. Popular campus events include "Something Every Friday," First Week, Festival of the Arts, Multicultural Film Festival, Haitian/ Dominican/CASA Cultural Night and Magic Triangle Jazz series. UMass Amherst has 324 official student organizations. The most popular are: music · theatre · political · service · recreation and special-interest groups. Intramural teams include: basketball · field hockey · flag football · ice hockey · soccer · softball · tennis · Ultimate Frisbee · volleyball · walleyball · wrestling. UMass Amherst is a member of the Atlantic 10 Conference (Division I), MAC (Division I, Football FBS), Hockey East Association (Division I) and CAA (Men's Lacrosse, DI).

America's
Best Colleges for
B Students

Academics and Learning Environment

UMass Amherst has 1,232 full-time and 146 part-time faculty members, offering a student-to-faculty ratio of 18:1. The most common course size is 10 to 19 students. UMass Amherst offers 212 majors with the most popular being psychology, biology and management. The school has a general core requirement. Cooperative education is available. All first-year students must maintain a 2.0 GPA or higher to avoid academic probation. Other special academic programs that would appeal to a B student include: self-designed majors · pass/fail grading option · independent study · double majors · dual degrees · accelerated study · honors program · Phi Beta Kappa · internships · distance learning certificate programs.

B Student Support and Success

UMass's General Studies program offers students the chance to develop skills like critical thinking, communication and learning skills. It consists of 14 required courses and assistance is possible through the Learning Commons and an academic advisor. A Learning Resource Center offers free help through tutoring, and supplemental instruction.

UMass Amherst provides dedicated guidance for: academic · career · personal · psychological · minority students · veterans · family planning. Annually, 89 percent of freshmen students return for their sophomore year. Approximately 20 percent of students pursue a graduate degree immediately after graduation. Companies that most frequently hire graduates from UMass Amherst include: PricewaterhouseCoopers LLP · KPMG · Ernst & Young · Teach for America · Raytheon · State Street Inc. · Aramark · Deloitte · General Electric · UMass · Hyatt Hotels · Macy's · TJX Companies Inc.

Support for Students with Learning Disabilities

UMass Amherst offers learning disabled students additional time to complete their degree, and a lightened course load. High school foreign language and math waivers are accepted. Students with learning disabilities will find the following programs useful: special classes · testing accommodations · untimed tests · extended time for tests · take-home exam · oral tests · exam on tape or computer · readers · typist/scribe · note-taking services · proofreading services · reading machines · tape recorders · early syllabus · diagnostic testing service · priority registration · waiver of math degree requirement · waiver of foreign language degree requirement. Individual or small group tutorials are also available in: time management · organizational skills · learning strategies · specific subject areas · study skills. An advisor/advocate from the LD program is available to students.

How to Get Admitted

For admissions decisions, non-academic factors considered: extracurricular activities · special talents, interests and abilities · character/personal qualities · volunteer work · work experience · geographical location · minority affiliation. A high school diploma is required, although a GED is also accepted for admissions consideration. SAT or ACT test scores are required of all applicants. *Academic units recommended:* 4 English, 3 Math, 3 Science, 2 Social Studies, 2 Foreign Language.

UNIVERSITY OF MASSACHUSETTS – AMHERST

Highlights

Admissions
Applicants: 35,868
Accepted: 22,556
Acceptance rate: 62.9%
Placed on wait list: 4,902
Enrolled from wait list: 106
Average GPA: 3.7
ACT range: 24-29
SAT Math range: 570-670
SAT Reading range: 540-640
SAT Writing range: Not reported
Top 10% of class: 28%
Top 25% of class: 69%
Top 50% of class: 97%

Deadlines
Early Action: 11/1
Early Decision: No
Regular Action: 1/15 (final)
Common Application: Accepted

Financial Aid
In-state tuition: $13,258
Out-of-state tuition: $27,974
Room: Varies
Board: Varies
Books: $1,000
Freshmen receiving need-based aid: 57%
Undergrads rec. need-based aid: 59%
Avg. % of need met by financial aid: 82%
Avg. aid package (freshmen): $14,197
Avg. aid package (undergrads): $15,247
Avg. debt upon graduation: $28,999

Prominent Alumni
Catherine 'Cady' Coleman, astronaut; Jeffrey C. Taylor, founder of Monster. com; Jack Welch, retired CEO of General Electric.

School Spirit
Mascot: Minutemen, Minutewomen
Colors: Maroon and white
Song: *Fight UMass*

485

How to Pay for College

To apply for financial aid, students should submit the following: Free Application for Federal Student Aid (FAFSA). UMass Amherst participates in the Federal Work Study program. *Need-based aid programs include:* scholarships and grants · general need-based awards · Federal Pell grants · state scholarships and grants · college-based scholarships and grants · private scholarships and grants. *Non-need-based aid programs include:* scholarships and grants · general need-based awards · state scholarships and grants · creative arts and performance awards · special achievements and activities awards · special characteristics awards · athletic scholarships · ROTC scholarships.

UNIVERSITY OF MEMPHIS

101 Wilder Tower, Memphis, TN 38152
Admissions: 800-669-2678 · Financial Aid: 901-678-4825
Email: recruitment@memphis.edu · Website: http://www.memphis.edu

From the College

"The University of Memphis was founded in 1912 by the Tennessee legislature and is one of only two doctoral research-extensive public universities in the state and is designated as "community engaged" by the Carnegie Foundation for the Advancement of Teaching. Home to students from all 50 states and 100 foreign countries, the University of Memphis strives to provide a close community for its students through its Learning Communities, Emerging Leaders Program, Honors Program, residence life and 140 student organizations. Our students are National Merit finalists, Goldwater Scholars, Emerging Leaders, Honors students and Merck Research scholars. They have won national competitions in robotics/artificial intelligence, music, journalism, investment challenges, moot court, architecture and mathematics. Men's basketball has a 20-year tradition of excellence, including repeated trips to the NCAA tournament and appearances in the famed Final Four.

"The UofM is comprised of five undergraduate colleges: arts and sciences, business, education, communication and fine arts and engineering, the University College, as well as a graduate school, law school, nursing school and a School of Audiology and Speech-Language Pathology. The University offers 15 bachelor's degrees in more than 50 majors and 70 concentrations, master's degrees in more than 45 subjects and doctoral degrees in 21 disciplines, in addition to the juris doctor (law) and specialist in education degrees. Our academic programs enable our students to compete at the highest level offering programs in education, psychology, philosophy, audiology and speech-language pathology, earthquake science, biomedical engineering and discrete mathematics, among others. The Loewenberg School of Nursing has a longstanding 100 percent first-time passage rate for state licensure, and the Cecil C. Humphreys School of Law graduates have the overall highest first-time bar exam passage of any law school in Tennessee. Our faculty in the College of Communication and Fine Arts has received Grammy Awards, Peabody Awards and CINE Eagle Awards. Within that college, the Rudi E. Scheidt School of Music is the only one in the Southeast region to offer a doctorate in music.

"The university is closely connected to the community via internships and research conducted in conjunction with area businesses and industries. The university is dedicated to lifelong learning and to making higher education accessible to as many people as possible. Toward that end, it makes significant use of online courses and offers classes at 34 off-site community locations and four satellite campuses in West Tennessee."

Campus Setting

University of Memphis, founded in 1912, is a comprehensive, public university. It changed its name from Memphis State University in 1994. A four-year institution, University of Memphis' campus covers 1,178 acres and has an enrollment of 21,480 students. Campus facilities include: art gallery · biological center · art and archaeological museums · Egyptian art and archaeology and technology institutes. University of Memphis provides on-campus housing that can accommodate 2,413 students. Housing options: coed dorms · women's dorms · men's dorms · sorority housing · fraternity housing · single-student apartments · married-student apartments · special housing for disabled students.

UNIVERSITY OF MEMPHIS

Highlights

University of Memphis
Memphis (Pop. 655,155)
Location: Major city
Four-year public
Founded: 1912
Website: http://www.memphis.edu

Students
Total enrollment: 21,480
Undergrads: 17,223
Freshmen: 3,514
Part-time students: 28%
From out-of-state: 5%
Male/Female: 40%/60%
Live on-campus: 13%
In fraternities: 12%
In sororities: 10%
Off-campus employment rating: Excellent
Caucasian: 51%
African American: 38%
Hispanic: 3%
Asian: 3%
Hawaiian or Pacific Islander: <1%
Native American: <1%
Mixed (2+ ethnicities): 3%
International: 1%

Academics
Calendar: Semester
Student/faculty ratio: 14:1
Class size 9 or fewer: 15%
Class size 10-29: 56%
Class size 30-49: 19%
Class size 50-99: 8%
Class size 100 or more: 2%
Returning freshmen: 77%
Six-year graduation rate: 44%

Most Popular Majors
Individual studies
Integrative studies
Nursing

Student Life and Activities

Most students (87 percent) live off campus. Popular campus events include Up 'til Dawn, Cultural Arts Series, Wednesday Night Live Series, major concerts and comedy, Domestic Violence Awareness Week, Why Do You Hate Me Week, debates, Homosexuality and Morality, Black History Month, Women's History Month and Black Scholars Breakfast. University of Memphis has 247 official student organizations. The most popular are: music · theatre · political, service and special-interest groups. University of Memphis is a member of the Conference USA (Division I, Football I-AA).

Academics and Learning Environment

University of Memphis has 887 full-time and 581 part-time faculty members, offering a student-to-faculty ratio of 14:1. The most common course size is 10 to 19 students. University of Memphis offers 124 majors with the most popular being individual studies, integrative studies and nursing and least popular being physics, African/African American studies and earth sciences. The school has a general core requirement. Cooperative education is available. All first-year students must maintain a 1.4 GPA or higher to avoid academic probation, and a minimum overall GPA of 2.0 is required to graduate. Other special academic programs that would appeal to a B student include: self-designed majors · pass/fail grading option · independent study · double majors · dual degrees · accelerated study · honors program · internships · distance learning certificate programs.

B Student Support and Success

The University of Memphis offers its students help through its Advanced Learning Center. The Learning Lab provides consultations, open forum learning, special topics training and educational seminars.

University of Memphis provides a variety of support programs including dedicated guidance for: academic · career · personal · psychological · minority students · military · veterans · nontraditional students · family planning · religious. University of Memphis offers remedial and refresher courses in: reading · writing · math · study skills. Annually, 77 percent of freshmen students return for their sophomore year. Approximately 18 percent of students pursue a graduate degree immediately after graduation. One year after graduation, 23 percent of graduates have entered graduate school. Companies that most frequently hire graduates from University of Memphis include: Cummins · Dell · FedEx · First Tennessee Bank · Hilton Hotels Corp. · International Paper · Nike · Pfizer Inc. · Phillip Morris · Medtronic · Merrill Lynch · Morgan Keegan · PricewaterhouseCoopers · Schering-Plough Corp. · Regions Financial Corp. · Thompson Dunavant · Wells Fargo · Williams Sonoma.

Support for Students with Learning Disabilities

Students with learning disabilities may take additional time to complete their degree and/or a lightened course load. According to the school, The LD/ADHD Program at University of Memphis promotes development and independence of students with LD and

ADHD through early intervention and education about disability-related functional limitations. Through counseling and coaching, students learn appropriate techniques and accommodation to compensate for functional limitations and move toward academic success. Students with learning disabilities will find the following programs at University of Memphis useful: remedial math · remedial English · remedial reading · tutors · learning center · testing accommodations · extended time for tests · take-home exam · exam on tape or computer · readers · typist/scribe · note-taking services · reading machines · tape recorders · texts on tape · early syllabus · diagnostic testing service · priority registration · waiver of foreign language and math degree requirement. Individual or small group tutorials are also available in: time management · organizational skills · learning strategies · specific subject areas · writing labs · math labs · study skills. An advisor/advocate from the Student Disability Services is available to students.

How to Get Admitted

For admissions decisions, non-academic factors considered: interview · extracurricular activities · special talents, interests and abilities · character/personal qualities · volunteer work · work experience · geographical location · religious affiliation/commitment · minority affiliation · alumni relationship. A high school diploma is required, although a GED is also accepted for admissions consideration. SAT or ACT test scores are required of all applicants. *According to the admissions office:* Admission of first-time freshmen is selective and based on a calculated index and an evaluation of the required high school curriculum completed.

How to Pay for College

To apply for financial aid, students should submit the following: Free Application for Federal Student Aid (FAFSA). University of Memphis participates in the Federal Work Study program. *Need-based aid programs include:* scholarships and grants · general need-based awards · Federal Pell grants · state scholarships and grants · college-based scholarships and grants · private scholarships and grants. *Non-need-based aid programs include:* scholarships and grants · general need-based awards · state scholarships and grants · creative arts and performance awards · athletic scholarships · ROTC scholarships.

UNIVERSITY OF MEMPHIS

Highlights

Admissions
Applicants: 6,107
Accepted: 4,088
Acceptance rate: 66.9%
Average GPA: 3.3
ACT range: 20-26
SAT Math range: 470-600
SAT Reading range: 460-610
SAT Writing range: 3-17
Top 10% of class: 16%
Top 25% of class: 43%
Top 50% of class: 75%

Deadlines
Early Action: No
Early Decision: No
Regular Action: Rolling admissions
Common Application: Not accepted

Financial Aid
In-state tuition: $7,410
Out-of-state tuition: $10,736
Room: $5,386
Board: $3,590
Books: $1,415
Freshmen receiving need-based aid: 63%
Undergrads rec. need-based aid: 69%
Avg. % of need met by financial aid: 75%
Avg. aid package (freshmen): $9,840
Avg. aid package (undergrads): $9,087
Avg. debt upon graduation: $23,601

Prominent Alumni
Bill Rhodes, chairman/president/CEO, AutoZone; Nancy Walton Laurie, philanthropist/founder of Cedar Lake Contemporary Ballet, owner of Providence Bank; Bill Laurie, philanthropist/former owner, St. Louis Blues.

School Spirit
Mascot: Tigers
Colors: Blue and white

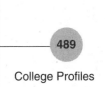

489

UNIVERSITY OF MISSISSIPPI

P.O. Box 1848, University, MS 38677-1848
Admissions: 800-OLEMISS (in-state)
Financial Aid: 800-OLEMISS (in-state)
Email: admissions@olemiss.edu · Website: http://www.olemiss.edu

From the College

"Founded in 1844, the University of Mississippi, known affectionately as Ole Miss, is the flagship university for the state of Mississippi. A world-class public research university, the institution has a long history of producing leaders in public service, academics and innovative research. Ole Miss is the state's largest university, with a major medical school, a nationally recognized law school and 15 academic divisions. It is home to one of the country's only two flagship programs in Mandarin Chinese, as well as an acclaimed MFA in Creative Writing program. The university's Sally McDonnell Barksdale Honors College has been named one of America's top three, its School of Accountancy ranks in the top 10 nationally for bachelor's, master's and doctoral programs, and its School of Pharmacy is home to the National Center for Natural Products Research, devoted to finding new drugs from plants and sea life. The Oxford campus is ranked as one of the nation's 10 safest.

"The University Museum, ranked as one of the 20 Best College Art Museums by *Complex Art & Design*, has notable collections of Southern folk art, Greek and Roman antiquities, 19th century scientific instruments and American fine art. The university also owns Rowan Oak, novelist William Faulkner's home and grounds, which is open to visitors. The J.D. Williams Library is home to the Blues Archive, one of the world's largest collections of blues recordings, memorabilia, photographs and sheet music and the National Library of the Accounting Profession, the world's largest collection of accountancy publications. The University Field Station includes 740 acres and more than 200 experimental ponds, plus laboratories, classrooms and an auditorium, providing faculty and students with a broad range of education and research opportunities in a broad spectrum of disciplines. The Center for Manufacturing Excellence, which combines curriculum from the schools of Engineering, Accountancy and Business Administration to educate students in a cross-disciplinary approach to manufacturing management, includes a 12,000-square-foot factory with full manufacturing lines for wood, metal and plastic fabrication."

Campus Setting

The University of Mississippi, founded in 1844, is a comprehensive, public institution. Programs are offered through the College of Liberal Arts, the Law and Medical Centers and the Schools of Accountancy, Business Administration, Education, Engineering, Applied Sciences and Pharmacy. Its 2,500-acre campus is located in Oxford, 70 miles southeast of Memphis. A four-year institution, University of Mississippi has an enrollment of 19,431 students. Although not originally a co-educational college, University of Mississippi has been co-ed since 1882. Campus facilities include: art galleries · museums. University of Mississippi provides on-campus housing options: women's dorms · men's dorms · sorority housing · fraternity housing · married-student apartments. Recreation and sports facilities include: fitness and aquatic centers · basketball, racquetball, sand volleyball and tennis courts · flag football, soccer and softball fields · disc golf and rebel challenge courses.

Student Life and Activities

Most students (68 percent) live off campus. Popular campus events include Welcome Week, Homecoming, Rumble in the Grove, Miss University Scholarship Pageant, Red and Blue Week, Greek Week, and Spring Fest. University of Mississippi has 275 official student organizations. The most popular are: music, theatre, political, service and special-interest groups. University of Mississippi is a member of the Southeastern Conference (Division I, Football I-A).

Academics and Learning Environment

University of Mississippi has 812 full-time and 176 part-time faculty members, offering a student-to-faculty ratio of 19:1. The most common course size is 20 to 29 students. University of Mississippi offers 126 majors. Elementary education, marketing and finance are the most popular. African American studies, linguistics and German are the least. The school has a general core requirement. Cooperative education is available. All first-year students must maintain a minimum GPA to avoid academic probation, and a minimum overall GPA of 2.0 is required to graduate. Other special academic programs that would appeal to a B student include: pass/fail grading option · independent study · double majors · accelerated study · honors program · internships · distance learning.

B Student Support and Success

The Academic Support Center at the University of Mississippi aids struggling students and those who have not yet declared a major. It helps with scheduling classes, exploring possible majors and fulfilling core requirements for a bachelor's degree. In addition, the center assists with questions or problems with student schedules, explanations of university policies and procedures as well as providing referrals to other offices as needed.

University of Mississippi provides support programs including dedicated guidance for: academic · personal · psychological. Additional counseling services include: science. Annually, 86 percent of freshmen students return for their sophomore year.

Support for Students with Learning Disabilities

According to the University of Mississippi, reasonable accommodations to verified students with disabilities are provided; accommodations are approved on an individual basis.

How to Get Admitted

For admissions decisions, non-academic factors considered: special talents, interests and abilities · character/personal qualities · state of residency. A high school diploma is required, although a GED is also accepted for admissions consideration. SAT or ACT test scores are required for some applicants. SAT Subject Test scores are not required. *Academic units recommended:* 4 Math, 4 Science, 2 Social Studies, 2 Foreign Language.

How to Pay for College

To apply for financial aid, students should submit the following: institution's own financial aid forms. University of Mississippi participates in the Federal Work Study program. *Non-need-based aid programs*

UNIVERSITY OF MISSISSIPPI

Highlights

University of Mississippi
Oxford, MS (Pop. 20,088)
Location: Small town
Four-year public
Founded: 1844
Website: http://www.olemiss.edu

Students
Total enrollment: 19,431
Undergrads: 16,677
Freshmen: 5,297
Part-time students: 6%
From out-of-state: 49%
Male/Female: 45%/55%
Live on-campus: 32%
In fraternities: 31%
In sororities: 36%
Off-campus employment rating: Good
Caucasian: 76%
African American: 15%
Hispanic: 3%
Asian: 2%
Hawaiian or Pacific Islander: <1%
Native American: <1%
Mixed (2+ ethnicities): 2%
International: 2%

Academics
Calendar: Semester
Student/faculty ratio: 19:1
Class size 9 or fewer: 15%
Class size 10-29: 53%
Class size 30-49: 15%
Class size 50-99: 13%
Class size 100 or more: 4%
Returning freshmen: 86%
Six-year graduation rate: 58%

Most Popular Majors
Elementary education
Marketing
Finance

491

College Profiles

UNIVERSITY OF MISSISSIPPI

Admissions
Applicants: 14,258
Accepted: 8,464
Acceptance rate: 59.4%
Average GPA: 3.5
ACT range: 21-27
SAT Math range: 490-600
SAT Reading range: 490-590
SAT Writing range: Not reported
Top 10% of class: 24%
Top 25% of class: 48%
Top 50% of class: 77%

Deadlines
Early Action: No
Early Decision: No
Regular Action: Rolling admissions
Common Application: Not accepted

Financial Aid
In-state tuition: $6,996
Out-of-state tuition: $19,044
Room: Varies
Board: Varies
Books: $1,200
Freshmen receiving need-based aid: 49%
Undergrads rec. need-based aid: 52%
Avg. % of need met by financial aid: 68%
Avg. aid package (freshmen): $10,052
Avg. aid package (undergrads): $7,890
Avg. debt upon graduation: $25,613

Prominent Alumni
Shepard Smith, anchor, Fox News; John Grisham, author; Larry Speakes, former White House Press Secretary for President Ronald Reagan.

School Spirit
Mascot: Ole Miss Rebels
Colors: Cardinal red and navy

include: scholarships and grants · special achievements and activities awards · ROTC scholarships.

UNIVERSITY OF NEVADA, LAS VEGAS

4505 South Maryland Parkway, Las Vegas, NV 89154
Admissions: 702-774-8658 · Financial Aid: 702-895-3424
Email: admissions@unlv.edu · Website: http://www.unlv.edu

From the College

"UNLV is an doctoral degree-granting institution of approximately 28,000 students and 2,900 faculty and staff. Founded in 1957, the university offers more than 220 undergraduate, master's and doctoral degree programs. UNLV is located on a 350-acre campus in southern Nevada and is classified in the category of research universities (high research activity) by the Carnegie Foundation for the Advancement of Teaching. UNLV's programs include the William F. Harrah College of Hotel Administration, William S. Boyd School of Law, an accomplished English department featuring a creative writing program and an international literary center, as well as Honors, environmental studies, architecture, health sciences, social work, business, physical therapy, liberal and fine arts, engineering and science programs. There are numerous research centers and interdisciplinary programs. UNLV is also home to the International Institute of Modern Letters.

"UNLV's main campus, located minutes away from the Las Vegas Strip, features a 300,000 square-foot library as its centerpiece. Among the university's newest facilities are a Science and Engineering Building, featuring more than 200,000 square feet of flexible laboratory and teaching space, offices, high-tech conference rooms and integrated research areas; Greenspun Hall, the home of the Greenspun College of Urban Affairs and broadcast studios for UNLV's radio and television stations and the UNLV Student Recreation and Wellness Center, a technologically advanced recreation, fitness and wellness facility. Additionally, the university is actively engaged in the development of "Midtown UNLV," a long-term, public-private endeavor to create a culturally diverse university district. UNLV's regional Shadow Lane campus stands on 18 acres in the heart of the downtown Las Vegas medical district. This campus is home to the UNLV School of Dental Medicine. UNLV's first international campus, UNLV Singapore, celebrated its eighth anniversary in 2014. Housed on the tenth and eleventh floors of the National Library of Singapore, a prestigious building comparable to the United States Library of Congress, UNLV Singapore offers undergraduate and graduate degree programs in hotel administration and hospitality management. Additional international campuses are planned."

Campus Setting

University of Nevada, founded in 1957, is a public co-educational university. Its 350-acre campus is located in Las Vegas, Nevada. A four-year institution, UNLV Las Vegas has an enrollment of 27,858 students. The campus facilities include: library · art galleries · recording studio and MIDI lab · recital hall · dental education complex · science and engineering complex · moot court facility · natural history museum · desert research institute · center for environmental studies · exercise physiology and cognitive interference lab. UNLV Las Vegas provides on-campus housing with 11 units that can accommodate 1,738 students. Housing options: coed dorms · special housing for disabled students · special housing for international students. Recreation and sports facilities include: football stadium · basketball and volleyball courts · physical education complex · student recreation and wellness center.

Student Life and Activities

Ninety-five percent of students live off campus. Students gather at the Student Recreation and Wellness Center, Student Union, Thomas Mack Center and Cox

UNIVERSITY OF NEVADA – LAS VEGAS

University of Nevada – Las Vegas

Las Vegas, NV (Pop. 596,424)
Location: Major city
Four-year public
Founded: 1957
Website: http://www.unlv.edu

Students

Total enrollment: 27,858
Undergrads: 23,099
Part-time students: 28%
From out-of-state: 15%
From public schools: 95%
Male/Female: 44%/56%
Live on-campus: 5%
In fraternities: 5%
In sororities: 3%
Off-campus employment rating: Excellent
Caucasian: 38%
African American: 8%
Hispanic: 23%
Asian: 16%
Hawaiian or Pacific Islander: 2%
Native American: <1%
Mixed (2+ ethnicities): 8%
International: 4%

Academics

Calendar: Semester
Student/faculty ratio: 22:1
Class size 9 or fewer: 6%
Class size 10-29: 53%
Class size 30-49: 23%
Class size 50-99: 13%
Class size 100 or more: 5%
Returning freshmen: 77%
Six-year graduation rate: 43%

Most Popular Majors

Hospitality/hotel administration
Business management
Education

Pavilion. Popular events include Charles Vanda Master Series, Barrick Lecture Series, University Forum Lecture Series, Moskow Distinguished Speaker Series, William S. Boyd School of Law Saltman Center for Conflict Resolution Lectures, UNLV Jazz Ensemble concerts and Las Vegas Philharmonic Concerts. University of Nevada - Las Vegas has 180 official student organizations. The most popular are: Academic clubs · sports clubs · International Civic Engagement & Advocacy. As for athletics, there are intramural teams available: badminton · basketball · bowling · cross-country running · football · golf · racquetball · soccer · softball · swimming and diving · tennis · track and field · volleyball. University of Nevada - Las Vegas is a member of the Mountain West Conference (Division I, Football I-A).

Academics and Learning Environment

University of Nevada - Las Vegas has 780 full-time and part-time faculty members, offering a student-to-faculty ratio of 22:1. The most common course size is 20 to 29 students. UNLV offers 188 majors with the most popular being hospitality/hotel administration, business management and education and least popular being Afro-American studies, health physics and romance languages. The school has a general core requirement. Cooperative education is available. All first-year students must maintain a 2.0 GPA or higher to avoid academic probation. Here are other academic programs a B student might be intrigued by: self-designed majors · pass/fail grading option · independent study · double majors · dual degrees · accelerated study · honors program · Phi Beta Kappa · internships · distance learning certificate programs.

B Student Support and Success

Student Support Services at UNLV helps students "overcome personal concerns, academic deficiencies and financial difficulties that could impair their chances of succeeding in college." It focuses on the development of good study habits and decision-making skills through tutoring and workshops on subjects such as study skills, time management, note taking, listening skills, reading and outlining textbooks, test-taking strategies, motivation, concentration and stress reduction. These services are free. An academic enrichment program for high school students called Upward Bound offers academic counseling, career exploration, tutoring, college admission testing workshops, motivation, personal development and concentration in computer literacy, English, foreign language, history, government, math and science. Upward Bound students are often involved in weekend or after-school instruction. During the summer, they can participate in daily classes emphasizing academic skills, study techniques and test preparation.

UNLV prides itself on its dedicated guidance for: academic · career · personal · psychological · minority students · veterans · non-traditional students · family planning · religious. Recognizing that some students may need extra preparation, UNLV offers remedial and refresher courses in: reading · writing · math · study skills. The average freshman year GPA is 3.3, and 77 percent of freshmen students return for their sophomore year. After college, many B students enter the workforce and approximately 16 percent pursue a graduate degree immediately after graduation. Among these students who enter the workforce, approximately 63 percent of them actually enter a field related to their major within six months of their graduation. The following list is a compilation of companies that most frequently hire graduates from UNLV: Clark County School District · Deloitte · Ernst & Young · Fairmont Hotel & Resorts · Four Seasons Hotels & Resorts · Hilton Hotels · Marriott International · Nevada Gaming Control Board · PricewaterhouseCoopers · Walt Disney World.

Support for Students with Learning Disabilities

UNLV is proud to offer a series of support programs specifically geared towards students dealing with learning disabilities. There are times when the college will grant additional time to students with learning disabilities so that they can complete their degree. The college may also offer a lightened course load to an LD student. These students will find the following list of programs rather helpful: tutors · learning center · testing accommodations · extended time for tests · take-home exam · oral tests · exam on tape or computer · readers · typist/scribe · note-taking services · reading machines · tape recorders · texts on tape · early syllabus · diagnostic testing service · priority registration · waiver of math degree requirement. Individual or small group tutorials are also available in: time management · organizational skills · learning strategies · specific subject areas · writing labs · math labs · study skills. An advisor/advocate from the Disability Resource Center is available to students.

How to Get Admitted

For admissions decisions, non-academic factors considered: state of residency. A high school diploma is required and a GED is not accepted for admissions consideration. SAT or ACT test scores are required of all applicants. *According to the admissions office:* Minimum combined SAT Reasoning score of 1040 (composite ACT score of 22), minimum of 3.0 GPA and Nevada Advanced High School Diploma required. *Academic units recommended:* 4 English, 3 Math, 3 Science, 3 Social Studies.

How to Pay for College

To apply for financial aid, students should submit the following: Free Application for Federal Student Aid (FAFSA) · institution's own financial aid forms. UNLV participates in the Federal Work Study program. *Need-based aid programs include:* scholarships and grants · general need-based awards · Federal Pell grants · state scholarships and grants · college-based scholarships and grants · private scholarships and grants. *Non-need-based aid programs include:* scholarships and grants · general need-based awards · state scholarships and grants · creative arts and performance awards · athletic scholarships.

UNIVERSITY OF NEVADA – LAS VEGAS

Highlights

Admissions
Applicants: 8,063
Accepted: 6,250
Acceptance rate: 77.5%
Average GPA: 3.3
ACT range: 19-24
SAT Math range: 450-560
SAT Reading range: 440-550
SAT Writing range: 1-8
Top 10% of class: 21%
Top 25% of class: 48%
Top 50% of class: 80%

Deadlines
Early Action: No
Early Decision: No
Regular Action: Rolling admissions
Common Application: Not accepted

Financial Aid
In-state tuition: $6,074
Out-of-state tuition: $19,984
Room: $5,880
Board: $4,644
Books: $1,400
Freshmen receiving need-based aid: 70%
Undergrads rec. need-based aid: 62%
Avg. % of need met by financial aid: 57%
Avg. aid package (freshmen): $8,765
Avg. aid package (undergrads): $9,204
Avg. debt upon graduation: $17,930

Prominent Alumni
Anthony Zuiker, television writer, CSI; Eric Whitacre, composer of choral, wind band/electronic music; Guy Fieri, author, co-owner of five restaurants, Food Network host.

School Spirit
Mascot: Rebel
Colors: Scarlet and gray

495

UNIVERSITY OF NEW HAVEN

300 Boston Post Road, West Haven, CT 06516
Admissions: 800-342-5864 · Financial Aid: 203-932-7315
Email: adminfo@newhaven.edu · Website: http://www.newhaven.edu

From the College

"The University of New Haven (UNH) is for students seeking quality education in liberal arts and in professionally oriented careers. We combine hands-on learning and a focused curriculum with a solid foundation in liberal arts and sciences. UNH brings practice into the classroom and the classroom into the workplace. We are committed to small classes and to tailoring coursework to everyday life in the selected field of study. Internships, special events and an experiential learning series enhance the UNH experience. Our most popular programs are: Forensic Science, Criminal Justice, Music and Sound Recording, Music Industry, Management of Sports Industries, Engineering, Fire Science, Dental Hygiene and the Biological Sciences."

Campus Setting

The University of New Haven, founded in 1920, is a private university. Programs are offered through the Schools of Arts and Sciences; Business Administration; Engineering; Hotel, Restaurant and Tourism Administration; and Public Safety and Professional Studies. Its 75-acre campus is located in West Haven, two miles from New Haven. A four-year institution, UNH has an enrollment of 6,555 students. The campus facilities include an art gallery and a library. UNH provides on-campus housing with 840 units that can accommodate 2,589 students. Housing options: coed dorms · single-student apartments. Recreation and sports facilities include: baseball, practice and softball fields · basketball, racquetball, handball and tennis courts · exercise and weight rooms · gymnasium · indoor track · stadium.

Student Life and Activities

Fifty-one percent of students live on campus. According to a school official, UNH has a family-like atmosphere with numerous community events and activities. This past year UNH had three major bands on campus for concerts. The variety of activities keep the students on campus during the weekends. In addition, because New Haven is a college town, there are many meeting places available off-campus. Where people go off-campus? Everywhere and anywhere. Popular gathering spots include the Student Center, Sports Spot, Beckman Recreation Center, Eddie's Bar and Century Diver. Popular campus events include Homecoming Weekend, Parents Weekend, Spring Fling Weekend, Black History Month, Latino Awareness Week, Bean House open mike nights, International Festival and International Coffee Hours. University of New Haven has 165 official student organizations. Influential groups on campus are Student Government, Student Committee on Programs and Events (SCOPE), Black Student Union, Latin American Student Association and the Fire Science Club. The following is for those interested in involvement with athletics or intramural teams: badminton · basketball · cheerleading/dance team · dodge ball · lightweight football · racquetball · soccer · softball · team handball · table tennis · tennis · volleyball. University of New Haven is a member of the Northeast-10 Conference.

Academics and Learning Environment

University of New Haven has 241 full-time and 379 part-time faculty members, offering a student-to-faculty ratio of 16:1. The most common course size is 20 to 29 students. University of New Haven offers 76 majors with the most popular being criminal justice, forensic science and psychology. The school has a general core requirement. Cooperative education is available. The B student might find these other academic programs appealing: independent study · double majors · dual degrees · accelerated study · honors program · internships · distance learning certificate programs.

B Student Support and Success

The Center for Learning Resources at UNH offers students support for writing assignments, plus sophomore-level core courses. It is made up of three labs: 1) Mathematics, Science and Business, 2) Writing and 3) Computer. In addition, the Office of Academic Services has many different programs. The Freshman Year Program is a one-credit seminar required for graduation. It helps to make the transition from high school to college. Academic Skills Counseling is offered individually and in small groups. The focus is on study and time management skills. Developmental mentoring assists students with developing the skills needed for college-level math and/or English.

University of New Haven provides a variety of support programs for its students, including dedicated guidance for: academic · career · personal · psychological · minority students · religious. Recognizing that some students may need extra preparation, University of New Haven offers remedial and refresher courses in: reading · writing · math · study skills. Annually, 76 percent of freshmen students return for their sophomore year. Approximately, 21 percent of students pursue a graduate degree immediately after graduation. One year after graduation, 35 percent of graduates have entered graduate school. Approximately 77 percent of students who enter the work force enter a field related to their major within six months of graduation.

Support for Students with Learning Disabilities

University of New Haven works hard to offer its learning disability students a plethora of support programs. If necessary, the college will grant additional time to LD students in order to complete their degree. Also, a lightened course load may be granted if deemed appropriate. According to the school, assisted technology is available, such as writing, talking word processors, graphic organizers and other services. LD students will be pleased to learn of the following programs: remedial math · remedial English · remedial reading · tutors · learning center · testing accommodations · untimed tests · extended time for tests · take-home exam · exam on tape or computer · readers · note-taking services · reading machines · tape recorders · texts on tape · early syllabus · diagnostic testing service · priority registration · waiver of foreign language and math degree requirement. Individual or small group tutorials are also available in: time management · organizational skills · learning strategies · specific subject areas · writing labs · math labs · study skills. An advisor/advocate from the Office of Disability Services and Resources is available to students.

How to Get Admitted

For admissions decisions, non-academic factors considered: interview · extracurricular activities · character/personal qualities · volunteer

UNIVERSITY OF NEW HAVEN

Highlights

University of New Haven
West Haven, CT (Pop. 55,404)
Location: Large town
Four-year private
Founded: 1920
Website: http://www.newhaven.edu

Students
Total enrollment: 6,555
Undergrads: 4,864
Part-time students: 9%
From out-of-state: 69%
Male/Female: 51%/49%
Live on-campus: 51%
Off-campus employment rating: Excellent
Caucasian: 52%
African American: 8%
Hispanic: 8%
Asian: 2%
Hawaiian or Pacific Islander: <1%
Native American: <1%
Mixed (2+ ethnicities): 1%
International: 7%

Academics
Calendar: 4-1-4 system
Student/faculty ratio: 16:1
Class size 9 or fewer: 6%
Class size 10-29: 72%
Class size 30-49: 20%
Class size 50-99: 3%
Class size 100 or more: -
Returning freshmen: 76%
Six-year graduation rate: 55%

Most Popular Majors
Criminal justice
Forensic science
Psychology

497

UNIVERSITY OF NEW HAVEN

Admissions
Applicants: 10,169
Accepted: 7,567
Acceptance rate: 74.4%
Average GPA: 3.3
ACT range: 20-25
SAT Math range: 470-580
SAT Reading range: 460-550
SAT Writing range: 1-11

Deadlines
Early Action: 12/1
Early Decision: No
Regular Action: Rolling admissions
Common Application: Accepted

Financial Aid
In-state tuition: $33,330
Out-of-state tuition: $33,330
Room: Varies
Board: Varies
Books: $1,000
Freshmen receiving need-based aid: 80%
Undergrads rec. need-based aid: 78%
Avg. % of need met by financial aid: 60%
Avg. aid package (freshmen): $21,697
Avg. aid package (undergrads): $20,633

Prominent Alumni
Dean Lombardi, president/general manager of the Los Angeles Kings; Craig Mortali, Emmy Award-winning producer at ESPN; David Beckerman, founder and CEO of Starter Corporation

School Spirit
Mascot: Charger
Colors: Gold and blue
Song: *UNH Fight Song*

work · work experience · state of residency. A high school diploma is required, although a GED is also accepted for admissions consideration. SAT or ACT test scores are required of all applicants. *Academic units recommended:* 4 English, 3 Math, 3 Science, 3 Social Studies, 2 Foreign Language.

How to Pay for College

To apply for financial aid, students should submit the following: Free Application for Federal Student Aid (FAFSA) · institution's own financial aid forms. University of New Haven participates in the Federal Work Study program. *Need-based aid programs include:* scholarships and grants · general need-based awards · Federal Pell grants · state scholarships and grants · college-based scholarships and grants. *Non-need-based aid programs include:* scholarships and grants · state scholarships and grants · special achievements and activities awards · athletic scholarships.

UNIVERSITY OF NEW MEXICO

1 University of New Mexico, Albuquerque, NM 87131-0001
Admissions: 505-277-8900 · Financial Aid: 505-277-8900
Email: apply@unm.edu · Website: http://www.unm.edu

From the College

"Noted for its beautiful campus and distinctive pueblo-style architecture, UNM offers more than 230 degree and certificate programs. In addition to housing the only medical, pharmacy, architecture and law schools in New Mexico, the university's Nursing and Midwifery program is ranked among the top five in the country, as is the UNM photography department. The UNM School of Law is prized for its faculty and student diversity, as well as being ranked among the top 10 in the nation for clinical training. UNM is home to the nation's largest long-term ecological research facility.

"While UNM is a leader in academics, UNM students are leaders of their campus and communities. The University of New Mexico is home to more than 400 student organizations, from cultural and religious to academic, political and service-oriented groups. The abundance of opportunities, and New Mexico's 310 days of sunshine each year, encourages students to explore the lifestyle of New Mexico. Culture, art, adventure and recreation are around every corner. Students hike, bike, snowboard and ski the Sandia Mountains and raft the Rio Grande River. Santa Fe and Taos are just to the north, White Sands National Monument and Carlsbad Caverns to the south. UNM is located in the center of Albuquerque, home to the Sandia National Laboratories and the world's largest hot air balloon fiesta. This is a place where a world-class research university blends rich history, amazing diversity and unexcelled natural beauty with cutting-edge education and discovery."

Campus Setting

The University of New Mexico, founded in 1889, is a public, comprehensive institution. Programs are offered through the Colleges of Architecture, Arts and Sciences, Dental Programs, Education, Engineering, Fine Arts, Nursing and Pharmacy, and the Schools of Management and Medicine. Its 769-acre campus is located in Albuquerque. A four-year institution, UNM has an enrollment of 28,592 students. The campus facilities include: library · art, anthropology, meteorite, geology and biology museums. UNM provides on-campus housing that can accommodate 2,400 students. Housing options: coed dorms · sorority housing · fraternity housing · single-student apartments · married-student apartments · special housing for disabled students · special housing for international students. Recreational offerings include aquatics, a challenge course (ropes course), intramural sports and fitness classes.

Student Life and Activities

Most students live off campus. Welcome Back Days, Red Rally, Homecoming, Hanging of the Greens, Lobo Day, Spring Storm and Fall Frenzy and the Cherry and Silver Game are popular events. University of New Mexico has 410 official student organizations. The most popular are: academic and departmental organizations · graduate organizations · military organizations · political organizations · service organizations · special-interest organizations · sport and recreation organizations · honorary organizations · student government organizations. For students possessing an interest in sports, there are intramural teams: archery · badminton · basketball · bowling · cross-country · flag football · golf · miniature golf · racquetball · soccer · swimming · volleyball · weightlifting. University of New Mexico is a member of the Mountain West Conference (Division I, Football I-A).

UNIVERSITY OF NEW MEXICO

University of New Mexico
Albuquerque, NM (Pop. 555,417)
Location: Major city
Four-year public
Founded: 1889
Website: http://www.unm.edu

Students
Total enrollment: 28,592
Undergrads: 22,416
Part-time students: 24%
From out-of-state: 13%
Male/Female: 44%/56%
Live on-campus: Not reported
In fraternities: 5%
In sororities: 6%
Off-campus employment rating: Good
Caucasian: 37%
African American: 3%
Hispanic: 44%
Asian: 3%
Hawaiian or Pacific Islander: <1%
Native American: 6%
Mixed (2+ ethnicities): 3%
International: 2%

Academics
Calendar: Semester
Student/faculty ratio: 20:1
Class size 9 or fewer: 16%
Class size 10-29: 55%
Class size 30-49: 14%
Class size 50-99: 10%
Class size 100 or more: 4%
Returning freshmen: 78%
Six-year graduation rate: 48%

Most Popular Majors
Business
Psychology
Elementary education

Academics and Learning Environment

University of New Mexico has 949 full-time and 478 part-time faculty members, offering a student-to-faculty ratio of 20:1. The most common course size is 20 to 29 students. University of New Mexico offers 206 majors with the most popular being business, psychology and elementary education. The school has a general core requirement. Cooperative education is available. All first-year students must maintain a 2.0 GPA or higher to avoid academic probation. B students will be intrigued by these academic programs: self-designed majors · pass/fail grading option · independent study · double majors · dual degrees · accelerated study · honors program · Phi Beta Kappa · internships · weekend college · distance learning certificate programs.

B Student Support and Success

UNM's Center for Academic Program Support offers free educational assistance through individualized peer tutoring (done by upper division undergraduates and graduate students) for courses numbered 100-499 as well as library and study strategies (by appointment only). Drop-in tutoring labs are available for biology, chemistry, physics, astronomy, writing, pre-calculus, statistics, calculus and engineering. In a new program called CAPS Across Campus, tutoring will be offered in the theater, library and student resident center commons room.

There are a variety of support programs available at University of New Mexico, including dedicated guidance for: academic · career · personal · psychological · minority students · veterans. Recognizing that some students may need extra preparation, University of New Mexico offers remedial and refresher courses in: reading · writing · math · study skills. Annually, 78 percent of freshmen students return for their sophomore year. This is a list of companies that most frequently hire graduates of University of New Mexico: Albuquerque Public Schools · Enterprise · Fidelity · Hewlett Packard · Intel Corp. · Presbyterian Hospital · Rio Rancho Schools · Sandia National Labs · State of New Mexico · University of New Mexico · University of New Mexico Hospital · Target · USDA · Verizon.

Support for Students with Learning Disabilities

Students handling learning disabilities will want to peruse these support programs offered at University of New Mexico. A lightened course load is available for LD students. Students coping with learning disabilities may want to research the following programs at University of New Mexico: remedial math · remedial English · remedial reading · tutors · learning center · testing accommodations · extended time for tests · take-home exam · readers · note-taking services · reading machines · tape recorders · texts on tape · videotaped classes · early syllabus · priority registration · waiver of math degree requirement. Individual or small group tutorials are also available in: time management · organizational skills · learning strategies · specific subject areas · writing labs · math labs · study skills. An advisor/advocate from the Accessibility Resource Center is available to students.

How to Get Admitted

For admissions decisions, non-academic factors considered: state of residency. A high school diploma is required, although a GED is also accepted for admissions consideration. SAT or ACT test scores are required of all applicants. *According to the admissions office:* Minimum 2.5 GPA required. *Academic units recommended:* 4 English, 4 Math, 3 Science, 2 Social Studies, 2 Foreign Language.

How to Pay for College

To apply for financial aid, students should submit the following: Free Application for Federal Student Aid (FAFSA). University of New Mexico participates in the Federal Work Study program. *Need-based aid programs include:* scholarships and grants · general need-based awards · Federal Pell grants · state scholarships and grants · college-based scholarships and grants · private scholarships and grants · Federal Nursing scholarships · United Negro College Fund. *Non-need-based aid programs include:* scholarships and grants · general need-based awards · state scholarships and grants · creative arts and performance awards · special achievements and activities awards · special characteristics awards · athletic scholarships · ROTC scholarships.

UNIVERSITY OF NEW MEXICO

Highlights

Admissions
Applicants: 11,995
Accepted: 6,799
Acceptance rate: 56.7%
Average GPA: 3.3
ACT range: 19-25
SAT Math range: 470-600
SAT Reading range: 470-610
SAT Writing range: Not reported

Deadlines
Early Action: No
Early Decision: No
Regular Action: Rolling admissions
Common Application: Not accepted

Financial Aid
In-state tuition: $6,447
Out-of-state tuition: $20,688
Room: Varies
Board: Varies
Books: Varies
Freshmen receiving need-based or merit-based aid: 98%
Avg. aid package (freshmen): Not reported
Avg. aid package (undergrads): Not reported

Prominent Alumni
Henry Crumpton, former director, Counter-terrorism at the State Department, and former CIA operative who designed the US strategy in Afghanistan; Edward Lewis, founder, Essence Communications; Joe Garcia, president, National Congress of American Indians.

School Spirit
Mascot: Lobos
Colors: Cherry and silver
Song: *Hail To Thee New Mexico*

UNIVERSITY OF NEW ORLEANS

2000 Lakeshore Drive, New Orleans, LA 70148
Admissions: 504-280-6595 · Financial Aid: 504-280-6603
Email: unopec@uno.edu · Website: http://www.uno.edu

From the College

"The University of New Orleans (UNO), a major urban university, provides essential support for the further development of the educational, economic, cultural and social well being of the New Orleans metropolitan area. Located in an international city, the university serves as an important link between Louisiana, the nation and the world. Its partnership approach strategically serves the needs of the region and builds on its success through mutually beneficial engagements with public and private bodies whose missions and goals are consistent with and supportive of the university's teaching, scholarly and community service missions. Focused local partnerships with public schools, government, foundations, business and civic groups enrich opportunities for learning and creative discovery as well as help enhance the opportunities for career and community growth. Graduate study and research are integral to the university's purpose. Doctoral programs will continue to focus on fields of study in which UNO has the ability to achieve national competitiveness and/or to respond to specific state / regional needs. UNO is categorized as an SREB Four-Year 2 institution, as a Carnegie Doctoral Intensive and as a COC/SACS Level VI institution. UNO will offer no associate degree programs. At a minimum, the university will implement Selective II admissions criteria. UNO is located in Region I."

Campus Setting

University of New Orleans, founded in 1958, is a public institution. Programs are offered through the Colleges of Business Administration, Education, Engineering, Liberal Arts, Sciences and Urban and Public Affairs, and the Metropolitan College. Its 195-acre campus is located in a residential section of New Orleans. A four-year institution, UNO has an enrollment of 9,323 students. The school also has a library with 896,000 books. UNO provides on-campus housing that can accommodate 1,426 students. Housing options: coed dorms · single-student apartments · married-student apartments · special housing for disabled students.

Student Life and Activities

Ninety percent of students live off campus. International Night is a popular campus event. University of New Orleans has 73 official student organizations. The most popular are: Louisiana Restaurant Association · Chess Club · UNO Filmmakers · Society for Earth and Environmental Science · Circle K · Rainbow Alliance. University of New Orleans is a member of the Sun Belt Conference (Division I, Football I-A).

Academics and Learning Environment

University of New Orleans has 289 full-time and 123 part-time faculty members, offering a student-to-faculty ratio of 21:1. The most common course size is 10 to 19 students. University of New Orleans offers 83 majors with the most popular being general studies, business administration and elementary education and least popular being Spanish, art history and music. The school has a general core requirement. Cooperative education is available. All first-year students must maintain a 2.0 GPA or higher to avoid academic probation. B students might want to research the following programs: self-designed majors · independent study · double majors · dual degrees · honors program · internships · weekend college · distance learning.

B Student Support and Success

UNO's Learning Resource Center offers free writing and math tutoring on both an individual and group basis. The computer lab has 24 workstations, and tutors are available for biology, business, chemistry, foreign language, psychology and physics. Much of the tutoring is performed by upperclassmen. Classes on time management, test taking, note taking and communication are offered, as are short workshops on test taking and note taking. A media library supplies videotapes and CD ROMs in math, science and liberal arts. The college's Writing Center guides students through their papers, while the Math Tutor Center and Study Hall assists students in math requirements to "maximize their math potential."

University of New Orleans is proud to offer its students a variety of options when it comes to support programs, including dedicated guidance for: academic · career · personal · psychological · minority students · military · veterans · family planning. The average freshman year GPA is 2.5, and 67 percent of freshmen students return for their sophomore year.

Support for Students with Learning Disabilities

Students with learning disabilities will be excited to learn that there are specific support programs available at University of New Orleans. ODS offers academic accommodations to students with documented disabilities. Tutoring and other content specific programming is open to all students through the Learning Resource Center or Counseling Services. LD students will want to research the following programs offered at University of New Orleans: learning center · testing accommodations · extended time for tests · take-home exam · exam on tape or computer · note-taking services · reading machines · tape recorders · texts on tape · early syllabus · priority registration. Individual or small group tutorials are also available in: time management · organizational skills · learning strategies · specific subject areas · writing labs · math labs · study skills. An advisor/advocate from the Office of Disability Services is available to students.

How to Get Admitted

For admissions decisions, non-academic factors considered: geographical location. A high school diploma is required, although a GED is also accepted for admissions consideration. SAT or ACT test scores are required of all applicants. *According to the admissions office:* Minimum 2.5 secondary school GPA, minimum ACT math score of 19 (SAT Reasoning math score of 460) and English score of 18 (SAT Reasoning English score of 450) with minimum ACT composite score of 23 (combined SAT Reasoning score of 1060) required.

How to Pay for College

To apply for financial aid, students should submit the following: Free Application for Federal Student Aid (FAFSA). University of New Orleans participates in the Federal Work Study program. *Need-based aid programs include:* scholarships and grants · general need-based awards · Federal Pell grants · state scholarships and grants · college-based scholarships and grants · private scholarships and

UNIVERSITY OF NEW ORLEANS

Highlights

University of New Orleans
New Orleans (Pop. 369,250)
Location: Major city
Four-year public
Founded: 1958
Website: http://www.uno.edu

Students
Total enrollment: 9,323
Undergrads: 7,144
Part-time students: 25%
From out-of-state: 9%
Male/Female: 50%/50%
Live on-campus: 10%
In fraternities: 2%
In sororities: 2%
Off-campus employment rating: Good
Caucasian: 56%
African American: 15%
Hispanic: 10%
Asian: 8%
Hawaiian or Pacific Islander: <1%
Native American: <1%
Mixed (2+ ethnicities): 3%
International: 4%

Academics
Calendar: Semester
Student/faculty ratio: 21:1
Class size 9 or fewer: 13%
Class size 10-29: 47%
Class size 30-49: 25%
Class size 50-99: 12%
Class size 100 or more: 3%
Returning freshmen: 67%
Six-year graduation rate: 32%

Most Popular Majors
General studies
Business administration
Elementary education

503

College Profiles

UNIVERSITY OF NEW ORLEANS

Admissions
Applicants: 3,197
Accepted: 1,610
Acceptance rate: 50.4%
Average GPA: 3.2
ACT range: 21-25
SAT Math range: 490-620
SAT Reading range: 470-590
SAT Writing range: Not reported
Top 10% of class: 16%
Top 25% of class: 41%
Top 50% of class: 66%

Deadlines
Early Action: No
Early Decision: No
Regular Action: Rolling admissions
Common Application: Accepted

Financial Aid
In-state tuition: $5,537
Out-of-state tuition: $19,147
Room: Varies
Board: Varies
Books: $1,200
Freshmen receiving need-based aid: 81%
Undergrads rec. need-based aid: 70%
Avg. % of need met by financial aid: 46%
Avg. aid package (freshmen): $10,506
Avg. aid package (undergrads): $8,762
Avg. debt upon graduation: $19,957

Prominent Alumni
Ellen DeGeneres, comedian and television host; Peter J. Fos, president of the University of New Orleans; John Larroquette, Emmy-winning actor.

School Spirit
Mascot: Privateers

grants. *Non-need-based aid programs include:* scholarships and grants · state scholarships and grants · athletic scholarships.

UNIVERSITY OF NORTH CAROLINA AT GREENSBORO

P.O. Box 26170, Greensboro, NC 27402
Admissions: 336-334-5243 · Financial Aid: 336-334-5702
Email: admissions@uncg.edu · Website: http://www.uncg.edu

From the College

"The University of North Carolina - Greensboro is is redefining the public research university for the 21st century. Our academic programs, research and partnerships contribute to a common goal: to be a responsive, engaged university focused on solutions to the problems of our times. Access and student success, interdisciplinary research, globalization and engagement are emphasized. As a doctoral-granting university, UNCG is committed to teaching based in scholarship and advancing knowledge through research. The College of Arts and Sciences and six professional schools offer challenging graduate and undergraduate programs in which students are mentored by outstanding teachers, including nationally and internationally recognized researchers and artists. Affirming the liberal arts as the foundation for lifelong learning, UNCG provides exemplary learning environments on campus and through distance education so that students can acquire knowledge, develop intellectual skills and become more thoughtful and responsible members of a global society."

Campus Setting

UNCG is a public liberal arts university founded in 1891, and became co-educational in 1963. Its 210-acre campus is located one mile from the center of Greensboro, NC. A four-year institution, UNCG has an enrollment of 17,707 students. The campus provides its students with a bountiful library, as well as an art museum. UNCG provides on-campus housing that can accommodate 5,014 students. Housing options: coed dorms · women's dorms · single-student apartments · special housing for international students. Recreation and sports facilities include: gymnasium · weight and exercise rooms · fitness course · athletic training facility · indoor swimming pool · dance studios · golf holes · tennis courts · soccer, softball and other field sports practice fields.

Student Life and Activities

Sixty-eight percent of students live off campus. UNCG has a large commuter population, reports the school newspaper. And of the on-campus residents, over 75 percent of them leave for the weekend. Popular off-campus gathering spots include Spring Garden Bar & Grill and New York Pizza. Popular campus events include UNCG Open House, athletic events, Students Taking Active Responsibility (STAR), Family Weekend, Spring Fling, intramural sports, Commuter Student Deli, Leadership Education and Development Seminars (LEAD Seminars), Career Days, Fitness Testing, Fall Kickoff, UNCG Theatre, Martin Luther King, Jr. Celebration, Office of Student Life Movie Series, International Festival, Outdoor Adventures, University Concert/Lecture Series and African American History Events. UNCG has 216 official student organizations. Student media organizations have widespread influence in student social life. The following are directed towards those students interested in intramural teams: basketball · flag football · indoor soccer · outdoor soccer · softball · volleyball. UNCG is a member of the Southern Conference (Division I).

Academics and Learning Environment

UNCG has 764 full-time and 240 part-time faculty members, offering a student-to-faculty ratio of 17:1. The most common course size is 20 to 29 students. UNCG offers 163 majors with the most popular being business administration, public health and

UNIVERSITY OF NORTH CAROLINA – GREENSBORO

University of North Carolina – Greensboro
Greensboro, NC (Pop. 277,080)
Location: Medium city
Four-year public
Founded: 1891
Website: http://www.uncg.edu

Students

Total enrollment: 17,707
Undergrads: 14,348
Freshmen: 3,475
Part-time students: 14%
From out-of-state: 7%
Male/Female: 35%/65%
Live on-campus: 32%
In fraternities: 4%
In sororities: 4%
Off-campus employment rating: Excellent
Caucasian: 57%
African American: 25%
Hispanic: 6%
Asian: 4%
Hawaiian or Pacific Islander: <1%
Native American: <1%
Mixed (2+ ethnicities): 4%
International: 2%

Academics

Calendar: Semester
Student/faculty ratio: 17:1
Class size 9 or fewer: 21%
Class size 10-29: 51%
Class size 30-49: 15%
Class size 50-99: 10%
Class size 100 or more: 3%
Returning freshmen: 74%
Six-year graduation rate: 55%

Most Popular Majors

Business administration
Public health
Psychology

America's
Best Colleges for
B Students

psychology and least popular being French, German and physics. The school has a general core requirement. Cooperative education is not offered. All first-year students must maintain a 1.8 GPA or higher to avoid academic probation, and a minimum overall GPA of 2.0 is required to graduate. Special academic programs that would appeal to a B student attending UNCG include: independent study · double majors · dual degrees · accelerated study · honors program · Phi Beta Kappa · internships · distance learning certificate programs.

B Student Support and Success

The Student Success Center has three divisions to help students succeed academically: the Learning Assistance Center, Resource Lab and Special Support Services. The Learning Assistance Center provides tutoring, academic skills assessment and counseling, academic workshops and a resource lab with computers, academic software and handouts. Tutoring is done on an individual basis for at least one hour a week or through small groups of no more than three students in sessions that last one and one-half to two hours a week. Walk-in tutoring is available also. The Resource Lab gives students a peaceful place to study and to receive tutoring. Students have access to computers, a textbook library and academic-skills assessment, as well as computer tutorials in math and foreign languages and handouts on academic skills like time management, note taking, textbook reading and test taking. In addition to this, the LAC works to help students increase their understanding of course content, enhance self-confidence and encourage positive attitudes toward learning. Special Support Services provides aid to students who are 1) first-generation college enrollees, 2) from low-income families or 3) have a documented disability. This program offers counseling, tutoring and a learning lab. A program known as Supplemental Instruction provides a series of weekly discussion/review sessions for students taking notoriously difficult courses. Each class is led by students who have successfully completed the course. According to the college, students who attend these supplemental classes attain grades that are one-third to one whole grade higher than the grades of those who do not participate.

UNCG is proud to offer its students a plethora of support programs including dedicated guidance for: academic · career · personal · psychological · minority students · family planning. Recognizing that some students may need extra preparation, UNCG offers remedial and refresher courses in: reading · writing · math · study skills. The average freshman year GPA is 2.8, and 74 percent of freshmen students return for their sophomore year. Among students who enter the work force, approximately 89 percent enter a field related to their major within six months of graduation.

Support for Students with Learning Disabilities

Students with learning disabilities, sometimes more commonly referred to as LD students, may desire to take part in support programs offered by UNCG. LD students will deem the following programs at UNCG extremely helpful: remedial English · remedial reading · tutors · learning center · testing accommodations · extended time for tests · oral tests · readers · note-taking services · reading machines · tape recorders · diagnostic testing service. Individual or small group tutorials are also available in: time management · organizational skills · learning strategies · specific subject areas · writing labs · math labs · study skills. An advisor/advocate from the Office of Disability Services is available to students.

How to Get Admitted

For admissions decisions, non-academic factors considered: state of residency. A high school diploma is required and a GED is not accepted for admissions consideration. SAT or ACT test scores are required of all applicants.

How to Pay for College

To apply for financial aid, students should submit the following: Free Application for Federal Student Aid (FAFSA). UNCG participates in the Federal Work Study program. *Need-based aid programs include:* scholarships and grants · general need-based awards · Federal Pell grants · state scholarships and grants · college-based scholarships and grants · private scholarships and grants. *Non-need-based aid programs include:* scholarships and grants · general need-based awards · state scholarships and grants · creative arts and performance awards · special achievements and activities awards · special characteristics awards · athletic scholarships · ROTC scholarships.

UNIVERSITY OF NORTH CAROLINA – GREENSBORO

Highlights

Admissions
Applicants: 10,154
Accepted: 5,909
Acceptance rate: 58.2%
Average GPA: 3.6
ACT range: 21-25
SAT Math range: 480-560
SAT Reading range: 470-560
SAT Writing range: 1-8
Top 10% of class: 22%
Top 25% of class: 48%
Top 50% of class: 84%

Deadlines
Early Action: No
Early Decision: No
Regular Action: Rolling admissions
Common Application: Not accepted

Financial Aid
In-state tuition: $3,932
Out-of-state tuition: $18,794
Room: $4,586
Board: $2,788
Books: $916
Freshmen receiving need-based aid: 79%
Undergrads rec. need-based aid: 80%
Avg. % of need met by financial aid: 56%
Avg. aid package (freshmen): $10,010
Avg. aid package (undergrads): $10,090
Avg. debt upon graduation: $24,595

Prominent Alumni
Tom Smith, musician and inductee, Jazz Education Hall of Fame; Claudia Emerson, Pulitzer Prize-winning author; Alejandro Moreno, retired Venezuelan international soccer player and MLS forward.

School Spirit
Mascot: Spiro the Spartan
Colors: Blue and gold
Song: *Blue and Gold*

507

UNIVERSITY OF OREGON

1226 University of Oregon, Eugene, OR 97403-1226
Admissions: 800-232-3825 · Financial Aid: 800-760-6953
Email: uoadmit@uoregon.edu · Website: http://uoregon.edu

From the College

"One of only 34 public institutions in the prestigious Association of American Universities, the University of Oregon is the state's flagship university. Academic quality is the cornerstone of the University of Oregon's identity as a public research university. Students are guided by faculty members renowned for both teaching and research, including 34 fellows of the American Association for the Advancement of Science and eight members of the American Academy of Arts and Sciences.

"Beginning in their freshman year, students take courses from faculty who are leaders in their respective fields, have opportunities to be involved in cutting-edge research in every academic discipline and work alongside prominent scholars, assisting with their work as well as conducting original research of their own. Freshmen have the option to enroll in over 60 different Freshman Interest Groups, special course groupings in which small groups of first-year students take two core courses that are connected through a third seminar course. In addition, Freshman Seminar classes allow students to explore topics in depth with some of Oregon's most prominent faculty members.

"Highly motivated students find opportunities for intellectual challenge in the Robert Donald Clark Honors College, the College Scholars program within the College of Arts and Sciences or research and honors programs within individual departments. Distinctive opportunities include the Warsaw Sports Marketing Center and the Lundquist Center for Entrepreneurship within the Lundquist College of Business; the Oregon Institute for Marine Biology, located on the Pacific Coast, offers the only marine biology degree in the Pacific Northwest; the Green Chemistry Laboratory and the Alice C. Tyler Instrumentation Center, the first green chemistry facilities of their kind in the nation; the Lorry I. Lokey Laboratories building that is encased in bedrock nineteen feet below the ground, providing an optimal setting for nanoscience research; extensive opportunities for overseas study and internships and Future Music Oregon, a center in the School of Music that explores sound and its composition through the innovative use of computers and new technologies.

"At the University of Oregon, more than 24,000 men and women study in idyllic, lush settings in the heart of the rugged Pacific Northwest where the dramatic Oregon coast is an hour's drive to the west, and the Cascade Mountains are an hour to the east, allowing easy access to both winter and summer sports and activities. The university's mid-range size gives it the ambience of a smaller institution, but with the benefit of the resources of a major research institution. The University of Oregon's 295-acre main campus is located in Eugene, nationally recognized as one of America's most livable cities, as well as one of its best college towns."

Campus Setting

The University of Oregon, founded in 1876, is a public and comprehensive liberal arts institution. Programs are offered through the College of Arts and Sciences, the Charles H. Lundquist College of Business, the College of Education and the Schools of Journalism, Music and Dance and Architecture and Allied Arts. Its 295-acre campus is located in Eugene, south of Portland. A four-year institution, University of Oregon has an enrollment of 24,473 students. The campus facilities include: library · museum of Art · Museum of Natural and Cultural History · Sports Marketing Center · Lundquist Center for Entrepreneurship · University of Oregon Many Nations Longhouse · Green Chemistry Laboratory and Instrumentation Center · Future Music Oregon · a computer music center in the School of Music. University of Oregon provides on-campus housing with 2,571 units that can accommodate 4,433 students. Housing options: coed dorms · sorority housing · fraternity housing · single-student apartments · married-student apartments · cooperative housing. Recreation and sports facilities include: student recreation center · swimming pool · indoor track · climbing wall · football stadium · basketball arena · track and field and softball complex · grass fields for practice.

Student Life and Activities

Eighty percent of students live off campus. Erb Memorial Union, the EMU amphitheater and the Memorial quad are popular gathering places for students. Cinco de Mayo Celebration, Hawaii Club Luau, Native American Pow Wow, Willamette Valley Folk Festival, Martin Luther King Events, InterMingle, athletic events, Miller Theatre Complex, Oregon Bach Festival, Concerts in Beall Hall, Jordan Schnitzer Museum of Art, Oregon Museum of Natural & Cultural History and Convocation are popular events. University of Oregon has 250 official student organizations. The most popular are: Many music, theater, political, service and special-interest groups. As far as athletics, there are intramural teams: badminton · basketball · cross-country · dodgeball · flag football · floor hockey · golf · racquetball · soccer · softball · swimming · tennis · track and field · volleyball · Ultimate Frisbee. The University of Oregon is a member of the PAC-12.

Academics and Learning Environment

University of Oregon has 1,029 full-time and 444 part-time faculty members, offering a student-to-faculty ratio of 19:1. The most common course size is 10 to 19 students. University of Oregon offers 200 majors with the most popular being business administration, psychology and sociology and least popular being printmaking, folklore and ceramics. The school has a general core requirement. Cooperative education is not offered. All first-year students must maintain a 2.0 GPA or higher to avoid academic probation. A B student should be made aware of the following: self-designed majors · pass/fail grading option · independent study · double majors · dual degrees · honors program · Phi Beta Kappa · internships · distance learning certificate programs.

B Student Support and Success

UO's Academic Learning Services offers a number of one-credit and multiple-credit courses each quarter to help with test taking, time management, communication skills and group dynamics. In the fall, the college offers "Get Savvy: Focus on Academic Success," a get-together geared to help students improve their study approaches, meet new people and even win prizes! Other workshops include "Active Learning," "Grammar Hour" and "Statistics." Math and Writing Labs are available, as is tutoring in small group or private

UNIVERSITY OF OREGON

Highlights

University of Oregon
Eugene, OR (Pop. 157,986)
Location: Medium city
Four-year public
Founded: 1876
Website: http://uoregon.edu

Students
Total enrollment: 24,473
Undergrads: 20,797
Freshmen: 4,994
Part-time students: 9%
From out-of-state: 43%
Male/Female: 48%/52%
Live on-campus: 20%
In fraternities: 13%
In sororities: 17%
Off-campus employment rating: Good
Caucasian: 64%
African American: 2%
Hispanic: 8%
Asian: 5%
Hawaiian or Pacific Islander: <1%
Native American: 1%
Mixed (2+ ethnicities): 6%
International: 13%

Academics
Calendar: Quarter
Student/faculty ratio: 19:1
Class size 9 or fewer: 11%
Class size 10-29: 52%
Class size 30-49: 17%
Class size 50-99: 12%
Class size 100 or more: 9%
Returning freshmen: 87%
Six-year graduation rate: 67%

Most Popular Majors
Business administration
Psychology
Sociology

509

UNIVERSITY OF OREGON

Admissions
Applicants: 21,938
Accepted: 16,206
Acceptance rate: 73.9%
Placed on wait list: 1,337
Enrolled from wait list: 359
Average GPA: 3.6
ACT range: 22-28
SAT Math range: 500-620
SAT Reading range: 490-620
SAT Writing range: 4-26
Top 10% of class: 25%
Top 25% of class: 64%
Top 50% of class: 94%

Deadlines
Early Action: 11/1
Early Decision: No
Regular Action: Rolling admissions
Common Application: Not accepted

Financial Aid
In-state tuition: $8,220
Out-of-state tuition: $28,305
Room: Varies
Board: Varies
Books: $1,050
Freshmen receiving need-based aid: 37%
Undergrads rec. need-based aid: 43%
Avg. % of need met by financial aid: 50%
Avg. aid package (freshmen): $10,200
Avg. aid package (undergrads): $10,172
Avg. debt upon graduation: $24,450

Prominent Alumni
Ken Kesey, writer; Ann Bancroft, first woman explorer to cross the North and South Poles; Phil Knight, founder and CEO of Nike.

School Spirit
Mascot: Ducks
Colors: Green and yellow
Song: *Mighty Oregon*

settings. Workshops to help prepare for standardized test preparation (GRE, GMAT, SAT, MCAT, etc.) are also offered.

B students will be interested to learn that University of Oregon provides a variety of support programs including dedicated guidance for: academic · career · personal · psychological · minority students · military · veterans · non-traditional students · family planning. The average freshman year GPA is 3.1, and 87 percent of freshmen students return for their sophomore year. The following is a list of companies that most frequently hire graduates from University of Oregon: Campus Point · Enterprise Rent-a-Car · Ernst & Young · First Investors · Fred Meyer · Jones & Roth · KPMG · Marine Corps · Nearby Nature · Peace Corps · Susan G. Komen Foundation · Teach for America · University of Oregon · Wells Fargo.

Support for Students with Learning Disabilities

B students with learning disabilities will want to investigate University of Oregon's support programs. When deemed necessary, the college will sometimes consider granting additional time to LD students to complete their degree or a lightened course load may be granted. High school foreign language waivers are accepted. High school math waivers are also accepted. According to the school, Paid tutoring groups offered in the Teaching and Learning Center are available to any student. The LD student will want to survey the following programs at University of Oregon: tutors · learning center · testing accommodations · untimed tests · extended time for tests · take-home exam · oral tests · readers · note-taking services · reading machines · tape recorders · priority registration. Individual or small group tutorials are also available in: time management · organizational skills · learning strategies · writing labs · math labs · study skills. An advisor/advocate from the Disability Services is available to students. This member also sits on the admissions committee.

How to Get Admitted

For admissions decisions, non-academic factors considered: extracurricular activities · special talents, interests and abilities · volunteer work · work experience · geographical location · minority affiliation. A high school diploma is required, although a GED is also accepted for admissions consideration. SAT or ACT test scores are required of all applicants. SAT Subject Test scores are required for some applicants. *Academic units recommended:* 4 English, 3 Math, 3 Science, 3 Social Studies, 2 Foreign Language.

How to Pay for College

To apply for financial aid, students should submit the following: Free Application for Federal Student Aid (FAFSA). University of Oregon participates in the Federal Work Study program. *Need-based aid programs include:* scholarships and grants · general need-based awards · Federal Pell grants · state scholarships and grants · college-based scholarships and grants · private scholarships and grants. *Non-need-based aid programs include:* scholarships and grants · general need-based awards · state scholarships and grants · creative arts and performance awards · special characteristics awards · athletic scholarships · ROTC scholarships.

UNIVERSITY OF PORTLAND

5000 North Willamette Boulevard, Portland, OR 97203
Admissions: 503-943-7147 · Financial Aid: 503-943-7311
Email: admissio@up.edu · Website: http://www.up.edu

From the College

"The University of Portland, Oregon's Catholic university, has received several national faculty awards from the Carnegie Foundation in recent years, among them the U.S. Professor of the Year (2000) and three Oregon Professor of the Year honors. Its faculty and students have earned many Fulbright, Marshall, Mitchell and Goldwater fellowships, and have received both the Oregon's Governor's Award for more than 10,000 hours of volunteer service annually and Washington Monthly magazine's national top ranking for service to the nation. The university is renowned for its extensive study-abroad programs (in Asia, Australia, Latin America and Europe), its cross-disciplinary entrepreneurship program, education, biology and theater programs, state-of-the-art nursing and science laboratories and its global business and environmental ethics majors—the latter the only one of its kind in the U.S. The university also sponsors a creative center for freshman support, savors its NCAA national champion women's soccer team (twice in four years), and has been dedicated for more than a century to creating a campus community where 'teachable moments' in and out of the classroom are not only prized but the true epiphanies sparking lifelong learning."

Campus Setting

The University of Portland, founded in 1901, is a private, church-affiliated institution. Programs are offered through the College of Arts and Sciences and the Schools of Business Administration, Education, Engineering and Nursing. Its 125-acre is located four miles from downtown Portland. A four-year institution, University of Portland has an enrollment of 4,036 students. Although not originally a co-educational college, University of Portland has been co-ed since 1951. The school is also affiliated with the Roman Catholic Church. The campus provides its students with a large library, as well as a museum. University of Portland provides on-campus housing that can accommodate 1,800 students. Housing options: coed dorms · women's dorms · men's dorms. Recreation and sports facilities include: aerobics · cardio and weight rooms · grass and artificial fields · gymnasium · swimming pool · tennis courts.

Student Life and Activities

Fifty-four percent of students live on campus. Espresso UP, Coffeehouse, Junior Parents Weekend, Service Plunge, International Night, Relay for Life, Dance of the Decades, Three Wise Monkeys Art Festival, Homecoming Dance and Guam Night are popular events. University of Portland has 60 official student organizations. The most popular are: accounting club · ActUP · American Chemical Society · American Society of Civil Engineers · Association for Computing Machinery · Institute of Electrical & Electronics Engineers · Investment Association · mechanical engineers club · Operations Management Association · Pre-Dental Student Association · social work club · Society of Women Engineers · Student Nurses Association · College Democrats · ecology club · College Republicans · Engineers Without Borders · English Society · Fair Trade Club · Feminist Discussion Group · Gay Straight Partnership · International Film Club · Latin American Solidarity Club · Literary Palaver Society · Mock Trial · music club · Roosevelt Institution Undergraduate Student Think Tank · Society of Sobriety · Spielfriek Society · Student Alumni Association · Student Led Unity Garden (SLUG) · Students for a Free Tibet · swing dance club · Tengokuno Anime · velo club. There are intramural teams available such as: basketball · dodgeball · flag

UNIVERSITY OF PORTLAND

University of Portland
Portland (Pop. 603,106)
Location: Major city
Four-year private
Founded: 1901
Website: http://www.up.edu

Students

Total enrollment: 4,036
Undergrads: 3,494
Freshmen: 835
Part-time students: 2%
From out-of-state: 71%
From public schools: 65%
Male/Female: 42%/58%
Live on-campus: 54%
Off-campus employment rating: Fair
Caucasian: 64%
African American: 1%
Hispanic: 10%
Asian: 10%
Hawaiian or Pacific Islander: 1%
Native American: <1%
Mixed (2+ ethnicities): 8%
International: 3%

Academics

Calendar: Semester
Student/faculty ratio: 14:1
Class size 9 or fewer: 12%
Class size 10-29: 56%
Class size 30-49: 31%
Class size 50-99: 1%
Class size 100 or more: -
Returning freshmen: 90%
Six-year graduation rate: 75%

Most Popular Majors

Nursing
Biology
Mechanical engineering

football · kickball · soccer · softball · Ultimate Frisbee · volleyball. University of Portland is a member of the West Coast Conference.

Academics and Learning Environment

University of Portland has 217 full-time and 115 part-time faculty members, offering a student-to-faculty ratio of 14:1. The most common course size is 20 to 29 students. University of Portland offers 46 majors with the most popular being nursing, biology and mechanical engineering and least popular being theology, music and physics. The school has a general core requirement as well as a religion requirement. Cooperative education is not offered. All first-year students must maintain a 2.0 GPA or higher to avoid academic probation. Here's a list of other special academic programs that might appeal to a B student: independent study · double majors · dual degrees · honors program · internships · certificate programs.

B Student Support and Success

The University of Portland's Academic Resources offers services that are extensive. An Integrated Writing Center, Speech Resource Center and Math Resource Center give information and advice for academic skills. The Shepard Freshman Resource Center is a one-stop place for first year students who want to know more about the campus and college life. The Learning Assistance program is geared to teach students' various learning strategies and skills. Counselors help guide students to improving learning skills like time management and prioritizing assignments, plus how to deal with overdue assignments, text anxiety, study overload and difficulty with reading and note taking.

University of Portland provides support programs and dedicated guidance for: academic · career · personal · psychological · religious. The average freshman year GPA is 3.3, and 90 percent of freshmen students return for their sophomore year. Regarding after college? Some enter the workforce and approximately 18 percent pursue a graduate degree following graduation. Organizations that most often hire graduates from University of Portland include: ACUMED · Adidas · Beaverton Public Schools · Bonneville Power Administration · Deloitte · Fidelity · Geffen Mesher · Gunderson · Hewlett Packard · Intel · KPMG · Legacy Health System · Merrill Lynch · Nike · Oracle · Oregon Health Sciences University · Pacificorp · Perkins & Company · Portland Public Schools · Providence · PricewaterhouseCoopers · Regence Blue Cross/Blue Shield · Smith Barney · State of Oregon · The Standard · Wells Fargo.

Support for Students with Learning Disabilities

Students coping with learning disabilities will be very interested to learn that University of Portland has several support programs available. Depending on the circumstances, the college may grant additional time to LD students to complete their degree. The college may also offer a lightened course load. Students with learning disabilities will want to be made aware of the following programs at University of Portland: extended time for tests · readers · note-taking services · reading machines · waiver of math degree requirement. Individual or small group tutorials are also available in: time management · organizational skills · learning strategies · writing labs ·

math labs · study skills. An advisor/advocate from the LD program is available to students.

How to Get Admitted

For admissions decisions, non-academic factors considered: interview · extracurricular activities · special talents, interests and abilities · character/personal qualities · volunteer work · work experience · state of residency · geographical location · religious affiliation/commitment · minority affiliation · alumni relationship. A high school diploma is required, although a GED is also accepted for admissions consideration. SAT or ACT test scores are required of all applicants. SAT Subject Test scores are considered, if submitted, but are not required. *According to the admissions office:* Minimum combined SAT score of 950 and minimum 2.8 GPA required. *Academic units recommended:* 4 English, 3 Math, 2 Science, 2 Social Studies.

How to Pay for College

To apply for financial aid, students should submit the following: Free Application for Federal Student Aid (FAFSA). University of Portland participates in the Federal Work Study program. *Need-based aid programs include:* scholarships and grants · general need-based awards · Federal Pell grants · state scholarships and grants · college-based scholarships and grants · private scholarships and grants. *Non-need-based aid programs include:* scholarships and grants · state scholarships and grants · athletic scholarships · ROTC scholarships.

UNIVERSITY OF PORTLAND

Highlights

Admissions
Applicants: 9,523
Accepted: 6,361
Acceptance rate: 66.8%
Average GPA: 3.6
ACT range: Not reported
SAT Math range: 540-650
SAT Reading range: 550-650
SAT Writing range: Not reported
Top 10% of class: 37%
Top 25% of class: 70%
Top 50% of class: 94%

Deadlines
Early Action: No
Early Decision: No
Regular Action: Rolling admissions
Common Application: Accepted

Financial Aid
In-state tuition: $38,350
Out-of-state tuition: $38,350
Room: $7,960
Board: $2,958
Books: $1,200
Freshmen receiving need-based aid: 68%
Undergrads rec. need-based aid: 65%
Avg. % of need met by financial aid: 70%
Avg. aid package (freshmen): $26,191
Avg. aid package (undergrads): $27,523
Avg. debt upon graduation: $27,164

Prominent Alumni
Fedele Bauccio, founder of Bon Appetit; John Heily, Pres/CEO Continental Mills; Donald Shiley, entrepreneur/inventor of the Shiley Heart Valve.

School Spirit
Mascot: Wally Pilot
Colors: Purple

UNIVERSITY OF REDLANDS

P.O. Box 3080, Redlands, CA 92373
Admissions: 800-455-5064 · Financial Aid: 909-748-8047
Email: admissions@redlands.edu · Website: http://www.redlands.edu

From the College

"The University of Redlands is a private, independent university committed to providing a personalized education that frees students to make enlightened choices. Redlands emphasizes academic rigor, curricular diversity and innovative teaching. Redlands fosters a community of scholars and encourages a pluralistic notion of values by challenging assumptions and stereotypes in both classes and activities. A Redlands education goes beyond training to embrace a reflective understanding of our world; it proceeds from information to insight, from knowledge to meaning. Welcoming intellectually curious students of diverse religious, ethnic, national and socio-economic backgrounds, the university seeks to develop responsible citizenship as part of a complete education. Redlands encourages a community atmosphere with exception opportunity for student leadership and interaction. For working adults, the university offers programs at convenient locations and times. Redlands blends liberal arts and professional programs, applied and theoretical study, traditional majors and self-designed contracts for graduation. Small classes enable each student to participate in class discussion, to work closely with professors and to receive extensive individual attention. Redlands remains sensitive to contemporary trends in society and challenges students to commit themselves to a lifetime of learning."

Campus Setting

Redlands, founded in 1907, is a private, liberal arts university. Its 140-acre campus is located in Redlands, 65 miles east of Los Angeles. A four-year institution, University of Redlands has an enrollment of 4,956 students. The campus facilities include: library · art gallery · center for communicative disorders · language lab · anthropology lab · physics laser photonics lab · geographic information system lab. University of Redlands provides on-campus housing with 30 units that can accommodate 1,572 students. Housing options include: coed dorms · women's dorms · men's dorms · sorority housing · fraternity housing · single-student apartments · special housing for disabled students. Recreation and sports facilities include: aquatic center · baseball, soccer and softball fields · fitness center · football stadium · golf country club · gymnasium · tennis court · track.

Student Life and Activities

Fifty-three percent of students live on campus. Popular campus events include the Feast of Lights and the Multicultural Festival. University of Redlands has 120 official student organizations. The most popular are: Accounting Club · Philosophy Club · Pre-Med Club (AMSA) · Student Athletic Advisory Committee · Wilderness Connections · Art Club · Dance Company · Astronomy Club · Glenn Wallichs Theatre Association · Improv Company · Mixed Blend · Music Educators National Conference (MENC) · Musical Theatre · Peer Theatre · Those Guys · Women's Ensemble · Amnesty International · Coalition for Non-Violent Activism · Biology Club · Collegians Activated to Liberate Life (CALL) · College Democrats · College Republicans · Mock Trial · Students for Environmental Action (SEA) · Big Buddies · Circle K · Habitat for Humanity · Maroon and Grey · Rotaract · Chemistry Club · Yeomen · Math Club · Economic Society · French Club · German Club. For those interested, there are intramural teams: basketball · cheerleading · football · racquetball

514

America's
Best Colleges for
B Students

· soccer · softball · table tennis · volleyball · water polo. University of Redlands is a member of the NCAA (Division II).

Academics and Learning Environment

University of Redlands has 202 full-time and 162 part-time faculty members, offering a student-to-faculty ratio of 15:1. The most common course size is 10 to 19 students. University of Redlands offers 43 majors with the most popular being business administration, liberal studies and psychology and least popular being French and philosophy. The school has a general core requirement. Cooperative education is not offered. All first-year students must maintain a 2.0 GPA or higher to avoid academic probation, and a minimum overall GPA of 2.0 is required to graduate. Academic programs that would intrigue a B student: self-designed majors · pass/fail grading option · independent study · double majors · honors program · Phi Beta Kappa · internships · certificate programs.

B Student Support and Success

The University of Redlands' Academic Support Services helps students develop and strengthen the skills they will need most for academic success, accomplishing this through academic counseling, subject tutoring, writing tutoring and a learning skills course. With academic counseling, students are encouraged to talk to their advisors when choosing a major, planning for possible study abroad and learning time management and study skills. The tutoring center provides time management calendars, study skills handouts and other materials. A learning skills course is offered each semester and covers time management, improving memory, understanding learning styles and developing positive attitudes and motivation. Time is spent discussing goal setting, career planning, test taking and note taking. Redlands also offers up to two hours a week of free peer tutoring. Students with documented learning disabilities may receive more. Writing tutors can be accessed on a drop-in basis. Students are able to receive help at all stages of their writing assignments from outlining to footnoting.

University of Redlands provides a variety of support programs, among them, dedicated guidance: academic · career · personal · psychological · religious. The average freshman year GPA is 3.0, and 87 percent of freshmen students return for their sophomore year. After college, many enter the workforce, but approximately 31 percent pursue a graduate degree immediately after graduation. One year after graduation, 10 percent of graduates have entered graduate school. These companies are a few that most frequently hire graduates from University of Redlands: Boys and Girls Club of Redlands · Disneyland · Ernst and Young · ESRI · Indy Mac Bank · Kiakonia Inc. · Let There Be Hope Foundation · McGladdry & Pullen · Northrup Grumman Space Technology · SAIC · Teach for America · Vavrinke · Wells Fargo Bank.

Support for Students with Learning Disabilities

Students with learning disabilities will want to research and perhaps get involved with these specific support programs. Sometimes, the college will grant additional time so that the LD student can finish their degree. A second option may be a lightened course load. High school foreign language waivers are accepted. High school

UNIVERSITY OF REDLANDS

Highlights

University of Redlands
Redlands, CA (Pop. 69,916)
Location: Large town
Four-year private
Founded: 1907
Website: http://www.redlands.edu

Students
Total enrollment: 4,956
Undergrads: 3,360
Freshmen: 724
Part-time students: 22%
From out-of-state: 27%
Male/Female: 44%/56%
Live on-campus: 53%
In fraternities: 13%
In sororities: 20%
Off-campus employment rating: Fair
Caucasian: 49%
African American: 5%
Hispanic: 25%
Asian: 4%
Hawaiian or Pacific Islander: 1%
Native American: 1%
Mixed (2+ ethnicities): 3%
International: 1%

Academics
Calendar: 4-4-1 system
Student/faculty ratio: 15:1
Class size 9 or fewer: 19%
Class size 10-29: 70%
Class size 30-49: 10%
Class size 50-99: 1%
Class size 100 or more: -
Returning freshmen: 87%
Six-year graduation rate: 63%

Most Popular Majors
Business administration
Liberal studies
Psychology

UNIVERSITY OF REDLANDS

Highlights

Admissions
Applicants: 4,501
Accepted: 3,099
Acceptance rate: 68.9%
Average GPA: 3.6
ACT range: 23-27
SAT Math range: 520-620
SAT Reading range: 510-610
SAT Writing range: Not reported
Top 10% of class: 28%
Top 25% of class: 64%
Top 50% of class: 91%

Deadlines
Early Action: 11/1
Early Decision: No
Regular Action: Rolling admissions
Common Application: Accepted

Financial Aid
In-state tuition: $42,836
Out-of-state tuition: $42,836
Room: Varies
Board: Varies
Books: $1,746
Freshmen receiving need-based aid: 82%
Undergrads rec. need-based aid: 84%
Avg. % of need met by financial aid: 87%
Avg. aid package (freshmen): $33,263
Avg. aid package (undergrads): $32,719
Avg. debt upon graduation: $32,035

Prominent Alumni
Cynthia J. Hoffman, chair, Department of Voice, The Julliard School; Gaddi H. Vasquez, U.S. Representative, United Nations Food and Agricultural Organization.

School Spirit
Mascot: Bulldogs
Colors: Maroon and gray
Song: *Och Tamale*

math waivers are also accepted. LD students will be very interested in the following programs at University of Redlands: tutors · testing accommodations · untimed tests · extended time for tests · take-home exam · oral tests · exam on tape or computer · readers · note-taking services · reading machines · tape recorders · early syllabus. Individual or small group tutorials are also available in: time management · organizational skills · learning strategies · specific subject areas · writing labs · math labs · study skills. An advisor/advocate from the Disability Services is available to students.

How to Get Admitted

For admissions decisions, non-academic factors considered: interview · extracurricular activities · special talents, interests and abilities · character/personal qualities · volunteer work · work experience · state of residency · geographical location · minority affiliation · alumni relationship. A high school diploma is required, although a GED is also accepted for admissions consideration. SAT or ACT test scores are required of all applicants. SAT Subject Test scores are not required. *Academic units recommended:* 4 English, 3 Math, 3 Science, 3 Social Studies, 3 Foreign Language.

How to Pay for College

To apply for financial aid, students should submit the following: Free Application for Federal Student Aid (FAFSA) · state aid form. University of Redlands participates in the Federal Work Study program. *Need-based aid programs include:* scholarships and grants · general need-based awards · Federal Pell grants · state scholarships and grants · college-based scholarships and grants · private scholarships and grants. *Non-need-based aid programs include:* scholarships and grants · state scholarships and grants · creative arts and performance awards · special achievements and activities awards · special characteristics awards.

America's
Best Colleges for
B Students

UNIVERSITY OF RHODE ISLAND

Newman Hall, 14 Upper College Road, Kingston, RI 02881-0806
Admissions: 401-874-7100 · Financial Aid: 401-874-5526
Email: admission@uri.edu · Website: http://www.uri.edu

From the College

"We are the largest university in the nation's smallest state, but with 13,000 under-graduates and 2,600 graduate students, URI is small enough to be friendly, intimate, safe and student-centered. Our students come from most states in the U.S. and dozens of countries all over the world. More than 100 undergraduate and 80 graduate degree programs, plus more than 100 student clubs and activities spark creativity and inspire our students' pioneering spirit. Perfectly located six miles from Rhode Island's coastal beaches and easy driving distances from Providence, Boston and New York, our picturesque rural setting is close enough to big-city culture to make anyone feel at home."

Campus Setting

URI, founded in 1892, is a public, comprehensive university. Programs are offered through the Colleges of Arts and Science, Business Administration, Engineering, Environmental and Life Sciences, Human Science and Services, Nursing and Pharmacy. Its 1,200-acre campus is located in Kingston, 30 miles south of Providence. A four-year institution, University of Rhode Island has an enrollment of 16,387 students. The school also has a library with over one million books. University of Rhode Island provides on-campus housing with 2,601 units that can accommodate 5,000 students. Housing options: coed dorms · sorority housing · fraternity housing · single-student apartments · married-student apartments · special housing for disabled students · cooperative housing. Recreation and sports facilities include: basketball, tennis and volleyball courts · fields · gymnasium · ice arena · swimming pool.

Student Life and Activities

Fifty-six percent of students live off campus. The Union, Fraternity houses, local dance clubs, bars and pool halls are hot spots for students. Popular campus events include First Night, Welcome Week, Winterfest, Springfest, Block Party, Oozeball, Greek Week, Rainville Awards Banquet, Ram Tours and Relay for Life. University of Rhode Island has 100 official student organizations. Greeks are influential in student life. If interested in sports, students should investigate some of these intramural teams: badminton · basketball · beach volleyball · billiards · bowling · flag football · floor hockey · golf · ice hockey · indoor soccer · soccer · softball · tennis · volleyball. University of Rhode Island is a member of the Atlantic 10 Conference (Division I, Football I-AA) and Colonial Athletic Association Eastern College Athletic Conferences (Division I, Football I-AA).

Academics and Learning Environment

University of Rhode Island has 682 full-time and 507 part-time faculty members, offering a student-to-faculty ratio of 16:1. The most common course size is 20 to 29 students. University of Rhode Island offers 222 majors with the most popular being nursing, psychology and communication studies. The school has a general core requirement. Cooperative education is offered. All first-year students must maintain a minimum GPA to avoid academic probation. Here are some other special academic programs that would appeal to a B student: pass/fail grading option · independent study · double majors · dual degrees · honors program · Phi Beta Kappa · internships · weekend college · distance learning.

517

College Profiles

UNIVERSITY OF RHODE ISLAND

University of Rhode Island
Kingston, RI (Pop. 6,974)
Location: Small town
Four-year public
Founded: 1892
Website: http://www.uri.edu

Students
Total enrollment: 16,387
Undergrads: 13,354
Part-time students: 11%
From out-of-state: 56%
Male/Female: 46%/54%
Live on-campus: 44%
In fraternities: 15%
In sororities: 15%
Off-campus employment rating: Good
Caucasian: 68%
African American: 5%
Hispanic: 9%
Asian: 3%
Hawaiian or Pacific Islander: <1%
Native American: <1%
Mixed (2+ ethnicities): 2%
International: 2%

Academics
Calendar: Semester
Student/faculty ratio: 16:1
Class size 9 or fewer: 10%
Class size 10-29: 58%
Class size 30-49: 21%
Class size 50-99: 6%
Class size 100 or more: 5%
Returning freshmen: 81%
Six-year graduation rate: 60%

Most Popular Majors
Nursing
Psychology
Communication studies

B Student Support and Success

URI's Academic Enhancement Center's motto is "Teaching Is Learning." This phrase reflects its belief that "learning happens best when the learner is engaged in teaching subject matter to others." Thus, students are helped through peer tutoring and study groups that focus both on general study skills topics as well as specific courses. The college advocates study groups that get together once a week and share responsibility for the material they are all learning. Students are encouraged to discuss class materials, work together to solve problems, compare notes and help each other to succeed. The URI Writing Center is free to all students who need help with all levels of writing. Additionally, the online assistance center has excellent materials to be read and/or downloaded.

There is dedicated guidance available at University of Rhode Island for the following: academic · career · personal · psychological · minority students · military · veterans · non-traditional students · family planning · religious. Additional counseling services include: graduate student counseling. Recognizing that some students may need extra preparation, University of Rhode Island offers remedial and refresher courses in: reading · writing · math · study skills. Other remedial services include: time management. Annually, 81 percent of freshmen students return for their sophomore year.

Support for Students with Learning Disabilities

Students with learning disabilities, also referred to as LD students, may want to investigate some of the support programs offered by University of Rhode Island. If deemed necessary, the college will sometimes grant additional time to LD students to complete their degree. A lightened course load is another available option. High school foreign language waivers are accepted. According to the school, Disability Services for Students coordinates accommodations and support for all students with disabilities. All accommodation requests are considered on a case-by-case basis and rely on complete documentation to substantiate the request. The following list of programs will appeal to LD students learning center · testing accommodations · extended time for tests · take-home exam · readers · typist/scribe · note-taking services · reading machines · tape recorders · special bookstore section · priority registration · waiver of math degree requirement. Individual or small group tutorials are also available in: time management · organizational skills · learning strategies · specific subject areas · writing labs · math labs · study skills. An advisor/advocate from the Disability Services for Students is available to students. This member also sits on the admissions committee.

How to Get Admitted

For admissions decisions, non-academic factors considered: extracurricular activities · special talents, interests and abilities · character/personal qualities · volunteer work · work experience · geographical location · minority affiliation · alumni relationship. A high school diploma is required, although a GED is also accepted for admissions consideration. SAT or ACT test scores are required of all applicants. *Academic units recommended:* 4 English, 4 Math, 4 Science, 4 Social Studies, 4 Foreign Language.

How to Pay for College

To apply for financial aid, students should submit the following: Free Application for Federal Student Aid (FAFSA). University of Rhode Island participates in the Federal Work Study program. *Need-based aid programs include:* scholarships and grants · general need-based awards · Federal Pell grants · state scholarships and grants · college-based scholarships and grants · private scholarships and grants. *Non-need-based aid programs include:* scholarships and grants · state scholarships and grants · creative arts and performance awards · special achievements and activities awards · athletic scholarships · ROTC scholarships.

UNIVERSITY OF RHODE ISLAND

Highlights

Admissions
Applicants: 20,907
Accepted: 15,844
Acceptance rate: 75.8%
Placed on wait list: 1,431
Enrolled from wait list: 279
Average GPA: 3.3
ACT range: 22-27
SAT Math range: 510-620
SAT Reading range: 490-590
SAT Writing range: 2-20
Top 10% of class: 19%
Top 25% of class: 47%
Top 50% of class: 83%

Deadlines
Early Action: 12/1
Early Decision: No
Regular Action: Rolling admissions
Common Application: Accepted

Financial Aid
In-state tuition: $10,878
Out-of-state tuition: $26,444
Room: $7,150
Board: $4,180
Books: $1,200
Freshmen receiving need-based aid: 63%
Undergrads rec. need-based aid: 70%
Avg. % of need met by financial aid: 59%
Avg. aid package (freshmen): $16,310
Avg. aid package (undergrads): $15,482
Avg. debt upon graduation: $31,141

Prominent Alumni
Christine Amanpour, anchor, ABC News' 'This Week'; Robert Ballard, famed undersea explorer, professor of oceanography at U of Rhode Island; Michael Fascitelli, CEO, Vornado Realty Trust, LP.

School Spirit
Mascot: Rams
Colors: Light blue and white
Song: *Rhode Island Bowm*

519

College Profiles

UNIVERSITY OF SAN FRANCISCO

2130 Fulton Street, San Francisco, CA 94117-1080
Admissions: 800-CALL-USF · Financial Aid: 415-422-2620
Email: admission@usfca.edu · Website: http://www.usfca.edu

From the College

"The core mission of the university is to promote learning in the Jesuit Catholic tradition. The university offers undergraduate, graduate and professional students the knowledge and skills needed to succeed as persons and professionals, and the values and the sensitivity necessary to be men and women for others. The university will distinguish itself as a diverse, socially responsible learning community of high quality scholarship and academic rigor sustained by a faith that does justice. The university will draw from the cultural, intellectual and economic resources of the San Francisco Bay area and its location on the Pacific Rim to enrich and strengthen its educational programs.'"

Campus Setting

University of San Francisco, founded in 1855, is a private, Jesuit Catholic University. Programs are offered through the Colleges of Arts and Sciences and Professional Studies, the McLaren College of Business and the Schools of Education, Law and Nursing. The 55-acre campus is located in San Francisco, three miles from downtown. A four-year institution, USF has an enrollment of 10,130 students. Although not originally co-educational college, USF has been co-ed since 1964. The school is also affiliated with the Roman Catholic Church. The campus provides its students with a large library, as well as a/an institute for Chinese-Western cultural history. USF provides some on-campus housing, comprising of seven units which can accommodate 2,300 students: coed dorms · women's dorms · single-student apartments. Recreation and sports facilities include a health and recreation center.

Student Life and Activities

Sixty-six percent of students live off campus. Homecoming, Founder's Week and Welcome Week are popular events on campus. University of San Francisco has 109 official student organizations. Student Leadership, Student Media and College Players have a strong presence in student social life. When it comes to sports, intramural teams are available: basketball · bowling · flag football · golf · lacrosse · racquetball · soccer · softball · swimming/diving · table tennis · tennis · volleyball. University of San Francisco is a member of the West Coast Conference (Division I).

Academics and Learning Environment

University of San Francisco has 461 full-time and 651 part-time faculty members, offering a student-to-faculty ratio of 15:1. The most common course size is 10 to 19 students. University of San Francisco offers 130 majors with the most popular being registered nursing/registered nurse, business administration/management and psychology. The school has a general core requirement as well as a religion requirement. Cooperative education is not offered. All first-year students must maintain a 2.0 GPA or higher to avoid academic probation, and a minimum overall GPA of 2.0 is required to graduate. The B student should be made aware of the following options: self-designed majors · pass/fail grading option · independent study · double majors · dual degrees · accelerated study · honors program · internships · distance learning certificate programs.

B Student Support and Success

The Learning Center at USF provides assistance to students through tutors in a variety of academic disciplines. The tutors are undergrads and graduate students who have excelled in certain academic areas and who have had special tutorial training. These students offer help on such topics as math, science, business, languages, computers, arts and general education. Study skills videos, textbooks and reference books are available, and the center also provides students a place to study that is peaceful and supportive. The Writing Center features tutors that tailor programs of instruction to meet each student's needs. The center's primary goal is to "guide students in developing their writing skills in rhetoric, style and correctness, through one-on-one interactive conferences with rhetoric and composition faculty who have been chosen to work as consultants."

University of San Francisco provides dedicated guidance for: academic · career · personal · psychological · minority students · non-traditional students · religious. Additional counseling services include: Learning Disabilities services. The average freshman year GPA is 3.2, and 88 percent of freshmen students return for their sophomore year. Some companies that most frequently hire graduates are: Deloitte · Enterprise Rent A Car · Ernst & Young · National Semiconductor · PricewaterhouseCoopers · Travelers Insurance · Wells Fargo.

Support for Students with Learning Disabilities

There are several options open to students with learning disabilities, specific support programs offered by University of San Francisco. For instance, the college may grant additional time to students with learning disabilities to complete their degree. Another choice would be a lightened course load. LD students will want to survey the following list of programs: tutors · learning center · testing accommodations · untimed tests · extended time for tests · take-home exam · oral tests · readers · note-taking services · reading machines · tape recorders · videotaped classes · diagnostic testing service · waiver of math degree requirement. Individual or small group tutorials are also available in: time management · organizational skills · learning strategies · specific subject areas · writing labs · math labs · study skills. An advisor/advocate from the Student Disability Services is available to students.

How to Get Admitted

For admissions decisions, non-academic factors considered: interview · extracurricular activities · special talents, interests and abilities · character/personal qualities · volunteer work · work experience · state of residency · minority affiliation · alumni relationship. A high school diploma is required, although a GED is also accepted for admissions consideration. SAT or ACT test scores are required of all applicants. SAT Subject Test scores are required for some applicants. *Academic units recommended:* 4 English, 3 Math, 2 Science, 3 Social Studies, 2 Foreign Language.

How to Pay for College

To apply for financial aid, students should submit the following: Free Application for Federal Student Aid (FAFSA). University of San

Highlights

University of San Francisco
San Francisco (Pop. 825,863)
Location: Major city
Four-year private
Founded: 1855
Website: http://www.usfca.edu

Students
Total enrollment: 10,130
Undergrads: 6,392
Freshmen: 1,333
Part-time students: 4%
From out-of-state: 29%
From public schools: 48%
Male/Female: 38%/62%
Live on-campus: 34%
In fraternities: 1%
In sororities: 1%
Off-campus employment rating: Excellent
Caucasian: 31%
African American: 3%
Hispanic: 19%
Asian: 19%
Hawaiian or Pacific Islander: <1%
Native American: <1%
Mixed (2+ ethnicities): 7%
International: 18%

Academics
Calendar: 4-1-4 system
Student/faculty ratio: 15:1
Class size 9 or fewer: 13%
Class size 10-29: 63%
Class size 30-49: 21%
Class size 50-99: 3%
Class size 100 or more: -
Returning freshmen: 88%
Six-year graduation rate: 69%

Most Popular Majors
Registered nursing/registered nurse
Business administration/management
Psychology

521

College Profiles

UNIVERSITY OF SAN FRANCISCO

Admissions
Applicants: 14,844
Accepted: 9,075
Acceptance rate: 61.1%
Average GPA: 3.6
ACT range: 23-27
SAT Math range: 540-640
SAT Reading range: 530-630
SAT Writing range: 6-35
Top 10% of class: 33%
Top 25% of class: 71%
Top 50% of class: 94%

Deadlines
Early Action: 11/15
Early Decision: 11/15
Regular Action: 1/15
Common Application: Accepted

Financial Aid
In-state tuition: $40,996
Out-of-state tuition: $40,996
Room: $8,950
Board: $4,370
Books: $1,600
Freshmen receiving need-based aid: 58%
Undergrads rec. need-based aid: 55%
Avg. % of need met by financial aid: 63%
Avg. aid package (freshmen): $32,310
Avg. aid package (undergrads): $28,727
Avg. debt upon graduation: $29,054

Prominent Alumni
Paul Otellini, president, Intel Corporation; Gordon Getty, business leader and philanthropist; Heather Fong, previous San Francisco Police Chief.

School Spirit
Mascot: Dons
Colors: Green, gold and white

Francisco participates in the Federal Work Study program. *Need-based aid programs include:* scholarships and grants · general need-based awards · Federal Pell grants · state scholarships and grants · college-based scholarships and grants · private scholarships and grants · Federal Nursing scholarships. *Non-need-based aid programs include:* scholarships and grants · state scholarships and grants · special achievements and activities awards · athletic scholarships · ROTC scholarships · University Scholars Program.

UNIVERSITY OF SOUTH CAROLINA – COLUMBIA

902 Sumter Street Access/Lieber College, Columbia, SC 29208
Admissions: 800-868-5872 · Financial Aid: 803-777-8134
Email: admissions-ugrad@sc.edu · Website: http://www.sc.edu

From the College

"Chartered in 1801 as South Carolina College, the University of South Carolina – Columbia blends historic charm with a 21st century attitude. The original campus, popularly known as the Horseshoe, is listed on the National Register of Historic Places. Today's students have access to world-class facilities, including the Strom Thurmond Wellness and Fitness Center and the world's largest "green" dorm. USC Columbia offers more than 350 undergraduate and graduate courses of study. Programs range from liberal arts and sciences to business, law, medicine and other professional studies. The international business program is very popular. Study abroad, undergraduate research and interdisciplinary programs of study are encouraged. The Honors College is strong."

Campus Setting

USC, founded in 1801, is a public, comprehensive university. Programs are offered through the Colleges of Business, Criminal Justice, Education, Engineering, Hospitality, Retail, & Sport Management, Journalism & Mass Communications, Library & Information Science, Liberal Arts, Nursing, Pharmacy, Science & Mathematics and Social Work; through the Schools of the Environment, Law, Medicine, Music and Public Health and through the South Carolina Honors College. Its 351-acre campus, including a pre-Civil War area listed on the National Register of Historic Places, is located in Columbia, in central South Carolina. A four-year institution, USC has an enrollment of 31,964 students. Although not originally a co-educational college, USC has been co-ed since 1893. The campus facilities include: library · museum · observatory · arboretum · green dorm with learning center focusing on sustainability · filtration research engineering demonstration unit. USC provides on-campus housing of 4,602 units, which accommodate 7,329 students. Housing options are as follows: coed dorms · women's dorms · men's dorms · sorority housing · fraternity housing · single-student apartments · married-student apartments · special housing for disabled students · special housing for international students. Recreation and sports facilities include: football, soccer and tennis stadium · basketball center · baseball and softball fields · golf club · natatorium · track and field · volleyball.

Student Life and Activities

Seventy-one percent of students live off campus. Popular campus events include Caught in the Creative Act: Writers Talk about their Writing, Garnet Jacket Classic Golf Tournament, Parents Weekend, Dance Marathon, Black History Month, Carolina Spirit Week & Tiger Burn, Homecoming Week, Carolina - Clemson Food Fight, First-Year Reading Experience and Carolina Cuisine at the McCutcheon House. USC has 387 official student organizations. The most popular are: music, theatre, political, service and special-interest groups. There are intramural sports teams such as: badminton · basketball · bench press · bowling · flag football · floor hockey · football · golf · indoor soccer · racquetball · sand volleyball · soccer · softball · swimming · tennis · track · tug-of-war · Ultimate Frisbee · volleyball · walleyball. USC is a member of the Southeastern Conference (Division I, Football I-A).

UNIVERSITY OF SOUTH CAROLINA – COLUMBIA

University of South Carolina – Columbia

Columbia, SC (Pop. 131,686)
Location: Medium city
Four-year public
Founded: 1801
Website: http://www.sc.edu

Students

Total enrollment: 31,964
Undergrads: 24,180
Part-time students: 7%
From out-of-state: 48%
Male/Female: 46%/54%
Live on-campus: 29%
In fraternities: 13%
In sororities: 28%
Off-campus employment rating: Good
Caucasian: 2%
African American: <1%
Hispanic: 10%
Asian: <1%
Hawaiian or Pacific Islander: 77%
Native American: 4%
Mixed (2+ ethnicities): 3%
International: 2%

Academics

Calendar: Semester
Student/faculty ratio: 18:1
Class size 9 or fewer: 15%
Class size 10-29: 56%
Class size 30-49: 19%
Class size 50-99: 7%
Class size 100 or more: 3%
Returning freshmen: 88%
Six-year graduation rate: 73%

Most Popular Majors

Biological sciences
Nursing
General experimental psychology

Academics and Learning Environment

USC has 1,560 full-time and 717 part-time faculty members, offering a student-to-faculty ratio of 18:1. The most common course size is 20 to 29 students. USC offers 254 majors with the most popular being biological sciences, nursing and general experimental psychology and least popular being Latin American studies, comparative literature and engineering science. The school has a general core requirement. Cooperative education is available. All first-year students must maintain a 2.0 GPA or higher to avoid academic probation. Here are several other academic programs that would appeal to a B student: self-designed majors · pass/fail grading option · independent study · double majors · dual degrees · accelerated study · honors program · Phi Beta Kappa · internships · weekend college · distance learning.

B Student Support and Success

At USC, where students are known as "Gamecocks," the Academic Center for Excellence provides free writing consultations, math tutoring and other services. Guidance from ACE coaches is offered in areas of time management, procrastination, reading comprehension, note taking, goal setting, test taking, motivation, anxiety management, concentration and information processing. In addition, USC has a site called "My Game Plan" that helps each student design a personal approach for achieving academic success in college. It includes a personal assessment, study strategies and much more.

USC provides a variety of support programs including dedicated guidance for: academic · career · personal · psychological · minority students · military · veterans · non-traditional students · family planning. Recognizing that some students may need extra preparation, USC offers remedial and refresher courses in: reading · writing · math · study skills. The average freshman year GPA is 3.3, and 88 percent of freshmen students return for their sophomore year. Companies that most frequently hire graduates from USC include: Information technology companies · education, government, and non-profit organizations · engineering firms · financial institutions · marketing and sales.

Support for Students with Learning Disabilities

Students with learning disabilities will be interested to learn that the USC offers specific support programs. The college may grant additional time to students with learning disabilities to complete their degree or even offer a lightened course load. Credit is given for remedial courses taken. High school foreign language waivers are accepted. LD students will find the following list rather helpful: untimed tests · extended time for tests · readers · note-taking services · reading machines · tape recorders. Individual or small group tutorials are also available in: time management · organizational skills · learning strategies · study skills. An advisor/advocate from the Student Disability Services is available to students.

How to Get Admitted

For admissions decisions, non-academic factors considered: extracurricular activities · special talents, interests and abilities · character/personal qualities · volunteer work · work experience · minority affiliation ·

alumni relationship. A high school diploma is required, although a GED is also accepted for admissions consideration. SAT or ACT test scores are required of all applicants. SAT Subject Test scores are not required.

How to Pay for College

To apply for financial aid, students should submit the following: Free Application for Federal Student Aid (FAFSA). USC participates in the Federal Work Study program. *Need-based aid programs include:* scholarships and grants · general need-based awards · Federal Pell grants · state scholarships and grants · college-based scholarships and grants · private scholarships and grants · Federal Nursing scholarships · United Negro College Fund · USC Opportunity Grant. *Non-need-based aid programs include:* scholarships and grants · general need-based awards · state scholarships and grants · creative arts and performance awards · special achievements and activities awards · athletic scholarships · ROTC scholarships.

UNIVERSITY OF SOUTH CAROLINA – COLUMBIA

Highlights

Admissions
Applicants: 23,035
Accepted: 14,844
Acceptance rate: 64.4%
Placed on wait list: 1,903
Enrolled from wait list: 3
Average GPA: 4.2
ACT range: 24-29
SAT Math range: 550-650
SAT Reading range: 540-630
SAT Writing range: Not reported
Top 10% of class: 30%
Top 25% of class: 66%
Top 50% of class: 94%

Deadlines
Early Action: 10/15
Early Decision: No
Regular Action: 12/1 (final)
Notification of admission by: 3/15
Common Application: Not accepted

Financial Aid
In-state tuition: $10,791
Out-of-state tuition: $18,461
Room: $5,988
Board: $2,921
Books: $994
Freshmen receiving need-based aid: 51%
Undergrads rec. need-based aid: 52%
Avg. % of need met by financial aid: 73%
Avg. aid package (freshmen): $12,650
Avg. aid package (undergrads): $13,332
Avg. debt upon graduation: $25,711

Prominent Alumni
Lindsey Graham, U.S. Senator; Darla Moore, financier/philanthropist; Gary Parsons, founder, XM Satellite Radio; Darius Rucker, country singer/philanthropist; Sterling Sharpe, football analyst, NFL Network.

School Spirit
Mascot: Cocky
Colors: Garnet and black
Song: *We Hail Thee Carolina*

525

College Profiles

UNIVERSITY OF TENNESSEE AT KNOXVILLE

320 Student Services Building, Knoxville, TN 37996
Admissions: 865-974-2184 · Financial Aid: 865-974-3131
Email: admissions@utk.edu · Website: http://www.utk.edu

From the College

"The University of Tennessee - Knoxville is a growing and vibrant university in a friendly urban setting. The university is consistently cited as a 'best buy' and great value and is committed to access and affordability. A wide range of scholarships helps to open doors for many qualified students to become Volunteers. The number of students who study abroad has soared in recent years with the rise in new scholarships, internships and service-learning opportunities around the world.

"The Haslam Scholars program, a premier honors program that admits fifteen of the nation's top students each year, provides undergraduates with exclusive benefits and funding to cover a study-abroad experience and a senior research thesis. The university's partnership with Battelle Corp. to manage the nearby Oak Ridge National Laboratory provides a wide array of research opportunities for students at all levels. As the nation's largest government science and energy lab, ORNL fuels the state's technology- and science-driven economy, providing unprecedented opportunities for UT students.

"The university has opened several state-of-the-art academic facilities, including the John D. Tickle Engineering Building, the Natalie L. Haslam Music Center and the Min Kao Electrical and Computer Engineering Building. A new outdoor RecSports Complex opened in 2013, and the first section of a new Student Union opened in 2015. The new Fred D. Brown Residence Hall opened in 2014. The university will replace six residence halls in the next five years. The new Sorority Village development has opened eleven houses on UT's scenic Morgan Hill.

"UT's campus has everything a student needs. From traditional sorority and fraternity organizations to professional societies, from archery and judo to rugby, water polo and every other sport in between, students can pursue any interest through more than 400 active clubs.

"UT students are known for their Volunteer spirit, both on game day and in the community. The Center for Leadership and Service sums up what it means to be a Vol through alternative spring and fall break service trips and other opportunities. Students are involved in outreach programs in areas such as health care, animal welfare, hunger and homelessness, city beautification, youth outreach, global issues and more.

"Just a few blocks away students can enjoy downtown Knoxville's diverse culture of music, eclectic foods, boutique shopping, arts and entertainment. Weekly farmers markets sell the freshest-tasting local food, and several galleries present work from UT visionaries and some of the world's most famous artists.

"UT is a member of the Southeastern Conference and has 18 men's and women's NCAA Division I teams. Students also enjoy Tennessee Smokies baseball and Ice Bears hockey games and nearby tourist destinations Gatlinburg, Pigeon Forge, Dollywood and the Great Smoky Mountains."

Campus Setting

UT is a public, research intensive university. Founded as a private college in 1794, it became the first campus of the University of Tennessee system in 1879. Programs are offered through the Colleges of Agricultural Sciences and Natural Resources, Architecture and Design, Arts and Sciences, Business Administration, Communication and Information, Education, Health and Human Sciences, Engineering, Law, Nursing, Social Work and Veterinary Medicine. Its 550-acre campus is located in Knoxville, just minutes from the Great Smoky Mountains National Park. A four-year public institution, UT has an enrollment of 30,030 students. Although not originally a co-educational college, UT has been co-ed since 1892. Campus facilities include: gallery · museum · gardens · international house · music hall · public policy and Black cultural centers. UT provides on-campus housing with 3,510 units that can accommodate 7,312 students. Housing options: coed dorms · women's dorms · men's dorms · fraternity housing · single-student apartments · married-student apartments · special housing for disabled students · special housing for international students. Recreation and sports facilities include: aquatic, athletic and recreational centers · basketball, handball, paddleball, sand volleyball and tennis courts · intramural and recreational sports fields · arena · baseball stadium · soccer complex · softball stadium · track.

Student Life and Activities

More than half of the students (63 percent) live off campus. As reported by a school representative, "Students have a large number of social and special interest groups to join. Every effort is made to expose students to music, theater and artistic venues that will foster personal growth and enhance the university experience." Popular on-campus gathering spots include the University Center, T-Rec and other sports/fitness facilities and The Strip. Popular campus events include Homecoming activities, Smokey's Howl, Cheerleading Competition, Box Car Races, Parade with Float and Miss Homecoming Queen Competition, All Sing Musical Competition, Carnicus (parodies and satire performance), Vol Night Long, Volapalooza, Volunteer Challenge, football and basketball games and other sports. UT has 412 official student organizations. Popular groups on campus include Student Government, Greeks, athletes, religious groups and sports clubs. Intramural teams include: basketball · billiards · bowling · cycling · fencing · field hockey · flag football · football · ice hockey · lacrosse · martial arts · rugby · sailing · sand volleyball · scuba diving · skiing · soccer · softball · swimming · tennis · volleyball · water polo · water skiing · weightlifting. UT is a member of the Southeastern Conference (Division I, Football I-A).

Academics and Learning Environment

UT has 1,734 full-time and 340 part-time faculty members, offering a student-to-faculty ratio of 17:1. The most common course size is 20 to 29 students. UT offers 235 majors with the most popular being biological sciences, psychology and logistics. The least popular majors are engineering physics, recreation and agricultural economics/business. The school has a general core requirement. Cooperative education is available. All first-year students must maintain a 2.0 GPA or higher to avoid academic probation. Other special academic programs that would appeal to a B student include: self-designed majors · independent study · double majors · dual degrees · honors program · Phi Beta Kappa · internships · distance learning.

UNIVERSITY OF TENNESSEE – KNOXVILLE

Highlights

University of Tennessee – Knoxville
Knoxville, TN (Pop. 182,200)
Location: Medium city
Four-year public
Founded: 1794
Website: http://www.utk.edu

Students
Total enrollment: 30,030
Undergrads: 21,182
Part-time students: 7%
From out-of-state: 11%
Male/Female: 51%/49%
Live on-campus: 37%
In fraternities: 14%
In sororities: 21%
Off-campus employment rating: Good
Caucasian: 80%
African American: 7%
Hispanic: 3%
Asian: 3%
Native American: <1%
Mixed (2+ ethnicities): 3%
International: 2%

Academics
Calendar: Semester
Student/faculty ratio: 17:1
Class size 9 or fewer: 7%
Class size 10-29: 54%
Class size 30-49: 23%
Class size 50-99: 9%
Class size 100 or more: 7%
Returning freshmen: 86%
Six-year graduation rate: 68%

Most Popular Majors
Biological sciences
Psychology
Logistics

527

College Profiles

UNIVERSITY OF TENNESSEE – KNOXVILLE

Highlights

Admissions
Applicants: 14,396
Accepted: 10,435
Acceptance rate: 72.5%
Average GPA: 3.9
ACT range: 24-29
SAT Math range: 520-650
SAT Reading range: 520-640
SAT Writing range: Not reported
Top 10% of class: 52%
Top 25% of class: 91%
Top 50% of class: 100%

Deadlines
Early Action: No
Early Decision: No
Regular Action: 11/1 (priority)
12/1 (final)
Notification of admission by: 3/31
Common Application: Accepted

Financial Aid
In-state tuition: $10,366
Out-of-state tuition: $28,556
Room: Varies
Board: Varies
Books: $1,582
Freshmen receiving need-based aid: 63%
Undergrads rec. need-based aid: 60%
Avg. % of need met by financial aid: 60%
Avg. aid package (freshmen): $13,727
Avg. aid package (undergrads): $12,126
Avg. debt upon graduation: $23,729

Prominent Alumni
Peyton Manning, NFL quarterback; Howard H. Baker, Jr., former senator, President Reagan's chief of staff, ambassador to Japan; Pat Summitt, all-time winningest NCAA Division I college basketball coach.

School Spirit
Mascot: Smokey: Blue-Tic Coon Hound
Colors: Orange and white
Song: *Rocky Top*

America's
Best Colleges for
B Students

B Student Support and Success

According to its website, UT offers "First Year Studies 101: a one credit course to introduce students to the university and resources, a Student Success Center: one stop shopping for academic referrals and resources, a Math Tutorial Center and Writing Center and a College academic advising center." Students are encouraged to "take a challenging curriculum of academic courses." UT offers this advice to those wishing to apply for acceptance: "Complete the personal statement with your application—it will be read! Letters of recommendation are not required but if you wish to include them, be sure that they are from teachers of academic subjects. Tell us about your academic challenges and successes. Tell about your special talents and abilities. UT welcomes B students with strong and diverse academic backgrounds."

UT provides a variety of support programs including dedicated guidance for: academic · career · personal · psychological · minority students · military · veterans · non-traditional students · family planning. The average freshman year GPA is 3.1, and 86 percent of freshmen students return for their sophomore year. Among students who enter the workforce, approximately 58 percent enter a field related to their major within six months of graduation. Companies that most frequently hire graduates from UT include: 21st Mortgage · ALSTROM Power · APL Logistics · Baker Hughes · CHEP USA · CIGNA Healthcare · Clayton Homes · Crowe Chizek and Company · Dell · Deloitte · Dixon Hughes · Dow Chemical Company · Eaton Electrical · Enterprise Rent-a-Car · Ernst & Young · ExxonMobil · Fed-Ex · Frito Lay · International Paper · Johnson & Johnson · Joseph Decosimo & Company · Kimberly-Clark · Knoxville Utilities Board · KPMG · Kroger · Manhattan Associates · Marriott Business Services · Newell Rubbermaid · Nissan · Pepsi Bottling Group · Pershing Yoakley · PricewaterhouseCoopers · Pugh & Company · Regions Bank · Shaw Industries Group · Siemens · Square D/ Schneider Electric · SPX Corporation · Target stores · Tennessee Valley Authority · University of Tennessee · Whirlpool · Wolseley North America.

Support for Students with Learning Disabilities

At UT, learning disabled students may request additional time to complete a degree and/or a lightened course load. High school foreign language and math waivers are accepted. According to the school, they do not have any separate admissions process for LD students. Eligibility for accommodations/services is established by the disability documentation provided by the student in accordance with institutional standards. Accommodations/services are coordinated through the Disability Services Office and are based on needs specified in the student's documentation. Other offices on campus may also provide services, some of which are not mandated by laws and/or regulations. Students with learning disabilities will find the following programs at UT useful: tutors · learning center · testing accommodations · extended time for tests · take-home exam · oral tests · exam on tape or computer · readers · typist/scribe · note-taking services · reading machines · tape recorders · texts on tape · early syllabus · diagnostic testing service · priority registration. Individual or small group tutorials are also available in: time management ·

organizational skills · specific subject areas · writing labs · math labs · study skills. An advisor/advocate from the LD program is available to students.

How to Get Admitted

For admissions decisions, non-academic factors considered: extracurricular activities · special talents, interests and abilities · character/personal qualities · volunteer work · work experience · geographical location · minority affiliation · alumni relationship. A high school diploma is required, although a GED is also accepted for admissions consideration. SAT or ACT test scores are required of all applicants. *According to the admissions office:* Minimum 2.0 GPA required; holistic review of all parts of the application.

How to Pay for College

To apply for financial aid, students should submit the following: Free Application for Federal Student Aid (FAFSA) · institution's own financial aid forms. UT participates in the Federal Work Study program. *Need-based aid programs include:* scholarships and grants · general need-based awards · Federal Pell grants · state scholarships and grants · college-based scholarships and grants · private scholarships and grants · Federal Nursing scholarships. *Non-need-based aid programs include:* scholarships and grants · general need-based awards · state scholarships and grants · creative arts and performance awards · special achievements and activities awards · special characteristics awards · athletic scholarships · ROTC scholarships.

UNIVERSITY OF THE PACIFIC

3601 Pacific Avenue, Stockton, CA 95211
Admissions: 800-959-2867 · Financial Aid: 209-946-2421
Email: admissions@pacific.edu · Website: http://www.pacific.edu

From the College

"The University of the Pacific is a study in contrasts. The community has the attitude of a California university and the pioneering spirit of the American West. But the campus looks like a school set in the countryside of New England, complete with old brick buildings, ivy and a lot of green spaces. In each of our 91 majors, students share the common experiences of mentoring faculty, small classes and guarantees of internships and graduation within four years."

Campus Setting

University of the Pacific, founded in 1851, is a private, comprehensive university. Programs are offered through the College of the Pacific; the Schools of Engineering, International Studies and Pharmacy; the Benerd School of Education; the Eberhardt School of Business and the Conservatory of Music. Its 175-acre campus is located in Stockton, 85 miles east of San Francisco. A four-year institution, University of the Pacific has an enrollment of 6,421 students. The school also has a library with 381,686 books. University of the Pacific offers on-campus housing with 1,445 units which can accommodate 2,205 students. Some other housing options: coed dorms · sorority housing · fraternity housing · single-student apartments · married-student apartments · special housing for disabled students. Recreation and sports facilities include: fitness center · gymnasium.

Student Life and Activities

More than half of students (54 percent) live off campus. Popular campus events include Diversity Week, Alumni Weekend, Homecoming, Festival of Lights and Founder's Day. University of the Pacific has 100 official student organizations. The most popular are: Academy of Student Pharmacists · Adult Learners · Advocating Animal Rights · American Institute of Graphic Design · American Society of Civil Engineers · American Society for Engineering Management · American Society of Mechanical Engineers · Amnesty International · Association for Computing Machinery · Association for Supervision and Curriculum Development · Association of Engineering Students · Biomedical Engineering Society · Bishop Scholars · Campus PACT · Celebrate Diversity · Circle K · College Republicans · Composers Club · Conservatory Student Senate · DDR club · Debate Society · Eberhardt School of Business Student Association · Human Resources Student Association · Institute of the Electrical and Electronics Engineers · Masters of Biology Society · mathematics and science club · Mathletics · MBA Student Association · Moonlight Puppeteers · multicultural engineering program · Music and Entertainers Industry Student Association · music management club · Music Therapy Association · National Association for Music Education · Navy League of the US-Pacific Council · Open Assembly of the School of International Studies · Orange Army · Pacific Ambassador Society · Pacific American Marketing Association · Pacific appreciation of hip hop culture club · Pacific Democrats · Pacific Forensics Society · Pacific speech & sports management club · Pagan Alliance · physical therapy · Project 30 Scholars · Residence Hall Association · School of Education Student Association · Snow bound · Social Justice Community · Society of Automotive Engineers · Society of Hispanic Professional Engineers · Society of Women Engineers · SPA · Sport Club Council · Student California Teachers Association · Student Athletic Training · Students for Environmental Action · Students

Teaching & Think Tank · The Council for Exceptional Children · United Cultural Council.

Academics and Learning Environment

University of the Pacific has 442 full-time and 365 part-time faculty members, offering a student-to-faculty ratio of 14:1. The most common course size is 10 to 19 students. University of the Pacific offers 80 majors. The school has a general core requirement. Cooperative education is available. All first-year students must maintain a 2.0 GPA or higher to avoid academic probation, and a minimum overall GPA of 2.0 is required to graduate. A B student should be made aware of the following special academic programs: self-designed majors · pass/fail grading option · independent study · double majors · accelerated study · honors program · internships.

B Student Support and Success

University of the Pacific's Retention Services offers tutoring, study skills sessions, peer mentoring, career counseling and academic counseling. Their student-to-student advising program has 40 undergrads that are there to help with time management, preparing for tests, choosing a major, meeting general education requirements and even dealing with homesickness.

University of the Pacific prides itself on providing a variety of support programs, including dedicated guidance for: academic · career · personal · psychological · veterans. Annually, 86 percent of freshmen students return for their sophomore year. For interested parties, the following are some companies that most frequently hire graduates from University of the Pacific: Accenture · Alcatel USA · American Express · AT&T Wireless · Biosource · California Human Development Corporation · Celebrity Cruise Lines · Cingular Wireless · Cisco Systems · Citgo Fund Services · Dresdner RCM Global Investors · Edward Jones · Enterprise · E-Trade · First Financial · Frito Lay · Gallo Wineries · Gap · General Mills · General Motors · George Simons International · Herzog Transit · Houston Astros · IRS · JET · Kaiser Permanente · Lawrence Livermore National Laboratory · Mervyns · Northwestern Mutual Financial · NY Life · Pacida International Maersk · PricewaterhouseCoopers · Quad Knopf · Rite Aid · Sandia National Laboratory · State of California · various school districts and non-profit organizations · Walgreens · Xerox.

Support for Students with Learning Disabilities

Some students, such as those with learning disabilities, may want to take advantage of specific support programs offered by University of the Pacific. Sometimes, the college will grant additional time to students with learning disabilities to complete their degree or a lightened course load may be offered. LD students will find the following programs at University of the Pacific extremely helpful: remedial math · remedial English · remedial reading · tutors · learning center · extended time for tests · reading machines · waiver of math degree requirement. Individual or small group tutorials are also available in: writing labs · math labs. An advisor/advocate from the Services for Students With Disabilities is available to students.

UNIVERSITY OF THE PACIFIC

Highlights

University of the Pacific
Stockton, CA (Pop. 297,984)
Location: Medium city
Four-year private
Founded: 1851
Website: http://www.pacific.edu

Students
Total enrollment: 6,421
Undergrads: 3,877
Part-time students: 3%
From out-of-state: 7%
Male/Female: 48%/52%
Live on-campus: 46%
In fraternities: 15%
In sororities: 16%
Off-campus employment rating: Good
Caucasian: 32%
African American: 1%
Hispanic: 3%
Asian: 19%
Hawaiian or Pacific Islander: 32%
Native American: <1%
Mixed (2+ ethnicities): 4%
International: 5%

Academics
Calendar: Semester
Student/faculty ratio: 14:1
Class size 9 or fewer: 26%
Class size 10-29: 55%
Class size 30-49: 15%
Class size 50-99: 4%
Class size 100 or more: -
Returning freshmen: 86%
Six-year graduation rate: 63%

UNIVERSITY OF THE PACIFIC

Highlights

Admissions
Applicants: 14,222
Accepted: 10,332
Acceptance rate: 72.6%
Placed on wait list: 1,100
Enrolled from wait list: 34
Average GPA: 3.5
ACT range: 22-29
SAT Math range: 530-680
SAT Reading range: 500-640
SAT Writing range: 11-29
Top 10% of class: 36%
Top 25% of class: 68%
Top 50% of class: 90%

Deadlines
Early Action: 11/15
Early Decision: No
Regular Action: Rolling admissions
Common Application: Accepted

Financial Aid
In-state tuition: $40,822
Out-of-state tuition: $40,822
Room: Varies
Board: Varies
Books: $1,746
Freshmen receiving need-based aid: 74%
Undergrads rec. need-based aid: 73%
Avg. aid package (freshmen): $28,021
Avg. aid package (undergrads): $29,290

Prominent Alumni
Alex Spanos, developer; Michael Olowokandi, professional basketball player; Janet Leigh, actress.

School Spirit
Mascot: Tigers
Colors: Orange and black
Song: *Tiger Fight Song*

How to Get Admitted

For admissions decisions, non-academic factors considered: extracurricular activities · special talents, interests and abilities · character/personal qualities · volunteer work · work experience · state of residency · geographical location · alumni relationship. A high school diploma is required, although a GED is also accepted for admissions consideration. SAT or ACT test scores are required of all applicants. SAT Subject Test scores are recommended but not required. *According to the admissions office:* Minimum grade average of 'B' in college-preparatory courses required. *Academic units recommended:* 4 English, 3 Math, 3 Science, 2 Social Studies, 2 Foreign Language.

How to Pay for College

To apply for financial aid, students should submit the following: Free Application for Federal Student Aid (FAFSA). University of the Pacific participates in the Federal Work Study program. *Need-based aid programs include:* scholarships and grants · general need-based awards · Federal Pell grants · state scholarships and grants · college-based scholarships and grants · private scholarships and grants · ACG · SMART. *Non-need-based aid programs include:* scholarships and grants · state scholarships and grants · special achievements and activities awards · special characteristics awards · athletic scholarships.

UNIVERSITY OF UTAH

201 Presidents Circle, Salt Lake City, UT 84112
Admissions: 800-685-8856 · Financial Aid: 800-685-8761
Email: admissions@utah.edu · Website: http://www.utah.edu

From the College

"The University of Utah offers competitive programs to meet the demands and expectations students will face after they graduate. These high standards attract students with a drive to accomplish goals and initiate new ideas, as seen by the large amount of businesses that start up from the University of Utah's alumni. Along with high academic performance, students that come to the U find a cooperative and friendly environment where students can have fun and learn together. With a beautiful outdoor environment, students have opportunities to participate in a wide variety of recreational activities. Whether in healthcare, science, humanities, social sciences or art, students are encouraged to share insights and work as a team. Students are working hard, and in a team, to meet the high standards of each program offered. The U encourages students to be innovative and achieve their goals through its faculty member's outstanding support, encouragement and instruction. The University of Utah gives students opportunities and lasting experiences in research, reason and recreation."

Campus Setting

The University of Utah, founded in 1850, is a public institution. Its 1,534-acre campus is located in Salt Lake City. A four-year institution, University of Utah has an enrollment of 32,077 students. The campus facilities include: library · theatre · dance center · fine arts and natural history museum · arboretum · cancer research center · research park · hospital · neuropsychiatric institute. University of Utah provides on-campus housing with 2,180 units that can accommodate 4,865 students. Housing options: coed dorms · sorority housing · fraternity housing · single-student apartments · married-student apartments · special housing for disabled students. Recreation and sports facilities include: courts · fields · gymnasium · recreation centers.

Student Life and Activities

Eighty-seven percent of students live off campus. According to the school, there is a diverse student body and thus there are many different cultural and ethnic events on campus for students. These include an independent film series, cultural awareness week, dance concerts and plays. In addition there are over 150 student clubs and organizations that students can join specific to their interests. Popular gathering places are the Port-O-Call Social Club, Bar-X, Lumpy's Social Club, the Bayou, The Park Cafe and The Pie. Tailgate Party at the Homecoming Game, Crimson Nights, Oktoberfest, Family Day, Friday Night Live, Union Film Festival, Union Art Gallery and the Union Bowling League Tournament are popular events on campus. University of Utah has 500 official student organizations. Greeks, the football team and the bar scene are heavy influences on student social life. Sports options include: basketball · billiards · bowling · dodgeball · flag football · golf · racquetball · sand volleyball · soccer · softball · table tennis · target shooting · tennis · Ultimate Frisbee. University of Utah is a member of the PAC-12.

Academics and Learning Environment

University of Utah has 1,387 full-time and 529 part-time faculty members, offering a student-to-faculty ratio of 13:1. The most common course size is 10 to 19 students. University of Utah offers 304 majors with the most popular being business adminis-

UNIVERSITY OF UTAH

University of Utah
Salt Lake City (Pop. 189,314)
Location: Medium city
Four-year public
Founded: 1850
Website: http://www.utah.edu

Students
Total enrollment: 32,077
Undergrads: 24,492
Freshmen: 3,853
Part-time students: 29%
From out-of-state: 26%
From public schools: 91%
Male/Female: 55%/45%
Live on-campus: 13%
In fraternities: 3%
In sororities: 4%
Off-campus employment rating: Excellent
Caucasian: 70%
African American: 1%
Hispanic: 9%
Asian: 5%
Hawaiian or Pacific Islander: 1%
Native American: 1%
Mixed (2+ ethnicities): 3%
International: 7%

Academics
Calendar: Semester
Student/faculty ratio: 13:1
Class size 9 or fewer: 11%
Class size 10-29: 46%
Class size 30-49: 20%
Class size 50-99: 15%
Class size 100 or more: 7%
Returning freshmen: 88%
Six-year graduation rate: 60%

Most Popular Majors
Business administration
Exercise/sport science
Biology

tration, exercise/sport science and biology and least popular being German, classics and university studies social/behavior science. The school has a general core requirement. Cooperative education is available. All first-year students must maintain a 2.0 GPA or higher to avoid academic probation. Special academic programs that might appeal to a B student are these: self-designed majors · pass/fail grading option · independent study · double majors · dual degrees · accelerated study · honors program · Phi Beta Kappa · internships · distance learning certificate programs.

B Student Support and Success

Students at the University of Utah can turn to PASS, or Programs for Academic Support, for help in subject areas. Through PASS, students receive free peer tutoring in physics, chemistry, science, some foreign languages and math. Sessions can be either one on one or in a group. Online tutoring has recently been expanded as well. A Self-Help Learning Lab features audio and videotapes, books and computer software for development of study skills. Assistance is available in reading, algebra, calculus, trigonometry, statistics, differential equations, chemistry, foreign language and more. Academic advising covers topics such as study skills and time management, effective listening and note taking, improving reading comprehension, test taking, test anxiety and learning style. Supplemental instruction is provided for the historically difficult entry-level classes.

University of Utah is proud to offer dedicated guidance for: academic · career · personal · psychological · minority students · military · veterans · non-traditional students · family planning. The average freshman year GPA is 3.1, and 88 percent of freshmen students return for their sophomore year. What about post-college? Many students dedicate themselves to the workforce. Approximately 18 percent of them pursue a graduate degree immediately after graduation. Once one year has passed since their graduation, 26 percent of graduates have entered graduate school, according to school reports. These are a handful of companies that most frequently hire these graduates: Deloitte · Ernst & Young · L-3 Communications · KPMG · Wells Fargo Financial · IBM.

Support for Students with Learning Disabilities

Those students with learning disabilities will be pleased to learn of these specific support programs. There are times when the college will grant additional time to students with learning disabilities to complete their degree. Another option available to LD students is a lightened course load. High school foreign language waivers are accepted. The following list should prove extremely helpful to LD students: tutors · testing accommodations · extended time for tests · take-home exam · oral tests · exam on tape or computer · readers · typist/scribe · note-taking services · reading machines · tape recorders · early syllabus · priority registration · waiver of math degree requirement. Individual or small group tutorials are also available in: time management · organizational skills · learning strategies · specific subject areas · writing labs · math labs · study skills. An advisor/advocate from the Center for Disability Services is available to students. This member also sits on the admissions committee.

How to Get Admitted

For admissions decisions, non-academic factors considered: interview · extracurricular activities · special talents, interests and abilities · character/personal qualities · state of residency · minority affiliation. A high school diploma is required, although a GED is also accepted for admissions consideration. SAT or ACT test scores are required of all applicants. SAT Subject Test scores are considered, if submitted, but are not required. *Academic units recommended:* 4 English, 2 Math, 3 Science, 2 Foreign Language.

How to Pay for College

To apply for financial aid, students should submit the following: Free Application for Federal Student Aid (FAFSA) · institution's own financial aid forms. University of Utah participates in the Federal Work Study program. *Need-based aid programs include:* scholarships and grants · general need-based awards · Federal Pell grants · state scholarships and grants · college-based scholarships and grants · private scholarships and grants · Federal Nursing scholarships · ACG · National SMART grant · TEACH grant. *Non-need-based aid programs include:* scholarships and grants · general need-based awards · state scholarships and grants · creative arts and performance awards · athletic scholarships · ROTC scholarships.

UNIVERSITY OF UTAH

Highlights

Admissions
Applicants: 11,354
Accepted: 9,281
Acceptance rate: 81.7%
Average GPA: 3.6
ACT range: 21-27
SAT Math range: 500-648
SAT Reading range: 483-620
SAT Writing range: 6-25
Top 10% of class: 21%
Top 25% of class: 48%
Top 50% of class: 83%

Deadlines
Early Action: No
Early Decision: No
Regular Action: Rolling admissions
Common Application: Not accepted

Financial Aid
In-state tuition: $6,929
Out-of-state tuition: $24,261
Room: $3,601
Board: $1,508
Books: $1,280
Freshmen receiving need-based aid: 44%
Undergrads rec. need-based aid: 46%
Avg. % of need met by financial aid: 59%
Avg. aid package (freshmen): $16,262
Avg. aid package (undergrads): $16,604
Avg. debt upon graduation: $36

Prominent Alumni
Willard Marriott, CEO, Marriott International; Ed Catmull, co-founder, PIXAR, president, Disney Feature Animation; John E. Warnock, co-founder/board chairman, Adobe Systems Inc.

School Spirit
Mascot: Swoop (red-tailed hawk)
Colors: Crimson and white
Song: *Utah Man*

535

College Profiles

UNIVERSITY OF VERMONT

South Prospect Street, Burlington, VT 05405-0160
Admissions: 802-656-3370 · Financial Aid: 802-656-5700
Email: admissions@uvm.edu · Website: http://www.uvm.edu

From the College

"Students at the University of Vermont benefit from a setting that combines the resources of a major research university with the intimate feeling of a liberal arts college. Renowned professors, rather than graduate assistants, are students' teachers and advisors, and many students assist their professors with their research projects. The nation's premier environmental university, UVM is located in Burlington, a small city regularly hailed as a top college town, surrounded by the mountains and lakes of the Vermont countryside. The university is noted for its academic programs and faculty, newly established Honors College, hands-on teaching, engaged student body and its quality of life."

Campus Setting

The University of Vermont, founded in 1791, is a public, comprehensive institution. Undergraduate programs are offered through the Colleges of Agriculture and Life Sciences, Arts and Sciences, Education and Social Services, Engineering & Mathematical Sciences and Nursing & Health Sciences, the School of Business Administration, and the Rubenstein School of Environment & Natural Resources. Outstanding undergraduates are invited to concurrent enrollment in the Honors College. The university also offers masters and doctoral programs through the Graduate College and the Doctor of Medicine through the College of Medicine. A four-year public institution, UVM has an enrollment of 12,723 students. Although not originally a co-educational college, UVM has been co-ed since 1871. The campus facilities include: library · art galleries · museums · center for cultural pluralism · research vessel · agricultural and environmental testing laboratory · agricultural experiment station · biomedical research complex · dairy farm and herd · entomology research laboratory · greenhouses · institute for ecological economics · horse-riding arena · horticultural research center. UVM provides on-campus housing of 3,204 units that can accommodate 6,141 students. Housing options: coed dorms · sorority housing · fraternity housing · single-student apartments · married-student apartments. Recreation and sports facilities include: gymnasium · fitness center · ice arena · basketball courts · handball/racquetball courts · natatorium · track · tennis courts · athletic fields (soccer · lacrosse · football · rugby · baseball/softball · field hockey).

Student Life and Activities

Half of students live on campus. UVM students are active - nearly 80 percent are involved in one or more academic, arts, athletic, environmental, media, cultural, political or service organizations. All first and second year students live on campus with many choosing special interest housing ranging from careers in medicine to live music to language and culture houses. While individuals tend to be passionate about their particular interests, the campus as a whole is noted for being exceptionally open and friendly. Many students arrive and nearly all leave with heightened appreciation and active concern for the natural environment. Popular gathering spots on campus include The Davis Center (atrium, fireplace lounges, game room, green roof and food court), 'Bailey Beach' (main library steps), the University Green, central campus amphitheater, Gucciardi fitness center and the Williams Hall fire escape for sunset views. Popular gathering spots off campus include Church Street Marketplace, Higher Ground (live music venue), local ski areas, North Beach and Waterfront Park.

Popular campus events include Fall Activities Fest, Homecoming and Family Weekend, the Hunger Banquet, Week of Welcome, Martin Luther King Celebration, Random Acts of Kindness Day (aka free hot dog day), Springfest, Community Works, hockey and basketball games, speakers and concerts. University of Vermont has 150 official student organizations. Groups that have a strong presence on campus include the Outing Club, Volunteers In Action (VIA), Vermont Student Environmental Program (VSTEP), Ski & Snowboard Club, fraternities and sororities, intramural leagues and club sports, Alternative Breaks (service trips), the Vermont Cynic (student newspaper), Free2Be and Feel Good (world hunger relief). For sports, there are intramural options: basketball · bowling · broomball · flag football · homerun derby · horseshoes · ice hockey · inner-tube water polo · racquetball · soccer · softball · tennis · volleyball · Wiffle ball. University of Vermont is a member of the American East Conference (Division I), Hockey East Association (Division I) and Eastern Intercollegiate Ski Association.

Academics and Learning Environment

University of Vermont has 602 full-time and 153 part-time faculty members, offering a student-to-faculty ratio of 17:1. The most common course size is 10 to 19 students. University of Vermont offers 168 majors with the most popular being business administration, psychology and English. The school does not have a general core requirement. Cooperative education is available. A minimum overall GPA of 2.0 is required to graduate. The B student may be interested in the following special academic programs: self-designed majors · pass/fail grading option · independent study · double majors · honors program · Phi Beta Kappa · internships · distance learning certificate programs.

B Student Support and Success

UVM has the Learning Cooperative, a place "where students help students learn." It offers individual tutoring, group study sessions and writing and learning skills conferences. The Learning Skills program is there to help students develop learning skills and study habits that lead to a successful college career. They do this through free tutoring and workshops. Along with individualized tutoring, the cooperative offers a number of group study sessions for the college's most traditionally difficult courses. A Writing Center helps with any class papers.

University of Vermont provides dedicated guidance for: academic · career · personal · psychological · minority students · military · veterans · non-traditional students · family planning · religious. Recognizing that some students may need extra preparation, University of Vermont offers remedial and refresher courses in: reading · writing · math · study skills. The average freshman year GPA is 3.0, and 86 percent of freshmen students return for their sophomore year. Among students who enter the workforce, approximately 60 percent choose to enter a field related to their major within six months of their graduation. This is a list of companies that most frequently hire graduates: Fletcher Allen Health Care · UVM · State of Vermont · Daymon Worldwide · AmeriCorps/VISTA · Mayo Clinic · Seventh Generation · State Street Bank · Dartmouth-Hitchcock Medical Center · Liberty Mutual · IBM ·

UNIVERSITY OF VERMONT

Highlights

University of Vermont
Burlington, VT (Pop. 42,282)
Location: Large town
Four-year public
Founded: 1791
Website: http://www.uvm.edu

Students
Total enrollment: 12,723
Undergrads: 10,912
Freshmen: 2,754
Part-time students: 11%
From out-of-state: 76%
From public schools: 70%
Male/Female: 44%/56%
Live on-campus: 50%
In fraternities: 6%
In sororities: 6%
Off-campus employment rating: Good
Caucasian: 83%
African American: 1%
Hispanic: 4%
Asian: 2%
Hawaiian or Pacific Islander: <1%
Native American: <1%
Mixed (2+ ethnicities): 3%
International: 2%

Academics
Calendar: Semester
Student/faculty ratio: 17:1
Class size 9 or fewer: 20%
Class size 10-29: 50%
Class size 30-49: 16%
Class size 50-99: 9%
Class size 100 or more: 5%
Returning freshmen: 86%
Six-year graduation rate: 76%

Most Popular Majors
Business administration
Psychology
English

537

College Profiles

UNIVERSITY OF VERMONT

Admissions
Applicants: 22,382
Accepted: 17,357
Acceptance rate: 77.5%
Placed on wait list: 2,288
Enrolled from wait list: 97
Average GPA: 3.5
ACT range: 24-29
SAT Math range: 540-650
SAT Reading range: 540-640
SAT Writing range: 9-39
Top 10% of class: 33%
Top 25% of class: 68%
Top 50% of class: 96%

Deadlines
Early Action: 11/1
Early Decision: No
Regular Action: 1/15 (final)
Notification of admission by: 3/31
Common Application: Accepted

Financial Aid
In-state tuition: $14,184
Out-of-state tuition: $35,832
Room: $6,844
Board: $3,558
Books: $1,200
Freshmen receiving need-based aid: 59%
Undergrads rec. need-based aid: 59%
Avg. % of need met by financial aid: 64%
Avg. aid package (freshmen): $21,812
Avg. aid package (undergrads): $21,296
Avg. debt upon graduation: $27,276

Prominent Alumni
Jody Williams, 1997 Nobel Peace Laureate for heading the International Campaign to Ban Land Mines; Jon Kilik, film producer, 'Malcolm X' and 'The Hunger Games'; John Dewey, educational philosopher.

School Spirit
Mascot: Rally Catamount
Colors: Green and gold
Song: *Champlain*

Mass General Hospital · Howard Center · Covidien · FairPoint Communications · Green Mountain Coffee Roasters · JP Morgan Chase · Burlington School District.

Support for Students with Learning Disabilities

There are a series of specific support programs available at the University of Vermont, which students with learning disabilities might be interested in. In order to complete their degree, the college may grant an LD student additional time. A second option for students with learning disabilities would be a lightened course load. High school foreign language waivers are accepted. LD students of the University of Vermont will find the following programs at University of Vermont useful: special classes · tutors · learning center · testing accommodations · extended time for tests · take-home exam · oral tests · substitution of courses · readers · note-taking services · reading machines · tape recorders · texts on tape · early syllabus · priority registration · priority seating · waiver of math degree requirement. Individual or small group tutorials are also available in: time management · organizational skills · learning strategies · specific subject areas · writing labs · math labs · study skills. An advisor/advocate from the ACCESS Academic Support Services is available to students.

How to Get Admitted

For admissions decisions, non-academic factors considered: extracurricular activities · special talents, interests and abilities · character/personal qualities · volunteer work · work experience · geographical location · minority affiliation · alumni relationship. A high school diploma is required, although a GED is also accepted for admissions consideration. SAT or ACT test scores are required of all applicants. SAT Subject Test scores are considered, if submitted, but are not required. *Academic units recommended:* 4 English, 4 Math, 3 Science, 3 Social Studies, 2 Foreign Language.

How to Pay for College

To apply for financial aid, students should submit the following: Free Application for Federal Student Aid (FAFSA). University of Vermont participates in the Federal Work Study program. *Need-based aid programs include:* scholarships and grants · general need-based awards · Federal Pell grants · state scholarships and grants · college-based scholarships and grants · private scholarships and grants · Federal Nursing scholarships. *Non-need-based aid programs include:* scholarships and grants · state scholarships and grants · creative arts and performance awards · special achievements and activities awards · special characteristics awards · athletic scholarships · ROTC scholarships.

UNIVERSITY OF WYOMING

1000 East University Avenue, Laramie, WY 82071
Admissions: 800-342-5996 · Financial Aid: 307-766-2116
Email: admissions@uwyo.edu · Website: http://www.uwyo.edu

From the College

"The University of Wyoming is the state's only public, four-year university which provides baccalaureate and graduate education, research and outreach services. UW combines major-university benefits and small-school advantages, with more than 180 programs of study set against the idyllic backdrop of southeastern Wyoming's rugged mountains and high plains. The main campus is located in Laramie, approximately two hours north of Denver. The university also maintains the UW/Casper College Center, nine outreach education centers across Wyoming and Cooperative Extension Service centers in each of the state's 23 counties and on the Wind River Indian Reservation."

Campus Setting

University of Wyoming, founded in 1886, is a public, multipurpose institution. Programs are offered through the Colleges of Agriculture, Arts and Sciences, Education, Engineering, Law, Health Sciences and Business. Its 780-acre campus is located in Laramie, in southeastern Wyoming, 50 miles west of Cheyenne, and 155 miles north of Denver, Colorado. A four-year institution, University of Wyoming has an enrollment of 12,778 students. The campus facilities include: library · art, geological, anthropology and insect museums · on site elementary school · Rocky Mountain and Solheim Herbarium · Spatial Data and Visualization Center · Williams Botany Conservatory · Learning Resource Center · National Park research center · Planetarium · State Veterinary Laboratory · Materials Characterization Lab · Cooperative Research Unit · Infrared Telescope · Star, Red Bullet and Elk Mountain Observatories · Survey Analysis Center · Institute of Environment & Natural Resources · Fishery and Wildlife Research Unit · American Heritage Center · Microscopy Facility. University of Wyoming provides on-campus housing, which comprises of 1,893 units. These units can accommodate 2,620 students. Housing options: coed dorms · sorority housing · fraternity housing · single-student apartments · married-student apartments · special housing for disabled students. Recreation and sports facilities include: athletic center · tennis courts · soccer fields · field house training rooms · gymnasium · pool · track · dance and weight rooms.

Student Life and Activities

Seventy-seven percent of students live off campus. Wyoming Union, Library Book & Bean, Coal Creek Coffee, Turtle Rock Cafe, Classroom Lounge and Prexys Pasture are popular gathering spots. Popular events include Friday Night Fever, theatre and dance performances, cultural programs, sports events, art exhibitions and the Border War. University of Wyoming has 241 official student organizations. Greeks, athletes and the student senate have a strong presence in student life. As for athletics, there are intramural teams: slam dunk contest · Hot Shot Competition · table tennis · basketball · tube water polo · wallyball · racquetball · billiards · track meet · wrestling · wiffleball · 4 on 4 volleyball · NCAA men's basketball pool · badminton · swim meet · indoor soccer · dodge ball · tennis · Home Run Derby · softball · intramural t-shirt design · golf scramble · bouldering · flag football · fantasy football league · outdoor soccer · golf tournament · paintball · ultimate frisbee · punt-pass and kick · miniature golf · home run contest · disc golf · floor hockey · 5K Fun Run · 3 on 3 basketball · bench press competition · free throw contest · bowling · sports trivia · volleyball. University of Wyoming is a member of the Mountain West Conference (Football FBS).

UNIVERSITY OF WYOMING

University of Wyoming
Laramie, WY (Pop. 31,681)
Location: Large town
Four-year public
Founded: 1886
Website: http://www.uwyo.edu

Students
Total enrollment: 12,778
Undergrads: 10,117
Part-time students: 18%
From out-of-state: 48%
Male/Female: 47%/53%
Live on-campus: 23%
In fraternities: 5%
In sororities: 5%
Off-campus employment rating: Good
Caucasian: 81%
African American: 1%
Hispanic: 6%
Asian: 1%
Hawaiian or Pacific Islander: <1%
Native American: 1%
Mixed (2+ ethnicities): 2%
International: 4%

Academics
Calendar: Semester
Student/faculty ratio: 14:1
Class size 9 or fewer: 14%
Class size 10-29: 56%
Class size 30-49: 20%
Class size 50-99: 6%
Class size 100 or more: 4%
Returning freshmen: 74%
Six-year graduation rate: 54%

Most Popular Majors
Nursing
Elementary education
Psychology

Academics and Learning Environment

University of Wyoming has 757 full-time and 81 part-time faculty members, offering a student-to-faculty ratio of 14:1. The most common course size is 10 to 19 students. University of Wyoming offers 179 majors with the most popular being nursing, elementary education and psychology. The school has a general core requirement. Cooperative education is not offered. All first-year students must maintain a 2.0 GPA or higher to avoid academic probation. These are some other special academic programs that would appeal to a B student include: self-designed majors · pass/fail grading option · independent study · double majors · dual degrees · accelerated study · honors program · Phi Beta Kappa · internships · distance learning certificate programs.

B Student Support and Success

Academic Services provides support for undergraduates through tutoring and study skills development. It includes a series of study skills workshops and individual advising. Student Success Services is a program designed for students who meet one of these three criteria: 1) first-generation college student, 2) low-income family or 3) documented disability, learning or physical. This support system offers individual and group tutoring, study skills workshops, individualized math assistance, career exploration and more to eligible students.

University of Wyoming provides a variety of support programs, among them dedicated guidance for: academic · career · personal · psychological · minority students · military · veterans · non-traditional students · family planning. The average freshman year GPA is 2.8, and 74 percent of freshmen students return for their sophomore year. Directly following college, many students enter the workforce. Approximately 19 percent pursue a graduate degree immediately after graduation. Among students who enter the workforce, approximately 55 percent enter a field related to their major within six months of their graduation. These are companies that most frequently hire graduates from University of Wyoming: Alaska Public Schools · Albany County Public Schools · American National Bank · AmeriCorps · Anadarko Petroleum Corporation · Baker Hughes · Banner Health Fairbanks · Bettis Labs · Bureau of Land Management · Burlington Northern · Casper Star Tribune · Centennial Mental Health Center Inc. · Chevron · CitiFinancial · Coffey Engineering & Surveying LLC · Conoco Phillips · CVS Pharmacy · Department of Defense · EchoStar · EMIT Water Discharge Tech. · EnCana Oil & Gas (USA) Inc. · Enterprise Rent-A-Car · Family First · First National Bank · Grooms and Harkins · Halliburton · Handel Information Tech. Inc. · HKM Engineering Inc. · Home Depot · Inberg-Miller Engineers · I.R.S / Criminal Investigation · I Tech · JELD-WEN · JR Engineering · J.R. Simplot Company · Kiewit · Liberty Mutual Insurance Co. · Lowes · Mayo Clinic Micron · Myriad Genetics Inc. · NAVAIR · Nebraska Public Power District · New Vision Charter · OCI · OppenheimerFunds Inc. · PacifiCorp · Peak Wellness · PCA Engineering Inc. · Pioneer Counseling Services · Puget Sound Naval Shipyard & IMF · Pure Energy · Questar Gas Company · Qwest Communications · Raytheon Company · Schlumberger · Shelton & Associates · Sun Health Corporation · State of Wyoming · Tait & Associates Inc. · Target ·

Trihydro Corporation · U.S. Military Branches · U.S. Peace Corps · Union Pacific Railroad · Union Telephone Company · Universal Forest Products Inc. · USDA · VA Medical Center · Walgreens · Wallace Engineering · Wells Fargo Financial · Williams Companies Inc. · WLC Eng. · Surveying & Planning · Wolseley's North American Division · WWC Engineering · Wyoming Department of Agriculture · Wyoming Department of Energy · Wyoming Dept. of Transportation.

Support for Students with Learning Disabilities

Students with learning disabilities should be made aware of some specific support programs offered by University of Wyoming. If deemed necessary, the college will grant additional time to students with learning disabilities in order to complete their degree. A lightened course load may also be granted to LD students. According to the school, Admissions does not inquire about disabling conditions in their application process; therefore no data is kept to respond to those items. UDSS does not track the number of applicants to the program, nor the numbers determined to be ineligible. Students with learning disabilities will want to investigate the following programs at University of Wyoming: tutors · learning center · testing accommodations · extended time for tests · take-home exam · oral tests · exam on tape or computer · readers · typist/scribe · note-taking services · reading machines · tape recorders · texts on tape · early syllabus · waiver of math degree requirement. Individual or small group tutorials are also available in: time management · organizational skills · learning strategies · specific subject areas · writing labs · math labs · study skills. An advisor/advocate from the University Disability Support Services is available to students.

How to Get Admitted

For admissions decisions, non-academic factors considered: state of residency. A high school diploma is required, although a GED is also accepted for admissions consideration. SAT or ACT test scores are required of all applicants. SAT Subject Test scores are not required. *According to the admissions office:* Minimum 3.0 GPA with minimum composite ACT score of 21 (combined SAT Reasoning score of 980) and completion of the success curriculum while attending secondary school. *Academic units recommended:* 4 English, 4 Math, 4 Science, 3 Social Studies, 2 Foreign Language.

How to Pay for College

To apply for financial aid, students should submit the following: Free Application for Federal Student Aid (FAFSA). University of Wyoming participates in the Federal Work Study program. *Need-based aid programs include:* scholarships and grants · general need-based awards · Federal Pell grants · state scholarships and grants · college-based scholarships and grants · private scholarships and grants. *Non-need-based aid programs include:* scholarships and grants · general need-based awards · state scholarships and grants · creative arts and performance awards · special achievements and activities awards · special characteristics awards · athletic scholarships · ROTC scholarships.

UNIVERSITY OF WYOMING

Highlights

Admissions
Applicants: 4,348
Accepted: 4,154
Acceptance rate: 95.5%
Average GPA: 3.5
ACT range: 22-27
SAT Math range: 510-620
SAT Reading range: 480-620
SAT Writing range: Not reported
Top 10% of class: 23%
Top 25% of class: 50%
Top 50% of class: 82%

Deadlines
Early Action: No
Early Decision: No
Regular Action: Rolling admissions
Common Application: Not accepted

Financial Aid
In-state tuition: $3,390
Out-of-state tuition: $13,620
Room: $4,160
Board: $5,595
Books: $1,200
Freshmen receiving need-based aid: 49%
Undergrads rec. need-based aid: 47%
Avg. % of need met by financial aid: 60%
Avg. aid package (freshmen): $9,334
Avg. aid package (undergrads): $9,119
Avg. debt upon graduation: $22,879

Prominent Alumni
Dick Cheney, former Vice President of the United States; Alan K. Simpson, former U.S. Senator; Ardis J. Meier, chief pharmacy consultant to USAF Surgeon.

School Spirit
Mascot: Cowboy Joe
Colors: Brown and gold
Song: *Ragtime Cowboy Joe*

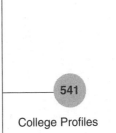

541

College Profiles

VALPARAISO UNIVERSITY

Kretzmann Hall, 1700 Chapel Drive, Valparaiso, IN 46383
Admissions: 888-468-2576 · Financial Aid: 888-468-2576
Email: undergrad.admission@valpo.edu · Website: http://www.valpo.edu

From the College

"All American colleges and universities bear a family resemblance to one another as they come from a common set of ancestors in Europe and colonial America. Within that larger family, Valparaiso University is neither a large research university nor a small liberal arts college. At the same time that it promotes a basic liberal arts curriculum, it features strong undergraduate colleges of Engineering, Nursing and Business Administration, a professional direction lacking in the conventional liberal arts college. Conversely, the university is not a cluster of professional colleges which merely pays lip service to the liberal arts. Education in the liberal arts is the foundation of every academic program, and the College of Arts and Sciences, the largest unit in the university, carries on many vital programs of its own. This combination of liberal and professional studies of such variety within an institution of modest size is rare in American higher education. Broad enough in curriculum and in variety of programs to be a university, still Valparaiso University emphasizes undergraduate teaching in the manner of the traditional small college, with many small classes and strong individual guidance. While the university focuses on undergraduate education, it maintains a modest graduate program as well as a law school. Valparaiso University is also a founding member of the Associated New American Colleges, a national consortium of small to mid-sized colleges and universities that are committed to the ideal of integrating liberal and professional studies. Valparaiso University's status as an independent Lutheran University supplies the rationale for this special combination of liberal and professional studies. No church body has control or authority over the university, which is owned and operated by the Lutheran University Association. Valparaiso is therefore both free and responsible to realize an educational ideal informed by the best traditions of Lutheran Christianity and of liberal and professional studies."

Campus Setting

Valparaiso University belongs to a small group of institutions of higher education that is characterized by the integration of liberal arts and professional studies. Students pursue majors in more than 70 fields of study in five colleges—Arts and Sciences, Business Administration, Engineering, Nursing and Christ College and the Honors College. Also part of the university are a Division of Graduate Studies and Continuing Education and the School of Law. Founded in 1859, Valparaiso University is located on 320 acres in northwest Indiana near the city of Chicago and the Indiana Dunes National Lakeshore on Lake Michigan. A four-year private institution, Valparaiso University has an enrollment of 4,508 students. The school is also affiliated with the Lutheran Church. Besides a library, the university also provides its students with the following facilities: art museum · center for the arts · chapel · audiovisual and language labs · virtual nursing learning center · Doppler radar facility · weather center · planetarium · observatory · scientific visualization lab · athletics recreation center. Valparaiso University provides on-campus housing with 1,050 units that can accommodate 2,026 students. Here are some housing options: coed dorms · women's dorms · fraternity housing · single-student apartments. Recreation and sports facilities include: basketball, racquetball, handball and tennis courts · baseball and softball fields · track · swimming pool · weight room · fitness center · golf course · bowling alley.

Student Life and Activities

Sixty-eight percent of students live on campus. Popular gathering spots include Harre

Student Union, Grinders Cyber Café and Athletics and Recreation Center. Popular campus events include Martin Luther King Jr. Day, Christ College Freshman Production, Homecoming Weekend, Siblings Weekend, JazzFest, Songfest, Battle of the Bands, International Dinners, Christ College Debates and Advent Vespers. Valparaiso University has 94 official student organizations. The most popular are: Acabellas · Alliance · American Chorale Directors Association · art club · Association for Women in Communications · German club · Spanish club · Lilly Scholars Network · Music Educators National Conference · Music Enterprise Student Association · Student Officials Association · VUCRU · VUDU Comedy · WVUR - Source 95 Radio · Pi Delta Chi-Deaconess club · Sigma Alpha Iota · Shakespeare Academy · ballroom · American Society of Civil Engineers · American Society of Mechanical Engineers · Institute of Electronic and Electrical Engineers · Engineers without Borders · National Weather Association · pre-medical arts club · public relations Student Society of America · Society of Automotive Engineers · Society of Physics Students · Society of Women Engineers · Storm Intercept Team · Independent Robotics Team · Delta Epsilon Chi - Business · Delta Sigma Pi - Business · fencing club · Intramural Advisory Council · Valparaiso Karate club · Ultimate Frisbee club · tennis club · Alliance · Alpha Phi Omega · Amnesty International · BACCHUS/GAMMA · Best Buddies · College Against Cancer · College Mentors for Kids · College Republicans · Council for Exceptional Children · Earthtones · Green Peas · Global Leaders Community · Habitat for Humanity · Honor Council · Meditation Group · Operation Smile · Political Action League · Pre-Law Society · Safe and Empowerment Board · Senior Planning Council · Student Alumni Association · Student Nurses Association · Student Senate · Students in Free Enterprise · Union Board · University Television · Mock Trial Team · outdoor club · biology club · chemistry club. For athletics, there are intramural teams such as: badminton · basketball, billiards · bowling · cheerleading · dodgeball · flag football · floor hockey · foosball · golf · kickball · racquetball · soccer · softball · swimming · table tennis · tennis · Ultimate Frisbee · volleyball · water basketball · wallyball. Valparaiso University is a member of the Horizon League (Division I) and Pioneer Football League (Division I, Football I-AA).

Academics and Learning Environment

Valparaiso University has 274 full-time and 127 part-time faculty members, offering a student-to-faculty ratio of 14:1. The most common course size is 10 to 19 students. Valparaiso University offers 107 majors with the most popular being nursing, English and biology and least popular being American studies, professional writing and international service. The school has a general core requirement as well as a religion requirement. Cooperative education is available. All first-year students must maintain a 2.0 GPA or higher to avoid academic probation. As for some other special academic programs that would appeal to a B student, there are: self-designed majors · pass/fail grading option · independent study · double majors · dual degrees · accelerated study · honors program · Phi Beta Kappa · internships · distance learning certificate programs.

B Student Support and Success

Valpo's Academic Success Center has a wide selection of helpful programs including tutoring, help sessions, study group sessions,

VALPARAISO UNIVERSITY

Valparaiso University
Valparaiso, IN (Pop. 32,014)
Location: Large town
Four-year private
Founded: 1859
Website: http://www.valpo.edu

Students
Total enrollment: 4,508
Undergrads: 3,251
Freshmen: 916
Part-time students: 4%
From out-of-state: 63%
Male/Female: 48%/52%
Live on-campus: 68%
In fraternities: 21%
In sororities: 19%
Off-campus employment rating: Good
Caucasian: 74%
African American: 5%
Hispanic: 7%
Asian: 2%
Hawaiian or Pacific Islander: <1%
Native American: <1%
Mixed (2+ ethnicities): 2%
International: 9%

Academics
Calendar: Semester
Student/faculty ratio: 14:1
Class size 9 or fewer: 13%
Class size 10-29: 66%
Class size 30-49: 17%
Class size 50-99: 3%
Class size 100 or more: 1%
Returning freshmen: 86%
Six-year graduation rate: 70%

Most Popular Majors
Nursing
English
Biology

543

College Profiles

VALPARAISO UNIVERSITY

Admissions
Applicants: 6,124
Accepted: 4,880
Acceptance rate: 79.7%
Average GPA: 3.7
ACT range: 23-29
SAT Math range: 510-620
SAT Reading range: 500-590
SAT Writing range: 2-20
Top 10% of class: 36%
Top 25% of class: 68%
Top 50% of class: 93%

Deadlines
Early Action: No
Early Decision: No
Regular Action: Rolling admissions
Common Application: Accepted

Financial Aid
In-state tuition: $33,680
Out-of-state tuition: $33,680
Room: $6,200
Board: $3,380
Books: $1,200
Freshmen receiving need-based aid: 77%
Undergrads rec. need-based aid: 74%
Avg. % of need met by financial aid: 75%
Avg. aid package (freshmen): $26,773
Avg. aid package (undergrads): $26,295
Avg. debt upon graduation: $31,891

Prominent Alumni
Rebecca Pallmeyer, District Judge, U.S. District Court, Chicago; Paul Sieving, Director, National Eye Institute; Cornell Boggs III, Senior Vice President, General Counsel and Corporate Secretary, Dow Corning.

School Spirit
Mascot: Crusaders
Colors: Brown and gold

academic advisement, learning assistance, learning enrichment workshops, career planning, student support groups and disability support services. The Peer Tutoring Program helps students one on one. The tutors have completed the courses for which they provide tutoring and receive recommendations from their professors.

Valparaiso University offers a variety of support programs, including dedicated guidance for: academic · career · personal · psychological · minority students · military · non-traditional students · religious. The average freshman year GPA is 3.1, and 86 percent of freshmen students return for their sophomore year. Here is a list of companies that most frequently hire graduates: Caterpillar · Enterprise · Mayo Clinic · Porter Hospital · Centier Bank · Harris Bank · Crowe Horwath · Peace Corps · Stryker · Gentex · ITT · Aldi · Walgreen's · CSI Technologies · Methodist Hospitals.

Support for Students with Learning Disabilities

Students with learning disabilities, sometimes referred to as LD students, may take advantage of specific support programs offered by Valparaiso University. According to the school, LD students should submit documentation to the DSS office following admission into the university. The following is a list of programs that LD students will find helpful: tutors · testing accommodations · extended time for tests · take-home exam · oral tests · readers · typist/scribe · note-taking services · tape recorders · texts on tape · early syllabus · priority registration · priority seating · waiver of math degree requirement. Individual or small group tutorials are also available in: time management · organizational skills · learning strategies · specific subject areas · writing labs · math labs · study skills. An advisor/advocate from the Valparaiso University Disability Support Services is available to students.

How to Get Admitted

For admissions decisions, non-academic factors considered: interview · extracurricular activities · special talents, interests and abilities · character/personal qualities · volunteer work · state of residency · religious affiliation/commitment · minority affiliation · alumni relationship. A high school diploma is required, although a GED is also accepted for admissions consideration. SAT or ACT test scores are required of all applicants. SAT Subject Test scores are not required. *Academic units recommended:* 4 English, 4 Math, 3 Science, 1 Social Studies, 2 Foreign Language.

How to Pay for College

To apply for financial aid, students should submit the following: Free Application for Federal Student Aid (FAFSA). Valparaiso University participates in the Federal Work Study program. *Need-based aid programs include:* scholarships and grants · general need-based awards · Federal Pell grants · state scholarships and grants · college-based scholarships and grants · private scholarships and grants. *Non-need-based aid programs include:* scholarships and grants · state scholarships and grants · creative arts and performance awards · special achievements and activities awards · special characteristics awards · athletic scholarships · ROTC scholarships.

VIRGINIA COMMONWEALTH UNIVERSITY

P.O. Box 842527, Richmond, VA 23284
Admissions: 800-841-3638 · Financial Aid: 804-828-6669
Email: ugrad@vcu.edu · Website: http://www.vcu.edu

From the College

"Virginia Commonwealth University is a public research university located in Richmond, the state capital of Virginia. VCU was founded in 1838 as the medical department of Hampden-Sydney College, becoming the Medical College of Virginia in 1854. In 1968, the General Assembly merged MCV with the Richmond Professional Institute, founded in 1917, to create Virginia Commonwealth University. Today, VCU enrolls more than 31,000 students in 222 degree and certificate programs and encompasses one of the largest academic health centers in the nation.

"VCU received $248 million in externally funded sponsored awards in fiscal year 2013 and has 33 graduate programs. VCU is designated as a research university with very high research activity by the Carnegie Foundation. A broad array of university-approved centers and institutes of excellence involving faculty from multiple disciplines in public policy, biotechnology and health care discoveries supports the university's research mission. VCU and the VCU Health System have been honored with prestigious national and international recognition for top-quality graduate, professional and medical care programs, reflecting a commitment to be among America's top research universities focused on student learning."

Campus Setting

Virginia Commonwealth, founded in 1838, is a public, research university. Programs are offered through the Centers for Environmental Sciences and Public Policy; the College of Humanities and Sciences and the Schools of Allied Health Professions, the Arts, Business, Dentistry, Education, Engineering, Mass Communications, Medicine, Nursing, Pharmacy and Social Work. Two campuses of 141 acres are both located in downtown Richmond. A four-year institution, Virginia Commonwealth University has an enrollment of 31,288 students. The university provides its students with a well-stocked library, as well as: gallery · life sciences building. Virginia Commonwealth University provides on-campus housing, which can accommodate 5,833 students. Housing options are: coed dorms · women's dorms · men's dorms · single-student apartments · special housing for disabled students · special housing for international students. Recreation and sports facilities include a sports medicine building.

Student Life and Activities

Seventy-five percent of students live off campus. Students enjoy gathering at the Student Commons, Shafer Court Area and the library. Popular campus events include Homecoming, Spring Fest, Welcome Week, Annual Fall Step Show, French Film Festival, VCU Block Party, Intercultural Festival, Family Day, Greek Week, Black History Month, Spring Fest and Career Fair. Virginia Commonwealth University has 583 official student organizations. The most popular are: Activities Programming Board · Literati · National Art Education Association · Shafer Alliance Theatre · American Choral Director's Association · Media · Art & Text Student Organization · Fall Block Step Show Planning Committee · Homecoming Committee · Intercultural Festival Planning Board · STRUT Planning Committee · Alternative Spring Break · Circle K · Habitat for Humanity · National Student Partnerships Richmond · Operation Smile · Powerful Beyond Measure · American Society of Interior Designers · International Interior Design Association · Amnesty International

545

College Profiles

VIRGINIA COMMONWEALTH UNIVERSITY

Highlights

Virginia Commonwealth University
Richmond, VA (Pop. 210,309)
Location: Medium city
Four-year public
Founded: 1838
Website: http://www.vcu.edu

Students
Total enrollment: 31,288
Undergrads: 23,657
Freshmen: 4,126
Part-time students: 16%
From out-of-state: 12%
Male/Female: 43%/57%
Live on-campus: 25%
Off-campus employment rating: Fair
Caucasian: 51%
African American: 18%
Hispanic: 7%
Asian: 12%
Hawaiian or Pacific Islander: <1%
Native American: <1%
Mixed (2+ ethnicities): 4%
International: 4%

Academics
Calendar: Semester
Student/faculty ratio: 17:1
Class size 9 or fewer: 7%
Class size 10-29: 54%
Class size 30-49: 22%
Class size 50-99: 9%
Class size 100 or more: 9%
Returning freshmen: 87%
Six-year graduation rate: 56%

Most Popular Majors
Biology
Psychology
Mass communication

· anime club · anthropology/archeology club · College Panhellenic Council · Interfraternity Council · National Pan-Hellenic Council · Network of Spiritual Progressive · Students for Sensible Drug Policy · Counselor Education Student Networking Association · Educational Leadership Doctoral Student Association · Guild of Graduate Students · Graduate Student Association · Graduate Writers Association · Siggraph Student Chapter · Sigma Phi Omega Association for Gerontology Epsilon Chapter · Black Ice · Cancer Awareness Team · Contemporary Craft Society · Diversity Theatre · Future Established Brothers & Sisters · Group Moda · Men Against Violence · Sexual Assault Dating Violence Education by Students · Project Reach · Quizbowl · Ramrass · The Philosophy Club · Alexandrian Society (history club). For athletics, there are intramural teams such as: badminton · basketball · dodgeball · kickball · light weight football · martial arts · racquetball · soccer · softball · table tennis · tennis · volleyball. Virginia Commonwealth University is a member of the Atlantic 10 Conference and Eastern Collegiate Athletic Conference.

Academics and Learning Environment

Virginia Commonwealth University has 2,170 full-time and 1,143 part-time faculty members, offering a student-to-faculty ratio of 17:1. The most common course size is 20 to 29 students. Virginia Commonwealth University offers 179 majors with the most popular being biology, psychology and mass communication. The school has a general core requirement. Cooperative education is available. All first-year students must maintain a 2.0 GPA or higher to avoid academic probation. The B student might want to be made aware of the following: self-designed majors · independent study · double majors · accelerated study · honors program · internships · distance learning.

B Student Support and Success

VCU has a College Success Program that works to "provide assistance to students that will help them attain their academic potential." Along with academic counseling and tutoring, students who need additional development in some academic areas are involved in a mandatory year-long program during their freshman year. The school also offers UNIV 101, An Introduction to the University, which is a one-credit class that guides students to resources and services, plus promotes the development of intellectual, personal and social skills. It examines learning styles and study skills as well.

Virginia Commonwealth University offers dedicated guidance for: academic · career · personal · psychological · minority students · military · veterans · non-traditional students · family planning · religious. Additional counseling services include: non-traditional student. Annually, 87 percent of freshmen students return for their sophomore year.

Support for Students with Learning Disabilities

There are specific support programs at Virginia Commonwealth University that will appeal to students with learning disabilities. Some options for LD students to take advantage of include a lightened course load, as well as additional time to complete their degree. Students with learning disabilities will find the following programs useful: tutors · learning center · testing accommodations · extended time for tests · take-home exam · oral tests · exam on tape or computer · readers · typist/scribe · note-taking services · reading machines · tape recorders · texts on tape · early syllabus · priority registration. Individual or small group tutorials are also available in: time management · organizational skills · learning strategies · specific subject areas · writing labs · math labs · study skills. An advisor/advocate from the Disability Support Services is available to students.

How to Get Admitted

For admissions decisions, non-academic factors considered: extracurricular activities · special talents, interests and abilities · character/personal qualities · volunteer work · work experience · state of residency. A high school diploma is required, although a GED is also accepted for admissions consideration. SAT or ACT test scores. *Academic units recommended:* 4 English, 4 Math, 4 Science, 1 Social Studies, 3 Foreign Language.

How to Pay for College

To apply for financial aid, students should submit the following: Free Application for Federal Student Aid (FAFSA). Virginia Commonwealth University participates in the Federal Work Study program. *Need-based aid programs include:* scholarships and grants · general need-based awards · Federal Pell grants · state scholarships and grants · college-based scholarships and grants · private scholarships and grants · Federal Nursing scholarships. *Non-need-based aid programs include:* scholarships and grants · state scholarships and grants · creative arts and performance awards · special achievements and activities awards · athletic scholarships.

VIRGINIA COMMONWEALTH UNIVERSITY

Highlights

Admissions
Applicants: 15,399
Accepted: 9,860
Acceptance rate: 64.0%
Placed on wait list: 607
Enrolled from wait list: 1
Average GPA: 3.6
ACT range: 21-26
SAT Math range: 500-600
SAT Reading range: 500-610
SAT Writing range: 4-20
Top 10% of class: 20%
Top 25% of class: 50%
Top 50% of class: 86%

Deadlines
Early Action: No
Early Decision: No
Regular Action: 1/15 (final)
Common Application: Accepted

Financial Aid
In-state tuition: $10,222
Out-of-state tuition: $27,671
Room: Varies
Board: Varies
Books: $1,375
Freshmen receiving need-based aid: 57%
Undergrads rec. need-based aid: 56%
Avg. % of need met by financial aid: 52%
Avg. aid package (freshmen): $11,574
Avg. aid package (undergrads): $9,984
Avg. debt upon graduation: $29,462

Prominent Alumni
Baruj Benacerraf, Nobel Prize winner in medicine; Debbie Matenopoulos, former co-host of *The View*; John C. Neal, CEO of Union Bank and Trust Company.

School Spirit
Mascot: Rams
Colors: Black and gold

547

VIRGINIA WESLEYAN COLLEGE

1584 Wesleyan Drive, Norfolk, VA 23502-5599
Admissions: 800-737-8684 · Financial Aid: 757-455-3345
Email: admissions@vwc.edu · Website: http://www.vwc.edu

From the College

"Virginia Wesleyan College is a small, private, liberal arts college located on the border of Norfolk and Virginia Beach. It focuses on creatively mixing core academic courses, extracurricular activities and opportunities to gain real-world experience through internships, fieldwork, study abroad and community service. Through the college's partnerships with businesses, government agencies and non-profit organizations, VWC's students explore various career paths, "shadow" professionals as they go about their work and take a hands-on approach to helping solve local community problems. VWC is affiliated with the United Methodist Church."

Campus Setting

Virginia Wesleyan, founded in 1961, is a private, church-affiliated, liberal arts college. Its 300-acre campus is located in Norfolk/Virginia Beach, 10 miles from downtown areas and 15 miles from the ocean. A four-year institution, Virginia Wesleyan College has an enrollment of 1,459 students. The school is also affiliated with the Methodist Church. Virginia Wesleyan College boasts a well-stocked library. The campus also has a center for the study of religious freedom and sacred music. Virginia Wesleyan College comes equipped with 350 on-campus units, which can accommodate 854 students in: coed dorms · women's dorms · sorority housing · fraternity housing · single-student apartments · special housing for disabled students · special housing for international students. Recreation and sports facilities include: baseball or softball complex · field hockey, lacrosse and soccer fields · basketball and tennis courts.

Student Life and Activities

With 60 percent of students living on campus, social activities abound. Popular campus events include Seafood Party in the Dell, Mud Games, Greek Week, village cookouts, poetry slams, Arts Alive, academic fair, Potato Drop, Celebration of Women's Voices, Native American fair, Marlin Spirit Pregame, Lake Taylor Music Festival, Lively in the Ivy Concert, Spring Fling, Homecoming, Airband, Intercultural Fashion Show, Comedy Club and Relay for Life. Virginia Wesleyan College has 65 official student organizations. The most popular are: Ambassadors · Traditional Music Society · Record Label DJs · step team · Electronic Music Society · Campus Kaleidoscope commuter club · Fairy Godmothers · Gay Straight Alliance · Circle K · Habitat for Humanity · Youth Matters · Order of Infinity · SVEA/NEA · IMAGINE · The Link · First Year Leadership Council · Honors and Scholars · Residence Hall Association · Wesleyan Activities Council · Greek Presidents · Relay for Life · Panhellenic Council · Interfraternal Council · SEAL · Beekeepers Association · College Republicans · Democracy Matters · Model UN · Young Democrats · Political Science Association · Society for the Advancement of Management · recreation majors club · psychology club · science club. For students interested in athletic involvement, there are intramural teams such as: basketball · canoeing · climbing wall · flag football · mud games · racquetball · running · soccer · swimming · volleyball. Virginia Wesleyan College is a member of the Old Dominion Athletic Conference (Division III).

Academics and Learning Environment

Virginia Wesleyan College has 92 full-time and 39 part-time faculty members, offering a student-to-faculty ratio of 13:1. The most common course size is 10 to 19 students. Virginia Wesleyan College offers 35 majors with the most popular being business, biology and criminal justice and least popular American studies, classical studies and Latin. The school has a general core requirement. Cooperative education is offered. All first-year students must maintain a 1.6 GPA or higher to avoid academic probation, and a minimum overall GPA of 2.0 is required to graduate. Here are a variety of other special academic programs that would appeal to a B student: self-designed majors · pass/fail grading option · independent study · double majors · dual degrees · accelerated study · honors program · internships · distance learning.

B Student Support and Success

The Learning Center at VWC offers tutoring and resource materials as well as study skills workshops. With a 13:1 student/teacher ratio, teachers are often willing to take the time to help students with one-on-one counseling and guidance. Career Services assists students with choosing a major and scheduling courses.

Virginia Wesleyan College prides itself on its dedicated guidance for: academic · career · personal · psychological · minority students · military · veterans · non-traditional students · family planning · religious. Recognizing that some students may need extra preparation, Virginia Wesleyan College offers remedial and refresher courses in the following: reading · writing · math · study skills. The average freshman year GPA is 2.6, and 67 percent of freshmen students return for their sophomore year. When it comes to after college, many students commit themselves to the workforce. Approximately 32 percent pursue a graduate degree immediately after their graduation. Some companies that most frequently hire graduates from Virginia Wesleyan College are these: American Funds Group · Chesapeake Public Schools · City of Virginia Beach · Landmark Communications · Norfolk Public Schools · Tidewater Community College · USAA · Virginia Beach Police · Virginia Beach Public Schools · Virginia Wesleyan College.

Support for Students with Learning Disabilities

Those students with learning disabilities may want to take advantage of specific support programs offered by Virginia Wesleyan College. Sometimes, the college will grant additional time to LD students so that they can complete their degree. A lightened course load may also be requested for the learning disabilities student. According to the school, students file the same application and apply to the Learning Center program separately. The Learning Center Coordinator serves as a consultant to the Admissions Committee. LD students may find the following list of support programs particularly helpful: remedial math · remedial English · tutors · learning center · testing accommodations · untimed tests · extended time for tests · oral tests · readers · typist/scribe · note-taking services · tape recorders · priority registration · waiver of foreign language degree requirement. Individual or small group tutorials are also available in: time management · organizational skills · learning strategies · specific subject areas · writing labs · math labs · study skills. An advisor/advocate from the Learning Center is available to students.

How to Get Admitted

For admissions decisions, non-academic factors considered: interview · extracurricular activities · special talents, interests and abilities ·

VIRGINIA WESLEYAN COLLEGE

Highlights

Virginia Wesleyan College
Norfolk, VA (Pop. 245,782)
Location: Medium city
Four-year private
Founded: 1961
Website: http://www.vwc.edu

Students
Total enrollment: 1,459
Undergrads: 1,459
Freshmen: 453
Part-time students: 8%
From out-of-state: 26%
Male/Female: 39%/61%
Live on-campus: 60%
In fraternities: 7%
In sororities: 3%
Off-campus employment rating: Good
Caucasian: 58%
African American: 23%
Hispanic: 6%
Asian: 1%
Hawaiian or Pacific Islander: <1%
Native American: 1%
Mixed (2+ ethnicities): 7%
International: 1%

Academics
Calendar: 4-1-4 system
Student/faculty ratio: 13:1
Class size 9 or fewer: 34%
Class size 10-29: 65%
Class size 30-49: 1%
Class size 50-99: -
Class size 100 or more: -
Returning freshmen: 67%
Six-year graduation rate: 44%

Most Popular Majors
Business
Biology
Criminal justice

VIRGINIA WESLEYAN COLLEGE

Highlights

Admissions
Applicants: 3,727
Accepted: 3,463
Acceptance rate: 92.9%
Average GPA: 3.3
ACT range: 18-24
SAT Math range: 450-570
SAT Reading range: 458-573
SAT Writing range: 2-10
Top 10% of class: 14%
Top 25% of class: 35%
Top 50% of class: 62%

Deadlines
Early Action: No
Early Decision: No
Regular Action: Rolling admissions
Common Application: Not accepted

Financial Aid
In-state tuition: $32,636
Out-of-state tuition: $35,636
Room: Varies
Board: Varies
Books: $1,000
Freshmen receiving need-based aid: 84%
Undergrads rec. need-based aid: 76%
Avg. % of need met by financial aid: 62%
Avg. aid package (freshmen): $22,062
Avg. aid package (undergrads): $19,980
Avg. debt upon graduation: $40,804

Prominent Alumni
Eric Asimov, chief wine critic at *The New York Times*; Michael Bay, film producer and direcror of the *Transformers* franchise; Bill Belichick, head coach of the New England Patriots; Denise Casper, U.S. District Court federal judge in Massachusetts.

School Spirit
Mascot: Marlin
Colors: Navy blue, silver, and white
Song: *Virginia Wesleyan College Alma Mater*

character/personal qualities · volunteer work · work experience · state of residency · alumni relationship. A high school diploma is required, although a GED is also accepted for admissions consideration. SAT or ACT test scores are required of some applicants. SAT Subject Test scores are considered, if submitted, but are not required. *According to the admissions office:* Minimum combined SAT Reasoning score of 900 required with rank in top half of secondary school class, and minimum 2.5 GPA recommended. SAT Reasoning scores may not be required of applicants with minimum 3.5 GPA. *Academic units recommended:* 4 English, 3 Math, 2 Science, 2 Foreign Language.

How to Pay for College

To apply for financial aid, students should submit the following: Free Application for Federal Student Aid (FAFSA) · state aid form. Virginia Wesleyan College participates in the Federal Work Study program. *Need-based aid programs include:* scholarships and grants · general need-based awards · Federal Pell grants · state scholarships and grants · college-based scholarships and grants · private scholarships and grants. *Non-need-based aid programs include:* scholarships and grants · general need-based awards · state scholarships and grants · creative arts and performance awards · special characteristics awards · ROTC scholarships · religious affiliation scholarships/grants; army ROTC scholarship/grants through affiliation with Old Dominion U.

550

WASHINGTON & JEFFERSON COLLEGE

60 South Lincoln Street, Washington, PA 15301
Admissions: 724-223-6025 · Financial Aid: 724-223-6019
Email: admission@washjeff.edu · Website: http://www.washjeff.edu

From the College

"Washington & Jefferson College has been ranked first in the country per capita for producing attorneys and third in the country for producing physicians and medical researchers. Routinely, 90 percent of our applicants to medical and law schools are admitted. More than 90 percent of seniors seeking employment find work in their fields or admission to graduate school before graduation. W&J offers students a personalized learning experience, with over 70 percent of classes having fewer than 20 students.

"Alumni around the world offer students networking opportunities in nearly every discipline. The result is student achievement of the highest caliber. Our students land research internships at the Pasteur Institute, Mayo Clinic and Los Alamos Labs, to name a few. W&J challenges our students by sending them to national meetings where their research is presented alongside that of professional researchers, graduate students and faculty from other institutions.

"More than half of our students take advantage of 40+ study abroad programs in countries such as Australia, China, France, Germany, Spain and South Africa. The Intersession term, a feature of our 4-1-4 academic calendar, allows students to take one course, intensively, during January. They may travel to London to study theatre, camp out in Africa to watch animals migrate or stay on campus to design robots or study with a prize-winning journalist.

"W&J was honored with the President's Honor Roll for Community Service with Distinction; students volunteer more than 15,000 hours a year in service to our community.

"W&J also has a strong tradition of producing student-athletes. The college fields 24 intercollegiate sports. W&J has graduated leaders in almost every field, from architecture to zoology."

Campus Setting

Washington & Jefferson College is a private, residential liberal arts and sciences college. Founded in 1781, the college is located on a 60-acre campus just 30 miles southwest of Pittsburgh. A four-year institution, Washington & Jefferson College has an enrollment of 1,328 students. Although not originally a co-educational college, Washington & Jefferson College has been co-ed since 1970. In addition to a large, well-stocked library, the campus facilities include: cell culture · isolator · neuropsychology · nuclear magnetic resonance (NMR) · language labs · laser scanning confocal microscope facility · atomic force microscope · mass spectrometer/gas chromatograph · microplate reader · X-ray diffraction unit · atomic absorption unit · refrigerated centrifuge · global learning unit · spectrometers · field station. Washington & Jefferson College provides on-campus housing with 843 units that can accommodate 1,385 students. Housing options: coed dorms · women's dorms · men's dorms · sorority housing · fraternity housing · single-student apartments · special housing for disabled students. Recreation and sports facilities include: natatorium · parks · stadiums · tennis courts · wellness center.

Student Life and Activities

Almost all students (94 percent) live on campus. Popular gathering spots include The Hub (Student Center), Swanson Wellness Center, Monticellos Coffee House,

WASHINGTON & JEFFERSON COLLEGE

Highlights

Washington & Jefferson College
Washington, PA (Pop. 13,555)
Location: Small town
Four-year private
Founded: 1781
Website: http://www.washjeff.edu

Students

Total enrollment: 1,328
Undergrads: 1,328
Freshmen: 326
Part-time students: 1%
From out-of-state: 27%
From public schools: 83%
Male/Female: 49%/51%
Live on-campus: 94%
In fraternities: 43%
In sororities: 46%
Off-campus employment rating: Good
Caucasian: 83%
African American: 3%
Hispanic: 3%
Asian: 3%
Hawaiian or Pacific Islander: <1%
Native American: <1%
Mixed (2+ ethnicities): 3%
International: 3%

Academics

Calendar: 4-1-4 system
Student/faculty ratio: 10:1
Class size 9 or fewer: 24%
Class size 10-29: 71%
Class size 30-49: 6%
Class size 50-99: -
Class size 100 or more: -
Returning freshmen: 88%
Six-year graduation rate: 77%

Most Popular Majors

Business/accounting
Psychology
History

Burnett, Technology Center, ski lodge/Barista in the Commons, cultural areas of Pittsburgh, local coffee shops and dining and Trinity Point. Popular events include Spring Concert, Homecoming Weekend, International Week, Street Fair, Family Weekend, Greek Week, V Day Monologues and Holiday Light-up Night. Washington & Jefferson College has 79 official student organizations. Greek Organizations, Athletic Teams, Student Activities Board, Asian Cultural Association, Black Student Union and club sports are influential groups on campus. For those interested in sports, there are intramural teams such as: basketball · billiards · bowling · cross-country · dodge ball · flag football · foul shooting · kickball · kickboxing · pilates · racquetball · slow pitch softball · soccer · street hockey · table tennis · tennis · triathlon · Ultimate Frisbee · volleyball · walleyball. Washington & Jefferson College is a member of the Presidents' Athletic Conference (Division III), Eastern College Athletic Conference, Empire 8 and Landmark Conference.

Academics and Learning Environment

Washington & Jefferson College has 114 full-time and 40 part-time faculty members, offering a student-to-faculty ratio of 10:1. The most common course size is 10 to 19 students. Washington & Jefferson College offers 33 majors. The most popular are business/accounting, psychology and history and the least popular are biophysics, art teacher education and music/general. The school has a general core requirement. Cooperative education is not offered. All first-year students must maintain a 2.0 GPA or higher to avoid academic probation. Other special academic programs that would appeal to a B student include: self-designed majors · pass/fail grading option · independent study · double majors · dual degrees · accelerated study · honors program · Phi Beta Kappa · internships.

B Student Support and Success

The Center for Learning and Teaching supports Washington & Jefferson students by providing peer-assisted learning in which study skills are taught by fellow students. In addition, assistance is also provided for areas such as memory and concentration, class participation, how to talk to your instructor, stress management and more. The Associate Director of the Center helps students assess their current academic skills by identifying strengths and weaknesses. Specific feedback is then given so that students know what areas to concentrate on within the Center.

Washington & Jefferson College provides a variety of support programs including dedicated guidance for: academic · career · personal · psychological · minority students · family planning · religious. The average freshman year GPA is 3.1. Approximately 39 percent pursue a graduate degree immediately after graduation, and 60 percent enter a field related to their major within six months of graduation. Companies that most frequently hire graduates from Washington & Jefferson College include: Altoona Hospital · American Eagle Outfitters · AT&T · Automated Security Alert Inc. · Bank of New York Mellon · Bechtel Bettis Inc. · Blue Grace Logistics · Brady Communications · Bucks County Schools · Bureau of Land Management · Carnegie Mellon University · Changes Property Staging · Chardon Laboratories · Cigna Group Insurance · Consol Energy · Federal Energy Regulatory Commission · Giant Eagle Pharmacy · JP Morgan Chase · Juniata School District · Kiddie Academy · Kids 'R' Us Childcare & Preschool · Kinex Pharmaceuticals · Klingensmith Healthcare · KPMG · Omega Federal Credit Union · Pathways of SW PA · Peace Corps · Penn Hills School District · Pittsburgh Logistic Services · PNC Bank · PPG - raw materials division · Precision Therapeutics Inc. · PricewaterhouseCoopers · Prince George County School District · Rivers Casino · Roadview Inc. · Schneider Downs · Shock Wave Solutions LLC · Sisterson & Company · Smith Elliot Kearns & Co. · SmithBarney · Standard Bank · Starcom · Thar Instruments - A Waters Company · The Kiski School · The Summit Academy · University of Pittsburgh · UPMC Presbyterian · UPMC-WPIC Pittsburgh Youth Study · US Air Force · US Army · US Marine Corps · Verizon Wireless · Walnut Ridge Memory Care · Walt Disney World · Washington & Jefferson College · Washington County Redevelopment Authority · Wells Fargo · West Mifflin Area School District · Wilhert Vault Company · Woodman of the World · World Marketing of America.

Support for Students with Learning Disabilities

Students with learning disabilities are granted extra time to complete a degree, and the chance to take a lightened course load. High school foreign language waivers are accepted. Students with learning disabilities may also want to utilize: tutors · learning center · testing accommodations · extended time for tests · take-home exam · oral tests · early syllabus · priority registration · priority seating. Individual or small group tutorials are also available in: time management · organizational skills · learning strategies · specific subject areas · writing labs · math labs · study skills. An advisor/advocate from the LD program is available to students.

How to Get Admitted

For admissions decisions, non-academic factors considered: interview · extracurricular activities · special talents, interests and abilities · character/personal qualities · volunteer work · work experience · geographical location · minority affiliation · alumni relationship. A high school diploma is required, although a GED is also accepted for admissions consideration. SAT or ACT test scores are considered, if submitted, but are not required. SAT Subject Test scores are considered, if submitted, but are not required. *Academic units recommended:* 4 English, 4 Math, 2 Science, 3 Foreign Language.

How to Pay for College

To apply for financial aid, students should submit the following: Free Application for Federal Student Aid (FAFSA). Washington & Jefferson College participates in the Federal Work Study program. *Need-based aid programs include:* scholarships and grants · general need-based awards · Federal Pell grants · state scholarships and grants · college-based scholarships and grants · private scholarships and grants · ACG and SMART grants. *Non-need-based aid programs include:* scholarships and grants · state scholarships and grants · special achievements and activities awards · special characteristics awards · Pittsburgh Promise scholarship.

WASHINGTON & JEFFERSON COLLEGE

Highlights

Admissions
Applicants: 7,176
Accepted: 2,851
Acceptance rate: 39.7%
Placed on wait list: 53
Enrolled from wait list: 5
Average GPA: 3.3
ACT range: 23-27
SAT Math range: 540-620
SAT Reading range: 510-610
SAT Writing range: Not reported
Top 10% of class: 37%
Top 25% of class: 70%
Top 50% of class: 94%

Deadlines
Early Action: 1/15
Early Decision: 12/1
Regular Action: Rolling admissions
Common Application: Accepted

Financial Aid
In-state tuition: $40,722
Out-of-state tuition: $40,722
Room: $6,390
Board: $4,494
Books: $800
Freshmen receiving need-based aid: 81%
Undergrads rec. need-based aid: 77%
Avg. % of need met by financial aid: 76%
Avg. aid package (freshmen): $30,900
Avg. aid package (undergrads): $29,320

Prominent Alumni
Roger Goodell, NFL Commissioner; Richard Clark, CEO of Merck; John Reed, former CEO, Citibank, president, New York Stock Exchange.

School Spirit
Mascot: Presidents
Colors: Red and black

WASHINGTON STATE UNIVERSITY

P.O. Box 645910, Pullman, WA 99164-5910
Admissions: 888-468-6978 · Financial Aid: 509-335-9711
Email: admiss2@wsu.edu · Website: http://www.wsu.edu

From the College

"Research opportunities: A growing number of undergraduate students participate in research with WSU professors, present papers at conferences, and publish their research findings in scholarly journals. More than 70 graduate degree programs attract inquisitive minds from around the world.

"Personal attention: A student to faculty ratio of 15:1 allows students to get to know their professors and receive individualized guidance. Dedicated advisors in the new University College help students assess their academic, personal and professional goals.

"Writing program for all majors: The nationally recognized Writing Program helps students across all disciplines to become more proficient writers. It has been named an Academic Program to Look For by *U.S. News & World Report's* America's Best Colleges for seven of the past nine years.

"Honors College: WSU is home to one of the most highly regarded public university honors colleges in the country, with a curriculum emphasizing global awareness and international impact. It immerses students in the study of international issues, builds their proficiency in a second language and encourages them to study abroad. Professors teach courses interactively, inspiring discussions among students. Honors students complete a senior year thesis and often conduct research as undergraduates.

"Communication: The Edward R. Murrow College of Communication is the only program in the Northwest that offers course sequences in all six communication fields: advertising, broadcasting, communication, communication studies, journalism and public relations. Students gain hands-on experience at campus television and radio stations, at the student newspaper and website and at a graphic design and publishing service for the community. The annual Edward R. Murrow Symposium brings renowned journalists and scholars to campus and connects students to industry professionals.

"Business: The College of Business is accredited at the baccalaureate, master's and doctoral levels by the Association to Advance Collegiate Schools of Business International, a distinction held by just two percent of the world's business schools. Programs in international business, entrepreneurship and hospitality business management are nationally ranked.

"Engineering: Senior design projects created through an industry partnership provide professional interaction and real-world experience.

"Organic agriculture: In 2006 WSU became the first university in the country to offer a major in organic agriculture. Students produce certified organic vegetables, fruit, herbs and flowers at the campus' certified organic teaching farm.

"Interior design: The state's only four-year program accredited by the Council for Interior Design Accreditation. The graduate program ranks in the Top Ten Best Programs in the U.S. according to Design Intelligence, a bimonthly journal for architecture and design professionals.

"Washington State conducts research that empowers students and improves people's lives. Motivated, high-achieving students work side by side with faculty, gaining insights and research experience. Across the university's 11 colleges, many academic programs rank among the nation's finest. Faculty researchers have earned international recognition in many fields, including the biological and physical sciences, engineering, mathematics, social sciences, humanities and the arts. Fortune 500 and other employers recruit the university's graduates."

Campus Setting

Founded in 1890, Washington State University is a top-tier public research university with four campuses, online degree programs and agricultural research and cooperative extension facilities throughout the state. The 620-acre main campus is located in Pullman, 75 miles south of Spokane. Regional campuses are located in Spokane, the Tri-Cities and Vancouver. Washington State University has an enrollment of 22,874 students. Beginning with a large library, the campus facilities also include: anthropology museum · arboretum · art museum · audio labs · behavioral lab · natural history museum · observatory · oil and gas processing laboratory · planetarium · herbarium and mycological herbarium · laboratory for biotechnology and bioanalysis · electron microscopy center · environmental research center · geoanalytical laboratory · music listening library · music recording studio · nuclear radiation center · planetarium · public and student-run television stations · state of Washington water research center · center for spectroscopy · speech and hearing clinic · vertebrate zoology museum.

Washington State University provides on-campus housing with 5,800 units that can accommodate 6,538 students. Housing options: coed dorms · women's dorms · men's dorms · sorority housing · fraternity housing · single-student apartments · married-student apartments · special housing for disabled students · special housing for international students. Recreation and sports facilities include: 18-hole championship golf course · stadium · indoor recreation center with cardio and weight equipment · basketball, volleyball, racquetball and badminton courts · roller hockey · indoor soccer · floor hockey inline skating · five-lane lap pool · leisure pool · spa · activity rooms · elevated four-lane running/walking track · climbing wall · gymnasiums · mat rooms and indoor tennis courts · indoor practice facility with full NCAA 200-meter track · triple jump pits · pole vault lanes · shot and disc arc · a 60-sprint track and roll-out turf system · playfields · sand volleyball courts · indoor swimming pools · track · outdoor recreation center with climbing gym and self-repair bike shop · walking and hiking trails.

Student Life and Activities

Seventy-four percent of students live off campus. According to a school representative, "Undergraduates comprise roughly half of the city of Pullman's population, with most living on or adjacent to campus. As a result, students of diverse social, economic and ethnic backgrounds from throughout the nation and scores of foreign countries come together as friends and neighbors. They rally as one behind Cougar athletes in Pac-12 games. They join one another in campus activities, like the Up All Night event series, with late-night movies, free popcorn and Ultimate Frisbee at midnight. Students find kindred spirits in more than 350 clubs. They play hard in intramural sports—one of the nation's largest programs of its kind—and work out side by side at the Student Recreation Center. They share music and laughter when big-name entertainers perform on campus. Together they donate more than 32,000 hours to help others through civic engagement. The unique shared experience of 'Cougs' forges lifelong bonds among fellow students and creates a worldwide network of support. WSU students can find even more

WASHINGTON STATE UNIVERSITY

Highlights

Washington State University
Pullman, WA (Pop. 31,359)
Location: Large town
Four-year public
Founded: 1890
Website: http://www.wsu.edu

Students
Total enrollment: 22,874
Undergrads: 19,554
Part-time students: 15%
From out-of-state: 14%
Male/Female: 48%/52%
Live on-campus: 26%
In fraternities: 19%
In sororities: 18%
Off-campus employment rating: Good
Caucasian: 68%
African American: 3%
Hispanic: 9%
Asian: 5%
Hawaiian or Pacific Islander: <1%
Native American: 1%
Mixed (2+ ethnicities): 6%
International: 4%

Academics
Calendar: Semester
Student/faculty ratio: 15:1
Class size 9 or fewer: 12%
Class size 10-29: 46%
Class size 30-49: 19%
Class size 50-99: 14%
Class size 100 or more: 10%
Returning freshmen: 84%
Six-year graduation rate: 67%

Most Popular Majors
Business, management, marketing/related support services
Social sciences
Health professions/related clinical sciences

555

College Profiles

WASHINGTON STATE UNIVERSITY

Highlights

Admissions
Applicants: 14,887
Accepted: 12,219
Acceptance rate: 82.1%
Average GPA: 3.3
ACT range: 20-26
SAT Math range: 460-580
SAT Reading range: 450-570
SAT Writing range: 1-11
Top 10% of class: 30%
Top 25% of class: 52%
Top 50% of class: 83%

Deadlines
Early Action: No
Early Decision: No
Regular Action: Rolling admissions
Common Application: Not accepted

Financial Aid
In-state tuition: $11,396
Out-of-state tuition: $24,478
Room: $6,858
Board: $4,418
Books: $960
Freshmen receiving need-based aid: 56%
Undergrads rec. need-based aid: 56%
Avg. % of need met by financial aid: 92%
Avg. aid package (freshmen): $16,949
Avg. aid package (undergrads): $16,861
Avg. debt upon graduation: $23,433

Prominent Alumni
Sherman Alexie, award-winning poet, author, screenwriter, director; Paul Allen, Microsoft co-founder, investor, philanthropist, founder of museums, brain science institute; Neva Martin Abelson, research physician, pediatrician, co-developer of Rh blood test.

School Spirit
Mascot: Cougar
Colors: Crimson and gray
Song: *Cougar Fight Song*

cultural and social activities, and another vast student population, just eight miles away at the University of Idaho in Moscow."

Popular gathering places for students are the Glenn Terrell Friendship Mall, a tree-lined campus hub amidst the library, Compton Union Building and academic buildings, Student Recreation Center, Martin Stadium, Ferdinand's Ice Cream Shoppe, The WSU Art Museum and the new 18-hole championship gold course. Popular campus events include the all-day concert festivals Cougfest (in the fall) and Springfest (in the spring), late-night weekend entertainment series "Up All Night," shows by big-name entertainers at Beasley Performing Arts Coliseum during Dad's Weekend in the fall and Mom's Weekend in the spring, Homecoming Celebration, the All-Campus Picnic, Pah-Loots-Pu Pow Wow and the annual National Lentil Festival. Washington State University has 380 official student organizations. WSU Cougar women's and men's intercollegiate athletic teams, Greek fraternities and sororities, student publications and the Student Entertainment Board all have a strong presence in student social life on campus. For those interested in sports, there are intramural teams such as: badminton · basketball · bowling · cribbage · dodgeball · flag football · golf · inner tube water polo · kickball · lawn games · racquetball · shuffleboard · soccer · softball · table tennis · tennis · triathlon · volleyball · ultimate disc · water polo · Wii tournaments. Washington State University is a member of the Pacific-12 Conference (Division I, Football I-A).

Academics and Learning Environment

For the B student, the learning environment of a college is just as important as the quality of its academic program. Washington State University has 1,242 full-time and 493 part-time faculty members, offering a student-to-faculty ratio of 15:1. The most common course size is 10 to 19 students. Washington State University offers 218 majors with the most popular being business, management, marketing/related support services, social sciences and health professions/related clinical sciences and least popular being physical sciences, public administration/social service professions and philosophy/religious studies. The school has a general core requirement. Cooperative education is available. All first-year students must maintain a 2.0 GPA or higher to avoid academic probation. Other special academic programs that would appeal to a B student include: self-designed majors · pass/fail grading option · independent study · double majors · dual degrees · accelerated study · honors program · Phi Beta Kappa · internships · distance learning certificate programs.

B Student Support and Success

WSU students go to the SALC, or Student Advising and Learning Center, for academic assistance. The staff at SALC provides advising, tutoring and other help. Academic Assistance offers services such as learning-strategies workshops, handouts, videos and a peer-tutorial program for one-on-one assistance in a wide range of subjects for an hourly fee. A two-credit elective class called the Freshman Seminar is designed to "help first-year students enhance critical thinking, research, writing and presentation skills as well as deal with transition issues faced when entering into the university." Students enrolled in this class develop a research project about the lessons learned in the course.

Washington State University provides a variety of support programs including dedicated guidance for: academic · career · personal · psychological · minority students · military · veterans · non-traditional students · family planning. The average freshman year GPA is 2.6, and 84 percent of freshmen students return for their sophomore year. Companies that most frequently hire graduates from Washington State University include: Abercrombie & Fitch · Alaska Airlines · Allstate Insurance Company · American Express · American Heart Association · Peace Corps · Planned Parenthood · PricewaterhouseCoopers · Safeco Insurance · Sacred Heart Medical Center · Safeway Inc. · Sarasota Avionics Inc. · Schlumberger · Schweitzer Engineering Laboratories Inc. · Sea Lane Biotechnologies · Sears · Ste. Michelle Wine Estates · Texas Instruments · The Seattle Times Company · The Vanguard Group · Virginia Mason Medical Center · Williams Sonoma · Windermere Real Estate.

Support for Students with Learning Disabilities

Students with learning disabilities may take advantage of specific support programs offered by Washington State University. If necessary, the college will grant additional time to students with learning disabilities to complete their degree. Also, a lightened course load may be granted to LD students. Students with learning disabilities will find the following programs at Washington State University useful: waiver of math degree requirement. Individual or small group tutorials are also available in: time management · organizational skills · learning strategies · specific subject areas · writing labs · math labs · study skills. An advisor/advocate from the Disability Resource Center is available to students.

How to Get Admitted

For admissions decisions, non-academic factors considered: extracurricular activities · special talents, interests and abilities · character/personal qualities · volunteer work · work experience · state of residency. A high school diploma is required, although a GED is also accepted for admissions consideration. SAT or ACT test scores are required of all applicants. *Academic units recommended:* 4 English, 4 Math, 2 Science, 3 Social Studies, 2 Foreign Language.

How to Pay for College

To apply for financial aid, students should submit the following: Free Application for Federal Student Aid (FAFSA). Washington State University participates in the Federal Work Study program. *Need-based aid programs include:* scholarships and grants · general need-based awards · Federal Pell grants · state scholarships and grants · college-based scholarships and grants · private scholarships and grants · Federal Nursing scholarships · United Negro College Fund. *Non-need-based aid programs include:* scholarships and grants · general need-based awards · state scholarships and grants · creative arts and performance awards · special achievements and activities awards · special characteristics awards · athletic scholarships · ROTC scholarships.

WELLS COLLEGE

170 Main Street, Aurora, NY 13026
Admissions: 800-952-9355 · Financial Aid: 315-364-3289
Email: admissions@wells.edu · Website: http://www.wells.edu

From the College

"Wells College is a co-educational, private, liberal arts college located on a 365-acre lakeside campus situated in the heart of the Finger Lakes Region of New York State in the historical village of Aurora. True to its heritage, Wells maintains a national reputation for academic excellence. The college prides itself on offering one of the most collaborative learning environments in higher education today. This is not your ordinary education. The Wells experience is deeply personal and intensely focused on superior academic achievement. Wells offers 23 majors and over 40 minors. With one professor for every ten students, professors really get to know everyone. The average class size has fourteen students and is taught seminar-style, with discussions taking precedence over lectures. Since 1868 we've been encouraging our students to stop outside the classroom. Why? Because the best education combines traditional studies with real-world experiences. Last year, the Wells Office of Career Services coordinated internships in twenty states, the District of Columbia, France and Senegal. By graduation, 97 percent of seniors had completed at least one internship. Your education won't stop at the edge of campus. Recent internships include: the White House, ABC Television, Aquarium of the Pacific, Rock and Roll Hall of Fame and Museum, Smithsonian Institution and many more. Wells also offers a study abroad program with affiliated programs in 18 different countries. Our staff will help you pursue your academic interests wherever they lead you.

"You might study ecosystems in Australia's Outback or work in labs, film studios or research hospitals anywhere in the world. Although the two most popular programs are in Florence and Paris you could study almost anywhere. We also work with affiliated institutions to make sure your learning opportunities are as rich and varied as possible. For example, if you find the perfect course at Cornell University or the London School of Economics, we'll do our best to get you there. There are many opportunities for you to develop your leadership skills through over 40 different organizations including a literary magazine and newspaper, music and drama groups and political organizations. Wells is a Division III member of the NCAA with intercollegiate women's teams in field hockey, lacrosse, soccer, basketball, softball, swimming and tennis and intercollegiate men's teams in soccer, lacrosse, basketball and swimming. We also have intercollegiate co-ed cross country and golf teams. Wells students are intellectually curious, open-minded and creative. They are comfortable expressing themselves, listening to others and sharing ideas. They are caring citizens of the world, eager to travel beyond the campus and outside their comfort zones. Wells students love to learn. If you love learning, you'll love the Wells experience."

Campus Setting

Wells, founded in 1868, is a private, co-educational, liberal arts college. Its 365-acre campus is located in Aurora, in central New York's Finger Lake region, 40 miles southwest of Syracuse. A four-year institution, Wells College has an enrollment of 532 students. Although not originally a co-educational college, Wells College has been co-ed since 2005. The campus facilities include: photography · social science · arts labs · art gallery · library · book arts center. Wells College on-campus housing options comprise of eight units, which can accommodate 615 students: coed dorms · women's dorms. Recreation and sports facilities include: cardio room · field hockey

· fitness center · gymnasium · indoor and outdoor tennis courts · lacrosse, soccer and softball fields · swimming pool.

Student Life and Activities

Ninty percent of students live on campus, so there are certainly a lot of social activities. Popular gathering spots include the Sommer Center and The Fargo. Popular campus events include Spring Weekend, Odd/Even Weekend, and Convocation. Wells College offers 50 clubs and organizations and encourages students to pursue their interests. The most popular of these clubs/organizations are: American Red Cross Club · Amnesty International · Appointed · Bell Ringer · Campus Greens · Cardinal · Chamber Singers · Concert Choir · Chronicle · College Democrats · College Republicans · Dance Collective · Early Music Ensemble · history society · Japanese club · literary society · Model UN · orchestra · Programming Board · Queers and Allies · Student Diversity Committee · Symposium club · Whirligigs · Women in Lifelong Learning · outdoor club · Student-Athlete Advisory Committee. Regarding those intrigued by sports, there are intramural teams such as: basketball · canoeing · cross-country skiing · fitness training · flag football · floor hockey · golf · indoor soccer · running · sailing · Ultimate Frisbee · volleyball. Wells College is a member of the North Eastern Athletic Conference (Division III).

Academics and Learning Environment

Wells College has 40 full-time and 25 part-time faculty members, offering a student-to-faculty ratio of 11:1. The most common course size is 10 to 19 students. Wells College offers 21 majors with the most popular being psychology, biology/biological sciences and English and least popular being women's studies, computer science and Spanish. The school has a general core requirement. Cooperative education is not offered. All first-year students must maintain a 2.0 GPA or higher to avoid academic probation. If interested, here are some other programs that might appeal to the B student: self-designed majors · pass/fail grading option · independent study · double majors · accelerated study · Phi Beta Kappa · internships.

B Student Support and Success

The First Year Experience (WLLS 101) is required for freshman enrolled at Wells. The course is designed to acquaint students with the four divisions of social sciences, humanities, sciences and fine arts and their connection to liberal arts. The class helps students to think, read and write critically, discuss complex issues, communicate effectively, use college resources precisely and learn as a group. It is taught in a combination of discussion and workshop.

A variety of support programs are available at Wells College, such as dedicated guidance for: academic · career · personal · psychological · minority students · non-traditional students · family planning · religious. The average freshman year GPA is 2.7, and 72 percent of freshmen students return for their sophomore year. Approximately 30 percent of students pursue a graduate degree immediately after graduation. School reports demonstrate that one year after graduation, 18 percent of graduates have entered graduate school. Approximately 35 percent of students who enter the work force enter a field related to their major within six months of graduation.

WELLS COLLEGE

Wells College
Aurora, NY (Pop. 722)
Location: Rural
Four-year private
Founded: 1868
Website: http://www.wells.edu

Students
Total enrollment: 532
Undergrads: 532
Freshmen: 161
Part-time students: 2%
From out-of-state: 32%
From public schools: 89%
Male/Female: 32%/68%
Live on-campus: 90%
Off-campus employment rating: Good
Caucasian: 64%
African American: 11%
Hispanic: 8%
Asian: 2%
Native American: 1%
Mixed (2+ ethnicities): 3%
International: 3%

Academics
Calendar: Semester
Student/faculty ratio: 11:1
Class size 9 or fewer: 39%
Class size 10-29: 60%
Class size 30-49: 1%
Class size 50-99: -
Class size 100 or more: -
Returning freshmen: 72%
Six-year graduation rate: 58%

Most Popular Majors
Psychology
Biology/biological sciences
English

WELLS COLLEGE

Admissions
Applicants: 2,217
Accepted: 1,321
Acceptance rate: 59.6%
Average GPA: 3.5
ACT range: 21-26
SAT Math range: 460-580
SAT Reading range: 470-590
SAT Writing range: 1-15
Top 10% of class: 32%
Top 25% of class: 64%
Top 50% of class: 86%

Deadlines
Early Action: 12/15
Early Decision: 12/15
Regular Action: 12/15 (priority)
3/1 (final)
Notification of admission by: 4/1
Common Application: Accepted

Financial Aid
In-state tuition: $35,200
Out-of-state tuition: $35,200
Room: Varies
Board: Varies
Books: $800
Freshmen receiving need-based aid: 88%
Undergrads rec. need-based aid: 99%
Avg. % of need met by financial aid: 90%
Avg. aid package (freshmen): $31,987
Avg. aid package (undergrads): $35,314
Avg. debt upon graduation: $39,964

Prominent Alumni
Dr. Margaret Pericak-Vance, medical geneticist; Lisa Marsh Ryerson, first alumna president of Wells College; Pleasant Thiele Rowland, founder of Pleasant Co./ American Girl Doll.

School Spirit
Mascot: Express
Colors: Red and white

Support for Students with Learning Disabilities

Students with learning disabilities may desire to take advantage of specific support programs offered at Wells College. The college will grant additional time, in some situations, to students with learning disabilities in order for them to complete their degree. A lightened course load is another option available to LD students. Students with learning disabilities will find the following list of programs at Wells College useful: tutors · extended time for tests · oral tests · note-taking services · tape recorders · waiver of math degree requirement. Individual or small group tutorials are also available in: writing labs · math labs. An advisor/advocate from the LD program is available to students.

How to Get Admitted

For admissions decisions, non-academic factors considered: interview · extracurricular activities · special talents, interests and abilities · character/personal qualities · volunteer work · work experience · state of residency · alumni relationship. A high school diploma is required, although a GED is also accepted for admissions consideration. SAT or ACT test scores are required of all applicants. SAT Subject Test scores are considered, if submitted, but are not required. *According to the admissions office:* Standardized tests are considered on sliding scale depending on GPA and rigor of secondary school curriculum and preparation. *Academic units recommended:* 4 English, 4 Math, 3 Science, 2 Social Studies, 2 Foreign Language.

How to Pay for College

To apply for financial aid, students should submit the following: Free Application for Federal Student Aid (FAFSA). Wells College participates in the Federal Work Study program. *Need-based aid programs include:* scholarships and grants · general need-based awards · Federal Pell grants · state scholarships and grants · college-based scholarships and grants · private scholarships and grants. *Non-need-based aid programs include:* scholarships and grants · state scholarships and grants.

WESLEYAN COLLEGE

4760 Forsyth Road, Macon, GA 31210-4462
Admissions: 800-447-6610 · Financial Aid: 888-665-5723
Email: admissions@wesleyancollege.edu
Website: http://www.wesleyancollege.edu

From the College

"Wesleyan College is forever first for women's education-striving for excellence, grounded in faith and engaged in service to the world. Founded in 1836 as the first college in the world for women, Wesleyan College offers an education that leads to lifelong intellectual, personal and professional growth. Our academic community attracts those with a passion for learning and making a difference. The Wesleyan experience has four cornerstones: Academics, Women, Faith and Community. We believe that real education is a lifelong endeavor, fueled by curiosity, challenge and discovery, providing a solid foundation for a lifetime of learning and growth. Mention the term 'women's college' and most people envision ivy-covered towers in the U.S. northeast. However, Wesleyan College in Macon, Georgia, a four-year liberal arts college founded in 1836, has the distinction of being the world's first degree-granting college for women. Today it is recognized as one of the nation's most diverse and affordable selective colleges. Students value the college's tradition of service, small classes, beautiful residence halls and picturesque campus. Wesleyan is committed to the goals of educating women to understand and appreciate the liberal and fine arts and preparing them for careers through high-quality professional programs."

Campus Setting

Wesleyan, founded in 1836, is a church-affiliated college for women. Its 200-acre campus is located in Macon, in central Georgia, 90 miles south of Atlanta. A four-year private college, Wesleyan College has an enrollment of 697 students. The school is also affiliated with the United Methodist Church. Facilities provided include: art and history museums · equestrian center · specialized labs · library. Wesleyan College does offer on-campus housing, which includes 361 units that can accommodate 622 students. Housing options are as follows: women's dorms · single-student apartments. Recreation and sports facilities include: athletic complex · gymnasium.

Student Life and Activities

Eighty-four percent of students live on campus, so there are abundant social activities. As reported by a school representative, "One of Wesleyan's strongest traditions is our class system. No, it's definitely nothing like the one Marx critiqued. It's based on a strong class-year system going back to the early 1900's. Each class is identified by a color and a mascot. They even have their own songs and cheers. Another one of our most popular traditions would have to be the annual class theatrics of STUNT. Performed each year since 1897, classes write, direct, act and produce their own skits to raise money for scholarships." Popular off-campus gathering spots include Ingleside Village Pizza, Starbuck's, The Stack, Joshua Cup and El Sombrero. Popular campus events include Homecoming, spring formal and STUNT. Wesleyan College has 44 official student organizations. Popular groups on campus include the Student Government Association, the Campus Activities Board and the Student Recreation Council. When it comes to sports, there are intramural teams like: basketball · dodgeball · fencing · fitness challenge · floor hockey · soccer. Wesleyan College is a member of the Great South Athletic Conference (Division III).

WESLEYAN COLLEGE

Wesleyan College
Macon, GA (Pop. 91,234)
Location: Medium city
Four-year private women's college
Founded: 1836
Website: http://www.wesleyancollege.edu

Students
Total enrollment: 697
Undergrads: 648
Freshmen: 119
Part-time students: 28%
From out-of-state: 12%
From public schools: 81%
Male/Female: 0%/100%
Live on-campus: 84%
Off-campus employment rating: Fair
Caucasian: 40%
African American: 29%
Hispanic: 4%
Asian: 1%
Hawaiian or Pacific Islander: <1%
Native American: <1%
Mixed (2+ ethnicities): 3%
International: 21%

Academics
Calendar: Semester
Student/faculty ratio: 11:1
Class size 9 or fewer: 52%
Class size 10-29: 47%
Class size 30-49: 1%
Class size 50-99: -
Class size 100 or more: -
Returning freshmen: 65%
Six-year graduation rate: 64%

Most Popular Majors
Business administration
Psychology
International business

Academics and Learning Environment

Wesleyan College has 50 full-time and 31 part-time faculty members, offering a student-to-faculty ratio of 11:1. The most common course size is 2 to 9 students. Wesleyan College offers 31 majors with the most popular being business administration, psychology and international business and least popular being communications, natural resources/conservation and foreign languages. The school has a general core requirement. Cooperative education is not offered. All first-year students must maintain a 2.0 GPA or higher to avoid academic probation, and a minimum overall GPA of 2.0 is required to graduate. The B student will be interested in the following programs: self-designed majors · pass/fail grading option · independent study · double majors · dual degrees · accelerated study · honors program · internships · weekend college.

B Student Support and Success

Students get abundant attention with class sizes generally being 19 and under. The school offers an Academic Center that provides free tutoring and counseling for students who may be struggling in their classes. Group and individual sessions are available year round, either by appointment or as on a drop-in basis. In addition, Wesleyan has a Writing Center for students who need assistance with any kind of writing project. The Computer Science Lab and Help Desk are also available and is staffed by peer tutors. It offers a quiet place to study, work on projects or conduct study groups. The director of the Academic Center also offers confidential counseling for academic issues with individual students.

Wesleyan College provides a variety of support programs, including dedicated guidance for: academic · career · personal · psychological · family planning · religious. Recognizing that some students may need extra preparation, Wesleyan College is willing to provide remedial and refresher courses in: reading · writing · math · study skills. The average freshman year GPA is 2.5, and 65 percent of freshmen students return for their sophomore year. How about when it comes to post-college? Approximately 32 percent pursue a graduate degree immediately after graduation. One year after graduation, school reports reveal that 30 percent of graduates have entered graduate school. Among those students who enter the workforce, approximately 28 percent of them enter a field that relates to their major within six months of graduation.

Support for Students with Learning Disabilities

Students with learning disabilities will be pleased to find that Wesleyan College offers a variety of specific support programs. If the situation calls for it, the college may grant additional time to students with learning disabilities to complete their degree. Another option open to LD students is a lightened course load. The following is a list that might prove helpful to those students with learning disabilities: tutors · learning center · testing accommodations · extended time for tests · oral tests · readers · note-taking services · priority registration · waiver of foreign language degree requirement. Individual or small group tutorials are also available in: time management · organizational skills · learning strategies · specific subject areas · writing labs · math labs · study skills. An advisor/advocate from the Academic Center is available to students.

How to Get Admitted

For admissions decisions, non-academic factors considered: extracurricular activities · special talents, interests and abilities · character/personal qualities · volunteer work · work experience · state of residency · alumni relationship. A high school diploma is required, although a GED is also accepted for admissions consideration. SAT or ACT test scores are required of all applicants. SAT Subject Test scores are not required. *According to the admissions office:* Minimum scores of 480 in critical reading and 440 in math (composite ACT score of 20 with scores of 20 in English and 18 in math) and minimum 2.0 GPA required. *Academic units recommended:* 4 English, 4 Math, 4 Science, 4 Social Studies, 4 Foreign Language.

How to Pay for College

To apply for financial aid, students should submit the following: Free Application for Federal Student Aid (FAFSA) · institution's own financial aid forms · state aid form · Non-custodian (Divorced/ Separated) Parent's Statement. Wesleyan College participates in the Federal Work Study program. *Need-based aid programs include:* scholarships and grants · general need-based awards · Federal Pell grants · state scholarships and grants · college-based scholarships and grants · private scholarships and grants · HOPE Scholarship · Georgia Tuition Equalization Grant Georgia LEAP Grant. *Non-need-based aid programs include:* scholarships and grants · general need-based awards · state scholarships and grants · creative arts and performance awards · special achievements and activities awards · special characteristics awards · United Methodist Church-related scholarships/grants.

WESLEYAN COLLEGE

Highlights

Admissions
Applicants: 779
Accepted: 338
Acceptance rate: 43.4%
Average GPA: 3.5
ACT range: 17-22
SAT Math range: 430-560
SAT Reading range: 450-570
SAT Writing range: 3-11
Top 10% of class: 32%
Top 25% of class: 55%
Top 50% of class: 87%

Deadlines
Early Action: No
Early Decision: 11/15
Regular Action: 5/1 (priority)
8/1 (final)
Common Application: Accepted

Financial Aid
In-state tuition: $19,750
Out-of-state tuition: $19,750
Room: Varies
Board: Varies
Books: $2,000
Freshmen receiving need-based aid: 66%
Undergrads rec. need-based aid: 65%
Avg. % of need met by financial aid: 71%
Avg. aid package (freshmen): $19,067
Avg. aid package (undergrads): $19,206
Avg. debt upon graduation: $31,776

Prominent Alumni
Toni Jennings, Lieutenant Governor of Florida; Sara Branham Matthews, microbiologist.

School Spirit
Mascot: Wolves
Colors: Purple and white
Song: *Hail Wesleyan*

563

WEST VIRGINIA UNIVERSITY

P.O. Box 6201, Morgantown, WV 26506-6201
Admissions: 800-344-WVU1 · Financial Aid: 800-344-WVU1
Email: go2wvu@mail.wvu.edu · Website: http://www.wvu.edu

From the College

"If you want to see where the world is going, follow West Virginia University (WVU). A tradition of academic excellence attracts exceptional high school seniors. WVU has produced 24 Rhodes Scholars, 36 Goldwater Scholars, 22 Truman Scholars and five members of *USA Today's* All-USA College Academic First team. Whether your goal is to be an aerospace engineer, reporter, physicist, athletic trainer, forensic investigator, pharmacist or CEO, WVU's 191 degree choices can make it happen. Student-centered initiatives extend learning beyond the classroom. Resident faculty leaders live next to the residence halls to mentor students, and WVUp All Night provides free food and activities on weekends. The Mountaineer Parents Club connects 20,000 WVU families, and a toll-free helpline leads to a parent advocate. The Student Recreation Center includes athletic courts, pools, weight/fitness equipment and a 50-foot indoor climbing wall. Students come from every West Virginia county, 50 states and Washington, DC and 100 countries because WVU encourages and nurtures diversity. As a major research institution, WVU averaged $176 million in sponsored research funding in the past two years. The campus is one of the safest in the nation, and the area's natural beauty provides chances to ski, bike, rock climb, hike and go white-water rafting."

Campus Setting

West Virginia University, founded in 1867, is a public, comprehensive institution. Programs are offered through the Colleges of Agriculture, Forestry and Consumer Sciences, Arts and Sciences, Business and Economics, Creative Arts, Engineering & Mineral Resources, Law and Human Resources & Education and the Schools of Dentistry, Journalism, Medicine, Nursing, Pharmacy and Physical Education. The two campuses, totaling 1,456 acres, are located in Morgantown and Evansdale, 75 miles south of Pittsburgh. A four-year institution, West Virginia University has an enrollment of 29,466 students. Although not originally co-educational college, West Virginia University has been co-ed since 1889. Besides a library, the campus facilities include: museums · arboretum · herbarium · planetarium · experimental farms · natatorium · coliseum · stadium · software development, fluidization, Black culture and research, cancer research, recreation and creative arts centers. West Virginia University's on-campus housing comprises of 16 units that can accommodate 5,781 students. Accommodation options are: coed dorms · women's dorms · men's dorms · sorority housing · fraternity housing · single-student apartments · married-student apartments · special housing for disabled students · special housing for international students. Recreation and sports facilities include: coliseum · football stadium · halls · intramural fields · natatorium · recreational center · swimming pool · track, baseball and soccer fields.

Student Life and Activities

Seventy-five percent of students live off campus. "Morgantown is a small city with cosmopolitan appeal, reports the student newspaper. "Major musical acts from the Ramones to Alan Jackson have played here recently, while artists and actors are showcased in WVU's Creative Arts Center. Even with easy access to Washington, DC and Pittsburgh, Morgantown is minutes away from recreational lakes, parks and wilderness." Popular student gathering spots include The Side Pocket Pub,

Mountainlair, the Student Union and Student Recreation Center. Popular campus events include Festival of Ideas, basketball games, FallFest, outdoor recreation trips, concerts by touring musical artists, football, Mountaineer Week and performing arts events at Creative Arts Center. West Virginia University has 400 official student organizations. Popular groups on campus include the student newspaper and campus radio station. West Virginia University is a member of the Big 12 (Division I, Football I-A) and Eastern Wrestling League (Division I).

Academics and Learning Environment

West Virginia University has 1,042 full-time and 590 part-time faculty members, offering a student-to-faculty ratio of 21:1. The most common course size is 20 to 29 students. West Virginia University offers 265 majors with the most popular being business, engineering and nursing. The school has a general core requirement. Cooperative education is available. All first-year students must maintain a 2.0 GPA or higher to avoid academic probation, and a minimum overall GPA of 2.0 is required to graduate. The following are other special academic programs that might appeal to a B student: self-designed majors · pass/fail grading option · independent study · double majors · accelerated study · honors program · Phi Beta Kappa · internships · weekend college · distance learning certificate programs.

B Student Support and Success

With almost 4,000 freshmen entering WVU each year, the school has designed a large program that provides students academic support. University 101 is a class geared to help freshmen adjust to university life and its demands. A passing grade in this course is required for graduation. In the fall semester, students also may take the SSS Orientation Course, which is designed to introduce them to academic requirements and acquaint them with how student support services can help. In assigning residence halls, the college places freshmen with similar majors and/or passions in the same dorm, enabling them to form peer study groups and meet others with the same interests. Other support systems include a math lab at the Learning Center and the availability of writing assistance through sessions geared to help with everything from letters to research papers. Free tutoring is available for most general classes in either one-on-one or study group sessions. Students who are still not sure about their major can get assistance through the Student Support Services professional staff of advisors.

West Virginia University prides itself on offering a variety of support programs, some of them being dedicated guidance for: academic · career · personal · psychological · minority students · military · veterans · non-traditional students · family planning. WVU recognizes that some students may need extra preparation and therefore offers remedial and refresher courses in: reading · writing · math · study skills. The average freshman year GPA is 2.5, and 77 percent of freshmen students return for their sophomore year. As for companies that most frequently hire graduates from West Virginia University, some of them include: Allegheny Energy · Department of the Treasury · Dow Chemical · Ernst & Young · FedEx Ground · Geico · Halliburton · Insight Global · KeyLogic

WEST VIRGINIA UNIVERSITY

Highlights

West Virginia University
Morgantown, WV (Pop. 31,000)
Location: Large town
Four-year public
Founded: 1867
Website: http://www.wvu.edu

Students
Total enrollment: 29,466
Undergrads: 22,757
Freshmen: 6,266
Part-time students: 8%
From out-of-state: 54%
Male/Female: 54%/46%
Live on-campus: 25%
In fraternities: 6%
In sororities: 5%
Off-campus employment rating: Good
Caucasian: 83%
African American: 4%
Hispanic: 3%
Asian: 2%
Hawaiian or Pacific Islander: <1%
Native American: <1%
Mixed (2+ ethnicities): 3%
International: 4%

Academics
Calendar: Semester
Student/faculty ratio: 21:1
Class size 9 or fewer: 17%
Class size 10-29: 45%
Class size 30-49: 20%
Class size 50-99: 11%
Class size 100 or more: 8%
Returning freshmen: 77%
Six-year graduation rate: 57%

Most Popular Majors
Business
Engineering
Nursing

565

College Profiles

WEST VIRGINIA UNIVERSITY

Admissions

Applicants: 16,079
Accepted: 13,713
Acceptance rate: 85.3%
Average GPA: 3.4
ACT range: 21-26
SAT Math range: 480-580
SAT Reading range: 470-570
SAT Writing range: Not reported
Top 10% of class: 20%
Top 25% of class: 45%
Top 50% of class: 79%

Deadlines

Early Action: No
Early Decision: No
Regular Action: Rolling admissions
Common Application: Accepted

Financial Aid

In-state tuition: $6,960
Out-of-state tuition: $20,424
Room: $4,956
Board: $4,626
Books: $1,100
Freshmen receiving need-based aid: 45%
Undergrads rec. need-based aid: 57%
Avg. % of need met by financial aid: 75%
Avg. aid package (freshmen): $6,616
Avg. aid package (undergrads): $7,271
Avg. debt upon graduation: $29,149

Prominent Alumni

Irene M. Keeley, U.S. district judge; Jerry West, NBA player and executive; Raymond J. Lane, former president/CO/chair, Oracle Corporation.

School Spirit

Mascot: Mountaineer
Colors: Old gold and blue
Song: *Hail West Virginia*

566

America's
Best Colleges for
B Students

Systems · KPMG · MC Dean · Microsoft · NAVAIR · NASA · Northrop Grumman · Northwestern Mutual Financial Network · Pepsi Bottling Group · PPG · PricewaterhouseCoopers · Siemens Energy · Sherwin Williams · United Bank · U.S. Department of Energy.

Support for Students with Learning Disabilities

West Virginia University prides itself on offering specific support programs geared towards students with learning disabilities. The university will, if seen as necessary, grant additional time to students with learning disabilities to complete their degree and/or offer a lightened course load. According to the school, The Mountaineer Academic Program is an academic enhancement program which provides student centered supplemental academic support services for students with disabilities. MAP Coaches provide consistency through regular contact and individualized support, accountability through weekly meetings, guidance to improve study skills, time management and organizational skills, and referrals and regular contact with various academic and personal support services. MAP Tutors provide individual content tutoring and support. LD students attending WVU will find the following list of programs useful: remedial math · tutors · learning center · testing accommodations · untimed tests · extended time for tests · take-home exam · oral tests · exam on tape or computer · readers · typist/scribe · note-taking services · reading machines · texts on tape · early syllabus · diagnostic testing service · priority registration · priority seating. Individual or small group tutorials are also available in: time management · organizational skills · learning strategies · specific subject areas · writing labs · math labs · study skills. An advisor/advocate from the Mountaineer Academic Program is available to students.

How to Get Admitted

For admissions decisions, non-academic factors considered: extracurricular activities · special talents, interests and abilities · work experience. A high school diploma is required, although a GED is also accepted for admissions consideration. SAT or ACT test scores are required of all applicants. SAT Subject Test scores are not required. *According to the admissions office:* English units should include composition, grammar and literature. Math units should include algebra I, algebra II and geometry. Electives in computer science, fine arts and humanities recommended. Minimum combined SAT Reasoning score of 910 (composite ACT score of 19) and minimum 2.0 GPA required of in-state applicants. Minimum combined SAT Reasoning score of 990 (composite ACT score of 21) and minimum 2.25 GPA required of out-of-state applicants. Higher requirements for some programs. *Academic units recommended:* 4 English, 4 Math, 3 Science, 3 Social Studies, 2 Foreign Language.

How to Pay for College

To apply for financial aid, students should submit the following: Free Application for Federal Student Aid (FAFSA) · state aid form. West Virginia University participates in the Federal Work Study program. *Need-based aid programs include:* scholarships and grants · general need-based awards · Federal Pell grants · state scholarships and grants · college-based scholarships and grants · private scholarships and grants. *Non-need-based aid programs include:* scholarships and grants · general need-based awards · state scholarships and grants · creative arts and performance awards · special achievements and activities awards · special characteristics awards · athletic scholarships · ROTC scholarships.

WESTERN CONNECTICUT STATE UNIVERSITY

181 White Street, Danbury, CT 06810
Admissions: 877-837-9278 · Financial Aid: 877-837-9278
Email: admissions@wcsu.edu · Website: http://www.wcsu.edu

From the College

"Western offers an array of programs–everything from an associate degree to a doctorate in instructional leadership–programs that empower your future and lead to success. Here, you'll find an outstanding learning environment in our small class sizes and an exceptionally qualified faculty who combine academic and practitioner perspectives."

Campus Setting

Western Connecticut State University, founded in 1903, is a public, comprehensive university. It has two campuses, the original, 34-acre campus located in downtown Danbury and a newer 364-acre campus west of the city's center. A four-year institution, Western Connecticut State University has an enrollment of 6,025 students. Although not originally a co-educational college, Western Connecticut State University has been co-ed since 1933. The school also has a library with 215,096 books. Housing options at Western Connecticut State University include 845 on-campus units which can accommodate 1,601 students. Housing options are: coed dorms · single-student apartments. Recreation and sports facilities include: athletic complex · baseball and softball fields · gymnasium · tennis courts.

Student Life and Activities

Seventy-six percent of students live off campus. Some popular campus events at Western Connecticut University include The President's Lecture Series, Bauhaus Art Club 'spoken word' events, English Society readings, Black Student Alliance summits and formals, German Studies Center talks, percussion ensemble performances, Concert Choir and Chamber Singers performances, Continuing 'Research Seminar' series, art department bus trips to New York City museums and department of social science 'The Social Hour'. Western Connecticut State University has 89 official student organizations. Popular groups on campus include fraternities and sororities, Catholic Campus Ministry, Jewish Student Association, Newman Club and West-Conn Christian Ministry. There are intramural teams available, such as: basketball · football · soccer · softball. Western Connecticut State University is a member of the Freedom Football Conference (Division III), Little East Conference (Division III), New England Women's Lacrosse Alliance (Division III) and New Jersey Athletic Conference (Division III).

Academics and Learning Environment

Western Connecticut State University has 213 full-time and 401 part-time faculty members, offering a student-to-faculty ratio of 14:1. The most common course size is 20 to 29 students. Western Connecticut State University offers 50 majors with the most popular being justice/law administration, management and psychology and least popular being medical technology and American studies. The school has a general core requirement. Cooperative education is available. All first-year students must maintain a 2.0 GPA or higher to avoid academic probation. Here are some other special academic programs that might appeal to a B student: self-designed majors · pass/fail grading option · independent study · double majors · dual degrees · honors program · internships · distance learning.

B Student Support and Success

Western Connecticut offers a Study Skills/Reading Lab to help students with skills such as reading, outlining, note taking, studying, time management, test taking, researching and word processing. The Math Clinic helps with everything from math skills to math anxiety. Tutors help student study for tests and solve homework problems. The Writing Lab provides assistance on writing, grammar, development, style, organization and mechanics.

Western Connecticut State University offers a variety of support programs. Some of these include dedicated guidance for: academic · career · personal · psychological · minority students · veterans · non-traditional students · family planning · religious. Additional counseling services include: Myers-Briggs Type Indicator (MBTI) · Strong Interest Inventory. Recognizing that some students may need extra preparation, Western Connecticut State University offers remedial and refresher courses in: reading · writing · math · study skills. Other remedial services include Educational Achievement and Access Program. The average freshman year GPA is 2.5, and 74 percent of freshmen students return for their sophomore year. How about what students do after college? Some do get involved with the workforce. Approximately two percent pursue a graduate degree immediately after graduation. One year after graduation, the school reports that five percent of graduated students have entered graduate school. This is a list of companies that most frequently hire graduates from Western Connecticut State University: ATMI · Bethel Board of Education · Brookfield Board of Education · Boehringer Ingelheim · Cardis · Citigroup · Costco Wholesale · Danbury Board of Education · Danbury Hospital · Deloitte · Ethan Allen · General Electric Capital Corporation · Hospital of Saint Raphael · IBM · KPMG · Mental Health Association of Connecticut · New Milford Board of Education · Norwalk Hospital · Ridgefield Board of Education · People's Bank · Saint Mary's Hospital · Scholastic Inc. · State of Connecticut · Waterbury Hospital · Western Connecticut State University.

Support for Students with Learning Disabilities

Some students, specifically those with learning disabilities, may take advantage of certain support programs offered by Western Connecticut State University. In some situations, the college will grant additional time to students with learning disabilities to complete their degree. Another option for the LD student is a lightened course load. LD students should consider the following programs: remedial math · remedial English · tutors · learning center · testing accommodations · untimed tests · extended time for tests · take-home exam · oral tests · exam on tape or computer · typist/scribe · note-taking services · reading machines · tape recorders · early syllabus · priority registration. Individual or small group tutorials are also available in: time management · organizational skills · learning strategies · specific subject areas · writing labs · math labs · study skills. An advisor/advocate from the LD program is available to students.

How to Get Admitted

For admissions decisions, non-academic factors considered: interview · extracurricular activities · special talents, interests and abilities ·

WESTERN CONNECTICUT STATE UNIVERSITY

Highlights

Western Connecticut State University
Danbury, CT (Pop. 82,807)
Location: Medium city
Four-year public
Founded: 1903
Website: http://www.wcsu.edu

Students
Total enrollment: 6,025
Undergrads: 5,492
Freshmen: 974
Part-time students: 20%
From out-of-state: 7%
From public schools: 85%
Male/Female: 47%/53%
Live on-campus: 24%
In fraternities: 3%
In sororities: 3%
Off-campus employment rating: Excellent
Caucasian: 68%
African American: 11%
Hispanic: 14%
Asian: 3%
Hawaiian or Pacific Islander: <1%
Native American: <1%
Mixed (2+ ethnicities): 1%
International: <1%

Academics
Calendar: Semester
Student/faculty ratio: 14:1
Class size 9 or fewer: 6%
Class size 10-29: 66%
Class size 30-49: 26%
Class size 50-99: 1%
Class size 100 or more: -
Returning freshmen: 74%
Six-year graduation rate: 44%

Most Popular Majors
Justice/law administration
Management
Psychology

569

College Profiles

WESTERN CONNECTICUT STATE UNIVERSITY

Highlights

Admissions
Applicants: 3,613
Accepted: 2,366
Acceptance rate: 65.5%
Average GPA: 3.4
ACT range: Not reported
SAT Math range: 440-540
SAT Reading range: 440-540
SAT Writing range: 1-10
Top 10% of class: 7%
Top 25% of class: 26%
Top 50% of class: 61%

Deadlines
Early Action: No
Early Decision: No
Regular Action: Rolling admissions
Notification of admission by: 12/1
Common Application: Accepted

Financial Aid
In-state tuition: $4,600
Out-of-state tuition: $14,886
Room: $6,432
Board: $4,674
Books: $1,300
Freshmen receiving need-based aid: 70%
Undergrads rec. need-based aid: 61%
Avg. % of need met by financial aid: 63%
Avg. aid package (freshmen): $7,920
Avg. aid package (undergrads): $7,767
Avg. debt upon graduation: $22,505

Prominent Alumni
Thurston Moore, musician for Sonic Youth; Jodi Rell, former Governor of Connecticut.

School Spirit
Mascot: Colonials
Colors: Dark blue, metallic copper and white

character/personal qualities · volunteer work · work experience · geographical location · alumni relationship. A high school diploma is required, although a GED is also accepted for admissions consideration. SAT or ACT test scores are required of all applicants. SAT Subject Test scores are recommended but not required. *According to the admissions office:* Minimum combined SAT Reasoning score of 1000, rank in top half of secondary school class and minimum 2.67 GPA recommended. *Academic units recommended:* 4 English, 3 Math, 2 Science, 1 Social Studies, 3 Foreign Language.

How to Pay for College

To apply for financial aid, students should submit the following: Free Application for Federal Student Aid (FAFSA) · institution's own financial aid forms. Western Connecticut State University participates in the Federal Work Study program. *Need-based aid programs include:* scholarships and grants · general need-based awards · Federal Pell grants · state scholarships and grants · college-based scholarships and grants · private scholarships and grants. *Non-need-based aid programs include:* scholarships and grants · state scholarships and grants · private scholarships/grants.

570

WESTERN NEW ENGLAND UNIVERSITY

1215 Wilbraham Road, Springfield, MA 01119-2684
Admissions: 800-325-1122, extension 1321
Financial Aid: 800-325-1122, extension 2080
Email: learn@wne.edu · Website: http://www.wne.edu

From the College

"Western New England University is committed to being a leader regionally and recognized nationally in providing integrated professional and liberal learning. The university is characterized by a synergy that results internally from the collaboration of its programs in Arts and Sciences, Business, Engineering, pre-Pharmacy and Law and externally from the strategic partnerships and alliances forged with the local and regional business, educational and civic community. All students are regarded as a resource in excellence whose special talents and attributes will be challenged by their educational program to assure success in their professional and personal development and lives."

Campus Setting

Western New England, founded in 1919, is a private, comprehensive, coeducational institution. Programs are offered through the Colleges of Arts and Sciences, Business, Engineering, Pharmacy (pending appropriate approvals) and the School of Law. Its 215-acre campus is located in a residential section of Springfield, 90 miles west of Boston. A four-year institution, Western New England University has an enrollment of 3,800 students. The school also has a library with 132,700 books. The on-campus housing of 765 units at Western New England University can accommodate 2,000 students. Housing options: coed dorms · single-student apartments · special housing for disabled students. Recreation and sports facilities include: athletic center · field · park · stadium.

Student Life and Activities

With sixty-five percent of students living on campus, there is a large selection of social activities. Some of the most popular social events during the year are Parent's Weekend, First Week and Senior Week. Western New England University has 60 official student organizations. The Student Senate and the Council of Peer Advisors are two of the influential groups on campus. As for sports, there are intramural teams: badminton · basketball · bocce · flag football · floor hockey · horseshoes · indoor soccer · inner-tube water polo · kickball · rock climbing · softball · table tennis · Ultimate Frisbee · volleyball. Western New England University is a member of the ECAC Hockey (Division III), New England College Wrestling Association (Division III), New England Football Conference (Division III), Commonwealth Coast Conference (Division III), New England Women's Lacrosse Alliance (Division III) and Pilgrim League (Division III).

Academics and Learning Environment

Western New England University has 221 full-time and 137 part-time faculty members, offering a student-to-faculty ratio of 13:1. The most common course size is 20 to 29 students. Western New England University offers 76 majors with the most popular being mechanical engineering, psychology and sport management and least popular being economics and philosophy. The school has a general core requirement. Cooperative education is not offered. All first-year students must maintain a 1.9 GPA or higher to avoid academic probation. As for some other special academic programs that might appeal to a B student, there are these: self-designed majors · independent

571

College Profiles

WESTERN NEW ENGLAND UNIVERSITY

Western New England University
Springfield (Pop. 153,552)
Location: Medium city
Four-year private
Founded: 1919
Website: http://www.wne.edu

Students
Total enrollment: 3,800
Undergrads: 2,667
Freshmen: 758
Part-time students: 6%
From out-of-state: 54%
Male/Female: 60%/40%
Live on-campus: 65%
Off-campus employment rating: Fair
Caucasian: 77%
African American: 5%
Hispanic: 8%
Asian: 3%
Hawaiian or Pacific Islander: <1%
Native American: <1%
Mixed (2+ ethnicities): 2%
International: 2%

Academics
Calendar: Semester
Student/faculty ratio: 13:1
Class size 9 or fewer: 18%
Class size 10-29: 76%
Class size 30-49: 6%
Class size 50-99: -
Class size 100 or more: -
Returning freshmen: 74%
Six-year graduation rate: 59%

Most Popular Majors
Mechanical engineering
Psychology
Sport management

study · double majors · accelerated study · honors program · internships · distance learning certificate programs.

B Student Support and Success

Information from Western New England University explains aspects of the school that are of interest to the B student: "Math and science tutoring centers, academic advisors, peer advisors, small classes (average 21-22); all professors are required to hold office hours. First year seminar course for freshmen students." Advice for prospective students includes these remarks: "Students should challenge themselves academically, show consistency in their grades and get involved in their school and community. When the Admission Office reviews a student's application, we calculate their transcript to obtain an overall GPA. We calculate all college prep courses (full credit) from freshmen to senior year. We look for a consistent performance over four years and we like to see students challenging themselves academically. Western New England University facilitates student learning."

Western New England University provides a variety of support programs. The university offers dedicated guidance for: academic · career · personal · psychological · minority students · military · veterans · non-traditional students · family planning · religious. Annually, 74 percent of freshmen students return for their sophomore year. Approximately 12 percent of students pursue a graduate degree immediately after graduation, and 79 percent enter a related field to their major within six months of graduation. Some companies that most frequently hire graduates from Western New England University are: AT&T · Deloitte · Various State and Local Police Departments · CDI Aerospace · BAE · Aetna · Cigna · Hamilton Sundstrand · MassMutual · Pratt & Whitney · PricewaterhouseCoopers · Raytheon · UPS.

Support for Students with Learning Disabilities

Students of Western New England University with learning disabilities may want to consider taking specific support programs. If deemed necessary, the LD student will receive additional time in order to complete their degree, as well as a lightened course load if desired. High school foreign language waivers are accepted. Students with learning disabilities may very well find the following programs at Western New England University useful: remedial English · remedial reading · tutors · learning center · extended time for tests · take-home exam · readers · typist/scribe · note-taking services · reading machines · tape recorders · texts on tape · early syllabus · priority registration · waiver of math degree requirement. Individual or small group tutorials are also available in: time management · organizational skills · learning strategies · specific subject areas · writing labs · math labs · study skills. An advisor/advocate from the WNEC Student Disability Services is available to students.

How to Get Admitted

For admissions decisions, non-academic factors considered: interview · extracurricular activities · special talents, interests and abilities · character/personal qualities · volunteer work · work experience · state of residency · minority affiliation · alumni relationship. A high school diploma is required, although a GED is also accepted for admissions consideration. SAT or ACT test scores are required of all applicants. SAT Subject Test scores are not required. *Academic units recommended:* 4 English, 4 Math, 2 Science, 2 Social Studies.

How to Pay for College

To apply for financial aid, students should submit the following: Free Application for Federal Student Aid (FAFSA) · federal income tax forms and W2(s). Western New England University participates in the Federal Work Study program. *Need-based aid programs include:* scholarships and grants · general need-based awards · Federal Pell grants · state scholarships and grants · college-based scholarships and grants · private scholarships and grants. *Non-need-based aid programs include:* scholarships and grants · state scholarships and grants · creative arts and performance awards · ROTC scholarships.

WESTERN NEW ENGLAND UNIVERSITY

Highlights

Admissions
Applicants: 5,988
Accepted: 4,881
Acceptance rate: 81.5%
Average GPA: 3.3
ACT range: 22-26
SAT Math range: 490-610
SAT Reading range: 470-570
SAT Writing range: Not reported
Top 10% of class: 17%
Top 25% of class: 44%
Top 50% of class: 74%

Deadlines
Early Action: No
Early Decision: No
Regular Action: Rolling admissions
Common Application: Accepted

Financial Aid
In-state tuition: $31,200
Out-of-state tuition: $31,200
Room: Varies
Board: Varies
Books: $1,240
Freshmen receiving need-based aid: 86%
Undergrads rec. need-based aid: 79%
Avg. % of need met by financial aid: 70%
Avg. aid package (freshmen): $24,995
Avg. aid package (undergrads): $23,023

Prominent Alumni
Kevin S. Delbridge, Senior Advisor, HarbourVest Partners LLC; Dennis M. Lind, Vice President, Design & Engineering, Walt Disney Parks & Resorts; Lisa Bachmann, Executive Vice President & Chief Operating Officer, Big Lots!

School Spirit
Mascot: Golden Bear
Colors: Blue and gold
Song: *The Time Has Come*

WESTMINSTER COLLEGE

South Market Street, New Wilmington, PA 16172
Admissions: 800-942-8033 · Financial Aid: 724-946-7102
Email: admis@westminster.edu · Website: http://www.westminster.edu

From the College

"It is the mission of Westminster College to bring to our students a world-class education that integrates the liberal arts with a major. We also pride ourselves in the manner in which extra- and co-curricular activities are integrated into the learning experience. The faculty take pride in the promotion of active and collaborative learning experiences. We enjoy a very high graduation rate with over seventy-six percent of our first year students graduating on time."

Campus Setting

Westminster, founded in 1852, is a church-affiliated, liberal arts college. Its 300-acre campus is located in New Wilmington, 65 miles north of Pittsburgh. A four-year private institution, Westminster College has an enrollment of 1,359 students and is affiliated with the Presbyterian Church (USA). Westminster College provides on-campus housing, which includes 700 units, accommodating 1,160 students. Housing options are as follows: women's dorms · men's dorms · fraternity housing. Recreation and sports facilities include: baseball, football, soccer and softball fields · fitness center · gymnasium · natatorium · indoor and outdoor track and field.

Student Life and Activities

Seventy-three percent of students live on campus. "Socially, fraternities provide the greatest amount of activity; culturally, there's not much happening, but Pittsburgh is close for concerts and museums," reports the Holcad. Popular on-campus gathering spots include fraternity houses, the student union and the campus pub; students gather off-campus at Seafood Express and Quaker Steak & Lube. Students flock to events including Homecoming, Christmas Vespers, Greek Week and Volley Rock. Westminster College has 69 official student organizations. According to the editor of the school newspaper, the most influential groups on campus are Christian organizations and the Greeks. There are intramural teams for students with an interest in athletics: aerobics · basketball · bowling · canoe racing · flag football · golf · indoor soccer · inner-tube water polo · kickball · racquetball · softball · table tennis · volleyball. Westminster College is a member of the Presidents' Athletic Conference (Division III).

Academics and Learning Environment

Westminster College has 98 full-time and 54 part-time faculty members, offering a student-to-faculty ratio of 11:1. The most common course size is 10 to 19 students. Westminster College offers 35 majors with the most popular being business administration, elementary education and biology and least popular being theatre, Spanish and philosophy. The school has a general core requirement. Cooperative education is not offered. All first-year students must maintain a 1.8 GPA or higher to avoid academic probation. For those B students interested, these programs are available: self-designed majors · pass/fail grading option · independent study · double majors · accelerated study · honors program · internships.

B Student Support and Success

The Westminster Plan provides a complete core curriculum in science, humanities, math, computer science and religion. All students graduate with two majors. Student-to-faculty ratio is 11:1, and most classes are no more than 19 students. The school emphasizes that it takes education seriously and that this is not a "party school." Westminster offers a First Year Program as well as the Next Chapter, a summer reading program for all incoming first-year students. The Learning Center is open for students who need assistance to "improve their academic performance."

Westminster College provides a variety of support programs including dedicated guidance for: academic · career · personal · psychological · minority students · non-traditional students · religious. Annually, 86 percent of freshmen students return for their sophomore year. These are some of the companies that most frequently hire graduates from Westminster College: Deloitte · NVR/ Ryan Homes · Montgomery County Public Schools · Seneca Valley School District · Sharon Regional Health System.

Support for Students with Learning Disabilities

For those students with learning disabilities, Westminster College offers several support programs. The college may see fit, depending upon the situation, to grant additional time to students with learning disabilities in order to complete their degree. Some options that might benefit LD students are these: remedial reading · tutors · learning center · untimed tests · extended time for tests · oral tests · readers · note-taking services · videotaped classes · priority registration · waiver of math degree requirement. Individual or small group tutorials are also available in: time management · organizational skills · learning strategies · specific subject areas · study skills. An advisor/advocate from the LD program is available to students.

How to Get Admitted

For admissions decisions, non-academic factors considered: interview · extracurricular activities · special talents, interests and abilities · character/personal qualities · volunteer work · work experience · state of residency · religious affiliation/commitment · minority affiliation · alumni relationship. A high school diploma is required, although a GED is also accepted for admissions consideration. SAT or ACT test scores are required of all applicants. SAT subject Test scores are not required. *Academic units recommended:* 4 English, 3 Math, 2 Science, 3 Social Studies, 2 Foreign Language.

How to Pay for College

To apply for financial aid, students should submit the following: Free Application for Federal Student Aid (FAFSA) · institution's own financial aid forms. Westminster College participates in the Federal Work Study program. *Need-based aid programs include:* scholarships and grants · general need-based awards · Federal Pell grants · college-based scholarships and grants · private scholarships and

WESTMINSTER COLLEGE

Highlights

Westminster College
New Wilmington (Pop. 2,467)
Location: Rural
Four-year private
Founded: 1852
Website: http://www.westminster.edu

Students
Total enrollment: 1,359
Undergrads: 1,306
Freshmen: 307
Part-time students: 4%
From out-of-state: 22%
From public schools: 90%
Male/Female: 41%/59%
Live on-campus: 73%
In fraternities: 35%
In sororities: 38%
Off-campus employment rating: Excellent
Caucasian: 83%
African American: 1%
Hispanic: 1%
Asian: <1%
Hawaiian or Pacific Islander: <1%
Native American: <1%
Mixed (2+ ethnicities): 2%
International: <1%

Academics
Calendar: Semester
Student/faculty ratio: 11:1
Class size 9 or fewer: 25%
Class size 10-29: 69%
Class size 30-49: 6%
Class size 50-99: 1%
Class size 100 or more: -
Returning freshmen: 86%
Six-year graduation rate: 77%

Most Popular Majors
Business administration
Elementary education
Biology

575

WESTMINSTER COLLEGE

Admissions
Applicants: 3,378
Accepted: 2,478
Acceptance rate: 73.4%
Average GPA: 3.5
ACT range: 20-25
SAT Math range: 460-570
SAT Reading range: 460-580
SAT Writing range: 1-14
Top 10% of class: 17%
Top 25% of class: 50%
Top 50% of class: 85%

Deadlines
Early Action: 11/15
Early Decision: No
Regular Action: Rolling admissions
Common Application: Accepted

Financial Aid
In-state tuition: $33,610
Out-of-state tuition: $33,610
Room: $5,480
Board: $2,660
Books: Varies
Freshmen receiving need-based aid: 87%
Undergrads rec. need-based aid: 81%
Avg. % of need met by financial aid: 80%
Avg. aid package (freshmen): $26,071
Avg. aid package (undergrads): $25,879
Avg. debt upon graduation: $34,870

Prominent Alumni
William N. Johnston, president of Wesley College; Andrew McKelvey, former chairman and CEO of Monster.com; Deborah Platt Majoras, former charirman of the Federal Trade Commission.

School Spirit
Mascot: Titans/Lady Titans
Colors: Blue and white
Song: *Victory*

grants. *Non-need-based aid programs include:* scholarships and grants · state scholarships and grants.

WHEELOCK COLLEGE

200 The Riverway, Boston, MA 02215
Admissions: 800-734-5212 · Financial Aid: 617-879-2443
Email: undergrad@wheelock.edu · Website: http://www.wheelock.edu

From the College

"Making the world a better place by educating people to improve the lives of children and families is the cornerstone of a Wheelock education. Wheelock's academic environment values excellence and equity, delivering an education that expands intellectual capabilities and provides students with the knowledge and skills needed to succeed in personal and professional life. What makes a Wheelock education distinctive is what is common across programs. No matter what is studied here at Wheelock, a student leaves a caring, creative and competent person with professional knowledge and skills and the confidence to apply learning to make a difference.

"Wheelock's Mission: to improve the lives of children and families. Wheelock's Vision: as a private college with a public mission, strive to be the premier college educating people to create a safe, caring and just world for children and families. As we have since 1888, we contribute to the vitality of families, communities and societies by: educating students who are well prepared academically and as practitioners with real-world experience -ready to be leaders and advocates, confident in their abilities and sought after in a wide range of careers; advocating for programs, policies and laws that enhance the quality of life for children and families. Wheelock's Values: we are committed to being a dynamic, rigorous and transformational learning, living and working community underpinned by theory, practice, research and advocacy. We infuse all we do with a focus on achievement, integrity, mutual respect, multiculturalism and diversity and social justice with a global perspective."

Campus Setting

A four-year private institution, Wheelock College has an enrollment of 1,378 students. Although not originally a co-educational college, Wheelock College has been co-ed since 1972. The school also has a library with 83,267 books. Wheelock College boasts on-campus housing with six units that can accommodate 630 students. Housing options: coed dorms · women's dorms · special housing for disabled students · cooperative housing.

Student Life and Activities

With 63 percent of students living on campus, there are plenty of social activities. On campus, students like to gather at the college center and the cafeteria. Popular activities include Spring Concert, Spring Formal, Oktoberfest, Explore Your Major Day, Black History Month, Red Sox games, *Vagina Monologues* and Fall Family Weekend. Wheelock College has 26 official student organizations. The most popular are: Best Buddies · Boston Association for the Education of Young Children · Campus Activities Board · Campus Association of Social Workers · Child Life Organization · dance team · Divine Harmony · drama club · Queer Co-Op · sign choir · Students Against Destructive Decisions · Math Mania.

Academics and Learning Environment

Wheelock College has 65 full-time and 26 part-time faculty members, offering a student-to-faculty ratio of 16:1. The most common course size is 10 to 19 students. Wheelock College offers 17 majors with the most popular being human development and social work. The school has a general core requirement. Cooperative education is not offered. All first-year students must maintain a 1.5 GPA or higher to avoid

WHEELOCK COLLEGE

Wheelock College
Boston (Pop. 636,479)
Location: Major city
Four-year private
Founded: 1888
Website: http://www.wheelock.edu

Students

Total enrollment: 1,378
Undergrads: 880
Freshmen: 217
Part-time students: 8%
From out-of-state: 39%
Male/Female: 12%/88%
Live on-campus: 63%
Off-campus employment rating: Good
Caucasian: 55%
African American: 11%
Hispanic: 11%
Asian: 3%
Hawaiian or Pacific Islander: <1%
Native American: <1%
Mixed (2+ ethnicities): 3%
International: 2%

Academics

Calendar: Semester
Student/faculty ratio: 16:1
Class size 9 or fewer: 21%
Class size 10-29: 79%
Class size 30-49: -
Class size 50-99: -
Class size 100 or more: -
Returning freshmen: 66%
Six-year graduation rate: 54%

Most Popular Majors

Human development
Social work

academic probation. As for some other special academic programs that might appeal to a B student, there are: pass/fail grading option · independent study · double majors · dual degrees · internships.

B Student Support and Success

According to Mike Akillian, assistant to the president of Wheelock, the college "has been providing a transformational education to students who aim to improve society by improving the lives of children and families." Akillian says that many of Wheelock's students focus on making contributions to society, electing to work in professions like education, social work, child life (in medical settings), juvenile justice and youth advocacy. "We believe it is our close collaboration with faculty, a blend of arts and sciences programs coupled with professional programs (most students graduate with double majors), a focus on mission and the integration of theory and scholarship with real-world practice that serves as a catalyzing force for change," says Akillian.

Wheelock College provides a variety of support programs including dedicated guidance for: academic · career · personal · psychological · non-traditional students. The average freshman year GPA is 3.1, and 66 percent of freshmen students return for their sophomore year. After college, approximately 60 percent pursue a graduate degree immediately after graduation and approximately 75 percent of students who enter the workforce get involved with a field related to their major within six months of graduation. Some companies that frequently hire graduates from Wheelock are: Boston Public Schools · Brookline Public Schools · Cambridge Public Schools · Framingham Public Schools · LEAP School · Kingsley Montessori · May Institute · South Bay · Children's Hospital · Mass. General Hospital · UMass Medical · New York Public Schools · Criterion Child Enrichment · Associated early Care and Education · Lawrence Public Schools · Lowell Public Schools · right Horizons · Quincy Public Schools · Stoughton Public Schools · Taunton Public Schools · Social Work PRN · Belmont Day School.

Support for Students with Learning Disabilities

Wheelock College offers students with learning disabilities special support programs. The college, after deeming it necessary, may grant additional time to students with learning disabilities to complete their degree. Another option open to LD students is a lightened course load. High school foreign language waivers are accepted. The following are some programs which students with learning disabilities might find pertinent: tutors · learning center · testing accommodations · untimed tests · extended time for tests · readers · typist/scribe · note-taking services · reading machines · tape recorders · texts on tape · early syllabus · priority registration. Individual or small group tutorials are also available in: time management · organizational skills · learning strategies · specific subject areas · writing labs · math labs · study skills. An advisor/advocate from the LD program is available to students.

How to Get Admitted

For admissions decisions, non-academic factors considered: interview · extracurricular activities · special talents, interests and abilities · character/personal qualities · volunteer work · work experience ·

state of residency · alumni relationship. A high school diploma is required, although a GED is also accepted for admissions consideration. SAT or ACT test scores are required of all applicants. SAT Subject Test scores are not required. *Academic units recommended:* 4 English, 3 Math, 3 Science, 2 Social Studies, 2 Foreign Language.

How to Pay for College

To apply for financial aid, students should submit the following: Free Application for Federal Student Aid (FAFSA). Wheelock College participates in the Federal Work Study program. *Need-based aid programs include:* scholarships and grants · general need-based awards · Federal Pell grants · state scholarships and grants · college-based scholarships and grants · private scholarships and grants. *Non-need-based aid programs include:* scholarships and grants · state scholarships and grants · special achievements and activities awards.

WHEELOCK COLLEGE

Highlights

Admissions
Applicants: 1,570
Accepted: 1,149
Acceptance rate: 73.2%
Average GPA: 3.1
ACT range: 14-25
SAT Math range: 450-540
SAT Reading range: 440-550
SAT Writing range: 2-8
Top 10% of class: 12%
Top 25% of class: 38%
Top 50% of class: 64%

Deadlines
Early Action: 12/1
Early Decision: No
Regular Action: Rolling admissions
Common Application: Accepted

Financial Aid
In-state tuition: $31,675
Out-of-state tuition: $31,675
Room: Varies
Board: Varies
Books: $880
Freshmen receiving need-based aid: 87%
Undergrads rec. need-based aid: 83%
Avg. % of need met by financial aid: 64%
Avg. aid package (freshmen): $24,890
Avg. aid package (undergrads): $21,783
Avg. debt upon graduation: $42,313

Prominent Alumni
Margaret Hamilton, actress who played the Wicked Witch in the *Wizard of Oz*; Philip R. Craig, author of the J.W. Jackson series.

School Spirit
Mascot: Wildcats

579

WHITTIER COLLEGE

13406 East Philadelphia Street, Whittier, CA 90608
Admissions: 888-200-0369 · Financial Aid: 562-907-4285
Email: admission@whittier.edu · Website: http://www.whittier.edu

From the College

"Whittier College is a residential, four-year, liberal arts institution where intellectual inquiry and experiential learning are fostered in a community that promotes respect for diversity of thought and culture. With 43 percent of its students from traditionally under-represented groups, and its federal designation as a Hispanic-Serving Institution, Whittier College remains one of the most diverse liberal arts schools in the nation. The college's location at the crossroads of Los Angeles and Orange Counties—Southern California's centers of urban and cultural life—provides opportunities to explore a full range of thought, cultures and talents.

"Recognized for its Whittier Scholars Program, interdisciplinary curriculum and emphasis on linking theory and practice, Whittier College's academic program is progressive; students gain a wide breadth of knowledge and the confidence to apply that knowledge. Working closely with professors and with the advantage of small class size, students have extensive undergraduate research opportunities, which atypically extend beyond the natural and physical sciences to include social sciences, humanities and the arts. Multitudes of students have become published authors through joint research endeavors and have actively participated in national professional conferences. Whittier faculty also embrace the educational advantages provided through experiential learning; a high percentage of students engage in off-campus study both locally and abroad, academically supported through research trips, fieldwork, service projects and professional internships.

"Popular with students is the January Interim session, an abbreviated but rigorous term that offers intense focus on subject matter, typically followed by a field trip to apply learning. Recent courses included travel to Mexico to study multinational management practices; Chile to analyze the politics of race, religion and gender in action; Paris to examine historical social construct through city planning; and Rome to explore origins of art and architecture. Whittier's 50-year association with the DIS-Copenhagen program remains the most popular semester abroad option, though recent choice destinations have included India, China, Egypt, Africa and South America.

"In particular, strong faculty-student relationships are forged here—through collaborative projects, mentoring and social interaction—that extend well beyond the college years and most often result in professional networking, graduate study references and career assistance later in life. Whittier graduates serve across a variety of sectors, including public service, education and social work, science and health, entrepreneurial business and the arts."

Campus Setting

Whittier College, founded in 1887, is a private, liberal arts college. Its 75-acre campus is located in Whittier, 18 miles east of Los Angeles. A four-year institution, Whittier College has an enrollment of 2,373 students. Campus facilities include: center for the performing arts · language resource center · image processing lab · analytical instrumentation and mass spectrometry lab · nuclear magnetic resonance spectrometry research lab. Whittier College provides on-campus housing with eight units that can accommodate 800 students. Housing options: coed dorms. Recreation and sports facilities include: aquatics center · fitness center · lacrosse and soccer fields · stadium · tennis courts.

Student Life and Activities

Fifty-one percent of students live on campus. Popular campus events include Sportsfest, Late Night Breakfast, Random Acts of Kindness Week, Diverse Identities Week, Asian Heritage Month, Black History Month, Hispanic Heritage Month, Spring Sing, Mona Kai, Luminarias, Helping Hands Day, Asian Night, Soul Food Night, Tardeada, Martin Luther King, Jr. Oratorical Contest and Hawaiian Islanders Club Lu'au. Whittier College has 68 official student organizations. The most popular are: Anthropology Club · International Relations Club · Les Copians (French Club) · Poet Democrats Club · Photography Club · Psychology Club · Reaching Equality and Diversity (READ) · Richard M. Nixon Republican Club · Society of Physics Students · Students for Community Medicine · Anime Ikkimasu · Whittier College Choir · Spanish Club · Break dancing Club · Whittier College Dance Team · Wickets and Balls (Cricket Club) · Intramural s · Artorian Order of the Knights of Pendragon (AOKP) · Art Club · Biology Club · Circle K · Coalition of Activist Leaders (COAL) · Consulting club · Economics Club. Whittier College is a member of the Southern California Intercollegiate Athletic Conference (Division III) and the Western Water Polo Association.

Academics and Learning Environment

Whittier College has 108 full-time and 59 part-time faculty members, offering a student-to-faculty ratio of 13:1. The most common course size is 10 to 19 students. Whittier College offers 31 majors with the most popular being Business Administration, Political Science and English and least popular being French, Music and Religious Studies. The school has a general core requirement. Cooperative education is not offered. All first-year students must maintain a 2.0 GPA or higher to avoid academic probation. Other special academic programs that would appeal to a B student include: self-designed majors · pass/fail grading option · independent study · double majors · internships.

B Student Support and Success

At Whittier's Center for Academic Success (CAS), tutoring is free and classes that have been identified as historically challenging for most students are supported through supplemental instruction. Students in group sessions review notes, practice quizzes and work to reinforce the knowledge and skills they need for the class. CAS also offers a class called Succeeding in College that helps students find out how to do well in school, both academically and personally. The class features individual exercises, cooperative learning, reading and lectures and is available each spring. Students who need assistance in the writing process can find all the help they need through the Writing Program.

Whittier College provides a variety of support programs including dedicated guidance for: academic · career · personal · psychological · minority students · family planning. The average freshman year GPA is 2.7, and 78 percent of freshmen students return for their sophomore year. About 20 percent pursue a graduate degree immediately after graduation, and about 40 percent do so within one year of graduation. Of those students who enter the workforce, about two-thirds enter a field related to their major within six months of graduation. Companies that most frequently hire

WHITTIER COLLEGE

Whittier College
Whittier, CA (Pop. 86,177)
Location: Large town
Four-year private
Founded: 1887
Website: http://www.whittier.edu

Students
Total enrollment: 2,373
Undergrads: 1,695
Freshmen: 446
Part-time students: 2%
From out-of-state: 23%
Male/Female: 44%/56%
Live on-campus: 51%
In fraternities: 9%
In sororities: 13%
Off-campus employment rating: Fair
Caucasian: 35%
African American: 5%
Hispanic: 42%
Asian: 9%
Hawaiian or Pacific Islander: <1%
Native American: 1%
Mixed (2+ ethnicities): 4%
International: 4%

Academics
Calendar: 4-1-4 system
Student/faculty ratio: 13:1
Class size 9 or fewer: 13%
Class size 10-29: 77%
Class size 30-49: 9%
Class size 50-99: -
Class size 100 or more: 1%
Returning freshmen: 78%
Six-year graduation rate: 66%

Most Popular Majors
Business administration
Political science
English

581

WHITTIER COLLEGE

Highlights

Admissions
Applicants: 4,380
Accepted: 2,771
Acceptance rate: 63.3%
Average GPA: 3.5
ACT range: 20-25
SAT Math range: 470-580
SAT Reading range: 460-570
SAT Writing range: 2-17
Top 10% of class: 23%
Top 25% of class: 39%
Top 50% of class: 89%

Deadlines
Early Action: 12/1
Early Decision: No
Regular Action: Rolling admissions
Common Application: Accepted

Financial Aid
In-state tuition: $41,246
Out-of-state tuition: $41,246
Room: Varies
Board: Varies
Books: $650
Freshmen receiving need-based aid: 79%
Undergrads rec. need-based aid: 79%
Avg. % of need met by financial aid: 77%
Avg. aid package (freshmen): $32,346
Avg. aid package (undergrads): $31,328
Avg. debt upon graduation: $27,752

Prominent Alumni
Richard M. Nixon, former US President; George and Geoff Stults, actors.

School Spirit
Mascot: Poets
Colors: Purple and gold

graduates from Whittier include: Beckman Coulter · Sony Pictures · Warner Brothers Entertainment · Wells Fargo · U.S. Congress · U.S. Department of State · University of Southern California Medical Center · Deloitte · Expeditors International · I Have a Dream Foundation · IBM Corporation · KMG Consultants · Smith Barney · Northrup Grumman Corp. · Peace Corps.

Support for Students with Learning Disabilities

According to the school, Whittier provides disability services, but does not offer a separate program for LD students. They complete the same requirements for admission as other students, and self-identify when they enter as freshmen or transfer students. However, LD students can access: special classes · tutors · learning center · testing accommodations · extended time for tests · take-home exam · oral tests · readers · note-taking services · reading machines · tape recorders · texts on tape · early syllabus · priority seating. Individual or small group tutorials are also available in: time management · organizational skills · learning strategies · specific subject areas · writing labs · math labs · study skills. An advisor/advocate from the Whittier College Disability Services is available to students.

How to Get Admitted

For admissions decisions, non-academic factors considered: interview · extracurricular activities · special talents, interests and abilities · character/personal qualities · volunteer work · work experience · geographical location · minority affiliation · alumni relationship. A high school diploma is required, although a GED is also accepted for admissions consideration. SAT or ACT test scores are required of all applicants. SAT Subject Test scores are considered, if submitted, but are not required. *Academic units recommended:* 4 English, 3 Math, 2 Science, 2 Social Studies, 3 Foreign Language.

How to Pay for College

To apply for financial aid, students should submit the following: Free Application for Federal Student Aid (FAFSA) · institution's own financial aid forms · state aid form. Whittier College participates in the Federal Work Study program. *Need-based aid programs include:* scholarships and grants · general need-based awards · Federal Pell grants · state scholarships and grants · college-based scholarships and grants · private scholarships and grants. *Non-need-based aid programs include:* scholarships and grants · state scholarships and grants · creative arts and performance awards · ROTC scholarships.

America's
Best Colleges for
B Students

WILKES UNIVERSITY

84 West South Street, Wilkes-Barre, PA 18766
Admissions: 570-408-4400 · Financial Aid: 570-408-2000
Email: admissions@wilkes.edu · Website: http://www.wilkes.edu

From the College

"Wilkes University combines opportunities of a large university with small-school atmosphere to offer students a unique educational experience. Rigorous scholarship, hands-on learning and individual attention open doors to more opportunities than you knew existed. With 38 majors, numerous minors, 18 athletic teams and 70-plus clubs and organizations, you can build your own future. You'll form meaningful relationships with inspiring professors, teachers and coaches. You'll likely even have some of their cell phone numbers."

Campus Setting

Wilkes is a private university. Founded as a junior college in 1933, it achieved college status in 1947, and university status in 1989. Its 25-acre campus is located in Wilkes-Barre, 20 miles from Scranton. A four-year institution, Wilkes University has an enrollment of 4,665 students. Among campus facilities, there are: · performing arts and sports centers · electron microscope · pharmacy information center · library · art gallery. Wilkes University provides on-campus housing that can accommodate 1,050 students and housing options include: coed dorms · women's dorms · men's dorms · single-student apartments. Recreation and sports facilities include: athletic center · basketball and tennis courts · football and soccer fields · field house · recreation and weight room.

Student Life and Activities

Fifty-six percent of students live off campus. Wilkes University has 70 official student organizations. The most popular are: choral club · Circle K · commuter council · Cue and Curtain · debating · film society · madrigal singers · men's and women's choruses · music ensembles · pep band · academic and community service clubs · special-interest groups. There are intramural teams for those wanting to be involved in sports. They are: basketball · golf · racquetball · soccer · softball · tennis. Wilkes University is a member of the Freedom Conference (Division III) and Middle Atlantic States Collegiate Athletic Conference (Division III).

Academics and Learning Environment

Wilkes University has 166 full-time and 212 part-time faculty members, offering a student-to-faculty ratio of 14:1. The most common course size is 10 to 19 students. Wilkes University offers 48 majors with the most popular being business administration, nursing and engineering and least popular being engineering management, theatre and foreign languages. The school has a general core requirement. Cooperative education is available. All first-year students must maintain a 1.7 GPA or higher to avoid academic probation. Some other special academic programs that might appeal to a B student are: self-designed majors · pass/fail grading option · independent study · double majors · dual degrees · honors program · internships · weekend college · distance learning.

B Student Support and Success

Wilkes has a deep interest in helping the B student achieve excellence through a dedicated faculty and personal tutoring. Admissions are based on secondary-school record, class rank and results of the SAT or ACT. Interviews are not required but highly recommended. Essays and letters of recommendation are not required but will be accepted and considered if submitted.

WILKES UNIVERSITY

Wilkes University
Wilkes-Barre (Pop. 41,243)
Location: Medium city
Four-year private
Founded: 1933
Website: http://www.wilkes.edu

Students
Total enrollment: 4,665
Undergrads: 2,388
Freshmen: 786
Part-time students: 9%
From out-of-state: 21%
Male/Female: 53%/47%
Live on-campus: 44%
Off-campus employment rating: Good
Caucasian: 77%
African American: 3%
Hispanic: 4%
Asian: 3%
Hawaiian or Pacific Islander: <1%
Native American: <1%
Mixed (2+ ethnicities): 3%
International: 7%

Academics
Calendar: Semester
Student/faculty ratio: 14:1
Class size 9 or fewer: 17%
Class size 10-29: 61%
Class size 30-49: 15%
Class size 50-99: 6%
Class size 100 or more: -
Returning freshmen: 78%
Six-year graduation rate: 58%

Most Popular Majors
Business administration
Nursing
Engineering

Wilkes University provides a variety of support programs including dedicated guidance for: academic · career · personal · psychological · minority students · military · veterans · non-traditional students. Recognizing that some students may require extra preparation, Wilkes University provides remedial and refresher courses in: reading · writing · math · study skills. The average freshman year GPA is 3.0, and 78 percent of freshmen students return for their sophomore year.

Support for Students with Learning Disabilities

When it comes to students with learning disabilities, they may take advantage of specific support programs offered by Wilkes University. For those wishing to complete their degree, the college will grant additional time to students with learning disabilities. The college also offers a lightened course load to LD students. Credit is given for remedial courses taken. High school foreign language and math waivers are accepted. Those students with learning disabilities may very well be interested in the following programs at Wilkes University: remedial math · remedial English · remedial reading · tutors · learning center · testing accommodations · extended time for tests · take-home exam · oral tests · readers · typist/scribe · note-taking services · reading machines · tape recorders · texts on tape · diagnostic testing service · priority registration. Individual or small group tutorials are also available in: time management · organizational skills · learning strategies · specific subject areas · writing labs · math labs · study skills. An advisor/advocate from the university is available to students.

How to Get Admitted

For admissions decisions, non-academic factors considered: interview · extracurricular activities · special talents, interests and abilities · character/personal qualities · volunteer work · work experience · state of residency · alumni relationship. A high school diploma is required, although a GED is also accepted for admissions consideration. SAT or ACT test scores are required of all applicants. SAT Subject Test scores are considered, if submitted, but are not required. *According to the admissions office:* Minimum combined SAT Reasoning score of 920 and rank in top three-fifths of secondary school class required. Minimum 2.5 GPA recommended. *Academic units recommended:* 4 English, 3 Math, 2 Science, 3 Social Studies.

Insight

Wilkes was founded to educate first-generation students. "What sets us apart from other colleges can't be measured by numbers on a page. Students succeed here because of the unique atmosphere and philosophy. At Wilkes you will find someone who believes in you," explains Mike Frantz, vice president of enrollment and marketing. "Our professors do everything they can to help students reach their goals. They even help them figure out what those goals are." According to Frantz, Wilkes is actively looking for reasons to include B students. "We look for signs of potential," he says. "Our faculty and staff truly take a deep interest in students' dreams and aspirations." For those students struggling with any particular skills, Wilkes offers individual tutoring as well as a staff that assists in career strategies and study skills. "We can take any students if they honestly express the desire to improve," explains Frantz. "This campus is full of passionate faculty who treat students as equals and challenge them to strive towards greater accomplishments."

How to Pay for College

To apply for financial aid, students should submit the following: Free Application for Federal Student Aid (FAFSA). Wilkes University participates in the Federal Work Study program. *Need-based aid programs include:* scholarships and grants · general need-based awards · Federal Pell grants · state scholarships and grants · college-based scholarships and grants · private scholarships and grants. *Non-need-based aid programs include:* scholarships and grants · state scholarships and grants · ROTC scholarships.

WILKES UNIVERSITY

Highlights

Admissions
Applicants: 3,120
Accepted: 2,500
Acceptance rate: 80.1%
Average GPA: Not reported
ACT range: Not reported
SAT Math range: 480-590
SAT Reading range: 450-560
SAT Writing range: 1-11
Top 10% of class: 21%
Top 25% of class: 53%
Top 50% of class: 80%

Deadlines
Early Action: No
Early Decision: No
Regular Action: Rolling admissions
Common Application: Accepted

Financial Aid
In-state tuition: $31,262
Out-of-state tuition: $31,262
Room: Varies
Board: Varies
Books: Varies
Freshmen receiving need-based aid: 89%
Undergrads rec. need-based aid: 80%
Avg. % of need met by financial aid: 71%
Avg. aid package (freshmen): $23,795
Avg. aid package (undergrads): $22,941
Avg. debt upon graduation: $36,961

Prominent Alumni
Catherine D. DeAngelis, first female editor of the *Journal of the American Medical Association*; Ellen Ferretti, secretary of Pennsylvania Department of Conservation and Natural Resources.

School Spirit
Mascot: Colonels
Colors: Blue and gold

585

College Profiles

WITTENBERG UNIVERSITY

P.O. Box 720, Springfield, OH 45501
Admissions: 800-677-7558, extension 6314 · Financial Aid: 800-677-7558
Email: admission@wittenberg.edu · Website: http://www.wittenberg.edu

From the College

"Wittenberg University provides a liberal arts education dedicated to intellectual inquiry and wholeness of person within a diverse residential community. Reflecting its Lutheran heritage, Wittenberg challenges students to become responsible global citizens, to discover their callings and to lead personal, professional and civic lives of creativity, service, compassion and integrity. Home to an award-winning faculty and to more than 50 majors and special programs, including interdisciplinary ones in East Asian Studies and Russian and Central Eurasian studies, Wittenberg requires community service to graduate. Every year, hundreds of students spend time in service locally and around the world, and many more go on to build homes with Habitat for Humanity, work in inner-city schools with Teach for America or enter the Peace Corps post-graduation. Wittenberg also supports a study-abroad program that annually sends students around the world. At the same time, Wittenberg graduates regularly land coveted positions in all fields as well as entry to prestigious graduate schools. The university also boasts one of the nation's most winning Division III athletics programs."

Campus Setting

Wittenberg, founded in 1845, is a church-affiliated, liberal arts university. Its 114-acre campus is located in Springfield, 25 miles northeast of Dayton, and 40 miles from Columbus. A four-year private institution, Wittenberg University has an enrollment of 1,979 students. Although not originally a co-educational college, Wittenberg University has been co-ed since 1874. The school is also affiliated with the Lutheran Church. The campus offers its students both a library and a gallery. When it comes to on-campus housing, Wittenberg University has 760 units, which can accommodate 1,797 students. Housing options: coed dorms · women's dorms · sorority housing · fraternity housing · single-student apartments · special housing for disabled students · special housing for international students. Recreation and sports facilities include: athletic arena · field house · fitness center · football, field hockey, lacrosse, soccer and softball fields · recreation center · tennis complex · track · stadium.

Student Life and Activities

With 83 percent of students living on campus, there is a lively social setting. "Since we are a small school, it's easy to make friends and find social events", reports the editor of the school newspaper. "There aren't many area bars, but there are many alternatives to parties, like Union Board cultural activities and sports." The Pub, fraternity houses, area bars and off-campus houses are the most frequented student gathering spots. Students enjoy events such as Witt Fest and Lil' Sibs Weekend. Wittenberg University has 120 official student organizations. Greeks, the Student Senate, athletes, the Union Board and Concerned Black Students have widespread influence on student social life at Wittenberg. For those students that would like to get involved with sports, the options are as follows: basketball · cheerleading · Chinese dance · crew · dance · dodgeball · flag football · hockey · indoor soccer · martial arts · outdoor caving · rugby · sand volleyball · softball · swing club · volleyball · Wiffle ball. Wittenberg University is a member of the North Coast Athletic Conference (Division III).

Academics and Learning Environment

Wittenberg University has 131 full-time and 65 part-time faculty members, offering a student-to-faculty ratio of 12:1. The most common course size is 10 to 19 students. Wittenberg University offers 40 majors with the most popular being biology, communication and education and least popular being accounting, French and geography. The school has a general core requirement as well as a religion requirement. Cooperative education is not offered. All first-year students must maintain a 1.8 GPA or higher to avoid academic probation, and a minimum overall GPA of 2.0 is required to graduate. Some programs that might appeal to a B student are: self-designed majors · pass/fail grading option · independent study · double majors · dual degrees · honors program · Phi Beta Kappa · internships.

B Student Support and Success

Wittenberg offers a First Year Experience program with Wittenberg Seminars or WittSems. These small courses introduce students to the core matters of "academic inquiry" through the skills of close reading, problem solving and critical thinking. They offer a Foreign Language Learning Center, Math Workshop and Writing Center to help students who are struggling with basic courses.

Wittenberg University provides a variety of support programs including dedicated guidance for: academic · career · personal · psychological · minority students · family planning · religious. The average freshman year GPA is 2.9, and 74 percent of freshmen students return for their sophomore year. Companies that most frequently hire graduates from Wittenberg University include: Cox Radio - Dayton · QBase Inc. · Environmental Protection Agency · Kentucky State Nature Preserves · Shadow Box Theatre · Abbott Nutrition · Diamond Exchange · Irwin Entertainment · Nextedge Technology Park · PricewaterhouseCoopers · Wittenberg University · Cincinnati Bell · Epic Systems · US Dept. of Veterans Affairs · Dayton Public Schools · ECC Group · Fulbright Association · Goddard School · Japan Exchange and Teaching Program (JET) · Newark City Schools · Springfield City Schools · Teach for America · Corporate Claims Management · George K. Baum & Company · Nationwide Insurance · Kroger Company · Clark County Dept. of Job & Family Services · Ohio Legislative Service Commission · The Indiana Republican Party · David M. Martin Company - LPA · Accreditation Council for Graduate Medical Education · AmeriCorps · Peace Corps · Federal Reserve Bank of New York · University of North Carolina Institute of Marine Science · International Luxury.

Support for Students with Learning Disabilities

Wittenberg University provides students with learning disabilities specific support programs. According to the school, students with disabilities are responsible for providing Academic Services with appropriate documentation of their disability (see documentation guidelines) and arranging an appointment to assess their needs. Following the appointment and the review of appropriate documentation, the Assistant Provost for Academic Services will make a determination of eligibility for disability services. Once accommodations have been finalized, students will receive letters for each of their professors listing their accommodations. Students

WITTENBERG UNIVERSITY

Highlights

Wittenberg University
Springfield, OH (Pop. 60,147)
Location: Large town
Four-year private
Founded: 1845
Website: http://www.wittenberg.edu

Students
Total enrollment: 1,979
Undergrads: 1,959
Freshmen: 584
Part-time students: 5%
From out-of-state: 30%
From public schools: 80%
Male/Female: 43%/57%
Live on-campus: 83%
In fraternities: 30%
In sororities: 33%
Off-campus employment rating: Fair
Caucasian: 81%
African American: 7%
Hispanic: 3%
Asian: 1%
Hawaiian or Pacific Islander: <1%
Native American: <1%
Mixed (2+ ethnicities): 4%
International: 2%

Academics
Calendar: Semester
Student/faculty ratio: 12:1
Class size 9 or fewer: 18%
Class size 10-29: 69%
Class size 30-49: 11%
Class size 50-99: -
Class size 100 or more: -
Returning freshmen: 74%
Six-year graduation rate: 63%

Most Popular Majors
Biology
Communication
Education

587

College Profiles

WITTENBERG UNIVERSITY

Admissions
Applicants: 5,160
Accepted: 4,612
Acceptance rate: 89.4%
Average GPA: 3.4
ACT range: 23-25
SAT Math range: 520-620
SAT Reading range: 520-620
SAT Writing range: Not reported
Top 10% of class: 22%
Top 25% of class: 49%
Top 50% of class: 81%

Deadlines
Early Action: 12/1
Early Decision: 11/15
Regular Action: Rolling admissions
Common Application: Accepted

Financial Aid
In-state tuition: $37,230
Out-of-state tuition: $37,230
Room: $5,056
Board: $4,680
Books: $1,000
Freshmen receiving need-based aid: 80%
Undergrads rec. need-based aid: 78%
Avg. % of need met by financial aid: 83%
Avg. aid package (freshmen): $31,935
Avg. aid package (undergrads): $31,471

Prominent Alumni
Sheila J. Simon, Lieutenant Governor, State of Illinois; Ronald Fook Shiu Li, founder of the Hong Kong Stock Exchange; Fred B. Mitchell, sports columnist, the *Chicago Tribune*.

School Spirit
Mascot: Tiger
Colors: Red and white

are encouraged to communicate the disability and special needs to course professors early in the term; however, this is left entirely to the individual's discretion. These students might find the following programs extremely helpful: tutors · extended time for tests · take-home exam · exam on tape or computer. Individual or small group tutorials are also available in: writing labs · math labs. An advisor/advocate from the LD program is available to students.

How to Get Admitted

For admissions decisions, non-academic factors considered: interview · extracurricular activities · special talents, interests and abilities · character/personal qualities · volunteer work · work experience · state of residency · alumni relationship. A high school diploma is required, although a GED is also accepted for admissions consideration. SAT or ACT test scores are considered, if submitted, but are not required. *Academic units recommended:* 4 English, 4 Math, 5 Science, 3 Foreign Language.

How to Pay for College

To apply for financial aid, students should submit the following: Free Application for Federal Student Aid (FAFSA) · state aid form · Non-custodian (Divorced/Separated) Parent's Statement · Verification form. Wittenberg University participates in the Federal Work Study program. *Need-based aid programs include:* scholarships and grants · general need-based awards · Federal Pell grants · state scholarships and grants · college-based scholarships and grants · private scholarships and grants. *Non-need-based aid programs include:* scholarships and grants · general need-based awards · state scholarships and grants · creative arts and performance awards · special achievements and activities awards · ROTC scholarships.

WOODBURY UNIVERSITY

7500 Glenoaks Boulevard, Burbank, CA 91510
Admissions: 818-252-5221 · Financial Aid: 818-252 5273
Email: admissions@woodbury.edu
Website: http://www.woodbury.edu

From the College

"Woodbury University is committed to providing the highest level of professional and liberal arts education. The integrated nature of our educational environment cultivates successful students with a strong and enduring sense of personal and social responsibility. Woodbury fosters academic excellence and individual development in an environment that honors the following values: integrity and ethical behavior, diversity, empowering students to determine and manage their own decisions, academic rigor, liberal arts-based professional education that effectively prepares students for careers and student focus in all aspects of the university's operations."

Campus Setting

Woodbury, founded in 1884, is a private university of business administration and professional design. Its 22-acre campus is located in Burbank, in the Los Angeles metropolitan area. A four-year institution, Woodbury University has an enrollment of 1,607 students. There are 91,897 books in the school library. As for the on-campus housing options at Woodbury University, there are 146 units that can accommodate 219 students. Housing options: coed dorms · single-student apartments. Recreation and sports facilities include: basketball court · swimming pool.

Student Life and Activities

The campus environment is affected by the fact that the great majority of students live off campus (88 percent). Woody's Cafe is a popular gathering spot. The University Gala, Winter Formal, Springfest and Commencement are popular events. Woodbury University has 26 official student organizations. The most popular are: American Institute of Graphic Arts (AIGA) · American Society of Interior Designers (ASID) · Architecture Student Forum · Business & Professional Women of Woodbury · Collegiate Entrepreneurs' Organization · communication club · Founders' Week · MBA Association · Midnight Breakfast · Organization Name Common Threads · Social Animals · Society of Accounting and Business · Society of Interior Architecture Students · Winter Formal · Woodstock.

Academics and Learning Environment

Woodbury University has 82 full-time and 189 part-time faculty members, offering a student-to-faculty ratio of 10:1. The most common course size is 10 to 19 students. Woodbury University offers 21 majors with the most popular being business/management, architecture and fashion design. The school has a general core requirement. Cooperative education is not offered. All first-year students must maintain a 2.0 GPA or higher to avoid academic probation. A list of programs that would appeal to a B student include: double majors · accelerated study · internships · weekend college.

Highlights

Woodbury University
Burbank, CA (Pop. 104,391)
Location: Major city
Four-year private
Founded: 1884
Website: http://www.woodbury.edu

Students
Total enrollment: 1,607
Undergrads: 1,357
Freshmen: 525
Part-time students: 14%
From out-of-state: 10%
Male/Female: 49%/51%
Live on-campus: 12%
In fraternities: 10%
Off-campus employment rating: Fair
Caucasian: 37%
African American: 4%
Hispanic: 29%
Asian: 9%
Hawaiian or Pacific Islander: 1%
Native American: <1%
Mixed (2+ ethnicities): 2%
International: 18%

Academics
Calendar: Semester
Student/faculty ratio: 10:1
Class size 9 or fewer: 24%
Class size 10-29: 75%
Class size 30-49: 1%
Class size 50-99: -
Class size 100 or more: -
Returning freshmen: 75%
Six-year graduation rate: 45%

Most Popular Majors
Business/management
Architecture
Fashion design

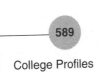

589

College Profiles

WOODBURY UNIVERSITY

Admissions
Applicants: 928
Accepted: 535
Acceptance rate: 57.7%
Average GPA: 3.1
ACT range: 19-25
SAT Math range: 445-550
SAT Reading range: 430-550
SAT Writing range: Not reported

Deadlines
Early Action: No
Early Decision: No
Regular Action: Rolling admissions
Common Application: Accepted

Financial Aid
In-state tuition: $34,448
Out-of-state tuition: $34,448
Room: $6,354
Board: $3,844
Books: $1,750
Freshmen receiving need-based aid: 65%
Undergrads rec. need-based aid: 87%
Avg. % of need met by financial aid: 53%
Avg. aid package (freshmen): $23,107
Avg. aid package (undergrads): $21,758
Avg. debt upon graduation: $35,216

Prominent Alumni
Helen Gurley Brown, editor in chief, *Cosmopolitan Magazine*.

America's
Best Colleges for
B Students

B Student Support and Success

Woodbury offers a variety of services to help B students through OASIS (Office of Academic Success and Instructional Services). Services include academic peer mentors, faculty advising and individual and small-group tutoring. The school also provides supplemental instruction for historically challenging courses in weekly study sessions. In addition, each freshman student is assigned a Student Orientation, Advising and Registration (SOAR) peer advisor who helps students with all aspects of college life.

Woodbury University provides a variety of support programs including dedicated guidance for: academic · career · personal · psychological. Annually, 75 percent of freshmen students return for their sophomore year. Companies that most frequently hire graduates from Woodbury University include: ABC · AmeriCorps · Bank of America · Bloomingdale's · Boeing · Brown & Brown LLP · Citibank · City of Los Angeles · Countrywide Mortgage · Disney · Dreamworks · DWP · Escada · First Commerce Bank · Gensler · Good Swartz · Guess · IKEA · JC Penney · LA County Office of Public Safety · LA Sheriff's Department · LA Superior Court · NBC · Nestle · Nickelodeon · Office Pavilion · Paramount · Port of Los Angeles · Shell Oil · State of California · Technicolor · Universal Studios · Warner Bros · Washington Mutual · Williams-Sonoma.

Support for Students with Learning Disabilities

Woodbury University offers specific support programs for those students with learning disabilities. The following are some programs at Woodbury University that will prove useful to these students: tutors · learning center · testing accommodations · untimed tests · extended time for tests · note-taking services · tape recorders · priority registration. Individual or small group tutorials are also available in: time management · organizational skills · specific subject areas · writing labs · math labs · study skills. An advisor/advocate from the LD program is available to students.

How to Get Admitted

For admissions decisions, non-academic factors considered: interview · extracurricular activities · volunteer work · work experience · state of residency · geographical location · alumni relationship. A high school diploma is required, although a GED is also accepted for admissions consideration. SAT or ACT test scores are required of all applicants. SAT Subject Test scores are recommended but not required. *According to the admissions office:* Minimum 2.5 GPA recommended. *Academic units recommended:* 4 English, 3 Math, 2 Science, 1 Social Studies, 2 Foreign Language.

How to Pay for College

To apply for financial aid, students should submit the following: Free Application for Federal Student Aid (FAFSA) · institution's own financial aid forms. Woodbury University participates in the Federal Work Study program. *Need-based aid programs include:* scholarships and grants · general need-based awards · Federal Pell grants · state scholarships and grants · college-based scholarships and grants · private scholarships and grants. *Non-need-based aid programs include:* scholarships and grants · state scholarships and grants.

XAVIER UNIVERSITY OF LOUISIANA

One Drexel Drive, New Orleans, LA 70125
Admissions: 877-XAVIERU · Financial Aid: 504-520-7517
Email: apply@xula.edu · Website: http://www.xula.edu

From the College

"Xavier University of Louisiana is Catholic and historically black. The ultimate purpose of the university is the promotion of a more just and humane society. To this end, Xavier prepares its students to assume roles of leadership and service in society. This preparation takes place in a pluralistic teaching and learning environment that incorporates all relevant educational means, including research and community service. So that they will be able to assume roles of leadership and service, Xavier graduates will be: prepared for continual spiritual, moral and intellectual development; liberally educated in the knowledge and skills required for leadership and service and educated in a major field so that they are prepared to complete graduate or professional school and to succeed in a career and in life."

Campus Setting

Xavier University, founded in 1915, is a church-affiliated, liberal arts institution. Its 29-acre, urban campus is located in New Orleans. A four-year private institution, Xavier University Louisiana is a historically black university with 3,121 students. The school is also affiliated with the Roman Catholic Church. The school also has a library with 261,000 books. As for on-campus housing at Xavier University Louisiana, there are 824 units that can accommodate 1,692 students. Housing options: coed dorms · women's dorms · men's dorms · special housing for disabled students. Recreation and sports facilities include: fitness center · gymnasium.

Student Life and Activities

Fifty-three percent of students live off campus, but there is still a vibrant atmosphere both on- and off-campus. The Student Union is a popular on-campus gathering spot. Popular campus events include Spring Fest, October Fest, Festival of Scholars and Greek shows. Xavier University of Louisiana has more than 175 official student organizations. The most popular are: music · theatre · political, service and special-interest groups. Xavier University of Louisiana is a member of the NAIA, Gulf Coast Athletic Conference.

Academics and Learning Environment

B students will appreciate Xavier's decent student-faculty ratio and class sizes. The university has 224 full-time and 26 part-time faculty members, offering a student-to-faculty ratio of 13:1. The most common course size is 20 to 29 students. Xavier University of Louisiana offers 47 majors with the most popular being biology, physical sciences and psychology and least popular being art education, economics and theology. The school has a general core requirement as well as a religion requirement. Cooperative education is available. All first-year students must maintain a 2.0 GPA or higher to avoid academic probation. Other special academic programs that would appeal to a B student include: independent study · double majors · dual degrees · accelerated study · honors program · internships.

B Student Support and Success

The Office of Academic Support Programs at Xavier provides academic assistance to students who need extra help. Services include one-on-one tutoring, academic counseling, study techniques, test-taking strategies, enrichment and development,

XAVIER UNIVERSITY OF LOUISIANA

Xavier University of Louisiana
New Orleans (Pop. 369,250)
Location: Major city
Four-year private
Founded: 1915
Website: http://www.xula.edu

Students
Total enrollment: 3,121
Undergrads: 2,504
Freshmen: 877
Part-time students: 5%
From out-of-state: 52%
From public schools: 24%
Male/Female: 28%/72%
Live on-campus: 47%
In fraternities: 1%
In sororities: 3%
Off-campus employment rating: Good
Caucasian: 4%
African American: 77%
Hispanic: 2%
Asian: 10%
Native American: <1%
Mixed (2+ ethnicities): 3%
International: 2%

Academics
Calendar: Semester
Student/faculty ratio: 13:1
Class size 9 or fewer: 21%
Class size 10-29: 62%
Class size 30-49: 11%
Class size 50-99: 5%
Class size 100 or more: 1%
Returning freshmen: 72%
Six-year graduation rate: 46%

Most Popular Majors
Biology
Physical sciences
Psychology

time management skills and referrals to the math, reading and writing labs. Tutoring services are free. The Math Lab helps student develop their mathematical abilities in an informal manner. The college states that the overall goal of the lab is to "increase each student's understanding of her or his course material. This takes time and active participation on the student's part." Students may also use the Reading Lab to read and study more effectively. Software can be utilized that helps improve vocabulary and comprehension skills. A Speech Lab is also available, as is a Writing Center website for online tutoring in the different stages of the writing process.

Xavier University of Louisiana provides a variety of support programs including dedicated guidance for: academic · career · personal · psychological · religious. Xavier also offers remedial and refresher courses in: reading · writing · math · study skills. The average freshman year GPA is 2.5, and 72 percent of freshmen students return for their sophomore year. After college, approximately 31 percent pursue a graduate degree immediately after graduation. Approximately 28 percent of the students who enter the workforce enter a field related to their major within six months of graduation. Companies that most frequently hire graduates from Xavier University of Louisiana include: 3M · Bernstein Global Wealth Management · Environmental Protection Agency · Federal Reserve Board of Governors · GEICO Insurance · Hilton Hotels (Corporate Office) · Inroads · JP Morgan Chase · Kellogg's · Randolph Air Force Base · Target · Walgreens (Retail Management) · Wells Fargo-Operations Division · Wells Fargo-Sales and Customer Service Group · Wells Fargo-Technology Group · Wells Fargo-Wholesale Banking Division.

Support for Students with Learning Disabilities

Some students, such as those with learning disabilities, may take advantage of specific support programs offered by Xavier University of Louisiana. If deemed necessary, the college will grant additional time to students with learning disabilities who wish to complete their degree. The following programs at Xavier University of Louisiana may prove useful to those students with learning disabilities: tutors · testing accommodations · untimed tests · extended time for tests · take-home exam · oral tests · typist/scribe · tape recorders · early syllabus · priority registration · waiver of math degree requirement. Individual or small group tutorials are also available in: time management · learning strategies · writing labs · math labs · study skills. An advisor/advocate from the LD program is available to students.

How to Get Admitted

For admissions decisions, non-academic factors considered: interview · extracurricular activities · special talents, interests and abilities · character/personal qualities · volunteer work · work experience · state of residency · alumni relationship. A high school diploma is required, although a GED is also accepted for admissions consideration. SAT or ACT test scores are required of all applicants. SAT Subject Test scores are recommended but not required. *Academic units recommended:* 4 Math, 3 Science, 1 Foreign Language.

How to Pay for College

To apply for financial aid, students should submit the following: Free Application for Federal Student Aid (FAFSA). Xavier University of Louisiana participates in the Federal Work Study program. *Need-based aid programs include:* scholarships and grants · general need-based awards · Federal Pell grants · state scholarships and grants · college-based scholarships and grants · private scholarships and grants · United Negro College Fund. *Non-need-based aid programs include:* scholarships and grants · state scholarships and grants · creative arts and performance awards · athletic scholarships · religious affiliation scholarships/grants.

XAVIER UNIVERSITY OF LOUISIANA

Highlights

Admissions
Applicants: 4,703
Accepted: 2,560
Acceptance rate: 54.4%
Placed on wait list: 44
Enrolled from wait list: 8
Average GPA: 3.4
ACT range: 20-26
SAT Math range: 420-550
SAT Reading range: 440-560
SAT Writing range: Not reported
Top 10% of class: 28%
Top 25% of class: 56%
Top 50% of class: 81%

Deadlines
Early Action: 10/15
Early Decision: No
Regular Action: Rolling admissions
Common Application: Accepted

Financial Aid
In-state tuition: $19,100
Out-of-state tuition: $19,100
Room: Varies
Board: Varies
Books: $1,200
Freshmen receiving need-based aid: 87%
Undergrads rec. need-based aid: 83%
Avg. % of need met by financial aid: 13%
Avg. aid package (freshmen): $21,644
Avg. aid package (undergrads): $20,877
Avg. debt upon graduation: $23,392

Prominent Alumni
Regina Benjamin, U.S. Surgeon General, Obama Administration; Alexis Herman, U.S. Secretary of Labor, Clinton Administration; Norman C. Francis, university president.

School Spirit
Mascot: Gold Rush
Colors: Gold and white

593

College Profiles

INDEX OF AMERICA'S BEST COLLEGES FOR B STUDENTS

America's Best Colleges
for B Students

INDEX OF COLLEGES BY LOCATION

Index

NEW JERSEY
Caldwell College, 120
Drew University, 166
Rider University, 364

NEW MEXICO
University of New Mexico, 499

NEW YORK
Adelphi University, 65
Alfred University, 80
Elmira College, 181
Hartwick College, 235
Hilbert College, 241
Manhattanville College, 280
Marymount Manhattan College, 286
Pace University, 335
Paul Smith's College, 341
Sarah Lawrence College, 381
St. Lawrence University, 416
SUNY - Purchase College, 421
Wells College, 558

NORTH CAROLINA
Campbell University, 122
Chowan University, 131
Guilford College, 223
High Point University, 238
Shaw University, 390
University of North Carolina - Greensboro, 505

OHIO
Bowling Green State University, 108
Hiram College, 244
Marietta College, 283
Muskingum University, 312
Ohio Northern University, 319
Ohio University, 322
Ohio Wesleyan University, 325
University of Cincinnati, 457
Wittenberg University, 586

OREGON
Oregon State University, 331
Southern Oregon University, 404
University of Oregon, 508
University of Portland, 511

PENNSYLVANIA
Albright College, 75
Drexel University, 169
Duquesne University, 172
Indiana University of Pennsylvania, 262
Lycoming College, 274
Seton Hill University, 387
Temple University, 435
Washington & Jefferson College, 551
Westminster College, 574
Wilkes University, 583

RHODE ISLAND
Bryant University, 117
Roger Williams University, 373
Salve Regina University, 378
University of Rhode Island, 517

SOUTH CAROLINA
Coastal Carolina University, 136
University of South Carolina - Columbia, 523

TENNESSEE
Fisk University, 193
University of Memphis, 487
University of Tennessee, 526

TEXAS
Angelo State University, 89
Schreiner University, 384
Texas Tech University, 438
University of Houston, 465

UTAH
University of Utah, 533

VERMONT
Champlain College, 128
Green Mountain College, 220
Norwich University, 315
University of Vermont, 536

VIRGINIA
Christopher Newport University, 133
George Mason University, 209
Hampden-Sydney College, 229
Hampton University, 232
Hollins University, 247
Longwood University, 268
Old Dominion University, 328
Radford University, 358
Randolph-Macon College, 361
Roanoke College, 370
Shenandoah University, 392

Sweet Briar College, 432
Virginia Commonwealth University, 545
Virginia Wesleyan College, 548

WASHINGTON
Evergreen State College, 187
Pacific Lutheran University, 338
Washington State University, 554

WEST VIRGINIA
Fairmont State University, 190
Shepherd University, 395
West Virginia University, 564

WISCONSIN
Alverno College, 86
Ripon College, 367

WYOMING
University of Wyoming, 539

598

America's Best Colleges
for B Students

CONTRIBUTORS

Shirley Bloomquist, MA, Ed M, NCC
College and Educational Counselor
sbloomqu@aol.com

Marilyn Emerson
Independent Educational Consultant
www.collplan.com
111 E. 85th Street
New York, NY 10028
212-671-1972 or
84 Old Farm Road North
Chappaqua, NY 10514
914-747-1760

Todd Fothergill
President of Strategies for College
www.strategiesforcollege.com

Marjorie Ann Goode
Educational Consultant/School Counselor
Start Early: College and Career Planning Services
agoode2003@yahoo.com

Laura Jeanne Hammond
Editor in Chief
Next Step Magazine
800-771-3117
www.nextstepmagazine.com
AIM screenname: nsmanswergirl

Todd Johnson
College Admissions Partners
2600 15th Street SW
Willmar, MN 56201
320-262-9955
todd@collegeadmissionspartners.com

Judith Mackenzie
Mackenzie College Consulting
4705 16th Avenue NE
Seattle, WA 98105
206-527-2287

Lynda McGee
College Counselor
Downtown Magnets High School
lmcgee00@aol.com

Maureen McQuaid
College Focus LLC
Independent Counselor
www.collegefocus.com
niep1@aol.com
650-343-3940

David Miller
Director of College Counseling
Stevenson School
www.rlstevenson.org

Laurie Nimmo
Career Center and College Admissions Coordinator/
Independent College Advising
Healdsburg, CA 95448
lnimmo@sonic.net

Terry O'Banion
Former President of the League for Innovation in the
Community College
www.league.org

Patrick O'Brien
Former Admission Officer and Consultant-
Ambassador for the ACT

Judi Robinovitz
Judi Robinovitz Associates and Educational
Consulting
www.scoreatthetop.com

Jennifer Tabbush, MBA, CEP
Headed for College
17328 Ventura Boulevard, Suite 216
Encino, CA 91316
818-996-9540
jtabbush@headedforcollege.com
www.headedforcollege.com

Sarah Wilburn
Campus Bound
617-769-0400
swilburn@campusbound.com
Campus Bound helps families across the country find
the right colleges, fill out all the applications and
apply for financial aid.

ABOUT THE AUTHOR

Tamra B. Orr is a full-time educational writer and author originally from Indiana and now living in the Pacific Northwest (where she takes a long look at the mountains every single day!). She is the author of more than 250 nonfiction titles for kids, teens and families. Her book, *Violence in Our Schools: Halls of Hope, Halls of Fear* (Scholastic), won the Best Nonfiction Book of the Year for Teens from the New York Public Library. She is also the author of *Ace the SAT Writing Even If You Hate to Write: Shortcuts and Strategies to Score Higher Regardless of Your Skill Level* (SuperCollege), *The Purple Cow Guide to Extraordinary Essays* (Scholastic) and *The Encyclopedia of Notable Hispanic-Americans* (Publications International).

Orr is involved in education in almost every imaginable way. She writes dozens of nonfiction books each year on a huge variety of topics (from face lifts to fire ants!) and she writes hundreds of stories and items for standardized tests for more than a dozen educational companies. She has a degree in Secondary Education and English from Ball State University in Muncie, Indiana. Orr has been married for more than half of her life to Joseph and together, they have four children ranging in age from 21 to 9. The three that are still living at home are all homeschooled (in between her writing and his messing around with old Volkswagens). Orr has appeared on numerous radio and television shows and has done countless book signings/appearances to promote her books and talk about a variety of issues within education. Since she was once so shy she almost flunked speech class in high school, this is still an amazing fact to her (and her parents!).

And to think she did all this . . . and was a mere B student!

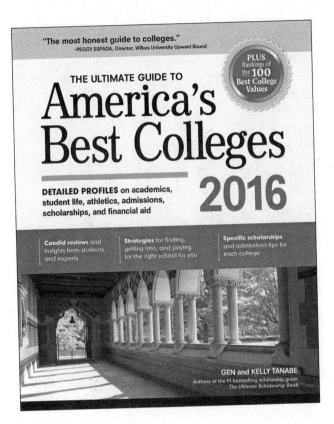

DETAILED PROFILES ON ACADEMICS, STUDENT LIFE, ATHLETICS, ADMISSIONS, SCHOLARSHIPS AND FINANCIAL AID

- Candid reviews and insights from students and experts
- Strategies for finding, getting into and paying for the right school for you
- Specific scholarships and admissions tips for each college

Get your copy at bookstores nationwide or from www.supercollege.com

ISBN13: 978-1-61760-071-5

Price: $23.99

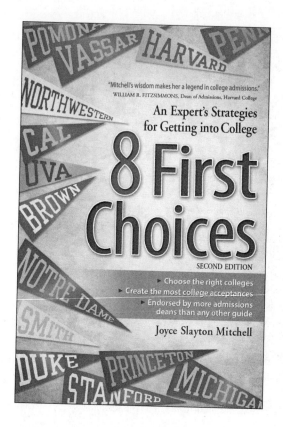

AN EXPERT'S STRATEGIES FOR GETTING INTO COLLEGE

- Choose the right colleges
- Create the most college acceptances
- Endorsed by more admissions deans than any other guide

Get your copy at bookstores nationwide or from www.supercollege.com

ISBN13: 978-1-61760-037-1

Price: $14.95

WRITE THE COLLEGE ADMISSION ESSAY THAT GETS YOU IN!

- 50 successful college essays—learn from the best
- Admission officers reveal exactly what colleges want to see in your admission essays
- 25 essay mistakes to avoid
- Complete instructions on crafting a powerful essay
- How to recycle your essay to save time
- Write the essay that will get you into your dream college

Get your copy at bookstores nationwide or from www.supercollege.com

ISBN13: 978-1-61760-038-8

Price: $14.95

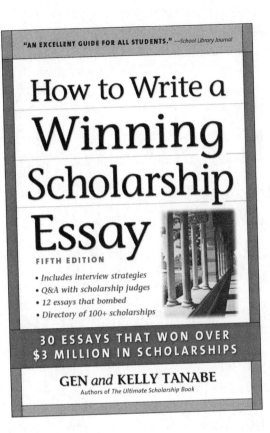

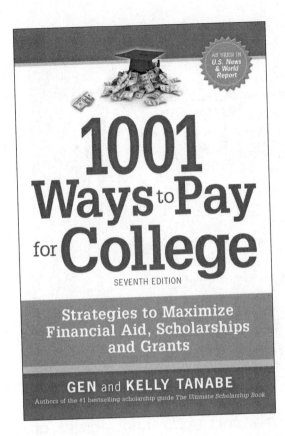

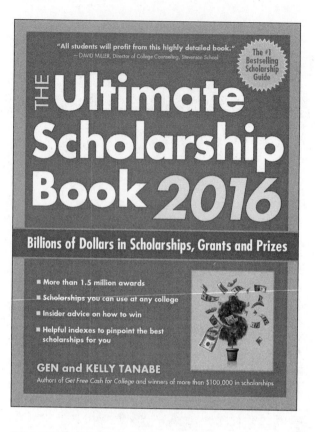

Home | About | Application Status | Scholarship Resources | Recent Winners | Contact

$1,000 Gen and Kelly Tanabe Scholarship

The Gen and Kelly Tanabe Scholarship is a merit-based program that helps students fulfill their dreams of a higher education. The scholarship is named for Gen and Kelly Tanabe, best-selling authors on education, whose generous donations fund this program.

Scholarship Application Form for Spring 2012
January 1 - July 31

Not ready to apply but don't want to forget?
Get our deadline reminder. See bottom of page.

First Name

Last Name

Gender ○ Male ◉ Female

Age [Select ▼]

Student Status [Select One ▼]

Street Address

City

State [------ ▼]

Zip Code

Email Address

Short Answer — Paste your essay into this space.

In 250 words or less, please submit an essay on one of the following:

1. Why do you deserve to win this scholarship? -OR-

2. Describe your academic or career goals. -OR-

3. Any topic of your choice.

Feel free to re-use an essay that you wrote in class, for college admission or another scholarship competition.

☑ I have read and agree to the Terms & Conditions and Privacy Policy.

[SUBMIT]

By submitting this application you affirm that you are the author of the above essay and all of the information is true and accurate.

Eligibility

9th-12th grade high school, college, or graduate student including adult students.

Legal resident of the U.S.

Currently in school or planning to start school within the next 12 months.

Deadlines

Spring Competition:
January 1 - July 31, 2012.

Fall Competition:
August 1 - December 31, 2012.

Selection & Award

Winners are chosen by committee, which bases its decision primarily on the submitted personal statement. The first place award is a $1,000 scholarship. The award can be used for tuition, room and board, required fees or any educational expense.

Home| About Us | Terms & Conditions| Privacy | Resources | Contact

APPLY FOR THE GEN AND KELLY TANABE SCHOLARSHIP

The Gen and Kelly Tanabe Scholarship is a merit-based program that helps students fulfill their dreams of a higher education. The program is open to 9th-12th grade high school, college, or graduate students including adult learners. Visit **www.gkscholarship.com** to apply.

GET MORE TOOLS AND RESOURCES FOR COLLEGE AT SUPERCOLLEGE.COM

Visit www.supercollege.com for more free resources on college admission, scholarships and financial aid. And, apply for the SuperCollege Scholarship.